VISUAL QUICKPRO GUIDE

FILEMAKER PRO 6 ADVANCED

FOR WINDOWS AND MACINTOSH

Cynthia L. Baron
Daniel Peck

Peachpit Press

Visual QuickPro Guide
FileMaker Pro 6 Advanced for Windows and Macintosh
Cynthia L. Baron and Daniel Peck

Peachpit Press
1249 Eighth Street
Berkeley, CA 94710
510/524-2178
800/283-9444
510/524-2221 (fax)

Find us on the World Wide Web at: http://www.peachpit.com
To report errors, please send a note to errata@peachpit.com

Peachpit Press is a division of Pearson Education
Copyright © 2003 by Cynthia L. Baron and Daniel Peck

Editors: Becky Morgan, Kate McKinley
Production Editor: Connie Jeung-Mills
Tech Editors: Tim Flynn, Julian Nadel of beezwax datatools
Compositor: Owen Wolfson
Indexer: Karin Arrigoni
Cover design: The Visual Group

Notice of Rights
All rights reserved. No part of this book may be reproduced or transmitted in any form by any means, electronic, mechanical, photocopying, recording, or otherwise, without the prior written permission of the publisher. For information on getting permission for reprints and excerpts, contact permissions@peachpit.com.

Notice of Liability
The information in this book is distributed on an "As Is" basis, without warranty. While every precaution has been taken in the preparation of the book, neither the author nor Peachpit Press, shall have any liability to any person or entity with respect to any loss or damage caused or alleged to be caused directly or indirectly by the instructions contained in this book or by the computer software and hardware products described in it.

Trademarks
Visual QuickStart Guide is a registered trademark of Peachpit Press, a division of Pearson Education

Throughout this book, trademarks are used. Rather than put a trademark symbol in every occurrence of a trademarked name, we state that we are using the names in an editorial fashion only and to the benefit of the trademark owner with no intention of infringement of the trademark.

ISBN 0-321-16219-6

9 8 7 6 5 4 3 2 1

Printed and bound in the United States of America

To the folks, who are always tickled to receive a new book.

To Shai, who makes all things possible.

To Dan, for a friendship whose legs get longer all the time.

—Cyndi

Sarah Boslaugh, my wife, for strength, love, and forbearance.

Cyndi Baron, my friend and partner for so many years.

Marjorie Baer, and our editors Becky Morgan and Kate McKinley at Peachpit Press.

Delfina Davis, Chris Gray, Stephen Gallagher, and Kevin Mallon at Filemaker Inc.

—Dan

Acknowledgements

To our seasoned Peachpit team, particularly Marjorie Baer, Becky Morgan, Connie Jeung-Mills, and Kim Lombardi.

And to our newcomer, Kate McKinley, an easy-going companion through the stretch.

To Kostia Bergman, for giving me someone to talk shop with in the halls of academe.

To the many good friends who remind me constantly why this work is worthwhile: the 3/16 group, the squeal & reel crowd, the Polaroid/PB connections. You know who you are, and why I treasure you.

And to the helpful, supportive folks at FileMaker, most particularly Kevin Mallon.

—Cyndi

For their inspiration and challenges: Richard Cohen, Linda Hammell, Nancy Senken, Ginger Cemelli, Carolyn Kostopoulos, Roz Goldfarb, Jessica Goldfarb, Daniel Kestenbaum, Ron Marx, Jeff Cohen, Marianne Carroll, Rob Getlan, Tim Neudecker, Stacy Kartegener, Larry Mayer, Lorin Sklamberg, Jessica Kligman, and Laurie Winfrey.

For tunes and sanity, my bandmates in the Buck Mountain Band: Bob & Sue Taylor and Carl Kirby. And in the Corn Family: Phil Levy, Sarah Carlton, and Jason Sypher.

For friendship, good times, and the occasional glass of wine: John Hatton, Ellen White, and Elizabeth White-Hatton at Cleff'd Ear Productions. Warren Argo, Maggie Brown, and Joan Green at the Festival of American Fiddle Tunes.

Henry Sapoznik, mayn bruder un banje rebbe.

And Andy Cemelli, whom I miss every day.

—Dan

TABLE OF CONTENTS

Chapter 1: **About FileMaker Pro 6**   **1**
FileMaker 6: Highlights of New Features 2
FileMaker Editions 6
Upgrading from pre–FileMaker 5.0 Versions 6
Using This Book 7

Chapter 2: **Organizing Data Efficiently**   **9**
About Relational Databases................... 10
Gathering Information 11
Creating a Field List......................... 13
Developing a Data Structure Strategy 14
Creating a Data Structure Chart............... 17
Field Design Tactics.......................... 18
Implementing Relationships 21
Testing Your Database....................... 22

Chapter 3: **Layout Enhancements**   **25**
Usability, Legibility, and Logical Grouping...... 26
Cross-Platform Issues 28
Using Format Painter........................ 31
Using Graphic Text.......................... 33
Formatting Elements as Buttons 36
Reusing Graphics 38
Entering Data in a Standard Layout 40
Cleaning Up a Layout for Printing 42
Creating and Formatting Value Lists........... 44
Validating Formats with Value Lists 45
Working with Conditional Value Lists.......... 47
Using Calculated Field Labels 49
Creating Field Masks......................... 51
Validating by Number of Characters 56
Copying Layouts............................ 58

Table of Contents

Chapter 4: Calculation Fields — 61
- Merging Fields Using Calculations 62
- Updating Auto-Entry Serial Numbers 67
- Formatting Labels or Envelopes 69
- Formatting Form-Letter Modules 72
- Augmenting a Form Letter 77
- Using GetField 82

Chapter 5: Creating Data Reports — 89
- Extending a Found Set 90
- Using Search Operators 92
- Creating an "Inverted" Search 94
- Creating Summary Layout Parts 95
- Using Counts and Averages 100
- Creating a Page Count 102
- Creating Running Totals 107
- Creating Sub-summary Reports 108
- Sorting Data for Sub-summary Reports 110
- Creating Modular Summary Reports 111
- Exporting Summary Data 113

Chapter 6: Creating Relationships — 117
- About Relationships 118
- Creating a Match Field in a Master File 120
- Lookup vs. Related Fields 122
- Using a Match Field to Choose a
  Related Record 125
- Using Calculated Match Fields 126
- Field Formatting with a Calculated
  Match Field 128
- About Repeating vs. Related Fields 131
- About Portals 132
- Sorting Data in Portals 135
- Summarizing Related Data 136
- About Self-Relationships 138
- Using a Portal for Navigation 140
- Searching for Self-Relationship Data 141
- Creating a Lookup with a Self-Relationship 142

Table of Contents

Chapter 7: Creating Simple Scripts   **145**
- Planning a Simple Script 146
- Storing Settings Before Scripting 147
- Using ScriptMaker 150
- Creating a Basic Script 153
- Creating Sub-scripts......................... 156
- Combining Sub-scripts 159
- Retaining Multiple Settings in a Script........ 161
- Extending or Constraining Found Sets
  - in a Script.............................. 164
- Using Sub-scripts for Multiple
  - Export Settings......................... 166
- Adding Comments to a Script................ 168
- Using External Scripts....................... 170
- Using Relative Paths........................ 173

Chapter 8: Working with Conditional Script Steps   **175**
- About Conditional Steps..................... 176
- Using the If Command 177
- Using If with Else 180
- About Status Functions 183
- Using Status Functions with If Steps.......... 185
- Using Loop in a Script....................... 190
- Using Counters to Control Loops.............. 192
- Controlling Scripts with User Input........... 195
- Creating Custom Dialog Boxes 198
- Password Protecting a Script................. 205
- Selecting for FileMaker Versions.............. 211
- Customizing Documents with If Steps 215

Chapter 9: Extending the Interface with Scripts   **227**
- Making a Find Layout with a Script 228
- Creating Script Buttons...................... 232
- Creating Interactive Buttons 234
- Deleting Records in a Related File 235
- Creating a Main Menu Layout................ 237
- Linking to the Main Menu................... 239
- Running Scripts from Fields 240
- Creating Interactive Error Messages 246
- Disabling Toolbars 250

vii

Table of Contents

Chapter 10: Script Troubleshooting — 253
- Testing Finished Scripts 254
- Fixing Typical Errors 256
- Creating an Error Trap Script 261
- Debugging Scripts 270
- Printing Scripts............................. 272
- Changing and Adapting Scripts 274

Chapter 11: FileMaker and Other Programs — 275
- Using Scripts to Send Email.................. 276
- Using Scripts to Send Bulk Email............ 279
- Using a Script to Open URLs................. 283
- Exporting Data to Static HTML Tables........ 285
- Exporting Formatted Text 286
- Using Excel Data in FileMaker 290
- Import from Excel Ranges 292
- Using AppleScript with FileMaker Scripting... 294

Chapter 12: Importing Data — 297
- Migrating to FileMaker 6 298
- Importing Data from Text Sources............ 301
- Batch Importing 307
- Batch-Importing from a Digital Camera (Mac OS X Only)........................ 309
- Importing with Scripts 312
- Setting the Next Auto-Entry Serial Number ... 314
- About FileMaker Mobile..................... 322
- Setting Up or Upgrading FileMaker Mobile.... 323
- Synchronizing from Mobile to Pro 327

Chapter 13: ODBC Import and Export — 331
- About FileMaker's ODBC Functions 332
- Sharing Databases Using ODBC 333
- About Importing ODBC Data 337
- Storing SQL Commands in Fields............. 338
- Using Calculations to Build Complex Queries.. 342
- Creating Dynamic SQL Queries 346

Chapter 14: Data Importing and Repairing — 351
- Cleaning Up Text Data before Importing 352
- Finding and Eliminating Duplicates 354
- Importing Data without Duplications......... 357
- Troubleshooting Problem Data............... 360
- Replacing Inconsistent Formatting 361
- Separating Parts of Data..................... 363

Chapter 15: Multi-User Files on a Network — 369
Setting Network Protocols 370
Setting Up Multi-User Files 372
Hiding Related Files.......................... 373
Creating an Opening Script 374
Restricting Access Privileges 379
Changing Password Access 382
Accessing Databases over the Internet 383
Testing Scripts for Access Problems 385

Chapter 16: Using FileMaker Pro Server — 389
Hosting Files on FileMaker Server 390
Optimizing Server Settings 393
Setting Up a Usage Log....................... 396
Managing Server Remotely 397

Chapter 17: Web Publishing — 401
Instant Web Publishing....................... 402
Configuring Databases for Web Access......... 403
Choosing a Layout Style 405
Suppressing Built-In Navigation in IWP 407
Creating Web Layouts 411
Creating a Web-Based Find Script 414
Switching Layouts with a Script 417
Web Display Considerations 419
Tracking Activity and Access 420
Accessing a File with a Browser 421
Enabling Remote Administration.............. 422
Restricting Database Access 423
Creating a Custom Home Page 424
Creating a Guest Book........................ 426
Testing Your Web Database................... 428
About Custom Web Publishing................ 429
Setting Up Custom Web Publishing............ 430
Creating a Template Format File............... 432
Prompting User Input with CDML............. 434
Providing Visitor Feedback 436
Searching for Data with CDML................ 438
Editing Data with CDML 440
Browsing Records............................ 444
Using the Web Security Database.............. 447
FM Developer's Edition....................... 449

Table of Contents

Chapter 18:	**FileMaker and XML**	**451**
	About XML	452
	Exporting from FileMaker with XML	454
	Importing into FileMaker with XML	456
	FileMaker, XML, and the Web	458
Appendix A:	**FileMaker and Third-Party Software**	**459**
	Web Integration	460
	Fax and Email	460
	Plug-Ins and Utilities	461
	Interface Design	462
Appendix B:	**FileMaker Resources**	**463**
	Mailing Lists	464
	Usenet	464
	Index	**465**

About FileMaker Pro 6

Welcome to the Visual QuickPro Guide to FileMaker Pro 6.

FileMaker is hands-down the simplest database program to pick up and use. You already know this, because you've benefited from its clarity and accessibility. You know and are comfortable with the FileMaker interface and its terminology (like fields, requests, lookups, and relationships). You can input records at lightning speed. You don't need the Help file to create and edit new fields and layouts, or to run effective finds and sorts. But if any of the above sounds like a foreign language to you, put this book down and pick up *FileMaker Pro 6 for Windows and Macintosh: Visual QuickStart Guide* by Nolan Hester, which will give you a solid grounding in the basic features and capabilities of FileMaker 6.

Now that you've been creating useful FileMaker projects, you've reached the point where you've realized that you don't know everything you'd like to know about FileMaker, and database development in general. You could be doing more, and maybe doing it better. We hope this book helps you to break through to the next level of FileMaker mastery. It offers tips, techniques, and examples of little-known features to help you perform remarkably sophisticated database tasks.

FileMaker 6: Highlights of New Features

Since version 5.0, FileMaker upgrades have conspicuously followed two themes: They've made an already-friendly interface cleaner and easier to use, and they've expanded FileMaker's ability to work in different environments and with different types of data. Version 6 continues confidently down these paths.

Because FileMaker Pro 6 uses the same file format as versions 5 and 5.5, you don't have to upgrade databases created in those versions, and multiuser files can be accessed by FileMaker 5, 5.5, or 6 simultaneously. The only caveat is that earlier versions will ignore features like the new script steps in FileMaker Pro 6. To avoid user confusion or database access problems, you may have to customize some scripts if you work in a mixed-version environment. See Chapter 8 for details.

Improved Interface Controls

FileMaker continues to clean up the small irritations that developers have often noted. In this release, more dialog boxes are resizable, particularly those that define relationships, like Lookup. Better yet, FileMaker remembers their shape and position on your desktop, no matter how many times you open and close the application.

And for the first time, FileMaker supports contextual menus in Windows and the Mac. Right-click (Windows) or Control-click (Mac) any object in any view, and a menu with a list of possible actions appears. The options are specific to the View you select. In all cases, this feature is a time-saving convenience because it eliminates the need to use pull-down menus or remember keyboard shortcuts. In one case, it's a true functional improvement. When you're in Browse mode, accessing a contextual menu allows you to sort in ascending or descending order, and by a value list, without having to wade through the Sort dialog box (**Figure 1.1**).

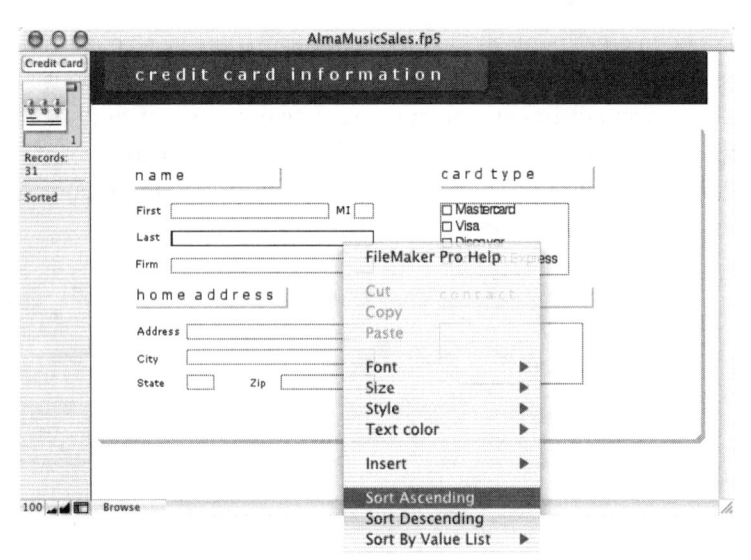

Figure 1.1 It doesn't matter which field you select to access the contextual menus. The Sort Ascending and Descending will always sort by the criteria you previously set in the Sort dialog box.

Figure 1.2 The Find/Replace dialog box allows you to do global search-and-replace tasks in all of your fields and records.

Format Painter

Anything that saves time in the often-laborious process of creating a good layout is welcome. FileMaker makes legions of us happy by adding the Format Painter to Layout View. It allows you to pick up the attributes of one object and clone them onto another object. If you change a label from 12-point Arial in black to 10-point Verdana in white, for example, you can click on one or more other labels and immediately apply the changes to all of them. This new feature is particularly useful for customizing a FileMaker template or for updating older layouts.

Improved Search Functions

For years, you could do sophisticated search-and-replace tasks in Microsoft Office applications from a single, well-formatted dialog box. In FileMaker, global updating and repair of text data was a far more complicated task requiring mastery of calculated fields. With this update, you can use the new Find/Replace dialog box (**Figure 1.2**) to search in one or all records and fields of a database. Changing dates and updating addresses is a breeze.

It's just as important to be able to modify a found set as it is to locate and change data. In previous versions, expanding or narrowing a found set by even one simple criteria took time and some planning, as well as knowledge of a host of search operators. FileMaker 6 brings welcome relief by offering two new menu options, Constrain Found Set and Expand Found Set, that let you adapt your original criteria quickly and painlessly.

Custom Dialog Boxes

The Show Message script step has always allowed a developer to communicate with a database user, but only in the most simplistic way. You had three limited button choices and a line of alert text. The new Show Custom Dialog script step has made Show Message obsolete. Show Custom Dialog includes the Show Message options, but allows you to create a custom dialog box that can include multiple user inputs, both in the dialog box itself and in a database field (**Figure 1.3**). This step allows sophisticated button actions, as well as allowing developers to augment security by creating scripts that will only run if the user has the appropriate password access.

Batch Import

If any one option was on everyone's wish list, it was probably the ability to important multiple data files at one time. This need has grown as more people use FileMaker for Web-based asset management. FileMaker 6 delivers the goods. You can now import a folder containing any single file type that FileMaker recognizes: text, JPEG, GIF, TIFF, even QuickTime files. You can even import files that are inside nested folders. Even better, you can import just the file references instead of full-sized images and movies—perfect for keeping track of visual assets in multiple folders on your disk.

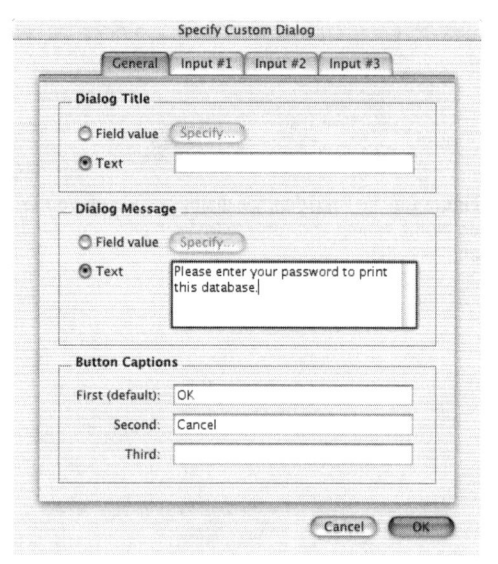

Figure 1.3 The Show Custom Dialog script step allows you to create a script that prompts a user for multiple inputs.

XML Import/Export

The most significant change in FileMaker 6 is its support of XML (Extensible Markup Language). XML is fast becoming one of the most important formats for structuring large, complicated volumes of data, because it offers designers and developers power, scalability, and flexibility. XML allows FileMaker developers to do everything they once did with CDML, and a great deal more. For example, you can import and export text and HTML pages using CSS to and from FileMaker. In addition, because XML is not a proprietary format as CDML is, many devices and applications are already XML-savvy. Opening up FileMaker to XML will make it easier to use FileMaker databases in custom Web applications and to access XML-coded data no matter how it's structured or where it resides.

Improved Web Companion Security

To further its goal of providing secure Web solutions for databases, FileMaker has rethought its Web Companion structure. In the FileMaker 6 folder is a new folder called "cdml_format_files" where you can store all your CDML or XML Web content. (You can still place images and databases wherever you'd like on your hard drive.) Once safely stashed, your coding is hidden from view by any browsers, because Web Companion processes the code before it's sent to a client computer. The code can't be copied, stolen, or even read.

Expanded OS Support

In the previous version, FileMaker earned the Windows 2000 logo–certification, which means that Microsoft certified it as a reliable, completely compatible application that would work flawlessly on both desktop and mobile Windows systems. In FileMaker 6, that logo-certification has been given for Windows XP as well. FileMaker also supports accessibility improvements in Windows XP, particularly the screen readers so necessary for the visually impaired.

Macintosh OS X users will be happy to know that FileMaker has fixed several (though not all) of the limitations they experienced in the prior version, although you'll need to be running at least OS 10.1 to take advantage of the changes. You'll also need to upgrade your system memory...in OS 10.1, FileMaker requires three times the free memory that it does in Windows or the Mac Classic OS. FileMaker 6 is faster and more responsive in OS X than 5.5 was. ODBC (Open Database Connectivity) support has been cleaned up. In 5.5, Macintosh OS X users needed to install a special plug-in to connect to ODBC databases, an extra step that has been eliminated in version 6. In addition, version 6 SQL (Structured Query Language) implementation is now consistent on all platforms. FileMaker has also provided a nice inducement for Mac Classic users who are contemplating moving to OS X. You can now import digital camera images directly into FileMaker, as easily as you can import them into iPhoto. This enhancement is a big time-saver for those of us who use FileMaker to help keep track of our images.

FileMaker Editions

There are four versions of FileMaker: the standard FileMaker Pro 6, the Unlimited version of the standard, FileMaker Server, and the DE (Developer's Edition).

FileMaker Pro 6 and FileMaker Pro 6 Unlimited are identical except for one key feature. The Web Companion in the standard version has a user limit of ten. A user is defined by the computer's IP address, not the user's log-in name, and the limit is in force for a 24-hour period.

FileMaker Server 5.5 is fully compatible with FileMaker version 6. It is a dedicated file server application for multiuser databases. We cover it in depth in Chapter 16. It can host only version 5.0 files and above, not earlier database versions.

FileMaker DE includes a standard version of FileMaker along with some utilities for advanced development work (like a program that can rename files and update all references in other files to the new name). It allows you to create an application-independent version of a FileMaker database. It also includes a vast array of technical information and documentation, particularly on Web integration, XML, and CDML.

Upgrading from pre–FileMaker 5.0 Versions

Upgrading to FileMaker 6 is quite painless. FileMaker automatically detects that a database was created in an earlier version and prompts you through the very short sequence of steps needed to update it. We do, however, have to warn you about two significant problems before you move all your old databases to the new version. First, a newly created database or one transferred from an earlier version of FileMaker Pro to the latest one isn't backward-compatible. That is, an .FM5 file can't be read in an older version and there is no way to resave it in one of the earlier formats. There's no going back. Keep copies of your files in the older format, and don't upgrade to FM6 at all if your database must be accessible on a computer that's not up to FileMaker 6's system requirements.

Second, because the standard FileMaker Pro version has some significant licensing restrictions for Web databases, you may need to choose between FileMaker Pro 6's enhanced usability and direct Web connections, and the limited access it provides. If you're a single user who wants to make your database accessible to a large number of people over the Internet, you should upgrade to the more powerful FileMaker Pro 6 Unlimited.

Using This Book

We hope you're no stranger to Peachpit's Visual QuickStart series. This book shares the QuickStart format, but differs in intent and material. QuickStart guides offer comprehensive feature-by-feature coverage of a software program. In this book we assume that you're familiar with how the program works because you're already using it. We also assume that you're a user who has the potential to become a FileMaker developer, but needs some guidance in making the jump between basic features and hard-core corporate development. Instead of exhaustive coverage of features, we concentrate on the practical ins and outs of situations you might run into while you work.

Because we're covering more complicated information, this book has some tasks that are a little longer than the QuickStart usual. We occasionally use sidebars to give you a little background on a topic, because we believe that when you have background knowledge it's easier to apply general instructions to your specific situation.

Windows and Macintosh

Although we've tended to use a lot of Windows screen shots to illustrate this book, it really doesn't matter what platform you use with FileMaker Pro. Except for an occasional dialog box and a few actions (like saving files and printing) that are different because of the operating system, everything in FileMaker is exactly the same everywhere.

With very few exceptions, any FileMaker Pro database will transfer seamlessly back and forth between the platforms, and can be updated over a network by people working on either type of computer. When one of these exceptions crops up (as they will in a few places) we'll point them out to you so you can be prepared.

Organizing Data Efficiently

To get the most out of any set of data, that data must be organized. Although this seems like an obvious statement, executing it is trickier than may initially appear. For every set of information there are dozens, maybe even multiple dozens of ways that information can be categorized, broken into pieces, and connected. Adding more complexity to the process, more than one of those ways may be the "right" way…depending on your goals. Almost every database can be made cleaner, more flexible, and easier to manipulate. Even if you've been creating FileMaker database files for some time, you can benefit from reexamining your process and structure for ways they can be augmented and improved.

About Relational Databases

FileMaker is a relational database program. That means two important things. First, it's a tool for taking a collection of information items and imposing a formal organization on them. (That's the part that makes it a database program.) All the earliest computer databases shared this characteristic, as, to some degree, do modern spreadsheet programs. Second, FileMaker allows you to fluidly retrieve, add to, and dynamically assemble that information in separate but connected database documents, without having to modify the initial database structure or create duplicate data entries. (That's the relational part.) Relational database programs are more flexible, sophisticated, and powerful than simple flat database programs.

Just because FileMaker allows you to create relational databases doesn't mean that every database you create using FileMaker will take full advantage of these features. In fact, most beginning users of FileMaker understand the database part of its capabilities long before they understand (and effectively use) the relational parts.

Dynamic data

One of the primary principles behind a relational database is that data should never be duplicated. If you create a file with one set of information, you shouldn't need to copy or reenter any of the field entries to create a new file. At most, you need a single duplicated field to act as the place where two sets of information "join." That join is also referred to as a *key field*, a category of unique information that identifies which records in one database refer to a particular record in another database. You can use this key field to display the data from the other database on a layout alongside the data in the first database.

A classic example used by database mavens to illustrate relational databases is a college course registration. Colleges can have thousands of students and hundreds of courses, so it would be really impractical to duplicate all the student information for each course roster. Instead, a course roster is created from a database of students, a database of faculty, and a database of courses. The course roster is the place where these separate entities join, with the course number serving as the field where the connections are made. We'll examine that scenario in greater detail later in this chapter.

Gathering Information

Database design can be enormously gratifying, particularly in its initial creative stages. As a developer, you can be equal parts designer and detective. You get to see information both globally and very specifically, as you speak to individual users and examine broad strategic issues. The decisions you make in structuring data can make an organization more efficient, its staff more comfortable and less frustrated in their work, and in some magical instances, can even lead to tangible business breakthroughs.

Of course, database developers don't always have the luxury of a clean slate. Every living database branches, grows, and can end up in desperate need of pruning—or even uprooting and replacing. Whether you're starting a database from scratch or retrofitting an existing one, the life expectancy of your database will be longer if it begins with careful and logical planning, based on solid research and discovery.

Before you begin to create fields and files, you should know:

- **The goal of the database.** Why is it needed or what problems will it solve? Here's where logic and common sense are most important. You want to create a database structure that provides not only a solution to the immediate problem, but also some room for growth. If there's already some form of database in place, examine how it began and developed. The history of an organization and its data can often provide clues to what the organization's future needs will be.

continues on next page

- **The people who will use the database.** Unless this database is your personal project, others will need to work with the information. What do they want to be able to do with the files? If there's an existing system in place, you should ask people what they would like to change to avoid perpetuating existing problems. Observe users as they work with the data as well. Sometimes people are unaware of how many unnecessary steps they perform, simply because they're so used to the old system that its shortcomings are not apparent to them. Your job is not only to organize data, but to make that data easy to read and access.

- **What information is important.** By using your own knowledge and/or interviewing the users, you should develop a list of required information categories. Within those categories, you will want to create a list of information specifics.

- **How your database will relate to other office systems.** Although some databases remain specialized islands, an organization's database is more likely to relate to several functions and business activities. Will users need to fax or email database information? Will the data be accessible over the Internet? Will the finance department want to use information from sales and marketing?

By examining all the facts and artifacts that show how information moves through the real world, you eventually develop a good concept of what your database will cover and how it will be structured.

Many databases are a replacement for existing systems. Functioning systems always depend on forms, records, and flat files, and so can you. Sometimes the only failing of the current system is that it's not computerized. If so, you can and should ground your structure firmly on a method that people already know. Base your initial categories and field headings on the existing format, then expand by looking for data that isn't yet being captured or presented successfully. For example, an organization may already track sales by individual but not by region. Capturing this information would enable them to have a better sense of the effectiveness of their sales force and their regional sales management.

Even if you're starting from scratch because the organization is new or this is the first attempt at capturing the information, you're probably not really breaking new ground. Others have likely created similar databases before. Ask around to discover what methods are being used in organizations similar to your own. One great source for templates or inspiration is the various sample files available at several FileMaker Internet sites. See Appendix B for specific URLs.

Creating a Field List

Once you have a collection of raw paper data and the input from anyone contributing information or requests you can implement, it's time to determine which major information topics you need to include in the database. In some cases, you'll already know how this information should be organized because you're copying an existing format. If so, you can skip directly to your data structure strategy. Otherwise, you need to list every data topic that might be important.

This sounds like a tall order, and indeed it is. Breaking down the data into its smallest parts is one of the hardest and most critical aspects of creating a good database. All too many files are flawed by a developer's tendency to lose patience or run out of time before breaking out the data sufficiently.

For example, one of the classic database errors is to create a field called Name, and to enter the person's entire name into it instead of breaking the information down into two or three fields (Last Name and First Name/MI or Last Name, First Name, and a separate Middle Initial field). It doesn't take too long before this error comes back to haunt you, because it prevents you from searching and sorting on the last name and denies you all sorts of elegant FileMaker tools for creating form letters. Fixing this error requires a rather complex script (see Chapter 14) and some additional tweaking to clean it up.

Looking at a field list

Although every field list is different, what they all share if done properly is a surprising length. A database can begin with a very limited field list, but as it becomes a tool you depend on, more and more fields get added.

Each time you add a field and enter more data into it, it's harder to be sure that every record contains parallel information and that this information has actually been input into the correct record. If you create a clear, well structured core that begins with all your most important field categories, you and the database users will have less work utilizing it later.

In our college database example, a quick listing of important information would look like this.

Student Last Name	Instructor Teaching Course
Student First Name	Credits per Course
Student Address	Instructor ID
Student City	Instructor Department
State	Instructor Last Name
Zip	Instructor First Name
Year Enrolled	Instructor Address
Birth date	City
Student Major	State
Student ID Number	Zip
Courses Taken	Phone
Credits Accumulated	Date Hired
Student Grades	Courses Taught
Course Numbers	Classes Running
Course Names	IDs of Students in Classes
Course Descriptions	Student Last Names
Course Prerequisites	Student First Names
Dept(s) Offering Course	Grades Earned in Class

Though this is a pretty long list, it still doesn't include everything the college would want to know. Even so, it's more than enough material to break into the categories that will become the actual database structure.

Developing a Data Structure Strategy

The most important part of creating a relational database is determining how you'll organize the data you've listed. The easiest way to visualize the task is to imagine your database as a series of spreadsheets. Each spreadsheet is a logical grouping of fields that belong together. Each individual column heading is a major category of information. Each row is a set of fields with entries in the columns. The column headings become the field headings in your database. Your mission is to match up the right set of column headings for each spreadsheet.

The best way to start this process is to segment the information into categories, and avoid putting too many columns in each category so you don't go crazy working with too many variables at once. Look for modules of information that can be logically grouped (**Figure 2.1**).

Let's continue with the college database. We have a class of data called Students. In the Student table listing, we'd certainly have the student name. But there are so many other pieces of information about the student to consider! The key thing to remember is that, although all this information is important, not all of it belongs in the Student spreadsheet table. For example, the Dean's office

Student Data
Student ID number
Student Last Name
Student First Name
Student Address
Student City
State
Zip
Phone Number
Major
Year Enrolled
Birthdate
High School Graduated
Region/Country
Course Numbers
Course Names
Credits Accumulated
Grade Point Average

Faculty Data
Instructor ID number
Department
Instructor Last Name
Instructor First Name
Instructor Address
City
State
Zip
Phone
Date Hired
Course Numbers
Course Names

Course Data
Course Numbers
Course Names
Course Descriptions
Course Prerequisites
Credits
Department

Class Data
Student ID number
Student Last Name
Student First Name, MI
Student Major
Course Number
Course Name
Credits
Instructor ID number

College Data
Departments
Majors
Course Numbers
Student ID numbers
Instructor ID numbers

Figure 2.1 The original list of possible data has been organized into logical groups.

Organizing Data Efficiently

probably already has a list of majors the college offers, broken out by the department that offers them. The Registrar's office certainly needs a separate database of courses for the student to choose from, as well as prerequisites for each class to prevent students from registering for a course they're not prepared to take. So these types of information are related to students, but aren't part of their primary information.

What does belong? Only the information that will remain intrinsic to the student no matter what happens during his or her college career: ID, birth date, addresses, phone numbers. Course-related information belongs in a different table, grade and credit information might belong in another. It's easier to create a lookup or a relationship between two tables to bring sets of information together than it is to separate information you've crammed together in one table. For example, although you'll need to know the courses students take and their grade point averages, the course information itself should be separate from the student records. The grade point average can be found by creating a calculation and a summary field that links to the database where final class grades are kept (**Figure 2.2**).

Student Data
Student ID number
Student Last Name
Student First Name
Student Address
Student City
State
Zip
Phone Number
Year Enrolled
Birthdate
High School Graduated
Region/Country

Course Numbers
Course Names
Credits Accumulated
Grade Point Average

Course Data
Course Numbers
Course Names
Course Descriptions
Course Prerequisites
Course Section Code
Credits per course
Instructor ID number

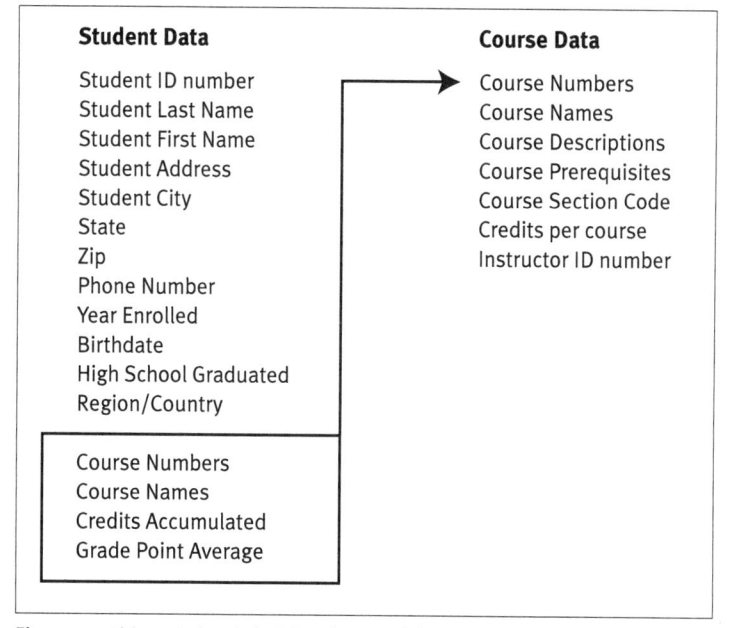

Figure 2.2 Although the circled data is part of the student information, it logically belongs in a separate file in the database.

Chapter 2

Since one student will take many courses, you'll want to create yet another file that contains the Student ID and the Course ID for each course in which the student enrolls. This is known as a "one-to-many" relationship (one student/many courses). In Chapter 6, you will see FileMaker techniques to create such relationships. For example, we could create a portal to list all of the courses for that student in a layout in the Student database, and use a summary of related fields to total the number of credits each student has earned (**Figure 2.3**).

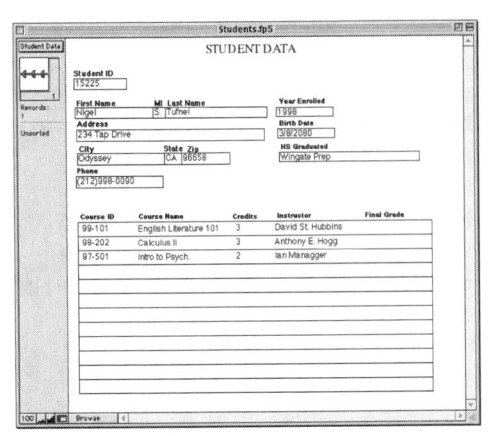

Figure 2.3 The Student Data file has a layout that includes a portal listing all the courses in which the student is currently enrolled.

FIELDS CREATED WITHIN INDIVIDUAL FILES

Student Data	Faculty Data	Course Data	Class Data
Student ID number	*Instructor ID number*	*Course Numbers*	Course Number
Last Name	*Last Name*	*Course Names*	Grades
First Name	First Name	*Credits*	Date
Major	Address	Descriptions	Student ID number
Address	City	Prerequisites	
City	State	Department	
State	Zip	Instructor ID number	
Zip	Phone		
Phone	Date Hired		
Year Enrolled			
Birthdate			
High School			
Region/Country			

FIELDS CREATED WITH LOOKUPS & RELATIONSHIPS

Student Data	Faculty Data	Course Data	Class Data
Course Numbers		Instructor Last Name	Course Name
Course Names			Student Last Name
Credits Accumulated			Student First Name
Grade Point Average			Student Major
			Instructor ID number
			Instructor Last Name
			Credits

Figure 2.4 No fields should have to be input twice in a well-designed database. The fields in italics will appear in other databases by setting up relationships or using lookups.

Creating a
Data Structure Chart

In our college database example, we've progressed through information gathering and categorizing data into fields, and have assigned the fields to categories that will be separate files in the database. Now we need to figure out what relationships each file should have to each of the other files in the database. The best way to visualize the relationships is to create a series of charts that represent the individual categories of information, then determine the relationship these groups should have to each other.

We have several files that will have a variety of relationships. The main ones are Students, Faculty, Courses, and Classes:

- **Students:** Contains the data related to each individual student. Except for grade-related information, this data should remain relatively static once it is input.

- **Courses:** Contains the data related to each course offered. Course information changes infrequently, so this is also a fairly stable file.

- **Faculty:** Contains the data related to each member of the faculty. Faculty can be added or deleted but, like the student and course files, will not change on a regular basis.

- **Classes:** Contains a list of running courses, along with the list of students taking them and the instructor who teaches each course. This list changes every semester and requires a separate record for each class taken by every student.

Note that we have begun to divide our list into fields that will contain records in the individual databases and fields that will depend on lookups or relationships to other databases. All of our duplications are here, as well as those fields that are unique but depend on data from other files—like the students' grade point averages and their accumulated credits, which will be calculated from their class data (**Figure 2.4**). We can use these organized field charts as blueprints for creating our database fields.

Field Design Tactics

The final step before moving to FileMaker and creating your database files is determining the fine points of your fields and relationships. A good strategy can be undermined by errors in tactical details—those important decisions that lead to a FileMaker implementation that's clear, flexible, and scalable.

Identifying key fields

Not all data is created equal. Certain types of information will be needed almost everywhere, while other types will rarely appear. Column headings that appear in multiple spreadsheet tables are good candidates for database key fields.

For example, in our imagined university database, a student's name or ID number will appear in many places: on the course roster, on the student's grade listing at the end of the term, and on the bursar's office listing of course payments. On the other hand, the student's phone number, while important in some situations, will hardly ever be needed outside the Student file listing itself. The name or ID number are good candidates for use as key fields; the phone number, which could easily change and is less useful, would not make a good key field. In your own database, you should always look for the most stable data to use as an identifier.

Choosing unique key fields

In our example, we've noticed that both the students' names and their ID numbers appear on multiple forms. They aren't, however, equally good candidates for use as a key field. For one thing, which part of the student name would you use? You certainly couldn't use the last name alone. Even first and last names are likely to be repeated.

Adding a middle initial can help, but any large college or university will have some duplications even using all three pieces. So, despite the constant recurrence of this information, it's not unique. The ID number, on the other hand, although not the first column in any spreadsheet list, is the only portion of the student data that can't be duplicated by any other student record. We use the same reasoning to choose our unique key fields for the other files in our database (**Figure 2.5**).

✔ Tip

- If a person's Social Security number is available, it is an ideal key field since only one person can have that number. To minimize input errors, always make sure that you specify the Social Security field as text, rather than number.

Organizing Data Efficiently

Student Data	Faculty Data	Course Data	Class Data
■ *Student ID number*	▲ *Instructor ID number*	● *Course Numbers*	● *Course Number*
Last Name	Last Name	Course Names	Grades
First Name	First Name	Credits	Date
Major	Address	Descriptions	Course Name
Address	City	Prerequisites	■ *Student ID number*
City	State	Department	Student Last Name
State	Zip	▲ *Instructor ID number*	Student First Name, MI
Zip	Phone		Student Major
Phone	Date Hired		Instructor ID number
Year Enrolled	Course Numbers		Instructor Last Name
Birthdate	Course Names		Credits
High School			
Region/Country			
Course Numbers			
Course Names			
Credits Accumulated			
Grade Point Average			

Figure 2.5 The key fields for each database are marked in this chart. The symbols identify which set of files will be connected by their key fields.

FIELD DESIGN TACTICS

19

Using global fields

Most database fields have different information for every record. Global fields, on the other hand, always contain the same information no matter which record or layout you are viewing. As you will see in Chapter 3, global fields are the best way to insert universal container data, like form letter text and graphic elements (logos, signatures, or special symbols). They're also the way to hold the information needed for data variables in calculations and scripts. As you examine your flowcharts, look for unchanging data elements that you can place into global fields.

In our college example, the school logo or a boilerplate affirmative action text disclaimer would do well as global fields. If you plan to create scripts that will require a loop counter, a global field would serve this purpose nicely.

✔ Tip

- Even if you don't have an immediate need for a global field, you can create one (or more) and hold it in reserve. This may save both time and inconvenience later, since FileMaker doesn't allow you to create new fields when multiple users are actively accessing a file. The same logic can apply to any types of fields, whether they be text, number, or container.

Using repeating fields

Generally speaking, you shouldn't. Whenever possible, build your database by creating relationships between files, and list your multiple entries in a portal. Repeating fields in FileMaker are leftovers from when it was a flat file database, not a relational one. Because repeating fields can contain multiple entries in the same field, they are fairly inflexible, can't be used in a relationship, and don't work well in calculations.

In Chapter 6, we examine some of the few instances when a repeating field can be useful.

✔ Tip

- One of the first things that you should notice in your field list is that some categories are duplicated, sometimes in more than one place. Once you've built the skeleton for one database (the simpler one, like the Faculty database in our example), you can copy the file, rename it, and update the field names for other similar files (like the Student file in our example). Then you can continue by adding the extra fields and relationships the second file requires.

Tracking fields

Depending on how active your database is and how many people use it, you might want to create fields that track the date and time changes to it were made. Creation and modification fields (created with Auto-Enter options), although not part of the data structure per se, can be invaluable tools for tracking records, as can a field that automatically enters the name of the database user who input or modified the record. In your courses and classes database, for example, you might have a kiosk-type setup with your database set to Entry Only so students could register themselves for classes. By time- and date-stamping these entries it would be easy to determine which students should be given precedence for a seat in a class with limited enrollment.

Implementing Relationships

When you created your flowchart of relationships, you outlined the most obvious places where the data in individual files would intersect. When it comes to implementing these relationships, you need to consider not just what the relationships will be, but how you want to express them in layouts and where you want them to join.

Thinking ahead about sorting and searching

When planning your database, you should be thinking about which pieces of information will be used to find certain records and which may be used to sort data. Then you can make sure that those pieces of data are in separate fields.

For example, you will probably want to sort and search using such criteria as Last Name (for alphabetical listings) or Zip (for mailings). That is why it is critical that these sets of data be in separate fields, and not combined with the first name or the city and state.

Another useful field is one listing the high school that a student graduated from, because you can generate reports that let you track them as alumni later. These fields should be included from the outset, so that you don't have to go back and laboriously enter the data later.

✔ Tip

- If you don't want your finds and sorts to take forever, look at your data relationships for likely search combinations before you break data into different files. Indexing is the key to a speedy search. Fields that are in portals can't be indexed, so FileMaker will take a lot longer to locate this related information.

Using key fields and relationships

Once the databases are created, you need to establish the relationships among them. In this example, we noticed early on that the Class data contained very little unique information. Therefore, it will have two main relationships: to the Student database (using the Student ID as the key field), and to the Course ID. The bulk of the data found in the Class database will be a result of lookups from the other related files. (The link to the Faculty database is indirect, since the Instructor ID field in Courses can be used to connect faculty information to the Class database.)

The Student ID will look up the rest of the student information and copy it into the class roster. At the end of the class, grades and credits earned will flow back to the Student database so that you can list which courses a student has taken, and summarize how many credits have accumulated. When you enter the Course ID in the Class database, the Course ID relationship will copy the course information (name, description, and credits) into the lookup fields (**Figure 2.6**).

Using lookups vs. relating data

By definition, building a relational database is based on the idea of using related data. Ordinarily, relating data is a much better strategy than relying on lookups, even though lookups are initially easier to create on the fly. One major problem with lookups is that they defeat one of the main purposes of a relational database, which is to avoid duplication of effort. Because you copy information from one file to another in a lookup, you freeze that data in the second file. Unless you update your lookup each time you change the original file (and we can hardly think of a worse waste of time), it's not long before the information is incomplete, flawed, and ultimately useless.

Despite these negatives, there are a few situations where you should plan to relate data using lookups. When a database entry needs to display related information that shouldn't be constantly updated, lookups are perfect. In our college example, once a course roster has been completed and the time period during which a student can drop or add a course elapses, data from the roster should become part of the student's historical information. That's why the Classes database is important: It combines selected student, course, and instructor information. When you create a new record in this database, the student ID number and course number are entered. By using a lookup from the Courses database to the Classes database for information like the instructor name and course credits, you have an archive from the time that the student took the course.

Testing Your Database

Now that you've divided your information into databases, figured out which fields belong in which files, and strategized the relationships and lookups, you're finally ready to create the FileMaker files themselves. Resist the temptation to think that your project is done. Once you have the architecture of the database set up, don't forget to test your decisions with some representative users before your structure is set in stone. You may discover that, although your structure makes perfect logical sense, it works at cross-purposes to some person's established workflow. Listen carefully to feedback, even if it means reconsidering some aspect of your structure. No matter how experienced you are, you always have something to learn from the people who will work with your creation every day.

Organizing Data Efficiently

Student Data

    Student ID number
    Last Name
    First Name, MI
    Major
Address
City
State
Zip
Phone
Year Enrolled
Birthdate
High School
Region/Country
    Grades
    Credits

Class Data

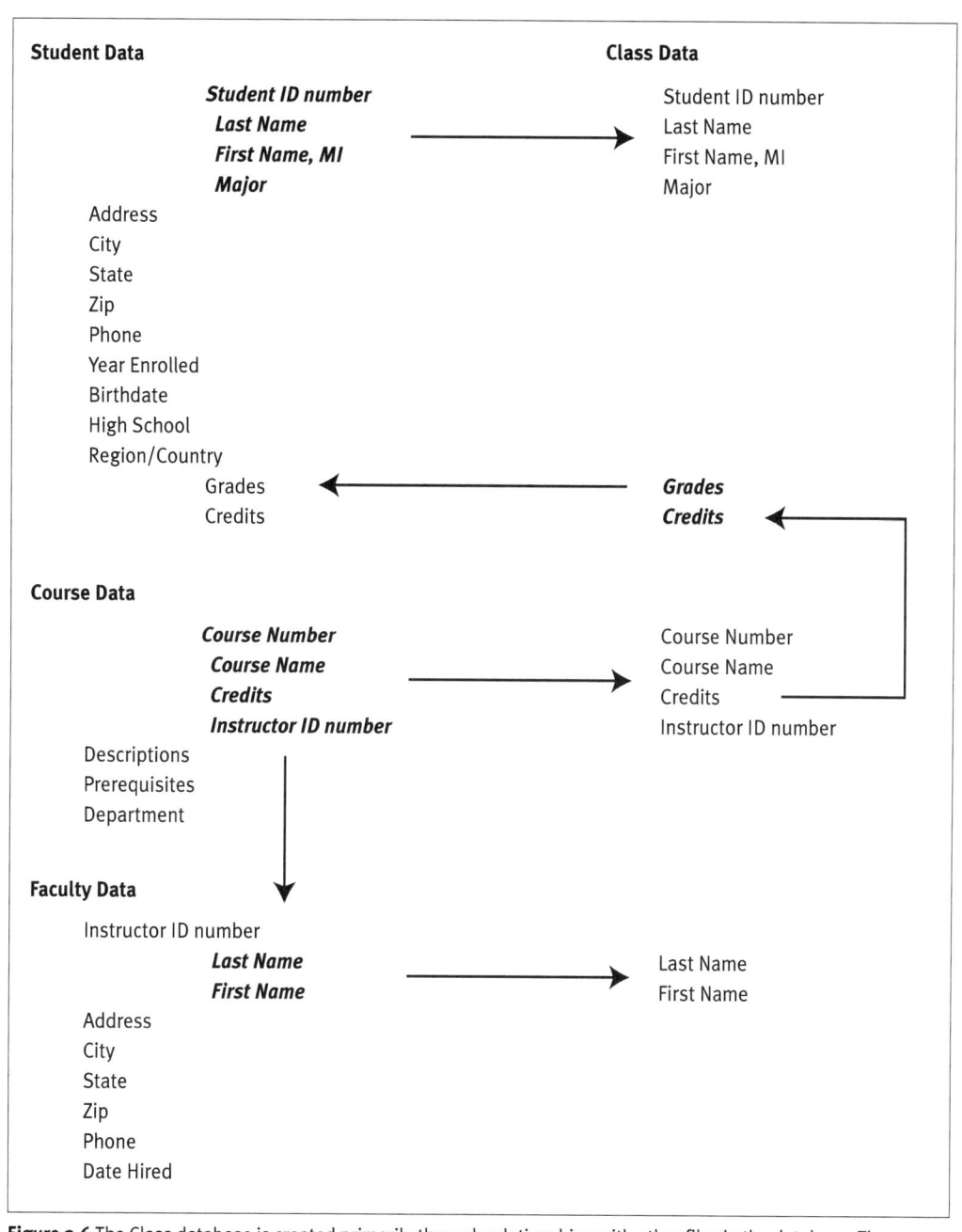

Student ID number
Last Name
First Name, MI
Major

Grades
Credits

Course Data

    Course Number
    Course Name
    Credits
    Instructor ID number
Descriptions
Prerequisites
Department

Course Number
Course Name
Credits
Instructor ID number

Faculty Data

Instructor ID number
    Last Name
    First Name
Address
City
State
Zip
Phone
Date Hired

Last Name
First Name

Figure 2.6 The Class database is created primarily through relationships with other files in the database. The arrows indicate the flow of information as lookups copy data to and from the Class database.

Layout Enhancements

FileMaker layouts are the connection between you, the database developer, and the users who will actually work with the database you've designed. An elegantly designed database with awkward layouts will lead to input errors that eat away at efficient use. Such a database can actually be less useful than the efforts of a beginner whose layouts are clear and carefully created. In this chapter, we'll explore several tools like pop-up lists and check boxes that facilitate data entry and viewing, as well as advanced techniques to help create properly constructed layouts, speed up data entry, eliminate entry errors, clarify the meaning of the data, and make the data easier to read.

Usability, Legibility, and Logical Grouping

Although a database developer doesn't have to be a graphic designer, it doesn't hurt to know a little bit about how people read and use information. When planning your layouts, consider how they can be optimized to avoid confusion. A few minutes of extra work on your part can save database users hours of frustration.

If you've planned your database with care, you've examined existing business forms and talked with people to find out how they use them. Once you've figured out what type of information you need to cover in a database, spend some time considering how that information should be visually arranged. For data-entry layouts especially, your field arrangement can be critical. Group fields of similar or sequential information together. Whenever possible, arrange fields to match the order of the raw material from which people using the database will work. If you don't, the data inputter is certain to miss or transpose information. For example, if a sales department uses contact sheets that provide phone numbers in the order voice, fax, then mobile, the layout you create should too.

People using the Latin alphabet read from left to right and top to bottom. If you need to create a layout with fields broken into two columns, separate the columns widely if the flow of information will fill one column before moving to the next. The opposite is true if your tab order will move left to right, then top to bottom (**Figure 3.1**).

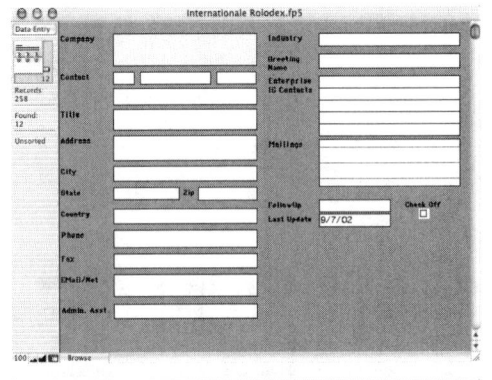

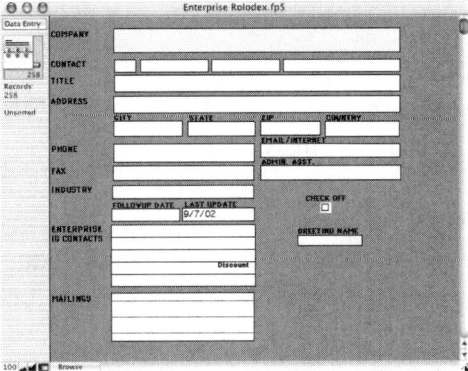

Figure 3.1 These layouts contain essentially the same fields, but differ in how their data will be added. In the top layout, information fills the left column, then moves to the right. The bottom layout moves left to right, then down line by line.

Layout Enhancements

Although FileMaker Pro gives you the useful option of changing the tab order of fields in a layout, use this feature wisely. People take breaks in the tedium of inputting, and it's much easier for them to lose their place in a layout whose tabs jump around the page.

If you've made several types of layouts and reports for a database, it's always a good idea to provide a menu of buttons linked with scripts to each of the layouts and reports. Just as you would in organizing fields, group similar types of button actions together, and provide headings for the groups to make it easy to recognize their functions (**Figure 3.2**). Organizing the main menu like this makes it easier to train new people and speeds up information processing even for accomplished users. We explore menu and button options in Chapter 9, "Extending the Interface with Scripts."

✔ Tip

- Avoid typing labels and other important information in all capital letters. Not only do they take up more space, but they're much harder to read than labels in upper- and lowercase, particularly if the labels are fairly close together (**Figure 3.3**).

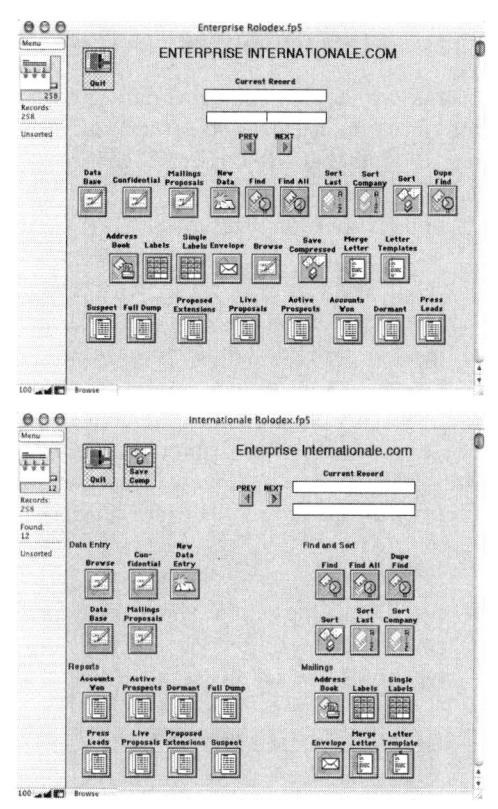

Figure 3.2 In the bottom main menu layout, reports and functions are organized by function. Use the Arrange > Set Alignment command to help you lay out your groupings on a menu page.

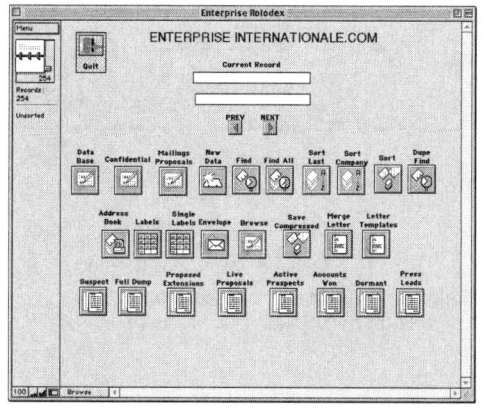

Figure 3.3 It takes people longer to recognize letterforms when they're all capital letters.

USABILITY, LEGIBILITY, AND LOGICAL GROUPING

27

Cross-Platform Issues

Since FileMaker Pro is a multiplatform and multiuser program, the same database may be running simultaneously on both Macintosh and Windows machines. A layout created on a Macintosh will look similar on a Windows machine, but some aspects, like fonts and colors, are displayed with slight variations. To make sure that people on both types of computers will be able to view and work comfortably with the database, you should consider screen sizes, font usage, and layout colors and graphics in designing a cross-platform database.

Although both the Macintosh OS 8.1 and newer and Windows 95 and newer operating systems support longer file names, a surprising number of people continue to work with older computers and operating systems. In order to assure compatibility across platforms, file names should adhere to the DOS/Windows 8.3 format, which limits a file name to only eight alphanumeric characters (no punctuation or spaces), and doesn't recognize any difference between capital and lowercase letters. Macintosh users must also add a file extension to the file name in order for the file or database to be recognized as valid on a Windows computer (**Figure 3.4**). If you don't follow this naming convention you may have to change the file name later on. Renaming a file can have serious consequences. Any relationships, scripts, and portals you've created with the old name will have to be re-created using the new one.

Cross-Platform Fonts

To ensure that your FileMaker database will read nicely on machines other than your own, use the fonts that are standard on most computers. Standardizing allows you to create a dependable look for your database no matter where it's running, and saves you the extra work and aggravation of having to change the fonts later. If you absolutely need to use fonts other than the standards, make sure that these fonts are installed on every machine that will use your database. If the font you use is not available on a computer running your database, another font will be substituted by the system software (see sidebar).

✔ Tip

- Avoid using the Outline and Shadow font styles available on the Macintosh. These type styles have no equivalent in Windows.

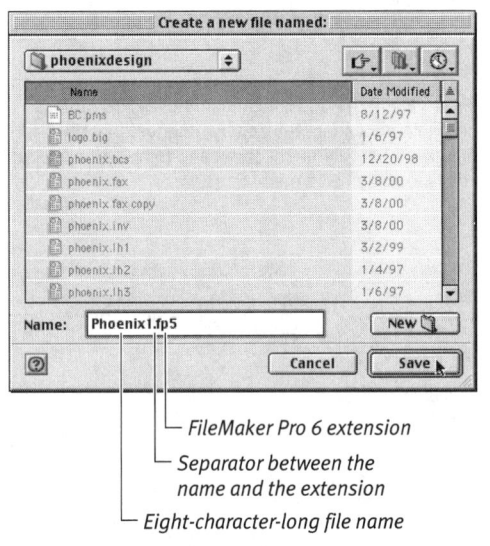

FileMaker Pro 6 extension
Separator between the name and the extension
Eight-character-long file name

Figure 3.4 This is the correct format for naming a cross-platform FileMaker Pro 6 database.

Layout Enhancements

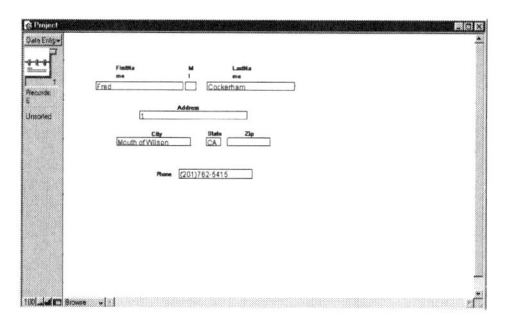

Figure 3.5 Text blocks created on a Macintosh may be displayed incorrectly in Windows if they use a typeface that isn't stored in the user's system.

Even when you use the standard fonts, some differences between Mac and Windows will still be obvious on-screen. Fonts are displayed somewhat larger in Windows than on the Mac. This means that the descenders (lower parts of the letters like *g* and *q*) and the first and last letters of a text block or field may be cut off (**Figure 3.5**). If you make your fields and text blocks slightly longer and higher you can avoid this problem. Setting text blocks (like field labels and other layout text) to Center alignment will also help avoid display problems, although that often makes for a less attractive print document. If the appearance of your output is important to you or your users, you should create two versions of your layouts—one for each operating system.

Font Equivalents

Every Windows or Macintosh operating system installs some basic fonts in its system folder. Some of them are only meant to be used in menus or for screen display. These are called system fonts. It's a bad idea to use system fonts (like the Mac's Geneva) in a cross-platform database because they have no equivalent font on the other side. Besides system fonts, each platform also includes some typefaces that are meant for print output. These fonts have equivalents that FileMaker will automatically substitute when the database is viewed on the other platform. These equivalents are:

Macintosh Fonts	**Windows Fonts**
Helvetica	Arial
Times	Times New Roman
Monaco	Courier
Courier	Courier

If you're working on a Macintosh but are creating a cross-platform database, you should install Microsoft TrueType fonts (downloadable from www.microsoft.com) and use Arial and Times New Roman to build your database rather than Helvetica and Times. Although FileMaker Pro will automatically substitute Arial for Helvetica, the two fonts just aren't the same. Labels you created in Helvetica will run longer in Arial, and your nicely designed layouts and letter text will become a patchwork of badly broken lines.

CROSS-PLATFORM ISSUES

29

Cross-Platform Colors

You will use colors in FileMaker layouts to shade the background of a layout or to highlight or contrast fields against the background. If the computers running your database can display 16,000 or more colors, the colors you use will appear essentially the same across platforms. Windows will render colors slightly darker than a Macintosh does, and colors chosen in Windows will appear lighter and slightly washed-out on a Mac. Simply avoid using the darkest and lightest shades in the color palette to get around this problem.

To use your database on older computers whose video capabilities are limited to 256 colors or to ensure color compatibility across platforms, set the color preference to the Web "color-safe" palette of 216 colors.

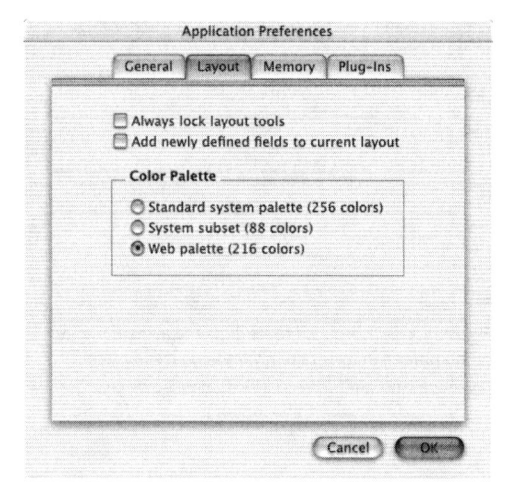

Figure 3.6 All cross-platform databases should have their document preferences set to "Web palette" to prevent using an unpredictable color by mistake.

To set the Color Palette:

1. Choose Edit > Preferences > Application (FileMaker Pro > Preferences > Application in Mac OS X).

2. When the Application Preferences dialog box appears, click the Layout tab.

3. Select "Web palette (216 colors)" in the Color Palette box (**Figure 3.6**) and click OK to close the dialog box.

✔ Tip

- Although it is possible to add custom colors to FileMaker, doing so increases the file size and slows the display redraw. As a rule, it's a bad idea.

Using Format Painter

Figure 3.7 The Format Painter will copy the formatting of a selected field to any other field.

Figure 3.8 Clicking the Web Address field applies the formatting from the Serial Key field to it.

FileMaker 6 provides a wonderful tool that copies the format of one layout element to one or many others. If you've created text with a particular format, you can apply that formatting to other text blocks (or fields). Not only is this tool a time-saver in creating new layouts, it's a winner for layouts that weren't originally designed for cross-platform uses. Change one instance of an object or piece of text to your desired cross-platform color or font, and you're a few clicks away from reconfiguring all the layouts in a database.

Format Painter copies different formatting depending on the element you chose:

◆ **Text:** Font, size, alignment, color

◆ **Fields:** Font, size, alignment, border thickness, fill pattern and color

◆ **Graphics:** Fill pattern and color, line thickness

✔ Tip

■ You can copy formatting from a part to a field, but you can't copy formatting from a field to a part.

This otherwise terrific new tool has only one unhappy feature. The Mac OS X version of FileMaker doesn't support toolbars, which means you can't double-click the icon to lock Format Painter for multiple uses. Fortunately, there's a work-around that keeps Format Painter locked each time you use it.

To copy a format to another element:

1. Choose View > Layout Mode (Control+L in Windows, Command+L on the Mac).

2. Click the element whose formatting you want to copy.

3. Choose Format > Format Painter or click the Format Painter tool (**Figure 3.7**).

4. Click the element to which you want to copy the format (**Figure 3.8**).

Chapter 3

To copy a format to multiple elements (not Mac OS X):

1. Choose View > Layout Mode (Control+L/Command+L).

2. Click the element whose formatting you want to copy.

3. Double-click the Format Painter tool to lock it (**Figure 3.9**).

4. Click the elements to which you want to copy the format.

5. When you're finished changing the formats, click a layout tool or press the Esc key.

To lock Format Painter in Mac OS X:

1. Choose FileMaker Pro > Preferences > Application (**Figure 3.10**).

2. When the Application Preferences dialog box appears, click the Layout tab.

3. Click the "Always lock layout tools" check box, then click OK (**Figure 3.11**).

When you use Format Painter, remember to click a layout tool or press the Esc key when you no longer want to copy formatting.

Figure 3.9 Once you click the Format Painter, it stays locked until you click a different tool.

Figure 3.10 Access the Preferences from the FileMaker Pro menu in OS X.

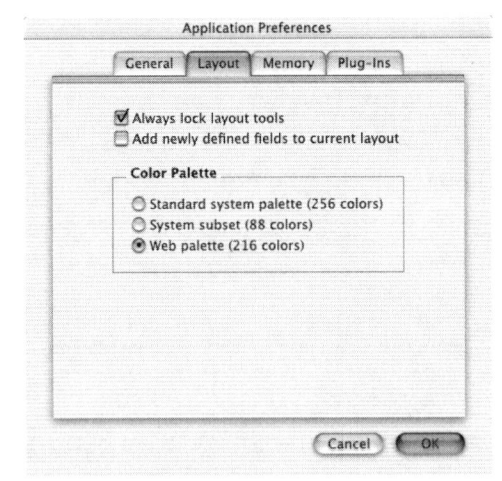

Figure 3.11 Select this preference, so that once you choose Format Painter it will always be locked until you choose a different tool.

Using Graphic Text

One method for displaying non-standard fonts in a layout is to create the text in a paint program. The text can be pasted into your layout as a graphic and will be displayed identically on any computer. This isn't a very efficient way to work if you have lots of text, but it's just fine for logo type or other graphics.

There are three ways to bring over graphic type—one for type you create yourself, another for inserting a graphic provided by someone else, and a third for when you don't want the graphic shape to be editable in the layout. This last option, which relies on a container field, is particularly useful if you're dealing with a logo that must look exactly as it was designed. Copied or inserted graphics are all too easy to stretch and compress without your realizing it. Graphics placed in a container field stay put.

To copy a graphic from a paint program into a layout:

1. Open your graphics program and create your type or open the document that already contains it.
2. Select the graphic, then copy it to the Clipboard (Control+C/Command+C).
3. Return to FileMaker and switch to Layout mode (Control+L/Command+L). Paste the graphic onto the layout (Control+V/Command+V).

✔ Tip

- If you'll need to print the logo or graphic text, create the original art at a print resolution of at least 300 dpi. Otherwise the outlines of your text or logo will look jagged and rough on paper.

Chapter 3

To import graphic text from a file:

1. Switch to Layout mode (Control+L/Command+L).

2. Choose Insert > Picture.

3. Navigate to the graphics file you want to insert. Once you find it, click Open.

   Your graphic will appear as a free-floating box. You can move or scale it like any other layout object.

To import uneditable graphic text:

1. Make sure you already have a graphic saved in one of the formats FileMaker can import, then go to the layout where you plan to add the graphic. Choose File > Define Fields (Control+Shift+D/Command+Shift+D).

2. When the Define Fields dialog box appears, type the name of your new field into the Field Name text box.

3. In the Type area of the dialog box, select the Container radio button, then click Create (**Figure 3.12**). The new field is added to the field list. Click Done.

4. Switch to Layout mode (Control+L/Command+L). From the layout tools on the left, choose Field and drag the field to its new position.

5. From the Specify Field dialog box that appears (**Figure 3.13**), choose the name of the container field you just created, uncheck the "Create field label" check box, and click OK.

6. Resize the field box to fit the graphic you'll be placing there.

7. Switch to Browse mode (Control+B/Command+B). Select the container field in your layout.

Figure 3.12 To place an uneditable graphic into a layout, create a new field, select Container as the field type, and click Create.

Figure 3.13 Uncheck "Create field label" when you put the field in your layout to avoid having a label on your graphic.

USING GRAPHIC TEXT

34

Layout Enhancements

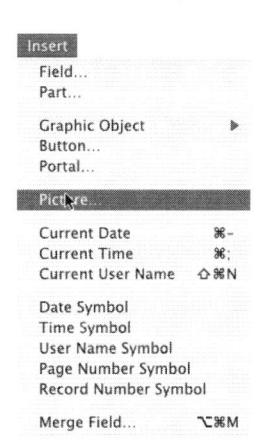

Figure 3.14 To place a graphic into a container field choose Insert > Picture.

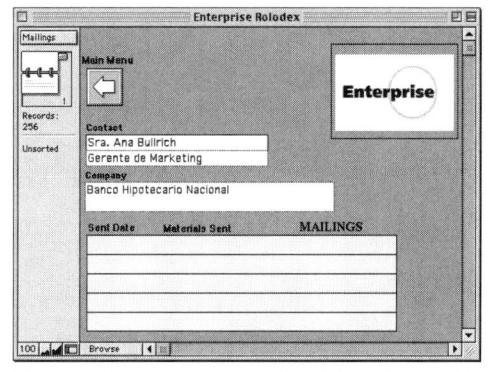

Figure 3.15 When you use Insert > Picture, the graphic is positioned in the center of the container.

8. Choose Insert > Picture (**Figure 3.14**) and navigate to the graphics file you want to insert. Once you find it, click Open. The graphic will be positioned in the center of your container field (**Figure 3.15**). If you don't like its position, return to Layout mode and move or resize the container field.

The text will now be a graphic in your layout. Keep in mind that the letters aren't really text. You can't edit or change them, except by returning to the graphics program.

✔ Tip

- If you're working in Classic on a Macintosh with FileMaker Pro 6 and use the Insert > Picture command, you may receive an error dialog box that says "Error −2804 occurred during initialization of Claris XTND system." If this message appears, you won't be able to insert graphics in FileMaker fields. This can happen if you (or a software installation program) turned off the XTND Power Enabler in the Extensions folder. FileMaker needs this Macintosh extension to process graphics in container fields. Just go the Extensions Manager, turn the extension back on, restart your machine, and try again. Your graphic should appear without a problem.

USING GRAPHIC TEXT

35

Chapter 3

Formatting Elements as Buttons

FileMaker's Button tool allows you to create a simple rectangular button and assign a command to it. But virtually any item in a layout can be formatted as a button (including fields). Creating a recognizable graphic for a custom button can help you quickly identify what the button does (**Figure 3.16**).

To use a graphic as a button:

1. Go to the layout where you'd like to place a button. Go to Layout mode (Control+L/Command+L). Follow the instructions in "To import graphic text from a file" on page 34 for copying or inserting a graphic in Layout mode.

2. Select the graphic you've copied or inserted into your layout, and choose Format > Button (**Figure 3.17**).

3. When the Specify Button dialog box appears, choose the command in the list that you wish to assign to the button, then click OK.

✓ Tip

- When you choose a command for your button, the Options box on the right will display check boxes or a drop-down list (**Figure 3.18**) if there are more choices for you to make. Otherwise, the Options area will be blank.

Figure 3.16 This button makes it clear that you'll leave the FileMaker program if you click it.

Figure 3.17 To make any graphic into a button, choose Format > Button.

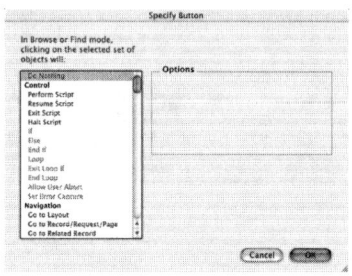

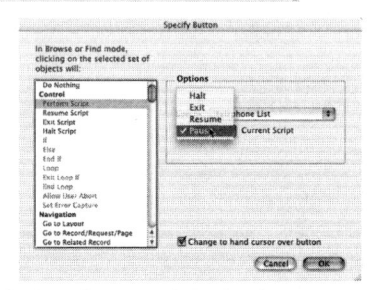

Figure 3.18 The Specify Button dialog box has a scrolling list of button actions, and can offer various options depending on the action chosen.

Layout Enhancements

Figure 3.19 Selecting Go to Layout from the command list brings up a drop-down list of all the layouts in your current database.

Figure 3.20 To switch to an individual record from a columnar layout, make one of the fields a button, then click on the field in Browse mode to go to the individual record.

One of the most helpful interface enhancements allows you to use a field as a button. If you make the Name field a button that switches to an individual record layout, you can click a name and be switched directly to the details layout.

To make a field into a button:

1. Go to the layout to which you'd like to add a field button, and enter Layout mode (Control+L/Command+L).

2. Click the field you want to make into a button.

3. Choose Format > Button.

4. When the Specify Button dialog box appears, click Go to Layout (**Figure 3.19**) in the Navigation section of the scrolling list.

5. From the drop-down list in the Options section, choose the layout to which you want to switch, then click OK.

   When you click the field button in Browse mode, the layout will switch and the data for the record you clicked will be displayed (**Figure 3.20**).

✔ Tips

- When a field is formatted as a button, you can't edit its contents by just selecting the field. If you want to be able to edit the field when you click it, you'll need to make that option part of a script you assign to the button. See Chapter 9 for more about attaching scripts to buttons.

- If you would like to use some FileMaker graphics without having to create your own, refer to Appendix A for information about commercially available button sets.

FORMATTING ELEMENTS AS BUTTONS

Reusing Graphics

If you need to use the same graphic in multiple layouts, the most convenient approach is to create a global field as a container. You can then use the graphic in any layout in the database.

To create a global container field:

1. Choose File > Define Fields (Control+Shift+D/Command+Shift+D).

2. When the Define Fields dialog box appears (**Figure 3.21**), name the field and choose the Global radio button from the Type section. Click Create.

3. When the Options dialog box appears, choose Container from the "Data type" drop-down menu (**Figure 3.22**). Click OK, then click Done.

4. Switch to Layout Mode (Control+L/Command+L), then switch to the layout where the container field will be displayed.

5. From the layout tools, choose Field and drag the field to its new position.

Figure 3.21 To make a global container field, be sure to choose Global as your field type, not Container.

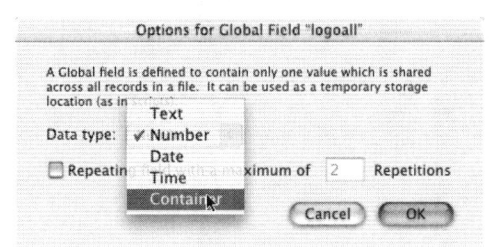

Figure 3.22 When you create a global field, FileMaker will ask you to choose the field data type.

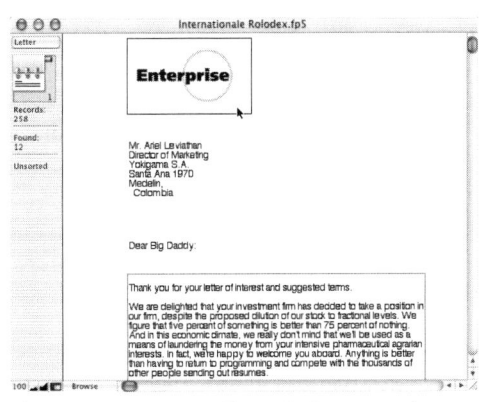

Figure 3.23 Use Insert > Picture in Browse mode to place a graphic into a global container field.

6. In the Specify Field dialog box that appears, choose the name of the global container field you just created and click OK. Resize the field box to fit the graphic you'll be placing there.

7. Change to Browse mode (Control+B/Command+B). Select the container field in your layout.

8. Choose Insert > Picture, and navigate to the graphics file you want to insert. Once you find it, click Open.

The field now contains the graphic. Since it's a global field, it will display and print the same graphic in every record (**Figure 3.23**).

✔ Tip

- If you've created a very clever FileMaker database, you may want to reuse it for other projects. If you choose File > Save a Copy As and choose Clone > No Data, you'll have a fresh copy of your database that you can rename. If you copy that clone to the FileMaker templates Folder (in the same folder as the FileMaker application) it will show up in the templates list when you choose File > New Database.

Chapter 3

Entering Data in a Standard Layout

Although you or someone else will have to type in most of the data for a FileMaker database, there a few ways to streamline the process. Not only will these shortcuts speed up data entry, but they will also help eliminate typing errors. Two of the most useful shortcuts are the Insert > From Index command and the value list.

To use Insert From Index, you'll first need a field whose options have been set to index its records. When you set a field to be indexed, FileMaker keeps track of the data every time you add a record to the field. Then, when you search for data, it checks the index rather than looking up the records themselves.

Indexing is a time-saving device, but it can have one little downside. Because an index file may contain a lot of data, if you're running FileMaker on a computer with a small hard drive you could run into space problems. If you have lots of storage space to burn, use the indexing function with confidence, because the search time it saves you definitely makes it worthwhile.

The Insert From Index command lets you access the index file directly. You can choose from a list of all entries that have already been entered into a specific field and paste the entry you want directly into the field. You can use this command to verify that your input is phrased identically to other records, and to decrease the trailing or initial spaces that can confuse an alphabetical sort. Insert From Index is particularly useful when using the Find mode to search for data, since by definition the data you're searching for already exists in that field.

To index an existing field:

1. Go to File > Define Fields.

2. In the Define Fields dialog box that appears, click the field name that you'd like to index and click Options (**Figure 3.24**).

3. When the Options dialog box appears, click the Storage tab (**Figure 3.25**).

Figure 3.24 Choose Options to access the indexing options for a field.

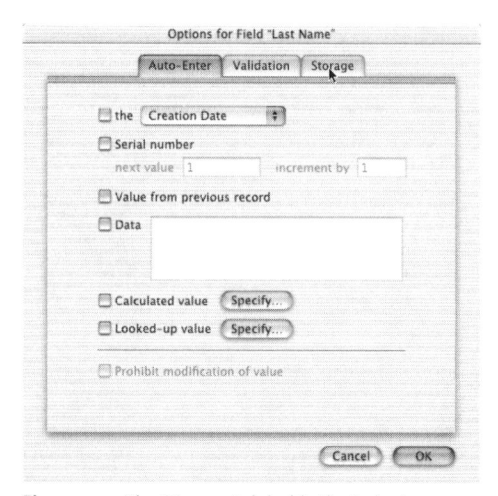

Figure 3.25 The Storage tab holds the indexing options.

Layout Enhancements

Figure 3.26 Choose On to start indexing a field.

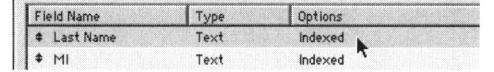

Figure 3.27 The field's options automatically update to show that the field is indexed.

Figure 3.28 To search for an existing entry without having to type it into a field, use Insert > From Index.

4. In the Indexing section of the Storage panel, click the On radio button, then click OK (**Figure 3.26**).

5. The field list will update to show that the field is now indexed (**Figure 3.27**). Click Done to close the Define Fields dialog box.

To paste an entry from the index:

1. Make sure you're in Find mode (Control+F/Command+F). Click inside the data entry field that you want, then choose Insert > From Index (Control+I/Command+I; **Figure 3.28**).

2. A list of each entry already made in that field will appear (**Figure 3.29**).

3. Double-click the desired entry to insert it into the data entry field.

Figure 3.29 Only entries appropriate to the field you've chosen will appear in the View Index dialog box.

ENTERING DATA IN A STANDARD LAYOUT

41

Chapter 3

Cleaning Up a Layout for Printing

Beginning FileMaker developers tend not to pay much attention to their layout design. Eventually, after wasting paper on blank or almost empty pages, or on layouts that don't fit properly on a standard page, a clean layout becomes more important. Two simple changes can make all the difference. First, you should design the layout to fit a standard paper size. Different page sizes give you different amounts of room, so you should set the page size before you construct the layout. It's surprisingly easy to do, and saves mental wear and tear.

The second step is a little more subtle. When you create a layout, you try to take into account the largest block of data a field will need to display or print. But by designing for the largest data, you often leave enormous holes in your printouts of pages whose data doesn't take up as much space. The Sliding/Printing option allows you to designate fields or layout elements that can move up if the fields above them are empty or contain less than the maximum data.

To create a layout to match your paper size:

1. Go to the layout to be printed.
2. Choose File > Page Setup (Macintosh) or File > Print Setup (Windows).
3. Choose the page size and orientation you want to print (**Figure 3.30**).
4. Choose View > Layout Mode.
5. Click and drag the Body Part tab until you see the dashed horizontal line that marks a page break (**Figure 3.31**). Drag the Body tab up slightly to cover this mark. If the part extends below the page break, you'll get an extra blank page every time you print.

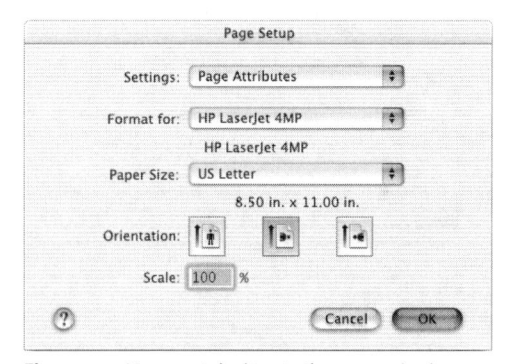

Figure 3.30 You must designate the paper size in Page/Print Setup before you add elements to the layout.

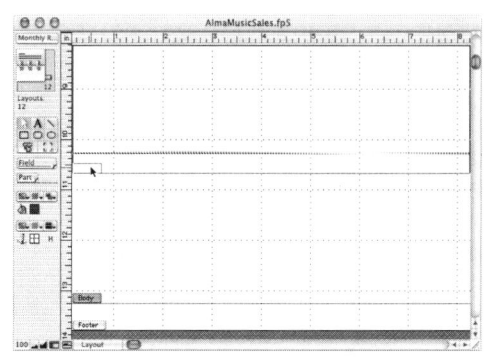

Figure 3.31 The dashed horizontal line on the layout shows where the bottom of the page is. The vertical one shows the right margin.

42

Layout Enhancements

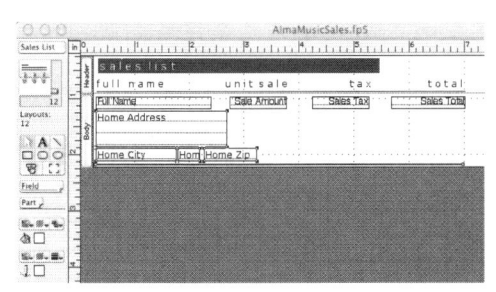

Figure 3.32 Select all the fields as well as any text or graphics that you want to slide up before selecting the Sliding/Printing dialog box.

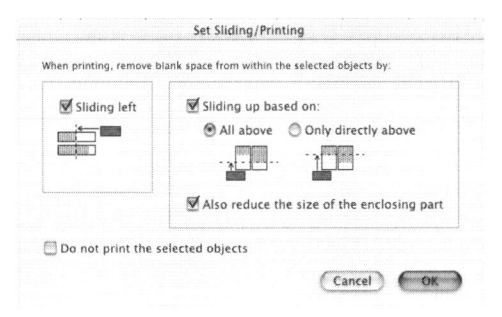

Figure 3.33 The "Also reduce the size of the enclosing part" option will save paper when the report is printed.

Figure 3.34 Even though the layout shows three lines in the Address field, it will shorten if the data entered has fewer lines. The Body part will also shrink with it.

To reduce the size of layout parts when sliding:

1. Choose View > Layout Mode (Control+L/Command+L).

2. Select the fields that you want to slide up. Be sure to include any text or graphics that you will want to slide up (**Figure 3.32**).

3. Choose Format > Sliding/Printing.

4. Click the "Sliding up based on" and "Also reduce the size of the enclosing part" check boxes (**Figure 3.33**). Click OK.

When you print or choose Preview mode, the fields or layout elements you chose will move up if the fields above them are shorter than the space you've allowed for them in the layout (**Figure 3.34**).

CLEANING UP A LAYOUT FOR PRINTING

43

Chapter 3

Creating and Formatting Value Lists

One of the most convenient ways to speed up data entry and eliminate mistakes is the value list. You can format a field to display a pop-up menu, pop-up list, radio buttons, or check boxes. These formats strategically narrow your users' choices, since they present only those options that you consider valid actions. Once a value list is created, it's available for every field in your database. For example, if you have several fields that will contain a Yes/No, you only have to create one Y/N value list.

Choosing a value list style

The value list style you choose should match the type of data you want to present. Styles are more than aesthetic or arbitrary choices. They affect how long it takes users to figure out what they should do next, and how easily they can do it. Choosing the wrong format negates the efficiency of creating a value list and leads to mistakes.

Radio Buttons

Use radio buttons when the choices you offer are both mutually exclusive and limited. For example, a radio button format is a good choice for a field containing the type of credit card used in a transaction.

Check Boxes

Use check boxes when the user can choose multiple items in field. A check box is also a good format for turning a choice on or off or for confirmation (like a check box next to Yes). Remember that the text next to the check box or radio button is the contents of a field, not the X or bullet that appears. In other words, you can't count, add, or otherwise manipulate the checks or radio buttons themselves. They're only a format to help the user navigate the field options you've set. If you change a check box field back to a standard

field, you'll only see the selected values for the record, not the whole group of choices (**Figure 3.35**).

Pop-up List

Use pop-up lists when the number of choices in the value list is very long. When the user clicks in a field with a pop-up list, they see a scroll bar. The user can either click on the scroll bar to advance the list or type the first letter or two to jump to an item.

Pop-up Menu

Use pop-up menus when there are more than three or four mutually exclusive choices, but few enough not to cover up something important beneath them when the pop-up menu opens.

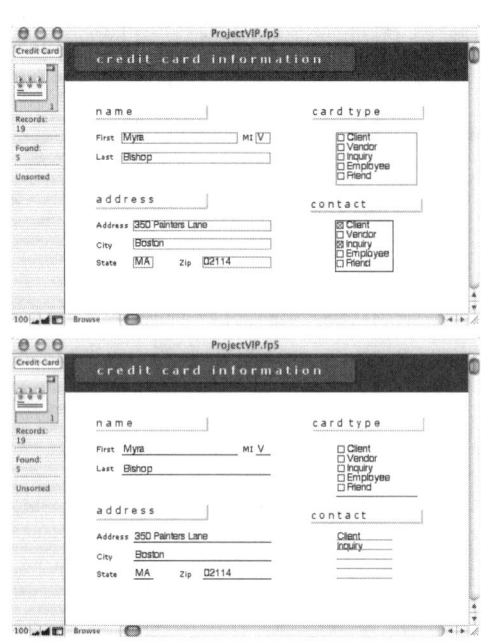

Figure 3.35 In this layout, the Contact section has five possible entries. When you change it back to a standard format, only the entries that had checks next to them still appear.

44

Validating Formats with Value Lists

People often use the pop-up menu format when another choice would be much more appropriate. If you've ever filled out a form on a Web page, you've probably seen a pop-up list with the abbreviations for all 50 states. Unless you live in Alabama, Alaska, Arkansas, or California, you probably find this format less convenient than if you simply typed in your state's two-letter abbreviation. If you release the mouse on the wrong choice you have to repeat the process. A scrolling pop-up list might be a good solution, or you can use a value list to validate user entries. If you create a value list with all the state abbreviations, it will compare the list against the entry to minimize errors.

Figure 3.36 To create a new value list, choose File > Define Value Lists.

Figure 3.37 Click New to define a new value list.

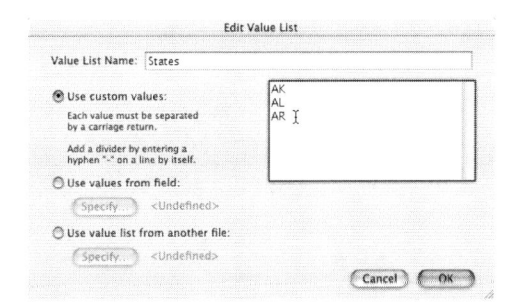

Figure 3.38 Every value must be typed on a separate line in a value list.

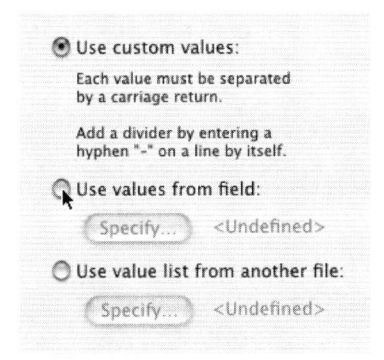

Figure 3.39 Choose "Use values from field" to select a field in the current database for your value list.

To use a value list for validation:

1. Go to the layout you'd like to format. Choose File > Define Value Lists (**Figure 3.36**).

2. When the Define Value Lists dialog box appears, click New (**Figure 3.37**). When the Edit Value list dialog box appears, give your value list a name.

3. Click inside the input box and type the items in your value list. Press Return (Mac) or Enter (Windows) between each value (**Figure 3.38**).

   Notice that you don't have to input every choice if you already have a field with this list in your database, or if you're using FileMaker Pro 6 and have typed the entries into a different database as a value list. If you have an existing value list you'd like to use, in the Edit Value List dialog box, choose either "Use values from field" or "Use value list from another file" to navigate to the existing field or value list (**Figure 3.39**).

continues on next page

45

Chapter 3

4. After you've typed the last entry or specified an existing value list, click OK and then Done.

5. Choose File > Define Fields (Control+Shift+D/Command+Shift+D).

6. In the scrolling list in the Define Fields dialog box, double-click the field you want to validate (**Figure 3.40**) and click Options.

7. When the Options box appears, click the Validation tab.

8. Choose the value list you just created from the "Member of value list" drop-down menu (**Figure 3.41**).

9. Click OK and then Done.

Now when you input data in the chosen field, FileMaker will check the input against the value list. If the value doesn't match the list, you'll see a dialog box (**Figure 3.42**) that alerts you to the error.

✔ Tips

- If you have a file that will have many value lists, or if you wish to use the same value list in several different files, you can create a database that contains just value lists and use them in any other file.

- If you specify a value list in a different database and move the primary file to another computer, remember to move the database file whose value lists you specified as well. If you don't, FileMaker won't be able to locate the value list to validate your input.

- If you have a database with lots of value lists, check the scrolling list first before naming your new value list to avoid similarities that might lead to confusion.

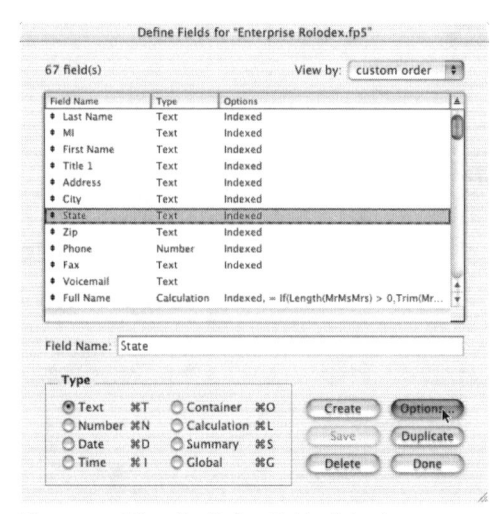

Figure 3.40 When the Define Fields dialog box appears, choose the field you want to validate from the field list.

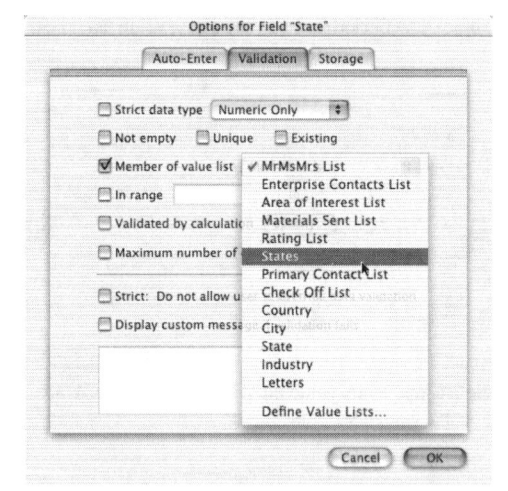

Figure 3.41 When you choose a value list, the check box next to "Member of value list" is automatically checked for you.

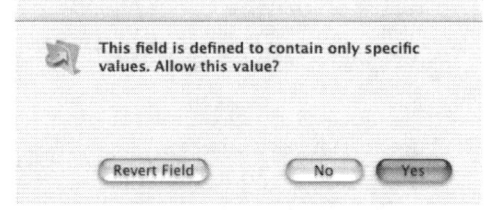

Figure 3.42 This dialog box allows the user to deliberately accept an error. You can eliminate this option by choosing strict validation in the Options dialog box when you define the field.

VALIDATING FORMATS WITH VALUE LISTS

Working with Conditional Value Lists

Value lists are an excellent tool in the battle against data errors, but they have some inherent limitations. The more possible entries you have, the less useful value lists become. FileMaker enhances value lists by allowing you to use fields in your database to dynamically alter the value list display.

Imagine you're creating a database of store branches for a nationally franchised company. They have offices in major cities in each state. Although the number of cities is limited, it still averages 15 per state, and some of them have similar names with different spellings (like Charleston and Charlestown), making the entries difficult to validate. To solve this problem, you could begin by creating a file with two fields: the states and their cities. Using this file as a value list, you can create a relationship between the state and city fields of the store branches. When you enter a state, only its cities appear as entry values.

To use a conditional value list:

1. Choose File > Define Relationships (**Figure 3.43**).

2. When the Define Relationships dialog box appears, click New (**Figure 3.44**).

3. In the Open File dialog box, select the file and click Open.

   The Edit Relationship dialog box will appear, and the name of your file will be inserted in the Relationship Name line. You can change it to something else, but it's a good idea to maintain the same name for your relationship and value list so you'll remember what the relationship is for.

4. Choose one match field from each of the two lists (**Figure 3.45**).

continues on next page

Figure 3.43 To connect a value list to a field, choose File > Define Relationships.

Figure 3.44 Click New to define a new relationship.

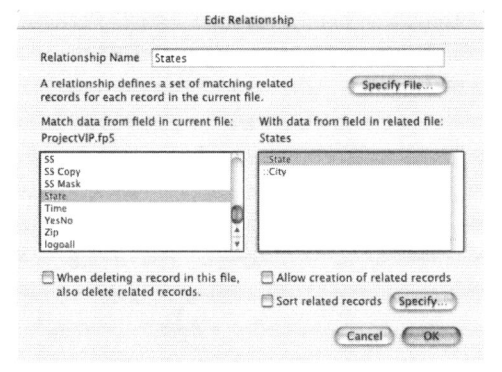

Figure 3.45 Select one field from the main database on the left, and a second field from the related field that will become the value list on the right.

Chapter 3

5. Click OK, then click Done to close the Define Relationships dialog box.
6. Choose File > Define Value Lists.
7. When the Define Value Lists dialog box appears, click New.
8. In the Edit Value List dialog box, type a name for the value list and click "Use values from a field."
9. When the Specify Fields dialog box appears, click "Only related values" and choose the relationship you defined above from the drop-down list (**Figure 3.46**).
10. In the left value column, click the field you'll want to display the subset of values. Click OK twice and then click Done.
11. Make sure you're in Layout mode (Control+L/Command+L), then go to the layout where the field you just selected is displayed.
12. Click on the field that will display the value list subset and choose Format > Field Format (**Figure 3.47**).
13. When the Field Format dialog box appears, click "Pop-up list" in the Style section and choose the list to be used (**Figure 3.48**). Click OK.

When you switch back to Browse mode and enter a value into the first field, the pop-up list will display only the subset of value options appropriate to that field. If there is no entry in the first field, the list in the second field will be blank.

✔ **Tip**

■ This technique will also work with pop-up menus, radio buttons, and check boxes.

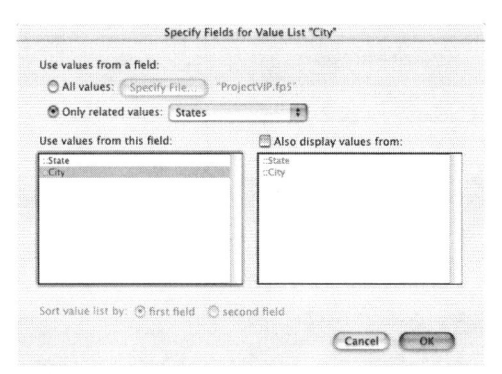

Figure 3.46 Be careful to specify the second field (the one that's dependent on the first input) when setting up the value list.

Figure 3.47 To make your value list subset appear as a group of choices in the correct layout field, choose Format > Field Format.

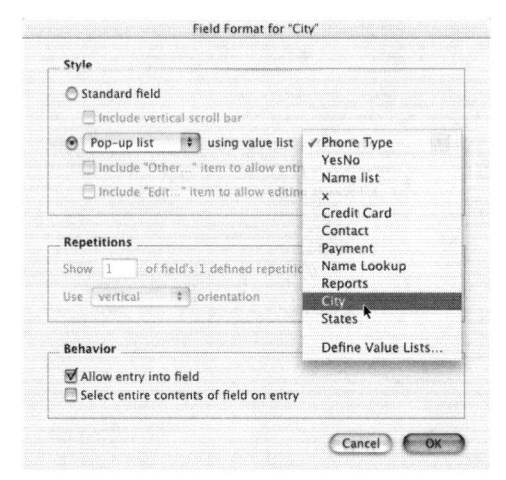

Figure 3.48 Choose the value list in the drop-down list.

48

Using Calculated Field Labels

When you design a layout, you usually include all fields that might be needed, even if some aren't always used. Major changes are best handled by creating another layout, but there can be times when you only need to include (or exclude) a specific field. For instance, you might have designed an invoice layout that includes a discount field. You would only want that field and its label to appear if there is a discount. (Otherwise the customer will want to know why they didn't get one.) By creating a calculated field that contains both the value and the label, you can customize the layout to automatically display or hide the field.

To create a calculated field label:

1. Choose File > Define Fields (Control+Shift+D/Command+Shift+D).

2. When the Define Fields dialog box appears (**Figure 3.49**), type a name into the Field Name text box. Choose Calculation as the type, and click Create.

3. When the Specify Calculation dialog box appears, in the functions list on the right double-click If (**Figure 3.50**).

4. In the Discount Display area, replace "test" in the If calculation by double-clicking it to make it the only highlighted parameter, then double-clicking IsEmpty in the Functions list.

5. With "field" highlighted in the calculation, double-click the field you want to designate in the fields list on the left side. This example uses the Discount field (**Figure 3.51**).

continues on next page

Figure 3.49 You create a calculation field by giving the field a descriptive name, selecting the Calculation radio button, and clicking Create.

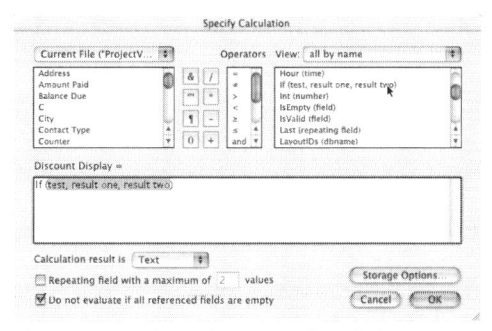

Figure 3.50 To place a function in the calculations text box, double-click it in the functions scrolling list. Functions are followed by parameters in parentheses, each of which needs to be specified.

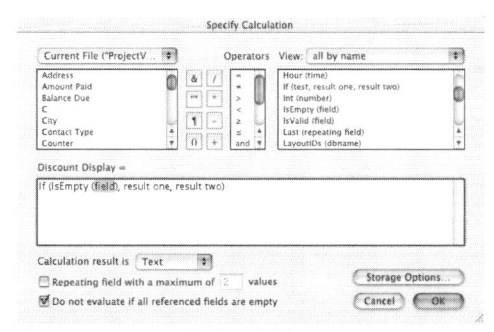

Figure 3.51 To specify what field to use in a calculation, double-click it in the field list on the left.

Chapter 3

6. Double-click "result one" to select it, then click the quotes button in the Operators keypad (**Figure 3.52**).

7. Double-click "result two" to select it, then click the quotes button again. Type the name of your label between the quotes. In this example, the label is "Discount."

8. Move your cursor between the last quote and the parenthesis and click the ampersand (&) button. Add the NumToText function by double-clicking it in the right functions list.

9. With "number" highlighted in the calculation, double-click the same field you chose in step 5. This example uses the Discount field.

10. Move your cursor between the two closing parentheses. Click the ampersand button, then the quotes button, and type % between the quotes.

11. Make sure to choose Text from the "Calculation result is" pull-down menu, and click OK (**Figure 3.53**). When you're finished, click Done to close the dialog box.

12. Go to the layout where the new field will be displayed and switch to Layout mode (Control+L/Command+L).

13. Add the new field to the layout.

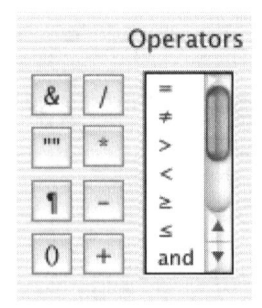

Figure 3.52 The most frequently used operators are controlled by the keypad.

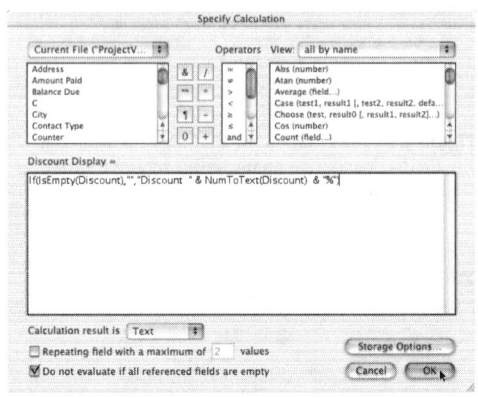

Figure 3.53 Click OK to save the finished calculation.

Layout Enhancements

Creating Field Masks

Many database programs have the ability to format data like phone numbers and Social Security numbers automatically. If you enter 2125551234 in the phone field, you'll see (212) 555-1234 instead. FileMaker Pro does not offer this feature, but you can mimic it in a layout. If you place a locked, formatted display field directly over an unlocked entry field, you mask the bottom field while still leaving it active. Connect the two fields with a calculation, and whatever value you enter displays properly in the field above it.

To create a field mask:

1. Go to a layout with a field you'd like to mask. Choose File > Define Fields (Control+Shift+D/Command+Shift+D).

2. When the Define Fields dialog box appears, select your existing field and change its type to Number if it was created as a text field. This example uses the Phone field (**Figure 3.54**).

3. Create a new field and add the word Mask in the Field Name line (like Phone Mask or Credit Card Number Mask). Select Calculation as the type and click Create (**Figure 3.55**).

4. When the Specify Calculation dialog box appears, click the quotes button and type (between the quotes (**Figure 3.56**).

continues on next page

Figure 3.54 To format a phone number, it must be a number field.

Figure 3.55 After you've verified that your Phone field is a number, create a new field for your mask by choosing Calculation as the type and clicking Create.

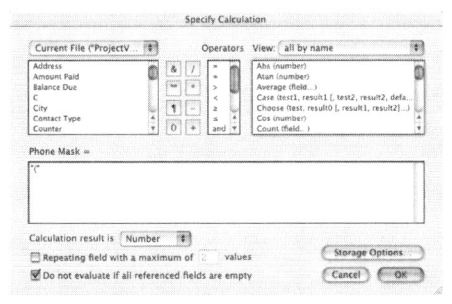

Figure 3.56 To make a parenthesis appear before the phone number, type it between quotes.

51

Chapter 3

5. Click to the right of the quotes and then click the ampersand button (**Figure 3.57**). Double-click Left in the function list on the right to add it to the calculation in the formula-builder window (**Figure 3.58**).

    Left will format the area code of the phone number by separating the first three numbers from the rest of the contents of the field.

6. Double-click "text" in the Left calculation to highlight it, then double-click Abs in the function list. "Abs" will replace "text" in the calculation (**Figure 3.59**).

    If the user enters a parenthesis at the beginning, FileMaker will assume that the number is a negative. The Abs function will return the entry as a positive.

7. With the first "number" highlighted in the formula builder, double-click Phone in the field list (**Figure 3.60**).

Figure 3.57 Click the ampersand (&) operator button to link functions together.

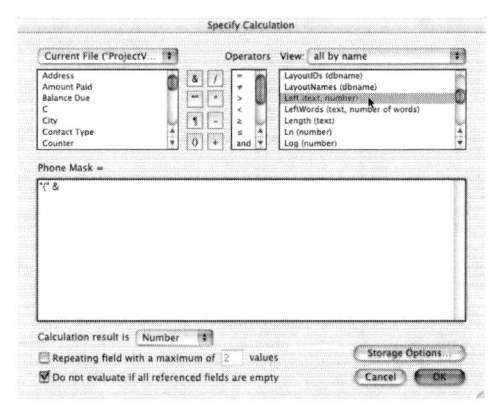

Figure 3.58 The Left function counts characters from the left of the field to separate them from the rest of the field contents.

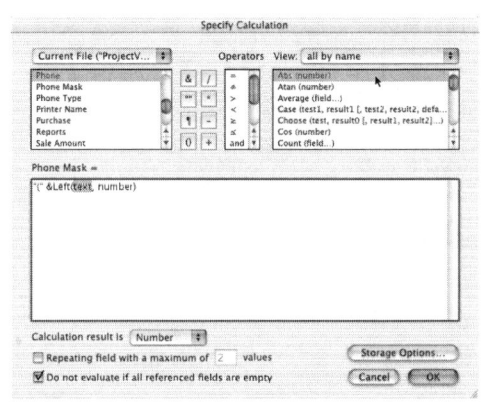

Figure 3.59 To replace a parameter with a function, select the parameter in the formula builder, then double-click the function in the function list.

Layout Enhancements

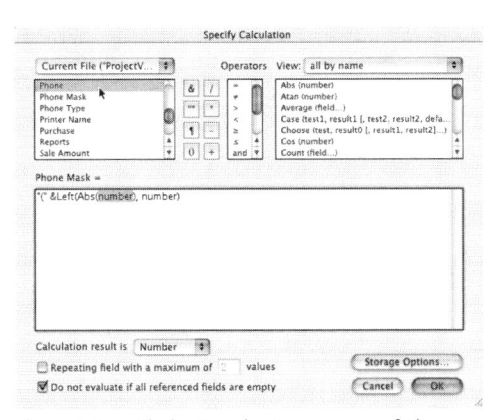

Figure 3.60 With the "number" parameter of Abs highlighted, select the field you want to connect to your mask.

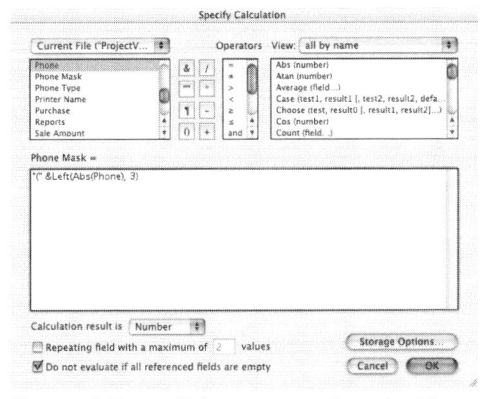

Figure 3.61 To specify how many numbers should display after the first parenthesis, replace the parameter with that quantity. (For an area code, type 3.)

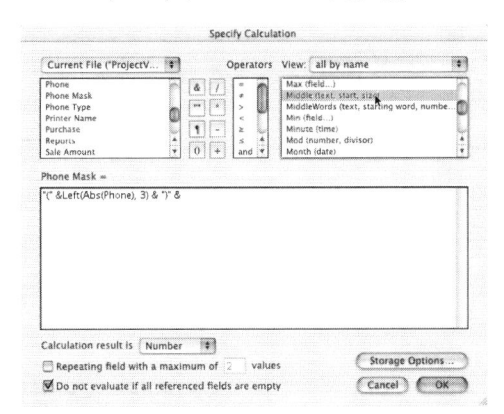

Figure 3.62 To add a function to a series of calculations, click the & button and then double-click the formula from the function list.

8. Highlight the remaining "number" and type 3 (**Figure 3.61**). The number parameter specifies how many numbers the Left function should put inside the parentheses. Since this is an area code, you type 3.

9. Move your cursor to the end of the formula. Click the & operator button, then the quotes operator button and type) inside the quotes.

10. Move your cursor to the end of the formula and click the ampersand button. Add the Middle function by double-clicking it in the right functions list (**Figure 3.62**).

    The Middle function works like the Left function, but instead of counting from the far left, begins counting at whatever character number you type in the "start" parameter, for the number of total characters you specify in the "size" parameter.

11. Use copy and paste to replace "text" in the Middle function with "Abs(Phone)" from the first part of the calculation.

continues on next page

CREATING FIELD MASKS

53

Chapter 3

12. Double-click "start" and replace it by typing 4, then select "size" and replace it by typing 3 (**Figure 3.63**). To designate the second part of the telephone number, the 4 specifies the fourth number in the sequence (in other words, after the area code). The 3 specifies how many digits will follow.

13. Move your cursor to the end of the formula. Click the ampersand button and then the quotes button. Type a hyphen (-) between the quotes

14. Move your cursor to the end of the formula, then click the ampersand button. Add the Right function by double-clicking it in the function list.

15. Replace "text" with "Abs(Phone)" again, then double-click "number" and replace it by typing 4.

16. Make sure your calculation result is set to Text, then click OK (**Figure 3.64**). When you're ready, click Done to close the Define Fields dialog box. You've finished creating the Mask field.

17. Go to the layout where you want the formatted field and switch to Layout mode (Control+L/Command+L).

18. Select your Phone field, or add it if necessary.

19. Duplicate the field by clicking and dragging it while holding down the Alt (Windows) or Option (Mac) key.

20. In the Specify Field dialog box, uncheck "Create field label" and select Phone Mask from the list (**Figure 3.65**), then click OK.

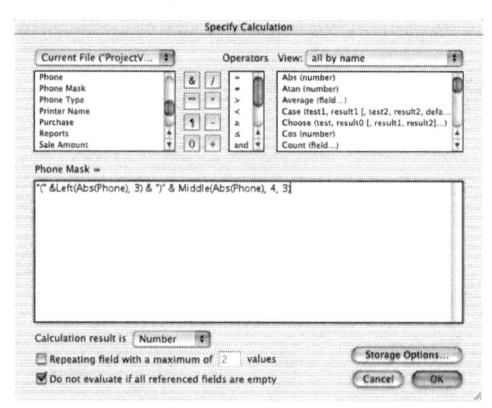

Figure 3.63 To specify the second part of the telephone number, replace "start" with 4 and "size" with 3.

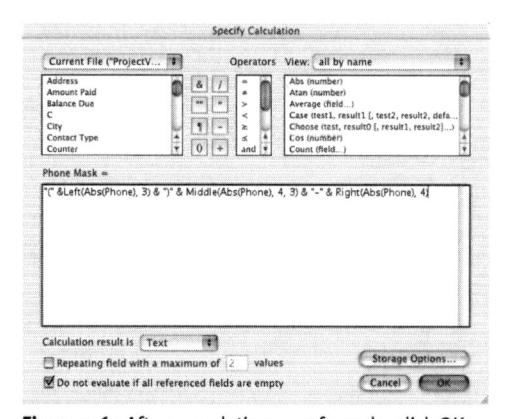

Figure 3.64 After completing your formula, click OK.

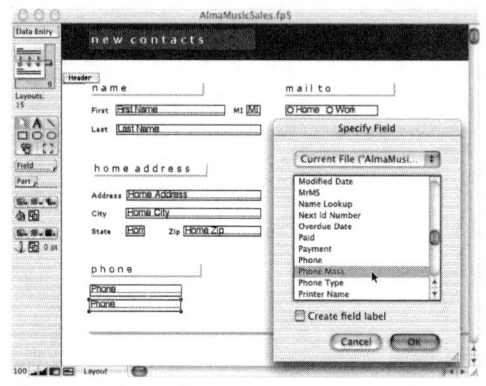

Figure 3.65 To avoid creating an unnecessary field label, uncheck the "Create field label" check box when you make the Mask field.

Figure 3.66 Lock a field by unchecking "Allow entry into field."

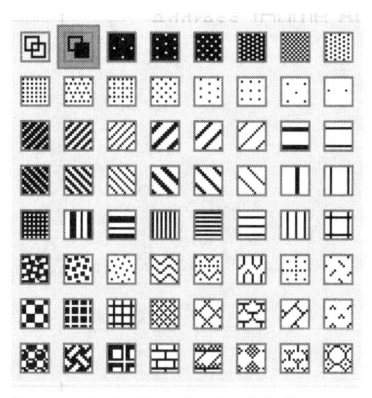

Figure 3.67 Setting the Mask field to opaque prevents the entry field beneath it from showing through.

21. While the Phone Mask field is selected, choose Format > Field Format (Control+Alt+F/Command+Option-F).

22. When the Field Format dialog box appears, uncheck "Allow entry into field," then click OK (**Figure 3.66**).

    This prevents data from being entered into the Mask field. When the user clicks on this field, the cursor will actually go into the entry field behind it.

23. Make sure that the Fill for the Mask field is set to Opaque (**Figure 3.67**).

24. Drag the Phone Mask field so that it is squarely on top of the Phone field.

When you switch to Browse mode and click on the Phone Mask field, the cursor will actually be in the Phone field.

✔ Tip

- Although the example puts parentheses around the area code, you can use the same strategy to separate numbers with periods, hyphens, or slashes instead.

Validating by Number of Characters

Some data, like phone numbers or Social Security numbers, must always have the same number of characters. But when users make simple errors—like adding hyphens in a phone number—they often don't know that they've done anything wrong. In the previous section, "Creating Field Masks," we showed you how to create a field mask to format a phone-number field. In order for the mask to work properly, the user must not enter more than 10 digits. This technique prevents such simple errors from taking place.

Figure 3.68 Open the file whose phone-number field you want to change.

To validate by number of characters:

1. Open a file with a phone-number field whose length you want to limit.

   We'll use the same file we worked with in "Creating Field Masks" (**Figure 3.68**).

2. Choose File > Define Fields (Control+Shift+D/Command+Shift+D).

3. When the Define Fields dialog box appears, double-click the Phone field.

4. When the Options dialog box appears, click the Validation tab.

5. Check the "Maximum number of characters" check box and enter 10 in the box to the right (**Figure 3.69**).

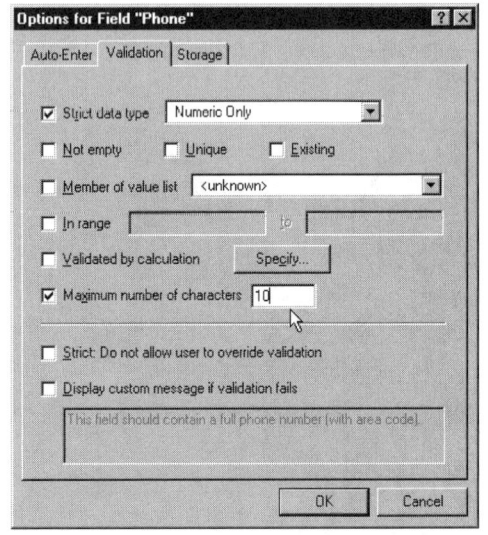

Figure 3.69 In the Validation panel of the Options dialog box, enter the maximum number of allowed characters.

Layout Enhancements

6. Click the "Strict: Do not allow user to override validation" check box (**Figure 3.70**).

7. If you want FileMaker to display a custom message when the user enters more than 10 characters, click the "Display custom message if validation fails" check box and type the message in the box below (**Figure 3.71**).

8. Click OK and then Done.

If the user enters more than 10 characters in the Phone field, FileMaker will display the alert message you entered in step 7 (**Figure 3.72**).

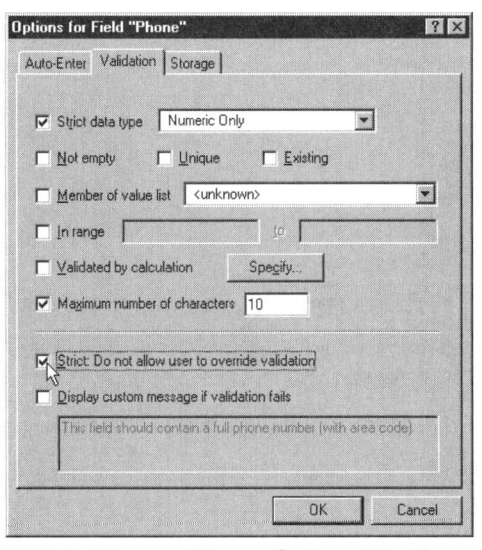

Figure 3.70 To prevent the user from overriding the validation alert, check the Strict option.

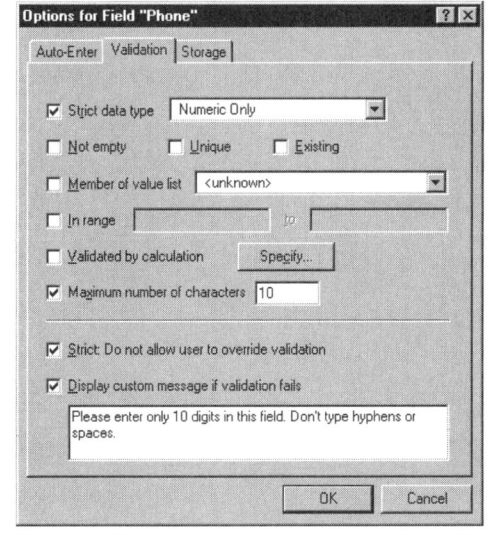

Figure 3.71 You can enter a custom message that will be displayed if the user enters more than the specified number of characters.

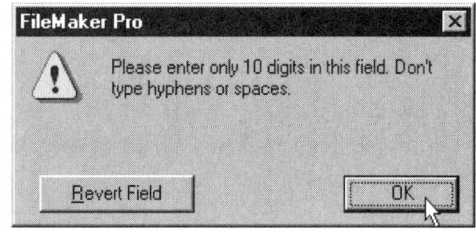

Figure 3.72 If the validation fails, the user will be prompted to change the input.

VALIDATING BY NUMBER OF CHARACTERS

Copying Layouts

You'll frequently want to duplicate an existing layout. If the layouts are in the same database, this is quite simple, but it may well be that the layout you want to duplicate is in another database. For example, you might have created an invoice layout for one client, and now you're building a database for a completely different company that has also asked for an invoice form. FileMaker does not have the capability to import layouts. But by using Copy and Paste, you can re-create most of a layout in another database.

Figure 3.73 Set the layout parts to match the layout you're copying.

To re-create a layout in another database:

1. In the database that will contain the layout, create a new layout, but don't add any fields.

2. Set up the blank layout so that it contains the same layout parts (Header, Body, Footer, etc.) as the layout to be copied (**Figure 3.73**). Use the rulers to make sure it has the same vertical size as the original layout.

3. Switch to Layout mode (Control+L/Command+L) and open the database containing the original layout.

4. Choose Edit > Select All (Control+A/Command+A).

5. Choose Edit > Copy (Control+C/Command+C) and switch back to the new database.

6. Make sure that you're still in Layout mode and choose Edit > Paste (Control+V/Command+V). All fields and text from the original layout will appear.

    The pasted items (fields and text) will still be selected, so you can click and drag everything to line them up in the new layout.

Layout Enhancements

Figure 3.74 Copied layout fields with no exact duplicate names will be blank, like Firm in this example.

If any of the field names differ from the original database, those fields will be blank on the new layout (**Figure 3.74**). You can double-click on the blank field boxes and the Specify Field dialog box will appear, allowing you to choose the correct name for that field.

✔ Tip

- Sometimes you may want to select just the fields (or text) on the original layout. Rather than individually selecting each item, try this:
    1. Click on one field (or text block).
    2. Press Control+Alt+A/Command+Option+A.

    All of the fields (or text) will be selected, but nothing else.

Keyboard Shortcuts

There are many commands in FileMaker that can be carried out without the mouse. Here are some of the most useful.

Control/Command+B	Browse mode	**LAYOUT MODE:**	
Control/Command+L	Layout mode	Control/Command+R	Group selected objects
Control/Command+F	Find mode	Shift+Control/Command+R	Ungroup selected objects
Control/Command+U	Preview mode	Control/Command+L	Lock selected objects
Shift+Control/Command+D	Define Fields	Shift+Control/Command+R	Unlock selected objects
Shift+Control/Command+F	Find & Replace	Control/Command+K	Align selected objects
BROWSE MODE:		Shift Control/Command+K	Set Alignment (dialog box)
Control/Command+S	Sort		
Control/Command+-	Insert current date		
Control/Command+;	Insert current time		
Control/Command+T	Omit record		
Shift+Control/Command+T	Omit multiple		

59

Calculation Fields

When you create a database, you break data into many separate fields because smaller bits of information are more flexible and easier to search. In layouts, however, you want to regroup these fields to re-create the original flow of text. With a calculation, you can combine the individual fields into a single element that formats the data exactly the way that you want.

Although a calculation field may seem like a lot of trouble initially, it's actually an elegant time-saver. Calculation fields offer powerful formatting capabilities for everything from labels and envelopes to form letters. If you combine them with FileMaker's text capabilities, you can frequently avoid having to use a separate word processor for standard letters and other types of bulk mailings.

Once you've created a calculation field you can place it in a layout like any other type of field. But that's where the similarities end. In a normal layout made up of many small fields, you have to laboriously select each field to change type size, font, or positions. Then, if one of the fields will sometimes be blank, you need to use the Sliding command to close up the space the blank field leaves behind. You can forget all that with a calculation field. Its combined information can be formatted as easily as it would be in Microsoft Word or AppleWorks. (In fact, considering Word, probably even easier.)

For frequent bulk mailings like monthly statements or special price promotions, a calculation field can make FileMaker a considerably better choice than other programs. Because a calculation field always refers back to the original fields for its information, addresses, area codes, and other all-too-changeable data will always update automatically once edited into the original record.

Merging Fields Using Calculations

Calculations provide an easy way to create a new field that's a collection of information from existing fields. Once you've merged the separate fields into one "super field," creating layouts gets much easier. Compare the ease with which you can align and reposition a calculation field to how you work with the individual fields, and we think you'll be convinced (**Figure 4.1**).

In these steps the calculation field Full Name combines the First Name, Middle Initial, and Last Name fields (with spaces in between) into a single field that you can place in any layout instead of the three separate fields. It also leaves out the Middle Initial (and the extra spaces around it) if a name doesn't contain one.

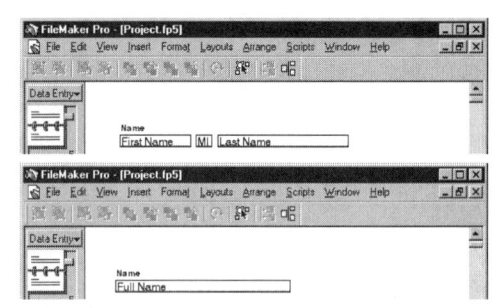

Figure 4.1 The layout on the top uses three text fields, the one on the bottom uses one calculation field. The printed document looks the same either way.

To merge fields:

1. Choose File > Define Fields (Control+Shift+D/Command+Shift+D).

2. When the Define Fields dialog box appears, type the name of your field in the Field Name text box, select the Calculation radio button, then click Create (**Figure 4.2**). In this example, we use Full Name.

3. The Specify Calculation dialog box appears. In the function list on the right, double-click the Trim function to begin the calculation in the formula box.

   Trim seeks out initial and trailing spaces that surround other text and "trims" them away from the text or number. The parameter "text" will be highlighted in the formula box (**Figure 4.3**).

Figure 4.2 Create a calculation field and call it Full Name.

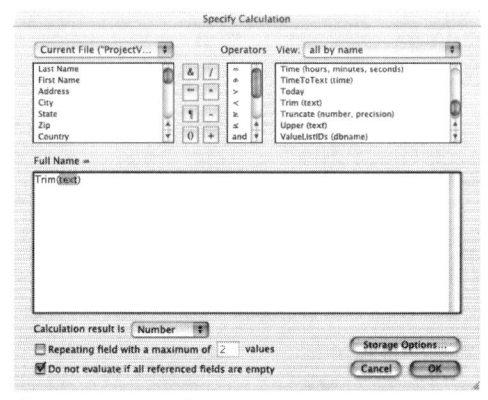

Figure 4.3 The Trim function removes any extra spaces entered before or after the text in a field.

Calculation Fields

4. The Trim function acts on the field that replaces its parameter. In the field list on the left, double-click the first of the fields you want to combine. This example uses First Name (**Figure 4.4**).

5. Click to the right of the parentheses. In the formula operators keypad, click the ampersand button (&) to add it to the formula box (**Figure 4.5**).

6. The quotes operator is used to add text characters to a calculation. In the Operators keypad, click the quotes button and type a space inside the quotes. Click to the right of the quotes and click the ampersand button again (**Figure 4.6**).

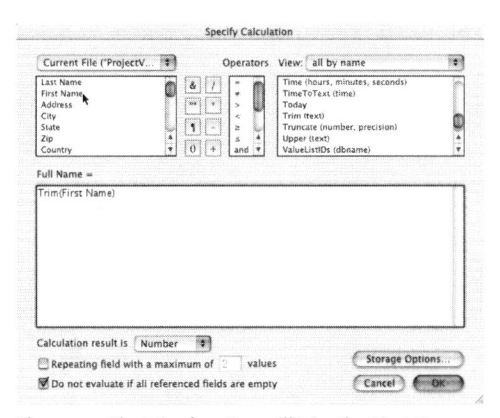

continues on next page

Figure 4.4 The Trim function will trim the First Name field in this example.

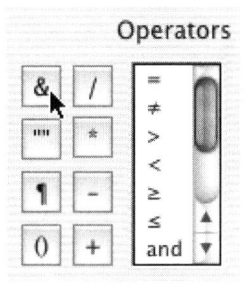

Figure 4.5 Choose the ampersand (&) operator to combine functions.

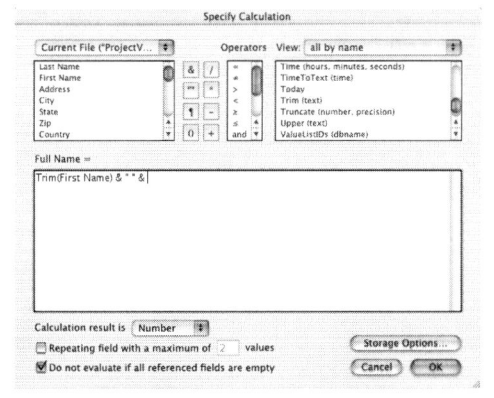

Figure 4.6 Type a space within the quotes in the formula box to add a space to the text.

MERGING FIELDS USING CALCULATIONS

63

Chapter 4

7. To leave out a field and its extra space when that field is empty, double-click If to choose it from the function list (**Figure 4.7**).

    If the name has a middle initial, you'll need to add it with a space after it. But some names don't have middle initials. You need a function that will allow for both possibilities. The If statement checks the field to see whether or not a situation exists. It can have two results: result one (if test is true) and result two (if test is not true).

8. In the formula box, double-click the "test" parameter in the If statement to select it. In the function list, double-click IsEmpty (**Figure 4.8**).

9. In the field list, double-click the next field you want to add to the calculation field.

    This example uses the MI field (**Figure 4.9**). The IsEmpty function looks at this field to see if there is anything in it.

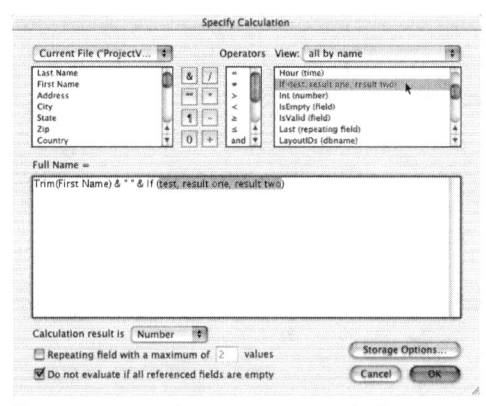

Figure 4.7 Use an If statement to test whether or not a field contains data.

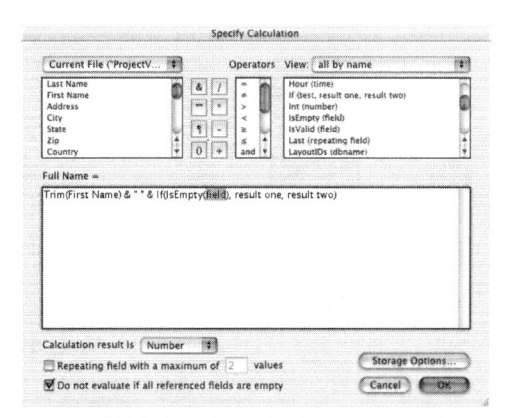

Figure 4.8 To test whether a field is empty, use the IsEmpty function as the test parameter.

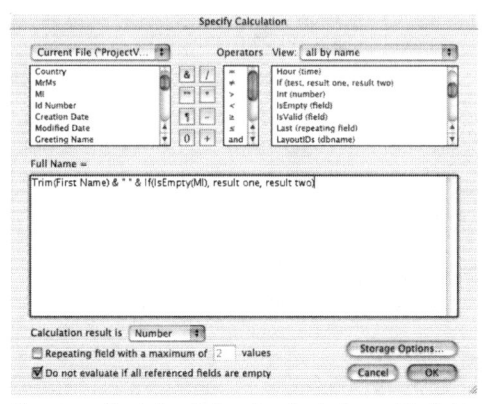

Figure 4.9 The IsEmpty function looks to see if a field has data in it.

Calculation Fields

10. In the formula box, double-click to highlight "result one." In the Operators keypad, click the quotes button to add a set of quotes to the calculation (**Figure 4.10**).

    By replacing the "result one" parameter with the quotes operator, without typing anything inside the quotes, you eliminate an empty field. (Much nicer than using the Sliding command!)

11. In the formula box, double-click to highlight "result two." In the function list, double-click Trim. The "text" parameter is highlighted in the formula box (**Figure 4.11**). Since you'll want to trim the second field if it has data in it, double-click the same field you chose in step 9 above.

    This example uses the MI field, so Trim will cut away any extra spaces around the middle initial if the full name has a middle initial in it.

12. In the formula box, click between the two parentheses, then click the ampersand button in the Operators keypad.

13. In the Operators keypad, click the quotes button. Type a space between the quotes, then click to the right of the parentheses and select the ampersand button from the Operators keypad (**Figure 4.12**).

    This adds a space after the middle initial if a name has one.

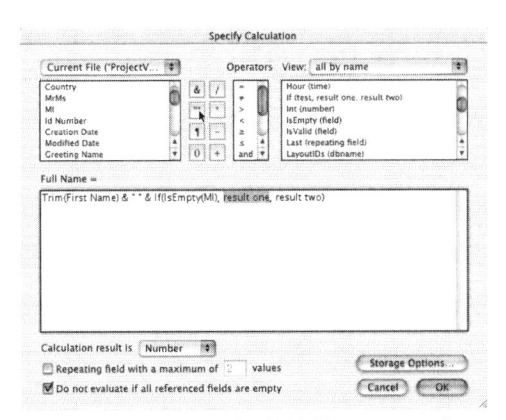

    continues on next page

Figure 4.10 To eliminate the field if it's empty, replace the "result one" parameter with the quotes operator and don't type anything inside the quotes.

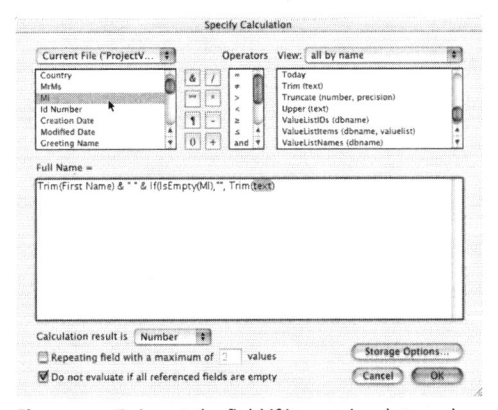

Figure 4.11 To insert the field if it contains data and trim any extra spaces around it, choose the Trim function and the field name.

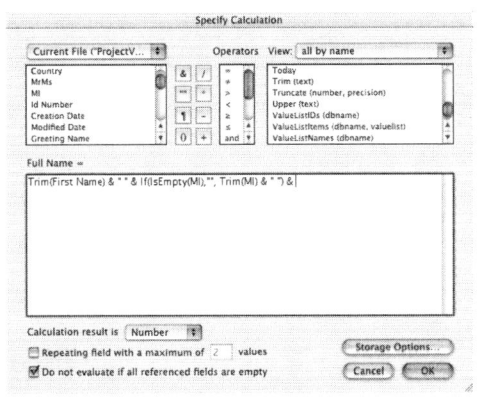

Figure 4.12 To add a space to the field text, put it between the quotes.

65

Chapter 4

14. In the function list, double-click Trim. With "text" highlighted in the formula box, select the next desired field from the field list.

    This example uses the Last Name field (**Figure 4.13**). In this case, you use the Trim function to eliminate leading spaces.

15. Set "Calculation result is" to Text since this calculation field won't contain any numerical calculations (**Figure 4.14**). Click OK, then click Done.

Now you have a completed formula in a field. When you place this field in a layout, it will display the full name on a record in Browse mode and also on a printout.

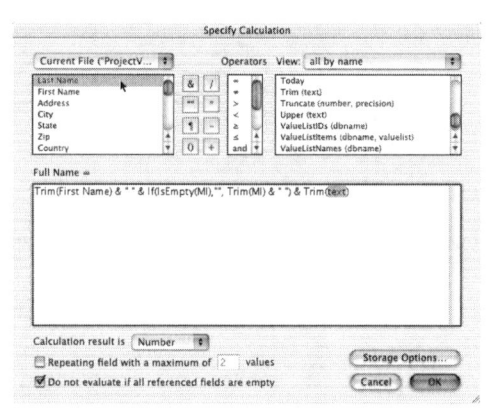

Figure 4.13 In this case, the Trim function eliminates leading spaces in Last Name.

✔ Tips

- When you select a function, FileMaker highlights its parameter in the calculation input box to prompt you to choose a field.

- This example can be customized to add fields at the beginning (like for Dr. or Mrs.), or a title field (like Chair or Accounts Payable) at the end. Remember to add a comma to the space between quotes before the ending title field.

- As calculations grow in complexity, they become increasingly difficult to read in the formula box. You can insert returns in long formulas to make them easier to read. FileMaker ignores the returns when evaluating the calculation (**Figure 4.15**).

- If you want to insert a return into the text result of a calculation, click the paragraph button in the Operators keypad (**¶**). Like all other characters you want to display as text, the paragraph marker must always be surrounded by quotes in the formula.

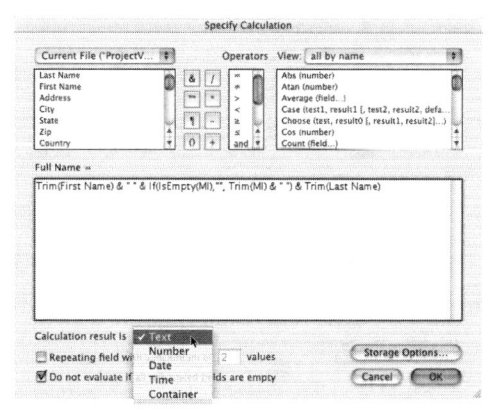

Figure 4.14 Use the drop-down menu to change the calculation result to Text.

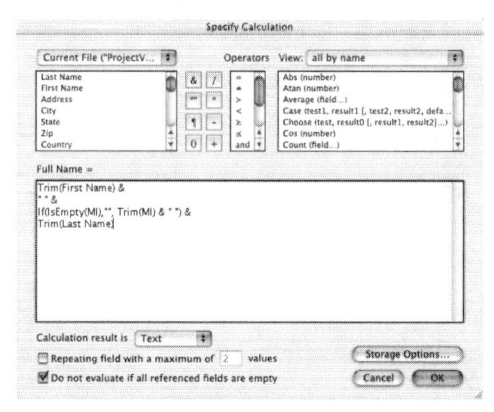

Figure 4.15 The same formula as in Figure 4.14 with returns inserted for readability.

MERGING FIELDS USING CALCULATIONS

Calculation Fields

Updating Auto-Entry Serial Numbers

When you delete a range of records in a database that uses an auto-enter serial number, you might like to be able to update the value of the next remaining serial number so there won't be a gap. With the Set Next Serial Value script step, FileMaker provides a delightfully simple way to do this.

In this script, we'll use a field called ID Number that contains the auto-enter serial number option. Since this script uses a Sort command, make sure that your serial number field is specified as a number field. Text fields will not sort properly.

Figure 4.16 The database is sorted by the ID Number field before the update is run.

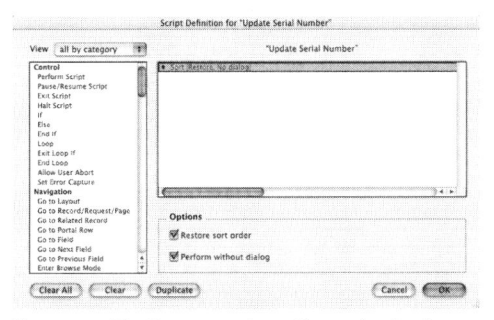

Figure 4.17 The Restore option will sort the database by the ID Number field every time the script runs.

To update serial numbers:

1. In the database with the auto-enter serial number, choose Records > Sort (Control+S/Command+S).

2. When the Sort Records dialog box appears, double-click ID Number in the field list on the left. Click Sort (**Figure 4.16**).

3. Choose Scripts > ScriptMaker.

4. When the Define Scripts dialog box appears, type Update Serial Number for the script name and click Create.

5. The Script Definition dialog box appears. In the step list on the left, double-click Sort in the Sort/Find/Print section to add it to the script-assembly window (**Figure 4.17**). Leave the "Perform without dialog" and "Restore sort order" options checked.

continues on next page

Chapter 4

6. In the Navigation section of the step list on the left, double-click Go to Record/Request/Page. In the Options area, choose Last from the Specify drop-down list (**Figure 4.18**).

7. In the Miscellaneous section of the step list, double-click Set Next Serial Value.

8. In the Options area, click Field. When the Specify Field dialog box appears, choose ID Number.

9. In the Options section, click the Specify button. When the Specify Calculation dialog box appears, double-click ID Number in the field list on the left.

10. Click the + operator button and then type 1 (**Figure 4.19**).

    This calculation tells FileMaker to add one to whatever is currently the highest serial number.

11. Click OK twice and then Done to finish.

    Whenever you delete multiple records, you can run this script to ensure that the serial number is updated.

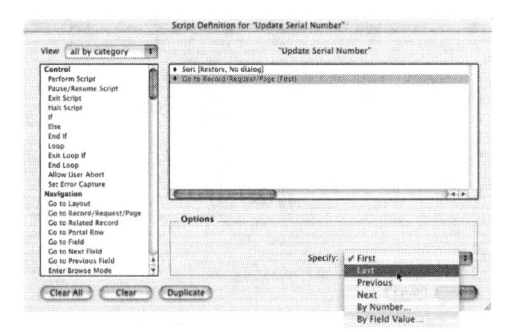

Figure 4.18 Since the database is sorted by the ID Number field, the last record contains the highest serial number.

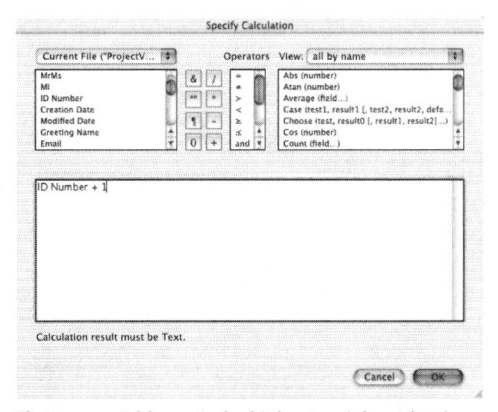

Figure 4.19 Add one to the highest serial number in the database to get the next value.

✔ **Tips**

- This method won't fill in holes in the serial number sequence—something you should never try to do. Related records in other files might be mistakenly connected to a new record with the old serial number.

- In FileMaker 5, dialog boxes like Define Fields and Define Calculation were made resizable, making it far easier to read long field and script definitions. But when you closed the dialog box, FileMaker did not remember the change and returned to the default size. In FileMaker 6 this annoyance is rectified. If you resize a dialog box, it will reopen at the new size the next time you use it.

Calculation Fields

Formatting Labels or Envelopes

Calculation fields can be combined with other fields to build more complex formulas. For example, once you have a Full Name calculation field, you can combine it with the address data to create a Label field. This field can become a building block for every layout that requires these fields to be used together. Not only will it make a label easy to position for printing, but the same field works nicely as a letter heading or Sold To field in an invoice. Just adjust the field fonts and sizes in each layout.

To create a label field:

1. Choose File > Define Fields (Control+Shift+D/Command+Shift+D).

2. When the Define Fields dialog box appears, type the name you'll use for your label field in the Field Name text box, select the Calculation radio button, then click Create. We use Label as the field name in this example.

3. When the Specify Calculation box appears, double-click the name of the full name calculation field you created in "To merge fields" on page 62—in our case, Full Name. In the Operators keypad, click the ampersand button.

4. In the Operators keypad, click the quotes button and then the paragraph (¶) button (**Figure 4.20**).

5. Click to the right of the quotes, then click the ampersand button and press Return (Mac) or Enter (Windows) (**Figure 4.21**).

6. In the function list on the right, double-click Trim.

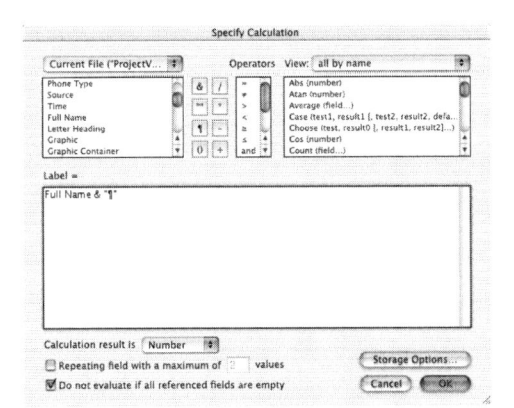

continues on next page

Figure 4.20 To put the first field on a line of its own, put a paragraph symbol between quotes.

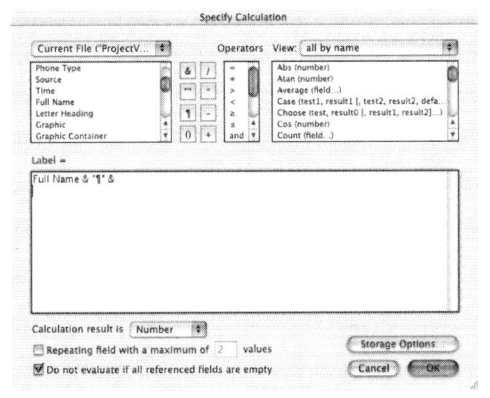

Figure 4.21 Just like in a word processing program, typing a return breaks the formula line.

7. With the "text" parameter highlighted in the formula box, double-click the next field to be used in the calculation. This example uses the Address field (**Figure 4.22**).

8. Click to the right of the parentheses. In the Operators keypad, click the quotes button and then the paragraph (¶) button.

9. Next you want to put the Address field on its own line in the label. Click to the right of the quotes, then click the ampersand button and press Return (Mac) or Enter (Windows).

10. In the function list, double-click Trim. Replace the "text" parameter by double-clicking City in the field list.

11. Click the quotes button and type a comma and a space inside the quotes. Click to the right of the quotes and click the ampersand button (**Figure 4.23**).

12. In the function list, double-click Trim. Replace the "text" parameter by double-clicking State in the field list. Click to the right of the quotes, and click the ampersand button in the Operators keypad.

13. Click the quotes button and type a space inside the quotes to add a space before the next field. Click to the right of the quotes and click the ampersand button.

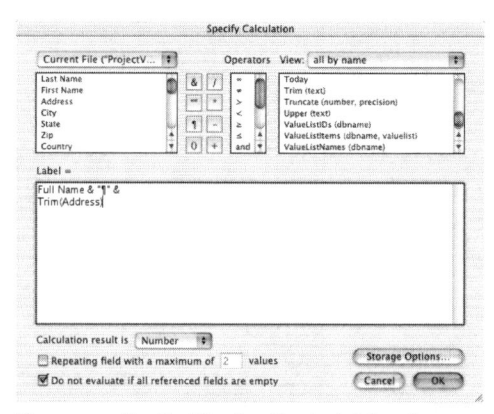

Figure 4.22 Use the Trim function to delete extra spaces around the address line.

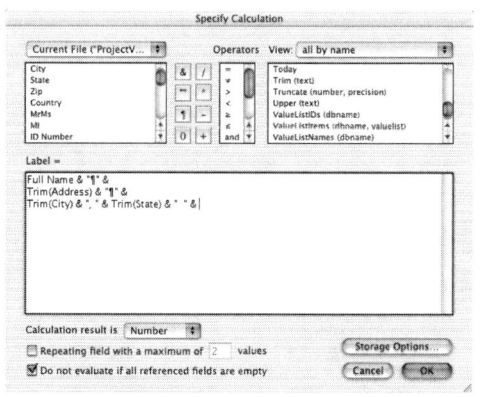

Figure 4.23 To insert a comma between two fields, use the quotes button and type a comma and a space inside the quotes.

Calculation Fields

14. In the function list, double-click Trim. Replace the "text" parameter by double-clicking Zip in the field list (**Figure 4.24**).

15. Set "Calculation result is" to Text and click OK. When you're finished, click Done.

Now you have a completed formula in a field. When you place this field in a layout, it will display three lines of text: the full name and two address lines.

✔ Tip

- If your addresses will sometimes include a country but not always, use the If function combined with IsEmpty to add the Country field as the last line of the formula. For information on how to do this, see steps 7–11 in "To merge fields" on page 62 (**Figure 4.25**).

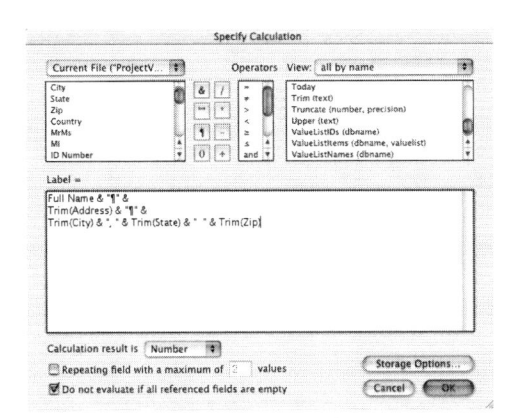

Figure 4.24 To string City, State, and Zip together on one line, use ampersands (&) between functions and don't insert the paragraph symbol.

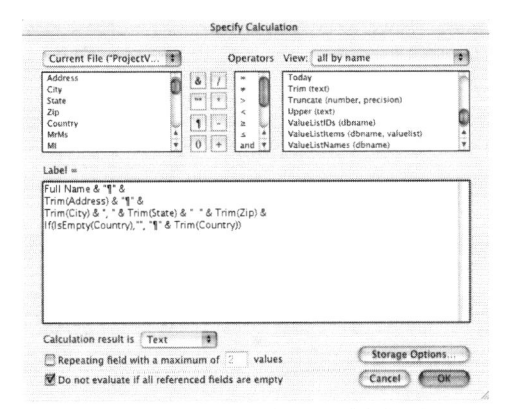

Figure 4.25 To add a Country line to a label, select the If function, and use IsEmpty to test the results. If the field contains data, the calculation will add a paragraph marker and the field contents. If it's empty, no extra line is inserted.

Chapter 4

Formatting Form-Letter Modules

If you've created form-letter layouts before, you know that it's relatively easy to use merge fields to personalize a standard letter. However, if you depend heavily on form letters, you still end up repeating the same tasks over and over when you use this tactic. Form letters usually follow the same basic concept—a salutation (Dear), a courtesy title (Mr., Ms., General, or Exalted Leader), and a last name. Then comes the body of the text, followed by a closing (Sincerely) and a signature name. Replace many of these form-letter elements with calculation fields and you can minimize duplications.

If you're clever about creating options with the all-purpose If function, you can trim the number of different layouts and letters you need to create as well.

For example, if you have a Greeting Name field, you can set your salutation to automatically create either a formal or informal heading. You'd still use If and IsEmpty functions to check for text in a field (like the MI field), but substitute the Greeting Name field instead. If there is no text in the Greeting Name field, the salutation would default to the standard formal format (Dear Mrs. Jones). If it is supplied, the less formal greeting name (a first name or a nickname) would be used (Dear Karen).

One of the most useful next steps in putting the Label calculation field to work is using it in a letter layout. Most well-composed letters include the addressee's name and address as a block of text (just like the label). Following that block of text is a date or a greeting line. Since the elements and their positions are standard, they're a prime target for another modular calculation field.

Calculation Fields

You can adapt the techniques below to create layouts such as business forms, statements, invoices, and other printouts that combine global, standard fields.

To create a standard letter heading:

1. Follow the steps in "To create a label field" on page 69.

2. Choose File > Define Fields (Control+Shift+D/Command+Shift+D).

3. When the Define Fields dialog box appears, type the name of your heading field in the Field Name text box, select the Calculation radio button, then click Create. We use Letter Heading as the field name in this example.

4. When the Specify Calculation box appears, double-click the name of your label calculation field—in our example, Label. In the Operators keypad, click the ampersand button.

5. In the Operators keypad, click the quotes button and then the paragraph button two or three times to create enough space between the heading address and the salutation. Click to the right of the quotes and click the ampersand button in the Operators keypad (**Figure 4.26**).

6. In the Operators keypad, click the quotes button. Between the quotes type Dear and a space. Click to the right of the quotes. In the Operators keypad, click the ampersand button (**Figure 4.27**).

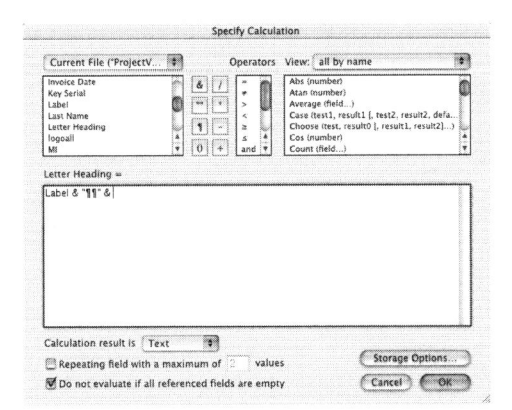

continues on next page

Figure 4.26 To create a letter heading, use the existing Label field, then add paragraph markers to separate the addressee information from the rest of the letter.

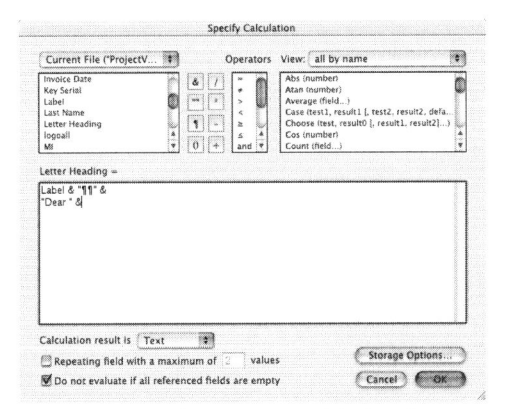

Figure 4.27 Put different portions of the heading calculation on different lines so you can read them easily later.

7. In the field list, double-click your courtesy title field. This example uses MrMs.

8. In the Operators keypad, click the ampersand button, then the quotes button. Type a space inside the quotes.

9. Click to the right of the quotes and click the ampersand button again (**Figure 4.28**).

10. In the function list, double-click Trim. With "text" highlighted in the formula box, double-click your Last Name field in the field list.

11. Click to the right of the parentheses. In the Operators keypad, click the ampersand button, then the quotes. Type a colon inside the quotes.

12. Make sure to select Text from the "Calculation result is" pull-down menu, then click OK, then Done.

You now have a standard letter heading and greeting in one field.

✔ Tip

- Once you get the hang of the concept, you can start combining modules of calculation fields to help you streamline your layout creation. For example, many invoices have two address sections: the ship-to address and the bill-to address. Sometimes these addresses are the same, but occasionally they're not. If you created one calculation field for the shipping address (usually the same as the label field), you can create another for a billing address. If the billing address exists, it will be inserted in the layout. If the billing calculation field is empty, the shipping address will be inserted instead.

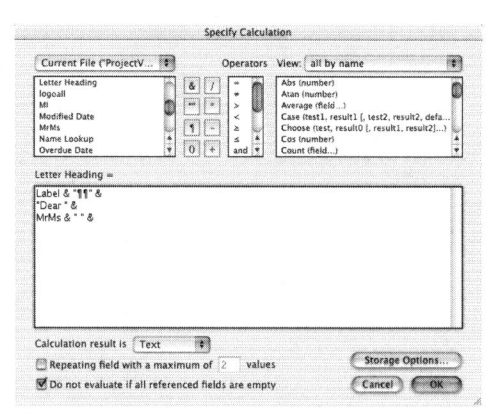

Figure 4.28 Always remember to add a space within quotes whenever you merge several text fields on one printed line.

Calculation Fields

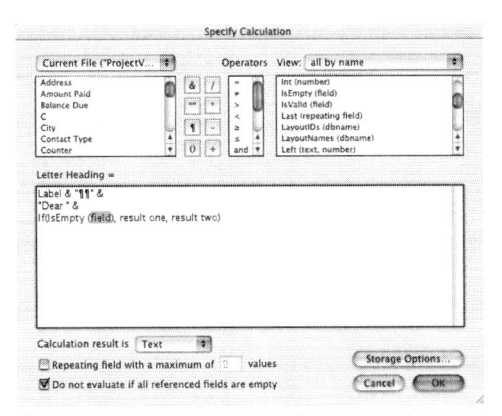

Figure 4.29 To create a formula that chooses between two options depending on whether there's data in a field, select the If function, then select IsEmpty as its test parameter.

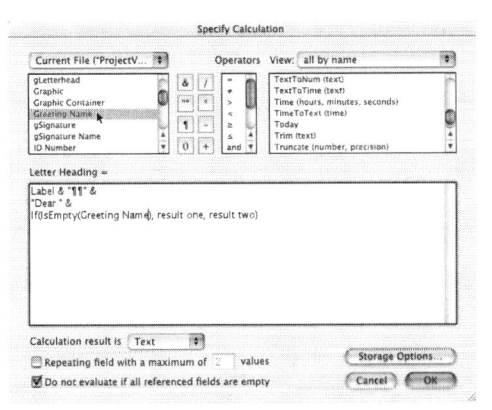

Figure 4.30 To use a Greeting Name if one exists, select it as the test parameter for IsEmpty.

To create a customizable letter heading:

1. Follow the steps in "To create a label field" on page 69.

2. Choose File > Define Fields (Control+Shift+D/Command+Shift+D).

3. When the Define Fields dialog box appears, type the name of your heading field in the Field Name text box, select the Calculation radio button, then click Create. We use Letter Heading as the field name in this example.

4. When the Specify Calculation box appears, double-click the name of your label calculation field—in our example, Label. In the Operators keypad, click the ampersand button.

5. In the Operators keypad, click the quotes button and then the paragraph button two or three times to create the visual space you'd like between the heading address and the letter salutation. Click to the right of the quotes again and click the ampersand button in the Operators keypad (**Figure 4.26**).

6. Click the quotes button. Type *Dear* and a space between the quotes. Click to the right of the quotes. In the Operators keypad, click the ampersand button (**Figure 4.27**).

7. Double-click If to choose it from the function list. In the formula box, double-click the "test" parameter in the If statement to select it. In the function list, double-click IsEmpty (**Figure 4.29**). The IsEmpty function looks at a field to see if it contains any data.

8. With the "field" parameter highlighted in the formula box, double-click Greeting Name in the field list (**Figure 4.30**).

continues on next page

Chapter 4

9. In the formula box, double-click "result one" to highlight it.

10. Double-click the courtesy title field in the field list.

11. In the Operators keypad, click the ampersand button, then the quotes button. Type a space inside the quotes.

12. Click to the right of the quotes and click the ampersand button.

13. Double-click Trim in the function list, which appears in the formula box with "text" highlighted, then double-click your Last Name field in the field list (**Figure 4.31**).

14. In the formula box, highlight "result two" and double-click the Trim function. With "text" highlighted in the formula box, double-click Greeting Name in the field list (**Figure 4.32**). Click to the end of the line.

15. In the Operators keypad, click the ampersand button, then click the quotes button and type a colon between the quotes.

16. Make sure your calculation is set to Text, then click OK. When you're finished, click Done.

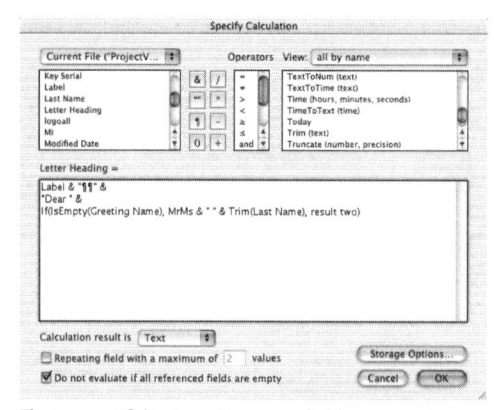

Figure 4.31 If the Greeting Name field is empty, the calculation will use the standard formal greeting of "Mr." or "Ms." plus a space and the last name.

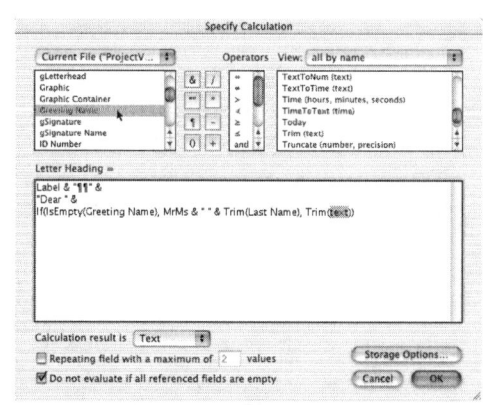

Figure 4.32 Choosing Greeting Name as the field for "result two" inserts it instead of the formal greeting whenever you want to use an informal name for the addressee.

Calculation Fields

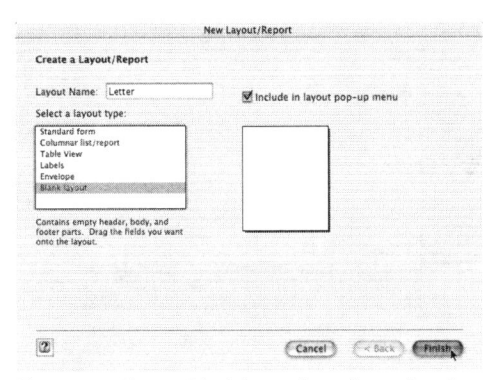

Figure 4.33 Choose Blank layout from the options in the New Layout dialog box.

Augmenting a Form Letter

If you have a letter heading calculation field, you can use it in a form letter layout. In fact, if you create the parts of the letter as separate fields, you'll have modules that will make future layouts increasingly easy to develop.

If you're using printed letterhead sheets for your form letters, skip steps 8–11 below, since you won't need a global container field if the logo is already printed on the paper.

To create a form letter with modular fields:

1. Go to the file where you want to create your new layout. First create a text global field to hold the body of your form letter and a container global field for the letterhead logo if you have one.

 We cover creating container global fields in the section "To create a global container field" in Chapter 3.

2. Choose View > Layout Mode (Control+L/Command+L), then choose Layouts > New Layout (Control+N/Command+N).

3. In the New Layout/Report dialog box, type the layout name (in this case, Letter) in the Layout Name box, and select Blank layout from the layout type list (**Figure 4.33**). Click Finish to create the layout.

 An empty layout with Header, Body, and Footer tabs will appear. By creating a blank layout you avoid adding unnecessary parts that you'll have to delete later.

continues on next page

77

Chapter 4

4. Select View > Graphic Rulers to turn on the horizontal and vertical rulers. Rulers will make it easier to set up your letter.

5. Click the Header part tab to select it. Drag it down until the header equals the margin you want at the top of your letter (**Figure 4.34**).

 In our example, we've left enough room to add a container field with our letterhead logo and some comfortable white space above it (**Figure 4.35**).

6. Click the Body tab and drag it down until it's at the 10½-inch (or 760-point) vertical mark. You'll see the dashed line indicating that you've reached the bottom of the page (**Figure 4.36**).

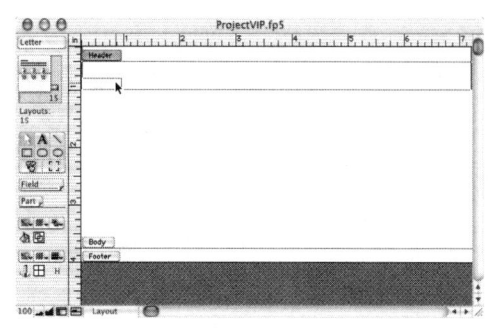

Figure 4.34 Drag the Header tab down to resize the part.

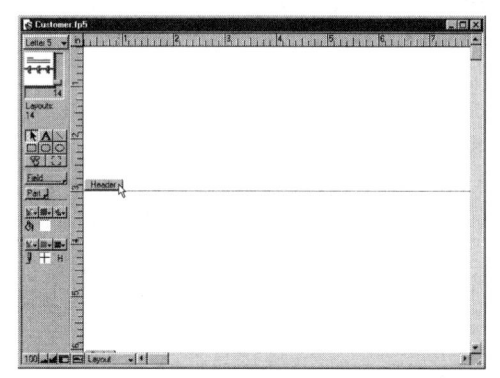

Figure 4.35 This Header part is 3 inches deep to allow for a margin and a letterhead logo.

Figure 4.36 Drag the Body tab down to the bottom of the page.

Calculation Fields

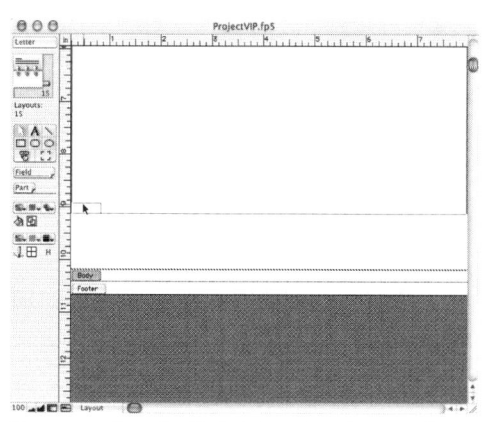

Figure 4.37 Drag the Body tab up to make room for a footer.

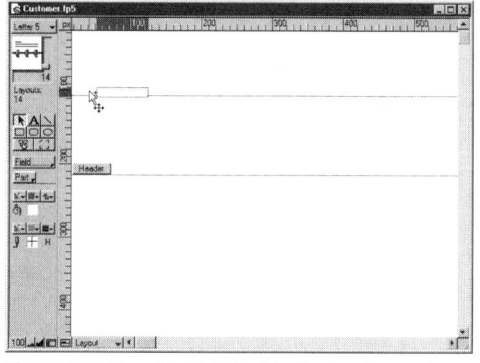

Figure 4.38 Drag the Field tool to the header to place your container field in the layout.

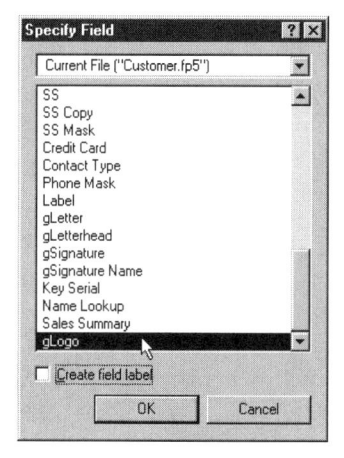

Figure 4.39 Choose the global container field from the field list in the Specify Field dialog box.

7. For most letters, you don't need a footer unless you have a letterhead design that has something printed at the bottom of the page. If you don't need a footer, drag the Footer tab up to delete it. If you do, drag the Body tab back up until you have enough room for the footer (**Figure 4.37**).

8. Scroll to the top of the layout. If you're going to use the global letterhead field, click the Field tool in the tool area on the left and drag it into the Header part (**Figure 4.38**).

9. When the Specify Field dialog box appears, uncheck the "Create field label" box.

10. Choose the global letterhead or logo field you created in step 1 and click OK (**Figure 4.39**). In our example, the field is called "gLogo."

11. Resize the field so it's big enough to display the entire letterhead or logo.

12. Click the Field tool and drag it into the Body part. When the Specify Field dialog box appears, choose Letter Heading.

continues on next page

AUGMENTING A FORM LETTER

79

Chapter 4

13. Now you need to know how much room to leave for the records in your database. To see a sample record, choose View > Show > Sample Data (**Figure 4.40**).

14. The first record in your database will appear in the Letter Heading field in the Body part on your layout (**Figure 4.41**). Unless you're sure the sample is the longest record, resize the field to allow for the longest and deepest address. You don't have to be precise, since you can always go back and change the layout later.

15. Click the Field tool and drag it into the layout below the Letter Heading field.

16. Choose your global letter field in the Specify Field dialog box. Resize the letter field to fill the rest of the Body part (**Figure 4.42**).

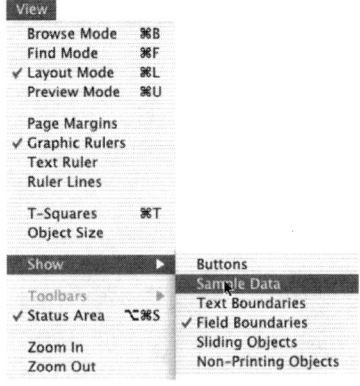

Figure 4.40 To make it easier to set the field sizes for your form letter, choose View > Show > Sample Data.

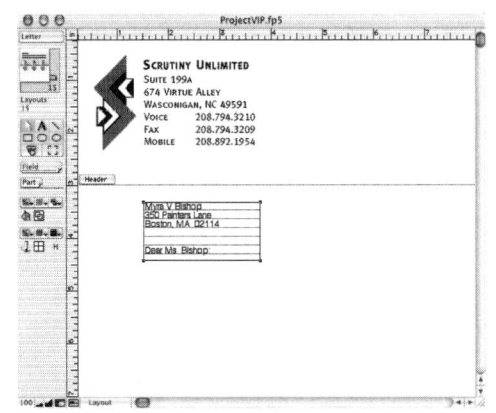

Figure 4.41 Show Sample Data makes setting the proper size of a field much easier by displaying the data instead of the field names.

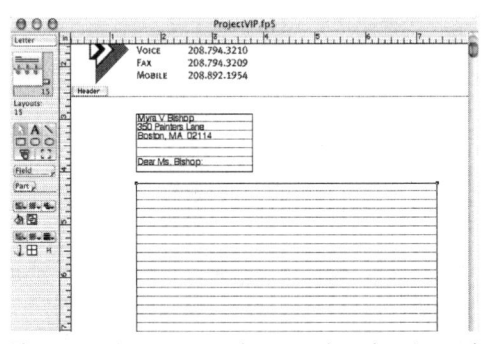

Figure 4.42 Leave a space between the salutation and the body of the letter.

Calculation Fields

Figure 4.43 To get rid of unused extra space you've left in your layout, choose Format > Sliding/Printing.

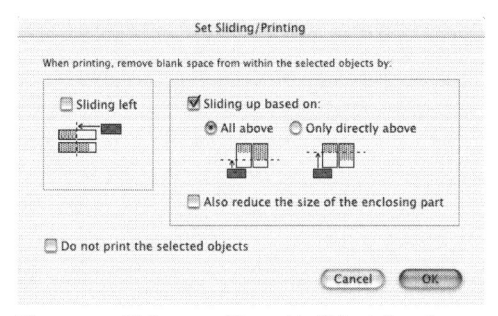

Figure 4.44 Sliding up will get rid of blank lines in the layout.

17. Shift-click to select both the Letter Heading and Letter fields in the layout, then choose Format > Sliding/Printing (**Figure 4.43**). Sliding will get rid of blank lines in the layout.

18. When the Set Sliding/Printing dialog box appears, click the "Sliding up based on" check box to prevent extra vertical spacing from being inserted because of differences in field record lengths. Click the "All above" radio button to take the longest Body part into account when aligning fields vertically below it (**Figure 4.44**).

19. Switch to Browse Mode (Control+B/Command+B). Click in the letter field and type the text of the letter.

✔ **Tips**

- The dashed line on a layout indicates the page break. Watch for it when you create a new layout! If the Body part extends past the page-break line, every letter will produce a blank page when you print it.

- It's a good idea to put a *g* at the beginning of a global field name as a reminder of its field type.

- To further automate your form letters, create a global container field for the signature. Scan a signature, add it to the global field, and place the field below the letter text.

- The fields that are set to slide will only do so when the layout is printed or in Preview mode (Control+U/Command+U). In Browse mode, the fields will show where they were placed on the layout.

- If you use many form letters, you may already have them as text in another application. Using FileMaker's batch processing (see Chapter 12), you can import multiple files of text at once, instead of retyping or cutting and pasting individual sections.

AUGMENTING A FORM LETTER

81

Using GetField

The new GetField function returns the contents of a specific field. At first glance, this function might not seem all that useful, since you could simply use any field name to get its contents.

But the magic is in how you apply GetField. If you put quotes around the field in GetField("Abracadabra"), nothing special happens, and you get the contents of the Abracadabra field.

But if you put the name of another field (say, Magic) into Abracadabra, then eliminate the quotes around the field name in GetField(Abracadabra), GetField won't return the word "Magic" in the calculation. Instead, you'll get the contents of the field Magic. Now that's useful!

In "Formatting Labels or Envelopes" earlier in this chapter, we showed you how to create a calculation field that combines name and address information into a single field that can be conveniently placed in a label or envelope layout. But databases often contain both home and work addresses, and people frequently prefer to be contacted at one address rather than the other. You could create yet another field for the preferred contact but it would be a nightmare to keep straight. Printing labels in two groups for work or home preferences is equally inconvenient. Using the GetField function, you can create a field to choose which address to use for the label.

To follow these steps, you'll need a database with separate fields for home and work addresses (**Figure 4.45**).

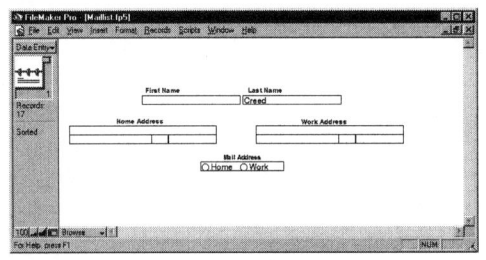

Figure 4.45 The address data for each record must appear in separate Home and Work fields.

Calculation Fields

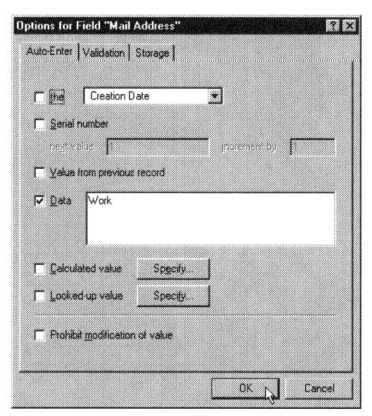

Figure 4.46 Set the Auto-Enter option for the Mail Address field. The Mail Label calculation won't be displayed properly unless the Data check box is selected.

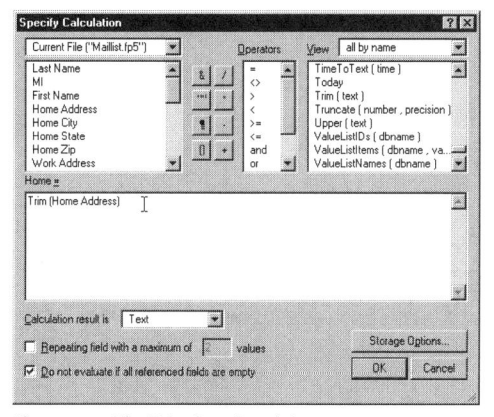

Figure 4.47 The Trim function deletes any spaces around the home address.

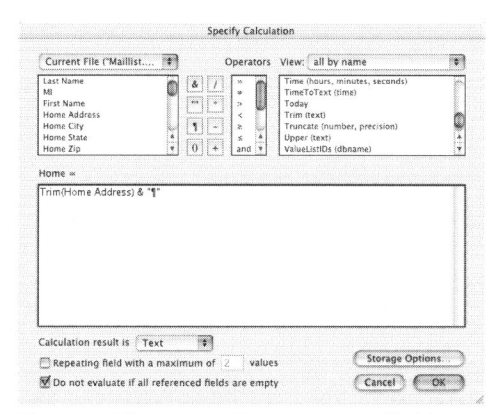

Figure 4.48 The paragraph operator puts all of the text that follows it on a new line.

To select a mailing address using GetField:

1. Choose File > Define Fields (Control+Shift+D/Command+Shift+D).

2. In the Define Fields dialog box, name the field Mail Address, choose Text as the type, and click Create.

3. Double-click the Mail Address field. When the Options dialog box appears, click the Auto-Enter tab.

4. Click the Data check box. Enter either Home or Work as the default value in the box to the right (**Figure 4.46**). Click OK.

5. In the Define Fields dialog box, type Home for the field name, choose Calculation as the type, and click Create.

6. When the Specify Calculation dialog box appears, double-click Trim in the function list on the right.

   Trim finds initial and trailing spaces around text and deletes them.

7. With the "text" parameter highlighted in the formula box, double-click the Home Address field in the field list. Click to the right of the parenthesis (**Figure 4.47**).

8. In the Operators keypad, click the ampersand button to add it to the formula box, then click the quotes button.

9. With the cursor still between the quotes, click the paragraph operator button (¶) (**Figure 4.48**).

continues on next page

83

Chapter 4

10. Click to the right of the quotes, then click the ampersand button and press Return (Mac) or Enter (Windows).

11. Next you want to put the city, state, and Zip code together on the second address line. In the function list, double-click Trim.

12. With the "text" parameter highlighted, double-click Home City in the field list. Click to the right of the parenthesis, then click the ampersand button.

13. Click the quotes button. Type a comma and a space between the quotes. Click to the right of the quotes, then click the ampersand button (**Figure 4.49**).

14. In the function list, double-click Trim. With the "text" parameter highlighted, double-click Home State in the field list. Click to the right of the parenthesis, then click the ampersand button.

15. Click the quotes button. Type a space between the quotes. Click to the right of the quotes, then click the ampersand button.

16. In the function list, double-click Trim. With the "text" parameter highlighted, double-click the Home Zip field in the field list.

17. Be sure to set "Calculation result is" to Text (**Figure 4.50**). Click OK to finish.

18. In the Define Fields dialog box, click the Home field and then click Duplicate.

19. Change the name of the duplicated field from Home Copy to Work and click Create (**Figure 4.51**).

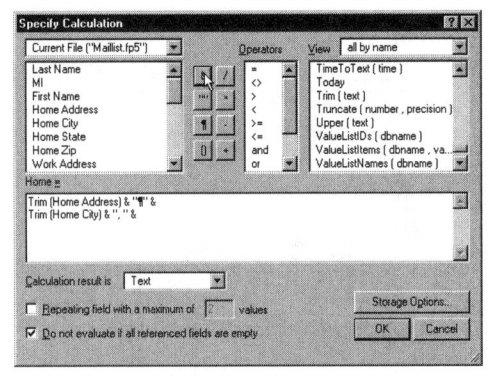

Figure 4.49 Text, spaces, and punctuation must appear within quotes if you want them to print as part of the address line.

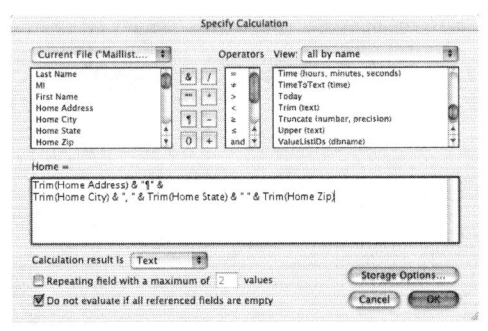

Figure 4.50 Since the fields in the calculation contain text, "Calculation result is" must be set to Text.

Figure 4.51 Duplicating the Home field and changing the calculation saves you from having to create the new field from scratch.

Calculation Fields

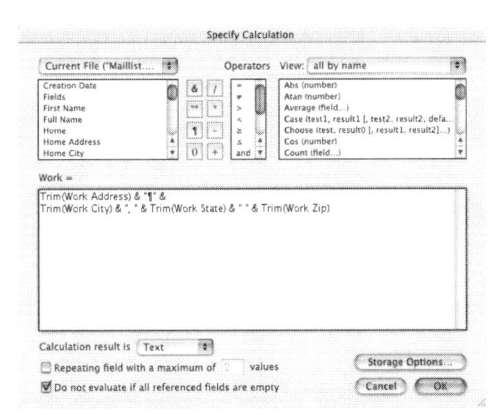

Figure 4.52 Change "Home" to "Work" throughout the calculation.

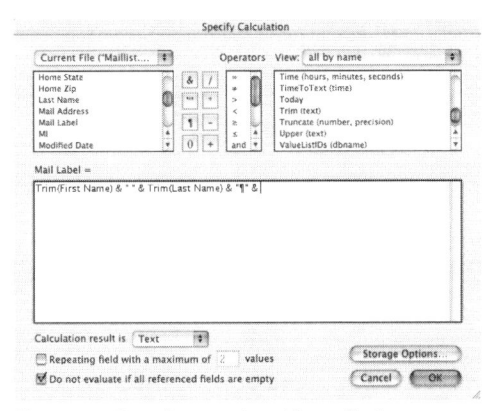

Figure 4.53 To make sure the address displays properly, use the Trim function to strip extra spaces from the field data.

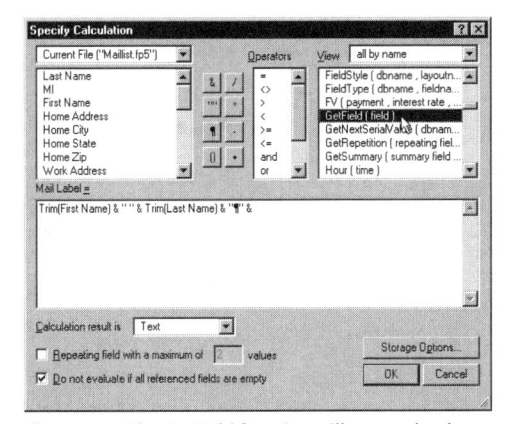

Figure 4.54 The GetField function will return the data from the field name you choose.

20. Double-click the Work field. When the Specify Calculation dialog box appears, change all the instances of "Home" to "Work" (**Figure 4.52**). Click OK.

    Now that we've set up the two calculations for home and work addresses, we need to write the calculation that will connect the person with the default address.

21. In the Define Fields dialog box, type Mail Label for the field name, choose Calculation as the type and click Create.

22. When the Specify Calculation dialog box appears, double-click Trim in the function list. With the "text" parameter highlighted, double-click the First Name field. Click to the right of the parenthesis, then click the ampersand button.

23. Click the quotes button, type a space between the quotes, then click to the right of the quotes. Click the ampersand button.

24. In the function list, double-click Trim. With the "text" parameter highlighted, double-click the Last Name field. Click to the right of the parenthesis and click the ampersand button.

25. Click the quotes button, then the paragraph button. Click to the right of the quotes and click the ampersand button (**Figure 4.53**). Press Return (Mac) or Enter (Windows).

26. In the function list, double-click the GetField function (**Figure 4.54**).

continues on next page

USING GETFIELD

85

Chapter 4

27. With the "text" parameter highlighted, double-click the Mail Address field in the field list (**Figure 4.55**).

28. Make sure that result is set to Text, click OK and then Done.

    We have our calculations, but we need to create a value list so we can choose between the Home and Work addresses.

29. Choose File > Define Value Lists. In the Define Value Lists dialog box, click New.

30. When the Edit Value List dialog box appears, type Mail Address for the Value List Name.

31. Click the "Use custom values" radio button. Enter Home and Work in the custom values box (**Figure 4.56**). Click OK and then Done.

32. Go to a layout that has the address fields. Choose View > Layout Mode (Control+L/Command+L).

33. Drag the Field tool into the layout. When the Specify Field dialog box appears, choose Mail Address (**Figure 4.57**).

34. Click the Mail Address field and choose Format > Field Format.

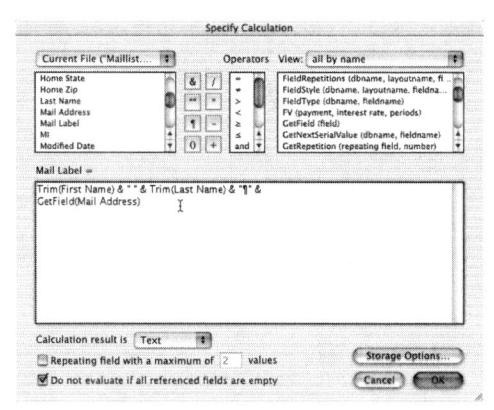

Figure 4.55 Don't put quotes around the field name in a GetField function, or GetField will return the name, not the contents.

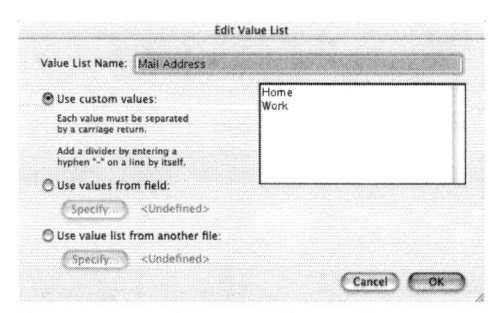

Figure 4.56 Enter the work and home address field names in the value list.

Figure 4.57 Specify the Mail Address field to add it to the same layout as the address fields; the user can easily choose which address to use for each record.

Calculation Fields

Figure 4.58 Because the field name used in GetField must match the data entered, set the Mail Address field to use radio buttons to prevent input errors.

35. When the Field Format dialog box appears, choose "Radio buttons" from the drop-down list and set "using value list" to Mail Address (**Figure 4.58**). Click OK.

36. Go to the label or envelope layout where the Mail Label field will be used. Choose View > Layout Mode (Control+L/Command+L). Drag the Field tool into the layout. When the Specify Field dialog box appears, choose Mail Label. Make the field large enough to display the address properly (**Figure 4.59**).

In each record, the Mail Label field will display the name and either the work or home address, depending on which you choose in the Mail Address field.

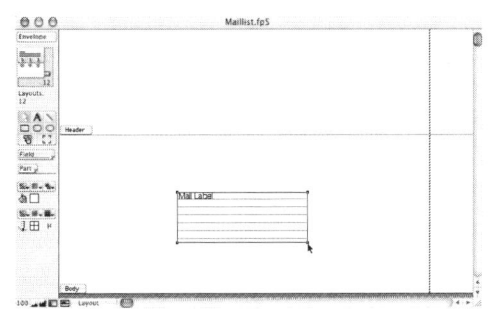

Figure 4.59 Add the Mail Label field to the label layout and size it to show all of the data.

FileMaker Pro and Two-Digit Dates

Unlike previous versions, FileMaker 6 uses a consistent set of rules to convert two-digit years into four-digit years in date fields. This is true for data entered manually and for imported data.

If the current date is in the first 10 years of the century (e.g., 2000–2009), FileMaker Pro converts two-digit years in the range 00–89 to dates in the current century, and 90–99 to dates in the previous century. In the future, when the current year is between 2010 and 2089, FileMaker Pro 6 will convert two-digit years to dates in the current century.

For the greatest accuracy, it is best to enter years using four digits whenever possible.

USING GETFIELD

87

Creating Data Reports

No matter how carefully you design a database or how accurately data is entered into it, your database remains an underutilized resource unless you can mine it for the precise information you need. Performing this effective information retrieval is a two-step process, covered in this chapter.

The first step is to isolate the set of information you need. You already know how to search on one field so that information will be organized in a specific way. Any time you need to see a mailing list by state or city, instead of alphabetically or in the order names were entered, you're performing a simple search. You may also know that you can add more criteria to a search in order to narrow down this information. For example, if you want to find which customers in Newport, Rhode Island, received mailings in April and June but not in May, and whether they purchased anything in response, a simple search is not enough. Fortunately, FileMaker Pro offers search tools for zeroing in on this exact set of information (known as the *found set*) and sort tools for organizing the found set in the most effective manner.

Once you've chosen a found set, you need to summarize it in a layout to display it for yourself and others. A summary report can show how many customers in the group responded, tell you how much they spent by month, and total the sales per individual—giving you quick feedback for decision-making.

Extending a Found Set

Once you have a found set, you might want to further refine it by finding records within the set or adding more records to the ones already found. In previous versions of FileMaker, you would use the Modify Last Find command, which would re-create the previous find criteria and allow you to modify them. That works just fine if your criteria are simple, but can create some serious issues if they were complex. For example, imagine that you had created a found set of customers in the six New England states with billings over $500 per year. Now you want to find out how many of this set spent more than $1,000. A simple task, but tedious. You'd have to select Modify Last Find and change the sales amount for all six requests to $1,000. But in FilcMakcr 6, you have the ability to find records within the previous find (Constrain Found Set) or in addition to it (Extend Found Set) when you use the Modify Last Find command.

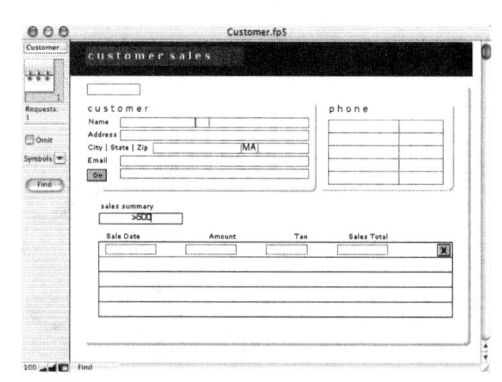

Figure 5.1 Enter the Find criteria to create the first found set.

In this example, we have a database with a State field, and another, called Sales Summary, that displays the Sales Amount fields in all records. We'll create a report of all New England customers who spent more than $500, and then use the Constrain Found Set command to create a separate report including just those customers who spent more than $1,000. As an alternative, we'll use Extend Found Set to add all the New York customers who spent more than $500 to the first found set.

To constrain a found set:

1. Choose View > Find Mode (Control+F in Windows, or Command+F in Mac).

2. Enter your criteria into as many fields as you need. In our example, we've entered MA in the State field and >500 in the Sales Summary field (**Figure 5.1**).

Creating Data Reports

Figure 5.2 Duplicate Request lets you input different criteria into fields you've already used.

Figure 5.3 When you select Constrain Found Set, you use the criteria in the second Find to locate records within the first found set.

3. Choose Requests > Duplicate Request (Control+D/Command+D; **Figure 5.2**).

4. Replace the old criteria with a new entry. In our case, we enter ME in the state field.

5. Repeat steps 3 and 4 for the rest of the criteria. In our example, we enter the other New England states (VT, CT, NH, RI).

6. Click the Find button to create the found set.

   Our found set has all the customers in New England who have spent more than $500. You can print your report for these records. Now you can narrow the result for only those customers with a sales amount greater than $1,000.

7. Choose View > Find Mode again. Enter >1000 in the Sales Summary field.

8. Choose Requests > Constrain Found Set (**Figure 5.3**).

   Our found set now contains only those customers who have spent more than $1,000.

To extend a found set:

1. Repeat steps 1–6 above to create the New England report set.

2. Choose View > Find Mode again. Enter >500 in the Sales Summary field and NY in the State field.

3. Choose Requests > Extend Found Set.

   The new found set will include all of the customers in New England *and* New York who have spent more than $500.

EXTENDING A FOUND SET

91

Chapter 5

Using Search Operators

FileMaker uses search operators to extend the power of Finds. "And" and "Or" searches are "big gun" tools that allow you to pull out large categories of data based on field names. Search operators are more like precision instruments. Using them, you can search for information that's more deeply buried in the database records themselves. These search operators are also very useful if you're not exactly sure what you're looking for but you know it has to be there. Mistyped entries, variant spellings, a checkbook discrepancy in the February balance—they can all be located with a well-chosen search operator.

The *range* operator is most often used to find a series of dates or numbers, but it's equally useful for an alphabetic search. In fact, most operators allow you to use letters in the same manner as numbers in finds. Try this with the range, greater than, and less than operators to search for items in different parts of the alphabet.

To use a search operator in a data search:

1. Switch to the layout you want, then choose View > Find Mode (Control+F/Command+F).

2. Click the field you wish to search. Type the first letter of the range.

3. In the status area on the left, click the Symbols arrow to choose the range operator from the drop-down menu (**Figure 5.4**). Type the last letter of the range, then click Find.

   In this case, typing A...M in the Last Name field will find all of the records where a check was paid to a supplier whose name begins with a letter in the first half of the alphabet (**Figure 5.5**).

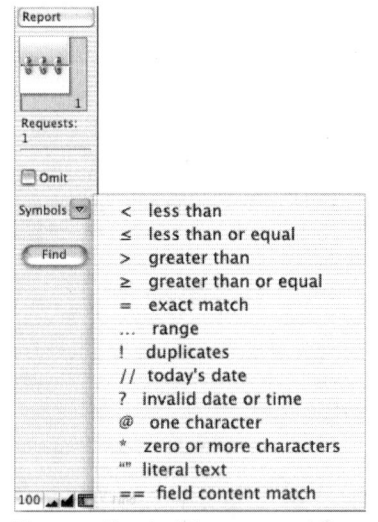

Figure 5.4 You don't have to search for operators on the keyboard; they're all listed in the Find status area.

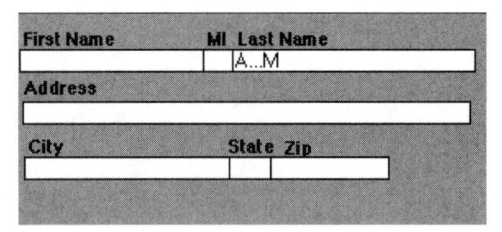

Figure 5.5 The range operator can be used to find ranges of letters, as well as dates or numbers.

Creating Data Reports

Figure 5.6 To find all entries that contain an ampersand (&) or other search operator, place quotes around the operator to change it from an operator to a plain text character.

Figure 5.7 By combining the "any character" wildcard (*) with the ampersand in quotes, you can find all entries with an ampersand in them no matter where in the field the ampersand appears.

✔ Tips

- Another way to search for a range that begins at the beginning of the alphabet would be to type ≤M in the Last Name field (use ≥N for the end of the alphabet).

- If you need to find an entry that includes one of the search operators (like an ampersand) place quotes around it. Quotes change an operator into a plain text character for search purposes (**Figure 5.6**). The combination of operators in this example will find all the entries with an ampersand anywhere in their Paid To field (**Figure 5.7**).

Search Operators

<	Finds values that are less than the search criteria	//	Finds records that have today's date in the field
≤	Finds values less than or equal to the search criteria	?	Finds records that have an invalid character in a date field
>	Finds values greater than the search criteria	@	Substitutes for a single character in search criteria (J@nes will find Jones, Janes, and Junes)
≥	Finds values greater than or equal to the search criteria	*	Substitutes for any number of characters in search criteria (J*nes will find Jones, Jarones, and Jinones)
=	Finds values that exactly match anywhere in the field	""	Finds records with an exact match for the criteria in quotes ("John Jones Jr.")
...	Finds values that fall within a range (e.g., 1/1/2000...1/31/2000)	==	Finds values that exactly match the search criteria
!	Finds records that have duplicate values in a field		

USING SEARCH OPERATORS

93

Creating an "Inverted" Search

You probably know that you can omit records from an existing found set. However, you can also use the process of elimination to create a found set made up only of records that don't match the Find criteria. Imagine that you're projecting your average monthly sales for a bank loan. You don't necessarily want to include the month you closed up shop and snorkeled in the Bahamas, so you'd want to create a report that omitted that period from the found set.

You can even create a single search that selects certain records and omits others. This combination lets you eliminate your vacation period while selecting only corporate purchase orders from the rest of the year's records.

To omit records from a search:

1. Switch to the layout you want to use for the search, then choose View > Find Mode (Control+F/Command+F).

2. Enter the search criteria you want to eliminate from the found set in the appropriate fields.

3. In the status area, check the Omit box (**Figure 5.8**), then click Find.

   The records that meet the search criteria will be omitted from the found set. In our example, the result would be a list of sales that excluded activity in the month of April.

To select and omit at the same time:

1. Switch to the layout you want to use for the search, then choose View > Find Mode (Control+F/Command+F).

2. Enter the search criteria for the records you want find in the appropriate fields.

3. Choose Requests > Add New Request (Control+N/Command+N). Enter the search criteria for the records you want to eliminate in the field, then click the Omit box. Click Find.

   The found set will display the records that meet the first search criteria (purchase orders, for example) but won't contain the records that also meet the criteria in the second request.

✔ Tips

- Watch the order of your combinations when you combine criteria that you want with criteria you want to eliminate.

- If a record meets the first criteria but also meets the omit criteria, it won't appear in your found set. For example, if your company doesn't accept purchase orders below $1,000, it would be useless to select purchase orders as the first criterion and then omit amounts below $1,000 from the set.

- If you create a complex Find combination or one that you will use frequently in the future, you can create a Perform Find (Restore) script to restore the last Find. We cover scripts in detail in Chapter 7.

Figure 5.8 Click the Omit box to exclude records instead of finding them.

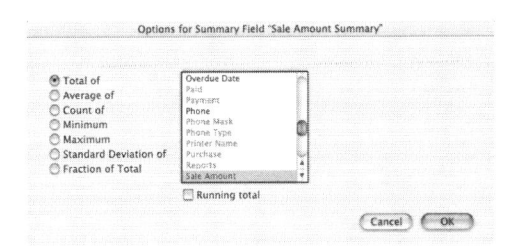

Figure 5.9 In the Options for Summary Field dialog box, you choose both the field to summarize and the form the summary will take.

Creating Summary Layout Parts

Once you have a found set, you can summarize it in a variety of ways. Using summary fields, you can count how many records were found and print the count in a report. You can create totals, averages, minimums, and maximums of number fields. If you are statistically inclined you can even create standard deviations.

Layouts with summary fields require a little more planning than those without them. A summary field is unique in that the same field will display different values, even in the same layout, depending on which part it appears in. A summary field defined as a total in the Trailing Grand Summary will display the total of that field for the entire found set. But the same field in the sub-summary layout part will only display the total for the sub-summary field.

To create summary fields:

1. Choose File > Define Fields (Control+Shift+D/Command+Shift+D). In the Define Fields dialog box, click the field to be summarized.

2. Change the field name by adding "Summary" to the end of it.

3. Click the Summary radio button.

4. Click Create (not Save).

5. When the Options for Summary Field dialog box appears, choose the type of summary you want (**Figure 5.9**). Click OK.

✔ Tip

- A summary field set to Count will return the number of records that have an entry in the summarized field.

Chapter 5

To create a layout with summary parts:

1. Choose View > Layout Mode (Control+L/Command+L). Choose New Layout (Control+N/Command+N).

   This automatically starts up the Layout Assistant. Based on the choices you make, the Layout Assistant creates the layout parts you need and places fields and their labels in a logical place within the parts.

2. In the New Layout/Report dialog box that appears, type a name for the layout and choose Columnar List/Report as the layout type (**Figure 5.10**). Click Next.

3. Click the Report with Grouped Data radio button. Check the Include Grand Totals box if you want to have totals for the entire report appear at the end (**Figure 5.11**). Click Next.

4. In the Specify Fields dialog box, double-click each available field to be included in the Body part of the report in order to place it in the Layout fields list. This example uses the Full Name, Sale Amount, Sales Tax, and Sales Total fields (**Figure 5.12**). When you're done, click Next.

5. In the Organize Records by Category dialog box, just click Next.

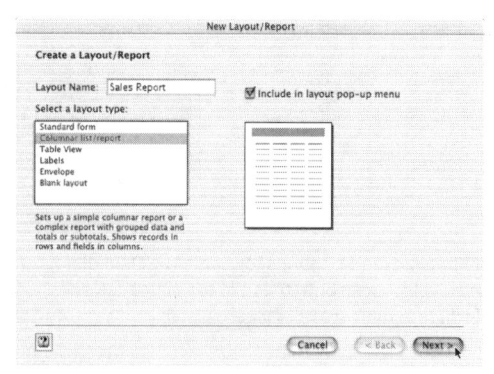

Figure 5.10 The Layout Assistant automates the process of creating a new layout.

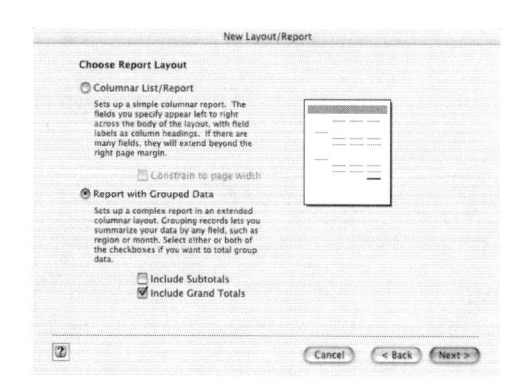

Figure 5.11 This layout example will include Grand Totals at the end of the report.

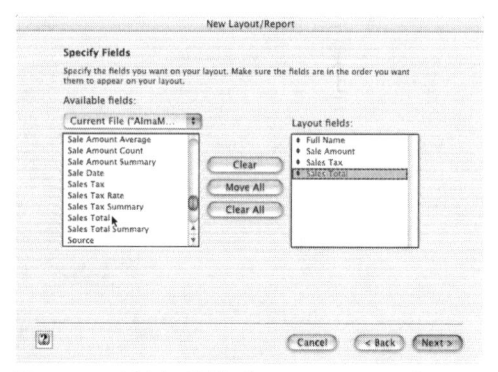

Figure 5.12 Add the fields that are not summaries to the Body part of the report.

Creating Data Reports

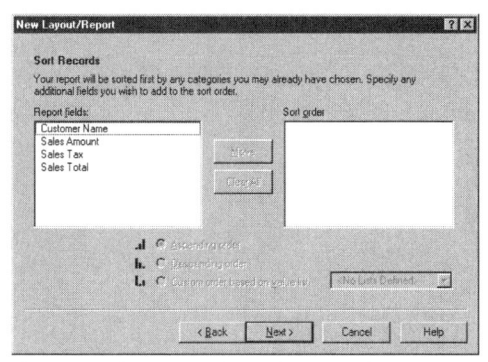

Figure 5.13 If you want to sort the report by one or more fields, choose them from the "Report fields" list.

Figure 5.14 This step adds the Summary fields that will display the grand totals in the Grand Summary part.

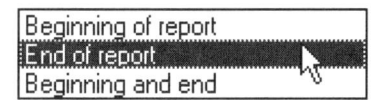

Figure 5.15 Choose the layout position for the summary totals from the "Grand total placement" drop-down menu.

6. If you wish to sort by any of the report fields listed in the Sort Records dialog box (**Figure 5.13**), double-click to select them. If you don't want to sort the report or if you're going to sort by other fields, leave the Sort order list empty. Click Next.

7. If you haven't yet created your summary fields, you can do so now by choosing Create Summary Field from the Summary Field drop-down menu in the Specify Grand Totals dialog box.

8. Select each of the summary fields you want to use, then click Add Grand Total to put each one into the Grand Total listing.

   We use summary fields that total sale amount, sales tax, and total sales (**Figure 5.14**).

9. From the "Grand total placement" drop-down menu, choose the position on the layout where you want the grand totals to appear (**Figure 5.15**).

   In this example, the totals will appear as a Trailing Grand Summary at the end of the report because we chose "End of report" from the drop-down menu. Click Next.

continues on next page

97

Chapter 5

10. In the Select a Theme dialog box, choose a color scheme for your report.

    If you're going to print the report on a black-and-white printer, play it safe with Default (no colors), or choose one of the themes with the word *print* in its title (**Figure 5.16**). Click Next.

11. In the Header and Footer Information dialog box, add any items like page numbers and data stamps that you wish to include in a specific place on the report by selecting them from the drop-down menus (**Figure 5.17**). Click Next.

12. To automatically create a script that will re-create the sort order you used for this summary and display the report in Preview mode, click the "Create a script" radio button and type a name for the script (**Figure 5.18**). (If you don't type a name, FileMaker will insert the layout name here.) If you don't want a script or plan to create your own, click "Do not create a script." Click Next.

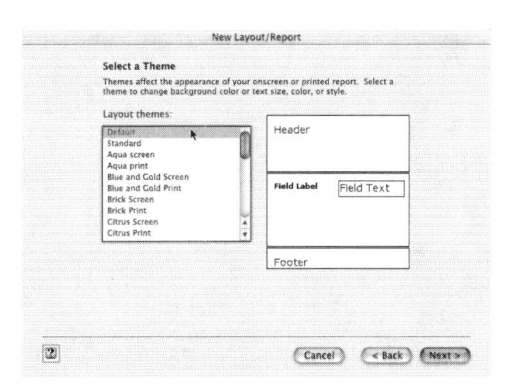

Figure 5.16 You can specify a color scheme for the report. If the report is to be printed on a laser printer, choose one of the print versions of the layout themes, or the black-and-white Default.

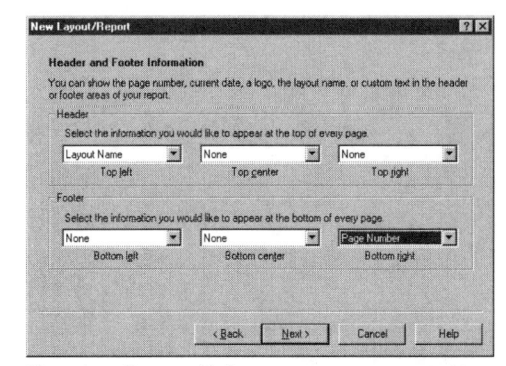

Figure 5.17 For a multiple-page report, you can add page numbers and titles to the footer or header.

Figure 5.18 You can create a script for this report automatically.

98

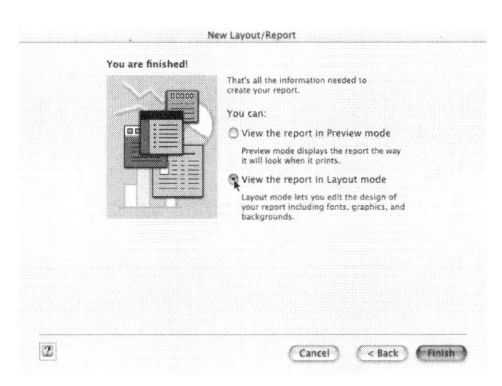

Figure 5.19 In Layout mode, you can fine-tune your report by reformatting fields and adding text.

13. If you want to see the report immediately, click the "View the report in Preview mode" radio button. If you want to fine-tune the layout, click "View the report in Layout mode" (**Figure 5.19**).

14. Click Finish to close the dialog box. Depending on which choice you made, your layout will be displayed in either Preview or Layout mode.

✔ **Tip**

- If you'd like your totals displayed at the beginning of a report instead of at the end, choose "Beginning of report" in step 9 above. If you've already created a report with a Trailing Grand Summary part, create a Leading Grand Summary part in Layout mode and place it at the top of the report, between the Header and Body parts. Then drag the summary fields to it and delete the Trailing Grand Summary.

Using Counts and Averages

Using an existing report with summary fields as a basis, you can easily add counts and averages. For example, if you have summary fields that track individual sales, total sales, and state sales tax, you can duplicate the summary total fields, rename them, and change their calculation result to add a summary field that counts the number of sales and the average sale amount.

To create counts and averages with a summary layout:

1. Choose File > Define Fields (Control+Shift+D/Command+Shift+D).

2. Duplicate the summary field that holds the total amount of the field you want to average (in this example, it's the Sale Amount Summary field). Change its name to something unique. Click Create (**Figure 5.20**).

3. Double-click the new field. When the Options dialog box appears, click the "Average of" radio button (**Figure 5.21**). Click OK.

4. To create another summary field that counts the number of sales, repeat steps 1 and 2. This time click the "Count of" radio button in the Options dialog box. Click OK to close the dialog box.

Figure 5.20 Duplicate the existing summary field, rename it, and change its calculation result from "Total of" to "Average of."

Figure 5.21 Duplicating an existing field and changing the calculation saves time in creating a summary field.

Creating Data Reports

Figure 5.22 Add the Sale Amount Average to the Trailing Grand Summary part to display the average of all sales in the report.

5. In Layout mode, choose the layout that will display the new fields. If it doesn't already have a Trailing Grand Summary part, create one by dragging the Part tool into the layout and choosing the Trailing Grand Summary radio button in the Part Definition dialog box. If the layout already has a Trailing Grand Summary part, click the bottom of the part and drag down to make room for the new fields.

6. Drag the Field tool into the Trailing Grand Summary part and add the Average field to display the average of all sales in the report (**Figure 5.22**). Click OK.

7. Drag the Field tool into the Trailing Grand Summary part again, and add the Count field to display the number of individual sales in the report. Click OK.

101

Creating a Page Count

When you print a multi-page document, you often set a header or footer in the application's print options to keep track of the total number of pages or how many pages you've printed. This information is particularly useful when you plan to send a report out for duplication, and it's invaluable if you need to keep the pages in order. FileMaker doesn't have a built-in function for the page total, so you'll need a bit of scripting to provide this useful information. If you've never scripted before, you'll find Chapter 7 useful in understanding what you're doing here.

To display a page count:

1. Choose File > Define Fields (Control+Shift+D/Command+Shift+D).

2. When the Define Fields dialog box appears, type the name of your field in the Field Name text box (we'll use the name gPageCount), select the Global radio button, then click Create (**Figure 5.23**).

   We use the name gPageCount as the field name in this example. The *g* at the beginning identifies the field as a global one.

3. Click Options. When the Options dialog box appears, set the data type to Number (**Figure 5.24**). Click OK, then Done.

4. Choose Scripts > ScriptMaker.

5. When the Define Scripts dialog box appears, type the script name and click Create (**Figure 5.25**).

   For this example, we use Set Last Page Number as the script name.

Figure 5.23 The field gPageCount is a Global field, so its value is the same in every record.

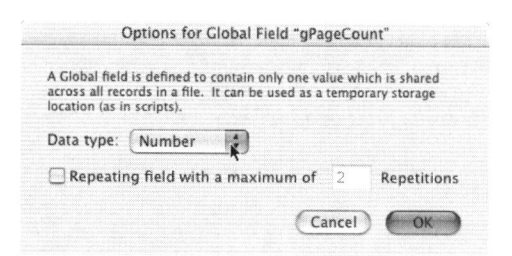

Figure 5.24 The data type of the global field must be Number to count the pages.

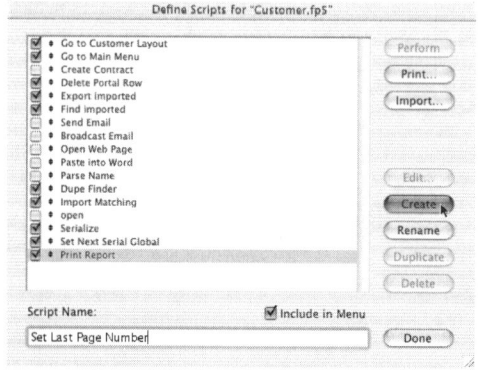

Figure 5.25 A script name should clearly describe what the script does.

Creating Data Reports

6. When the Script Definition dialog box appears, double-click Go to Layout in the Navigation section of the script step list on the left (**Figure 5.26**).

7. From the Specify drop-down menu in the Options section at the bottom, choose the layout in which you want to display the page count (**Figure 5.27**).

8. In the Navigation section of the step list on the left, double-click Enter Preview Mode. In the Options section, uncheck the Pause box.

   You don't need a Pause after you enter Preview mode, because you won't need to check the layout before continuing.

9. In the Navigation section of the step list on the left, double-click Go to Record/Request/Page. In Options, choose Last from the Specify drop-down menu (**Figure 5.28**).

10. Scroll down to the Fields category in the step list on the left, then double-click Set Field (**Figure 5.29**).

continues on next page

Figure 5.26 The Go to Layout script step opens the layout you specify.

Figure 5.27 The script must first go to the layout you want to print.

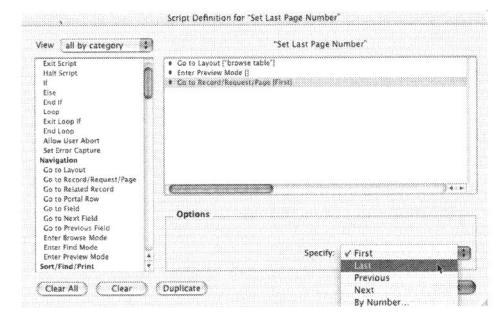

Figure 5.28 The Go to Page (Last) step will go to the last page in the report.

Figure 5.29 The Set Field step allows you to insert a calculation into a specified field.

103

Chapter 5

11. In Options, click the Field (Windows) or Specify Field (Mac) button.

12. When the Specify Field dialog box appears, choose the field name—in our example, gPageCount (**Figure 5.30**). Click OK to close the box and return to the Script Definition window.

13. In Options, click the Specify button.

14. When the Specify Calculation dialog box appears, click the View drop-down menu and scroll down to choose "Status functions" (**Figure 5.31**).

15. In the list of status functions, scroll down to Status (CurrentPageNumber) and double-click it (**Figure 5.32**). Click OK to return to the Script Definition dialog box.

    This Set Field step replaces whatever is in the global field with the page number FileMaker finds.

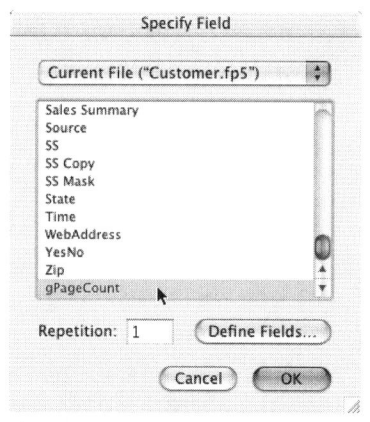

Figure 5.30 The gPageCount field will display the total number of pages.

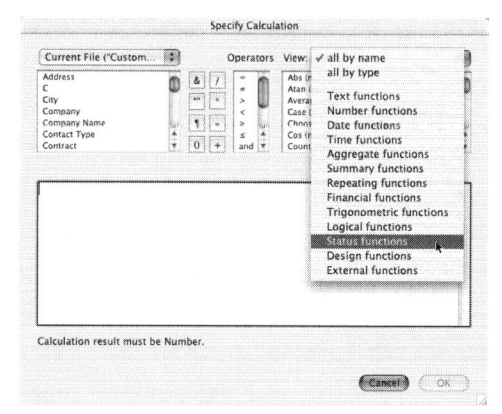

Figure 5.31 Status functions are only available when that option is chosen in the View drop-down menu.

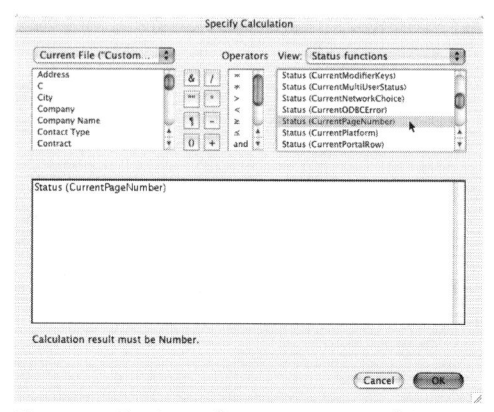

Figure 5.32 The Status (CurrentPageNumber) function returns the number of the page being displayed.

Figure 5.33 The Go to Page (First) step returns to the first page so you can see the report from the beginning.

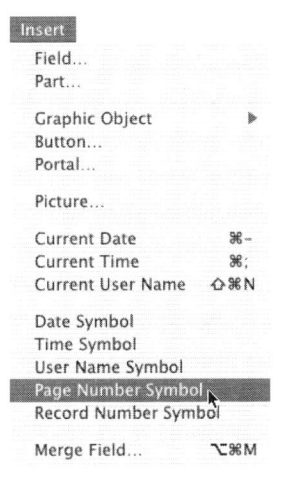

Figure 5.34 The Page Number Symbol will be replaced with the current page number from 1 to 99.

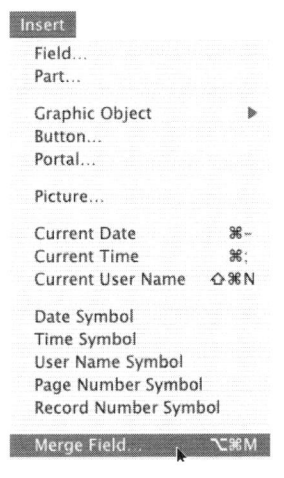

Figure 5.35 The Insert > Merge Field puts a field in a string of text on the layout.

16. In the script step list on the left, double-click Go to Record/Request/Page again, and leave it set to First (**Figure 5.33**). Click OK and then Done to finish.

    Next we add the global field and accompanying text to a layout.

17. Switch to the layout you chose in step 7. Choose View > Layout Mode (Control+L/Command+L).

18. In the status area on the left, click the Text tool, then click in the Header part of the layout.

19. Type Page and a space. Choose Insert > Page Number Symbol (**Figure 5.34**).

20. Type a space, then of and another space. Choose Insert > Merge Field (Control+Alt+M/Command+Option+M; **Figure 5.35**).

continues on next page

21. When the Specify Field dialog box appears, scroll down to your global field (ours is gPageCount) and double-click to insert it in the layout (**Figure 5.36**).

    When you run this script, you'll see the current page number and the total page count on each page in Preview mode (**Figure 5.37**).

✔ **Tip**

- It's always a good idea to put the field type somewhere in the name of a summary field, so you can easily recognize its purpose.

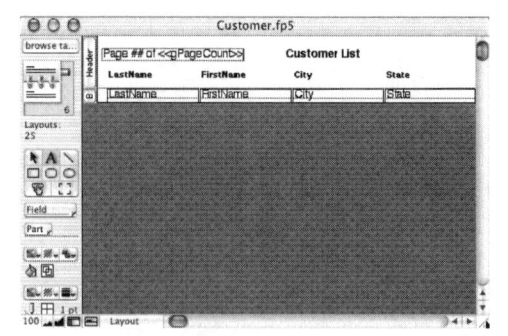

Figure 5.36 The field gPageCount will display the total number of pages on each page.

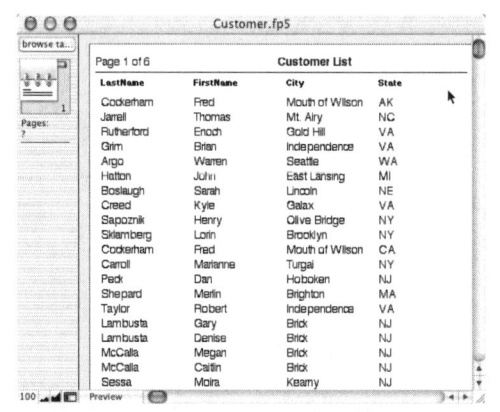

Figure 5.37 The page number and count will only appear in Preview mode.

Creating Running Totals

If you create a database to manage your checkbook, it's convenient to see the balance after each entry. This incremental update is called a *running total*. You can use a running total summary field to display a total for each record instead of just the total for all records.

To create running totals:

1. Choose File > Define Fields (Control+Shift+D/Command+Shift+D).

2. In the Define Fields dialog box, enter a name, choose Summary as the type, and click Create.

3. When the Options dialog box appears, choose the "Total of" radio button and check the "Running total" box below the list of fields (**Figure 5.38**). Click OK.

4. Repeat steps 2 and 3 for as many running total fields as you need.

   In our example, we create two summary fields: one for deposits and one for withdrawals.

5. To display the running balance, you need to create a calculation field that subtracts the withdrawal field from the deposit field. Open the Define Fields dialog box, type a name in the Field Name box, click the Calculation radio button, and click Create.

6. In the Specify Calculation dialog box, double-click the first field (in this example, Running Deposit) from the field list on the left, click the minus button in the Operators keypad, then double-click the second field—in this example, Running Withdrawal (**Figure 5.39**). Click OK, then Done.

7. In Layout mode, switch to the layout where you want the running total to appear. Add the Running Balance field to the Body part of a column layout or to a standard layout (**Figure 5.40**). Switch to Browse mode to see the balances.

Figure 5.38 To add running-total summaries for a field, check the "Running total" box when you create the summary field.

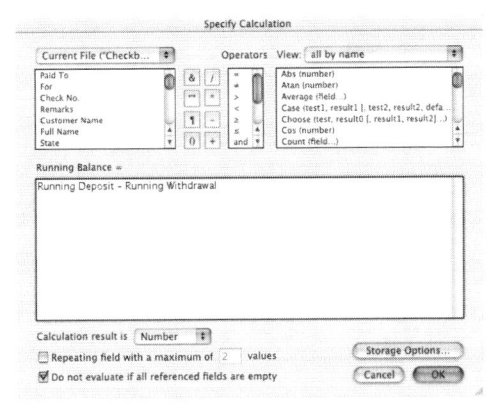

Figure 5.39 For a running checkbook balance, create a calculation field that subtracts the total withdrawals from the total deposits.

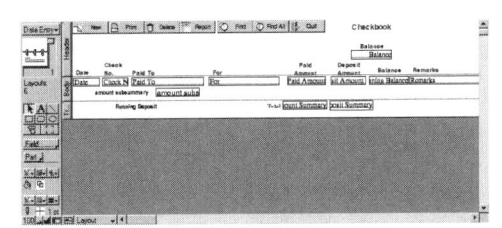

Figure 5.40 The Running Balance field displays the current balance for each record.

Creating Sub-summary Reports

FileMaker has the power to take you beyond simple totals. Using the Sub-summary layout part, you can produce reports that display subtotals for any field. For example, you can create a report that shows sales totals broken out by state and, within each state, broken out by payment type.

You'll need to manually add a Sub-summary part to a layout. Although you can create a Sub-summary part with the Layout Assistant when you first design a layout, the Assistant can't be used to modify existing layouts.

To add a Sub-summary part to a layout:

1. Choose View > Layout Mode (Control+L/Command+L). Switch to the layout to which you want to add sub-summaries.
   This example uses the Sales Report layout created in "To create a layout with summary parts," earlier in this chapter.

2. Click the Part tool and drag it onto the layout. In this example we add the sub-summaries to the Trailing Grand Summary (**Figure 5.41**).

3. When the Part Definition dialog box appears (**Figure 5.42**), click the "Sub-Summary when sorted by" radio button, then choose the field for which you want subtotals from the scrolling list (this example uses the State field). Click OK.

4. The Sub-summary part is now in the layout, but the Trailing Grand Summary part is too small and the fields that were in it are now in the Sub-summary part (**Figure 5.43**). Resize the Trailing Grand Summary part to accommodate the moved fields.

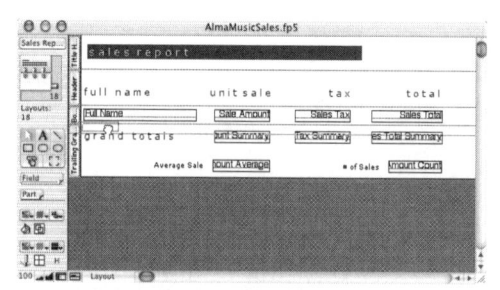

Figure 5.41 Drag the Part tool to the place in the layout where the Total field should appear.

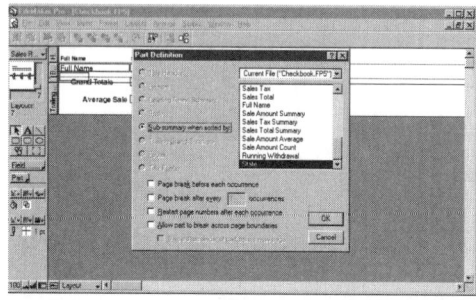

Figure 5.42 In the Part Definition dialog box, choose the field name from the scrolling list.

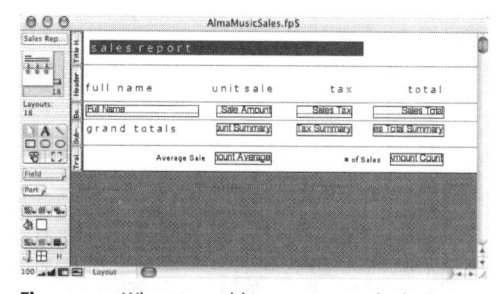

Figure 5.43 When you add a new part to the layout, the part below it will shrink.

Creating Data Reports

Figure 5.44 Drag with the Control or Option key to copy the summary fields and position them in both the Sub-summary and Trailing Grand Summary parts.

Figure 5.45 Add to the Sub-summary part the field by which the summary fields will be sorted.

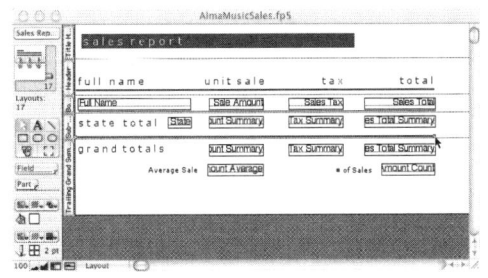

Figure 5.46 The report will be easier to read with horizontal lines separating the sections.

5. Select the totals fields and their text labels. Hold the Control (Windows) or Option (Mac) key and drag them back down where they belong (**Figure 5.44**).

   This technique keeps the fields aligned, as well as duplicating them so they appear in two different layout parts. In the Sub-summary part, they will display subtotals for each state. In the Grand Summary part they will display totals for the entire report.

6. Edit any duplicated field labels or other text you need to change to match one of the parts.

7. Drag the Field tool into the Sub-summary part. When the Specify Field dialog box appears, choose the first field by which you want the sub-summaries to be sorted. In this example, we chose State (**Figure 5.45**).

✔ Tips

- To add more subtotals, repeat steps 2–6, specifying different fields for the sort and duplicating the summary fields in the new Sub-summary parts.

- To make a report easier to read, you can add horizontal lines below the header text and the sub-summaries. Click on the Line tool, hold down the Shift key (to keep the line straight) and draw the lines in the Header and Sub-summary parts (**Figure 5.46**). You can use the Control/Option-drag technique to duplicate the horizontal lines (or any other layout element).

Sorting Data for Sub-summary Reports

If you go directly to Preview mode after adding Sub-summary parts to a report, the subtotals will not appear. Before you preview, you must sort the database to match the order of the sub-summaries in your layout.

The key to using sub-summaries is sorting the database in the right order. In this example, the database must be sorted first by state, then by last name.

To sort data for sub-summary reports:

1. Since you can't sort records in Layout mode, switch to either Browse or Preview mode. Choose Records > Sort (Control+S/Command+S).

2. When the Sort Records dialog box appears, double-click the first field you want to sort by, which should be the first sub-summary in the layout. (You could also highlight the field, then click Move.) This example uses the Work State field for the first sort (**Figure 5.47**).

3. If you added more than one sub-summary, double-click the fields in the same order that the parts appear in the layout.

4. Select a radio button to determine how your sort will be arranged (ascending or descending order), and click Sort.

5. After sorting the sub-summary fields, you can sort the fields that appear in the Body part (**Figure 5.48**).

Figure 5.47 Choose as your first sort field the one for the first Sub-summary part on the layout.

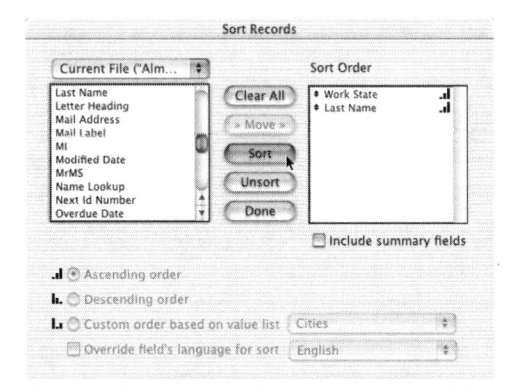

Figure 5.48 After you sort the sub-summary field(s), you can choose the sort order for the records in the Body part.

Creating Data Reports

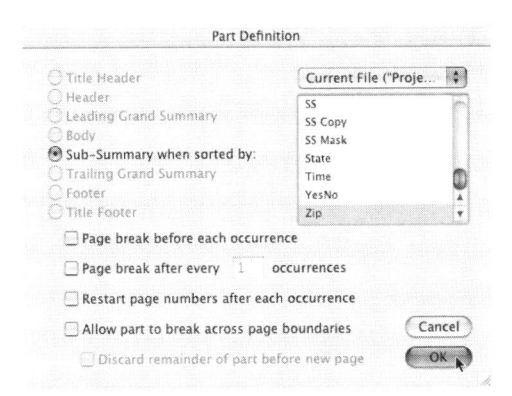

Figure 5.49 The database must be sorted by the proper field when using a Sub-summary part.

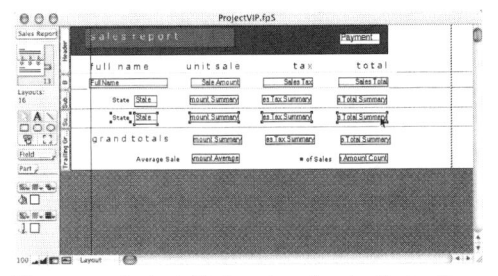

Figure 5.50 Control-/Option-dragging duplicates the selected fields.

Figure 5.51 Change the State field to Zip in the new part.

Creating Modular Summary Reports

After you go to all the trouble of setting up a report with sub-summaries, you'll probably want to show different summaries without having to create a new report for each one. A sub-summary part does not appear on a printout unless the database is sorted by the corresponding field, so you can easily make one layout work for multiple reports.

In the example above, we created a sub-summary report that displayed subtotals by state. By adding another Sub-summary part to the same layout, we can display the same report summarized by Zip code.

To select summary data by sort criteria:

1. Go the same sales report layout you used in the previous section.

2. Choose View > Layout Mode (Control+L/Command+L).

3. In the status area on the left, click the Part tool and drag it into the layout below the Sub-summary by state part.

4. When the Part Definition dialog box appears, choose the Zip field from the scrolling list of fields on the right (**Figure 5.49**).

5. Select all of the fields in the first Sub-summary part. Holding the Control (Windows) or Option (Mac) key, drag the fields into the new part (**Figure 5.50**).

6. In the new Sub-summary part, double-click the State field.

7. When the Specify Field dialog box appears, choose the Zip field. Change the field label text to Zip (**Figure 5.51**).

continues on next page

111

Chapter 5

8. Choose View > Browse Mode (Control+B/Command+B).

9. Choose Records > Sort (Control+S/Command+S).

10. When the Sort Records dialog box appears, click Clear All. In the scrolling list of fields on the left, double-click Zip and then Last Name. Click Sort (**Figure 5.52**).

11. Choose View > Preview Mode. The data will display the records with summaries by Zip code (**Figure 5.53**).

You can add as many sub-summary parts as you like to a layout. Only those whose field is the current top Sort field will be displayed.

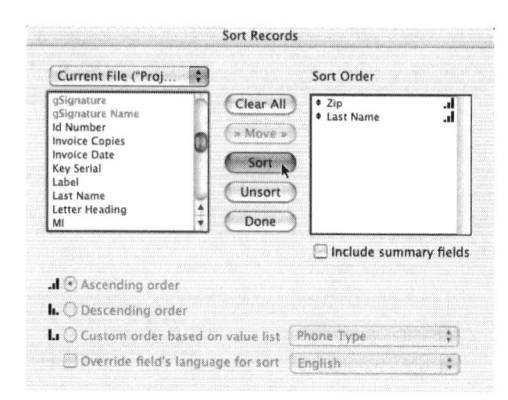

Figure 5.52 The Zip field must be first in the Sort order.

Figure 5.53 Sub-summary parts are only displayed in Preview mode or when printed.

Exporting Summary Data

The report described above may be useful to you when printed out. But suppose you want to use the totals in another program?

Using the Export Records command, you can create a file that contains the same information that is in the printed report, including the subtotals. This file can be opened in a spreadsheet or word processor, or imported into your accounting software for invoicing. Once you have it in another application, the data is completely editable. It can be used to create quarterly or annual reports in a layout program like QuarkXPress, or to define charts in Excel or PowerPoint.

Figure 5.54 For exporting to spreadsheets, choose WK1 (Windows) or WKS (Mac).

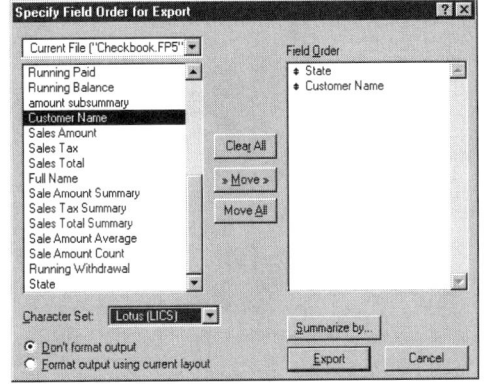

Figure 5.55 The first fields should be the fields that are used in the sort, followed by the summary fields.

To export summary data:

1. Make sure you've sorted your data properly by following the procedure in "To sort data for sub-summary reports" earlier in this chapter.

2. Choose File > Export Records. When the Export Records to File dialog box appears, choose a file type from the "Save as type" drop-down menu (**Figure 5.54**). In this example, it will be a spreadsheet, so we'll choose WK1 (Windows) or WKS (Mac). Type a name for the file, choose a destination folder, and click Save.

3. When the Specify Field Order for Export dialog box appears, double-click the names of all the fields you want to export. This moves the fields into the Field Order list. Remember to choose the Summary fields as well (**Figure 5.55**).

   Windows users will need to make a selection from the Character Set drop-down menu if they're exporting to a file that will be read in another operating system. If you're working on a Mac, your Specify Field Order dialog box won't have this menu.

continues on next page

Chapter 5

4. Click the "Summarize by" button; the Summarize by dialog box lists the sort fields. Click to the left of the field names so that a checkmark appears—don't just click the field name (**Figure 5.56**). Click OK to return to the Specify Field Order dialog box.

5. All the sub-summary fields will have joined the fields you chose in step 3. If you wish to have the numbers formatted to match the current layout, click the "Format output using current layout" radio button (**Figure 5.57**). Click Export to save the exported file.

6. If you open the exported file in Excel, it won't display column headers. You'll have to add them manually (**Figure 5.58**).

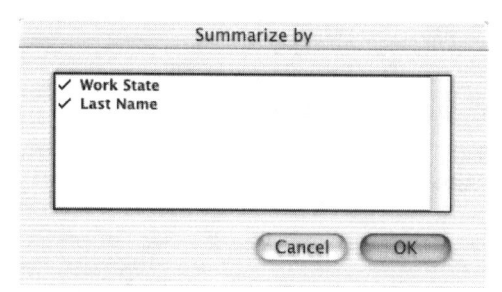

Figure 5.56 Make sure that the checkmark appears to left of the field name.

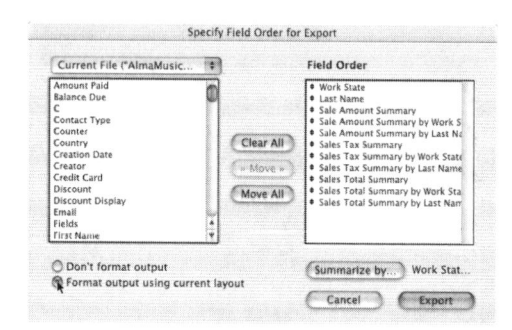

Figure 5.57 You can choose to format the numbers in the export file as they are in the current layout.

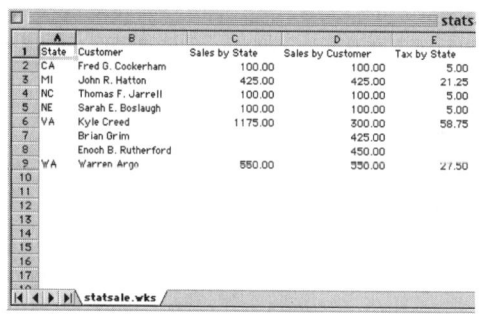

Figure 5.58 Add column headers to an exported FileMaker spreadsheet file.

Creating Data Reports

Figure 5.59 When you right-click (Windows) or Control-click a header in Table View, you can sort by that field.

✔ Tips

- If you're going to use the exported file in a word processor, choose TAB (Windows) or tab-separated (Mac).

- If you're working on a Mac, add the correct extension to the exported file name if you'll need to use it in Windows. (The Windows version of FileMaker adds the extension automatically.) For a spreadsheet, add .WK1. For a word processing document, add .TXT.

- As with Finds, after you export a file, you can create an Export Records (Restore Export Order) script to re-create the same field exports in the future.

- If you need to maintain the field labels as column headings in your exported file, try exporting your files in either Merge (MER in Windows) or DBF format. If you use one of these formats, be sure to check the labels carefully once you open the exported file. Merge brings over the labels, but replaces any spaces with underscores. DBF maintains the spaces, but has a 10-character maximum limit per label.

- FileMaker 6 lets you sort with a mouse click in Table View. Right-click (Windows) or Control-click (Macintosh) the header of the field you want to sort by. Choose Ascending or Descending and your database is sorted by that field (**Figure 5.59**). Isn't that convenient?

115

CREATING RELATIONSHIPS

Every file starts its life as a free-floating entity, managing a specific set of data and separate from other files. This is fine if the file meets all your database needs, but frequently it doesn't. As you discover new information to track, you create additional files to contain it. The time inevitably comes when you realize that some of the information in one file could be profitably used in another one.

Perhaps you've planned out all the possible connections your files could make and have built them to share data. Hats off to you if you have! In reality, such clarity usually comes with experience. You're probably working with files that were created before you discovered all the ways they might interconnect.

FileMaker doesn't require you to own a crystal ball. In fact, a database file that's too full of fields becomes cumbersome to update and takes too long to search. By creating relationships between files, you can painlessly join multiple sets of data without having to duplicate information. Once connected, the merged information can be displayed and manipulated as if there were only one database file.

About Relationships

The concept of a database relationship can seem more complex than it really is. FileMaker relationships are based on one very down-to-earth concept: that information can be shared in many ways. It can flow one way (like a TV station broadcasting the news) or two ways (like a reporter interviewing someone by phone), or use some combination (like the interviewee talking to the reporter at the same time she's using a videocam to broadcast to the Internet).

In a group of database files, you might have a mailing list containing names and addresses and a second file that tracks customer invoices. You want to display the name and address information from the mailing list in the invoice file. Like the broadcasting station, the mailing list is the information source. The invoice file, like the TV, is the information destination. It's receiving information but not giving anything back.

Using FileMaker, there's nothing to prevent the receiving file from opening a two-way communication or becoming the information source for another file. All FileMaker files have a peer-to-peer relationship, meaning that they're all capable of being sources or receivers of information, or both.

In FileMaker terminology, when a file is playing the role of a receiver, it's called a *master file*, because it's the focus of the information transfer. The file broadcasting its information is called the *related file*. Although we'll use these terms when necessary, they tend to confuse the issue because they aren't descriptive of what's actually going on. Instead, we'll refer to the master file as the *receiver* or *destination file*, and the related file as the *source file*.

The examples in this chapter are based on two model files. One is a customer file containing each client's name and address data. The other is a sales file with one entry for each client's purchase. The sales file (the master file or receiver) will use the data from the customer file (the related file or source).

Defining a Master File

To define a file as either source or receiver, you need to create a key field—which FileMaker calls the *match field*—that is common to both files. Each record in the source file must have a unique match field, so that the receiving file can identify which record is which.

There can only be one instance of a match field in the source file, while there could be any number of occurrences of it in the master. This is referred to as a One-to-Many relationship.

There are two common methods for creating a match field. The easiest is to create a serial number field, using the Auto-Enter field option to assign a sequential number to every new record you create.

To create a serial number match field:

1. In the source file, choose File > Define Fields. When the Define Fields dialog box appears, type a name for the match field, click the Number radio button, then click Create. In this example, the field name is Key Serial. When you're done, double-click the new field name.

2. When the Options dialog box appears, click the Auto-Enter tab. Click the check box for Serial number. If this is a new database without any existing records, click the box for "Prohibit modification of value" to prevent anyone from altering this field by mistake (**Figure 6.1**). If this is a database with existing records, leave this box unchecked for now. Click OK and then Done.

Creating Relationships

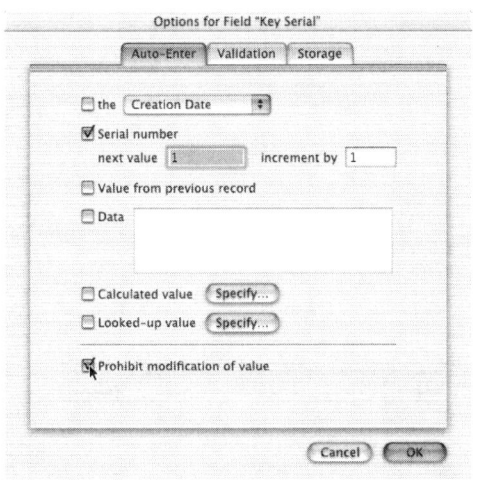

Figure 6.1 Prohibiting modification prevents the auto-entered value from being changed.

Figure 6.2 Add the serial match field to the layout so you can update existing records.

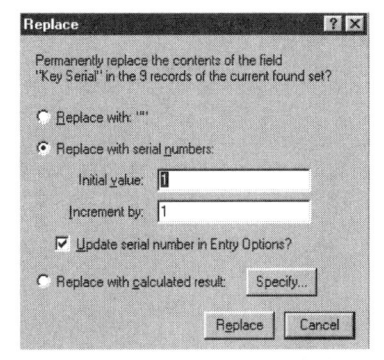

Figure 6.3 The Replace command allows you to update the beginning number in the auto-entry sequence.

3. If this is a new database without existing records, you've finished. If you are adding this field to a database that already has records in it, you'll have to add serial numbers to the existing records before you can enter new ones. To do so, choose View > Layout Mode (Control+L/Command+L).

4. Drag the Field tool to the layout and choose your serial number field name from the scrolling list in the dialog box (**Figure 6.2**).

5. Choose View > Browse Mode (Control+B/Command+B).

6. Click in the serial number field. Choose Records > Replace (Control+=/Command+=).

7. When the Replace dialog box appears, click the "Replace with serial numbers" radio button (**Figure 6.3**). Click Replace.

   The existing records now have sequential numbers in the serial number field, and the field definition has been updated to enter the next serial number with one higher than your last record.

8. Return to File > Define Fields and double-click the serial number field name.

9. When the Options dialog box appears, choose the "Prohibit modification of value" check box. Click OK, then Done.

✔ Tip

- Not all types of fields can be used as match fields. Container fields can't ever be match fields. Global and Summary fields can be used as match fields in the destination file, but not in the source.

119

Chapter 6

Creating a Match Field in a Master File

To use data from the source file you've created a match field in, you also need a match field in a master (destination) file. Once you have both match fields, you define a relationship that links the master to the source.

Figure 6.4 Define a relationship in the master (receiver) file, not the source file.

To create a match field in a master file:

1. In the destination file, go to File > Define Fields.

2. Define a new number field and name it. This example is named Key Serial to match the source field of the same name. Click Create, then Done.

3. Choose File > Define Relationships.

4. When the Define Relationships dialog box appears, click New (**Figure 6.4**).

5. In the Open File dialog box choose the source file by either double-clicking or selecting it and clicking Open. In this example the file is Customers.FP5 (**Figure 6.5**).

6. In the Edit Relationship dialog box, Relationship Name already displays the name of the file chosen in step 5. (You can change it if you want.) In the "Match data from field in current file" scrolling list, click the serial field. In our example, it's Key Serial (**Figure 6.6**).

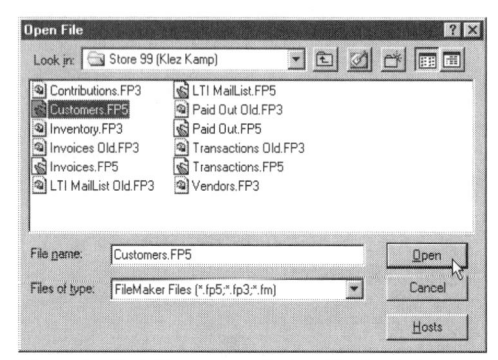

Figure 6.5 To define a new relationship, begin by choosing the source file.

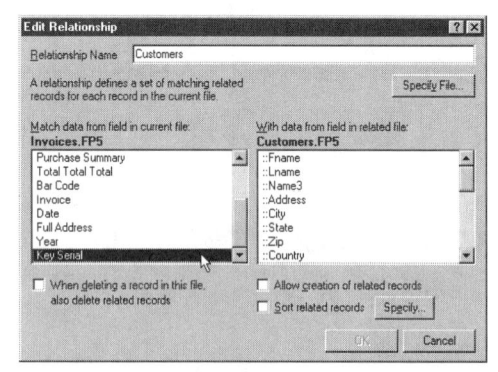

Figure 6.6 Choose the match field for the master file from the left scrolling list.

120

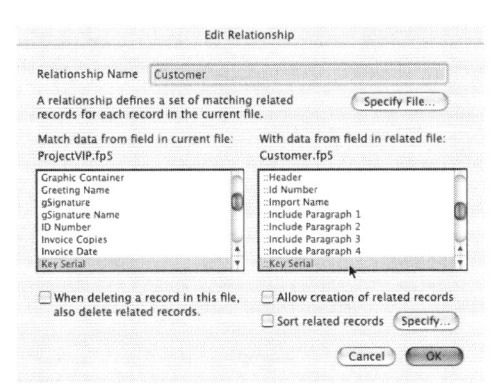

Figure 6.7 Choose the related source field from the right scrolling list.

7. In the "With data from field in related file" scrolling list, choose the name of the serial field in the source file (**Figure 6.7**). Click OK and then Done.

✔ Tips

- To create a relationship using a calculated field, repeat the steps in "To create a match field in a master file," substituting the name of the calculated field for the serial match field.

- Give the match field in the master file the same name as the match field in the source. The names don't *have* to be the same to create a relationship, but it makes it easier to remember which fields are related.

- Watch your field types! Match fields must be the same type of field.

Lookup vs. Related Fields

Once you've established a relationship between files, you can choose between two methods for using the source file data. With the first method, you use the Lookup function to copy the actual data from a field in the source file to a field in the receiver file. Alternatively, you can display the source file data directly by placing its fields on a layout (or using them in a calculation) in the receiver file.

If you choose Lookup, when you enter a value in the source file's match field, the data in the specified fields is copied into fields in the receiver file. Once you've copied the files, however, if the data in the source changes, the data in the receiver file won't update. This might be useful if, for example, you want to maintain the customer's shipping address at the time of the sale.

If you choose to display the source data in the master file layouts without copying it, any changes made to the source *will* be reflected in the master file. The fields displayed in the layout are the *actual* fields in the source database, not a copy. If a customer moves and you update your records, all the entries in both databases will show the new address, no matter when the entries were originally made.

To create lookup fields:

1. Open your master file and choose File > Define Fields.

2. When the Define Fields dialog box appears, type a name for the first field, make it a text or number field (depending on what you need), and click Create.

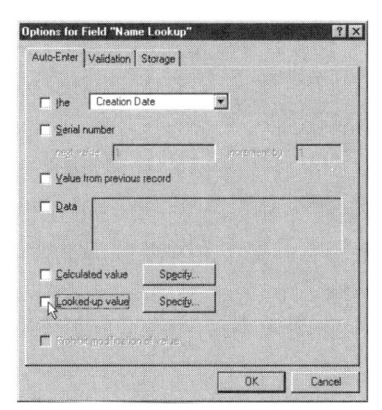

Figure 6.8 To copy data from the source file into a field in the current database when a new record is created, check the Looked-up value check box.

Figure 6.9 Choose a relationship from the Lookup dialog box list, or choose Define Relationships to create a new one.

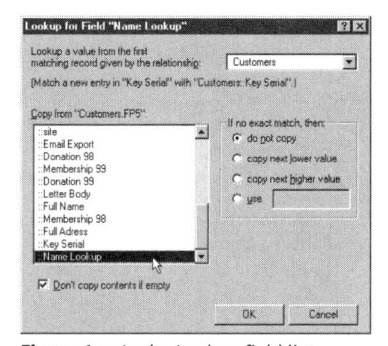

Figure 6.10 In the Lookup field list, choose the field in the source file from which the data will be copied.

3. Repeat step 2 for every field from the source database that you need to duplicate. These fields will hold the data that will be copied from the source file. Use the same field names for these destination fields that you used in the original source file.

4. When you've finished creating the new fields, double-click the first field name.

5. The Options dialog box appears with the Auto-Enter tab displayed. Check the "Looked-up value" check box (**Figure 6.8**). The Lookup dialog box opens.

6. From the drop-down menus, choose the relationship you created for the two files. In our example, it's Customers, which we created in "To create a match field in a master file" on page 120 (**Figure 6.9**).

7. The "Copy from" field list will become active. Choose the field to be copied from the source file (**Figure 6.10**). Click OK, then OK again to close the Options box.

8. Repeat steps 4–7 for each field that will contain looked-up data, then click Done.

✔ **Tip**

■ You can update data in the master file that you entered with a Lookup. To do this, click in the match field in the layout and choose Records > Relookup. The database will copy the related data from the source into all lookup fields using that match field for the relationship. If you only want to update certain records, do a search for those records and then choose Records > Relookup. Only records in the current found set will be updated.

Chapter 6

To use related fields in a layout:

1. Go to the layout in which you want to display the related fields. Choose View > Layout Mode (Control+L/Command+L).

2. Drag the Field tool onto the layout to bring up the Specify Field dialog box.

3. From the drop-down menu above the field lists, choose the relationship you wish to use (**Figure 6.11**).

4. The field list will display the fields in the source database (**Figure 6.12**). Choose the field you want and click OK.

5. Repeat steps 2–4 for each field you want to use.

   The related fields on the layout will have field names preceded by two colons (::). The double colons indicate that the fields are from a relationship, not from the current file (**Figure 6.13**).

✔ Tips

- A database can have many relationships. You can use a field from any relationship in a layout. Just choose the relationship in the Specify Field dialog box before choosing the field name.

- The source match field can have multiple entries, separated by returns. As long as the match field in the destination field is the same as any of the entries in the source match field, the relationship will work.

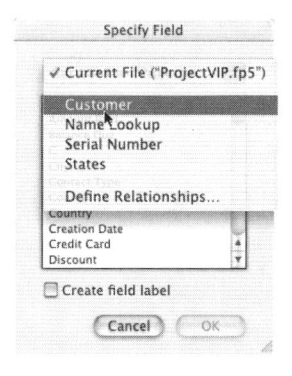

Figure 6.11 Choose the relationship that will be used to display the data for this field.

Figure 6.12 After you choose a relationship, the Specify Field list changes to display the source file's field list.

— Double colon before field name

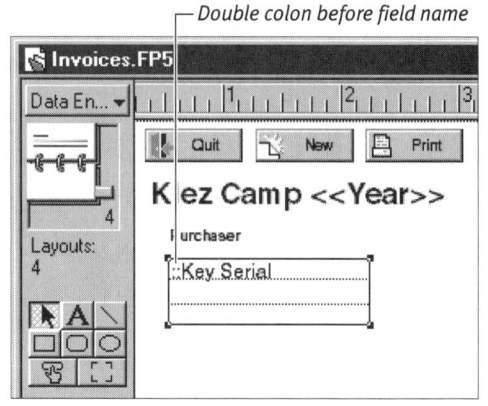

Figure 6.13 Every field in a layout that depends on a relationship will have two colons in front of its name.

Creating Relationships

Figure 6.14 Enter the value in the match field for the related record.

Figure 6.15 The related data won't appear until you click another part of the layout or press Enter or Return.

Using a Match Field to Choose a Related Record

Once you have a relationship between two files and have created lookup fields (or added related fields to the layout), you can bring data from the source to the receiver file.

The simplest (though not necessarily best) way to transfer data is to type the serial number value directly into the match field.

To use a match field to choose a related record:

1. Go to a layout that has a related field and switch to Browse mode.

2. Create a new record (Control+N/ Command+N).

3. Type the customer's serial number (from the Customer file) into the serial number field. In our example, the field is Key Serial (**Figure 6.14**).

4. Click someplace else on the layout or hit Enter/Return. The related data will now appear in all the fields (**Figure 6.15**).

✔ Tip

- Related values will change if another value is entered in the match field. To update a single record, change or clear the serial number value and then re-enter it.

Using Calculated Match Fields

A serial number match field ensures that you won't create duplicate key values. However, it's much more useful for establishing a relationship between existing records than for new ones. In fact, it can be downright irritating if you try to use it for a new invoice. To create a new customer record, you have to know (or manually look up) the customer's serial number. Although you could look up serial numbers in the database, this is obviously not very efficient.

As an alternative, you can create a calculated match field that uses the data in the source file to uniquely identify which record is being chosen. The following example may need a little tweaking for your individual needs. If you have a very large database, for example, you may have to add the street address or phone number field to create a unique record for each customer.

To create a calculated match field:

1. In the source file, choose File > Define Fields (Control+Shift+D/Command+Shift-D).

2. When the Define Fields dialog box appears, type a name for the field, make it a Calculation, and click Create.

   In this example, we call the field Name Lookup (**Figure 6.16**).

3. When the Specify Calculation dialog box appears, enter the following formula in the Specify Calculation dialog box (**Figure 6.17**). If necessary, substitute your own field names for the ones in our example calculation.

   Trim(Fname) & " " & Trim(Lname) & " "& Trim(City) & " " Trim(Zip)

Figure 6.16 Name Lookup will be the unique match field for each customer record.

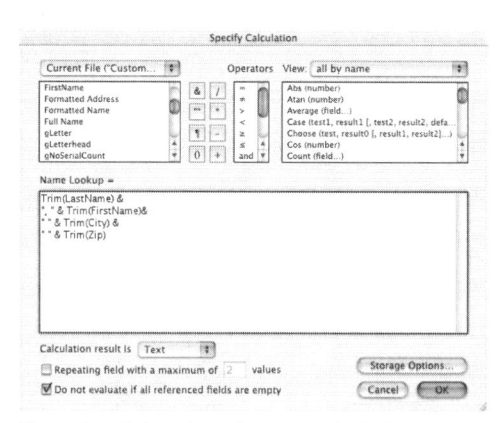

Figure 6.17 Enter returns between calculation elements to make reading the formula easier.

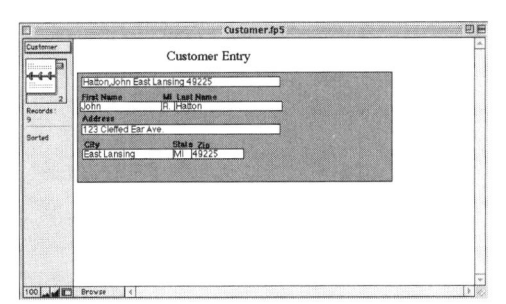

Figure 6.18 This calculated lookup field will contain the Last Name, First Name, City, and Zip code with punctuation.

Notice that there are spaces between the quotes of the formula, and that we've added returns to make the formula easier to read.

4. Click OK, then click Done. Add this new field to a layout. It will contain a first and last name, city, and Zip code, all correctly separated by spaces and punctuation (**Figure 6.18**).

✔ Tips

- For more details, see "Merging Fields Using Calculations," in Chapter 4.

- To create a relationship using a calculated field, repeat the steps in "To create a match field in a master file" on page 120, substituting the name of the calculated field for the serial match field.

- When you create a calculated key field, keep in mind that FileMaker only indexes the first 20 characters of each word in the text that results from the formula (for example, "Dick Tracy, Metropolis 07307"). The maximum total characters the program indexes is 60, including spaces. So if the total number of characters goes above the limit and two fields share the same first 20 characters, you could easily have errors in your lookup. You can avoid this problem by using only those fields that are most likely to provide a unique result. Eliminate the ones (like the State field if you're using a Zip field) that you don't need.

Field Formatting with a Calculated Match Field

Using the calculated field technique combined with a drop-down list format allows the user to choose the customer from a list of names rather than numbers. You will need to make one change to the relationship as it was shown in "To create a calculated match field" on page 126. It's more efficient to list the customers in alphabetical order by last name, so you'll want to re-sort before you create the drop-down value list.

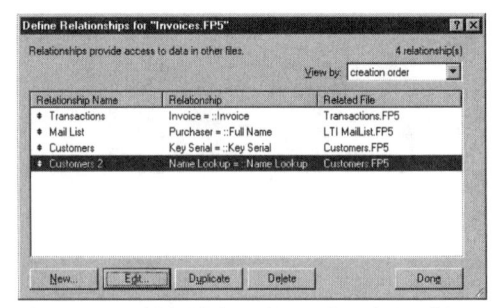

Figure 6.19 Double-click to choose the relationship that uses your calculated match field from the Define Relationships listing.

To add a drop-down list to a match field:

1. Go to the receiver file and switch to the layout that holds your calculated match field. Choose File > Define Relationships.

2. When the Define Relationships dialog box appears, double-click the relationship that you established by creating a calculated field.

   In this example, we use Name Lookup (**Figure 6.19**).

3. When the Edit Relationship dialog box appears, click the "Sort related records" check box (**Figure 6.20**).

4. In the Specify Sort dialog box, double-click a field to define the sort criteria.

   In this example, we use Last Name (**Figure 6.21**). Click OK, then OK again, then click Done.

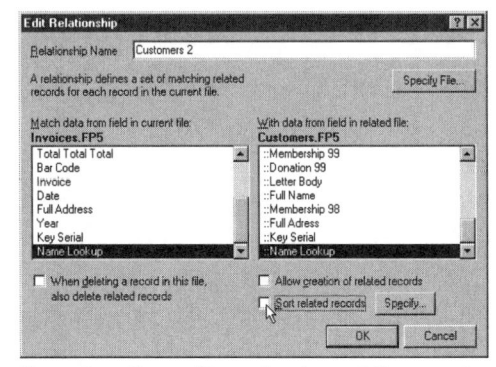

Figure 6.20 Choose "Sort related records" to organize the files in the match field.

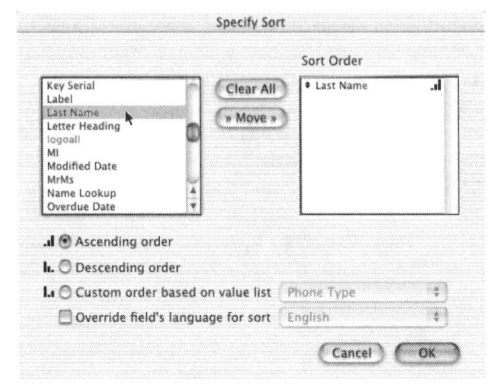

Figure 6.21 To choose the way a match field will be sorted, select the field you want to sort on from the Specify Sort list.

Creating Relationships

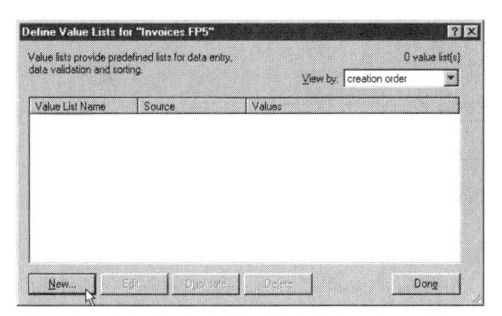

Figure 6.22 The Define Value Lists dialog box will be empty if you have never used it in the file before.

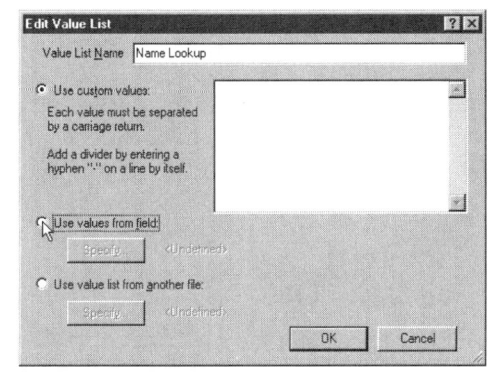

Figure 6.23 Give the value list the same name as the calculated field to make it easy to remember their connection.

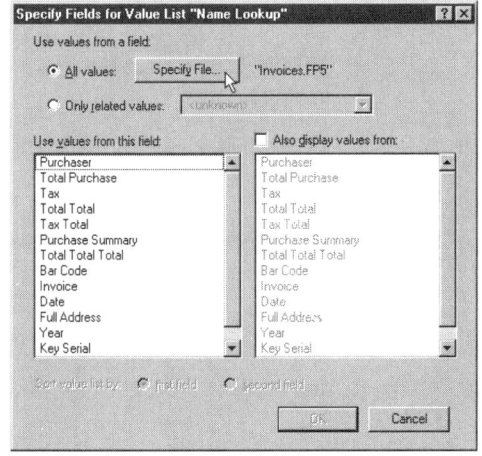

Figure 6.24 Click Specify File to choose the source database.

5. Choose File > Define Value Lists. When the Define Value Lists dialog box appears, click New (**Figure 6.22**).

6. When the Edit Value List dialog box appears, give the value list the same name as your calculated match field and click the "Use values from field" radio button (**Figure 6.23**).

7. The Specify Fields for Value List dialog box will appear with the name of your master file in quotes at the top. Click Specify File (**Figure 6.24**).

8. In the Open File window, navigate to the source file and double-click to select it.

9. The Specify Fields for Value List dialog box will appear again. In the list on the left, click to select the calculated match field. In our example, it's Name Lookup (**Figure 6.25**). Click OK, then OK again, then Done.

continues on next page

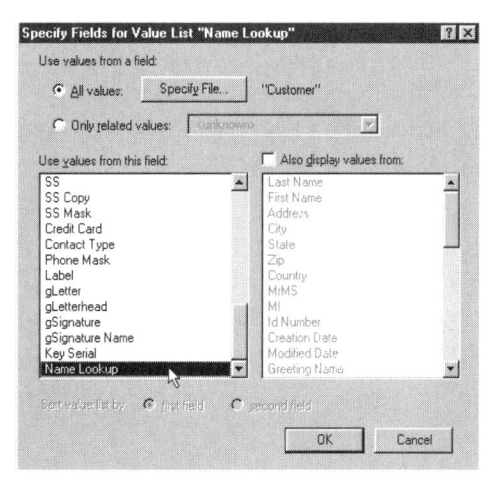

Figure 6.25 The fields in the related database will be in this scrolling list.

129

Chapter 6

10. Go to the data entry layout and switch to Layout mode (Control+L/Command+L).

11. From the tools on the left, choose the Field tool and drag it onto the layout to add the calculated match field to the layout (**Figure 6.26**).

12. Click this field to select it and choose Format > Field Format (Control+Alt+F/Command+Option+F).

13. When the Field Format dialog box appears, click the "Pop-up list" radio button and choose the calculated match field from the "using value list" pop-up on the right (**Figure 6.27**). Click OK.

14. If you are using lookup fields, verify that they are defined to copy data using the Name Lookup relationship. (See "To create lookup fields," page 122.) If you are displaying related data, make sure that the fields are from the correct relationship.

15. Return to Browse mode and create a new record (Control+N/Command+N).

16. Click in the match field. It will display a list of names from the source field of the same name in the Customer database. Click the name you want (**Figure 6.28**).

    All of the related (or lookup) fields will fill with the values from the related record of the name you chose (**Figure 6.29**).

✔ Tip

- In a pop-up list, you can type the first letter or two to go right to the first item that begins with those letters.

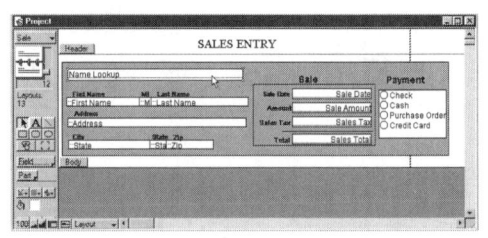

Figure 6.26 Use the calculated match field to choose the related record.

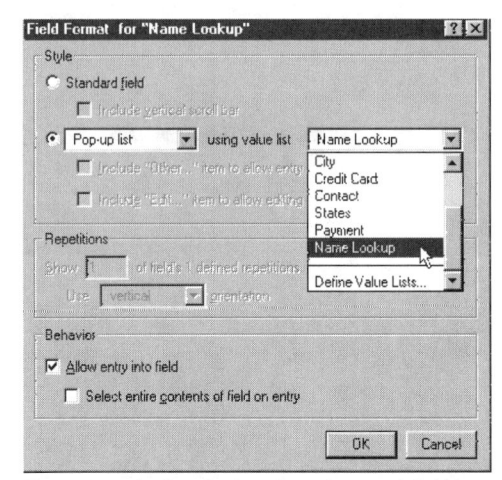

Figure 6.27 The list of values from the match field in the source database is displayed in the pop-up.

Figure 6.28 The list of customer names will appear in alphabetical order by last name.

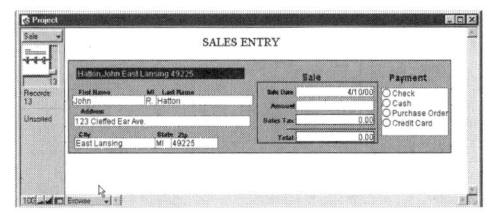

Figure 6.29 When you choose a name in the Name Lookup list, all of the related fields display the values from the source database.

Creating Relationships

Figure 6.30 A repeating field for phone number can contain all of the numbers for a particular person in a single field.

Figure 6.31 A related field with the same number of repetitions as a typical phone field can contain the designations for each number, yet allow you to search or collect the entries individually.

About Repeating vs. Related Fields

Many FileMaker users are excited when they discover the FileMaker repeating field. It seems to save time while you're defining fields—a boring stage for many in creating a database. A repeating field allows you to group multiple entries into one field, but have them appear on a layout as if they were separate entries. One practical use for a repeating field might be for people with more than one email address. Repeating fields allow you to avoid the tedium of making several fields labeled "email 1," "email 2," and so on.

On the other hand, most accomplished FileMaker developers use repeating fields sparingly or not at all, because you can accomplish many of the same things much better through the use of related fields. Repeating fields have significant disadvantages. In general, they are treated as one indivisible unit. You can only sort repeating fields by their first entry and you can't create subtotals for particular entries. Although there is a calculation formula to pry out a particular repetition from the rest (GetRepetition), in general individual items in repeating fields are very difficult to extract for a report.

For all of these reasons, whenever you're considering using a repeating field, ask yourself whether a related database makes more sense. (It usually does.)

✔ Tip

- Phone numbers are a frequent use for a repeating field because you can enter all of the numbers for a particular person in one place (**Figure 6.30**). On the other hand, instead of creating a repeating field, you could create a text match field as both a relationship and a label for each phone number (**Figure 6.31**).

About Portals

Portals are a tool for accessing multiple files in another database without having to actually copy the data. They are a supercharged alternative to creating a relationship and placing a source field in a receiver field's layout.

Using a portal, you can display fields from all of another file's records without duplicating information or bloating a database with information that lives in another place. Take our two example files, Customer and Sales. You could create a portal in the Customer file to list all of the purchases made by each customer (**Figure 6.32**). Once you have a portal, you can even use it to create new records in a related field. (See "Creating Related Data with Portals" later in this chapter for more details.)

Figure 6.32 A portal can be used to show a list of all related records contained in another file.

To create a portal:

1. Go to the master file layout where the portal will be added and switch to Layout mode (Control+L/Command+L).

   Make sure the layout has enough room for the portal (**Figure 6.33**). If it doesn't, drag the Body tab down to resize the part.

2. Click the Portal tool. Click on the layout and drag the pointer out and down to size.

3. In the Portal Setup dialog box that appears, click the drop-down list and choose the relationship for this portal (**Figure 6.34**).

4. If you haven't yet created a relationship, choose Define Relationships from the drop-down list and follow the instructions in "To create a match field in a master file" on page 120, then return to the Portal Setup dialog box.

5. In the Format section of the Portal Setup dialog box, type in the number of rows you want to display.

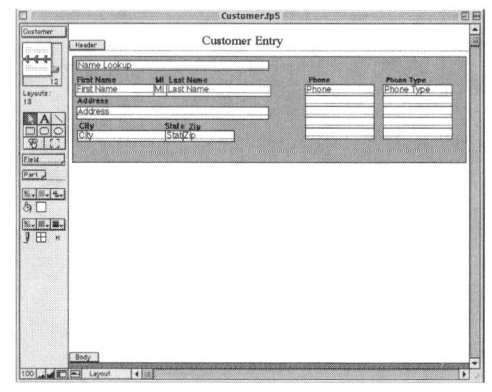

Figure 6.33 If you need more room in a layout to add a portal, drag the Body tab down to enlarge the part.

Figure 6.34 You can either choose an existing relationship or create a new one.

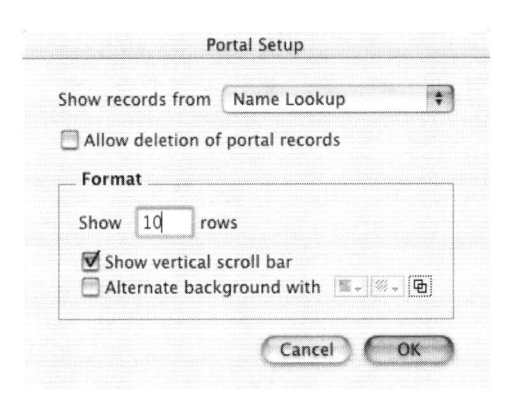

Figure 6.35 Add a scroll bar so the user can access all records regardless of the number of portal rows you choose.

Figure 6.36 The portal lists all purchases found in the source file that were made by this customer.

6. Click the "Show vertical scroll bar" check box (**Figure 6.35**). This allows the user to access all the records if there are more records than rows. Click OK.

7. With the portal selected on the layout, follow the steps in "To use related fields in a layout" on page 124 to add fields to the top row of the portal with the Field tool.

   You only need to add fields to the top row, since the portal will repeat them for as many related records as there are in the source file.

8. Switch back to Browse mode to see the records in the portal (**Figure 6.36**).

✔ **Tip**

- When you add fields in a portal, make sure that your field labels are outside the portal or they will be repeated with every related record that appears in the layout list instead of appearing only once as headings.

Chapter 6

Creating Related Data with Portals

When you create a relationship, one of the options is "Allow creation of related records" (**Figure 6.37**). If this option is checked, you can use the source file to create new records in the destination file.

To enter data in related files using portals:

1. Go to the master file layout where the portal will be added, and switch to Layout mode (Control+L/Command+L).

2. Make sure the layout has enough room for the portal. If it doesn't, drag the Body tab down to resize the part.

3. Click the Portal tool. Click on the layout and drag the pointer out and down to size.

4. Choose File > Define Relationships.

5. When the Define Relationships dialog box appears, double-click the relationship to bring up the Edit Relationship dialog box.

6. Make sure that "Allow creation of related records" is checked. Click OK and then click Done.

7. Switch to Browse mode (Control+B/Command+B) if you aren't there already.

8. Click in a field in the first blank row of the portal (**Figure 6.38**). Enter data in any of the fields in that row.

    The data you entered is contained in a new record in the related database.

9. You can switch to the related database to see the new record (**Figure 6.39**).

    The key field in the new record of the related file is automatically filled in with the data in the current record of the source.

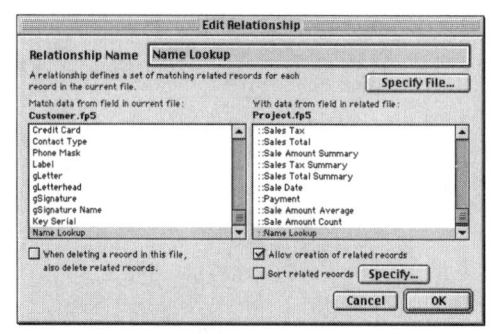

Figure 6.37 Check "Allow creation of related records" to use the source file to create new records in the destination file.

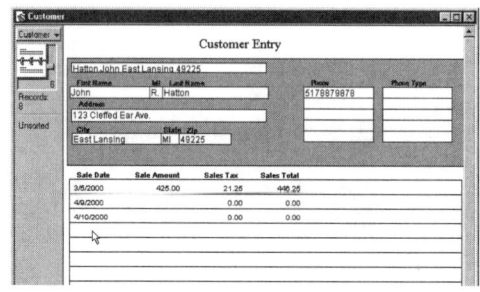

Figure 6.38 When the first blank row in a portal is clicked, a new record is created in the related database and the new data you enter is added to the record.

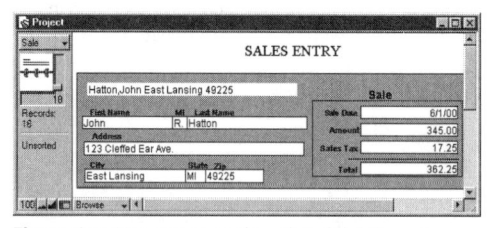

Figure 6.39 You can go to the related database to see the contents of the new record.

✓ Tip

- Portals make serial number key fields very useful. Instead of having to manually input a serial number to bring up a customer record, a portal will enter the serial number automatically. Just be sure to create serial number match fields (as shown on page 118 in "To create a serial number match field") before you create the portal in your layout.

Creating Relationships

Sorting Data in Portals

There is no way to specify a sort method in a portal once you're in a layout. If you want to view the portal data sorted by one of its fields, you need to specify this option in the relationship itself.

To sort data in portals:

1. Choose File > Define Relationships.

2. When the Define Relationships dialog box appears, select the relationship your portal uses and click Edit.

3. When the Edit Relationship dialog box appears, click "Sort related records" (**Figure 6.40**).

4. In the Specify Sort dialog box, double-click the field(s) to sort (**Figure 6.41**). You can specify ascending, descending, or custom sort for each field. Click OK.

   Portals based on this relationship will now display the related records sorted by the criteria and the order you specified.

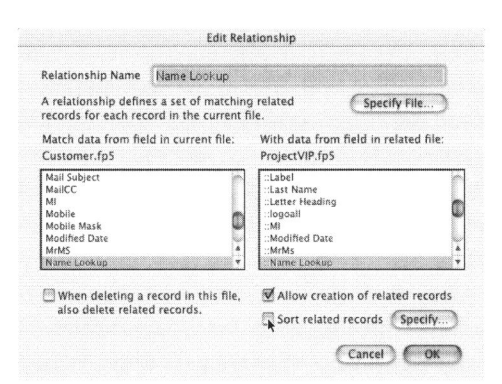

Figure 6.40 Click "Sort related records" to choose a field to sort the portal records.

Figure 6.41 You can specify ascending, descending, or a custom order for each sort field.

135

Summarizing Related Data

Summary functions work on related fields in a layout just as they do on the non-related fields in the database. You can summarize the contents of a portal's data using a calculation field to create an account statement for individual clients, for example.

To summarize related data:

1. Open your master file and go to the layout that holds your portal. Choose File > Define Fields.

2. When the Define Fields dialog box appears, type a name for the field, click the Calculation radio button, then click Create.

   In this example, the field name is Sales Summary (**Figure 6.42**).

3. In the Specify Calculation dialog box, double-click an aggregate function from the function list on the right.

   Depending on what type of information you want, you can use Sum, Average, Count, Max, Min, StDev, or StDevP. In our example, we've chosen Sum because we want to add all of the records.

4. Click the drop-down menu above the field list on the left and select the relationship for the field you want to summarize (**Figure 6.43**).

   The field list will change to display the fields in the source file. Because they're related fields, their names begin with a double colon.

5. In the field list, double-click the field you want to summarize (**Figure 6.44**).

Figure 6.42 Related fields can be summarized with a calculation field.

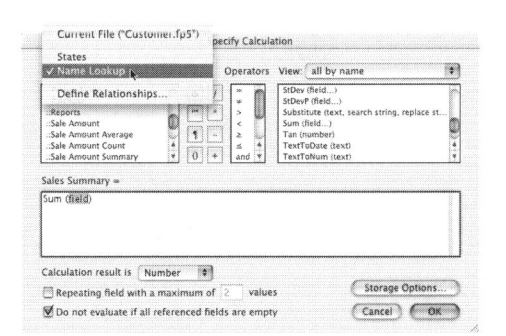

Figure 6.43 Before you choose a field, choose the relationship from the drop-down menu to switch the field list to the source file.

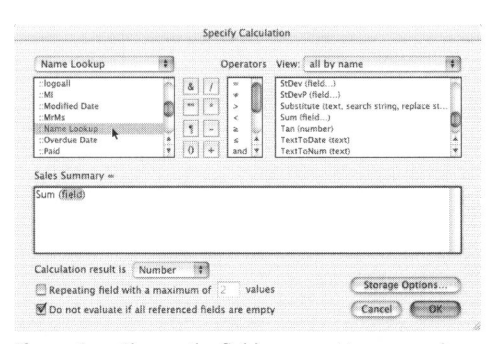

Figure 6.44 Choose the field you want to summarize from the field list on the left.

136

Creating Relationships

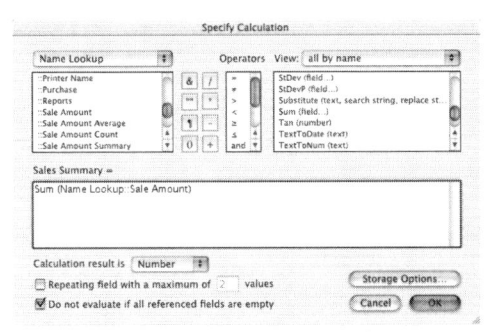

Figure 6.45 Enter the related field in the function between the parentheses.

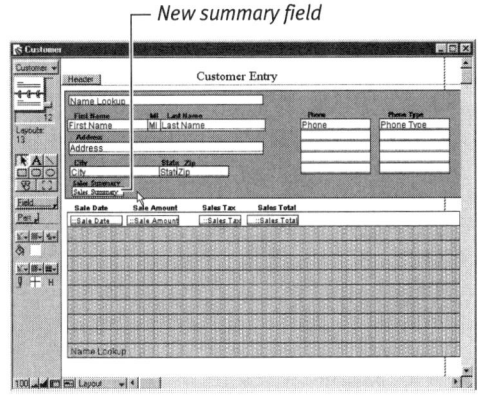

Figure 6.46 Put the summary calculation field in the layout body, not in the portal.

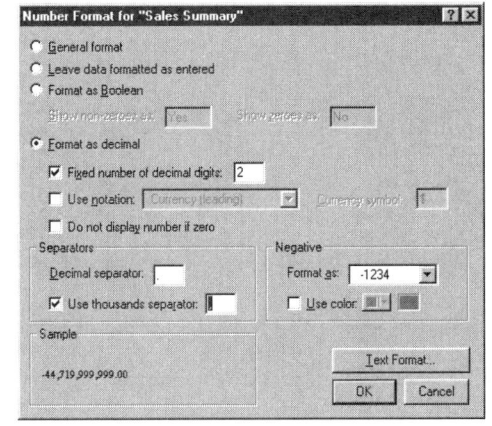

Figure 6.47 You can format the summary field to display in any standard number format.

6. The two related field names (the one in the master file and its related field in the source) will appear in the formula box (**Figure 6.45**).

7. Leave the calculation result set to Number. Click OK and then Done.

8. Switch to Layout mode (Control+L/Command+L) and add the field to the layout outside the portal.

   In our example, we've added a Sales Summary field (**Figure 6.46**).

9. Choose Format > Number.

   When the Number Format dialog box appears, you can specify the exact format in which you want the summary information to appear (**Figure 6.47**).

   In this case, we chose the "Format as decimal" radio button and set it to display the number to two decimal places. We also used a comma to set off the thousands column.

10. Switch to Browse mode to see the total for that record in the summary field (**Figure 6.48**).

Figure 6.48 The summary calculation field displays the total for the current record.

SUMMARIZING RELATED DATA

137

Chapter 6

About Self-Relationships

Not only can you relate one file to another, you can also relate records within a file to each other. This is called a self-relationship. There are lots of situations where self-relationships are useful. If you have a database of contact names, many of whom work for the same company, you can create a self-relationship in a portal to list everyone working for the same company on each individual employee's record. Self-relationship portals can be defined as buttons to switch between records. You can also use a self-relationship to do simple finds, create summary fields, and even create lookups to speed up data entry.

To create a self-relationship:

1. Choose File > Define Relationships.

2. When the Define Relationships dialog box appears, click New.

3. In the Open File dialog box, double-click the name of the current file (**Figure 6.49**). In this case, the file is called Contacts.fp5.

4. In the Edit Relationship dialog box, enter a relationship name.

   In this example, we use the Company field, so we've named the relationship Company.

5. Click the same field in both field lists (**Figure 6.50**).

6. If it's not already checked, click the "Sort related records" check box. Click Specify to bring up the Specify Sort dialog box.

7. In this example, we'll set the Sort criteria to Last Name by double-clicking to choose it (**Figure 6.51**). Click OK, OK again, and then Done.

Figure 6.49 To create a self-relationship, choose the current file name in the Open File dialog box.

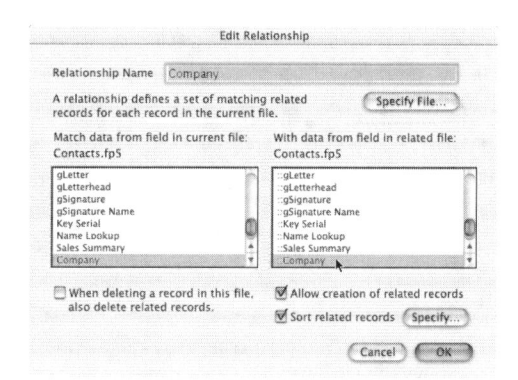

Figure 6.50 Choose the same field name in both field lists.

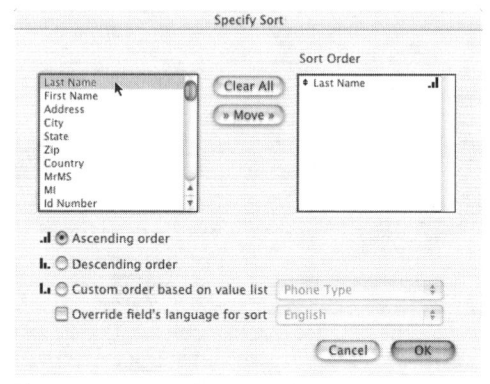

Figure 6.51 You can choose any field to sort the relationship.

Creating Relationships

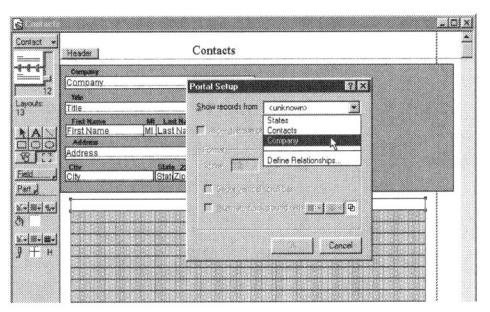

Figure 6.52 Choose the relationship that the portal will use to choose records.

Figure 6.53 Add fields into the first row of the portal using the Field tool.

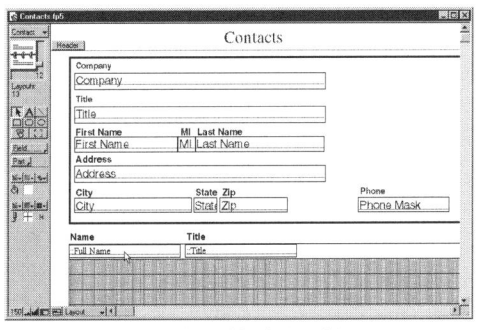

Figure 6.54 Choose the self-relationship you want to display from the drop-down menu.

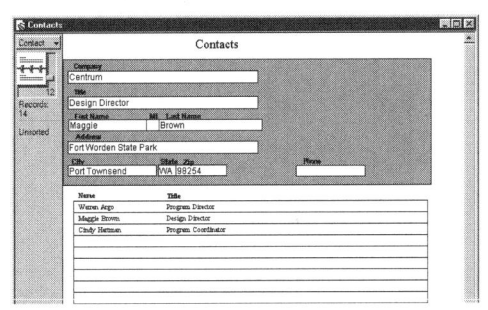

Figure 6.55 In Browse mode, the portal will display the fields from the related records.

To display and access self-relationship data:

1. Switch to the layout that will display the related data and choose View > Layout Mode (Control+L/Command+L).

2. Make sure the layout has enough room for the portal. If it doesn't, drag the Body tab down to resize the part.

3. Click the Portal tool. Click on the layout and drag the pointer out and down to size.

4. In the Portal Setup dialog box that appears, click the drop-down menu and choose the relationship for this portal (**Figure 6.52**).

5. Select the Field tool and drag it to the portal to add a field.

6. When the Specify Field dialog box appears, make sure you use the right relationship to choose the fields (**Figure 6.53**).

   In this case, we'll add Full Name and Title (**Figure 6.54**).

7. Switch to Browse mode to view the portal with the related data (**Figure 6.55**).

   The names listed in the portal are from the records where the company name is the same as the current record.

✔ Tip

- Once a self-relationship has been created, you can use the Go to Related Record command in the Navigation portion of the Specify Button dialog box to jump to a specific related record. You can also choose just the related records as if you had done a search for the contents of the match field in the current record.

ABOUT SELF-RELATIONSHIPS

139

Using a Portal for Navigation

By making a portal field into a button, you can quickly switch between records by just clicking the field.

To use a portal for navigation:

1. Go to a layout with the self-relationship portal and switch to Layout mode (Control+L/Command+L).

   In this example, we use the company portal we created in "To display and access self-relationship data" on page 139.

2. Click one of the self-relationship portal fields. In this example, we use Full Name (**Figure 6.56**). Choose Format > Button.

3. In the Specify Button dialog box, scroll down to the Navigation section and select the type of location you want to connect your button to (**Figure 6.57**).

4. In the Options section on the right, select the relationship in the Specify drop-down menu (**Figure 6.58**). Click OK.

5. Switch to Browse mode. Click a Name field in the portal. You'll now see the record for the name you selected.

✔ Tip

- When you make a field into a button, you can no longer use the field to edit data. However, once you click the field/button, FileMaker brings you to the related record where you can make changes.

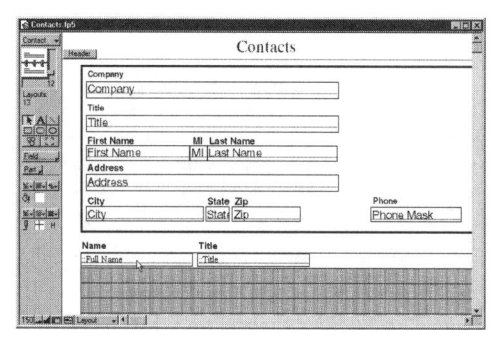

Figure 6.56 Select a field in the portal to make into a button.

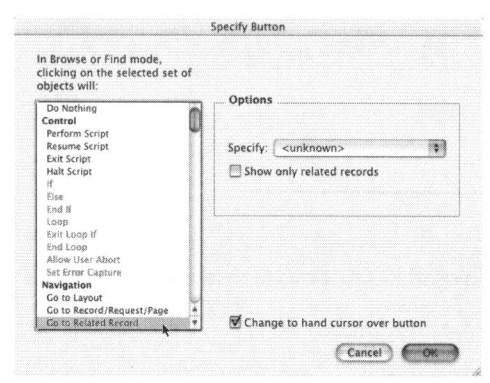

Figure 6.57 Select the button address type from the Navigation section. We choose Go to Related Record.

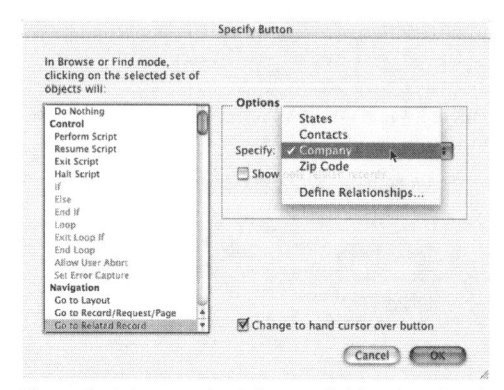

Figure 6.58 Connect the Full Name field to the related source file.

Searching for Self-Relationship Data

Instead of using a portal field as a button, you can create a separate button in the portal and use it to perform a search in the self-relationship records.

To search for self-relationship data:

1. Go to a layout with the self-relationship portal and switch to Layout mode (Control+L/Command+L).

2. Click the Button tool, then click and drag on the layout to size and place the button (**Figure 6.59**). The Specify Button dialog box appears.

3. In the list on the left, scroll to the Navigation section and select the Go to Related Record command.

4. In the Options section on the right, choose the relationship (we use Company).

5. Check the "Show only related records" box (**Figure 6.60**). Click OK.

6. At the flashing cursor, type a title for the button. You can also resize and add color if needed.

   When you switch to Browse mode and click the button, the found set of company records will appear in the portal.

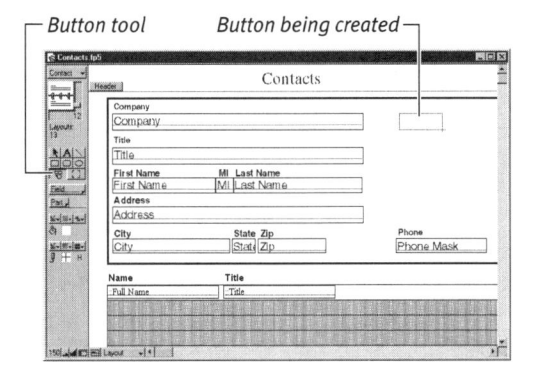

Figure 6.59 Use the Button tool to create a button on the layout.

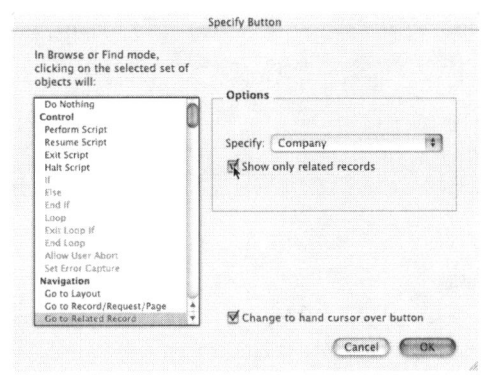

Figure 6.60 "Show only related records" acts like a Find command.

Creating a Lookup with a Self-Relationship

By using a self-relationship to do a lookup, you can save yourself lots of repetitive input and decrease typing errors. Many types of information, like a Zip code and the city and state combination it represents, must always be the same. If you use the most specific information (in this case, the Zip code) to define the relationship, you can automatically insert the other two fields' contents.

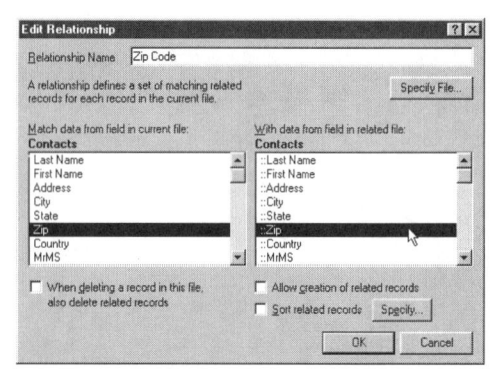

Figure 6.61 This relationship will use Zip as the key field.

To create a lookup with a self-relationship:

1. Choose File > Define Relationships.

2. When the Define Relationships dialog box appears, click New.

3. In the Open File dialog box, double-click the name of the current file. In this case, the file is called Contacts.fp5.

4. In the Edit Relationship dialog box, type in a relationship name.

   Since we're looking up records based on the Zip code, that's what we've named our relationship.

5. Click the same field in both field lists. In this example, we've chosen the Zip field (**Figure 6.61**).

6. Leave the "Sort related records" check box unchecked because you don't need to specify a sort. Click OK and then Done.

7. Choose File > Define Fields.

8. In the Define Fields dialog box, double-click the first field you want to look up. In our example, it's City.

9. The Options dialog box appears with the Auto-Enter tab in front. Click the "Looked-up value" check box (**Figure 6.62**).

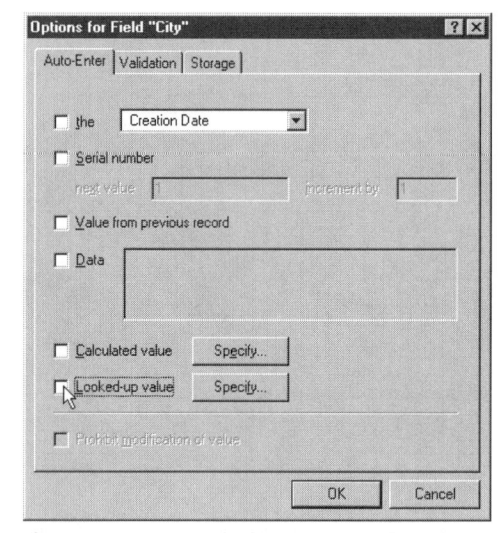

Figure 6.62 To create a lookup based on a field, choose "Looked-up value" from the Options dialog box.

142

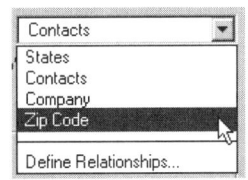

Figure 6.63 Use the Zip Code relationship to do the lookup.

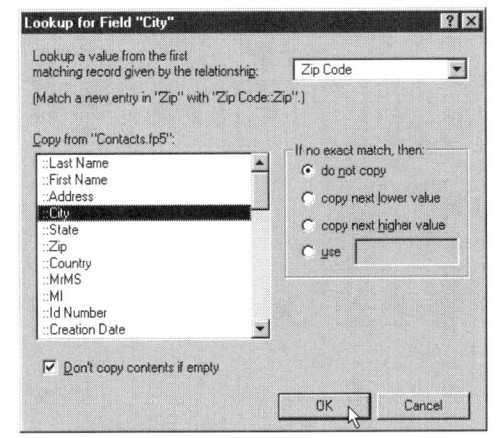

Figure 6.64 Don't copy the values for City and State if the zip code isn't exactly the same.

Figure 6.65 You can choose to create a new tab order, or edit the existing one.

10. When the Lookup dialog box appears, click the drop-down menu at the top to choose the self-relationship you just created (**Figure 6.63**).

11. Click the City field in the list. Make sure that "If no exact match, then" is set to "do not copy" and the "Don't copy contents if empty" check box is checked (**Figure 6.64**).

    In our example, selecting these options ensures that if there is an existing record with the same Zip code, the city and state that match it will be filled in automatically. If there isn't a record with that Zip code, nothing will be copied, so you can fill in the fields manually. Click OK, then OK again.

12. Repeat steps 8–11 if you have a second field to look up. In our example, we use the State field. Click Done when you're finished.

13. Go the layout where the data will be entered. Switch to Layout mode.

14. Choose Layouts > Set Tab Order.

15. The Set Tab Order dialog box appears. If your layout doesn't have a tab order already, choose the "Create new tab order" radio button. Otherwise, select "Edit tab order" (**Figure 6.65**).

continues on next page

16. Click inside the arrows on the fields to change or create the tab order so that the number in the Zip field is lower than the numbers in the City and State fields (**Figure 6.66**).

17. Changing the tab order prompts you to enter the Zip code before the city and state, so that the lookup can take place.

18. In the Set Tab Order dialog box, click OK.

✔ **Tips**

- The Tab Order setting does not control the order if the user is using the mouse to move between fields. You can put a text reminder on the layout telling the user to go to the Zip field before City and State.

- Instead of using the Zip code in the above example, you could use the same technique with a relationship based on the Company field. Then you could set lookups for Address, City, State, and Zip to avoid even more repetitive input.

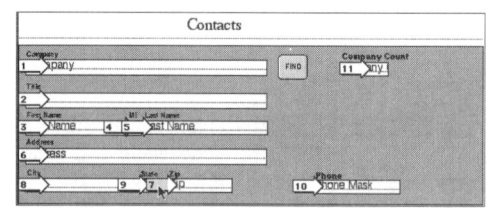

Figure 6.66 The tab order is set to bring you to the Zip Code field before City and State.

CREATING SIMPLE SCRIPTS

Databases are powerful things, but they sure can be tedious to set up and manipulate. Sometimes it seems as if you're using the same darned combination of mouse clicks and menu commands over and over. Why can't FileMaker learn how you work and do some of these functions for you? You may be surprised to discover that it can, if you're willing to take just a little time to train it by using scripts.

At its most basic level, a script is just a list of things you want FileMaker to do for you, written in exactly the order you want to have them done. It's like leaving a To Do list with an efficient helper, so that you can mentally "walk away" and return to find the tasks crossed off.

FileMaker scripts are patient, so if you need one to wait for more information before proceeding, you can build in a pause. They're also modular, so you can start with very simple lists and add more items to them as they occur to you. One script can be used together with other scripts, making a complex master script that efficiently automates many actions with one simple button. And once you've created a working script, it's foolproof. You'll never have to start over again because you chose the wrong drop-down menu, or forgot to change your page setup before printing.

We think scripting is addictive. Once you grow accustomed to planning them out, hundreds of different script combinations will occur to you. For instance, you can move records automatically between different files, click one button to sort and print files in a monthly report, and then export the result to Excel. If it can be done manually, chances are there's a script command to do it for you.

Planning a Simple Script

You never just launch into FileMaker and create databases and make fields "on the fly." If you did, you'd be sure to waste lots of time later correcting your mistakes, adding fields (and then the data for them) and adapting layouts. Creating a script is very much like creating a new database. If the end result is successful, it's because you carefully considered your goals and strategies first.

Begin by thinking about how you work. Ask yourself, "What things do I do in FileMaker that waste time, typing, and mouse clicks because I always have to repeat them?" Make a list of these tasks. (If nothing occurs to you at the moment, open your database and start working!) For example, you might have, "Print out a list of accounts over 30 days past due."

You should temporarily skip any tasks that require you to choose between options at some point in the process (we'll get to those later). Of the tasks that remain, look for one that mostly involves several menu commands in sequence. Make a list of the main menu bar commands you choose when you do the task, in the order in which you do them.

When we look at the steps we take to get our overdue accounts statement, our list contains:

- Find records
- Sort records
- Go to the overdue accounts layout
- Print the layout

That's a good beginning, but always go back and look at the steps carefully to see if there are any you've missed. In this first list, we've forgotten that we need to set up the page for printing so the proper page size and orientation are used. Our revised list now reads:

- Find records
- Sort records
- Go to the overdue accounts layout
- Set the printing options
- Print the layout

There's one last step that you might not think about when you look at your process. Once you've finished printing, you don't usually need the printing layout on the screen. In fact, you probably want to return to whatever you were doing before you printed the overdue accounts statement. So the last step in the list should be:

- Go back to where you started

Once you've listed all your steps, look closely at the list for things you can group together. The nice thing about scripts is that you don't necessarily have to tackle them all at once, from start to finish. You can start with very small, short tasks and build up to more complex functions by adding new steps to the beginning, end, or even the middle of a script.

Storing Settings Before Scripting

Looking at a list of steps you want to combine into a script, you'll probably notice that several steps depend on others. For example, if you want to print a report, you have to set up your printing options first. If you want to sort records, you have to find them first. The order in which you do things really does matter. This may seem pretty obvious when you look at it now, but it's actually easy to lose sight of this concept when you plan a script.

Settings like page size or sort order are easy to leave out, but you could get incorrect results if you've forgotten to consider them. Unless you tell it otherwise within the script steps, FileMaker will apply its most recently used settings, even if they're not appropriate for what you have in mind. Imagine how irritated you'd be if you set a script in motion to print your 50-page accounts payable, only to find the data cut in two because the page setup specified portrait instead of landscape orientation.

To protect you from these frustrations, FileMaker allows you to store your settings when you create a script. Several script steps give you the option to Restore:

- **Perform Find:** Restores all the criteria for a find request, including any combination of omitted items.

- **Sort:** Restores the sort criteria for the records.

- **Import Records:** Restores the name of the file and its records, as well as any connections you've made between the imported and current files.

- **Export Records:** Restores the name of the file you're exporting to, the specific records you're exporting, as well as any export options you've set.

- **Page/Print Setup:** Restores page size, print percentage, number of copies, and other printer-specific print settings.

Chapter 7

In order to take full advantage of the Restore option, create all the settings you need just before creating the script. Don't assume that you know what these settings are. If you've done any work in FileMaker between the time you created your script pre-sets and when you sit down to make the script, create the pre-sets again.

To create pre-sets for a script:

1. Open your database and go to the layout you need to find your records.

   In our example, we create the pre-sets for accounts over 30 days, so we need our Sales Entry layout.

2. Choose View > Find Mode.

3. Enter the find criteria and click Find (**Figure 7.1**).

   In our example, we're searching for files with a sale date earlier than January 1, 2000.

4. Choose Records > Sort (Control+S/Command+S).

5. When the Sort Records dialog box appears, double-click fields in the scrolling list on the left to move them to the Sort Order list on the right, then click Sort (**Figure 7.2**).

   In our example, we sort by last name to get an alphabetical list of the overdue accounts.

6. Click the Layout drop-down menu in the toolbar and switch to the layout you'll use to print the report (**Figure 7.3**).

Figure 7.1 If you want to use the Perform Find [Restore] step in your script, you must create a Find request before creating the script.

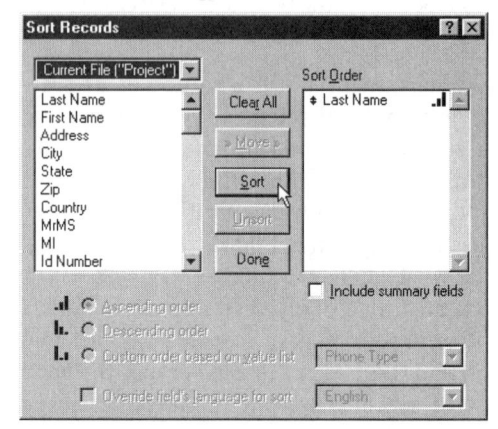

Figure 7.2 The Sort order in use when you create a script will be used when the Sort [Restore] step is included.

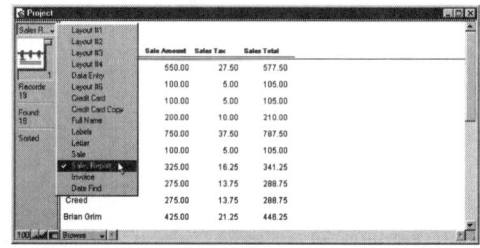

Figure 7.3 The Go to Layout step will use whatever layout you were in just before you created the script.

STORING SETTINGS BEFORE SCRIPTING

148

Creating Simple Scripts

7. Choose File > Print Setup (Page Setup on Macintosh). Set the print options needed for the script. Click OK (**Figure 7.4**).

8. Choose File > Print.

9. In the Print dialog box, click the Print drop-down list and choose "Records being browsed" (**Figure 7.5**). Click OK. At this point, the basic pre-sets for the script you've planned are complete.

✔ Tip

- FileMaker doesn't retain a previous sort order after a find. Anytime you execute the Find command, you must re-sort the database. Always remember to include the Sort command after a Find command in a script.

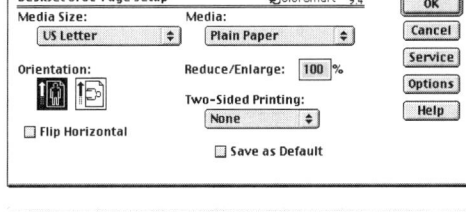

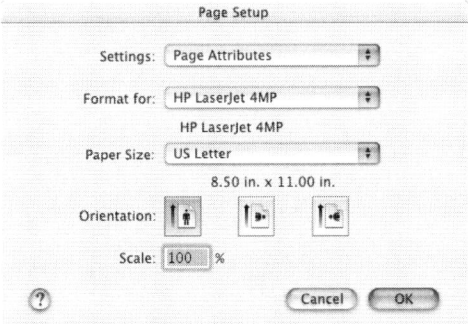

Figure 7.4 Print Setup options for Windows and Macintosh.

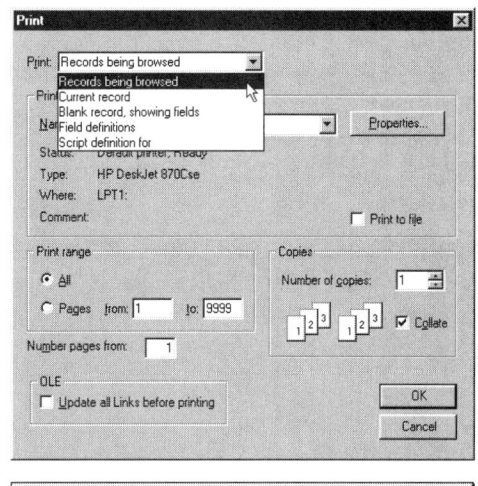

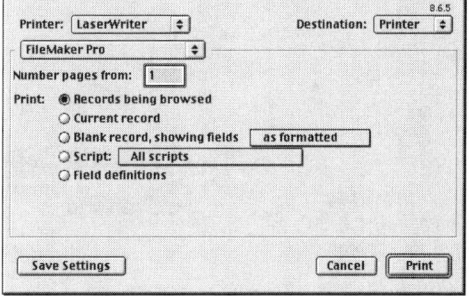

Figure 7.5 Windows and Macintosh Print dialog boxes.

STORING SETTINGS BEFORE SCRIPTING

149

Chapter 7

Using ScriptMaker

ScriptMaker is a module inside FileMaker for assembling scripts. Anyone who has ever had to do scripting for other purposes (like creating a roll-over with JavaScript) will appreciate the simplicity and clarity of the two ScriptMaker dialog boxes.

Define Scripts (**Figure 7.6**) manages existing scripts. If you check the box next to a script, it will appear as an option in the Scripts menu. Otherwise, only the ScriptMaker module will appear in the Scripts menu (**Figure 7.7**). This feature lets you run an existing script at any time.

Script Definition (**Figure 7.8**) provides a working space for editing and creating new scripts.

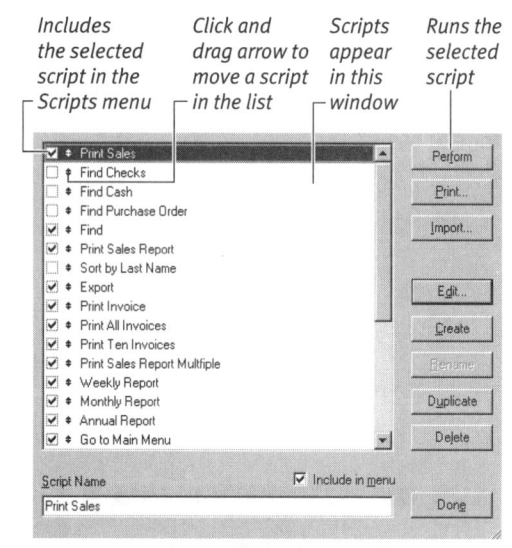

Includes the selected script in the Scripts menu
Click and drag arrow to move a script in the list
Scripts appear in this window
Runs the selected script

Figure 7.6 The Define Scripts dialog box is where you manage scripts you've already created.

Figure 7.7 In the first menu, we chose to have the script appear as a menu option. In the second menu, we didn't.

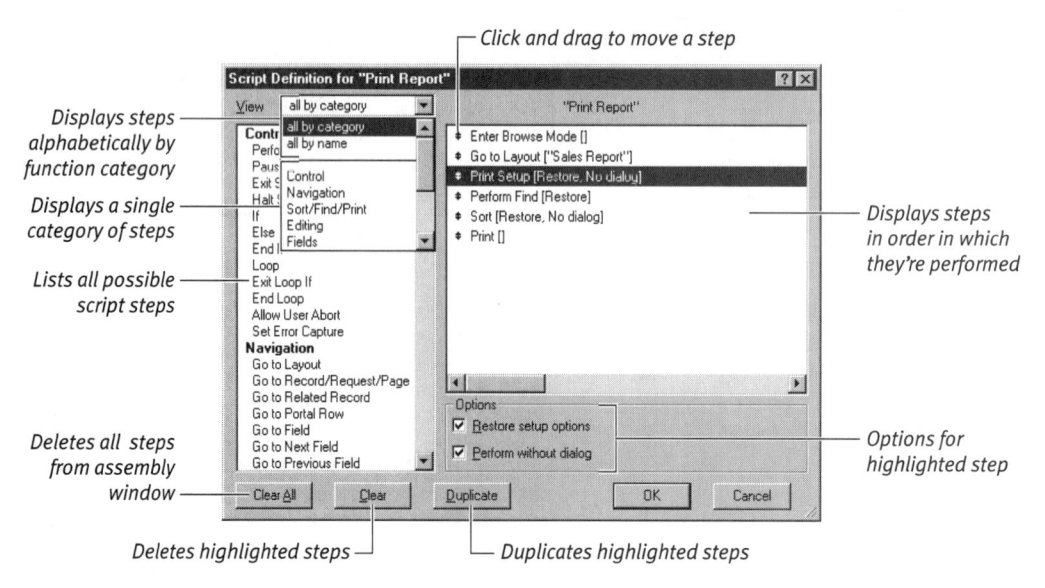

Click and drag to move a step
Displays steps alphabetically by function category
Displays a single category of steps
Lists all possible script steps
Deletes all steps from assembly window
Deletes highlighted steps
Duplicates highlighted steps
Displays steps in order in which they're performed
Options for highlighted step

Figure 7.8 The Script Definition dialog box is where you build or edit scripts.

150

Creating Simple Scripts

To duplicate a script:

1. Choose Scripts > ScriptMaker.

2. In the Define Scripts list of scripts, highlight the name of the script you want to duplicate.

3. Click Duplicate. The script copy will appear at the end of the list (**Figure 7.9**).

If you wish to adapt an existing script, the best strategy is to duplicate the script, then rename it and edit in the change.

To rename a script:

1. Choose Scripts > ScriptMaker.

2. In the Define Scripts list of scripts, highlight the name of the script you want to rename.

3. Type the new name in the Script Name box to make the Rename button active, then click Rename (**Figure 7.10**).

To delete a script:

1. Choose Scripts > ScriptMaker.

2. In the Define Scripts list of scripts, highlight the name of the script you want to delete.

3. Click Delete. When the warning dialog box appears, click Delete again.

Figure 7.9 A duplicated script appears at the end of the Define Scripts window list.

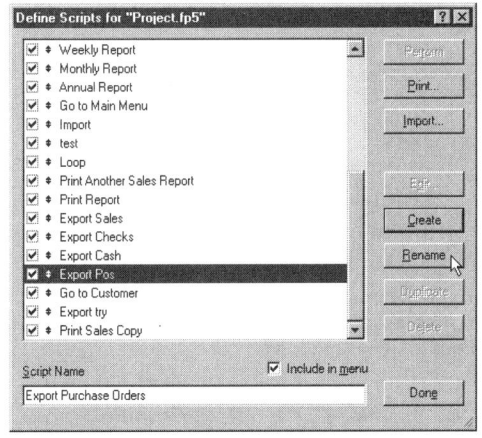

Figure 7.10 You can't choose Rename until you've edited the name of a script.

To edit a script:

1. Choose Scripts > ScriptMaker.

2. In the Define Scripts list of scripts, highlight the name of the script you want to edit.

3. When the Script Definition dialog box appears, make whatever script changes you need, then click OK.

   If you're modifying a script that has restored settings (like Find or Sort), a dialog box will appear that gives you the option of keeping or replacing each pre-set (**Figure 7.11**). In our example, only our Print Setup information has changed.

4. If you've changed any of the settings and want to use the new ones, click the Replace radio button for those settings. Otherwise, click the Keep radio button. When you've finished, click OK.

✔ Tips

- You can run any of the first 10 scripts listed in the menu by holding the Control (Windows) or Command (Mac) key and typing a number from 1 to 0 (**Figure 7.12**). You can rearrange the list to put different scripts in the top 10 by clicking the double arrow before the script name and dragging up or down (**Figure 7.13**).

- If you rename a script, ScriptMaker updates the script name in every other script that refers to it so that all your other scripts continue to work properly.

Figure 7.11 If you edit a script with restored settings, you can choose whether to keep the original settings or change them to the current settings.

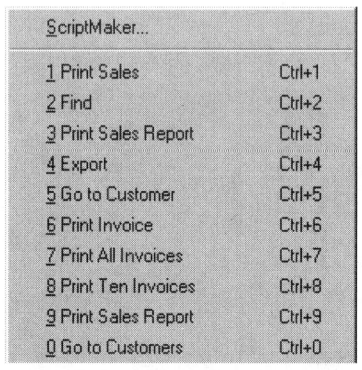

Figure 7.12 You can run the first 10 scripts in the Script menu by pressing Control/Command and a number key.

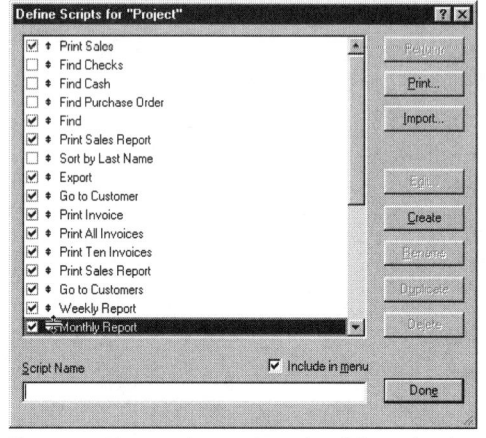

Figure 7.13 You can change the order of the scripts by clicking and dragging the double arrows.

Creating a Basic Script

Every script step consists of two parts—the step name, which is a description of what it does, and the step options inside brackets. If the brackets are empty, the step doesn't have any options selected. If there are no brackets, the step has no options available. If a step has options, their settings can be changed. Highlighting the step in the assembly window on the right displays its options below.

A newly added step is highlighted in the assembly window. New steps are added immediately below the highlighted step, so you should be careful not to select an earlier step in the window. If you do, any new steps you select will be inserted after the highlighted step, not after the last step in the window.

In this example, we'll create a script that finds records, sorts them, and prints a report from a specified layout. In creating this script, we've already followed the steps in "To create presets for a script" earlier in this chapter.

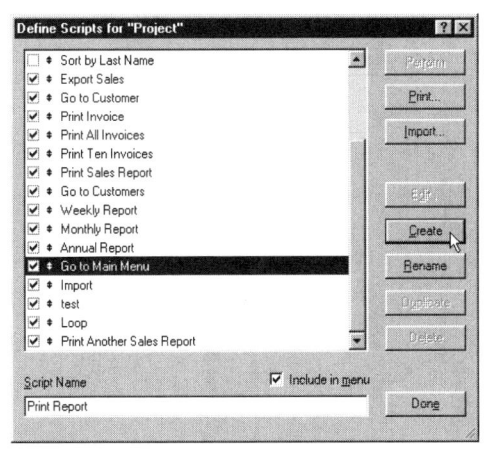

Figure 7.14 Script names should describe the script's function.

Figure 7.15 Go to Layout switches to the layout in use when the script was created.

To create a basic script:

1. Choose Scripts > ScriptMaker.

   When the Define Scripts dialog box appears, type a descriptive name for the script and click Create (**Figure 7.14**).

2. The Script Definition dialog box appears. Scroll down to the Navigation category in the left window and double-click Go to Layout (**Figure 7.15**) to select it.

   If you check the "Refresh window" box under Options, FileMaker will update the layout display for each change. Most of the time this just slows the script down, although it can sometimes be useful if you want to check how a script runs.

continues on next page

Chapter 7

3. In the Options section, choose the layout you want to use for the script from the Specify drop-down menu (**Figure 7.16**).

4. Scroll down to the Sort/Find/Print category in the left window and double-click Perform Find (**Figure 7.17**).

   In the Options section, leave the "Restore find requests" box checked. This setting restores the Find criteria in use when you created the script.

5. From the Specify drop-down menu in the Options section, choose Replace Found Set (**Figure 7.18**).

   Extend Found Set and Constrain Found Set allow you to expand or narrow an already existing found set. (See Chapter 5 for more about extending and constraining.)

6. In the Sort/Find/Print category in the left window, double-click Sort.

   This step sorts the records using the sort criteria you defined when you created the script.

7. In the Options section, leave the "Restore sort order" and "Perform without dialog" boxes checked (**Figure 7.19**).

   "Perform without dialog" means that the sort step will be carried out without displaying the Sort dialog box.

Figure 7.16 Since the layout name is in brackets, it can be changed to any other layout in the database.

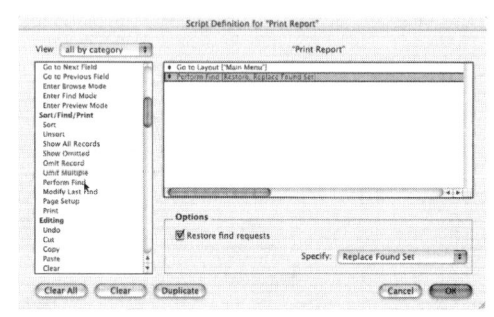

Figure 7.17 Perform Find enters Find mode and lets you change the criteria to either find all the records in the database, or just some of them.

Figure 7.18 Replace Found Set performs a normal find, creating a new found set from your criteria.

Figure 7.19 The Restore option will use the settings in place when the script is created.

154

Creating Simple Scripts

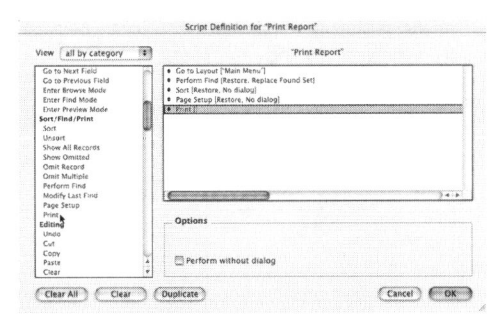

Figure 7.20 The brackets after Print are empty because the "Perform without dialog" option below is not checked.

Figure 7.21 Add the Go to Layout [original layout] step at the end of the script so you end up back where you started when the script is finished.

Figure 7.22 The Beep script step will play the system Alert sound.

8. In the Sort/Find/Print category in the left window, double-click Page Setup. As above, leave the "Restore setup options" and "Perform without dialog" boxes checked.

9. In the Sort/Find/Print category in the left window, double-click Print (**Figure 7.20**).

   To print using the settings defined in the previous steps, check the "Perform without dialog" box in Options. To choose printing options each time you run the script, leave this box unchecked.

10. Scroll to the Navigation category in the left window and double-click Go to Layout to add this step to the end of the script (**Figure 7.21**). Leave its Option set to "original layout."

    This step will return you to the layout you were in before you ran the script.

11. Click OK to save the script and return to the Define Scripts dialog box. Click Done.

✔ Tips

- The Show All Records script step makes all the records in your database available for printing. Select it to make sure that all records in the database will print in a layout.

- If you want a script to let you know that a particular step is complete (or that the script is finished), you can add a beep to it at the appropriate place in the script. The Beep step can be found in the Miscellaneous category. It uses whatever sound file has been selected as the operating system's Alert sound (**Figure 7.22**).

155

CREATING A BASIC SCRIPT

Chapter 7

Creating Sub-scripts

You can create small sub-scripts that do one or two specialized tasks, then combine them with a more generic larger script to execute a variety of actions. These scripts may only contain one step apiece, but they allow you to retain a variety of settings without having to re-search or re-sort each time you want to create a variation on one script idea. For example, if you frequently have to sort your files by last name, you can pre-set your database with this sort, then create a sub-script that only has a Sort step in the script. Then you can add this sub-script to any other script—for updating accounts payable or analyzing account payment patterns—as you need it. We use this strategy to create a search script for payments by check.

Figure 7.23 To use the restore option, you must do a search before creating the script.

To create a sub-script to find records:

1. Go to Find mode. Go to the layout that contains the fields you need for your search. Input your criteria in the layout and click Find in the status area. In our example, we go to the Sales layout and search for all sales that were paid by Check (**Figure 7.23**).

2. Choose Scripts > ScriptMaker.

3. When the Define Scripts dialog box appears, type Find Checks in Script Name and click Create (**Figure 7.24**). The Script Definition dialog box will appear.

4. Scroll down to the Sort/Find/Print category in the left window and double-click Perform Find. Leave "Restore find requests" checked in Options to maintain the find criteria. Leave Replace Found Set selected in the Specify drop-down menu (**Figure 7.25**). Click OK.

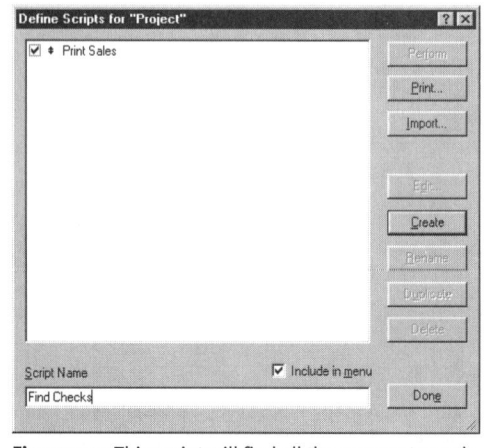

Figure 7.24 This script will find all the payments made by check.

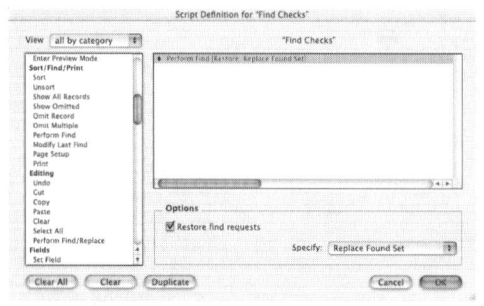

Figure 7.25 This script will restore the current find request.

156

Creating Simple Scripts

Figure 7.26 A separate script is required for each find request.

Figure 7.27 The sort script restores the sort order, so it doesn't require the dialog box.

5. Click Done to finish. You now have a script that will just find all of the records that were paid by check.

6. To create scripts for other types of payment, follow these steps but substitute other payment types. In our example, we created a total of four small scripts sorted for cash, purchase orders, and credit cards as well as Check (**Figure 7.26**).

To create a sub-script to sort records:

1. Choose Records > Sort.

2. Sort the records by the criterion that you want. For this example, we'll use last name.

3. Choose Scripts > ScriptMaker.

4. When the Define Scripts dialog box appears, type Sort by Last Name in Script Name and click Create.

5. When the Script Definition dialog box appears, scroll down to the Sort/Find/Print category in the left window. Double-click Sort to move it to the assembly window. Leave both option boxes checked (**Figure 7.27**). This creates a small sub-script that will sort data by the Last Name field.

continues on next page

✔ Tips

- Sometimes you create sub-scripts and forget what settings you used for them, or you inherit scripts from other people who have worked on your database. To discover what search settings or sort settings are restored with a script, you must actually run the script. Once the script is finished, go to Browse mode, then choose Records > Modify Last Find to see what search criteria are entered in the layout (**Figure 7.28**). To see the sort criteria, choose Records > Sort instead. To avoid having to backtrack, see "Adding Comments to a Script" later in this chapter.

- Sub-scripts can take up precious room in the Scripts menu list. If you don't expect to use any of the sub-scripts by themselves, uncheck the "Include in menu" box next to the name in the Define Scripts dialog box (**Figure 7.29**).

Figure 7.28 Records > Modify Find Request brings up the layout used for the original search with its search criteria indicated. This is the Payment field, showing that the search criterion was "check."

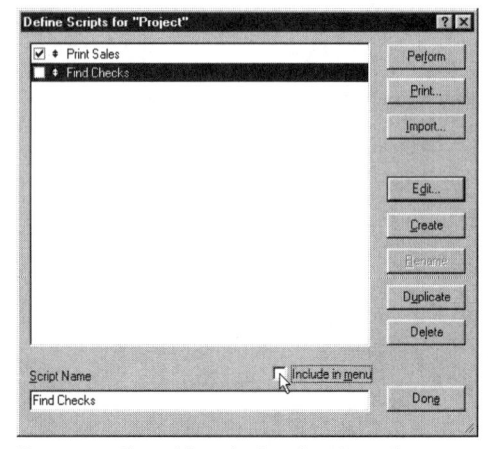

Figure 7.29 Since this script is only going to be used as a sub-script, it doesn't need to appear in the Scripts menu.

Creating Simple Scripts

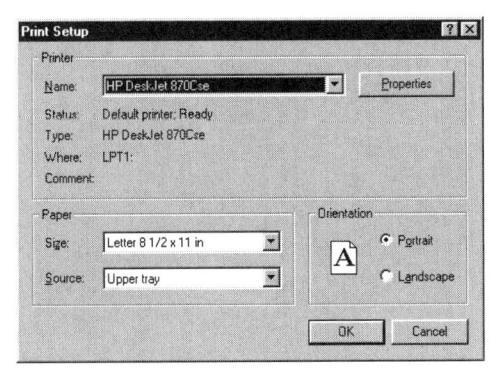

Figure 7.30 You must set the Print/Page Setup options before creating the script.

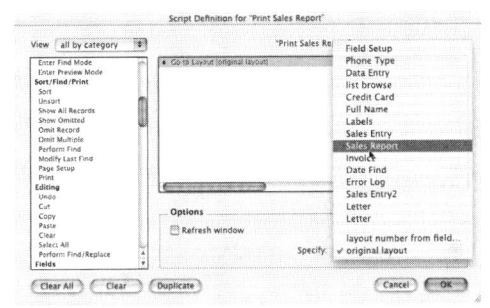

Figure 7.31 Specify a layout in the Go to Layout script step.

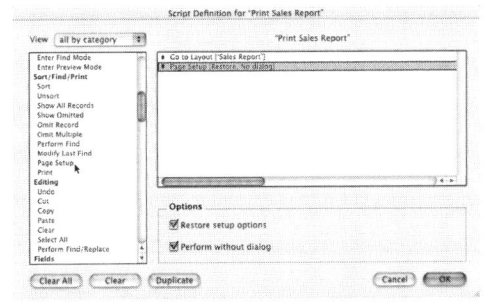

Figure 7.32 Restore will use the Print/Page Setup options in use when the script was created.

Combining Sub-scripts

In "To create a sub-script to find records," we created several sub-scripts. Because they're small and modular, we can swap them in and out to create customized master scripts that do essentially the same things for a wide variety of different criteria. For this example we'll create a script that combines a find sub-script and a sort sub-script, then prints the result.

To create a master script:

1. Go to the layout you want to use for your report. Choose File > Print Setup/Page Setup.

2. Set the options for printing this report (**Figure 7.30**).

3. Choose Scripts > ScriptMaker.

4. When the Define Scripts dialog box appears, type Print Sales Report in the Script Name box and click Create.

5. The Script Definition dialog box will appear. In the step list on the left, scroll down to the Navigation section and double-click Go to Layout.

6. In the Options section, choose your report layout from the Specify drop-down menu (**Figure 7.31**). In our example, we use Sales Report.

7. Double-click Print Setup/Page Setup in the Sort/Find/Print section. Leave both Options boxes checked (**Figure 7.32**).

continues on next page

159

Chapter 7

8. In the step list on the left, double-click Perform Script in the Control section to add it to the assembly window.

9. In the Options section, choose Find Checks from the Specify drop-down menu (**Figure 7.33**).

10. Double-click Perform Script again.

11. In the Options section, choose Sort by Last Name from the Specify menu (**Figure 7.34**).

12. In the step list on the left, scroll to the Sort/Find/Print section and double-click Print. You can choose to have the Print dialog box appear by unchecking the "Perform without dialog" box (**Figure 7.35**).

13. Click OK to add the script to the Define Scripts listing, then click Done.

Figure 7.33 Choose the script to perform from the Specify drop-down menu.

Figure 7.34 The sort script must be run after the find script.

Figure 7.35 If the "Perform without dialog" check box is unchecked, the report will print to the current printer after prompting the user.

Retaining Multiple Settings in a Script

Although you can simply edit the Options in a master script to change the sub-scripts you perform, it's more sensible to combine many similar actions into one script that automatically does them all at once. For example, in "To create a sub-script to find records," we created four separate sub-scripts that broke out sales by different types of payment. Chances are that we'd like to print all four reports at once. Since FileMaker can't handle more than one set of restore options per script, you can't simply search for one criterion, add a Perform Find step, then repeat. Instead, ScriptMaker uses sub-scripts to keep all the settings separate from each other, and Perform Script to call them up when you need them.

In this example, we make a copy of the script we created in "To create a basic script." By duplicating and editing the original script steps, we make a new script that finds, sorts, and prints several different reports. Although we create four report variations in our sample script, there's no limit to how many variations you can create in one script.

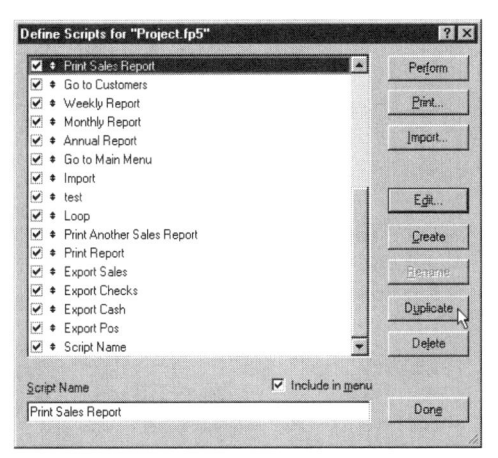

Figure 7.36 To edit an existing script, select it from the scrolling list in the Define Scripts dialog box, then duplicate and rename it.

To retain multiple finds and sorts in scripts:

1. Choose Scripts > ScriptMaker.

2. When the Define Scripts dialog box appears, highlight the script name you want to use as a template in the script window and click Duplicate. In our example, we chose Print Sales Report (**Figure 7.36**).

3. Change the script name, then click Rename. Click Edit.

continues on next page

Chapter 7

4. When the Script Definition dialog box appears, click the step Perform Script [Sub-scripts, "Find Checks"] in the assembly window on the right. Hold down the Shift key and click the final Print step (**Figure 7.37**).

   This step selects the three steps in the script that we will want to duplicate for all of our reports.

5. Click the Duplicate button as many times as you have report variations. All the highlighted steps will be reproduced multiple times at the end of the list (**Figure 7.38**).

6. Click to highlight the first duplicated Perform Script [Sub-scripts, "Find Checks"] step. Choose "Find Cash" from the Specify menu (**Figure 7.39**).

7. Click to highlight the next duplicated Perform Script [Sub-scripts, "Find Checks"] step. Choose "Find Purchase Orders" from the Specify menu.

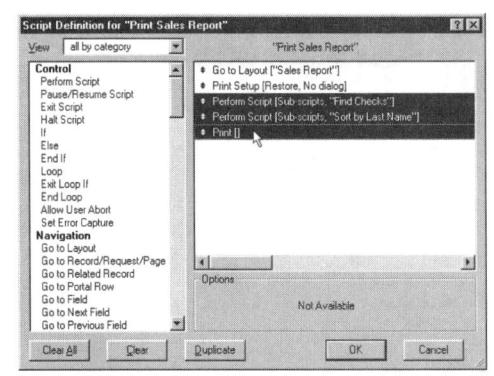

Figure 7.37 You can duplicate multiple steps in a script by Shift-clicking to select them, and then using the Duplicate button.

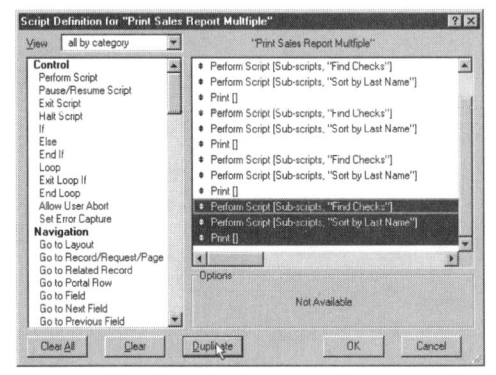

Figure 7.38 Duplicated script steps will appear at the end of the current list.

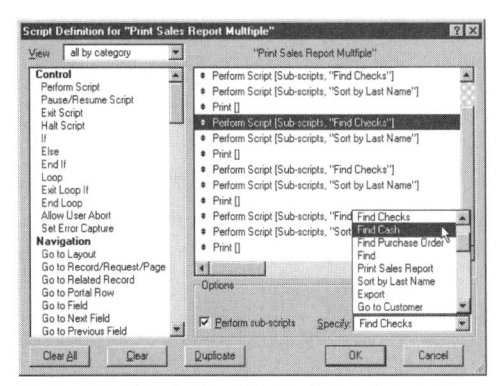

Figure 7.39 After duplicating steps, just change the Options for each variation.

Creating Simple Scripts

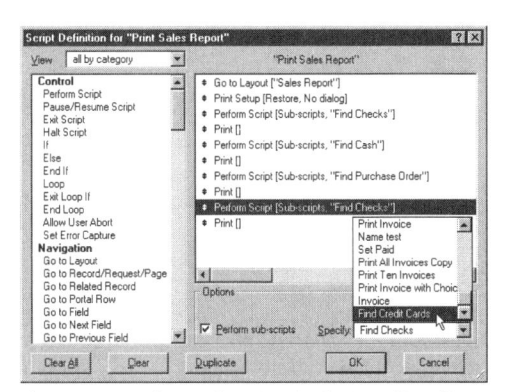

Figure 7.40 Replace sub-scripts in the Specify pull-down menu.

Figure 7.41 Click the Keep radio button to retain the same settings for the script.

8. Click to highlight the last duplicated Perform Script [Sub-scripts, "Find Checks"] step. Choose "Find Credit Cards" from the Specify menu (**Figure 7.40**).

9. Click OK to finish.

10. A dialog box will appear asking if you want to Keep or Replace the Page Setup information (**Figure 7.41**). Click the Keep radio button and then click OK.

11. Click Done. When you run it, the new script will print four reports, each with a different set of records, but all sorted by Last Name.

Extending or Constraining Found Sets in a Script

In Chapter 5, we showed you how to constrain or extend existing found sets. This capability is also available in any script that uses the Perform Find step. Using the basic script that we created earlier in this chapter, we can use Perform Find to constrain or expand the found set that's in place when the script is run.

In "Creating a Basic Script," we created a script that finds all of the records with a date before 1/1/2000 and then sorts the records and prints a report. If you'd like to be able to use that script but limit the printed report to a particular state, you can use the Constrain Found Set option.

To extend or constrain found sets in a script:

1. Choose Scripts > ScriptMaker.

2. Double-click the Print Report script you created in "Creating a Basic Script" earlier in this chapter.

3. When the Script Definition dialog box appears, click the Perform Find step in the assembly window on the right.

4. From the Specify pop-up menu, choose Constrain Found Set (**Figure 7.42**).

5. Click OK. In the dialog box, choose the Replace radio button for Find Requests (**Figure 7.43**). Click Done to finish.

6. Before you run the script, choose View > Enter Find Mode (Control+F/Command+F). Enter the abbreviation for a state in the State field (or any other criteria you would like to use) and click Find. When you run the script, it will only find the records with a date before 1/1/2000 that are contained in the existing found set.

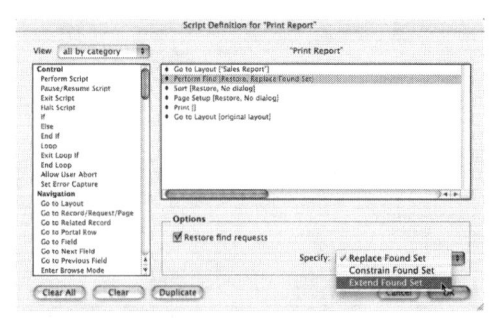

Figure 7.42 The Perform Find script step can be used to constrain or extend found sets.

Figure 7.43 When you edit an existing script, you must choose Replace for retained settings that have been changed.

Creating Simple Scripts

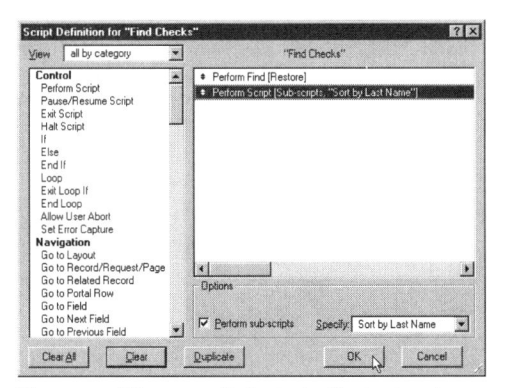

Figure 7.44 When you eliminate duplicate steps by incorporating them in sub-scripts, the master script is much easier to understand.

✔ Tips

- You can select multiple non-contiguous steps in a script by using the Control/Command key instead of Shift.

- Copying multiple steps in a script and editing them makes it easy to combine scripts, but it also makes for scripts that are long and hard to read. In the examples above, all our scripts are individually sorted by last name. Your scripts will be cleaner and more professional if you combine the find and the sort steps together into one script, and eliminate the duplicated sort steps entirely from the master script. Your master script for printing reports will then be shorter and much easier to understand (**Figure 7.44**). Remember that the scripts must run in the right order, with the sort command coming after the find step.

Chapter 7

Using Sub-scripts for Multiple Export Settings

In Chapter 5, we showed you how to export data to a spreadsheet or accounting program. You can use the sub-script strategy you learned in "To create a sub-script to find records" to create sub-scripts for different export settings. In this example, we create the sub-script that holds one export pre-set.

To create sub-scripts for multiple export settings:

1. Choose File > Export Records.

2. When the Export Records to File dialog box appears, type a name for the export file, choose a file format from the drop-down menu and click Save (**Figure 7.45**).

   The name you choose in this step isn't important, because you can choose a different one in the script itself. You must name the file something, however, or FileMaker won't let you proceed!

3. When the Specify Field Order for Export dialog box appears, double-click the fields in the left window that you want to export to the new file (**Figure 7.46**).

4. Click Export to create the file on your disk. You've now created the pre-sets you'll need for your export script.

5. Choose Scripts > ScriptMaker.

6. When the Define Scripts dialog box appears, type a name in the Script Name box and click Create.

7. The Script Definition dialog box will appear. In the step list on the left, scroll down to the Records category and double-click Export Records (**Figure 7.47**). Leave "Restore export order" checked to retain the settings you created in steps 2 and 3.

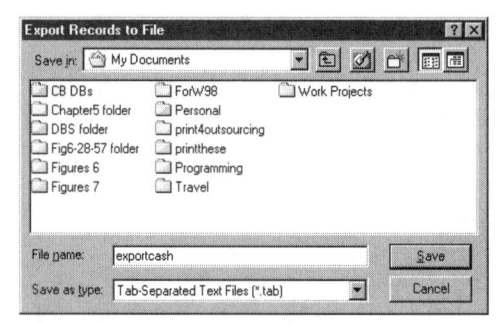

Figure 7.45 Choose a file format and specify a name for the export file.

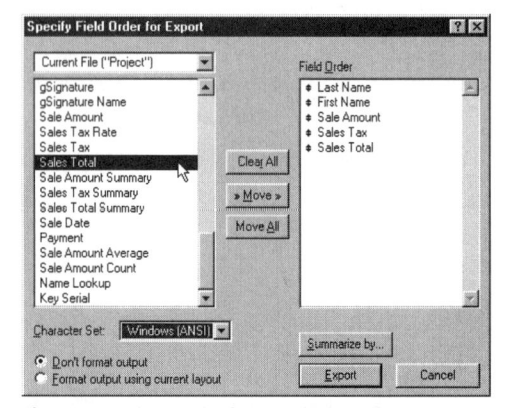

Figure 7.46 Choose the fields to be included in the export.

Figure 7.47 Check "Restore export order" to use the same fields in the same order as the last export.

166

Creating Simple Scripts

Figure 7.48 If you check Specify, you can set a file name that will be used every time the export script runs.

Figure 7.49 Clicking File lets you choose a different file name for your export file.

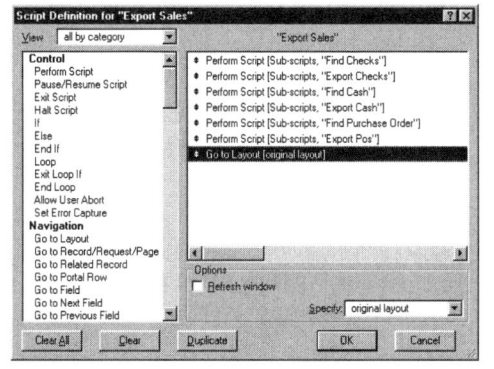

Figure 7.50 The combined master script will find and then export each set of records separately.

8. Under Options, check the Specify box to choose a file name that will be used for the export file (**Figure 7.48**).

9. When the Export Records to File dialog box appears, specify a file name for your export file. Click Save.

   If you don't specify a file name, you'll be prompted for one when the script runs, even if "Perform without dialog" is checked.

10. The script step will display the name and file type of the export file. Click OK to finish.

    You can repeat these steps to create new exports and their associated scripts.

✔ Tips

- You can change the file name you specify for your export script at any time by returning to ScriptMaker and editing the script. First, highlight Export Records in the assembly window. In Options, click the Specify File (Mac) or File (Windows) button **Figure 7.49**). This brings up the Export Records to File dialog box again, allowing you to select a new file name.

- Once you've created several export sub-scripts, you can combine them into a master script to create and export different sets of data. For example, at the end of a quarter you might need to move your account sales data both to an accounting program and an Excel spreadsheet. A master script allows you to export the same data in both formats at the same time. To do this, follow the steps in "To retain multiple finds and sorts in scripts" on page 161 to create a script that uses a series of Perform Script steps (**Figure 7.50**).

167

Adding Comments to a Script

One of FileMaker's serious scripting weaknesses is that it doesn't provide an automatic way to see the settings it stores with the script. If you create a script and then forget its criteria, or have to troubleshoot someone else's scripting, you have to run the script first to restore the settings. This is particularly irritating if the script includes printing a very long report or series of records. Either you temporarily clear the print step (and then have to remember to put it back!) or you waste a stack of paper.

Even worse, if all of the fields that were used for the search don't appear in the current layout, you won't see an accurate picture of the settings, nor will you have any clue that this is the case.

"There must be a better way," you're thinking. And there is, although it does require additional work on your part. You can insert comments in a script as a reminder of what the steps do. In fact, you can add any information as a comment, not just find and sort criteria. For this example, we add comments to a sub-script.

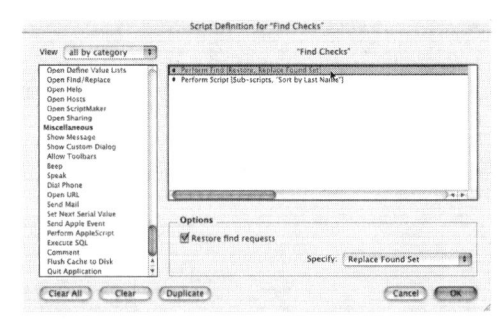

Figure 7.51 Select steps that will need explanations later.

Figure 7.52 Choosing the Comment step adds a new line beneath the step you want to annotate.

To add comments to a script:

1. Choose Scripts > ScriptMaker.

2. In the Define Scripts list of scripts, highlight the name of the script you want to annotate and click Edit.

3. When the Script Definition dialog box appears, select the step you want to explain in the assembly window (**Figure 7.51**).

4. Scroll down to Miscellaneous in the step list, and double-click Comment (**Figure 7.52**). A new line beginning with a # symbol is inserted after the step.

Figure 7.53 Type your comment in the Specify dialog box.

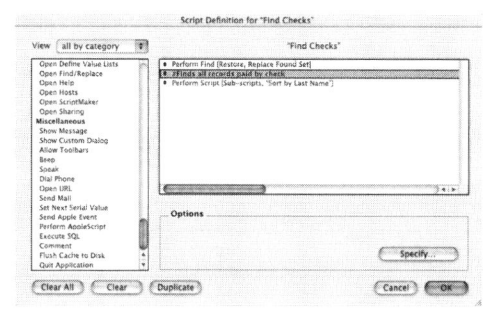

Figure 7.54 Your typed comment is inserted after the # sign.

5. Click Specify to open the Specify input window.

6. Type the text of your comment. Although you can type as much as you want, keeping the comment short and sweet is best so it will fit on one line in the script-assembly window (**Figure 7.53**). When you're finished click OK.

7. The comment will appear in the script steps list (**Figure 7.54**). Click OK.

8. A dialog box will appear asking if you want to keep or replace the settings. Click the Keep radio button and then click OK.

✔ **Tips**

- If you create a comment that's too long to fit in the script's step list, it will be cut off in the assembly window because ScriptMaker doesn't wrap long sentences to the next line. Double-click the comment to read all of it.

- The # symbol that begins a comment line in ScriptMaker is a visual cue to let programmers and scripters know that the rest of the line that follows isn't a step in the script. It's used in almost every scripting and programming language, not just for FileMaker. Comments aren't considered steps because they don't perform any actions.

- When you include comments in your scripts, they're displayed in bold type. When you print scripts, comments will be printed in italics.

ADDING COMMENTS TO A SCRIPT

Chapter 7

Using External Scripts

In "Combining Sub-scripts" we ran scripts from inside a master script. However, all of the sub-scripts we used were in the same file as the master script. Scripting also allows you to run scripts in other files. Doing this allows you to access data from a second file while working in the first database. Using a script to switch to another file is much simpler than selecting the file from the Window menu, then choosing a layout. If the second file is not already open, the script will open it and then run the external script.

In this example, we create a master script that switches from the Project file (where sales data is maintained) to the Customer layout in the Customer file (where customer data is kept). You might use this script to get contact information from a new customer's invoice in the sales file and transfer it to your customer database.

To run a script in another file:

1. Go to the file that will be called by the external script. In our example, we use the Customer database.

2. Choose Scripts > ScriptMaker.

3. When the Define Scripts dialog box appears, type a name for the script and click Create (**Figure 7.55**).

4. The Script Definition dialog box will appear. In the step list on the left, double-click Go to Layout in the Navigation section to add it to the script-assembly window.

5. In the Options section, choose your report layout from the Specify drop-down menu (**Figure 7.56**). In this example, we choose Customer. Click OK, then Done.

    When this script runs, it will open the Customer database if it isn't already open and then switch to the Customer layout.

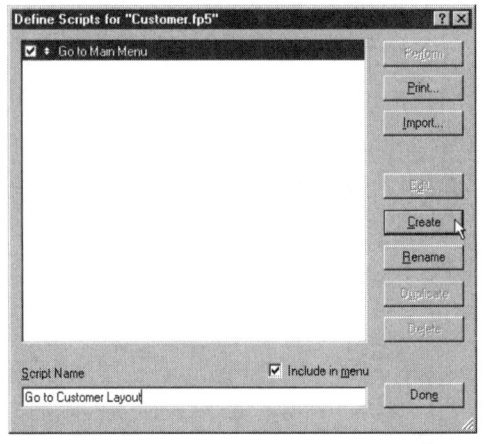

Figure 7.55 Use a script name that describes what the script will do.

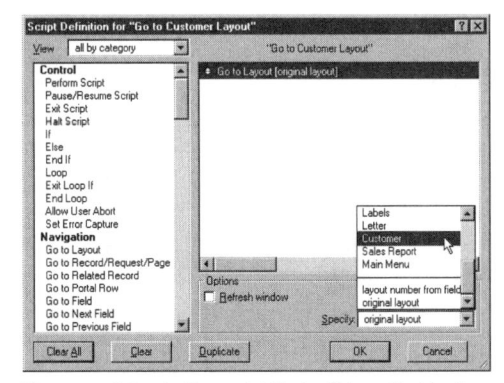

Figure 7.56 Create the script that will be called by the external script.

170

Creating Simple Scripts

Figure 7.57 Create the external script that will call the layout script in the other database.

Figure 7.58 Choose External Script instead of one of the current file's scripts listed below it.

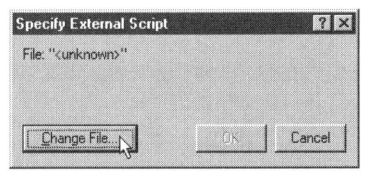

Figure 7.59 Click Change File to replace the File "< unknown >" setting with the name of the other file.

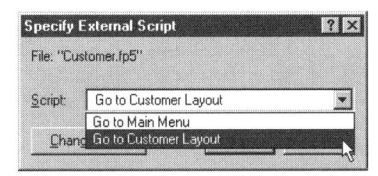

Figure 7.60 The Script pop-up menu now lists all of the scripts in the external file.

6. Open the file in which you will create the script that calls the external script. In our example, we use Project.

7. Choose Scripts > ScriptMaker.

8. When the Define Scripts dialog box appears, type the script name and click Create (**Figure 7.57**).

9. When the Script Definition dialog box appears, click Clear All to delete the default script.

10. In the step list on the left, double-click Perform Script in the Control section.

11. In the Options section, choose External Script from the Specify drop-down menu (**Figure 7.58**).

12. When the Specify External Script dialog box appears, click Change File (**Figure 7.59**).

13. In the Open File dialog box, navigate to the FileMaker database you used in steps 1–5 above. Double-click to select it.

14. In the Specify External Script dialog box, choose the script that you want to run from the Script drop-down menu (**Figure 7.60**). Click OK.

The external script will display the name of the external file that you chose. It won't show you the script name (**Figure 7.61**).

continues on next page

Chapter 7

15. To prevent you from forgetting which external script you're using, create a comment for this step. In the Miscellaneous section of the step list, double-click Comment. A new line beginning with a # symbol is inserted after the step (**Figure 7.62**).

16. Click Specify to open the Specify input window.

17. Type the text of your comment and click OK to add it to the script assembly window. Click OK, then Done.

    When this script is run, it opens the Customer layout in the Customer database, where you can edit or add data.

✔ **Tip**

- When the last command in a script performs another script, the script sequence will end when the second script finishes. As a result, you'll end up in the layout and database where the external script ran, not in the original layout and database where you ran the master script. A common technique to return you to the other database is to use Go to Layout [original layout] as the last step in a script (**Figure 7.63**). This technique will work even if the sub-script was in another file.

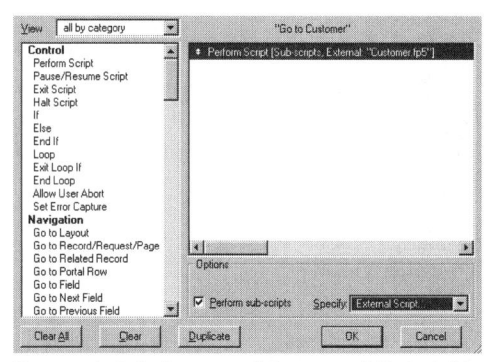

Figure 7.61 Only the name of the external file is visible in the script step, not the name of the script.

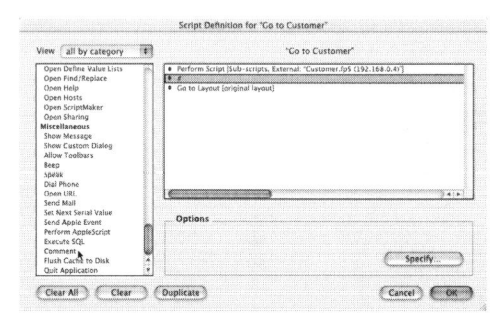

Figure 7.62 Write a comment showing the name of the external script.

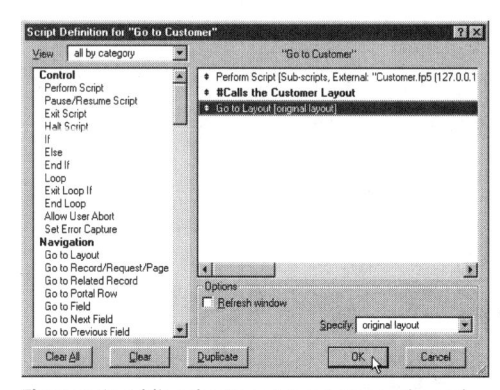

Figure 7.63 Adding the Go to Layout step to the end of a script returns you to the database and layout from which you ran the script.

Using Relative Paths

When you use a script function that references a second file, FileMaker looks in the folder that held the file at the time that the script was created. If it doesn't find the file, the program searches your hard drive and then all the mounted network volumes for a file of the same name. Since there's always a good possibility that another file by the same name might be found on a network drive, you could end up running your script on a completely different file. Yikes! A potential disaster for all concerned, since FileMaker wouldn't notify you of the substitution.

All this nasty business can be avoided with one quick check box. If you choose FileMaker's relative path option and the related file is not where FileMaker expects it, the Open File dialog box will open, giving you the chance to specify the correct file.

"Save relative path only" appears as a script option for opening or closing files with a script, and when you import records, create value lists, or perform scripts on an external file.

To open a file with a relative path:

1. Choose File > Define Relationships.
2. When the Define Relationships dialog box appears, click New (**Figure 7.64**).

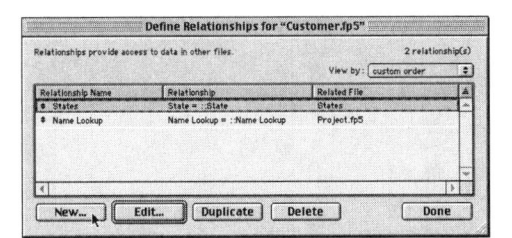

continues on next page

Figure 7.64 Create a new relationship in the Define Relationships dialog box.

3. When the Open File dialog box appears, leave the "Save relative path only" box checked (**Figure 7.65**). Double-click the file to create the new relationship.

4. When the Edit Relationship dialog box appears, choose the matching fields for the relationship and any options that are necessary (**Figure 7.66**). Click OK and then Done.

✔ **Tip**

- To open a file on a host server, choose File > Open Remote. You'll go directly to the Hosts dialog box. The Open Hosts script step offers the same convenience.

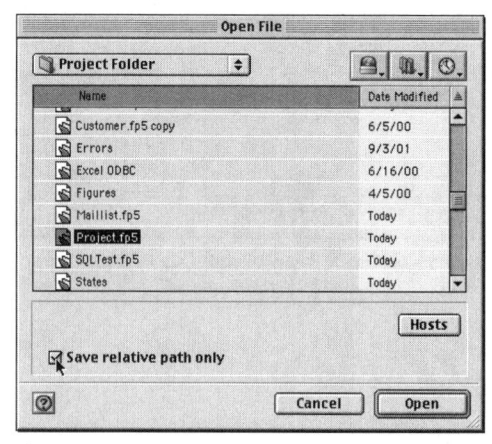

Figure 7.65 Your chances of using the wrong file are minimized when you open a file using a relative path.

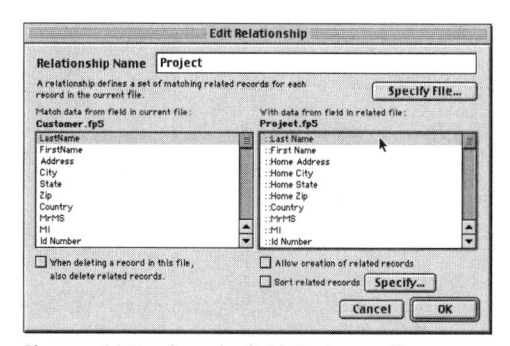

Figure 7.66 Match up the fields in the two files.

Working with Conditional Script Steps

Simple scripting is basically a time- and finger-saver. It automates menu items, batch-processes straightforward procedures like sorting and printing, and with the use of comments, helps you keep track of your own procedures. But if you never reach beyond a step-by-step record of your actions, you miss out on some of the best reasons to script.

Every time you work with FileMaker, you have to make choices based on the task and what you want to accomplish. When you check an account listing against a database of paid invoices, you act one way when you find a paid invoice (pay bills) and another when you discover that the account is still outstanding (send out past due statements). Wouldn't it be nice if you didn't have to spend the time matching up accounts and actions? By adding conditional steps to a script, you can kiss such chores goodbye. Conditional steps allow you to create "smart" scripts that make your decisions by examining options and following the guidelines you provide.

About Conditional Steps

Look closely at a simple, menu-driven script step. It's just a series of terse commands. "Go to this layout," "Find these records," or "Sort this file." The script has no contingency plan. Add a conditional step, and the script can ask the question "Under what condition should I perform this command?" More to the point, it can answer the question by examining the options you've provided.

What makes a step conditional? That word of possibilities: if. In ScriptMaker, If is always followed by a condition. Conditions are very much what you might think they are: the situation under which the script can act. "If the account is based in Boston," "If the part is listed in inventory," and "If it's after March 31" are all examples of conditional statements. When the phrase following the If is true (it's a Boston account, the part is in inventory) the script will execute any commands that follow the If step. When the answer is no, the script may execute a different command or do nothing, depending on how you've structured the rest of the If command.

If you don't add to the If, the script will end without doing anything. You can, however, add an Else step inside the If. FileMaker will do whatever follows the Else step if the answer to the If is negative.

To figure out whether you need a simple If or an If combined with Else, write down what you'd like to have happen. For example, if you want a script to print a statement if there's a balance due in the account, you'd say:

```
If there's a balance due,
Print a statement.
```

Since there isn't anything you want to do as an alternative to printing, you need a simple If step.

On the other hand, if you want a script to mark the Paid field with a Y or N depending on whether or not there's a balance due in the account, you'd say:

```
If there's a balance due Enter Y.
If there's not a balance due Enter N.
```

In this case, you have two different actions you want to take place when the script runs. Because of that, your If command will need an Else step inside it.

Working with Conditional Script Steps

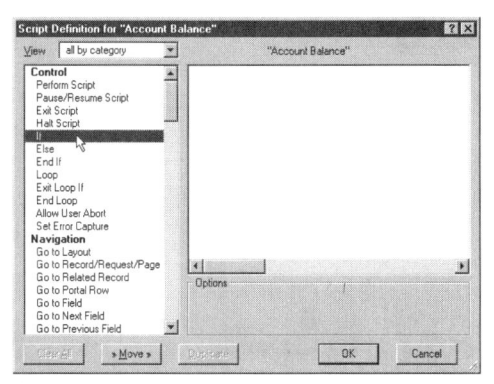

Figure 8.1 Double-click If to add it to the assembly window.

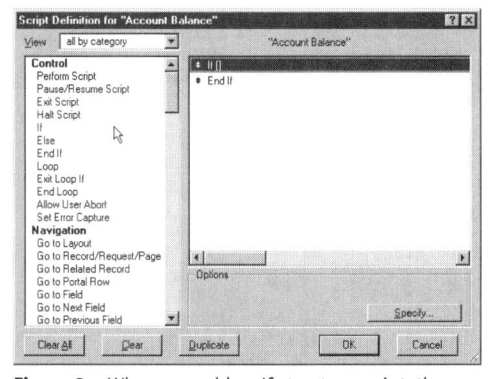

Figure 8.2 When you add an If step to a script, the End If is added automatically.

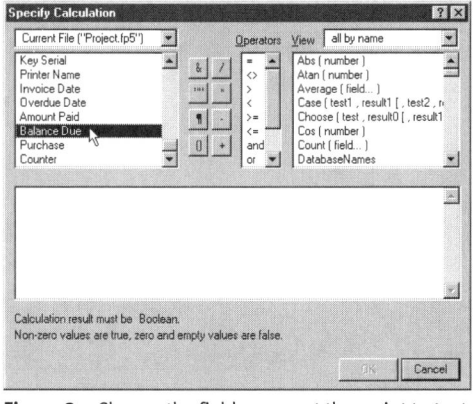

Figure 8.3 Choose the field you want the script to test in the If statement.

Using the If Command

Once you've figured out what kind of conditional step you need, you create the script in ScriptMaker. The syntax for a simple If statement to print a statement isn't much more complex than plain English.

To use the If command step:

1. Choose Scripts > ScriptMaker.

2. When the Define Scripts dialog box appears, type a name for the script (in this case Account Balance) and click Create.

3. The Script Definition dialog box will appear. Under the Control category in the left window, double-click If (**Figure 8.1**).

   When you add If to a script, you'll see two lines in the script steps: If and End If (**Figure 8.2**). End If is added by default every time you choose If to mark the place in the script where the If steps end. Everything you want in your If statement must be placed between If and End If.

4. In the Options section, click Specify to bring up the Specify Calculation dialog box.

   The If step uses the same formula builder you use to create a calculation field (see Chapter 4).

5. In the field list on the left, scroll to find your field (we use Balance Due). Double-click to add it to the formula box (**Figure 8.3**).

continues on next page

177

Chapter 8

6. Choose the greater than (>) symbol from the Operators scrolling list by double-clicking it.

7. Type 0 (zero), then click OK (**Figure 8.4**). The Script Definition dialog box now displays the highlighted If statement with its condition (**Figure 8.5**).

8. In the step list on the left, double-click the action you want performed. In this example, we choose Perform Script, because we want to run a print statement script we created (**Figure 8.6**).

   The new step is added below the If step. It's also indented from the left to show that it's inside the If step. This line is just a standard script command. (For more information about Perform Script, see Chapter 7.) Any script steps can be placed inside an If step—even another If step.

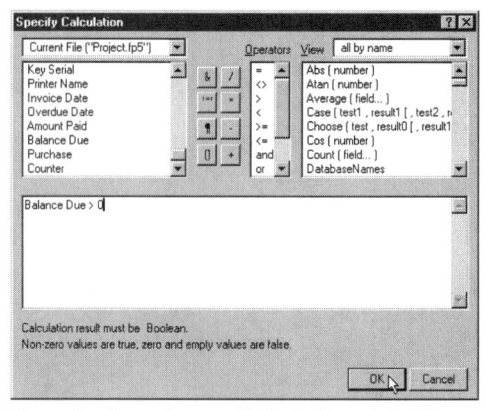

Figure 8.4 Type a 0 manually in the formula builder.

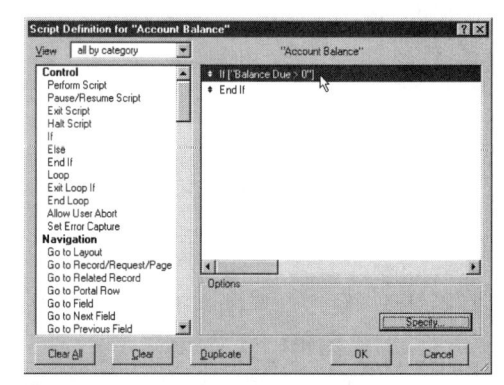

Figure 8.5 Your conditional statement is added automatically to the If statement brackets.

Figure 8.6 Steps inside other steps are indented.

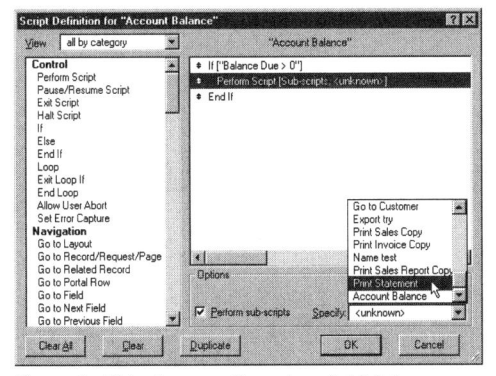

Figure 8.7 This step runs the sub-script Print Statement.

9. In the Options section, choose the script you want performed if there's a balance due (**Figure 8.7**). Since you don't have anything else you want the script to do if there's no balance due, the If statement is finished.

10. Click OK, then Done to close ScriptMaker.

✔ **Tip**

- You can just type the condition in the formula box for a statement as simple as "Balance Due > 0". However, when you start creating more complicated scripts, or if your fields have somewhat long names, it's better to stick to selecting field names and operators, as well as functions, from the scrolling lists. Computer programs aren't very good at intuiting what you want. You must have a field that exactly matches what's in the conditional statement so that FileMaker can check its value. One of the hardest and most time-draining aspects of scripts is that they frequently won't work right simply because you didn't catch a typing error.

Using If with Else

Sometimes you want the script to do something when the answer to the If condition isn't yes. You use an Else step within an If so the script will choose a different action when the If statement isn't true. Else steps are only executed if the condition is not true. Otherwise, they're ignored.

This script uses If and Else to change data in the Paid field for each record.

To use If and Else to modify data:

1. Choose Scripts > ScriptMaker.

2. When the Define Scripts dialog box appears, type a name for the script (in this case Set Paid) and click Create.

3. The Script Definition window appears. Under the Control category in the left window, double-click If.

4. In the Options section, click Specify to bring up the Specify Calculation dialog box (**Figure 8.8**).

5. In the field list on the left, scroll to find your field (we're using Balance Due). Double-click to add it to the formula box.

6. Choose the greater than (>) symbol from the Operators scrolling list by double-clicking it.

7. Type 0 (zero), then click OK. The Script Definition dialog box now displays the highlighted If statement with its condition.

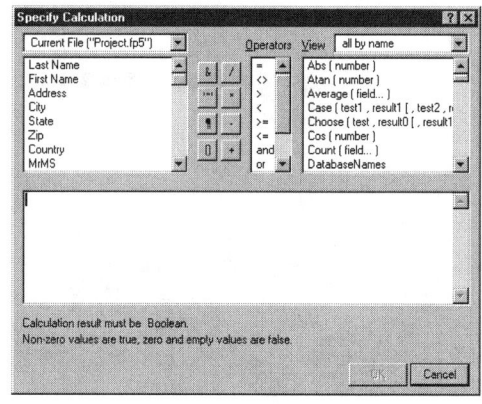

Figure 8.8 When you choose Specify, ScriptMaker brings up the Specify Calculation dialog box.

Working with Conditional Script Steps

8. In the step list on the left, double-click the action you want performed. In this example, we choose Set Field from the Fields section (**Figure 8.9**). It replaces the contents of a field with whatever you choose.

9. In Options, click the Field (Windows) or Specify Field (Mac) button (**Figure 8.10**).

10. When the Specify Field dialog box appears (**Figure 8.11**), choose the field name (in our example, we choose Paid). If you don't yet have the field you need, click Define Fields to create it. Click OK to close the box and return to the Script Definition window.

11. In the Options section, click the Specify button.

continues on next page

Figure 8.9 Choose Set Field to insert new information into an existing field.

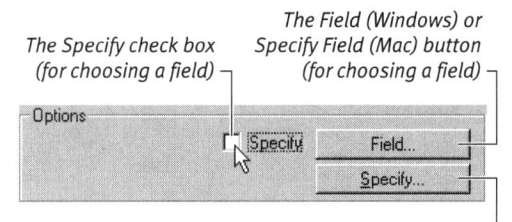

Figure 8.10 The Specify check box allows you to specify the field you want to change.

Figure 8.11 Choose or create the field you want in the Specify Field dialog box.

181

Chapter 8

12. When the Specify Calculation window appears, click the quotes operator button (""), then type an N between the quotes. Click OK to close the dialog box (**Figure 8.12**).

    At this point, your script checks to see if the balance in the account is more than 0. If it is, the script marks the Paid field with an N for not paid.

13. In the step list, double-click Else to add it to the assembly window (**Figure 8.13**).

14. Repeat steps 8–11 above.

15. When the Specify Calculation window appears, click the quotes operator button (""), then type a Y between the quotes. Click OK to close the dialog box (**Figure 8.14**).

    Now your script marks the Paid field with a Y for paid if there was no balance due.

16. Click OK, then Done to close ScriptMaker.

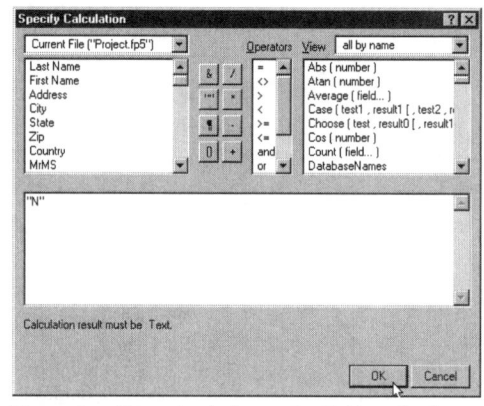

Figure 8.12 If there's a balance, Set Field marks the Paid field with an N for not paid.

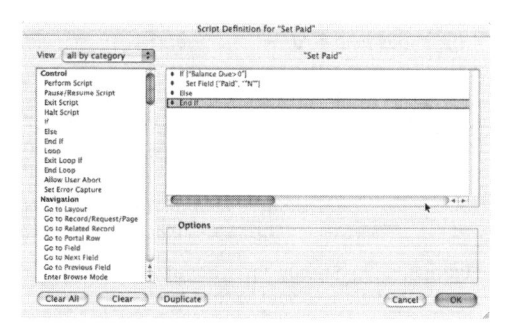

Figure 8.13 Else follows If in a script.

Figure 8.14 The finished If/Else script.

About Status Functions

Status functions are a special group of formulas that capture what's going on while you're working. They can peek at FileMaker's current settings and preferences, such as what mode it's in, what file is currently open, or what layout is active. Status functions can also check out information about your computer, like what version of the OS you're running, which user is currently logged in, or what the computer sees as the current date.

Being able to extract this type of data may initially seem pointless—or too advanced. Not so. For example, imagine that you wanted to write a script that would set different preferences or allow different levels of access to data depending on who is using the computer. Or you wanted to insert the current date into an invoice or statement layout. Only a status function can pry this information out of the computer and make it available to the script.

There's a generic status function in the Specify Calculation dialog box, but it's much more useful to use the specific function you need.

To see the available status functions:

1. Choose File > Define Fields.

2. When the Define Fields dialog box appears, input a field name and choose Calculation as the type. Click Create. Since this is just a test, you can use any field name.

3. When the Specify Calculation box dialog box appears, click the View drop-down menu, scroll down, and select "Status functions." The list of specific status functions will take the place of all the generic functions.

Applying Status Functions

If you're having problems visualizing how these status functions might be used, here are some practical suggestions to start your imagination working:

Date and Time
Use date and time functions in scripts to time-stamp changes and additions.

Current Message Choice
Make a user's choice the condition for an If/Else statement.

CurrentLayoutName
CurrentMode
CurrentUserName
Good for scripting custom navigation within a database. You can really fine-tune what each user sees and where they go in the database with these tools. CurrentUserName is also great for identifying which user is using which of your scripts.

CurrentFoundCount
Use this function to determine whether or not a scripted Find had the desired results. If you use it in combination with Set Error Capture [On] it will enable a script to return a custom result for a scripted Find.

CurrentSystemVersion
CurrentPlatform
These can be invaluable if you have to adjust your scripts for older operating systems, fine-tuning printing issues between Macs and Windows, or keeping specialized FileMaker plug-ins straight on the different platforms.

Commonly Used Status Functions

Although there are dozens of status functions in the function list, some of them are much more useful than others. These are some of our favorites, which we use frequently in scripts we create.

Date & Time

Status (CurrentDate)
The current date according to your computer.

Status (CurrentTime)
The current time according to your computer.

Script

Status (CurrentError)
The error code for the most recent error.

Status (CurrentMessageChoice)
A number that stands for one of three possible buttons a user can choose from an alert message. All three can be changed using the Show Message step in a script.
1 = first button (default)
2 = second button
3 = third button

Status (CurrentScriptName)
The name of the script that's currently running.

Field & Layout

Status (CurrentFieldName)
The name of the active field.

Status (CurrentLayoutName)
The name of the current layout.

Status (CurrentPortalRow)
The number of the current portal row. If no portal is selected, this number will be 0.

Status (CurrentRepetitionNumber)
The number of the current repetition in a repeating field.

Database

Status (CurrentFileName)
The name of the current file.

Status (CurrentFoundCount)
The number of records in the current found set.

Status (CurrentRecordCount)
The number of records in the database.

Status (CurrentMode)
0 = Browse mode
1 = Find mode
2 = Preview mode
3 = Printing in progress

Status (CurrentSortStatus)
0 = unsorted
1 = sorted
2 = partially sorted

Multi-User

Status (CurrentMultiUserStatus)
0 = single user
1 = multi-user
2 = multi-user from a guest computer or server

Status (CurrentGroups)
The group (or groups) that the current user is a member of, based on the current password.

Status (CurrentUserName)
The name of the current FileMaker Pro user.

System Settings

Status (CurrentSystemVersion)
The version of the current operating system.

Status (CurrentPlatform)
1 = Macintosh OS 9 or earlier
-1 = Macintosh OS X
2 = Windows 95 or 98
-2 = Windows NT or Windows 2000

Status (CurrentPrinterName)
The name of the current printer, printer type, and network zone (Mac) or Port Name (Windows).

Working with Conditional Script Steps

Using Status Functions with If Steps

Combining a status function with a conditional step, we can create a script that automatically adds the current date to an invoice, calculates the net 30 date when it will become overdue, then prints the invoice. Before you create the script, remember to set the Print/Page Setup options for the invoice.

To date and print an invoice using status functions:

1. Choose Scripts > ScriptMaker.

2. When the Define Scripts dialog box appears (**Figure 8.15**), type a name for the script (in this case Print Invoice) and click Create.

3. The Script Definition dialog box will appear. Under the Control category in the left window, double-click If.

4. In the Options section, click Specify to bring up the Specify Calculation dialog box. In the function list on the right, double-click the IsEmpty function (**Figure 8.16**).

   IsEmpty checks whatever field you put in the parentheses to see if there is data in it.

5. In the field list on the left, double-click Invoice Date. Click OK to close the Specify Calculation box.

   This section of the script checks the Invoice Data field to see if you've already entered anything in it (**Figure 8.17**).

6. Scroll down to the Field category in the left window and double-click Set Field.

7. In the Options section, click the Specify check box.

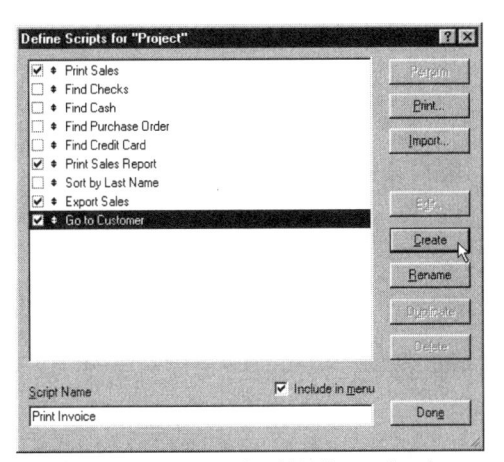

continues on next page

Figure 8.15 Script names should indicate what the script will do.

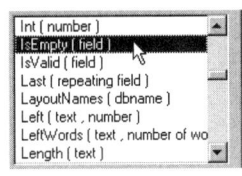

Figure 8.16 IsEmpty checks for data in a field.

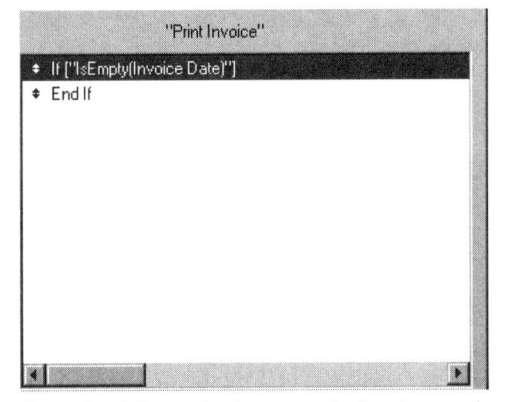

Figure 8.17 IsEmpty checks to see whether the record has an Invoice Date.

Chapter 8

8. When the Specify Field dialog box appears, choose the same field name you used in the If step. Click OK (**Figure 8.18**).

9. In the Options section, click the Field (Windows) or Specify Field (Mac) button.

10. When the Specify Calculation window appears, click the View drop-down menu, scroll down, and choose Status Functions (**Figure 8.19**).

11. In the list of status functions, double-click the Status(CurrentDate) function (**Figure 8.20**). Click OK.

    This portion of the script will check the computer's settings and enter the current date in the Invoice Date field.

12. The Set Field step in the script-assembly window should be highlighted. Click the Duplicate button. A copy of the step appears below the original (**Figure 8.21**).

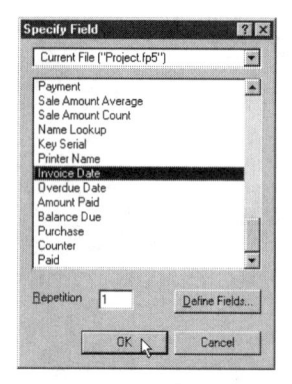

Figure 8.18 The fields in IsEmpty and the Set Field step must match.

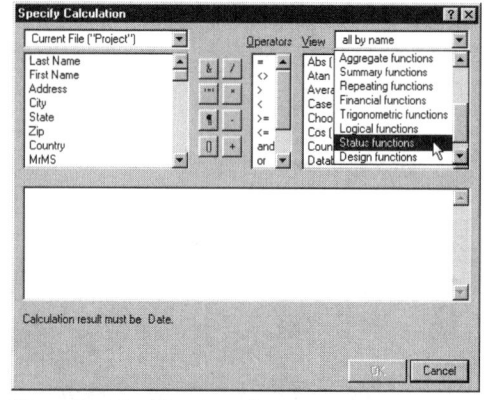

Figure 8.19 The View drop-down menu lets you choose functions by category.

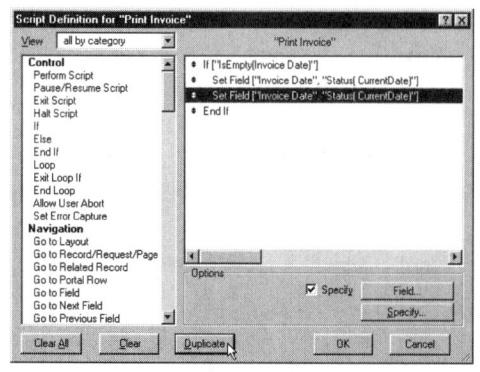

Figure 8.21 Since this step is almost the same as the previous, duplicating it is easier than creating it.

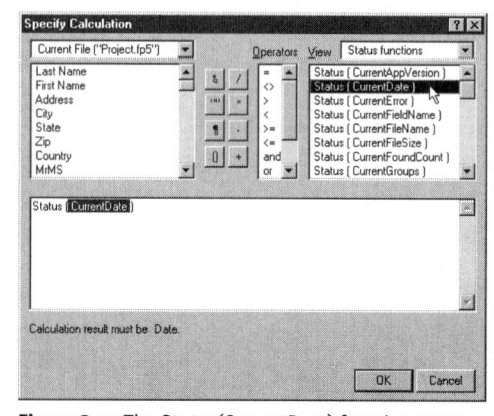

Figure 8.20 The Status(CurrentDate) function returns the computer's current date.

186

Working with Conditional Script Steps

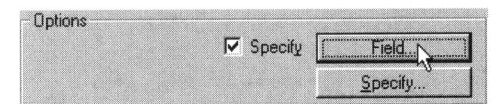

Figure 8.22 Click the Field button to edit a field you've previously specified.

Figure 8.23 The duplicated step needs to have a new field chosen.

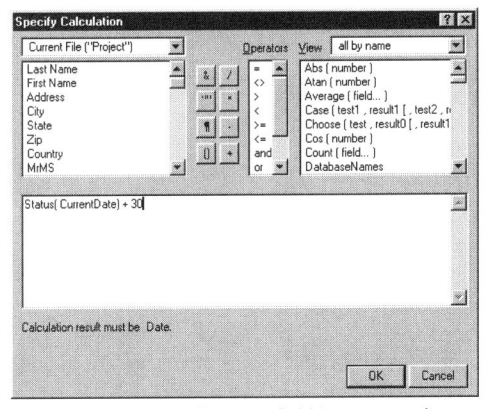

Figure 8.24 The Overdue Date field is set to 30 days after the current date.

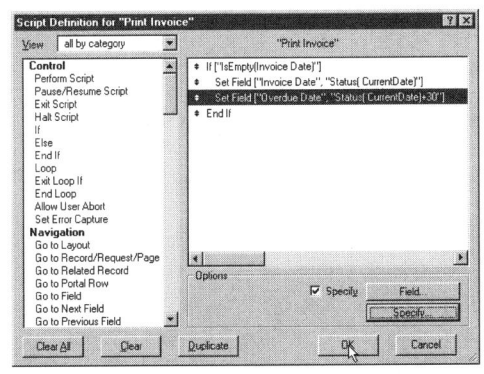

Figure 8.25 The duplicated and edited Set Field step.

13. We need to edit this step so that it will change the data of a different field. In the Options section, click the Field/Specify Field button (**Figure 8.22**).

14. When the Specify Field dialog box appears, choose the field (in our example, Overdue Date). Click OK (**Figure 8.23**).

The second Set Field step now looks at a different field.

15. In the Options section, click the Specify button.

16. When the Specify Calculation window appears, click inside the formula box just after Status(CurrentDate) and type +30 (**Figure 8.24**). Click OK.

This script line checks the status of the current date, adds 30 days to it, and inserts that date into the Overdue Date field (**Figure 8.25**).

continues on next page

USING STATUS FUNCTIONS WITH IF STEPS

187

Chapter 8

17. In the script-assembly window, click to select the End If step.

18. Scroll down to the Navigation category in the left window, and double-click Go to Layout (**Figure 8.26**).

19. In the Options section, choose Invoice from the Specify drop-down menu (**Figure 8.27**).

    This step switches the mode from its current status to Layout, and chooses the Invoice layout.

20. Scroll down to the Sort/Find/Print category in the left window, and double-click Print Setup (Windows) or Page Setup (Mac). Leave the options checked (**Figure 8.28**).

21. In the left step window, double-click Print.

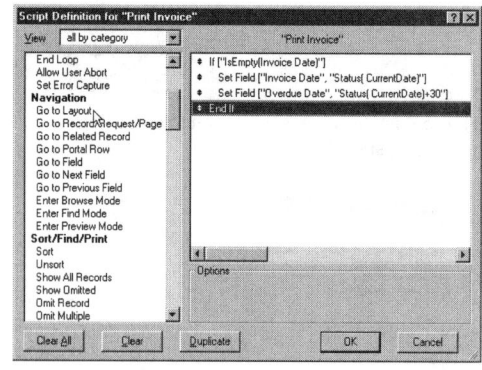

Figure 8.26 Select End If to add Go to Layout to the end of the script.

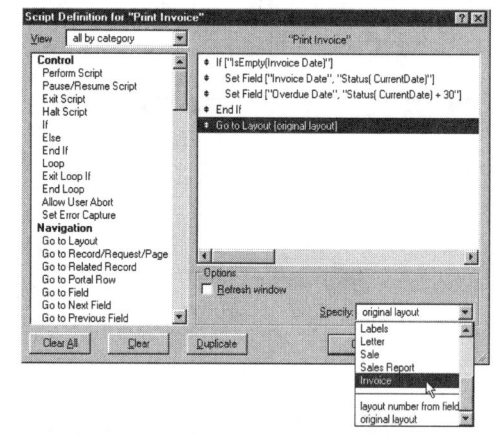

Figure 8.27 The script switches to the Invoice layout before printing.

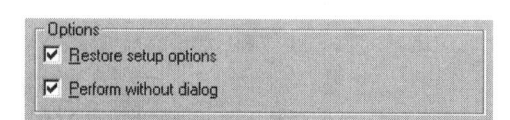

Figure 8.28 The Restore option will ensure that the invoice prints using the correct Page/Print Setup.

Working with Conditional Script Steps

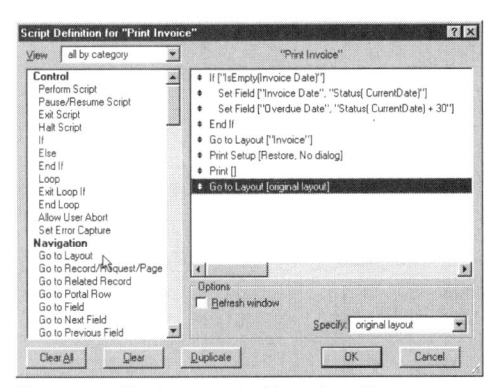

Figure 8.29 The last step in this script will return you to the layout where the script started.

Figure 8.30 Insert Current Date is an alternative to Set Field with a status function.

22. In the left step window under the Navigation category, double-click Go to Layout. Leave Specify set to "original layout" (**Figure 8.29**).

    This last part of the script returns you to the original layout.

23. Click OK, then Done.

✔ Tip

- There's a step called Insert Current Date that some people use instead of Set Field and the Status(CurrentDate) function (**Figure 8.30**). But Insert Current Date requires that the field where the date is entered be on the current layout. Set Field is a better choice because it works even if the field is not on the layout. Good script design makes the fewest assumptions about the database's current state.

189

Chapter 8

Using Loop in a Script

If the whole purpose of scripting is to automate repetitious actions, the Loop step is probably the ultimate scripting command. Any steps you nest (create inside) in a Loop will continue until the loop runs out of records or you tell it to stop.

The script in "To date and print an invoice using status functions" prints invoices one record at a time. That's nice, but you still have to sit at your computer and run each record individually. Place the Print Invoice script inside a loop that prints automatically whenever it finds a balance in an account, and you can completely automate your invoicing process.

Figure 8.31 When you choose the Loop step, End Loop will be added automatically.

To use Loop to print invoices:

1. Choose Scripts > ScriptMaker.

2. When the Define Scripts dialog box appears, type a name for the script (in this case, Print All Invoices) and click Create.

3. The Script Definition dialog box will appear. In the step window on the left, double-click Loop (**Figure 8.31**).

   As with If and End If, FileMaker automatically inserts both Loop and End Loop in the script-assembly window.

4. In the left window, double-click If (**Figure 8.32**).

   Notice that If and End If are indented under the Loop step to indicate that they're running inside the Loop step.

5. In the Options section, click Specify.

6. When the Specify Calculation window appears, choose Balance Due from the field list on the left.

7. Click the greater than (>) operator button and type a 0 (**Figure 8.33**). Click OK.

   So far, this script looks to see if the Balance Due field is greater than 0.

Figure 8.32 Since the If step is inside the loop, it will be executed for each loop.

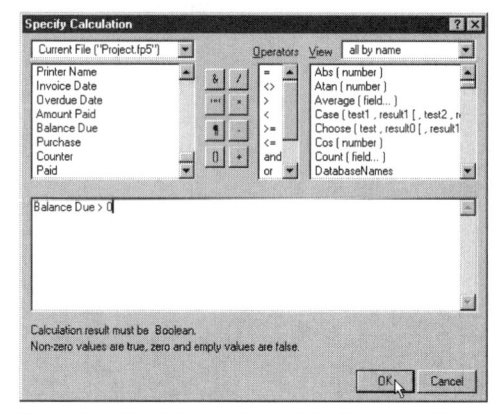

Figure 8.33 The Print Invoice script will only run if there is a balance greater than 0.

Working with Conditional Script Steps

8. In the left window, double-click Perform Script.

   Perform Script is indented one more level than the If statement, and two indents more than Loop (**Figure 8.34**). This structure is a visual clue to help you keep track of complicated nested scripts.

9. In the Options section, choose Print Invoice from the Specify drop-down menu (**Figure 8.35**).

   If there's a balance in the first record, FileMaker will follow the steps in the Print Invoice script.

10. To make sure that the next script steps are inserted after the If statement, click to select End If in the script-assembly window.

11. Scroll down to the Navigation category in the left window and double-click Go to Record/Request/Page.

12. In the Options section, click the "Exit after last" check box and choose Next from the Specify drop-down menu (**Figure 8.36**).

    These options tell the script to go to the next record in the database until it comes to the last one.

13. Click OK, then Done.

✔ **Tip**

- When creating a looping script with printing steps, remember to leave No Dialog chosen as the option in the Print command. Otherwise, the script will pause and ask you to click OK every time!

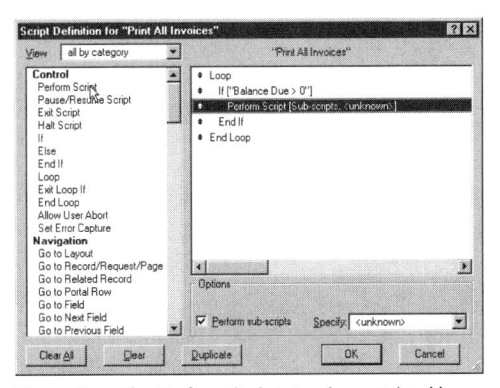

Figure 8.34 The Perform Script step is contained by both the Loop and the If steps.

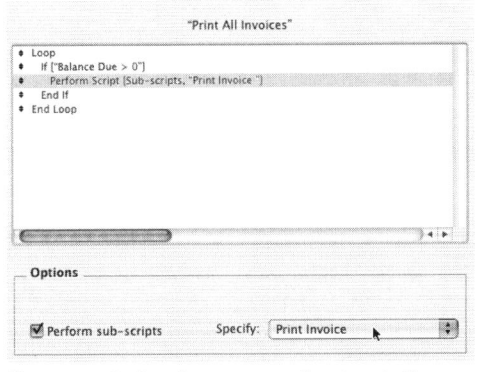

Figure 8.35 Rather than re-create the steps in the Print Invoice script, you can run it as a sub-script.

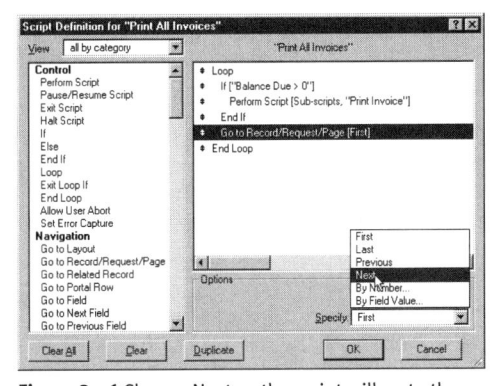

Figure 8.36 Choose Next so the script will go to the next record.

191

Using Counters to Control Loops

Just as the If step is made more flexible and dynamic by the addition of Else, so is looping improved by the Exit Loop If step. If you don't want a loop to continue through every record in your database (and lots of times you really don't!), Exit Loop If provides a way to target your loop to a specific number or group of records.

There are many ways to define your exit point, but one of the most elegant methods is with a counter. Counters do precisely that: You can set them to start at zero, or any other number you need. When it comes to loops, counters are particularly useful in keeping track of how many times a loop has run, allowing you to stop it after as few or as many iterations as you need. For example, in this script we use a counter with the Exit Loop If to print only 10 invoices at a time.

Figure 8.37 You can define new fields when creating scripts.

To use a loop to print multiple invoices:

1. Choose Scripts > ScriptMaker.

2. When the Define Scripts dialog box appears, type a name for the script (in this case, `Print Ten Invoices`) and click Create.

3. When the Script Definition dialog box appears, scroll down to the Fields category in the left window and double-click Set Field.

4. In the Options section, click the Field (Windows) or Specify Field (Mac) button.

5. When the Specify Field dialog box appears, click Define Fields (**Figure 8.37**).

192

Working with Conditional Script Steps

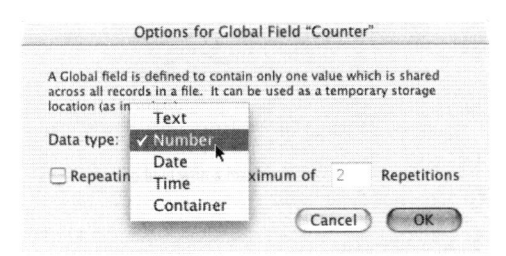

Figure 8.38 Counter is a global field with a Number data type.

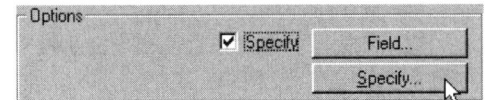

Figure 8.39 Choose Specify to access the Specify Calculation dialog box.

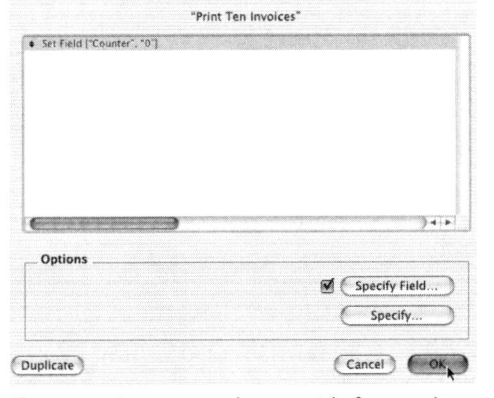

Figure 8.40 Counter must be set to 0 before running the script.

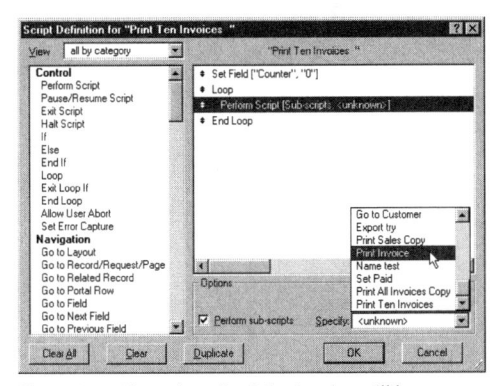

Figure 8.41 The sub-script Print Invoice will be executed in each loop.

6. When the Define Fields dialog box appears, type Counter for the field name and choose Global as the Type. Click Create.

7. In the Options dialog box, choose Number from the "Data type" pop-up menu (**Figure 8.38**).

8. Click OK and then Done.

9. Choose Counter from the list of fields in the Specify Fields dialog box, then click OK.

10. In the Options section, click the Specify button (**Figure 8.39**).

11. When the Specify Calculation window appears, type a 0 and click OK.

    You now have a global counter field that will start counting from 0 in each record it finds (**Figure 8.40**).

12. In the left window, double-click Loop and then double-click Perform Script.

13. In the Options section, choose Print Invoice from the Specify pop-up menu (**Figure 8.41**).

14. Scroll down to the Fields category in the left window and double-click Set Field.

15. In the Options section, click the Field/Specify Field button. When the Specify Field dialog box appears, choose Counter, and click OK.

16. In the Options section, click the Specify button.

continues on next page

Chapter 8

17. When the Specify Calculation window appears, scroll to Counter in the field list on the left and double-click to select it. Type +1 to the right of the field name. Click OK (**Figure 8.42**).

   The script will go to the Counter field and add one to whatever number is in the field.

18. In the left window, double-click Exit Loop If (**Figure 8.43**).

19. In the Options section, click Specify.

20. In the Specify Calculation dialog box, scroll to Counter in the field list on the left and double-click to select it. Click greater than (>) in the Operators list and type 10 (**Figure 8.44**). Click OK.

21. Click OK, then Done. The script will start by setting Counter to 0, then it will print an invoice, add 1 to Counter, and exit the loop (and script) after the 10th invoice.

✔ **Tip**

- When a user (or a script the user is running) makes an entry in a global field in a multi-user database, that value only appears in that user's database. Other users do not see the value and can use other values in the same field.

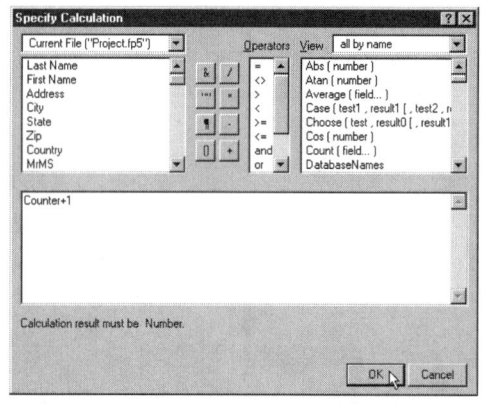

Figure 8.42 Counter is increased by 1 after each invoice is printed.

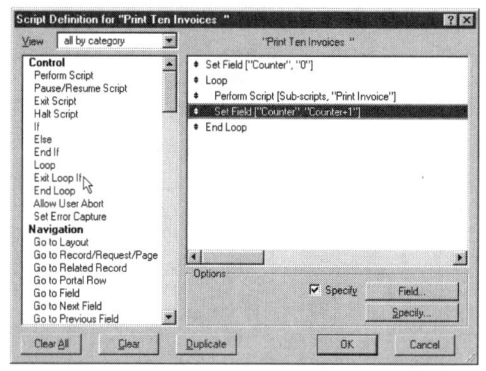

Figure 8.43 Choose Exit Loop If while the Set Field step is selected.

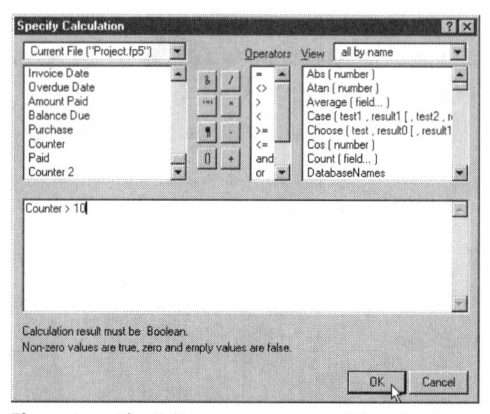

Figure 8.44 The Exit Loop tests to see if Counter has reached 10. If it has, the loop is exited.

Working with Conditional Script Steps

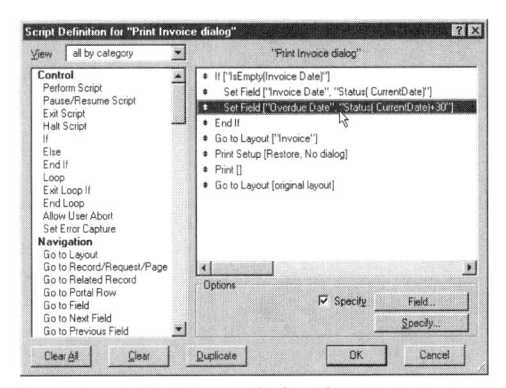

Figure 8.45 Select the step before the one you want to insert.

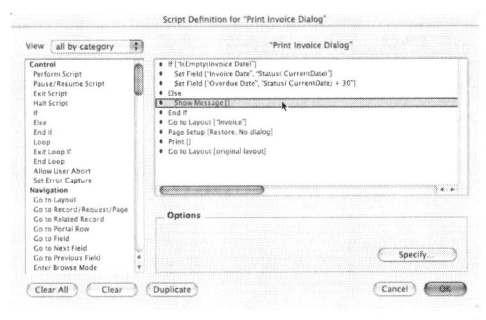

Figure 8.46 Show Message is used to display text and get input from the user.

Controlling Scripts with User Input

You can use the Show Message script step to prompt a user entry to control a script. The message text you enter will be displayed in a dialog box.

Using the Print Invoice script, we can add a step that checks whether there is an Invoice Date and, if there is, asks you if you want to print the invoice anyway. This will prevent unintentional duplicate invoices. You can include If steps within other If steps (nested Ifs). Just as steps in an If are run only when the preceding If is true, a nested If is evaluated only when the first If is true.

If the user chooses the Print button, the script will execute the rest of the steps. If the user chooses Don't Print, the script will stop.

To control scripts with user input:

1. Choose Scripts > ScriptMaker.

2. In the Define Scripts dialog box, click the script to which you want to add user controls. In our case, it's the Print Invoice script. Give it a slightly different name and click Create (which makes a new script), then click Edit. This keeps your original script intact, which can be very useful if you make a mistake as you edit.

3. When the Script Definition dialog box appears, click the second Set Field step in the assembly window (**Figure 8.45**).

4. In the step window on the left, double-click Else.

5. Scroll down to the Miscellaneous category in the left window and double-click Show Message (**Figure 8.46**).

continues on next page

195

Chapter 8

6. In the Options section, click Specify. The Specify Message dialog box opens (**Figure 8.47**).

   This dialog box will generate a customized message and buttons in your operating system's standard format. The dialog box can have up to three labeled buttons.

7. In Message Text, type:

   This record looks like it's already been invoiced. Do you want to print another copy?

8. Under Button Captions, type Print in the First (default) box and type Don't Print in the Second box (**Figure 8.48**). Click OK.

   When you run the script, these choices will generate your custom message (**Figure 8.49**).

9. In the step list on the left, double-click If.

10. In the Options section, click Specify.

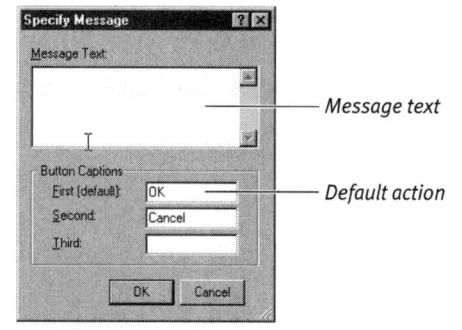

Figure 8.47 You can enter text to create a customized message and set of buttons. OK and Cancel are the default choices, but you can replace them with custom text.

Figure 8.48 Designate your message choices in the Specify Message dialog box.

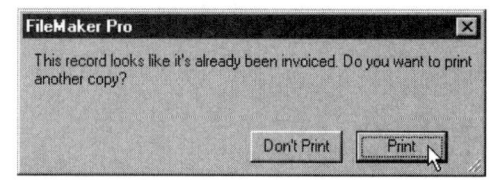

Figure 8.49 This custom dialog box will display when you run the script.

196

Working with Conditional Script Steps

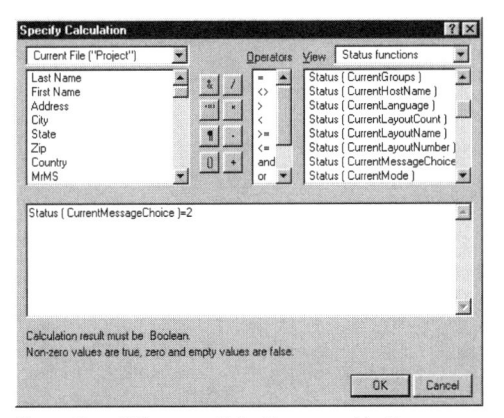

Figure 8.50 If the user clicks the second button, Status(CurrentMessageChoice) will equal 2.

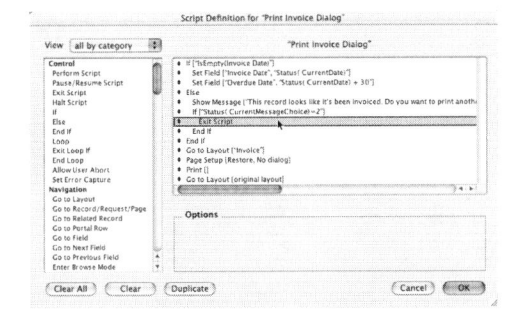

Figure 8.51 The "2" in this step refers to the second button choice in the dialog box.

11. When the Specify Calculation box dialog box appears, click the View drop-down menu and scroll down to "Status functions." Click to select it and display the detailed status functions list. Double-click Status (CurrentMessageChoice). Click to the right of it in the formula box and type =2 (**Figure 8.50**). Click OK.

12. In the step list on the left, double-click Exit Script.

    This If step looks at which button was clicked. If the second (Don't Print) button was clicked, the script ends without printing anything (**Figure 8.51**).

13. Click OK, then OK again to keep your print settings. Click Done to finish.

    When you run this script, FileMaker will look for an Invoice Date and print an invoice if it doesn't find one. If there is an Invoice Date, the alert message will ask if you want to print a second one.

Creating Custom Dialog Boxes

In "To control scripts with user input" in the previous section, we use the Show Message step to give the user information and provide a simple choice between going forward or canceling. Show Message is a clean and simple way to communicate simple information or prompt the user to choose between two opposite actions, but it's otherwise severely limited. If you need more complex user interaction, you should use the Show Custom Dialog script step instead. It allows you to create a dialog box that can gather text input from the user into fields. A dialog box created using the Show Custom Dialog step can display up to three fields into which the user can enter values.

To illustrate how useful Show Custom Dialog can be, we'll create a script that displays a dialog box prompting the user to enter any combination of the contents of the Last Name, City, and State fields to perform a find. The script will use global fields to capture the user input and set the find criteria from the contents of these global fields.

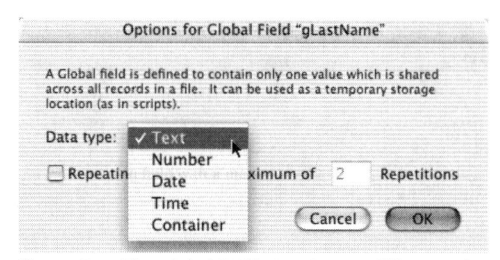

Figure 8.52 The global field gLastName will be used to get the user's input for the Find step.

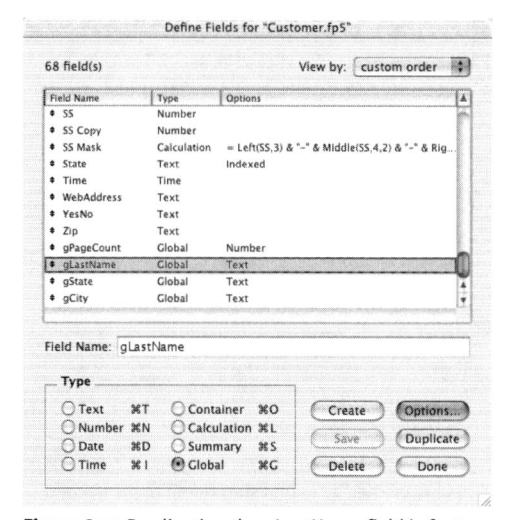

Figure 8.53 Duplicating the gLastName field is faster than creating the new field from scratch.

To customize a dialog box for user input:

1. Choose File > Define Fields.

2. When the Define Fields dialog box appears, type `gLastName` in the Field Name box, choose Global as the field type, and click Create.

3. When the Options dialog box appears, specify Text as the data type (**Figure 8.52**). Click OK.

4. Repeat steps 2 and 3 to create gCity and gState global fields (**Figure 8.53**). Click Done.

5. Choose Scripts > ScriptMaker.

Working with Conditional Script Steps

6. In the Define Scripts dialog box, type a name for the script (we use Dialog Find) and click Create.

7. When the Script Definition dialog box appears, scroll down to the Miscellaneous section in the step list on the left and double-click Show Custom Dialog (**Figure 8.54**).

8. In the Options section, click Specify.

9. The Specify Custom Dialog dialog box opens. Under Dialog Title, enter the text for the title of the dialog box (**Figure 8.55**).

10. Under Dialog Message, enter the text of the dialog box message. In our example, we give the user explicit instructions on how to use the dialog box (**Figure 8.56**).

11. The Button Captions section has default button names already inserted. If you want to rename any of the buttons, highlight the text and type the new caption (**Figure 8.57**).

continues on next page

Figure 8.54 The Show Custom Dialog step is an enhanced version of Show Message.

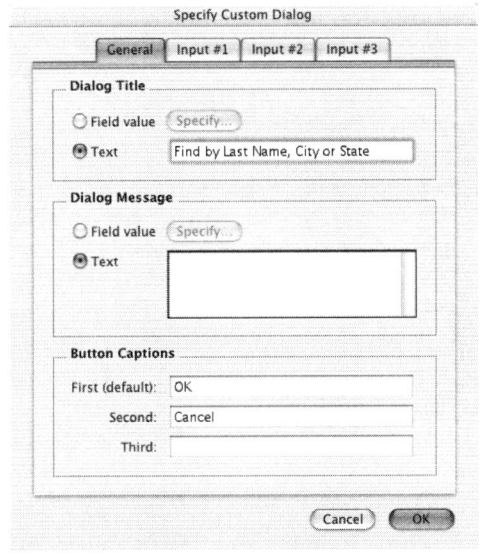

Figure 8.55 Keep the dialog box title short and to the point.

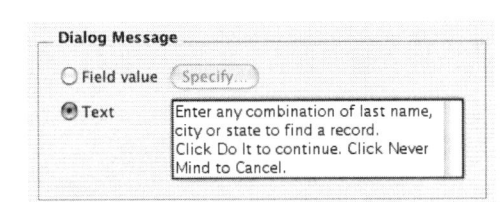

Figure 8.56 The dialog message should contain a brief, clear explanation of the dialog box function.

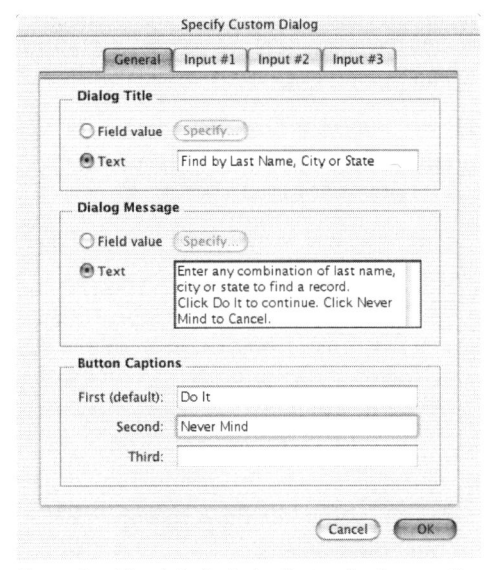

Figure 8.57 The defaults in the Button Captions section can be customized to fit your needs.

Chapter 8

12. Click the Input #1 tab. Check "Enable field input."

13. When the Specify Field dialog box appears, double-click the gLastName field.

14. In the Label Name input box, enter Last Name for the field label (**Figure 8.58**).

15. Click the Input #2 tab. Repeat steps 12–14 for the gCity field.

16. Click the Input #3 tab. Repeat steps 12–14 again, this time for the gState field. Click OK to return to the Script Definition dialog box.

17. In the step window on the left scroll up to the Control section. Double-click If.

18. In the Options section, click Specify.

19. When the Specify Calculation dialog box appears, click the View drop-down menu and scroll down to "Status functions." Click to select it and display the detailed status functions list.

20. In the list of status functions, double-click the Status(CurrentMessageChoice) function (**Figure 8.59**).

21. In the formula box, click to the right of the status function and type =2 (**Figure 8.60**). Click OK.

22. In the step window on the left, double-click Exit Script.

    This If step looks at which button you clicked. If you chose the second button (Never Mind), it cancels the script without any action.

23. To make sure that the next script steps are inserted after the If statement, click to select End If in the script-assembly window.

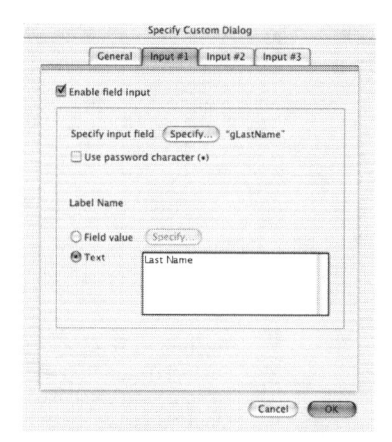

Figure 8.58 The label for an input field should match the standard field name, not the global field name, to avoid user confusion.

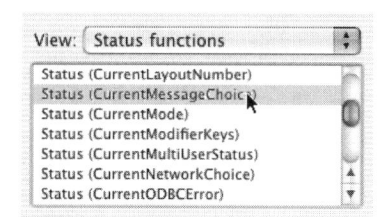

Figure 8.59 This status function returns 1 for the first button, 2 for the second button, and 3 for the third button in a custom dialog box.

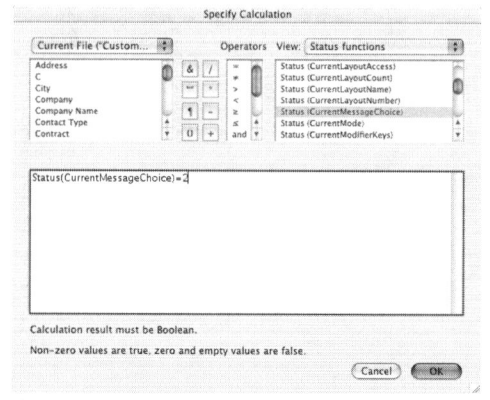

Figure 8.60 If the user clicks the second button to cancel, Status(CurrentMessageChoice) will return the number 2, telling the script to Cancel.

Working with Conditional Script Steps

Figure 8.61 Since this script will perform a new find, the Pause and Restore options are not needed.

Figure 8.62 Less frequently used operators are listed in a scrolling list, rather than as buttons.

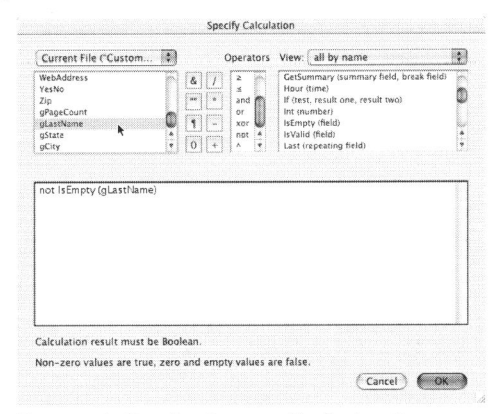

Figure 8.63 If no data is entered in the Last Name field, it will not be used in the find.

24. Under the Navigation category of the left window, double-click Enter Find Mode. Uncheck the Pause and "Restore find requests" boxes (**Figure 8.61**).

25. We need to set the find criteria to use values only for the fields the user selects. In the step window on the left, double-click If.

26. In the Options section, click Specify.

27. When the Specify Calculation dialog box appears, double-click not in the Operators list (**Figure 8.62**).

28. In the function list, double-click IsEmpty.

29. Replace the text parameter by double-clicking gLastName in the field list (**Figure 8.63**). Click OK.

30. In the step window on the left, scroll down to the Fields category and double-click Set Field. In the Options section, click the Field (Windows) or Specify Field (Mac) button.

31. When the Specify Field dialog box appears, double-click to choose Last Name.

32. In the Options section, click the Specify button.

continues on next page

CREATING CUSTOM DIALOG BOXES

201

33. When the Specify Calculation dialog box appears, double-click gLastName in the field list. Click OK (**Figure 8.64**).

    If the user has typed anything into the Last Name section of the custom dialog box, this portion of the If step transfers it to the LastName field.

34. Click the If step you created in step 25. Hold down the Shift key and the select the Set Field and End If steps. Click the Duplicate button twice (**Figure 8.65**).

35. Double-click the second of the three identical If steps. When the Specify Calculation dialog box appears, highlight "gLastName" after IsEmpty and double-click to replace it with gCity. Click OK.

36. In the script-assembly window, double-click the second of the three Set Field steps. When the Specify Field dialog box appears, double-click the field City.

37. In the Options section, click the Specify button. When the Specify Calculation dialog box appears, change the field from gLastName to gCity. Click OK.

38. Repeat steps 35–37, changing the fields in the last If and Set Field steps to gState and State (**Figure 8.66**).

39. To make sure that the next script steps are inserted after the If statement, click to select End If in the script-assembly window.

Figure 8.64 The script enters the contents of the gLastName field in the Last Name field in Find mode.

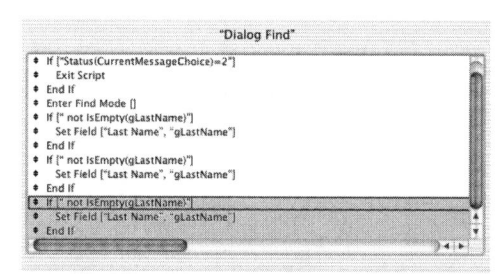

Figure 8.65 Since the steps are just about the same for all three sections, the Duplicate button is easier than creating the individual steps.

Figure 8.66 After you duplicate the steps, only the field specifications have to be changed.

Working with Conditional Script Steps

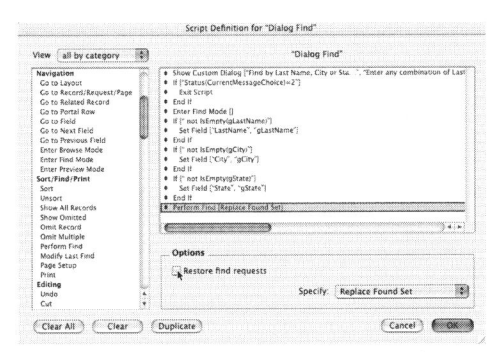

Figure 8.67 The Restore option is not used in this script.

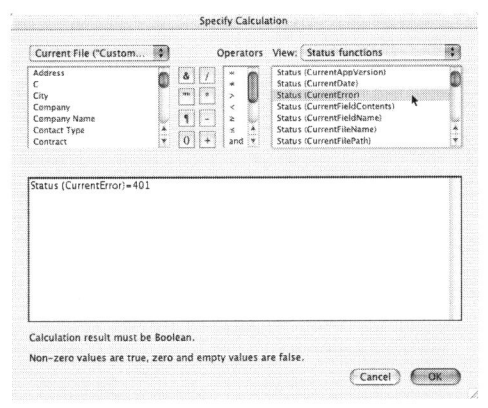

Figure 8.68 Error 401 is returned when no records match the find criteria.

Figure 8.69 Since the user has only one option, only one button caption is required.

40. In the step window on the left, scroll to the Sort/Find/Print category and double-click Perform Find. Uncheck the "Restore find requests" box (**Figure 8.67**).

    Now we'll add another If section to alert the user if there are no records found. Otherwise, if no records are found, the user gets dumped into the generic No Records Found dialog box, which would be confusing.

41. In the step window on the left, scroll up to the Control category and double-click If. In the Options section, click the Specify button.

42. When the Specify Calculation dialog box appears, click the View drop-down menu and scroll down to choose "Status functions."

43. In the list of status functions, double-click Status(CurrentError).

44. Click after the close parentheses and type =401 (**Figure 8.68**). Click OK.

    Error 401 is returned when no records match the find criteria.

45. In the step window on the left, scroll down to the Miscellaneous category. Double-click Show Message. In the Options section, click Specify.

46. When the Specify Message dialog box appears, type a message to be displayed when no records are found. In the Button Captions section, delete "Cancel" from the Second box (**Figure 8.69**). Click OK to close the Specify Message dialog box.

    continues on next page

CREATING CUSTOM DIALOG BOXES

203

Chapter 8

47. In the step window on the left, scroll up to the Sort/Find/Print category and double-click Show All Records.

    If no records are found, this step will reset the database to display all records.

48. After the find is performed, we need to clear all three global fields. In the step window on the left, scroll down to the Fields category and double-click Set Field.

49. In the Options section, click Field/Specify Field.

50. When the Specify Field dialog box appears, double-click to choose gLastName.

51. In the Options section, click Specify. When the Specify Calculation dialog box appears, click the quotes button in the Operators keypad (**Figure 8.70**). Click OK.

52. Click the Set Field step you just created. Click Duplicate twice.

53. Double-click the first of the new Set Field steps. When the Specify Field dialog box appears, change the field to gCity.

54. Repeat step 53 to replace the last global field with gState (**Figure 8.71**). Click OK and then Done to finish.

    When the script is run, the user will see a dialog box in which to enter the find requests (**Figure 8.72**). If they click Do It, the script will perform the find. If no records are found, the Show Message step will tell them so. Either way, at the end the script will clear the global fields so the data entered won't appear the next time the script is run.

Figure 8.70 The empty quotes clear the contents of the field.

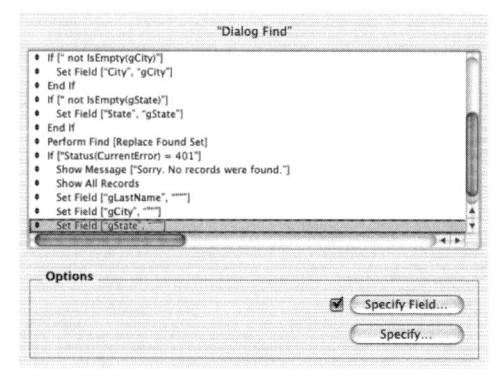

Figure 8.71 All three global fields should be cleared before the script is done.

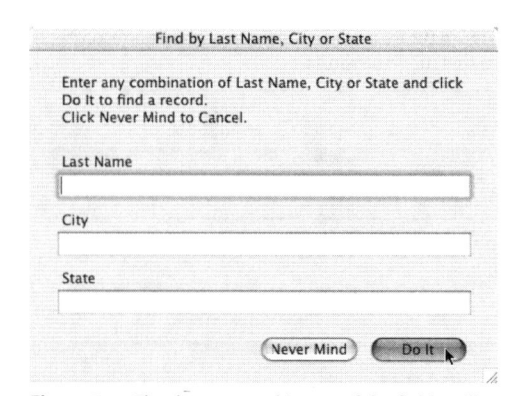

Figure 8.72 The data entered in any of the fields will be used to create the find request.

204

Working with Conditional Script Steps

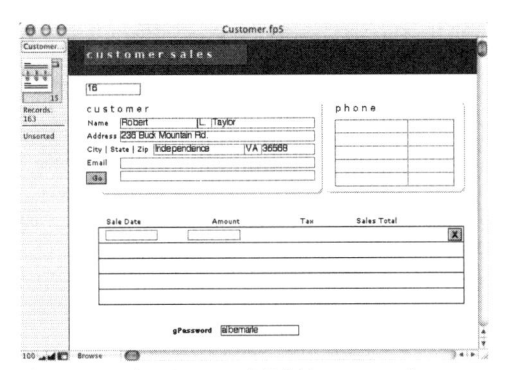

Figure 8.73 The gPassword field is temporarily placed in a layout to set a password.

Password Protecting a Script

Show Custom Dialog is a tremendously useful script step, because you can adapt its options to a wide variety of needs. For example, there are many scripts that, if run by inexperienced people or run in error, can permanently harm your database. A custom dialog box that requires the user to enter a password to run a script lets you add an extra level of security to powerful scripts.

In this example, we create a script that can be called from other scripts to determine whether the user should be allowed to run them.

To set up password protection for a script:

1. Choose File > Define Fields.

2. When the Define Fields dialog box appears, enter *gPassword* for the field name, make it a Global type, and click Create.

3. When the Options dialog box appears, set the data type in the drop-down menu to Text. Click OK.

4. With the gPassword field selected, press Duplicate. Change the name to gGetPassword and click Save. Click Done to close the Define Fields box.

5. Choose View > Layout Mode. Drag the Field tool onto any layout. In the Specify Field dialog box, choose gPassword.

6. Choose View > Browse Mode. Click in the gPassword field and enter the password for authorized users (**Figure 8.73**).

continues on next page

205

Chapter 8

7. Choose View > Layout Mode. Select the gPassword field and its label and press the Delete key.

   We added the gPassword field to the layout just to enter the password data. We removed it to hide the password we entered.

8. Choose Scripts > ScriptMaker.

9. In the Define Scripts dialog box, type **Admin Password** for the Script Name and click Create.

10. When the Script Definition window appears, scroll down to the Miscellaneous category and double-click Show Custom Dialog.

11. In the Options section, click the Specify button.

12. In the Specify Custom Dialog dialog box, enter a title in the Dialog Title text input box. In our example we use Enter Password.

13. In the Dialog Message text input box, enter instructions for the user.

14. Under Button Captions, delete "Cancel" from the Second text input box (**Figure 8.74**).

15. Click the Input #1 tab. Click the "Enable field input" check box.

16. When the Specify Field dialog box appears, double-click the gGetPassword field.

17. Click the "Use password character" check box. Enter **Password:** in the Label Name box (**Figure 8.75**). Click OK to return to the Script Definition dialog box.

18. In the step window on the left, scroll up to the Control category and double-click If.

19. In the Options section, click the Specify button.

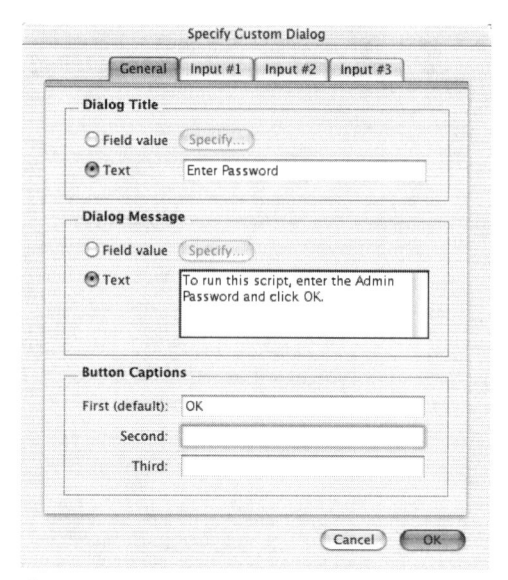

Figure 8.74 Since the user has no alternative actions in this dialog box, delete the second button caption.

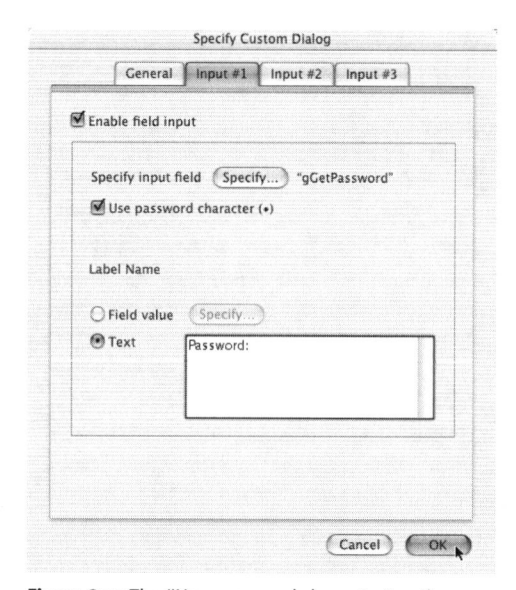

Figure 8.75 The "Use password character" option substitutes bullets for the password the user enters.

Working with Conditional Script Steps

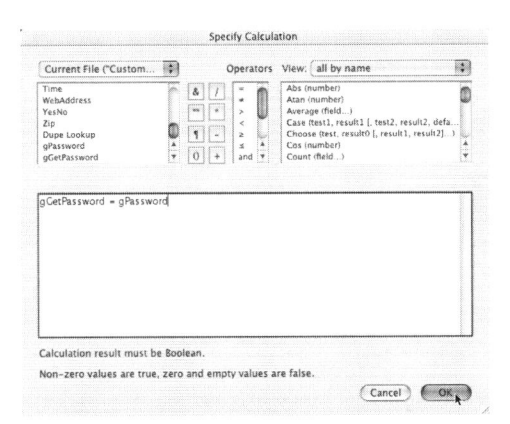

Figure 8.76 The script checks to see if the password the user entered matches the contents of the gPassword field.

Figure 8.77 Set Field allows you to erase the typed password to maintain security.

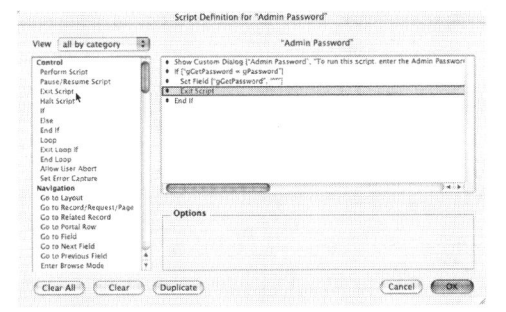

Figure 8.78 If the password is correct, the Exit Script step returns control to the script the user originally tried to run.

20. When the Specify Calculation dialog box appears, double-click the gGetPassword field in the field list on the left.

21. In the Operators list, double-click the = operator. In the field list on the left, double-click gPassword. Click OK to return to the Script Definition dialog box (**Figure 8.76**).

22. In the step window on the left, scroll down to the Fields category and double-click Set Field.

23. In the Options section, click the Field (Windows) or Specify Field (Mac) button. When the Specify Field dialog box appears, double-click gGetPassword.

24. In the Options section, click the Specify button. When the Specify Calculation dialog box appears, click the quotes button in the Operators section. Click OK.

    By selecting the quotes but not typing anything within them, you reset the gGetPassword field to erase the password from it (**Figure 8.77**).

25. In the step window on the left, scroll up to the Control category and double-click Exit Script (**Figure 8.78**).

26. In the step window on the left, double-click Else.

27. In the step window on the left, scroll down to the Miscellaneous category and double-click Show Message.

28. In the Options section, click the Specify button. Enter the message the user will see if the password they enter is incorrect.

continues on next page

207

Chapter 8

29. In the Button Captions section, delete "Cancel" from the Second text box. Click OK to return to the Script Definition dialog box (**Figure 8.79**).

30. Click the Set Field step you created in step 22. Click Duplicate. Drag the new step below the Show Message step (**Figure 8.80**).

31. In the step window on the left, scroll up to the Navigation category and double-click Go to Layout. Leave the option set to "original layout."

32. In the step window on the left, scroll up to the Control category and double-click Halt Script (**Figure 8.81**).

    If the user didn't enter the correct password, they will see the dialog box telling them that they can't run the script. The Halt Script step will exit both this script and the one that called it.

33. Click OK and then Done to finish.

Figure 8.79 If the password is not correct, the Show Message step will inform the user.

Figure 8.80 If the password is incorrect, you still need to clear the field so the user can try again.

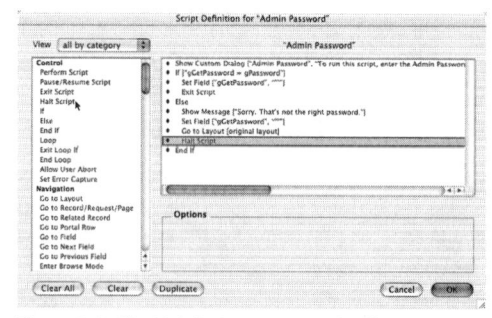

Figure 8.81 The Halt Script step cancels all running scripts, so control does not return to the original script.

Working with Conditional Script Steps

Figure 8.82 Putting the Admin Password script at the beginning of another script prevents that script from running without the proper password.

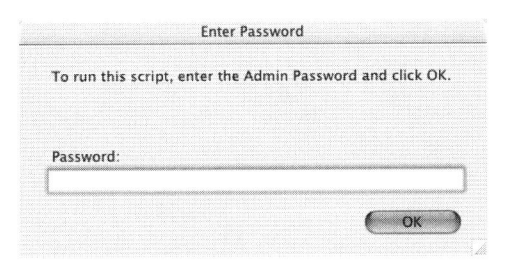

Figure 8.83 The user must enter the proper password or they can't run the script.

To password-protect a script:

1. Choose Scripts > ScriptMaker. In the Define Scripts dialog box, double-click the script you want to protect.

2. The Script Definition dialog box appears. In the script-assembly window, select the first step in the script.

3. In the step window on the left, double-click Perform Script.

4. Drag the Perform Script step up so it becomes the first step in the script.

5. In the Options section, from the Specify drop-down menu, choose the Admin Password script you just created in "To set up password protection for a script" (**Figure 8.82**). Click OK and then Done to finish.

When the user selects the protected script, the Admin Password script runs first (**Figure 8.83**). If the user doesn't enter the correct password, the protected script won't run.

continues on next page

PASSWORD PROTECTING A SCRIPT

209

Chapter 8

✔ Tips

- Although they're terribly addictive, try to avoid the temptation of too many nested If statements. They become next to impossible to follow in the script editor, guaranteeing lots of wasted time if you have to troubleshoot them.

- The first button in a Show Message or Show Custom Dialog dialog box is always the default choice. If you press Enter instead of clicking a button when the message box is displayed, the Status(CurrentMessageChoice) function will react as if you chose the default button. Protect your users from unpleasant accidents by choosing the least destructive option as the default choice.

Custom Dialog Limitations

The Show Custom Dialog dialog box has a nifty feature. Any of the text titles (Dialog Title, Dialog Message, and Label Names) can be set to the contents of a global field rather than using fixed text entered by you in ScriptMaker. So you can store captions in global fields and change them without editing the script.

However, there are some text-length limits, which vary by OS. To ensure the best cross-platform compatibility, here are some good rules for maximum lengths:

- Dialog Title: 55 characters

- Dialog Message: 181 characters

- Field Labels: 60 characters

- Button Captions: 9 characters

- The maximum number of characters that can displayed in any input field is 31.

Working with Conditional Script Steps

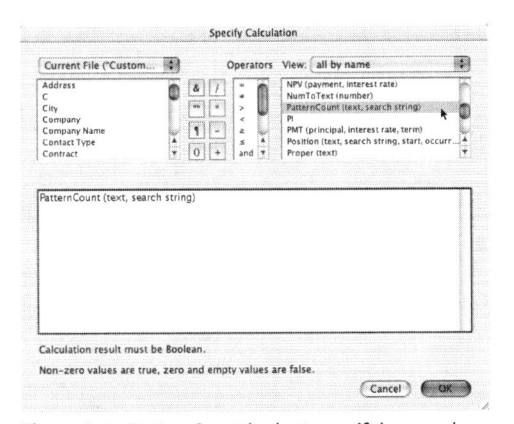

Figure 8.84 PatternCount looks to see if the search string exists in the text.

Selecting for FileMaker Versions

If you use features like Show Custom Dialog that are only available in FileMaker 6, a user who opens the file in version 5 or 5.5 won't be able to use them. Worse, a script may launch and then fail when it reaches an unsupported step. When you can't be sure that all users are running the same version, create a script that identifies the version in use and takes appropriate action before a script using new features can run.

You can determine which version the current user is running with the Status(CurrentVersion) function. This function returns text indicating the running FileMaker version. You can make this script the first step of any script that uses a version 6–only function to protect users from getting lost in a script that won't run.

Sometimes you can get the same result with a script that uses version 5 or 5.5 functions instead of version 6 ones. Combine the Check Version script with an If step, and you can seamlessly launch an alternate script when the Check Version script discovers an older version.

To determine the user's version before a script runs:

1. Choose Scripts > ScriptMaker.

2. In the Define Scripts dialog box, type Check Version for the script name and click Create.

3. The Script Definition dialog box appears. In the step list on the left, double-click If.

4. In the Options section, click Specify.

5. The Specify Calculation dialog box appears. In the functions list on the right, scroll down to PatternCount and double-click it (**Figure 8.84**).

continues on next page

211

Chapter 8

6. In the script-assembly box, double-click the field parameter "text" after PatternCount.

7. In the View drop-down menu, choose Status functions. Double-click the Status(CurrentAppVersion) function (**Figure 8.85**).

8. In the script-assembly box, select the words "search string." Click the quotes operator button. Type Pro 6 between the quotes (**Figure 8.86**).

9. Click to the right of the parentheses. Double-click the less than (<) operator. Type 1, then click OK (**Figure 8.87**).

10. In the step list on the left, scroll down to the Miscellaneous category and double-click Show Message.

11. In the Options section, click the Specify button.

12. When the Specify Message dialog box appears, type the message that the user will see if they aren't running FileMaker Pro version 6.

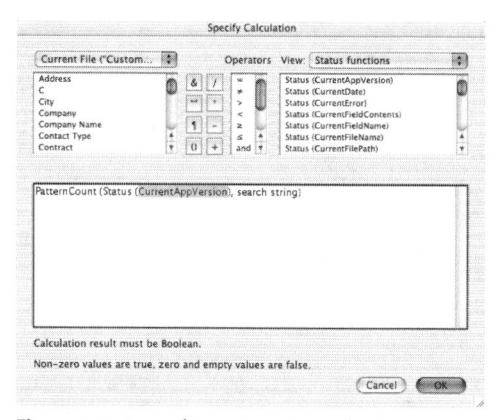

Figure 8.85 Status(CurrentAppVersion) returns text indicating the version of FileMaker being run by each user.

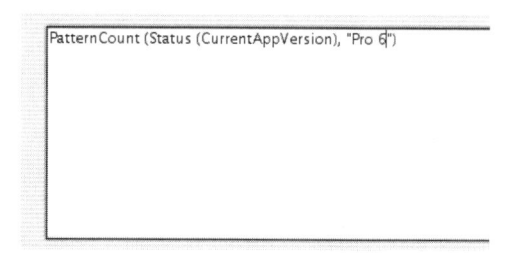

Figure 8.86 If the user is running FileMaker 6, the function will return "Pro 6."

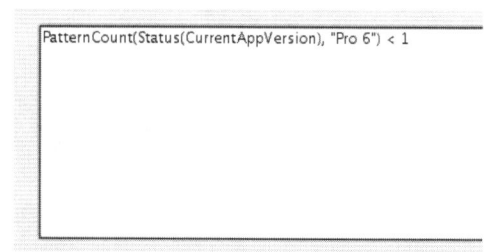

Figure 8.87 If the user is running an earlier version of FileMaker, "Pro 6" will not be in the text returned by Status(CurrentAppVersion).

Working with Conditional Script Steps

Figure 8.88 Only the first button will be used in this Show Message step, so the second caption is deleted.

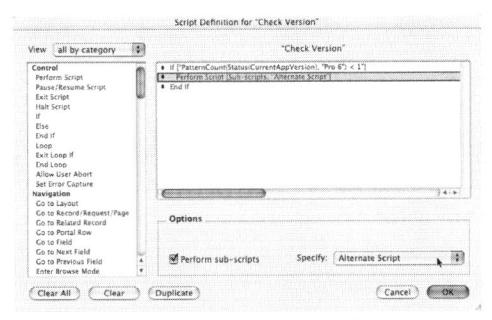

Figure 8.89 The Perform Script step will run an alternate script if the version is not 6.

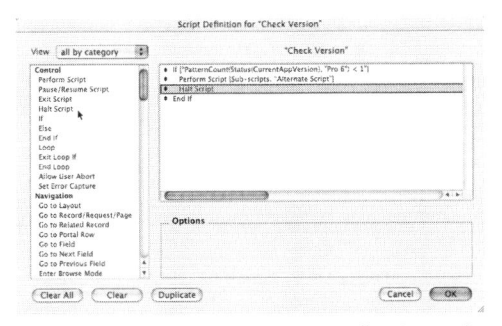

Figure 8.90 The Halt Script step stops all scripts and sub-scripts.

13. In the Button Captions section, delete "Cancel" from the Second text input box (**Figure 8.88**). Click OK.

14. In the step list on the left, double-click Halt Script. Click OK and then Done to finish.

This script checks for the FileMaker version. If it isn't version 6, it warns the user and stops the script from running.

To specify an alternate script for a different version:

1. Follow steps 1–9 in the previous task, "To determine the user's version before a script runs."

2. In the step list on the left, double-click the Perform Script step.

3. In the Options section, choose the script you want to substitute for the one with version 6 features from the Specify pop-up menu (**Figure 8.89**).

4. In the step list on the left, double-click Halt Script (**Figure 8.90**). Click OK and then Done to finish.

    You need the Halt Script step even if you run an alternate script. Without it, the alternate script would run, then return to the Check Version script, which would then go back to the original script.

213

Chapter 8

To check version for a specific script:

1. Choose Scripts > ScriptMaker. In the Define Scripts dialog box, double-click a script that uses a feature specific to FileMaker Pro 6.

2. The Script Definition dialog box appears. In the script assembly window, select the first step in the script.

3. In the step list on the left, double-click Perform Script.

4. Drag the Perform Script step up so it becomes the first step in the script.

5. In the Options section, choose the Check Version script (with or without an alternative script) you created above from the Specify drop-down menu (**Figure 8.91**). Click OK and then Done to finish.

   When the script is run, the Check Version script will run first. If the FileMaker running is not version 6, the user will either see the message or the alternate script will run instead.

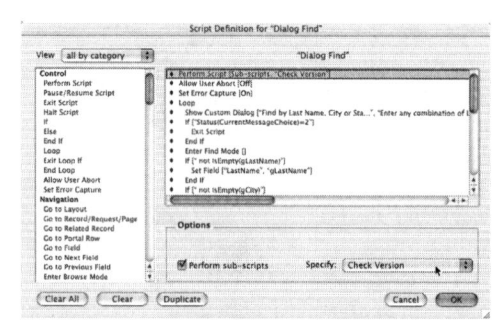

Figure 8.91 The Perform Script step runs the Check Version script before running the script with a version 6 feature.

Customizing Documents with If Steps

One of the things small businesses and free agents regularly do is generate repetitive documents. Whether it be contracts, form letters, or promotions, you build a "customized" document by combining relevant paragraphs of boilerplate text and specific names and addresses from a database. You end up keeping several versions of the same basic stuff around, and then you have to manually edit each one to customize it for a specific mailing or legal document.

Although you might automatically reach for a word processing program for these kinds of projects, think again. You can crank up FileMaker's scripting muscle to generate your documents with far less pain. It's true that the set-up involves several separate tasks and will take a little time, but if you deal frequently with contracts (or any other text-based form with several modular variations), you'll find the results worth the effort.

The document script has some prerequisites before it will work its magic. First, you need several global fields to hold the boilerplate text paragraphs and modular choices. The text itself can be typed directly into the fields or cut-and-pasted from any existing text document. Second, you need to create two layouts: one to hold your mix-and-match templates and another formatted as a finished document. We'll create the fields and layouts before creating the script to put it all together.

Once you have your building blocks, you can design a script that constructs a document by combining the boilerplate text with the choices you make from the template elements.

To build the formatted document efficiently, see "To create a label field" in Chapter 4. We'll use this calculated field to include a complete name and address field in the document the script creates.

To create modular text fields:

1. Choose File > Define Fields.

2. When the Define Fields dialog box appears, type **Paragraph 1** in the Field Name box, choose Global as the field type, and click Create (**Figure 8.92**).

continues on next page

Figure 8.92 Paragraph 1 is a Global field that will contain the text of the first boilerplate paragraph.

215

Chapter 8

3. In the Options dialog box, choose Text as the data type and click OK (**Figure 8.93**). This creates a field to hold one paragraph of modular text.

4. Repeat steps 2 and 3 for as many additional modular paragraphs as you need.

   In our example, we create a total of four global fields, named Paragraph 1 through 4 (**Figure 8.94**).

5. In the Define Fields dialog box, type `Include Paragraph 1` in the Field Name box, choose Text as the field type, and click Create. This creates a field to use as a check box for choosing Paragraph 1.

6. Repeat step 5 to create as many check box fields as you just created fields for modular paragraphs.

   In our example, we create a total of four text fields, named Include Paragraph 1 through 4 (**Figure 8.95**).

7. We need one field to contain the compiled text that the script creates. Type the document's name in the Field Name box, choose Text for the field type, and click Create. Click Done to close the Define Fields box.

   In our example, we're building a contract, so our field name for the compiled text is Contract.

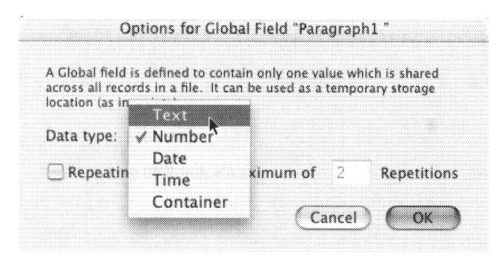

Figure 8.93 This Global field will contain text.

Figure 8.94 Increase the name of each paragraph by one as you add them.

Figure 8.95 There should be as many Include Paragraph fields as there are Paragraph fields.

Working with Conditional Script Steps

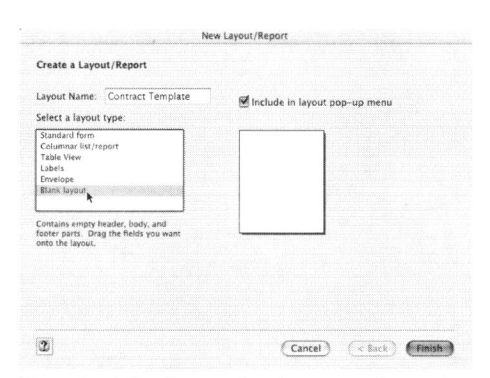

Figure 8.96 Use the template layout to select and edit the contents of the Paragraph fields.

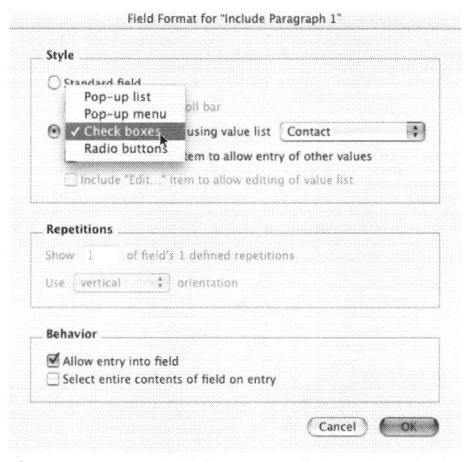

Figure 8.97 Use check boxes to tell the script which paragraphs to include.

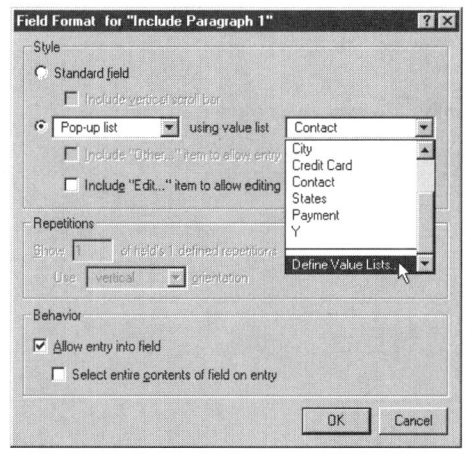

Figure 8.98 You'll need to define a Value List for the check boxes.

To create a template layout:

1. Choose View > Layout Mode (Control+L/Command+L).

2. Choose Layouts > New Layout (Control+N/Command+N).

3. In the New Layout dialog box, type a name for the layout in the Layout Name box and select "Blank layout" for the layout type (**Figure 8.96**). We named our example Contract Template. Click Finish.

4. In the blank layout, drag the Header and Footer tabs up so they disappear, then drag the Body tab down to fill the window.

5. Drag the Field tool onto the layout to bring up the Specify Field dialog box. Double-click Include Paragraph 1 in the field name list.

6. Click the Include Paragraph 1 field on the layout.

7. Choose Format > Field Format (Control+Shift+F/Command+Shift+F) to access the Field Format dialog box.

8. In the Style section, select the second radio button and choose "Check boxes" from the drop-down menu (**Figure 8.97**).

9. From the "using value list" drop-down menu, choose Define Value Lists (**Figure 8.98**).

continues on next page

217

Chapter 8

10. When the Define Value Lists dialog box appears, click New.

11. In the Edit Value List dialog box, type Y as the Value List Name, and type Y in the "Use custom values" box (**Figure 8.99**). Click OK.

    The single value in the value list will be displayed in the layout as one check box.

12. Click Done to close the Define Value Lists dialog box, then click OK.

13. In the layout, resize the Include Paragraph 1 field so that only the check box is visible (**Figure 8.100**).

    The check box field you've just created will allow you to include the first paragraph of text when the script runs.

14. Drag the Field tool onto the layout to bring up the Specify Field dialog box. Double-click Paragraph 1 in the field name list (**Figure 8.101**).

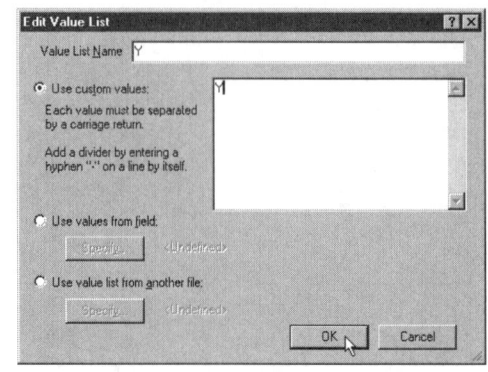

Figure 8.99 This Value List only needs a single value, Y.

Figure 8.100 You only need to see the check box for this field.

Figure 8.101 Edit the Paragraph fields in this layout.

Working with Conditional Script Steps

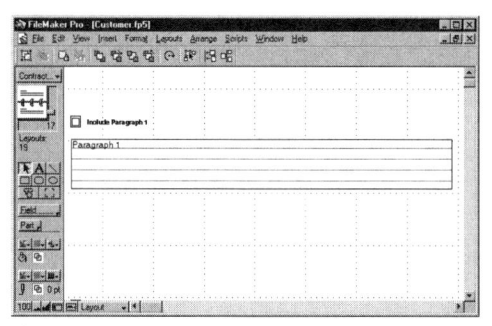

Figure 8.102 Make the field large enough for the paragraph text.

Figure 8.103 Add all of the Paragraph and Include fields to the layout.

15. Resize this field to fit the paragraph, then arrange the label, check box field, and Paragraph 1 field as you'd like them on the page (**Figure 8.102**).

16. Repeat steps 6–15 for as many paragraph fields as you created (**Figure 8.103**). Or see the tip on the next page.

17. Choose View > Browse Mode.

18. Enter the text for each paragraph of the document in their respective Paragraph fields. You can type this text in or paste it in from an existing text document.

We now have a group of modular paragraphs that we can mix and match to create a customized document when we run our script.

continues on next page

CUSTOMIZING DOCUMENTS WITH IF STEPS

219

Chapter 8

✔ Tips

- Although you can create the check boxes and paragraph fields separately, frankly that's pretty tedious. It's faster to Shift-click the Include Paragraph 1 field, its label, and the Paragraph 1 field to select them all, then hold down Alt (Windows) or Option (Mac) as you drag the mouse (**Figure 8.104**). Arrange the duplicated layout items below the first group in the layout. Double-click each layout item and select the next field name in the Specify Field dialog box to match the next paragraph (**Figure 8.105**). Remember to edit the paragraph numbers on the labels as well.

- If you're creating a boilerplate document that people other than yourself might use, it's a good idea to add some instructions to the template layout (**Figure 8.106**).

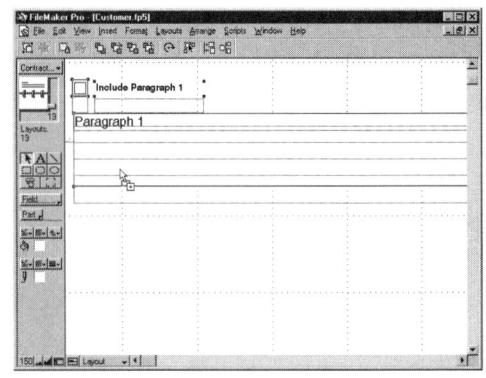

Figure 8.104 Alt- or Option-dragging a field retains the size and formatting in the copied field.

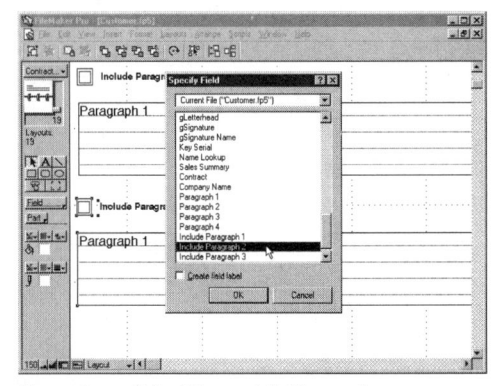

Figure 8.105 Select the next field name in sequence.

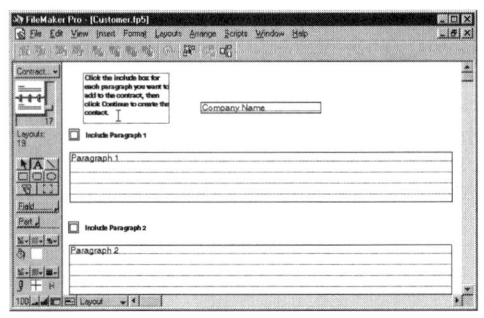

Figure 8.106 Add text to explain how to use the layout.

Working with Conditional Script Steps

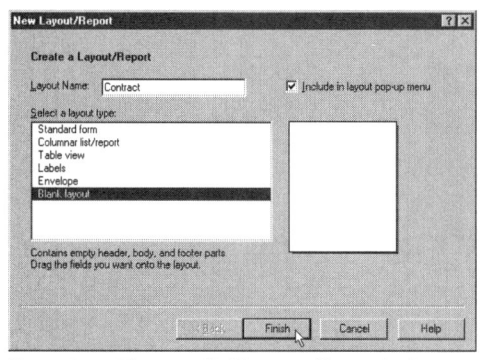

Figure 8.107 The compiled layout will contain the assembled text.

Figure 8.108 Don't add field labels, since this layout will be printed.

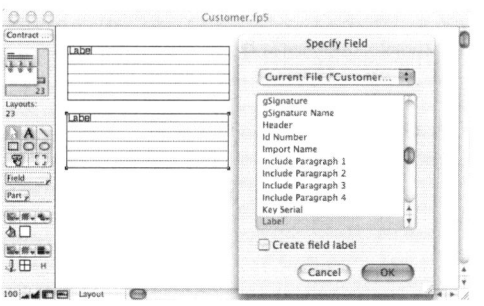

Figure 8.109 Double-click to specify another field.

To create a layout for the compiled document:

1. Choose View > Layout Mode.

2. Choose Layouts > New Layout (Control+N/Command+N).

3. In the New Layout dialog box, type a name in the Layout Name box and select "Blank layout" for the layout type. Click Finish (**Figure 8.107**).

4. In the blank layout, drag the Header and Footer tabs up so they disappear, then drag the Body tab down to fill the window.

5. Drag the Field tool onto the layout. In the Specify Field dialog box, uncheck the "Create field label" check box and double-click Label (**Figure 8.108**).

6. Alt-drag (Windows) or Option-drag (Mac) the Label field to the layout to duplicate it. In the Specify Field dialog box, choose the field you created to hold your compiled document (**Figure 8.109**).

continues on next page

221

Chapter 8

7. Resize the fields to fit their text (**Figure 8.110**).

8. Click the Text tool and add any additional text that you want to appear on the document when it's printed (**Figure 8.111**).

To create a modular document script:

1. Choose Scripts > ScriptMaker.

2. Type a script name in the Script Name box and click Create.

   We use Create Contract, because that's what we're doing in our example.

3. The Script Definition dialog box will appear. In the step list on the left, scroll down to the Navigation category and double-click Enter Browse Mode.

4. In the Navigation category of the step list, double-click Go to Layout. In the Options section, choose your template layout from the drop-down menu (**Figure 8.112**).

   When the script runs, this step will bring you to the layout we created in "To create a template layout" earlier in this section.

5. In the step list on the left, double-click Pause/Resume Script.

   This step halts the script, allowing you to choose which paragraphs to include.

6. In the Field category of the step list, double-click Set Field. In the Options section, click the Field (Windows) or Specify Field (Mac) button. When the Specify Field dialog box opens, choose the compiled text field (in our example, Contract) by double-clicking it.

Figure 8.110 The fields need to be large enough for all of the text.

Figure 8.111 Use the Text tool to add text to the layout.

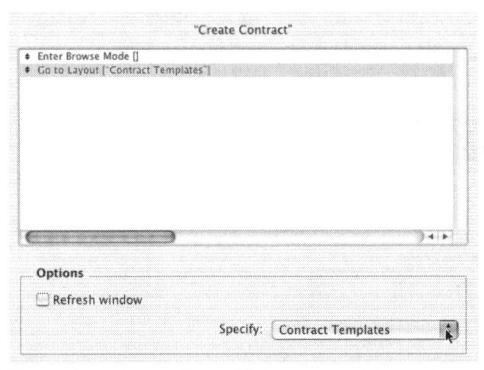

Figure 8.112 The script will bring you to the template layout.

Working with Conditional Script Steps

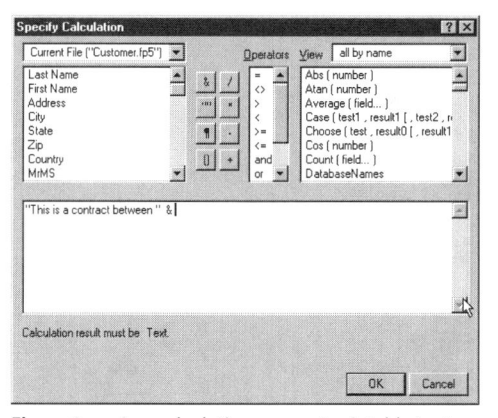

Figure 8.113 In a calculation, you put printable text in quotes.

Figure 8.114 The introductory text will include the full name of the customer.

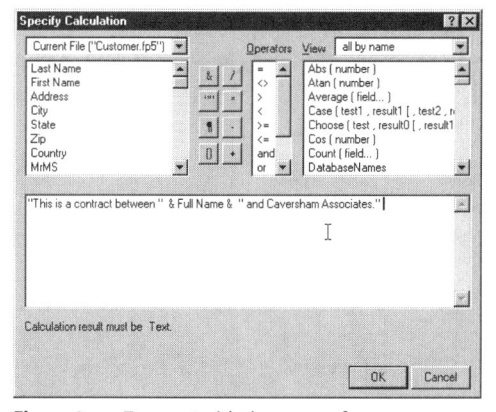

Figure 8.115 Type *and* with the name of your company in quotes.

7. If you want to include the name of a person from a database within the text, click the Specify button to bring up the Specify Calculation dialog box.

    In our example, we're creating a contract, so we'll create a calculation to insert a name in the right place in the contract text.

8. Click the quotes operator. Inside the quotes, type your opening text (in our case, we use "This is a contract between"), followed by a space at the end of the phrase. Click to the right outside the quotes and then click the ampersand (&) operator button (**Figure 8.113**).

9. In the field list on the left, double-click the Full Name field. Click the ampersand button again (**Figure 8.114**).

    The Full Name field is a calculation field that combines the First Name, Last Name, and Middle Initial fields into one. See Chapter 4 for more on calculation fields.

10. Click the quotes operator button and type *and* between the quotes. (There's a space before and after the and.)

    After the space, we've typed the name of the company followed by a period to complete the typical contract phrase (**Figure 8.115**).

    continues on next page

223

Chapter 8

11. Click to the right of the quotes, then click the ampersand button, the quotes button, and the paragraph button (**Figure 8.116**). Click OK to return to the Script Definition window.

    This complex-looking field is just a text line that inserts a name from the database in the right place in a sentence.

12. In the step list on the left, double-click If. In the Options section, click Specify.

13. In the Specify Calculation dialog box, double-click the Include Paragraph 1 field.

14. Type ="Y" and click OK (**Figure 8.117**).

15. In the step list on the left, double-click Set Field.

16. In the Options section, click the Field/Specify Field button to bring up the Specify Field dialog box, then double-click Contract in the list.

17. In the Options section, click the Specify button to bring up the Specify Calculation dialog box. Double-click Contract in the field list on the left.

18. Click the ampersand button, then double-click the Paragraph 1 field (**Figure 8.118**).

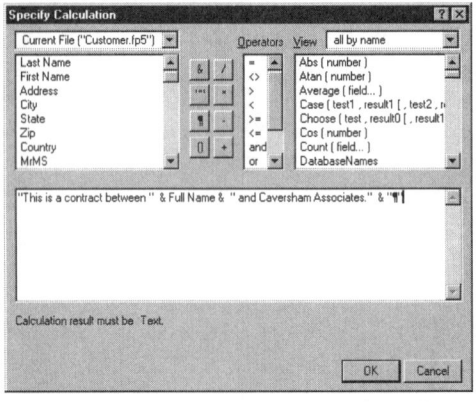

Figure 8.116 The finished calculation combines the text entered with the contents of the Full Name field to create the opening paragraph of a contract.

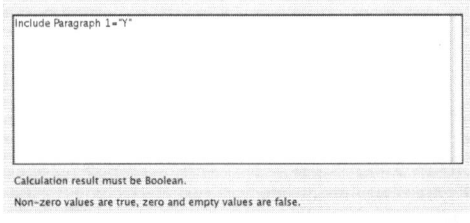

Figure 8.117 If the Include Paragraph field is checked, the contents of the field are actually Y.

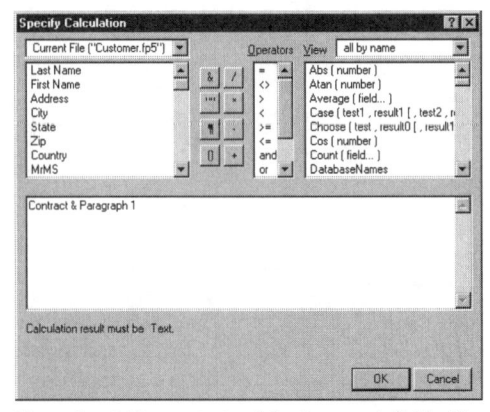

Figure 8.118 The contents of the Paragraph field will be added to the field holding the compiled text.

Working with Conditional Script Steps

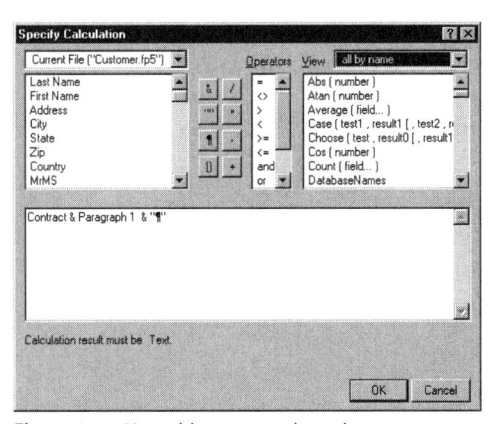

Figure 8.119 You add a paragraph marker to space down to the next paragraph.

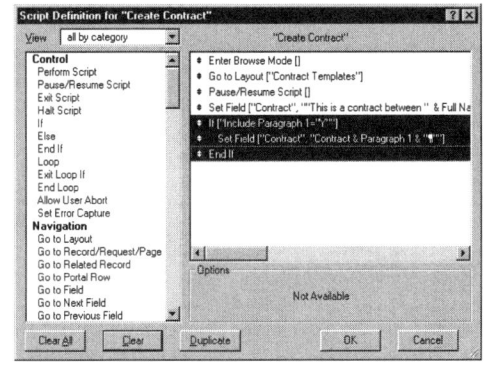

Figure 8.120 Duplicating the steps is easier than adding them manually.

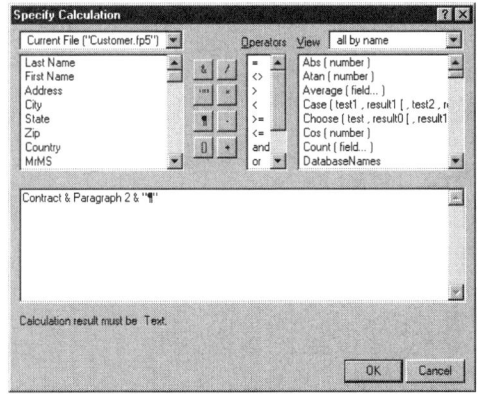

Figure 8.121 Change the number to indicate the second paragraph.

19. Click the ampersand button, then the quotes button. Click between the quotes and then click the paragraph button (**Figure 8.119**). Click OK to return to the Script Definition window.

    This If step adds the first paragraph if you check it in the template layout.

20. In the script-assembly window, click the If step, hold down the Shift key and click End If. Click the Duplicate button (**Figure 8.120**).

21. Double-click the duplicate If step. When the Specify Calculation dialog box appears, change the 1 to 2, then click OK.

22. Click the duplicate Set Field step. In the Options section, click Specify. When the Specify Calculation dialog box appears, change the 1 to 2, then click OK (**Figure 8.121**).

    continues on next page

225

Chapter 8

23. Repeat steps 20–22 for as many additional paragraphs as you created. In our example, we do this for numbers 3 and 4 (**Figure 8.122**).

24. In the step list on the left, double-click Go to Layout. In the Options section, choose the layout for the compiled document (in our case, Contract) from the Specify drop-down menu. Click OK and then Done to finish.

When you run the script, it goes to the template layout and waits for you to make choices. It finishes by switching to the second layout, where it compiles your choices into a text document. You can make additional changes to the text before printing.

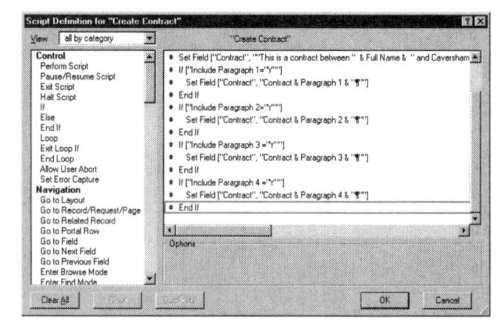

Figure 8.122 Add and modify a set of Ifs for each paragraph in the contract.

Extending the Interface with Scripts

Although you're pretty comfortable with FileMaker, you may not be the only person who uses your files. Other people may not be as savvy as you are, or may be such occasional users that they never memorize the FileMaker commands. You can make it easier for others to work with your files by creating a custom interface for them.

This may seem a little daunting. After all, real interface design is pretty challenging, since it involves both graphics and programming skills. But you don't have to have strong skills in either of these areas to create a mini-interface of common tasks in FileMaker. Scripts and buttons make it easy to create navigation bars, buttons, and menus to insulate others from commands—and also protect your database from well-intentioned errors. Even if everyone who uses the database is a FileMaker whiz, they'll appreciate these shortcuts. Clicking a single button is always easier than accessing one (or more) menu commands.

Chapter 9

Making a Find Layout with a Script

Because setting up a find request takes time and typing, you'll frequently find yourself creating scripts that hold your typical search criteria. But you can't always predict what the criteria will be, although you might be able to predict the category. For example, every once in a while you may want to print out a record of your receivables. For those occasions you can create a generic date-search script with its own layout that generates a report when it's done. Once you have the script, you can run it from the menu bar, or from any layout that contains a script button you create.

To create a layout for searching:

1. If the script you're creating requires a sort, perform the sort. If this script will use a Print command, set the Print/Page Setup to the desired settings.

2. Choose View > Layout Mode (Control+L/Command+L).

3. Choose Layouts > New Layout (Control+N/Command+N). In the New Layout dialog box, type a name for the layout. For this example, we'll use Date Find.

4. Choose "Blank layout" as the layout type and click Finish (**Figure 9.1**).

5. Drag the Header and Footer parts up until they disappear, since we only need the Body part.

6. Drag the Field tool into the layout. In the Specify Field dialog box that appears, choose your date field. Here, we add Sale Date (**Figure 9.2**).

7. Using the Text tool, add directions on how to use the layout and arrange the text and field on the layout page (**Figure 9.3**).

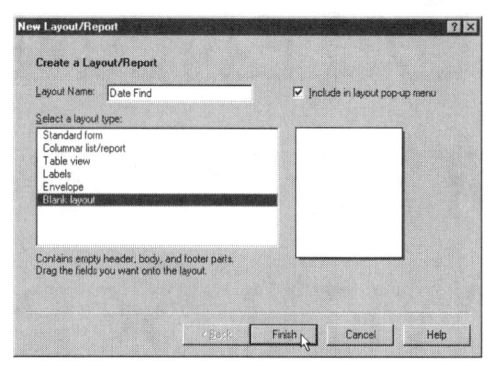

Figure 9.1 Since only one field will be used in this layout, choose "Blank layout."

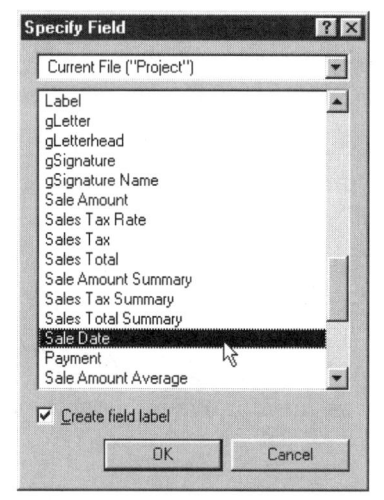

Figure 9.2 Choose the field for the find criteria in the Specify Field dialog box.

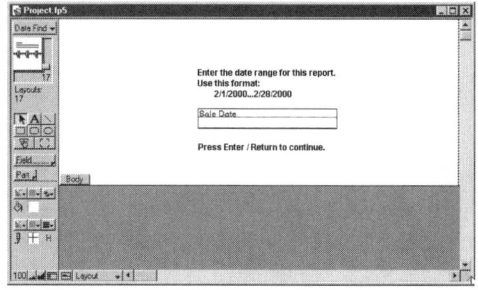

Figure 9.3 Add directions in the layout to explain how to use it.

228

Extending the Interface with Scripts

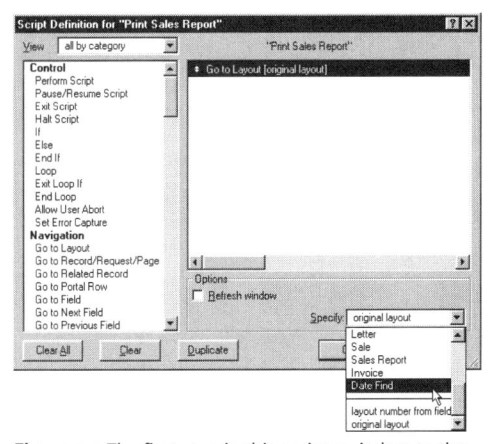

Figure 9.4 The first step in this script switches to the Date Find layout.

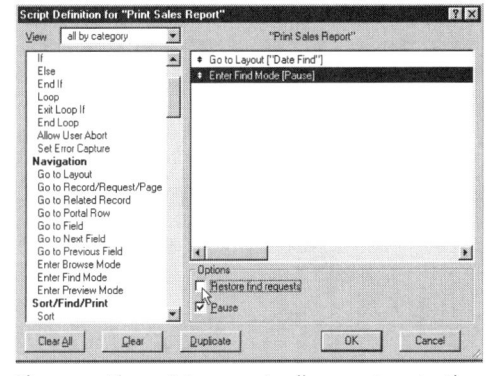

Figure 9.5 The script pauses to allow you to enter the find criteria.

Figure 9.6 Since you'll enter new find criteria each time, don't use the Restore option.

Next we'll create the script to do the find request and print the result.

8. Choose Scripts > ScriptMaker. In the Define Scripts dialog box, type a name for the script. (We use Print Sales Report.) Click Create.

9. The Script Definition dialog box appears. In the step list on the left, double-click Go to Layout.

10. Under Options, choose the layout you just created from the Specify drop-down menu (**Figure 9.4**).

11. In the Navigation section of the step list on the left, double-click Enter Find Mode.

12. Under Options, uncheck the "Restore find requests" box. Leave the Pause box checked (**Figure 9.5**).

    Since you'll choose different dates each time the script runs, you don't want to use the Restore option. The Pause option makes the script wait for your input before continuing.

13. In the Sort/Find/Print section of the step list on the left, double-click Perform Find. Uncheck the "Restore find requests" box (**Figure 9.6**).

continues on next page

229

MAKING A FIND LAYOUT WITH A SCRIPT

14. If you want to use a sort, double-click Sort in the list of steps and leave the "Restore sort order" box checked (**Figure 9.7**).

15. In the step list on the left, double-click Go to Layout.

16. Under Options, choose the layout in which you want the found set to appear from the Specify drop-down menu (**Figure 9.8**).

17. Under Sort/Find/Print in the step list on the left, double-click Print Setup (Page Setup on the Mac). Leave the "Restore setup options" and "Perform without dialog" boxes checked (**Figure 9.9**).

   This step will set the Print/Page Setup options for the printing in the next step.

Figure 9.7 If the script will use a sort, you can check the Restore option.

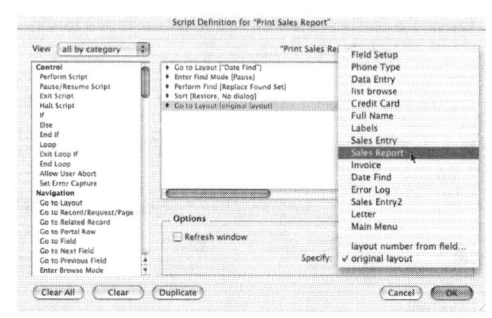

Figure 9.8 This script will switch to the Sales Report layout before printing.

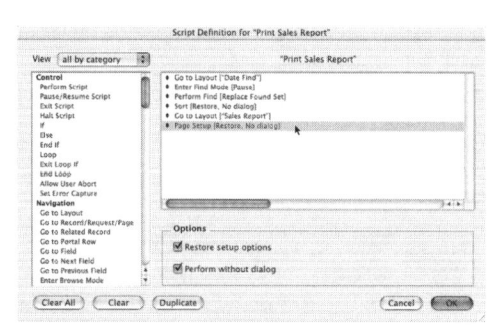

Figure 9.9 The Print/Page Setup with the Restore option will create the correct print settings.

Extending the Interface with Scripts

Figure 9.10 If the "Perform without dialog" box is checked, you won't be prompted before printing.

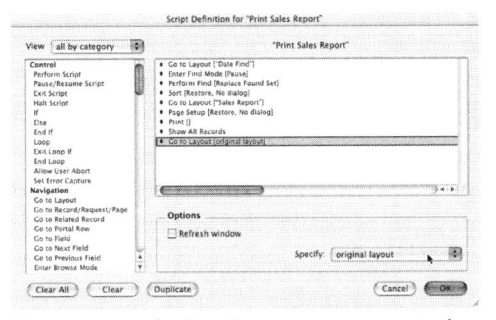

Figure 9.11 Use the Go to Layout step to return to the layout you were in when you ran the script.

18. In the step list on the left, double-click Print. If you want to see the Print dialog box, uncheck the "Perform without dialog" box (**Figure 9.10**).

19. In the step list on the left, double-click Show All Records.

    This will reset the database to All Records after you've finished printing the found set.

20. In the step list on the left, double-click Go to Layout. Leave the options untouched (**Figure 9.11**).

    This step will return you to the layout from which the script was run.

21. Click OK, then Done.

231

Chapter 9

Creating Script Buttons

Although you can run any script from the Script menu list, it's a better idea to use script buttons. Naturally, it's easier to click once than to click, drag, and select. But script buttons are more than a lazy way to save a couple of seconds. For one thing, it's easy to forget which script belongs with a layout. And if other people use your database they could make a remarkable mess of it by running the wrong script at the wrong time.

To create a button for a script:

1. If you're not already there, enter Layout mode and switch to the layout where you want to place the button.

2. Click the Button tool (**Figure 9.12**).

3. Dragging the cursor on the layout creates the button and brings up the Specify Button dialog box. In the list on the left, click Perform Script.

4. Under Options, choose the script name from the Specify drop-down menu and click OK (**Figure 9.13**).

5. The button will appear in the layout with the text cursor flashing (**Figure 9.14**). Type a descriptive label, then select the text and format it as desired.

6. Switch to Browse mode and click the new button to test the script.

✔ Tips

- You're not limited to the default look of a FileMaker button. The tools used for creating graphics can also be used to change the thickness or color of the lines and the color or fill pattern of a button.

- If you use a graphic element to create a button (instead of the Button tool), click the graphic and choose Format > Button to specify what the button does.

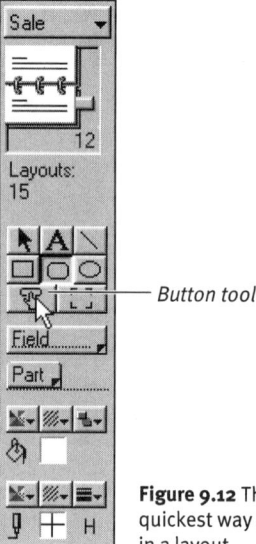

Figure 9.12 The Button tool is the quickest way to create a new button in a layout.

Figure 9.13 After you add the button to the layout, specify the action the button will perform.

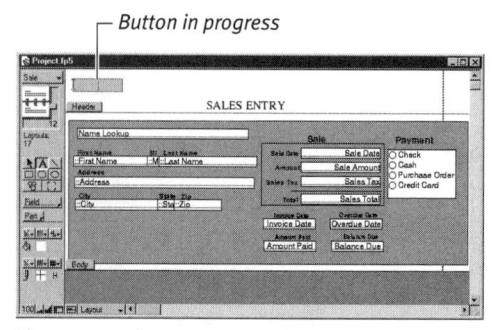

Figure 9.14 When you create a button, FileMaker automatically switches to the Text tool for input.

About Buttons

There are many ways to make buttons for your interface. The easiest is to just use the Button tool, which does a reasonable job of making simple text buttons with geometric shapes. You can also use premade art. Some earlier versions of FileMaker included sample graphic buttons (**Figure 9.15**), but unfortunately FileMaker 6 doesn't. If you have an older version of FileMaker, you can still use these samples in the new version. In addition, you'll find contact information in Appendix A for premade button sets that you can download.

If you own a graphics program and are artistically inclined, you can design unique button icons. Intelligently designed graphical elements can enhance a button's usefulness. A printer icon is much more universally recognized than text that says "Print."

If you decide to make custom graphics for your FileMaker databases, follow the same guidelines you would if you were creating them for the Internet. Buttons that use many colors, are very big, or are complex take longer to display on the screen, and a lot longer to open on a networked multiuser database. Each time the user switches screens, the local computer needs to download the layout elements from the server and redraw them.

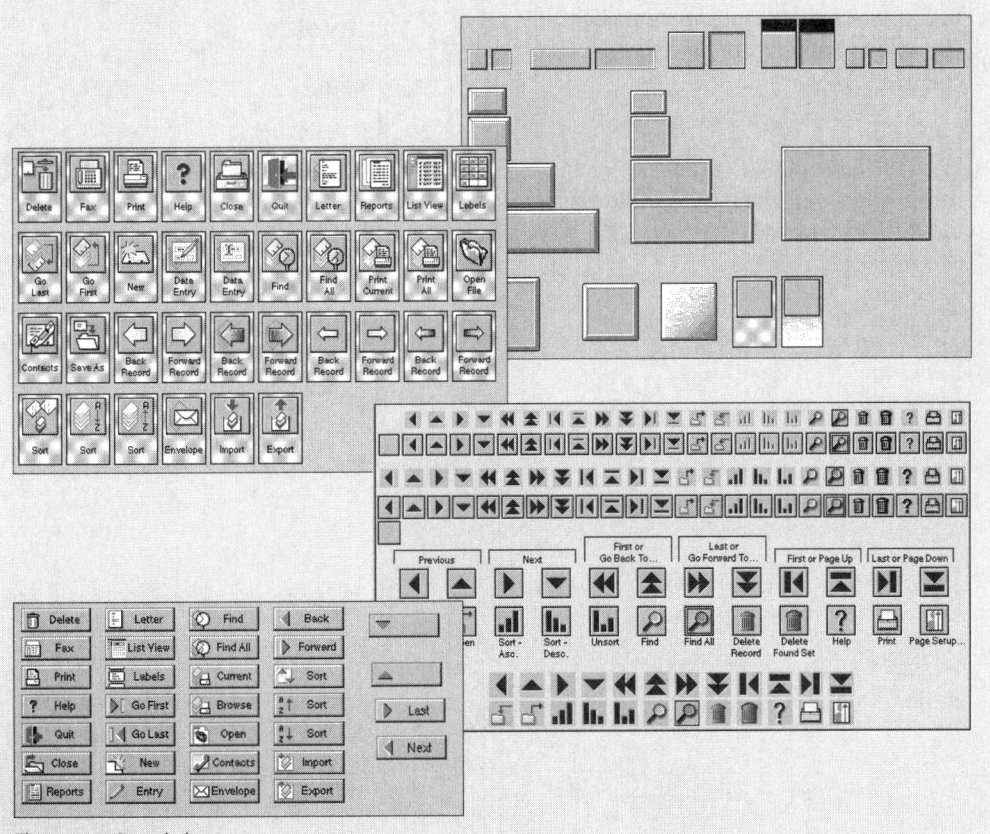

Figure 9.15 Sample buttons.

Chapter 9

Creating Interactive Buttons

When layout elements are formatted as buttons, it isn't always obvious to users that a particular element is indeed a button. This problem arises frequently when you've formatted a field as a button. FileMaker lets you provide a visual clue by turning the cursor into a hand icon when it rolls over a button.

To change a cursor to a hand icon:

1. Choose View > Layout Mode.
2. Click a button.
3. Choose Format > Button.
4. In the Specify Button dialog box, click "Change to hand cursor over button" (**Figure 9.16**).
5. Click OK.

   With the hand cursor option set, when the cursor is over the button in Browse mode, the arrow will change to a hand (**Figure 9.17**).

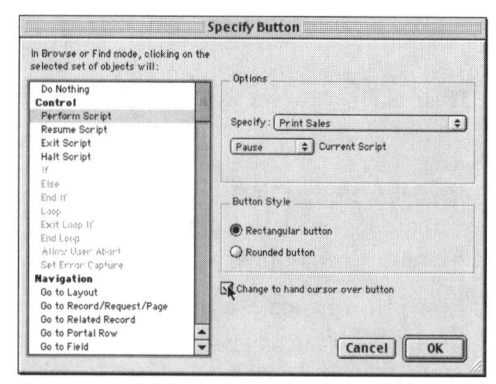

Figure 9.16 Turn on the hand cursor option for each button in the Specify Button dialog box.

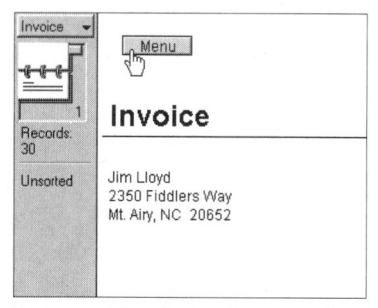

Figure 9.17 With the hand cursor option set, users will have a visual cue to guide them to a layout's buttons.

234

Extending the Interface with Scripts

Figure 9.18 The portal must be set to allow deletion of rows.

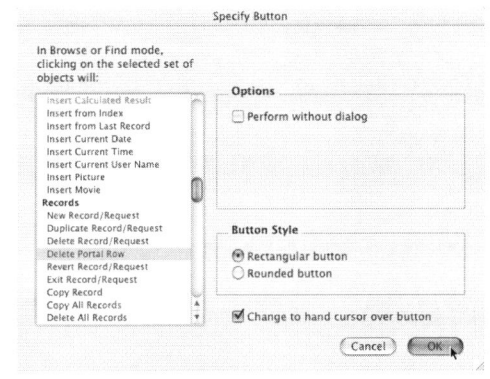

Figure 9.19 You want to have a warning before the row is deleted, so leave the "Perform without dialog" option unchecked.

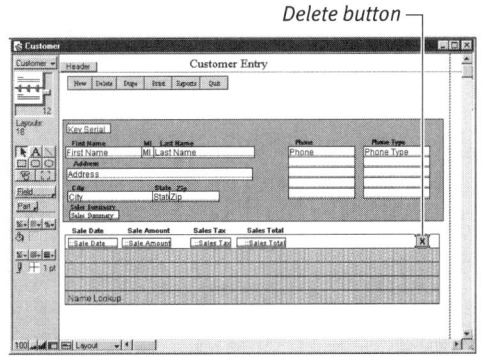

Delete button

Figure 9.20 The bold X gives you a visual cue as to what the button does.

Deleting Records in a Related File

When you create records using a portal (see "About Portals" in Chapter 6), you may want to be able to delete specific records (portal rows) in the other file. For example, if a customer cancels an order, you'll need to remove the entry from the sales database. Rather than going to the related file and searching for the record to delete, you can create a button to delete the record without leaving the first file.

To delete records in a related file:

1. Go to the layout that contains the portal. Choose View > Layout Mode (Control+L/Command+L).

2. Double-click the portal. When the Portal Setup dialog box appears, make sure that the "Allow deletion of portal records" box is checked (**Figure 9.18**). Click OK.

3. While in the portal, follow the steps in "To create a button for a script" earlier in this chapter, but in the Specify Button dialog box, scroll down to the Records section and choose Delete Portal Row (**Figure 9.19**). Do not check "Perform without dialog" because you want to be able to cancel the choice if you've made a mistake.

   When you click the button a dialog box appears. If you click Delete, the portal row and its related record will be deleted from the other database. If you click Cancel, it won't be.

4. At the flashing cursor, type X (the universal icon for Delete). To add emphasis, make the X bold (**Figure 9.20**).

   continues on next page

235

Chapter 9

5. Choose View > Browse Mode (Control+B/Command+B).

6. Test the button by clicking it in any row that you want to delete. The warning dialog box will appear to confirm the deletion (**Figure 9.21**).

✔ **Tips**

- If the layout in which you put a button is one you use for printing, the button will print out too. To hide the button when you print, switch to Layout mode and select the button. Choose Format > Sliding/Printing. Click the "Do not print the selected objects" check box and then OK (**Figure 9.22**). The button will appear on the layout but won't appear on printouts.

- Add a series of buttons to a layout, either grouped vertically along the left side (**Figure 9.23**) or horizontally along the top (**Figure 9.24**), to create a button bar. Put this group of buttons in the layout you use most to speed up access to other layouts and scripts. You can put a button in those other layouts that switches back to the main layout.

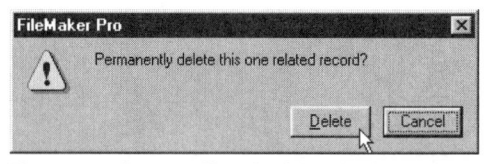

Figure 9.21 The row will not be deleted unless you confirm the choice.

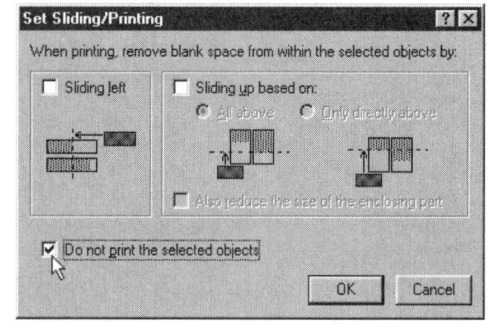

Figure 9.22 If a layout element is formatted with the "Do not print the selected objects" option on, it will appear in Browse mode but not in Preview mode or on printouts.

Figure 9.23 Buttons can be grouped vertically along the left side of the layout.

Figure 9.24 If the layout won't scroll, you can place the buttons in a row at the top of page.

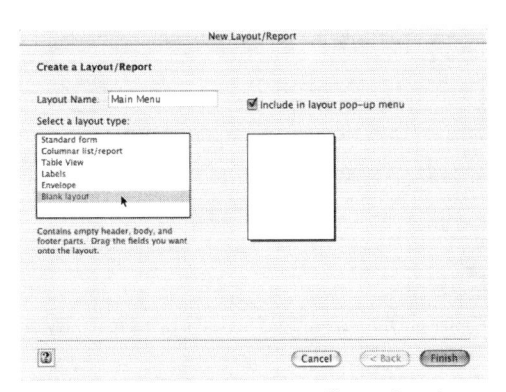

Figure 9.25 Since the Main Menu will contain only buttons, begin with a blank layout.

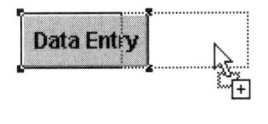

Figure 9.26 Control- or Option-dragging allows you to create one button and then duplicate it, retaining its size and formatting.

Creating a Main Menu Layout

If you have a really large or complex database with several files and dozens of layouts, the simple task of navigating from one place to the next can become difficult. A button bar can help, but once your database gets really cumbersome, all the buttons you need will take up too much space in a layout—space you need for real work. When this happens, you can create a Main Menu layout that contains only buttons. The buttons will take you to the most important layouts (like Data Entry) or execute scripts that search or print reports. Each of the other layouts in the database need contain only one button that returns you to the Main Menu.

To create a Main Menu layout:

1. Choose View > Layout Mode (Control+L/Command+L).

2. Choose Layouts > New Layout (Control+N/Command+N).

3. In the New Layout dialog box, type a name for the layout. (We use Main Menu.) Choose "Blank layout" as the layout type (**Figure 9.25**). Click Finish.

4. Drag the Header and Footer parts up until they disappear, since we need only the Body part, then drag the Body tab down to make room for the buttons you're going to add.

5. Follow the steps in "To create a button for a script" earlier in this chapter to add a button to the layout.

6. Select the new button. Holding down the Control/Option key, drag to duplicate the button, changing the labels and scripts for each one (**Figure 9.26**). Repeat this step as many times as necessary to create the total number of buttons for the layouts and scripts you use frequently.

continues on next page

7. Arrange the buttons on the page and add labels and headings. It's a good idea to group functions logically so you won't waste time later reading every button to find the one you want (**Figure 9.27**).

   You now have a layout with buttons that link you around your database. All that's left is to create a script you can use to link your other layouts back to the Main Menu.

8. Choose Scripts > ScriptMaker. In the Define Scripts dialog box, type a name for the script. (We use Go to Main Menu.) Click Create.

9. The Script Definition dialog box appears. In the step list on the left, double-click Go to Layout.

10. Under Options, choose Main Menu from the Specify drop-down menu (**Figure 9.28**). Click OK, then Done.

11. In layouts in the same database file as the Main Menu, follow the steps in "To create a button for a script" earlier in this chapter to add a button to the layout.

12. In the Specify Button dialog box, select Go to Layout from the list on the left and Main Menu from the Specify drop-down menu under Options (**Figure 9.29**). Label the button Main Menu.

13. Repeat this step for every layout you need to link to the Main Menu.

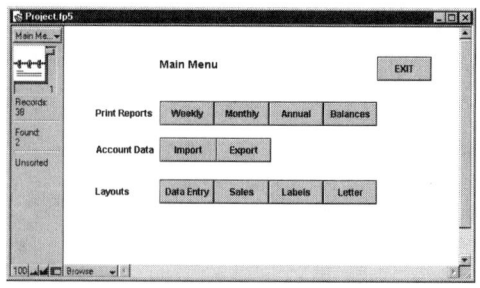

Figure 9.27 Group buttons logically to make it easy to use them later.

Figure 9.28 Choose the layout you want to go to when you click the button.

Figure 9.29 Buttons in other layouts will run the Go to Main Menu script.

Extending the Interface with Scripts

Figure 9.30 Set the Perform Script step to run a script in another file.

Figure 9.31 You must specify the file that contains the external script.

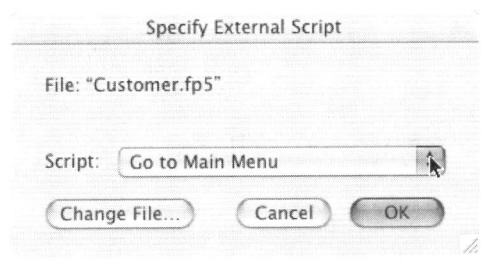

Figure 9.32 Specify the script to run in the other file.

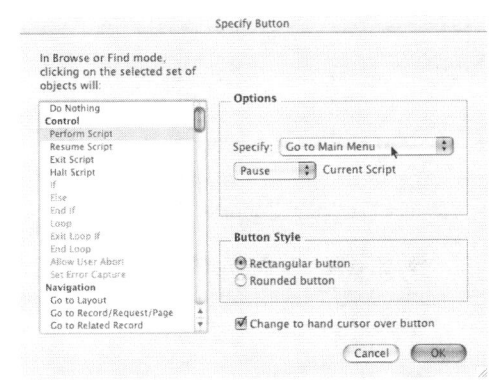

Figure 9.33 To switch to a particular layout in another file, you must perform a script.

Linking to the Main Menu

If you create a Main Menu, you'll quickly discover its fatal weakness. You can almost instantaneously jump from the Main Menu to someplace else, but getting back to it is another story. To avoid confusion, you should also provide easy access back from the linking layouts, especially those in different databases than where the Main Menu itself is placed.

To link to Main Menu from layouts in different files:

1. Go to an external file that you want to link to from the Main Menu. Choose Scripts > ScriptMaker.

2. In the Define Scripts dialog box, type a name for the script. We use Go to Main Menu. Click Create.

3. The Script Definition dialog box appears. In the step list on the left, double-click Perform Script.

4. From the Specify drop-down menu, choose External Script (**Figure 9.30**).

5. In the Specify External Script dialog box, click the Change File button (**Figure 9.31**).

6. When the Open File dialog box appears, navigate to the file with the Main Menu layout and double-click to select it.

7. In the Specify External Script dialog box, choose the Go to Main Menu script from the drop-down menu of scripts in the external file (**Figure 9.32**). Click OK, OK again, then Done.

8. Follow the steps in "To create a button for a script" earlier in this chapter to add a button to the layout in the external file. In the Specify Button dialog box, select Perform Script from the list on the left and choose the Go to Main Menu script (**Figure 9.33**).

239

Running Scripts from Fields

Three or four buttons are efficient, but as you add more buttons your layout will start to look (and feel) cluttered and cramped. You'll be back where you started, having to negotiate too many chaotic choices. Although you could make a Main Menu page, not all databases lend themselves to this solution. If you have a database with many reports, for example, you might be better off creating one field with a drop-down list of choices.

Before you can create this script, you'll need a global field formatted as a drop-down list, and a list of scripts you want to use for the value list.

To make a formatted global field:

1. Choose File > Define Fields.

2. In the Define Fields dialog box, type a name for the field (we use Reports). Choose Global for the field type (**Figure 9.34**). Click Create.

3. When the Options dialog box appears, choose Text as the data type, then click OK (**Figure 9.35**). Click Done.

4. This field will automatically be added to your layout. Next we'll create a value list of script names to display in the field.

5. Go to the layout where you want to place this button. Choose View > Layout Mode (Control+L/Command+L).

6. Drag the Field tool into the layout. Choose Reports in the Specify Field dialog box (**Figure 9.36**). Click the Reports field and choose Format > Field Format (Control+Alt+F/Command+Option+F).

Figure 9.34 Reports is a global field, so its contents are the same in every record.

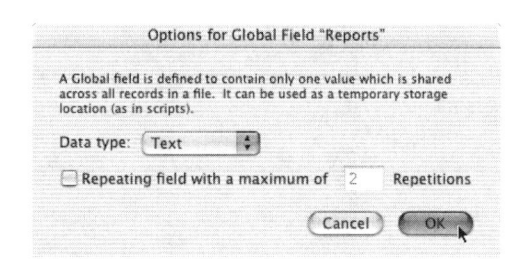

Figure 9.35 The Reports field will contain text.

Figure 9.36 Specify Reports when you add the field to the layout.

Extending the Interface with Scripts

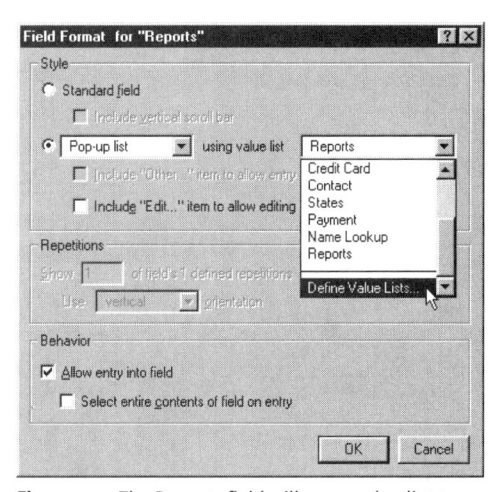

Figure 9.37 The Reports field will use a value list to display the choices.

7. When the Field Format dialog box appears, click the "Pop-up list" radio button. From the value list drop-down menu, choose Define Value Lists (**Figure 9.37**).

8. When the Define Value Lists dialog box appears, click New (**Figure 9.38**).

9. When the Edit Value List dialog box appears, give the value list the same name as you gave the global field (we use Reports).

10. Click inside the "Use custom values" box and type the names of the scripts that you want to choose from (**Figure 9.39**). Click OK. Click Done and then click OK to finish.

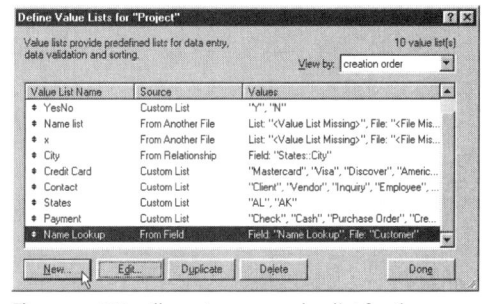

Figure 9.38 You'll create a new value list for the names of the scripts.

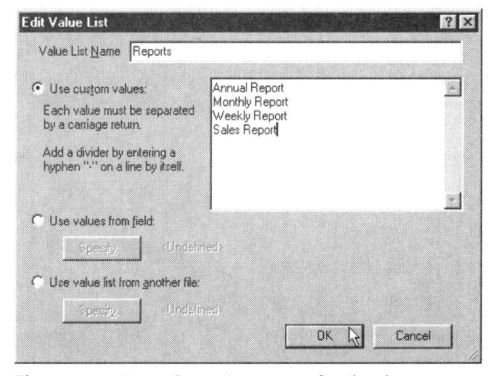

Figure 9.39 Enter the script names for the drop-down list.

You now have the global field placed in a layout, with all of the choices listed in a drop-down menu. All you need now is the script to run these choices for you.

To make a script to run scripts:

1. Choose Scripts > ScriptMaker. In the Define Scripts dialog box, type a name for the script. (We use Choose Report.) Click Create.

2. The Script Definition dialog box appears. In the step list on the left, double-click Go to Field. Under Options, click Specify.

3. When the Specify Field dialog box appears, select Reports (**Figure 9.40**). Click OK.

4. In the step list on the left, double-click Pause/Resume Script.

   This step makes the script wait while you select a report from the drop-down menu.

5. In the step list on the left, double-click If. Under Options, click Specify.

6. In the field list on the left in the Specify Calculation dialog box, double-click Reports.

7. Double-click the = operator, then click the quotes. Within the quotes, type the name of the first report you added to the value list in your global field—ours was Annual Report (**Figure 9.41**). Click OK to close the dialog box.

8. In the step list on the left, double-click Perform Script.

9. From the Specify drop-down menu under Options, choose the script that matches your first report (**Figure 9.42**).

   Our If step says that if you choose Annual Report from the drop-down menu, the script called Annual Report will run.

Figure 9.40 Before it can do anything else, the script must be in the Reports field.

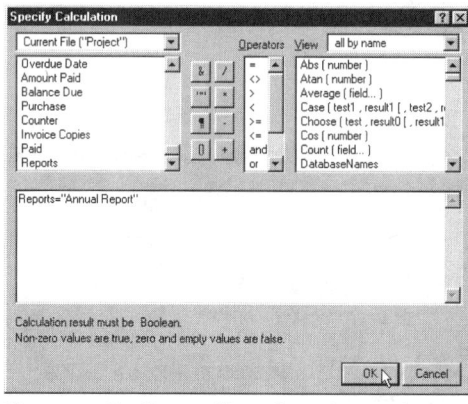

Figure 9.41 The If step will run the script you choose. Specify the first report in your value list by typing it within the formula quotes.

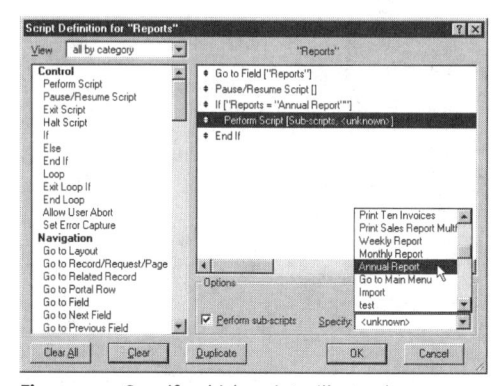

Figure 9.42 Specify which script will run when you choose the report.

Extending the Interface with Scripts

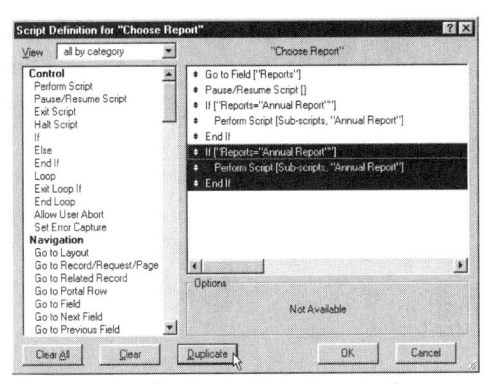

Figure 9.43 Duplicating the If step is easier than creating additional ones from scratch.

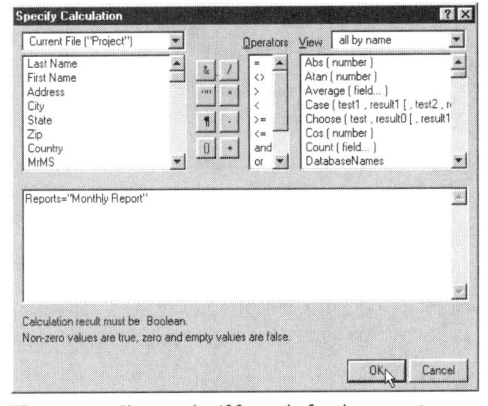

Figure 9.44 Change the If formula for the new steps.

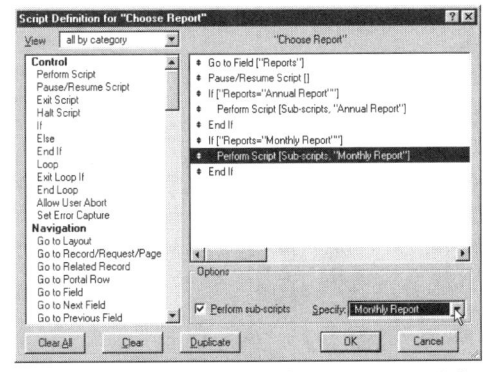

Figure 9.45 Edit each If and Perform Script step. Make sure they always match each other.

10. In the assembly window, click the If step, hold down the Shift key and click End If. Click Duplicate to make a second copy of the entire If sequence (**Figure 9.43**).

11. Double-click the new If step to bring up the Specify Calculation dialog box.

12. Edit the report name in the formula box to match your second script (**Figure 9.44**). Click OK.

13. Click the new Perform Script step.

14. From the Specify drop-down menu under Options, select the script that matches the report name you just typed (**Figure 9.45**).

continues on next page

243

Chapter 9

15. Repeat steps 10–14 for as many reports as you want in the drop-down menu.

16. Highlight the last End If step in the script-assembly window (**Figure 9.46**). In the step list on the left, double-click Go to Layout. Leave "original layout" as the selected option (**Figure 9.47**).

17. Click OK. If "Include in menu" is checked in the Define Scripts dialog box, uncheck it (**Figure 9.48**).

Click Done to finish.

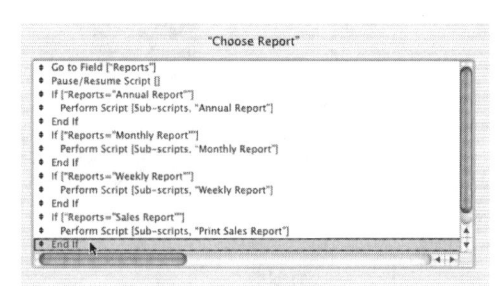

Figure 9.46 A new step is added after a highlighted step.

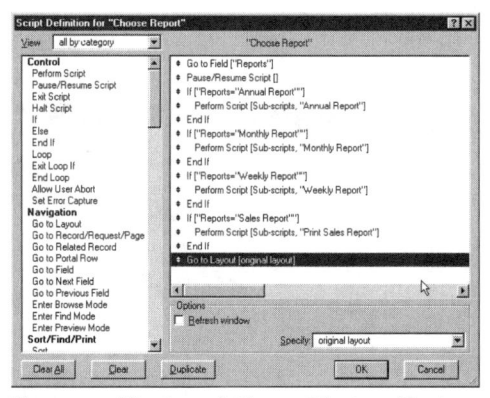

Figure 9.47 After the script is run, this step will return you to the layout you were originally in.

Figure 9.48 This script will run only when you click its button, so there's no point in having it appear in the Script menu.

Extending the Interface with Scripts

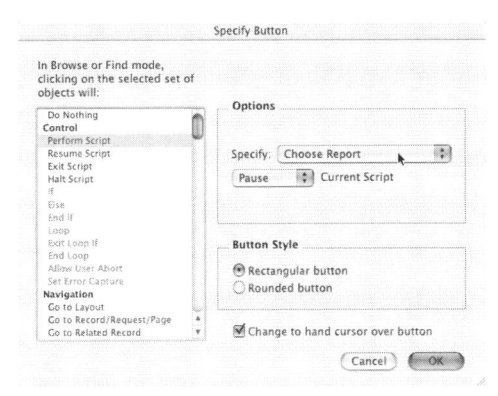

Figure 9.49 Format the field as a button that runs the Reports script.

Figure 9.50 Add instructions to the layout to clarify what the button does.

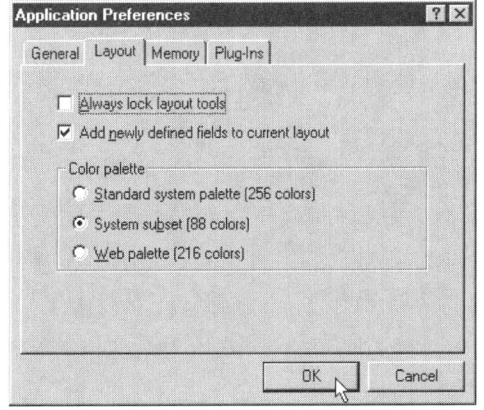

Figure 9.51 This choice automatically adds new fields to whatever layout is in use.

Now that we have a script, we need to connect it to the Reports field by making the field a button.

To make a field into a button that runs a script:

1. Click the field you want to run the script (in our example, it's the Reports field) and choose Format > Button.

2. In the scrolling list on the left, click Perform Script.

3. Under Options, select the script you just created (in our example, Choose Report) from the Specify drop-down menu (**Figure 9.49**). Click OK.

4. Use the Text tool to add helpful instructions to the layout (**Figure 9.50**).

✔ Tip

- To speed up the process of adding new fields to an existing layout, choose Edit > Preferences > Application. Click the Layout tab and check "Add newly defined fields to current layout" (**Figure 9.51**). Now you can go to the layout where you want a field, define the new field, and see it appear automatically in the layout. This is much more convenient than the manual method of defining each field, then returning to the layout, clicking the Field tool, and dragging it to define the field.

245

Chapter 9

Creating Interactive Error Messages

When a script runs and encounters an error, FileMaker usually displays an error message on the screen. Using the script step Set Error Capture, you can replace this generic statement with a message that not only alerts you to the problem, but provides options for a solution. For this example, we create a message prompt that appears when no records are found by a search script.

Figure 9.52 This script goes to a layout, enters Find mode, and performs a new search.

To show error messages with customized choices:

1. Choose Scripts > ScriptMaker. Double-click a script with a Perform Find step in it, or create a new one. Our example is called Find Date (**Figure 9.52**).

2. In the assembly window, select the script step above the steps you want. In our example, we select the step above the Perform Find step (**Figure 9.53**).

3. In the step list on the left, double-click Set Error Capture. By default, On is selected under Options (**Figure 9.54**).

   Turning on Error Capture tells FileMaker to take note of the error code for any error that occurs.

4. While the Set Error Capture step is selected in the assembly window, double-click Loop in the step list on the left.

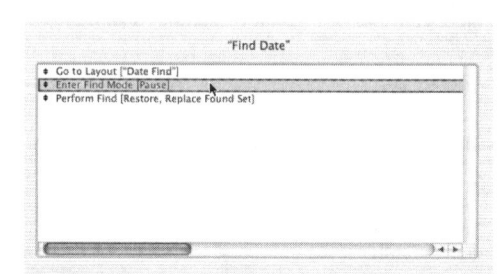

Figure 9.53 New steps are inserted after the selected step.

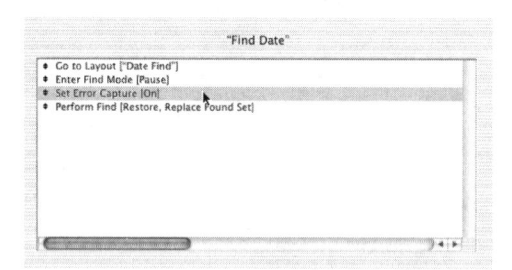

Figure 9.54 Use Set Error Capture to turn off FileMaker's own messages.

246

Extending the Interface with Scripts

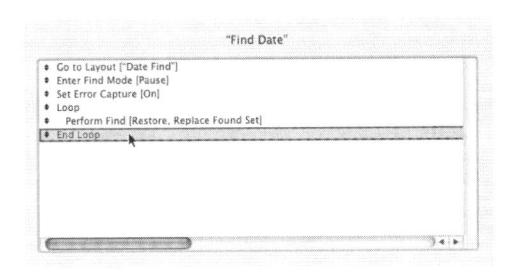

Figure 9.55 Loop will repeat the steps before End Loop.

Figure 9.56 Exit Loop If must occur after the step or steps that might create an error.

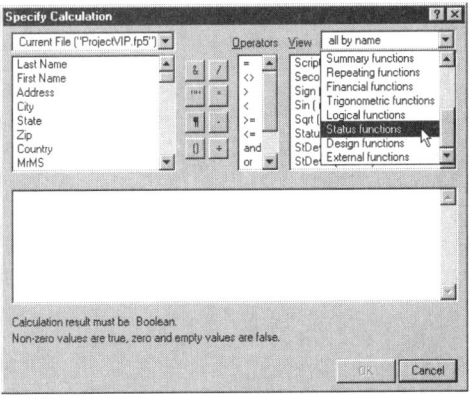

Figure 9.57 Choose Status Functions to see only the status functions.

5. Click the double arrow to the left of the End Loop step and drag it to the end of the script (**Figure 9.55**).

   The Loop step indents anything you put between it and End Loop so you can easily see what takes place inside the Loop.

6. In the assembly window, select the Perform Find step. In the step list on the left, double-click Exit Loop If (**Figure 9.56**). Click Specify to open the Specify Calculation dialog box.

7. In the Specify Calculation dialog box, choose "Status functions" from the View drop-down menu to access the detailed list of status functions (**Figure 9.57**).

continues on next page

CREATING INTERACTIVE ERROR MESSAGES

247

Chapter 9

8. Double-click the Status(CurrentError) function (**Figure 9.58**). Click to the right of the formula and type =0 (**Figure 9.59**). Click OK.

   The script is now set to exit the loop if there is no error.

9. In the Miscellaneous section of the step list on the left, double-click Show Message. Under Options, click Specify.

10. When the Specify Message dialog box appears, type your custom error message in the Message Text box.

11. Double-click in the First (default) box and replace the OK with "Try Again," or another short phrase that will fit on the button. Leave Cancel in the Second box. Click OK (**Figure 9.60**).

    When you create a search that turns up no records matching your find criteria, your error message will be displayed (**Figure 9.61**).

12. In the step list on the left, double-click If. Under Options, click Specify to access the Specify Calculation window.

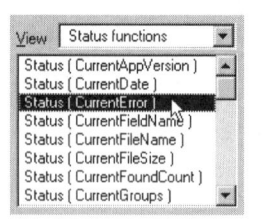

Figure 9.58 Status(CurrentError) looks to see if anything has gone wrong.

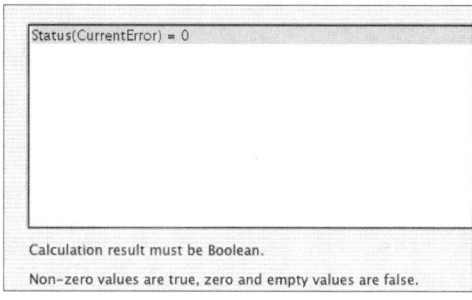

Figure 9.59 Status(CurrentError) is 0 if there is no error.

Figure 9.60 You can customize the message and the buttons that will appear in the error dialog box.

Figure 9.61 Your message will appear when a user uses search criteria that don't match the records in the file.

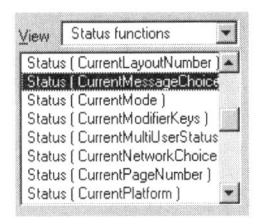

Figure 9.62 Double-click a function to transfer it to the formula box.

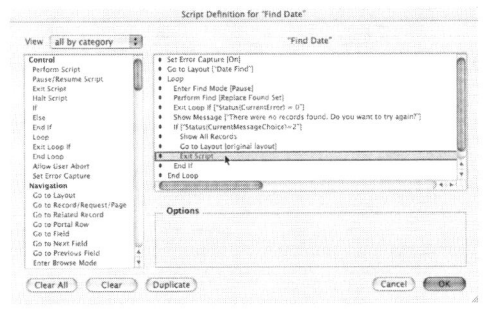

Figure 9.63 If the second button (Cancel) is clicked, the script will exit the loop and return you to the original layout, with all records displayed.

13. From the View drop-down menu, choose "Status functions," then double-click the Status(CurrentMessageChoice) function (**Figure 9.62**).

14. Click to the right of the parentheses and type =2. Click OK.

    The second message button is Cancel, so this script step says that if you choose Cancel in the dialog box, the If step will end.

15. In the Sort/Find/Print section of the step list on the left, double-click Show All Records.

16. In the Navigation section of the step list on the left, double-click Go to Layout.

17. In the step list on the left, double-click Exit Script (**Figure 9.63**).

    These last three steps say that if you don't choose Cancel, the script will reset the file, return you to the layout, and exit the script so you can try again.

    After the End Loop, you can add any commands you want to take place after a successful find.

18. When you're finished, click OK, then Done.

Disabling Toolbars

There may be times, especially in multiuser settings, when you do not want users to have access to the formatting toolbars. With a single script step, you can control whether the toolbars will be available.

In Macintosh OS X, this section is not relevant. For technical reasons known only to Apple, FileMaker toolbars aren't available in OS X. This may be corrected in the future, but as of OS X version 10.2, no toolbars will appear.

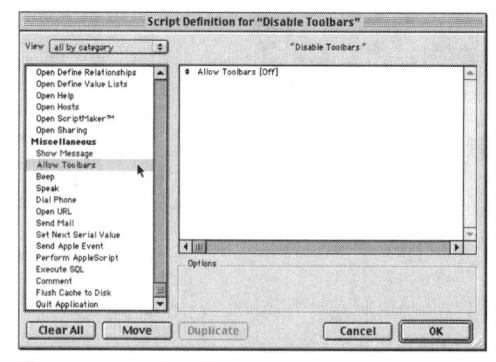

Figure 9.64 Setting Allow Toolbars to Off prevents a user from turning on any toolbars.

To disable toolbars:

1. Choose Scripts > ScriptMaker.

2. When the Define Scripts dialog box appears, type `Disable Toolbars` as the script name and click Create.

3. In the Miscellaneous section of the step list, double-click Allow Toolbars.

4. Leave the option set to Off (**Figure 9.64**). Click OK and then Done.

5. Choose Edit > Preferences > Document.

6. Click the General tab of the Document Preferences dialog box. In the "When opening" section, check the "Perform script" box and choose the Disable Toolbars script (**Figure 9.65**). Click OK.

7. When the database opens, all the options in the Toolbars menu will be disabled (**Figure 9.66**).

If you want to turn toolbar access back on, duplicate the script, change its name to Enable Toolbars and switch the option to On. When that script runs, toolbar access is enabled.

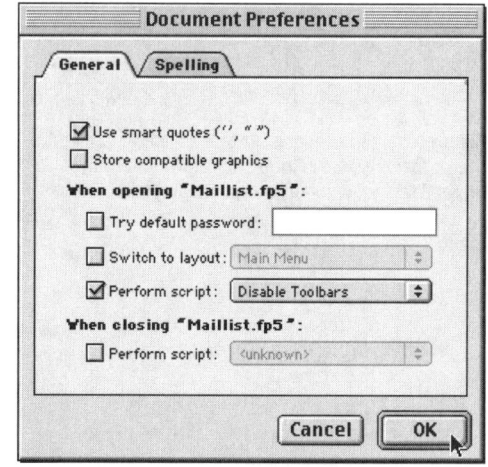

Figure 9.65 Setting the Disable Toolbars script to run when the file opens will disable access automatically.

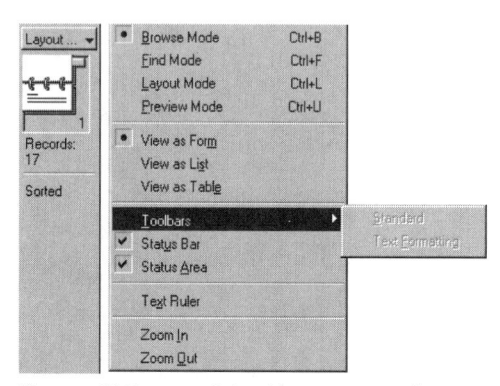

Figure 9.66 Users won't be able to access toolbars after you run the Disable Toolbars script.

Toggle Window Script Options

When you're scripting for both Macintosh and Windows users, you may have noticed that it's irritating to open a file that's been used in one operating system (OS) after the window has been optimized for the other. You can make sure that a window will cover the entire screen when it opens by using the Toggle Window(Maximize) script step in any OS. It allows you to make sure that your database window looks and feels consistent no matter where it's opened.

The commands for minimizing/hiding a window differ depending on which operating system you're using to write the script. Fortunately, the option you choose translates properly when the database is used on a different OS (**Figure 9.67**).

Minimize and Hide

- **Minimize** (Windows) Turns the window into a desktop icon
- **Hide** (Mac OS) Makes the current database window invisible. This is equivalent to choosing Hide Window in the menu bar.

Maximize, Restore, and Unzoom

- **Maximize** Resizes the window to fill the full screen
- **Restore** (Windows) Returns the window to the size it was before minimizing
- **Unzoom** (Mac OS) Returns the window to the size it was before it was hidden

Zoom

- **Zoom** Restores the window to a previously defined size.

Zoom and Unzoom should not be confused with Set Zoom Level, which changes the magnification level of the current screen, but not the size of the window.

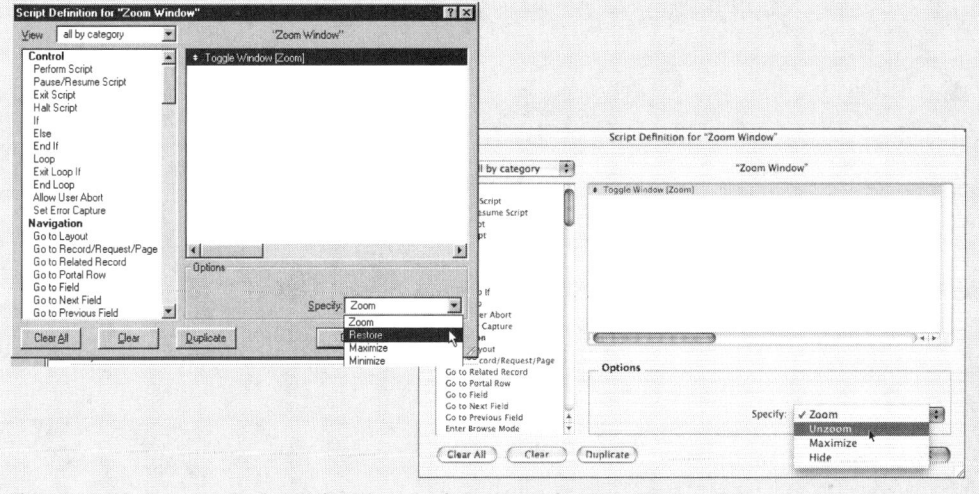

Figure 9.67 The Restore step in Windows is properly interpreted as Unzoom on a Mac.

Script Troubleshooting

10

A script may look fine while you're working on it, but when you run it the results may surprise you: The wrong records print out in the wrong format, the script quits without doing anything, or refuses to quit at all. Sometimes an error is merely an easily fixed annoyance, like forgetting to sort a small found set before creating the script. Other times it wastes reams of paper and printing time, abandons an untrained user in an unfamiliar layout, or permanently corrupts a good database by altering records.

Although scripting looks easy (and often is), the more steps you add, the more likely it is that you've overlooked something. This is particularly true if you have conditional statements and loops. The debugging process can be challenging, especially if you're relatively new to the concept of scripting in general. The best way to prevent script errors is to assume that you're fallible. Build error-checking steps into your process, and the script will give you debugging feedback as it runs. If an error does occur, a well-written script gives you action options, branches to another part of the script or simply exits before something irretrievable happens.

Testing Finished Scripts

It's wise to test a script you've written to see if it performs as intended. However, even test runs can be dangerous if you don't take precautions. Procedures like modifying data in fields or deleting records can't be undone. Follow good testing procedures and you'll never experience the sinking feeling that comes with a misplaced or missing step.

After the script is run, check to see that the proper records were found, that you end up at the correct layout, that the records are properly sorted, or any other results that you intended are properly done.

To test a new script:

1. Choose File > Save a Copy As to make a copy of the database before running the script.

   This first step is the most critical one. If a script modifies data, deletes records or involves any other actions that can't be undone, you should never, ever test it on your only copy of a current database. If all goes as planned, you can delete the copy of the file right after the test.

2. In the Create Copy (Windows)/Create a copy named (Mac) dialog box, choose "copy of current file" in the Save a (Windows)/Type (Macintosh) drop-down menu (**Figure 10.1**). Click Save.

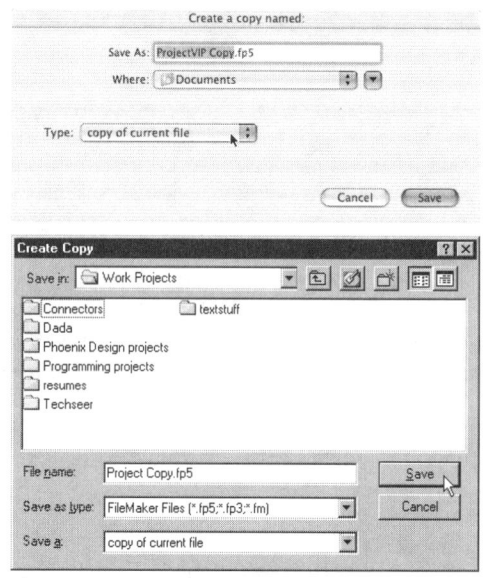

Figure 10.1 The Create a copy named (Mac) or Create Copy (Windows) dialog box lets you save a copy of your file before testing scripts that can alter data.

Script Troubleshooting

3. Choose Scripts > ScriptMaker.

4. In the Define Scripts dialog box, highlight the script in the window and click Perform to test it by running it in the original file (**Figure 10.2**).

   If the script itself seems to run without errors, check the result—layout, printouts, or records—to make sure they're correct.

5. If everything is OK, you're finished. If you find anything wrong, close the file or quit FileMaker. Delete the altered original file. Rename the copy with the original file name.

6. Choose Scripts > ScriptMaker and see "Debugging Scripts" later in this chapter.

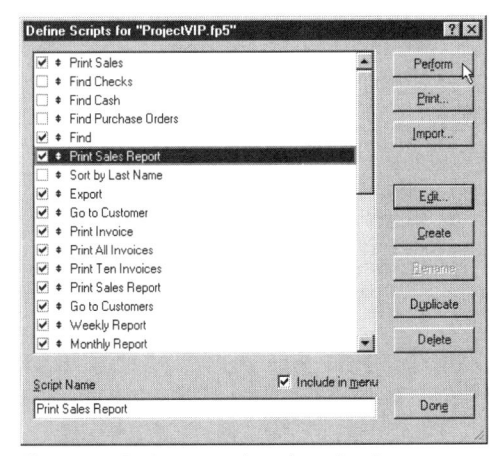

Figure 10.2 Perform runs the selected script.

Chapter 10

Fixing Typical Errors

Some errors are classics: They crop up in every new scripter's efforts and are all very easily fixed. Before you try troubleshooting your scripts from scratch, check this group of suggested problems and their solutions.

To fix missing or wrong records:

1. If the troublesome script is supposed to find a certain set of records, re-create the find, then choose Scripts > ScriptMaker.

2. In the Define Scripts dialog box, double-click the script you want to check.

3. In the Script Definition dialog box, click OK.

4. In the dialog box, click the Replace radio button in Find Requests (**Figure 10.3**).

5. Click OK, then Done.

To fix an incorrect sort:

1. If your script has any Find steps, make sure your find pre-sets are done before the Sort command, then redo your sort.

2. Sort the records, then choose Scripts > ScriptMaker.

3. In the Define Scripts dialog box, double-click the script you want to check.

4. In the Script Definition dialog box, click OK.

5. In the dialog box, click the Replace radio button in Sort Order (**Figure 10.4**).

6. Click OK, then Done.

Figure 10.3 Update the restored find and choose Replace for Find Requests.

Figure 10.4 Click Replace for the sort after you've updated it, or the script definitions won't change.

Figure 10.5 Set the Print/Page Setup options, open the script, and choose Replace when closing.

To fix an incorrect print format:

1. Choose File > Print/Page Setup.

2. Set the print options you want, click OK, then choose Scripts > ScriptMaker.

3. In the Define Scripts dialog box, double-click the script you want to check.

4. In the Script Definition dialog box, click OK.

5. In the dialog box, click the Replace radio button in Print/Page Setup (**Figure 10.5**).

6. Click OK, then Done.

✔ Tip

- The Restore option of the Print/Page Setup step also restores the setting in the Print dialog box that determines what will print—just the current record or each of the records being browsed. If your script is printing more files than you expect, check your printing pre-sets as well as your find and sort settings.

Chapter 10

To make a script end on a different layout:

1. Choose Scripts > ScriptMaker.

2. In the Define Scripts dialog box, double-click the script.

3. In the Script Definition dialog box, highlight the last script step in the assembly window (**Figure 10.6**).

4. In the Navigation section of the step list on the left, double-click Go to Layout.

5. Under Options, choose the layout you want the script to end on from the Specify drop-down menu (**Figure 10.7**). If you want the script to end in the same layout you were in before you ran the script, leave the default, "original layout," specified.

6. Click OK, then OK again in the Keep/Replace dialog box, then Done.

✔ Tip

- If you end a script with a sub-script, the sub-script, in effect, becomes the main script. This can be confusing if the sub-script calls information from another file, because it will leave you in the external file, not the one you ran the script from in the first place. The solution is simple: Add a Navigation script step to the end of the main script. We recommend Go to Layout, using the default option of "original layout" (**Figure 10.8**).

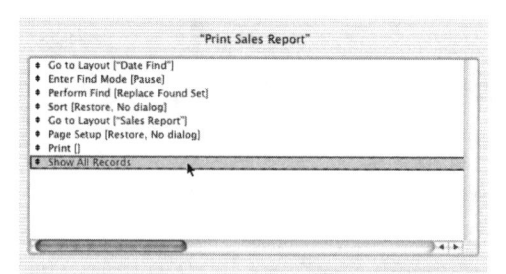

Figure 10.6 You need to select a step to ensure that your new command is inserted in the right place.

Figure 10.7 You can choose any layout as the ending place for the script.

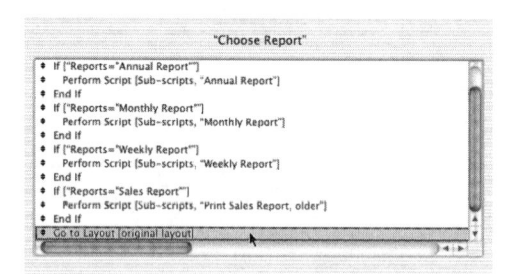

Figure 10.8 If there are no steps after a Perform Script step, the script will not return to the original layout.

258

Script Troubleshooting

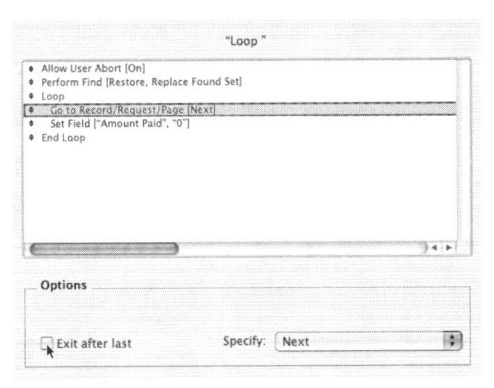

Figure 10.9 Make sure that the script exits after the last record.

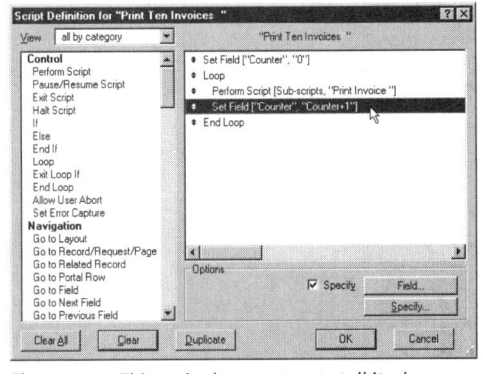

Figure 10.10 This script has no step to tell it when to end.

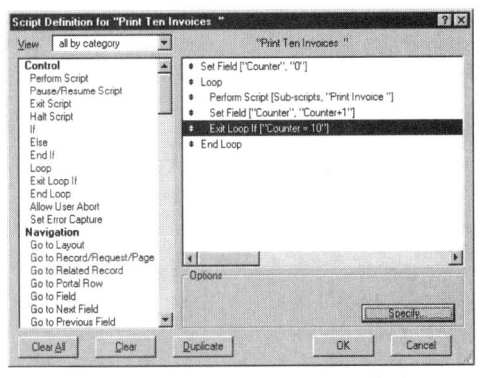

Figure 10.11 Looping scripts need to be told when to exit.

To fix a loop that won't end:

1. Choose Scripts > ScriptMaker.

2. In the Define Scripts dialog box, double-click the script.

3. In the Script Definition dialog box, look for a Go to Record/Request/Page step. If you see one, click to select it.

4. Under Options, check the "Exit after last" check box (**Figure 10.9**). Click OK, then OK again if the Keep/Replace dialog box appears, then Done.

5. If you have no Go to Record/Request/Page step, look for an Exit Loop If step. If you don't find one, click to select the step above the End Loop step (**Figure 10.10**).

6. In the step list on the left, double-click Exit Loop If.

7. Under Options, click Specify to bring up the Specify Calculations dialog box and specify the circumstances under which you want the script to end.

   In our example, we have the loop exit when the counter reaches 10 (**Figure 10.11**).

8. Click OK, then OK again if the Keep/Replace dialog box appears, then Done.

continues on next page

FIXING TYPICAL ERRORS

259

Chapter 10

✔ Tips

- The Allow User Abort script step (**Figure 10.12**) controls whether you can cancel a running script. When you're creating and testing scripts that contain loops, add it as the first line of your script and set its option to On. When the script runs, you can stop it by pressing Escape (Windows) or Command+period (Macintosh). If you have sub-scripts in your script that call steps you might want to cancel, you'll need to place an Allow User Abort step in them and turn it on as well.

- You can cause yourself problems if you cancel a script before it finishes. Caught in mid-stream, an unfinished script leaves an inconsistent database with some records processed and some untouched. To avoid creating problems instead of solving them, remember to turn the Allow User Abort option to Off after you've finished troubleshooting. Otherwise, if your script has a step in it that already includes a pause for input (like a Find request), a Cancel button will appear in the status area and someone could click Cancel instead of Continue (**Figure 10.13**).

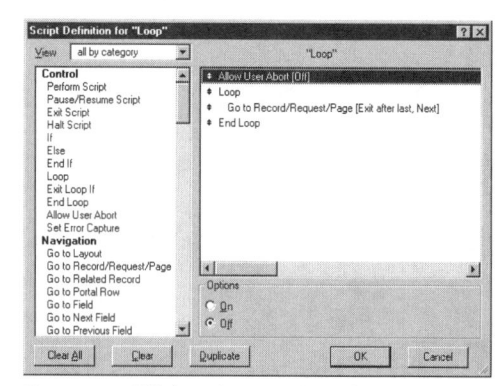

Figure 10.12 This loop has no Exit condition, so it will never end unless you can manually cancel the script.

Figure 10.13 When Allow User Abort is on, the Cancel button appears in Find mode.

Creating an Error Trap Script

FileMaker doesn't always tell you that a scripting error has occurred, or what the error is. For example, if a script has a restored sort that uses a field that is no longer in the database or a Go to Layout step that calls for a deleted or renamed layout, the script will behave unpredictably. Not having a clue to what's wrong with the script, you can waste precious time just narrowing down the nature of the error. To avoid this exasperating experience, create a script that reacts when it finds an error, looks up the error number, and uses the information to give you feedback on what happened.

This script relies on status functions for its effectiveness. A status function takes the pulse of what's happening on your computer at any given time. The Status (CurrentError) function specifically identifies any error code FileMaker generates. FileMaker offers a complete list of Status (CurrentError) numbers in its Help file. We'll use this to create the database of error numbers and descriptions that the error trap script displays.

Once we have the database, we'll create a connection between it and the file whose scripts you want to check, create a layout to display error codes, and write the script you add to existing scripts to test them. Although this process is specific to capturing error codes, parts or all of it can be adapted to create online help for new users or supply read-only information from a Rolodex or customer database in another file.

To create an error trap database from tabular text:

1. Choose Help > Contents and Index.

2. In the Index tab of the Help Topics dialog box (**Figure 10.14**), type err in the box.

   This jumps you to the error messages topic in the index.

3. Double-click "error messages" in the index. On the Mac, this will open a list of subtopics below "error messages." In Windows, this brings up the Topics Found dialog box. Double-click Status (CurrentError) function (**Figure 10.15**).

4. When the Reference page appears, scroll down to the Error Codes list (**Figure 10.16**). Select all the error codes in the list.

5. Copy the list, then close the Help window and launch a word processing program.

6. Create a blank document in the word processor, and paste the list into it.

7. Save the file with Text Only as the file type (**Figure 10.17**) to create a file with no formatting in it, just text and numbers, which can be imported into FileMaker as data for fields.

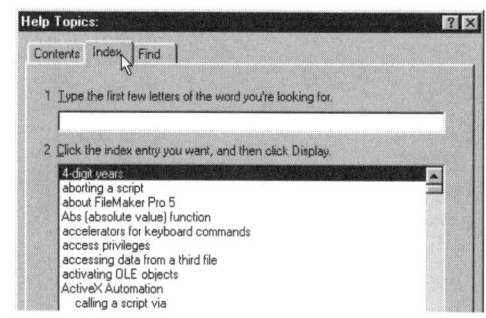

Figure 10.14 Click the Index tab to bring up an alphabetical list of Help topics.

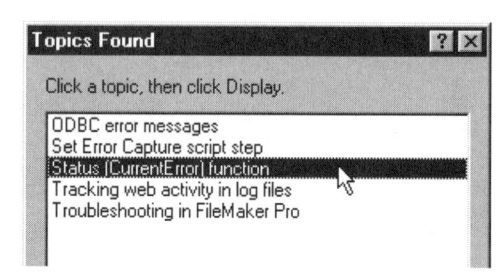

Figure 10.15 Double click Status (CurrentError) to see the list of error numbers and descriptions.

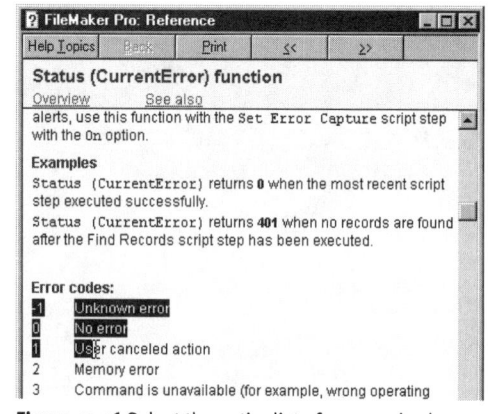

Figure 10.16 Select the entire list of error codes by dragging the mouse down to the end.

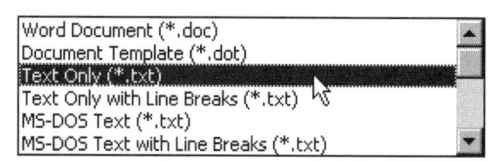

Figure 10.17 Save the file as Text Only so that you can import it into FileMaker.

Script Troubleshooting

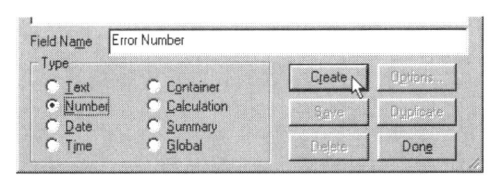

Figure 10.18 Create the field for the error codes and make it a number type.

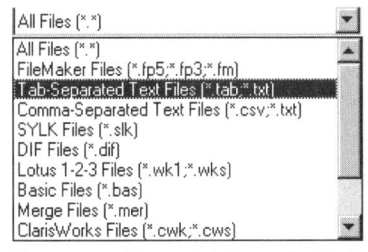

Figure 10.19 Choose Tab-Separated Text Files to keep the error numbers separate from their explanations.

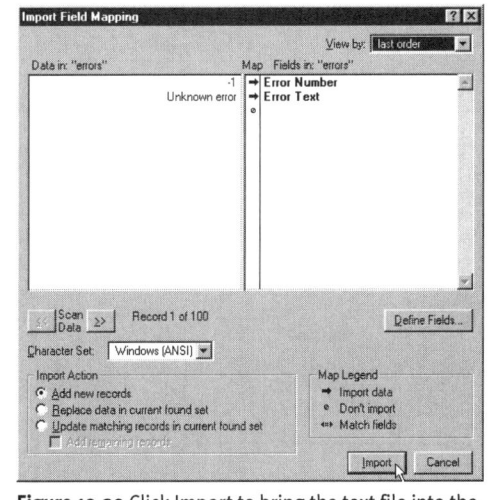

Figure 10.20 Click Import to bring the text file into the database file.

Figure 10.21 The error codes and their matching descriptions will appear in each record.

8. In FileMaker, choose File > New Database. If the template dialog box appears, choose the empty file radio button. Give the file a name and click Save.

9. When the Define Fields dialog box appears, name the field you'll use for the error code (we use Error Number). Select Number as the field type and click Create (**Figure 10.18**).

10. Name the field you'll use for the error description (we use Error Text) for the next field name. Select Text as the field type and click Create. Click Done to finish.

11. FileMaker will add these two fields to Layout #1.

12. Choose File > Import Records > File.

13. In the Open File dialog box, navigate to the text file that holds your error codes and click to select it. Choose Tab-Separated Text Files in the drop-down menu (**Figure 10.19**). This file type eliminates all text formatting except the tabs between the error numbers and their text. Click Open.

14. When the Import Field Mapping dialog box appears, click Import (**Figure 10.20**). The Errors database now contains a record for each Status (CurrentError) code, along with the text description of each error (**Figure 10.21**).

263

To relate the data of one file to another file:

1. In the database whose scripts you want to check for errors, choose File > Define Fields (Control+Shift+D/Command+Shift+D).

2. Enter a field name (we use gError Number), select Global as the field type, and click Create.

3. When the Options for Global Field dialog box appears, choose Number as the data type (**Figure 10.22**). Click OK, then Done to finish.

4. We need to create a relationship to look up the error number description. Choose File > Define Relationships.

5. When the Define Relationships dialog box appears, click New.

6. When the Open File dialog box appears, navigate to the database of error codes and double-click to select and open it (**Figure 10.23**).

7. In the list on the left side of the Edit Relationship dialog box (**Figure 10.24**), click the global field you just created (ours is gError Number). In the list on the right, click the Error Number field. Click OK and then Done.

8. To display the script errors, you need a layout. Choose View > Layout Mode (Control+L/Command+L).

9. Choose Layouts > New Layout (Control+N/Command+N).

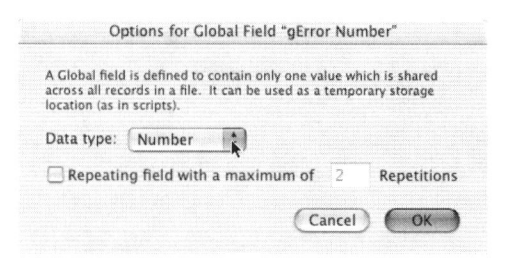

Figure 10.22 Since the gError Number field will contain an error code, choose Number as its type.

Figure 10.23 The relationship will look up the descriptions in the Errors database.

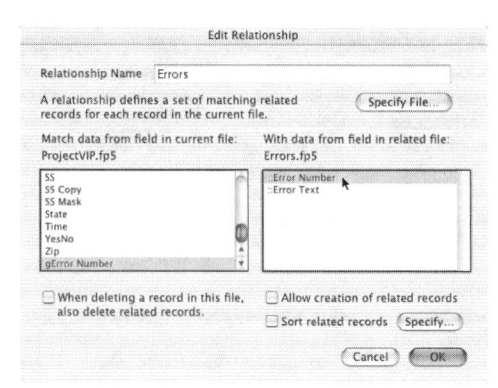

Figure 10.24 The match field for this relationship is gError Number.

Script Troubleshooting

Figure 10.25 Add the gError Number field to the Errors layout to see the error number.

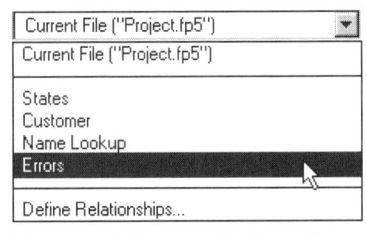

Figure 10.26 Change to the Errors file to add the Error Text field to the layout.

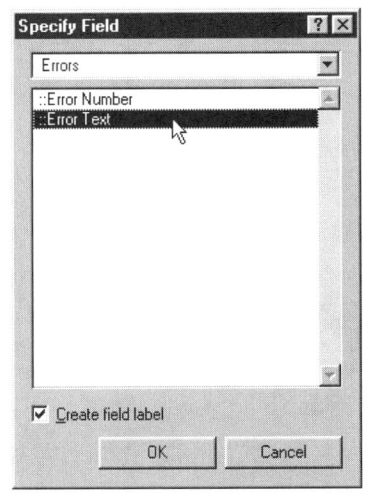

Figure 10.27 The Error Text field will display the error description for the code in the global field.

10. In the New Layout/Report dialog box, type a layout name (we use Error Description). Click "Blank layout" in the "Select a layout type" list. Click Finish.

11. Click the Header tab and drag up until it disappears. Do the same with the Footer tab to leave Body as the only part in your layout.

12. Drag the Field tool into the layout. When the Specify Field dialog box appears, double-click the global field (**Figure 10.25**).

13. In the layout, Control/Option drag the global field to duplicate it. In the Specify Field dialog box, click the Current File drop-down menu and choose Errors (**Figure 10.26**).

14. In the Specify Field dialog box, double-click the Error Text field (**Figure 10.27**).

    You can resize the Error Text field to allow enough room to read the error description. Use the Text tool to add instructions for anyone else who might need to check scripts (**Figure 10.28**).

Figure 10.28 Allow enough room for the Error Text field to display the longest error description.

265

Chapter 10

To create an error trap script:

1. To create the actual error-trapping script, choose Scripts > ScriptMaker.

2. In the Define Scripts dialog box, type a name for the script (we use Error Trap). Click Create.

3. The Script Definition dialog box appears. In the step list on the left, double-click If.

   An If step allows you to test whether or not an error exists.

4. Under Options, click Specify to bring up the Specify Calculation dialog box. In the field list on the left, scroll to gError Number and double-click.

5. In the operators list, click <>. Type a 0 in the formula box (**Figure 10.29**). Click OK.

   This step tells FileMaker to follow certain instructions if the error code number is anything other than zero. (An error code of zero means that there is no error.)

6. In the step list on the left, double-click Go to Layout. Under Options, choose the layout you just created (ours is Error Description) from the drop-down menu (**Figure 10.30**).

7. In the step list on the left, double-click Pause/Resume Script (**Figure 10.31**).

   This step pauses the script to allow you to read the description of the error.

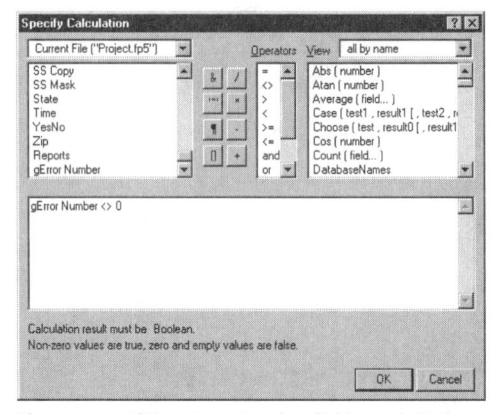

Figure 10.29 If the gError Number field equals 0, then no error occurred and none of the subsequent steps will be executed.

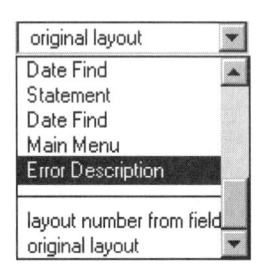

Figure 10.30 If an error has occurred, the script will go to the Error Description layout.

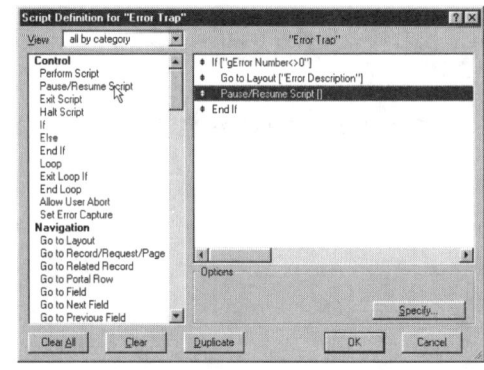

Figure 10.31 The Pause/Resume step waits to let you read the description.

Script Troubleshooting

8. In the step list on the left, scroll down to Fields and double-click Set Field (**Figure 10.32**).

9. Under Options, click the Field button to bring up the Specify Field dialog box; then choose your global field (**Figure 10.33**).

10. Under Options, click Specify to bring up the Specify Calculation window. In the formula box, type a 0. Click OK (**Figure 10.34**).

    This Set Field step resets the global field so the old error won't still be displayed after it's no longer relevant.

11. In the step list on the left, scroll up to Navigation and double-click Go to Layout. From the Specify drop-down menu, choose a layout that you want to switch to after the script finds an error.

12. In the step list on the left, double-click Halt Script to stop all scripts from running (**Figure 10.35**). Click OK and then Done to finish.

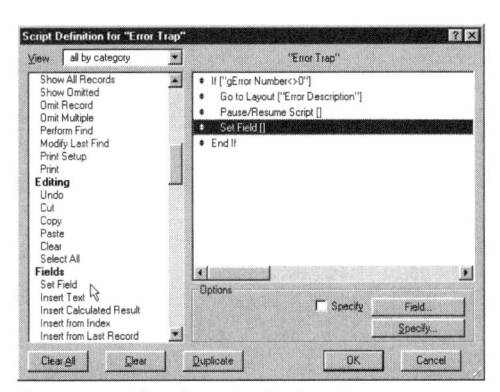

Figure 10.32 After the script displays the error description, you'll want to reset gError Number to 0.

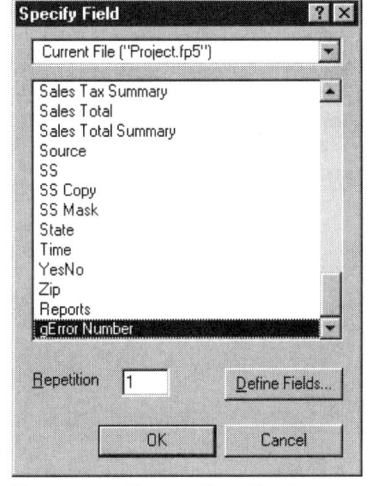

Figure 10.33 Choose gError Number as the field to reset.

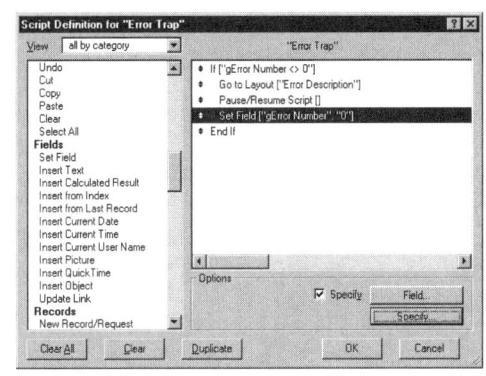

Figure 10.34 "gError Number" is the name of the field, and 0 is the value that clears the field.

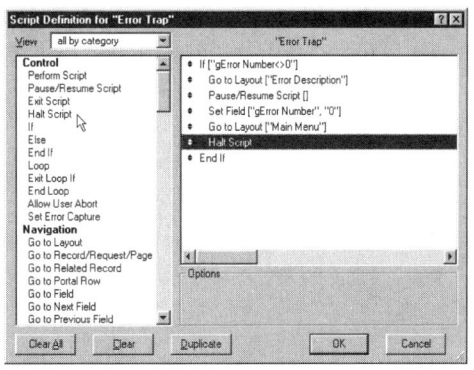

Figure 10.35 The Halt Script step stops both the Error Trap script and the script that called it.

267

Now that you've created a script to explain errors, you need another script that captures the errors themselves and runs the error trap script when they occur.

To use an error trap script in another script:

1. Choose Scripts > ScriptMaker.

2. In the Define Scripts dialog box, double-click a script that you want to test.

3. Click the first step in the Script Definition assembly window. In the step list on the left, double-click Set Error Capture and move it up until it's the first line of the script (**Figure 10.36**).

4. Select the step in the assembly window that may be causing an error. For this example, we use the Sort step.

5. Scroll down to the Fields section of the step list on the left and double-click Set Field.

6. Under Options, click the Field button (**Figure 10.37**). When the Specify Field dialog box appears, choose the global field created in "To relate the data of one file to another file" earlier in this chapter, then click OK.

7. Under Options, click the Specify button to bring up the Specify Calculation dialog box.

8. In the View drop-down menu on the right, scroll down to "Status functions" and click to select it.

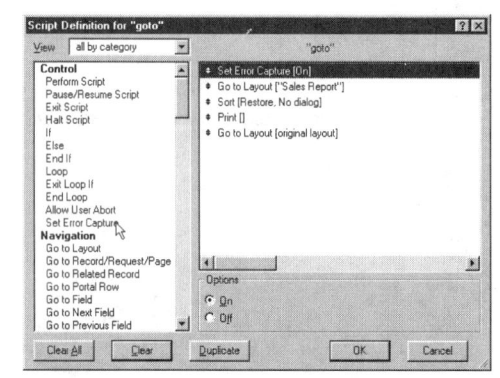

Figure 10.36 In the original script, Set Error Capture must be set to On for the Error Trap script to work.

Figure 10.37 Specify the field to set by clicking Field or checking the Specify check box.

Script Troubleshooting

9. Double-click the Status (CurrentError) function (**Figure 10.38**). Click OK.

   This Set Field step replaces whatever is in the global field with the error number FileMaker finds.

10. In the step list on the left, double-click Perform Script. Under Options, choose the Error Trap script (**Figure 10.39**).

11. Click OK, then OK again to keep your pre-sets.

12. Highlight the script you just added the Error Trap to, and click Perform to run it.

If everything goes well, the script will run without an error code, meaning that there's nothing functionally wrong with your script. If there's a problem that causes a FileMaker error, you'll see it in the Error layout and the script will pause.

✔ Tip

- Sometimes a perfectly good script goes bad because one of the elements it needs—like an external file—has been moved. To guard against such problems, you can use Show Message (see "To show error messages with customized choices" in Chapter 9). This step allows you to offer the option of manually locating the missing file in the Open File dialog box if the script doesn't initially find it.

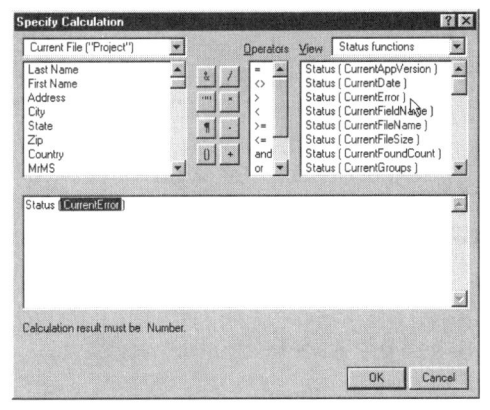

Figure 10.38 The field gError Number is set to Status (CurrentError) before the Error Trap script is run.

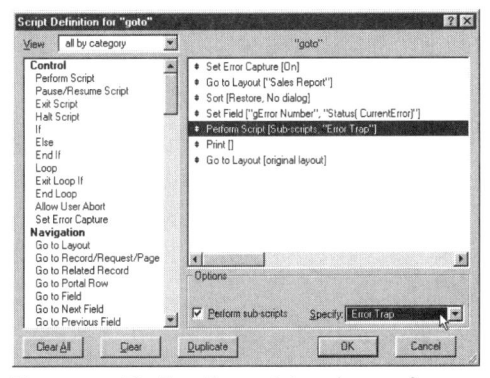

Figure 10.39 The Error Trap script can be run after any step that might generate an error.

Chapter 10

Debugging Scripts

Debugging is the process of figuring out what the error message you're getting actually means, how it relates to what you've done in your script, and what you need to do to correct it. Although an error capture script can help you with the first step, you have to apply that knowledge to your specific situation.

In addition, not all script problems generate error codes. Everything in the script can be technically correct (no missing fields, no endless loops, no problem sorts) and still not do what you want it to do. When that happens, you need to debug the script from scratch.

There are three major places to check when a script goes wrong:

- **The pre-sets.** The easiest error to make is forgetting to set your sort, find, or print options before creating the script. Checking your pre-sets is the first debugging step if you have no error codes but your script doesn't give you the records you expect.

- **Step order.** It's easy to add a step in the wrong place, particularly if you're adapting an existing script. Using the Pause Script, Halt Script, and Exit Script steps, you can stop a script at any stage to isolate the problem.

  Pause Script stops everything until you click Continue or Exit in the status area. You can set several Pause Script steps in strategic places in a long script to help you figure out where to concentrate your debugging efforts. The Exit step stops a running sub-script and returns you to the main script. This helps you figure out whether your problems are in the main script or are really based in the sub-script it uses. The Halt step brings all scripts to an end at whatever point you place it. Halt is particularly useful for troubleshooting loops.

- **Conditional statements.** Even the best script-makers occasionally put the item they want as the Else condition into the If step instead. When you have a nested If script (one If step inside another), it's all too easy to get confused. An error-trapping script is particularly useful in troubleshooting an If statement.

To see pre-sets in existing scripts:

1. Run the script through to the end.

2. Choose Records > Sort (Control+S/Command+S).

3. When the Sort Records dialog box appears, the setting that appears in Sort Order (**Figure 10.40**) is the one that was used by the script.

You can also use this technique to view restored settings for Page/Print Setup, Find, Import, and Export by using the relevant menu choices in step 2.

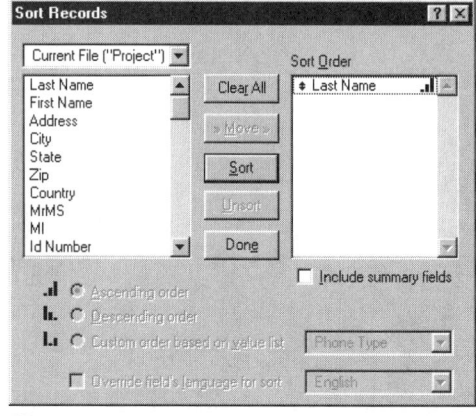

Figure 10.40 When you do a manual sort, the default sort order will be the same as the last sort.

Script Troubleshooting

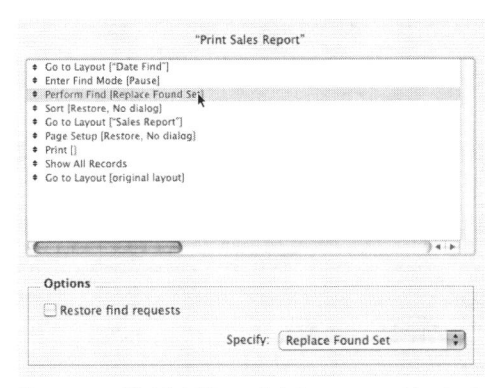

Figure 10.41 Highlight the script step you want to check.

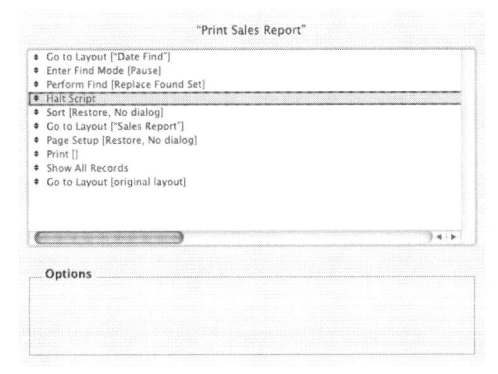

Figure 10.42 The Halt command will stop a script where ever you place it.

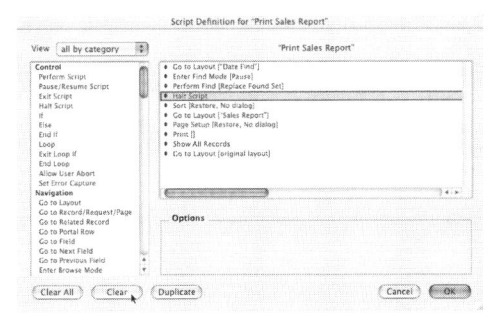

Figure 10.43 After you've debugged the script, remove the Halt step.

To use the Halt, Pause, or Exit Script commands:

1. Choose Scripts > ScriptMaker.

2. Double-click the script you want to check. Our example, Print Sales Report, has a restored find, and we want to check which records the script found.

3. In the assembly window in the Script Definition dialog box, click to select the step that you want to check. In our example, it's Perform Find (**Figure 10.41**).

4. Double-click Halt Script in the step list on the left (**Figure 10.42**). Click OK, and then OK again in the Keep/Replace dialog box.

5. In the Define Scripts dialog box, click Perform to run the script.

   The script will end where you inserted the Halt step. Check the conditions at that point to see if there is a problem.

6. Choose Scripts > ScriptMaker and return to the Script Definition dialog box to make any changes.

7. Repeat steps 5 and 6 until your script runs perfectly.

8. When you're finished, return to the Script Definition dialog box. Click the Halt step that you inserted. Click Clear (**Figure 10.43**).

9. Click OK and then Done.

✔ Tips

- To use Pause or Exit Script, substitute these commands for the Halt step.

- There's no way to see the restored find request in ScriptMaker. But you can insert an Exit Script step after the Perform Find (Restore) and then use the Modify Last Find command manually to see what the restored find criterion is.

271

Chapter 10

Printing Scripts

Once you've debugged a script, particularly if it's a long and complex one, you can print it out for future reference. Having printed copies makes it easier to locate a script you want to use as a basis for a new script, particularly if you run several related files or different databases. It also makes it easy to reconstruct a complicated script if something nasty happens to your database and you have to reconstruct it from an earlier version. You can print scripts individually or all at once.

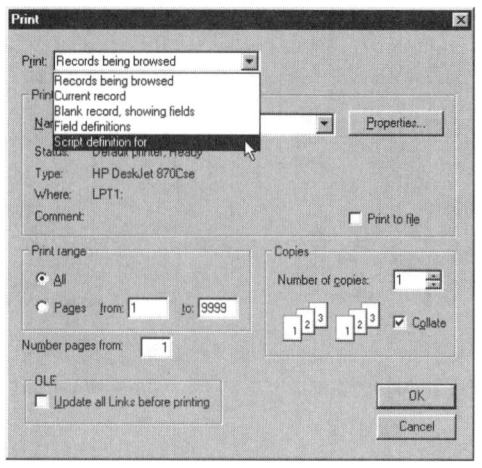

Figure 10.44 Set the Print option to "Script definition for."

To print a script in Windows:

1. Choose File > Print.
2. In the Print drop-down menu, choose "Script definition for" (**Figure 10.44**).
3. In the script drop-down menu, leave the default "all scripts" or choose a specific script to print (**Figure 10.45**).
4. Click OK to print the script(s).

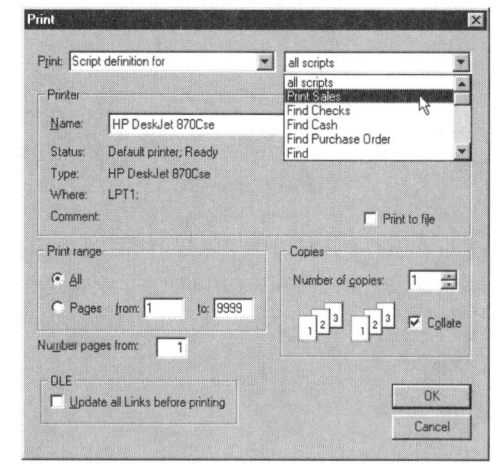

Figure 10.45 You can choose to print all of the scripts in the database or just one.

Script Troubleshooting

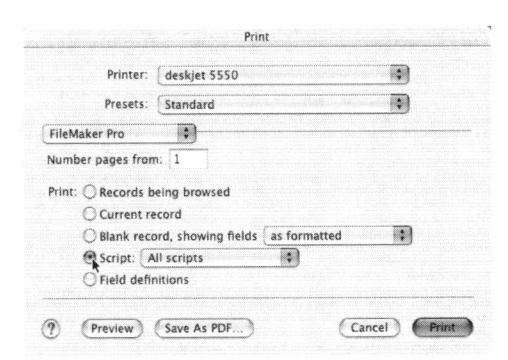

Figure 10.46 The Print Script radio button will print the script definitions.

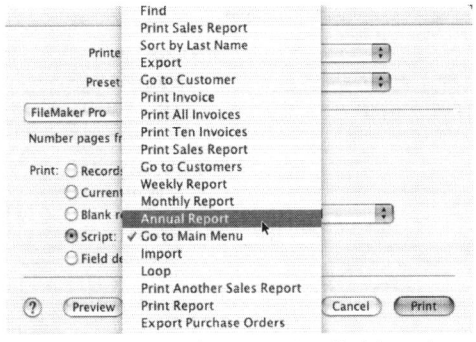

Figure 10.47 You can choose to print all of the scripts in the database or just one.

To print a script on the Macintosh:

1. Choose File > Print.

2. In the Print: section at the bottom of the dialog box, click the Script radio button (**Figure 10.46**).

3. In the Script drop-down menu, leave the default "All scripts" or choose a specific script to print (**Figure 10.47**).

4. Click OK to print the script(s).

PRINTING SCRIPTS

273

Changing and Adapting Scripts

There are only so many different ways you can sort and print a report. Rather than re-create the scripting wheel every time, it makes a lot more sense to duplicate an already debugged script, then adapt it for new uses.

To change pre-sets for a script:

1. Create new Find, Sort, or Print settings.

2. Choose Scripts > ScriptMaker. In the Define Scripts dialog box, double-click the script you want to change.

3. In the Script Definition dialog box, click OK.

4. In the dialog box that appears, choose which settings to keep and which to replace, and click OK. Click Done to finish.

To adapt an existing script:

1. If the new script involves restored Find, Sort, or Print settings, set these manually before working on the script.

2. Choose Scripts > ScriptMaker. In the Define Scripts dialog box, click to select the script on which you want to base the new script. Click Duplicate (**Figure 10.48**).

3. Type a new name for the script and click Rename (**Figure 10.49**).

4. Double-click the new script name to bring up the Script Definition dialog box. Make any changes that are required.

5. Click OK when you're finished. If there are restored settings in the script, choose which settings to keep and which to replace in the dialog box, and click OK (**Figure 10.50**). Click Done to finish.

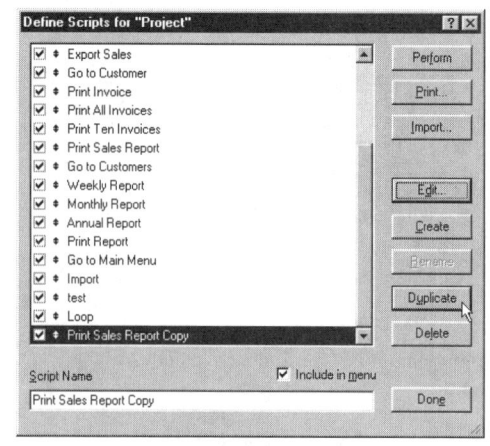

Figure 10.48 When you duplicate a script, it will create a script with the same name plus "Copy."

Figure 10.49 Make sure that you click Rename and not Create.

Figure 10.50 Click Replace for the restored settings that you want to change.

FileMaker and Other Programs

Whenever you import or export a spreadsheet file, you're using FileMaker to communicate with other software. This transfer of information is important, but it's limited and indirect. You're forced to create a new file in a format that both programs can read, and only unformatted text and numeric information is transferable. Sometimes that's enough, like when you just want to export a list of names and numbers. But when tempting data sits out of reach in industrial-strength databases while you re-create the parts you need, you can really feel hemmed in by these limitations.

Rest assured—there are work-arounds for many applications. In some cases FileMaker itself provides links to other information, either with its built-in flexibility or through plug-ins that come with it. Scripting is also key to unlocking access to other programs, their formats, and their data. Using scripting, you can not only transfer files to and from other programs, you can embellish the information with formatting and manipulate the programs themselves.

Using Scripts to Send Email

FileMaker isn't an email program, but you can make it act as if it were. If you're using one of the following email applications as your default email software, FileMaker can access it from within your database.

MACINTOSH	WINDOWS
Eudora	Eudora
Claris Emailer	Exchange
Outlook	Outlook
Entourage	All MAPI-compliant email programs

You'll notice a glaring omission. Unfortunately, AOL software does not work directly with FileMaker's Send Mail scripting command. However, Macintosh AOL users can use Claris Emailer to send mail from FileMaker. There are also third-party FileMaker add-ons that can circumvent the need to use an email application. See Appendix A for download information.

If you have fields for an email address and an Internet URL in a contact database, FileMaker scripting can give you direct access to your customers. First you need to set up an email-message layout, then set up the script that will actually send the message.

Before you follow these instructions, add three additional text fields to the database file you plan to use: cc:, Subject, and Body. With these fields, you'll be able to create a FileMaker layout similar to the window you use to send mail in your email software.

To create an email layout:

1. Choose View > Layout Mode (Control+L/Command+L).

2. Choose Layouts > New Layout/Report (Control+N/Command+N).

3. When the New Layout/Report dialog box appears, give the layout a name (we use Email). Click "Blank layout" in the "Select a layout type" menu. Click Finish.

4. Drag the Header and Footer tabs up until they disappear. Drag the Body tab down to fill the screen.

5. Drag the Field tool into the layout. Choose your email address field from the Specify Field dialog box (**Figure 11.1**). Click OK.

6. Holding the Control/Option key, drag the Email Address field to duplicate it.

7. When the Specify Field dialog box appears, double-click the cc: field to choose it (**Figure 11.2**).

Figure 11.1 Add the email address field to the Email layout by choosing it in the Specify Field dialog box.

Figure 11.2 After duplicating the first field, specify a different field for the copy.

FileMaker and Other Programs

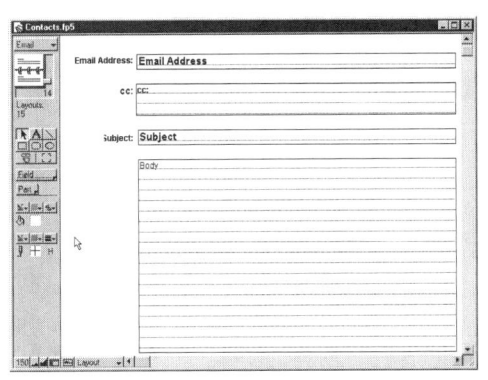

Figure 11.3 Enlarge the fields to allow room for the longest sections you expect to need.

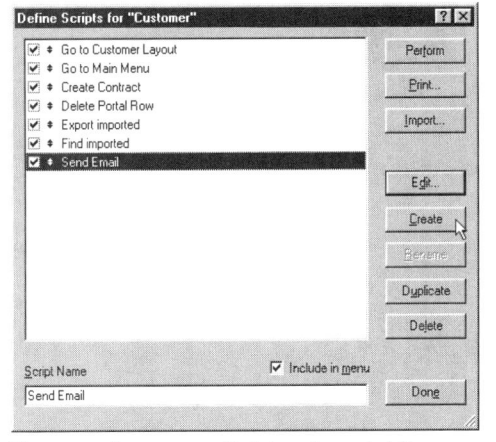

Figure 11.4 Type a name that describes what the script does.

Figure 11.5 Add the Send Mail step to the script.

8. Repeat steps 6 and 7 for the Subject and Body fields.

 When creating the Body field, uncheck the "Create field label" check box.

9. Resize all the fields as necessary to allow enough room for addresses and the text of an email message (**Figure 11.3**).

To use these fields to compose and send a message, see "To create an email script" below.

To create an email script:

1. Choose Scripts > ScriptMaker.

2. In the Define Scripts dialog box, enter a name for your script (we use Send Email). Click Create (**Figure 11.4**).

3. The Script Definition dialog box will appear. In the script step list on the left, scroll down to Miscellaneous and double-click Send Mail (**Figure 11.5**).

4. In the script assembly box, double-click the Send Mail step to bring up the Specify Mail dialog box.

5. In the To: section, click the Field Value radio button (**Figure 11.6**).

continues on next page

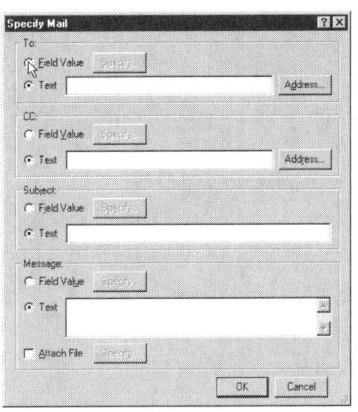

Figure 11.6 Choose Field Value to use an email address from your database.

277

Chapter 11

6. When the Specify Field dialog box appears, choose your email address field from the scrolling list. Under Records, click the "Use current record" radio button (**Figure 11.7**). Click OK.

7. Repeat steps 5 and 6 for the cc:, Subject, and Message sections, choosing the appropriate fields in the Specify Fields dialog box (**Figure 11.8**). Click OK to finish.

   When you return to the Script Definition dialog box, the Send Mail script line will include the name of your subject field in quotes (**Figure 11.9**).

8. Check "Perform without dialog" under Options to queue or send the messages without having to interact with the email program itself (**Figure 11.10**).

   If you leave this box unchecked, the message will open in your email program and wait for you to manually send it. If you expect to send attachments occasionally, you might prefer to leave the box unchecked so you can do this selectively in the email program.

9. Click OK, and then Done to finish. When you run the script, FileMaker will send the data you entered into the appropriate fields in your email program.

✔ **Tip**

- To add a Send button so you can run the script with one click from the email layout, follow the instructions in "To create a button for a script" in Chapter 9.

Figure 11.7 Since you'll only want to send email to the person in the open record, choose the "Use current record" setting.

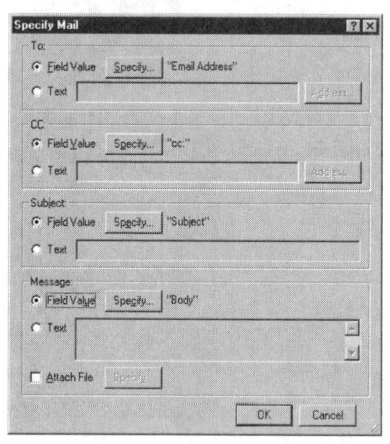

Figure 11.8 To use the contents of the fields to fill in the email data, specify each field.

Figure 11.9 Send Mail selects your subject line as the email reference information.

Figure 11.10 If you want to review the contents of the message in your email program before it is sent, leave the "Perform without dialog box" unchecked.

278

FileMaker and Other Programs

Using Scripts to Send Bulk Email

By adapting the script created in "To create an email script" in the previous section, you can create a script to send email to every person in an entire database or within a found set.

To send bulk email:

1. Follow the steps in "To create an email script."

2. If you want to send bulk email to only a subset of people, do a find to create a found set of the contacts you want to reach.

3. Choose Scripts > ScriptMaker.

4. In the Define Scripts dialog box, click the script you just created, and then click Duplicate (**Figure 11.11**).

5. Rename the script, then click Rename. We call our new script Broadcast Email.

6. Double-click the new script to open the Script Definition dialog box.

7. In the script assembly window on the right, click the Send Mail step.

8. Because bulk email can be interpreted as spam (junk email) or cause embarrassment if you run this script by mistake, we'll insert a dialog box to confirm that you really want to run this script. In the script step list on the left, scroll down to Miscellaneous and double-click Show Message (**Figure 11.12**).

9. Move the Show Message step above Send Mail, then double-click it (**Figure 11.13**).

continues on next page

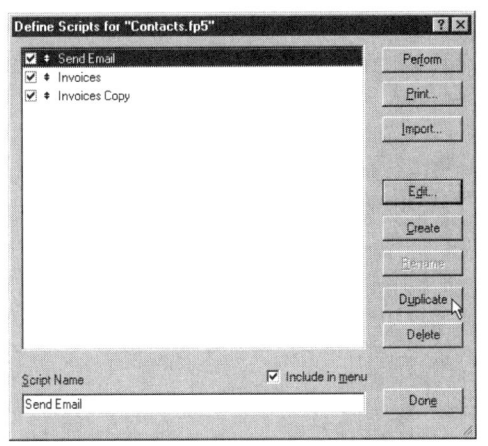

Figure 11.11 Since this script is very similar to an existing one, it's easier to duplicate the original and edit it than to create a new script from scratch.

Figure 11.12 Use Show Message to add a dialog box prompt to confirm that you want to send bulk email.

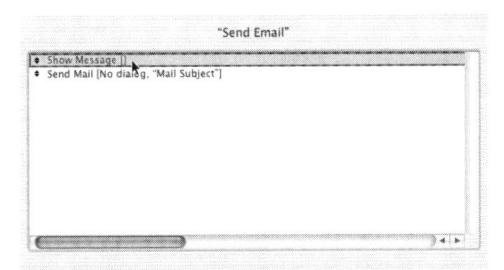

Figure 11.13 Your message should appear before your Send Mail step takes place.

279

Chapter 11

10. When the Specify Message dialog box appears, type a message like "Are you sure you want to send this email to everyone?" in the Message Text box (**Figure 11.14**).

11. In the Button Captions section, type No in the First (default) box and Yes in the Second box (**Figure 11.15**). Click OK.

12. In the script step list on the left in the Script Definition dialog box, scroll up to the Control section and double-click If (**Figure 11.16**). In the Options section, click Specify.

13. When the Specify Calculation dialog box appears, click the View drop-down menu on the right and choose "Status functions."

14. In the list of status functions, double-click the Status (CurrentMessageChoice) function (**Figure 11.17**).

Figure 11.14 The message text warns that the email will be sent to everyone in the found set.

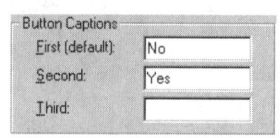

Figure 11.15 The default is set to No, the least dangerous choice.

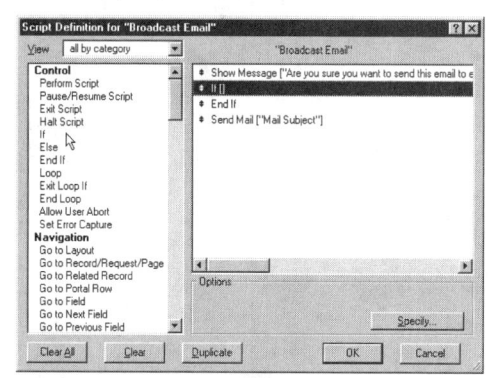

Figure 11.16 The If step will check which button the user clicked and act accordingly.

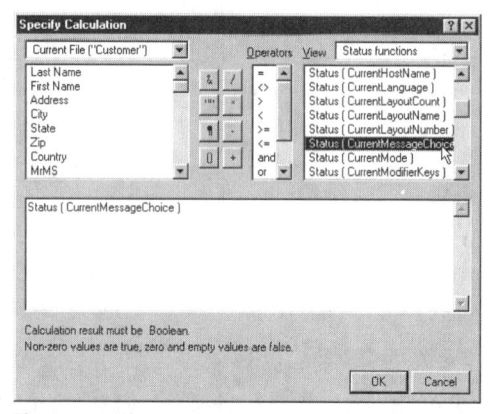

Figure 11.17 The CurrentMessageChoice status function returns a number corresponding to the button you click in the message box.

280

FileMaker and Other Programs

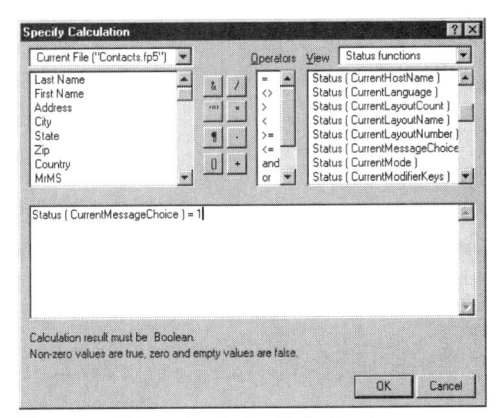

Figure 11.18 The value for the No button is 1.

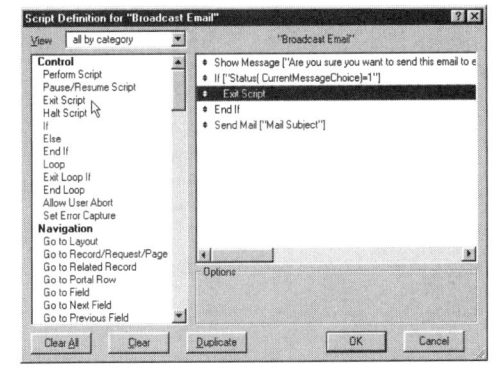

Figure 11.19 If the choice is No, the script ends without sending the email.

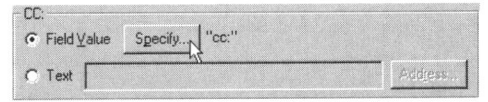

Figure 11.20 The Field Value for the cc: option is where you'll put the bulk mail addresses.

15. Click to the right of the parentheses. Double-click the = operator button, then type 1 (**Figure 11.18**). Click OK.

    This step sets the default choice to No, so you won't send bulk email unless you're certain you want to.

16. In the script step list on the left, double-click Exit Script (**Figure 11.19**). In the script assembly window, double-click the Send Mail step.

17. When the Specify Mail dialog box appears, click the Specify button in the cc: section (**Figure 11.20**).

18. When the Specify Field dialog box appears, choose your email address field from the scrolling list.

continues on next page

281

19. Click the "Use all records in found set" radio button (**Figure 11.21**).

20. Click OK to save the change. Click OK to close the Specify Mail dialog box, OK again and then Done.

When you run this script, the message you typed in the Show Message dialog box appears (**Figure 11.22**). If you click No, nothing will happen. If you click Yes, FileMaker creates an email message addressed to the person in the current record with the addresses of everyone else in the found set entered in the cc: section (**Figure 11.23**).

✔ Tips

- If you've already added a Send button to the Email layout, add a Broadcast button to the same layout to make it easy to choose between the two scripts.

- Normally when sending bulk email, you would want to put the list of addresses in the bcc: (blind carbon copy) line so that the recipients will not be able to see the addresses for the other recipients. Since FileMaker does not have a bcc option, the list of email addresses will be visible. If your list is very long, or private, uncheck the "Perform without dialog" option in the Send Mail script step. You can then cut and paste the list from the cc: to the bcc: line in your email application.

- Sometimes when you're sending email, you'll want to attach a file. If you do this all the time, return to the script and double-click the Send Mail step to reopen the Specify Mail dialog box. Click the Attach File box in the Message section (**Figure 11.24**). When the Open dialog box appears, navigate to the file you want to attach, click OK to save the change, then exit ScriptMaker.

Figure 11.21 "Use all records in found set" will insert all the current email addresses into the cc: section of the email.

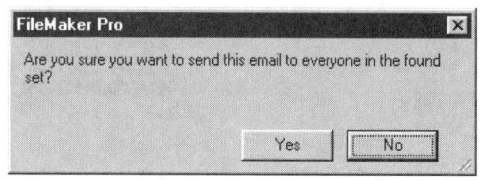

Figure 11.22 Without the message, you could send bulk email by mistake.

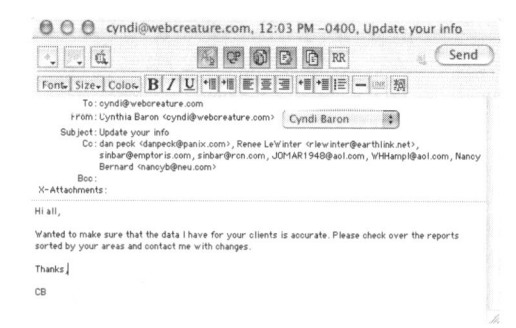

Figure 11.23 The cc: section contains all the addresses except the current record.

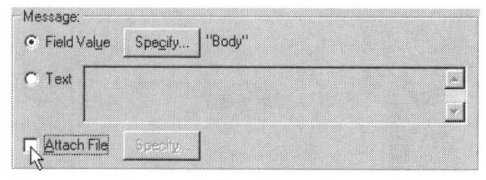

Figure 11.24 You can bulk-mail attachments by choosing the Attach File check box.

FileMaker and Other Programs

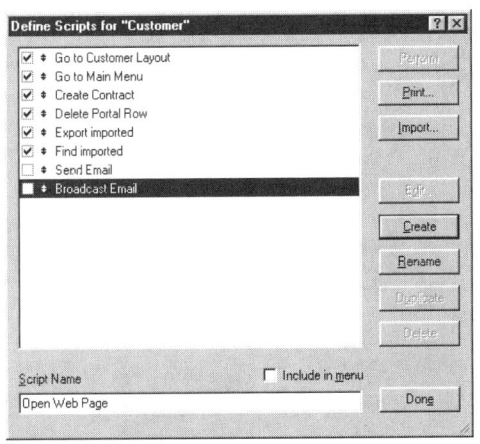

Figure 11.25 Create a new script to open a Web page in a browser.

Figure 11.26 The Open URL step tells your default browser software to open.

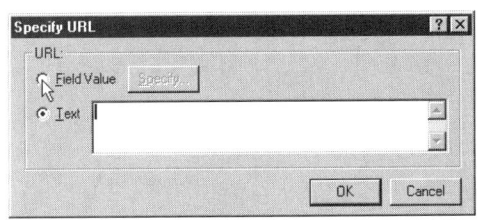

Figure 11.27 The Specify URL dialog box will open the URL for the current record.

Using a Script to Open URLs

Many of the companies and people in your contact list have a Web page. If it lists pricing, products, or other useful data, you might want to have easy access to it when you examine the customer accounts. If you have a URL field for the entry, you can create a script to open the Web page in your default browser.

To use a script to open a Web page:

1. Choose Scripts > ScriptMaker.

2. In the Define Scripts dialog box, name the new script (we use Open Web Page). Click Create (**Figure 11.25**).

3. The Script Definition Dialog appears. In the step list on the left, scroll down to Miscellaneous and double-click Open URL (**Figure 11.26**).

4. Under Options, click the "Perform without dialog" check box, then click the Specify button.

5. When the Specify URL dialog box appears (**Figure 11.27**), click the Field Value radio button.

continues on next page

283

Chapter 11

6. In the Specify Field dialog box, double-click the field that contains Web addresses (ours is URL; **Figure 11.28**). Click OK.

   If necessary, you can click the Define Fields button to create a URL field.

7. Click OK to save the script, then Done to finish.

✔ Tips

- To add a convenient button that will run the script, follow the instructions in "To create a button for a script" in Chapter 9. Although you can name this button anything you'd like, "Go" is short, sweet, and familiar to anyone using the Internet (**Figure 11.29**).

- Although we used a Web URL in this example, you can use this script to open an FTP site or any other type of address that an Internet utility (like Fetch or Gopher) understands. As long as the field data is properly formatted, the script will open the appropriate application.

Figure 11.28 Specify the field that contains your Web addresses.

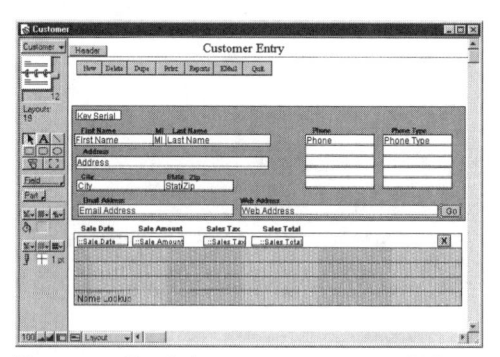

Figure 11.29 The Go button appears on many Web pages.

Exporting Data to Static HTML Tables

In Chapter 17, we show you how to use FileMaker directly on the World Wide Web. But sometimes you just want to export data from FileMaker to a simple HTML table. If that's all you need to do, you can create a file with data and HTML Table tags using the Export command.

To create an HTML table:

1. In the database with the table data, sort the records as you want them to appear.

2. Choose File > Export Records.

3. In the Export Records to File dialog box, type a name for the export file and choose HTML Table Files as the Save as type (**Figure 11.30**). Click Save.

4. The Specify Field Order for Export dialog box will appear. In the field list on the left, double-click to choose the fields you want to include in the table (**Figure 11.31**). Click Export.

If you open the exported HTML file in your Web browser, it will appear as a table (**Figure 11.32**). The actual contents of the file are in HTML code that can be inserted into any other Web page (**Figure 11.33**).

Figure 11.30 Choosing HTML Table Files formats the field contents with an HTML <TABLE> tag.

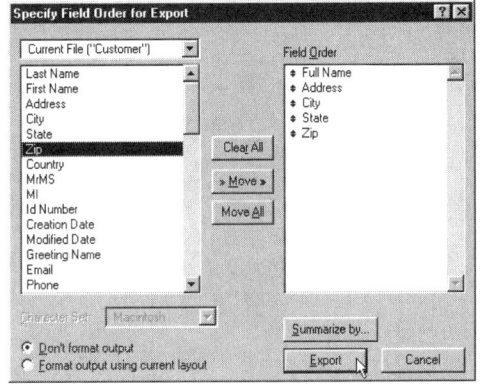

Figure 11.31 Choose the fields you want to export to the table.

Figure 11.32 The exported file appears with the HTML <TABLE> tag defaults.

Figure 11.33 The new file contains field data surrounded by HTML code.

Exporting Formatted Text

When you use the Export command in FileMaker, you create a text file without any of the formatting specifications that you created in your layouts.

Using calculation fields, you can embellish that raw data if you're exporting the text to a program like QuarkXPress that supports formatting tags. Being able to control typographic setup when you export records can improve your communication with a designer who's using the material to create an annual report, or simply save your own precious time by not having to redefine basic hierarchies of information in a page layout program.

As an example of how to export Quark-style tags, we'll add tags to name and address fields to make the names bold and the addresses italic.

To include format tags in exported text:

1. In the file you want to export as formatted text, choose File > Define Fields (Control+Shift+D/Command+Shift+D).

2. In the Define Fields dialog box, type a field name (we use Formatted Name). Click the Calculation radio button for field type (**Figure 11.34**). Click Create.

3. When the Specify Calculation dialog box appears, click the quotes operator button. Double-click the <> brackets operator (**Figure 11.35**). Insert your cursor within the brackets and type B.

    The <> operator is also the universally recognized symbol for a font formatting tag. Formatting tags act as toggles, so this <B> turns on the bold style.

4. Click to the right of the quotes and click the ampersand (&) button (**Figure 11.36**).

Figure 11.34 You need a calculation to specify formatting tags.

Figure 11.35 The <> symbol can be found in the Operators list.

Figure 11.36 Use the & button to connect different portions of a formula.

Figure 11.37 The comma and space must be inside quotes.

Figure 11.38 The second bold tag turns off the bold style.

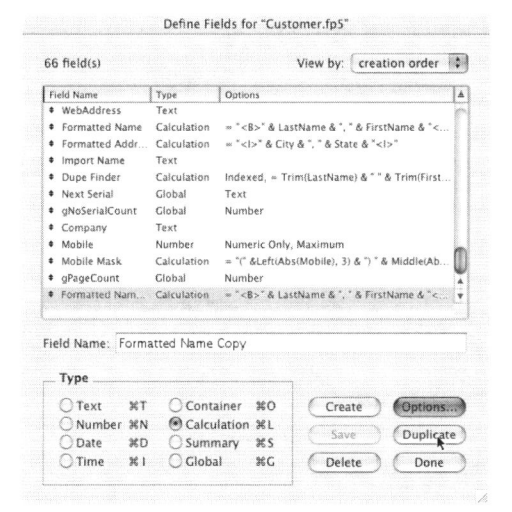

Figure 11.39 Duplicating and changing the Formatted Name field is easier than creating the second field from scratch.

5. Click to the right of the ampersand. Double-click the Last Name field in the field list.

6. Click the ampersand button and then the quotes button. Type a comma and a space between the quotes (**Figure 11.37**).

   You must put quotes around any non-field characters so they won't be mistaken for a field or operator.

7. Click to the right of the quotes and click the ampersand button. Double-click the First Name field in the field list.

8. Click the ampersand button and then the quotes button. Double-click the <> operator. Insert your cursor within the brackets and type B (**Figure 11.38**). This second formatting tag toggles the bold style off. Click OK.

   This first formula creates a format that will make the field text export like this: **Smith, Patti**

9. When the Define Fields dialog box returns, click the Formatted Name field and click Duplicate (**Figure 11.39**).

continues on next page

287

Chapter 11

10. Change the field name to Formatted Address and click Create (**Figure 11.40**). Double-click the Formatted Address field.

11. In the Specify Calculation dialog box, change both <B>s to <I>s (**Figure 11.41**). Doing this changes the toggled style to italic.

12. Select the Last Name field in the formula and double-click the City field in the field list (**Figure 11.42**).

13. Select the First Name field in the formula and double-click the State field in the field list (**Figure 11.43**). Click OK, and then Done to finish.

    The address information will export in this format: *New York City, NY*

Figure 11.40 Save your edited changes.

Figure 11.41 Change the bold tags to italic tags by editing the letter inside the angle brackets.

Figure 11.43 The completed formula replaces the formatting tags and fields with new ones.

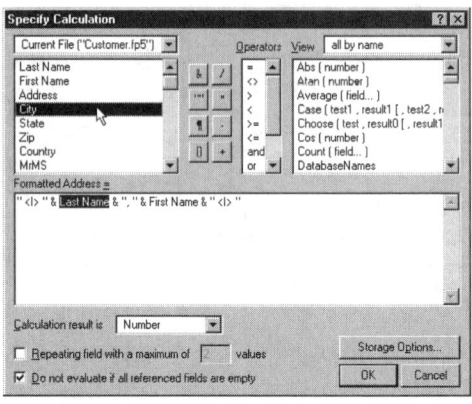

Figure 11.42 Select only the field name, then replace it with a different field.

288

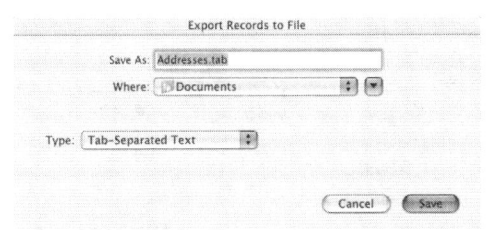

Figure 11.44 Choose Tab-Separated Text as the file type to insert tabs, not spaces, between each field.

Figure 11.45 Specify the formatted fields, not the original ones, for export.

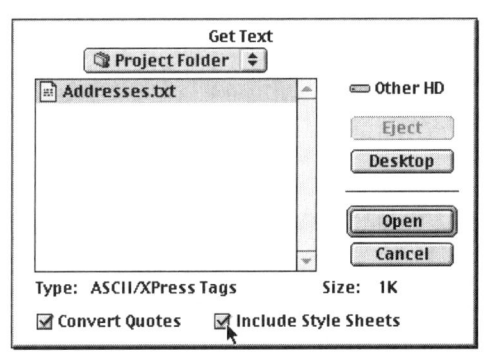

Figure 11.46 Include Style Sheets will interpret the formatting tags properly when the text is placed in a Quark document.

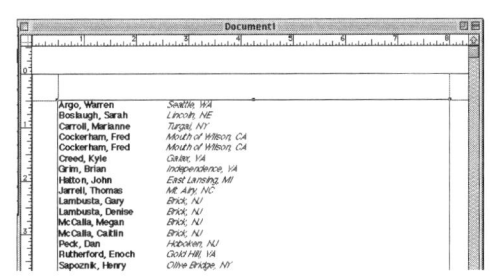

Figure 11.47 This is how the imported text will look in Quark.

To export formatted fields to a text file:

1. Once you have a calculation that adds format tags to your data, choose the records to export and sort them.

2. Choose File > Export Records.

3. In the Export Records to File dialog box, type a name for the export file. Click in the file type drop-down menu and choose Tab-Separated Text (**Figure 11.44**). Click Save.

4. In the Specify Field Order for Export dialog box, double-click the Formatted Name and Formatted Address fields in the field list on the left. Click Export (**Figure 11.45**).

You now have a text file that you can import into QuarkXPress just as you would any other text document. When you place the text in Quark, make sure that the Include Style Sheets option is checked (**Figure 11.46**).

When placed in Quark, the list will automatically be formatted in bold and italics (**Figure 11.47**).

✔ Tip

- You can expand this technique to include any formatting options. Consult the documentation of the page layout program you use for a complete list of available tags.

Chapter 11

Using Excel Data in FileMaker

The FileMaker company has done a great job of making FileMaker and Excel files easily interchangeable. For example, in Chapter 5 in "To export summary data," we show how easy it is to save FileMaker databases as worksheet files using the File > Export Records command.

But did you know that you can also open Excel files directly in FileMaker to create a new database? This allows you to create a new FileMaker file with all of the spreadsheet data included. You can use column headers from the Excel file to automatically create FileMaker field names. Use the drag-and-drop feature in both Windows and the Mac OS, and the whole process can be virtually effortless.

To create a FileMaker database from an Excel file:

1. In Windows Explorer or the Macintosh Finder, arrange your windows or desktop so that you can access the Excel file and the FileMaker program icon (or a shortcut/alias) at the same time (**Figure 11.48**).

2. Drag the Excel file icon on top of the FileMaker program icon (**Figure 11.49**). Doing this launches FileMaker and automatically opens the First Row Option dialog box.

    If you don't have a FileMaker program icon on your desktop, start FileMaker and choose File > Open. Choose Microsoft Excel Files in the drop-down list (**Figure 11.50**). Double-click the name of the Excel file.

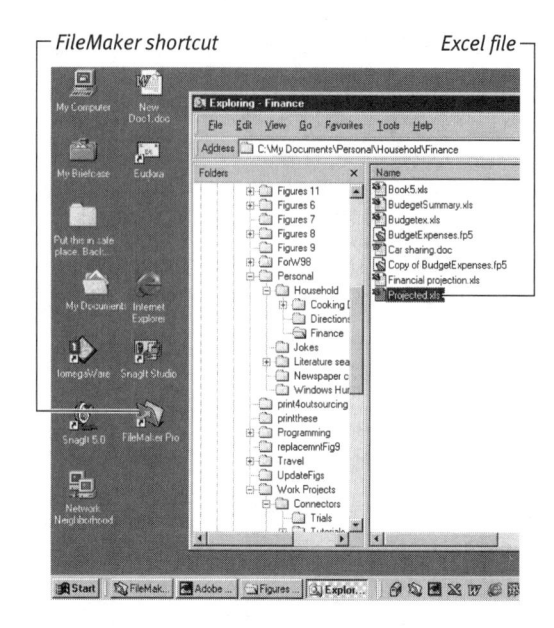

Figure 11.48 Windows Explorer is open to the Excel file, and the FileMaker program alias is on the desktop.

Figure 11.49 Use drag-and-drop to launch the Excel spreadsheet as a FileMaker file.

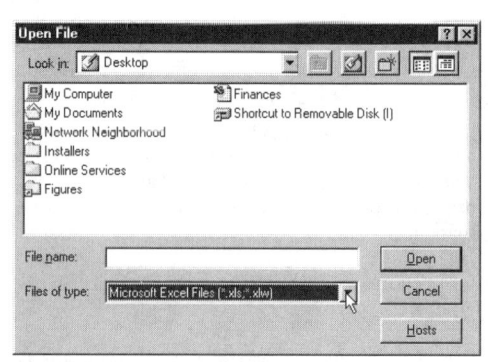

Figure 11.50 Choose Excel as the file type to see all the available Excel files.

290

FileMaker and Other Programs

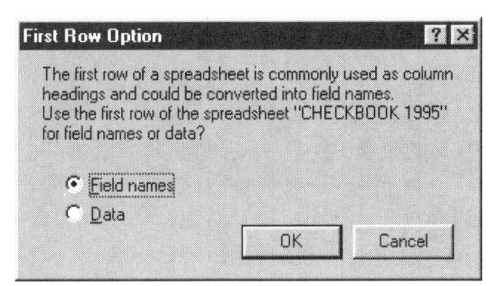

Figure 11.51 Choose "Field names" to use data in the first row of the spreadsheet as the field names in the new database.

Figure 11.52 The field names will be taken from the first row in the spreadsheet if you chose that option.

3. In the First Row Option dialog box, click the "Field names" radio button if you want to use the first row in the spreadsheet as your field names (**Figure 11.51**). If not, click the Data button. Click OK.

4. In the "Name converted file" dialog box, type a name for the new database. Click Save.

5. The new FileMaker database will open with all of the data from the spreadsheet.

If you choose the "Field names" option in step 3, the field names will be created from the first row of the spreadsheet (**Figure 11.52**). Otherwise, your fields will be given generic letter/number codes (F1, F2, F3, etc.) as field names, which you can edit in the Define Fields dialog box.

✔ **Tip**

- If you convert an Excel spreadsheet that contains formulas into a database, the formula results will be displayed in the fields, not the formulas themselves. Alas, Excel formulas don't translate into FileMaker calculations

Import from Excel Ranges

There are a multitude of situations in which you need only a specific portion of a spreadsheet as FileMaker data. When you bring in the entire spreadsheet, you have to match fields, delete extra information, and clean up the data. That's a lot of extra work, and it's completely unnecessary. If you've been clever in Excel and named ranges for printing reports or for organizing data, FileMaker will recognize these ranges and allow you to import one range at a time.

To import data ranges from Excel:

1. Choose File > Import Records > File (to insert data in a existing file) or File > Open (to create a new database).

2. When the Open File dialog box appears, select the Excel file containing named ranges that you want to import.

3. When the Specify Excel Data dialog box appears, click the Display Named Ranges radio button (**Figure 11.53**).

4. Click the name of the range to be imported. Click OK.

5. In the First Row Option dialog box, click the button to indicate whether the first row of the range contains field names or data (**Figure 11.54**). If you're creating a new file and choose Data, the Name Converted File dialog box will appear. Name the file and click Save.

    The Excel spreadsheet columns will automatically be converted to fields named F1 through FN, which you can rename in the Define Fields dialog box.

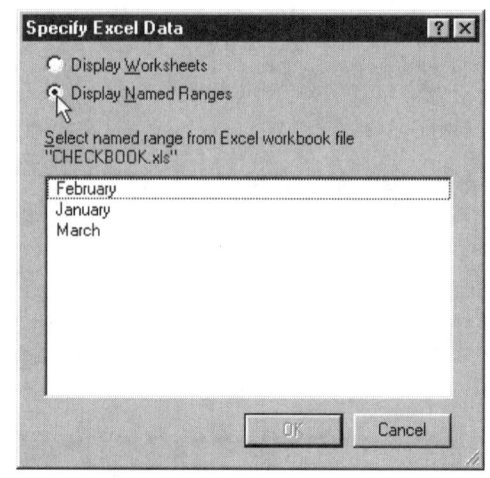

Figure 11.53 When you choose an Excel file with named ranges, you can select which one to import.

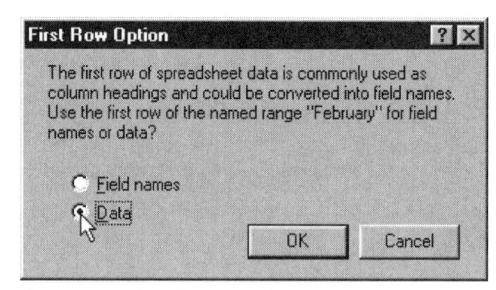

Figure 11.54 If the first row of the named range contains field names, leave the "Field names" radio button selected to eliminate them from the import.

FileMaker and Other Programs

Figure 11.55 Move the FileMaker field names to match the Excel data being imported.

6. If you're creating a new file and choose "Field names" in the First Row Option dialog box, or if you're importing into an existing database file, the Import Field Mapping dialog box will appear.

7. In the Import Field Mapping dialog box, match up the data from the Excel file on the left with the existing field names on the right.

8. In the Import Action section in the lower left, choose whether the imported data will add new records or replace or update existing records. Click Import (**Figure 11.55**).

✔ Tip

- If you're using Excel, you'll import your data with Excel's import wizard. Look at the data in the wizard to see if any of the fields is a Zip code. If so, use the wizard to set that field to text format or else Excel will strip the leading zeroes when you import.

293

Using AppleScript with FileMaker Scripting

Although AppleScript itself is outside the scope of a FileMaker Pro book, it's definitely worth a mention because it allows you to combine FileMaker scripting with almost limitless ability to affect Macintosh Finder functions (like automatically backing up FileMaker databases at specific times of day), and to initiate actions in other AppleScript-aware programs—from simply cutting and pasting text between applications to mining your Netscape cache for interesting GIF files.

Figure 11.56 This script name describes what its AppleScript does.

This example uses a simple script that copies the contents of a FileMaker field, switches to Microsoft Word, and pastes the text into a document.

To send an Apple Event to another Mac application:

1. Choose Scripts > ScriptMaker.

2. In the Define Scripts dialog box, name the new script (we use Paste into Word). Click Create (**Figure 11.56**).

3. The Script Definition dialog box appears. In the script step list on the left, double-click Go to Layout. From the Specify drop-down menu under Options, choose the layout that holds the field data you want to copy. Our example uses the Contract layout (**Figure 11.57**).

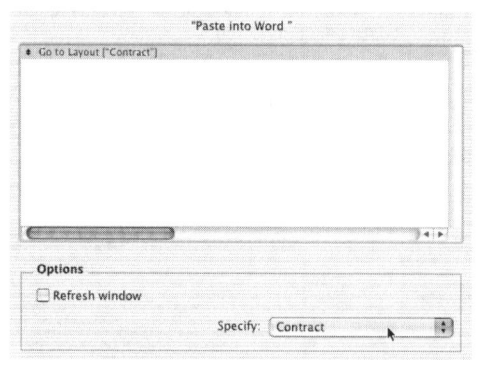

Figure 11.57 For the Copy step to work properly, the field whose contents you want to copy must appear in the layout you specify.

4. In the step list on the left, scroll down to the Editing section and double-click Copy.

5. Click Specify Field to bring up the Specify Field dialog box and double-click Contract to choose it from the field list. Leave "Select entire contents" checked unless you want to edit the field (**Figure 11.58**).

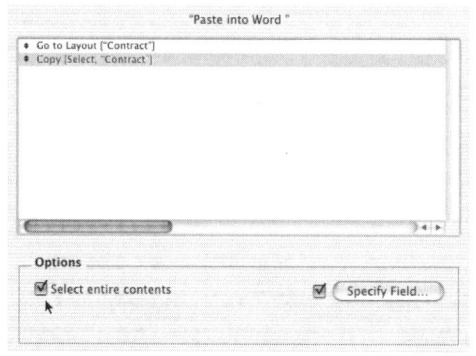

Figure 11.58 Leave "Select entire contents" checked to copy the entire contents of the field.

294

FileMaker and Other Programs

Figure 11.59 The Perform AppleScript step allows you to enter commands that are executed by AppleScript.

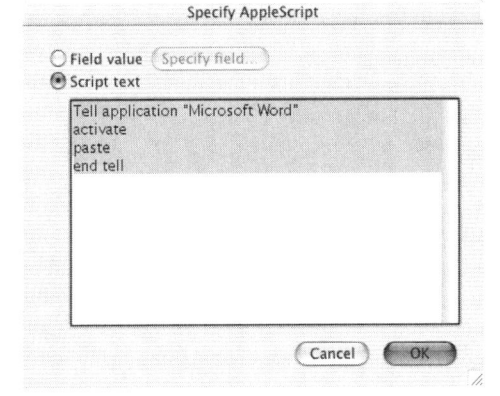

Figure 11.60 These AppleScript commands switch to Microsoft Word and paste data into its current document.

6. In the script step list on the left, scroll down to Miscellaneous and double-click Perform AppleScript (**Figure 11.59**).

7. Under Options, click Specify.

8. When the Specify AppleScript dialog box appears, type your AppleScript (**Figure 11.60**).

9. Click OK, and then Done to finish.

✔ Tips

- Although AppleScript is a very powerful tool for connecting FileMaker with other applications, it is not cross-platform. If you open a database file that uses AppleScript on a Windows computer, the scripts won't work.

- To learn more about how to use FileMaker with AppleScript, check *AppleScript for Applications: Visual QuickStart Guide,* by Ethan Wilde, published by Peachpit Press.

295

IMPORTING DATA

No good program is an island, and FileMaker 6 proves that with its increasing network of bridges. No area of database support has been ignored. Heading the list are connections between your desktop and the rest of the world. FileMaker's ongoing commitment to streamlining user tasks is evident from the vast range of ways you can move information into your database. Transferring scripts from file to file, importing pieces of Excel worksheets, and the beauty of batch-importing are only a sample. To add to the options, FileMaker Mobile provides an easy to way to carry your database in your pocket.

In this chapter, we show you how to access and apply this wide range of import and connection features. In Chapter 18, we'll cover importing with XML.

Migrating to FileMaker 6

Files created in 5.0 or 5.5 need no migration at all. Just open them in FileMaker 6 as you would in the earlier versions. If you don't use any of the new features, the file will continue to work perfectly in all three versions, because they all use the same file format: .fp5.

But even if you're upgrading from an older release, you'll find that it's very easy to convert to FileMaker 6. Before converting, you'll want to open the file in the earlier version and save a compressed copy just in case you (or someone else) still need to examine the database in its original format.

To compress a copy of a file:

1. Open your database in FileMaker 3 or 4.
2. Choose File > Save a Copy As.
3. In the Create Copy/Save dialog box, choose "compressed copy" from the Type/Save a drop-down menu (**Figure 12.1**). Click Save.

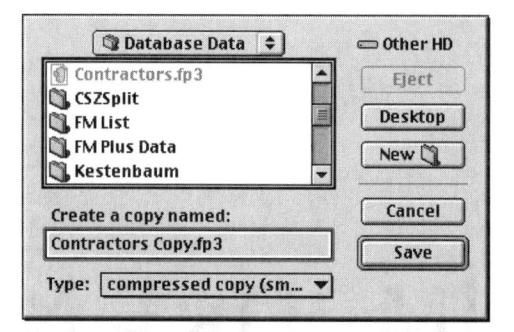

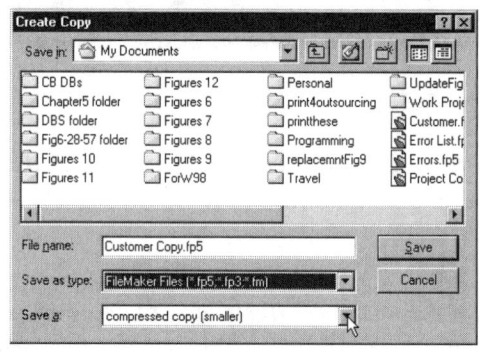

Figure 12.1 You should save a compressed copy of the old file before you convert to FileMaker 6.

Importing Data

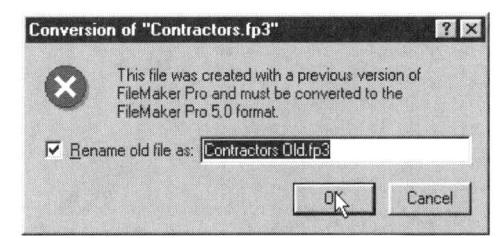

Figure 12.2 FileMaker saves a backup copy of the old file.

Figure 12.3 Click Save in the "Name converted file" dialog box to convert the old file into the .fp5 format.

To convert earlier databases to FileMaker 6:

1. Launch FileMaker 6.

2. Choose File > Open.

3. In the Open File dialog box, double-click the file you want to convert.

4. In the Conversion dialog box, you'll see the default name under which FileMaker will save a copy of the file in its original version. You can either type a new name, or just click OK to accept the default name (**Figure 12.2**). Click OK.

5. In the "Name converted file" dialog box, leave the default name and click Save (**Figure 12.3**).

   The file will open in FileMaker 6. There will also be a backup copy saved with the name chosen in step 4.

6. A file converted from earlier versions of FileMaker will be exactly the same in version 6 as it was in the original. All calculations, layouts, relationships, and scripts will be intact. However, this new file is no longer compatible with older FileMaker versions. If this database is used by other people on your network, make sure that they all have FileMaker 5, 5.5, or 6 installed or they won't be able to use the new file.

About Data File Types

Although FileMaker can import a variety of file types, the most common are text files. Not all word-processed document files are text files—in fact, most of them aren't. Text files are a special subset of files that contain only ASCII text. ASCII text contains only text, numbers, and basic punctuation—no special characters and no font, format, or layout information. Because they're so simple, ASCII text files are readable on every type of computer, and virtually every application that works with data can produce text files. This universal readability makes text format the best choice for transferring data between different applications.

By convention, text file names end with .txt on most operating systems. Although the Macintosh Classic OS doesn't add a file extension at the end of its file names, it still recognizes .txt files.

Although text files can't contain real formatting, they can carry a couple of special characters that make them useful for data transfer as well as straight text. These characters allow for line returns and tabs. Most programs that support ASCII text as well as their own formatting have an option for saving files with these two important characters (**Figure 12.4**). Some programs call this file type "Tab-delimited text," while others use "Text Only with Line Breaks." ("Delimited text" is another name for letters and numbers with tabs—or commas—separating the fields and returns separating the records.)

Other common file formats you're likely to encounter when importing data are DIF and DBF, both of which FileMaker recognizes. DBF and DIF file names should end with .dbf and .dif, respectively.

DIF files are usually created by spreadsheets. Unlike plain text files, DIF files retain any field names they contain. DBF files are created in a format that dates back to the venerable grandparent of all modern databases, Dbase. Many database programs can both export and import DBF files. Like DIF files, DBF files retain the field name information.

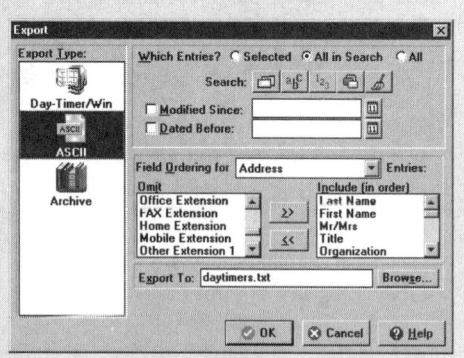

Figure 12.4 This Day-Timer database has the option of saving as an ASCII file.

Importing Data from Text Sources

Some files from other applications (like Microsoft Excel) can be imported into FileMaker without much fuss. But to import data from most programs, you need to create intermediate files in a format readable by both FileMaker and the original program. (See "About Data File Types" on the previous page, and refer to your software's documentation for instructions on exporting files.)

Although text files are a universal output format, they don't usually contain field names. You have to determine field order either by looking at the data in the original program or by examining the data after you import it. Fortunately, FileMaker has a wonderful field-mapping feature right in the Import dialog box that allows you to match imported data to your existing FileMaker fields.

To import text data files:

1. With the database you want to import into open, choose File > Import Records > File.

2. When the Open File dialog box appears, choose the format of the exported file from the "Files of type" drop-down menu. Navigate to the file and double-click to import it (**Figure 12.5**).

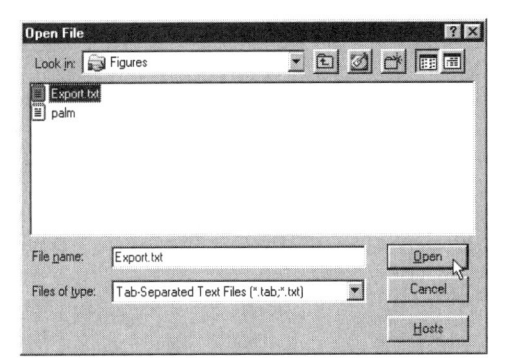

continues on next page

Figure 12.5 When you choose a file type, only files of that type will appear in the Open File dialog box.

Chapter 12

3. If the export file includes field names, you'll see them in the Import Field Mapping dialog box (**Figure 12.6**). If not, you'll see the data from the first record (**Figure 12.7**). Click the field names on the right and move them up or down to match the data (or field names) on the left (**Figure 12.8**).

Figure 12.6 If there are field names in the import file, they will appear as the data of the first record, although they may not match up with your fields on the right.

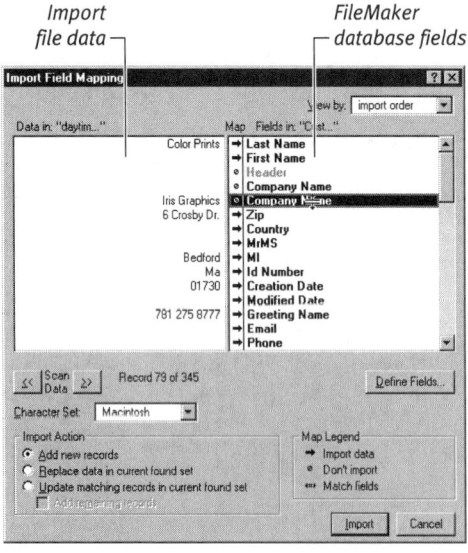

Figure 12.8 Drag the FileMaker field names to correspond to the data that will be imported into them.

Figure 12.7 If there are no field names in the import file, you will see the data in the first record instead.

Importing Data

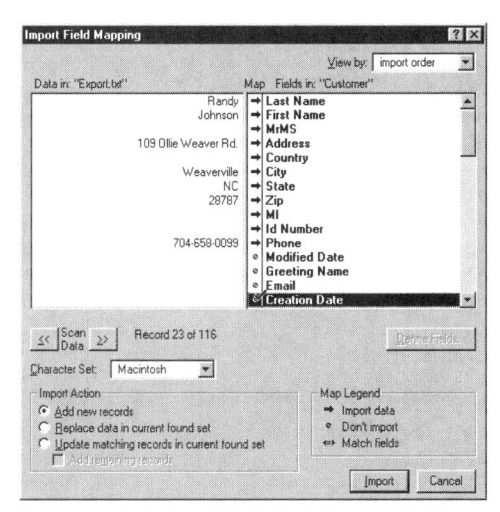

Figure 12.9 Indicate which fields to import with the arrows in the Map column.

4. For each field that you want to import, turn on the arrow in the Map column by clicking it. If there are fields that you don't want to import, click the arrow off (**Figure 12.9**).

To help you locate all the match fields, examine the rest of the data in the import file by clicking the Scan Data buttons (**Figure 12.10**). If you find information that doesn't match any current fields, click the Define Fields button (**Figure 12.11**). This will bring you to the Define Fields dialog box, where you can create a new field to hold the data.

continues on next page

Figure 12.10 The Scan Data buttons let you see any records in the import file.

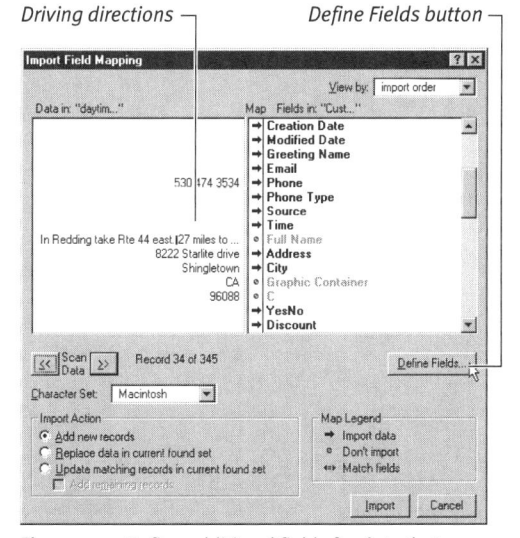

Figure 12.11 Define additional fields for data that don't match your current database. In this example, we need to add a Directions field.

303

Chapter 12

5. When you're satisfied that the field mapping is correct, click Import.

6. In the Import Options dialog box, click the "Perform auto-enter options while importing" check box if you want the database to do lookups or add serial numbers to the new records (**Figure 12.12**). Click OK to start the import.

   When the import is complete, the database will show the imported data as a found set. Check the data carefully. If you find that all the fields didn't match up properly, choose Records > Delete Found Records to delete all the imported records and try again—FileMaker will remember the last field import order, and you can adjust it as necessary.

7. If the imported file had field names, the first record will display them. Delete this record (**Figure 12.13**).

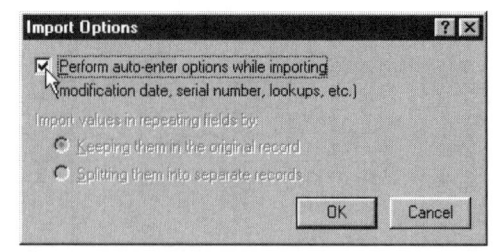

Figure 12.12 You can have the imported data update any lookups or other auto-enter settings.

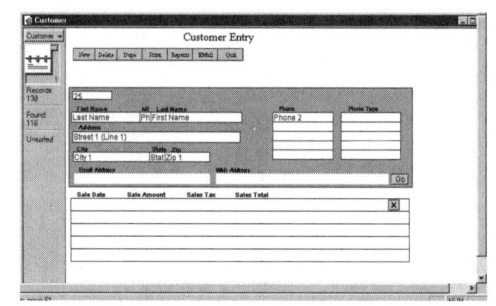

Figure 12.13 If the field names were imported with the data, delete that record.

Importing Data

Figure 12.14 In a spreadsheet, columns are the fields and rows are the records.

Figure 12.15 If you want to create field names in a spreadsheet, insert a row at the top and type the field names.

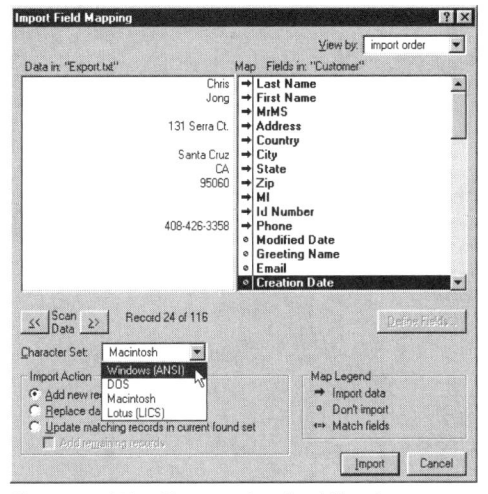

Figure 12.16 The Character Set should be the same as the operating system running the FileMaker database.

✔ Tips

- If the data in a file you're importing doesn't match your existing FileMaker structure, give the information a thorough looking-over in a spreadsheet program like Excel before you continue. Spreadsheet programs display tab-delimited data in columns. Each column corresponds to a field and each row to a record (**Figure 12.14**). You can insert a row at the top of the spreadsheet to create field names, making the match-up process a little easier (**Figure 12.15**). You can also make global search-and-replace changes, then save the data as an Excel file to retain the field names when you import.

- For Windows users: If you're importing a text file from a Mac or an old DOS application, FileMaker can usually determine the correct character set automatically. If it doesn't, you can manually set the correct Character Set in the Import dialog box (**Figure 12.16**).

Batch Importing

One of the most tedious tasks in the database world is having to transfer information from another program to FileMaker one item at a time. That's how FileMaker users had to import groups of files prior to version 6. You could cut and paste individual text blocks, or you could import images or media into container fields one by one. With batch importing—the ability to import the entire contents of a folder into an existing database—FileMaker becomes a powerful asset-management tool for everything from Web sites to retail inventory.

To import multiple files in a folder:

1. Choose File > Import Records > Folder.

2. The Folder of Files Import Options dialog box appears. In the Folder Location section, click Specify (**Figure 12.17**).

3. In the Choose a Folder dialog box, navigate to the folder whose contents you want to import. Click Choose to select the folder. If there are other folders with content that you don't want to import, uncheck the "Include all enclosed folders" check box.

4. In the File Type section, click to the select the type of file you want to import, then click OK.

5. When the Import Field Mapping dialog box appears, match the image information with the fields that will hold it (**Figure 12.18**). Click Import.

   Only the information with arrows in the Map column will actually be transferred to the file.

6. The Import Options dialog box appears. Set any import options you need, then click OK.

Figure 12.17 Specify allows you to navigate to the folder you want to import.

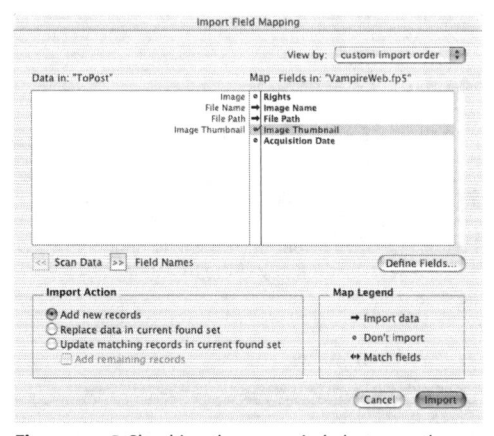

Figure 12.18 Checking the open circle between the data and the field tells FileMaker that the data should be transferred.

Importing Data

✔ Tips

- If you've saved space by importing only the path reference for an image, you can still see the image quickly. In Browse mode, right-click (Windows) or Control-click (Mac OS X) the path to bring up a contextual menu that will let you open the file in the appropriate application.

- Unfortunately, there's no way to import just an image thumbnail without importing the image as well. Batch import them both, then go to Define Fields. In the Define Fields dialog box, highlight the Image field and click Delete, then OK. The field and all the imported images will disappear, leaving only the image thumbnails, and a much tinier database.

Batch-Importing Guidelines

Although batch importing is very easy, it can require some fancy mental footwork to be an elegant solution instead of a horrific muddle. Some important hints for importing multiple files:

You can't generate a brand-new database from the contents of a folder. The database already has to exist and have fields available for the new content.

All the items will be imported into the same field. Be sure to delete from the folder any files that belong in a different category.

Text files must all be simple text-only files. They can't contain embedded images or charts. Any formatting (like font or point size) won't transfer.

No FileMaker database can exceed 2 GB in size. This is an easy limit to exceed when you're batch-importing photographs. Consider importing just the file path and information instead of the image itself.

When you batch-import to update or replace data, records and incoming files have to match. If there are more files in a folder than there are records to hold them, the extra files will be ignored when the import takes place.

Be very careful when batch-importing replacement files. Create a found set of the records whose data you'll be replacing, and make sure that it is sorted correctly for the incoming files.

And most important: Unless it's a brand-new file, always make a backup of your database before you import, particularly if you'll be replacing or updating data, not just importing new files from scratch. The more material you import, the worse mess your file can become if you've overlooked something in your preparation.

Batch-Importing from a Digital Camera (Mac OS X Only)

Batch importing is the perfect way to transfer into FileMaker a collection of images that are already on your computer. But what if you have a digital camera filled with images? It would be nice to avoid the two-step process of uploading, then batch-importing.

But there's more at stake than a few extra minutes' work. Your images also invisibly hold useful information, like the dates they were shot and many of the camera settings you used to shoot them. All of that EXIF (Exchangeable Image File) information disappears when you download unless you can transfer it directly into a program that can read and archive it. So if you have to batch-import from a folder, the file information is already gone.

Mac OS X users don't have to lose that useful data. They can import images directly from camera to database.

In this example, we use one of FileMaker's most useful templates to create an instant database for our camera import. This database template already has fields for capturing not only the image itself, but all of the EXIF file data.

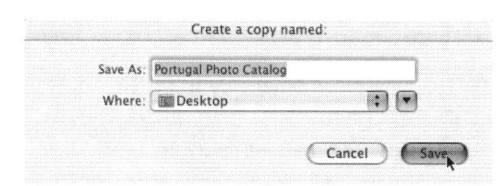

Figure 12.19 FileMaker won't let you use the original template, only a copy of it.

To import images from a digital camera:

1. Attach your camera to your Mac and launch FileMaker Pro.

2. Choose File > New Database.

3. When the New Database dialog box appears, select Home from the drop-down menu. In the list of templates, double-click Photo Catalog.

4. When the "Create a copy named:" dialog box appears, rename the database file. Click Save (**Figure 12.19**).

Importing Data

Figure 12.20 The Method section allows you to import the actual images or only information about where to find the images on the disk.

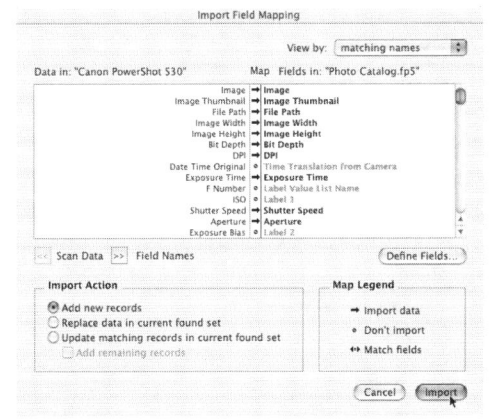

Figure 12.21 The FileMaker template and the incoming EXIF data should match up perfectly with no work on your part.

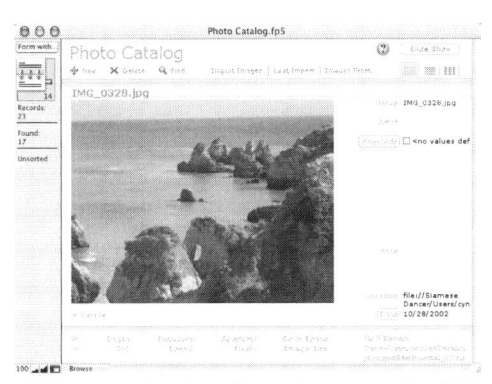

Figure 12.22 FileMaker will size the image to fit within the container field of the catalog template.

5. Choose View > Browse Mode. Choose File > Import Records > Digital Camera.

6. The Photo Import Options dialog box appears. In the Download section, click the "All images" radio button to transfer everything in the camera to the database. Click OK.

   As with a regular folder batch import, you can import the actual photos into the database, or only the reference information (**Figure 12.20**).

7. When the Import Field Mapping dialog box appears, match up the incoming information with the database fields. Click Import (**Figure 12.21**).

8. When the Import Options dialog box appears, set any auto-enter options, then click OK.

9. The Import dialog box will appear, giving you a status bar of your files as they import. When all of the photos have been downloaded, you can view them in the database (**Figure 12.22**).

BATCH-IMPORTING FROM A DIGITAL CAMERA

309

Chapter 12

Once an image is imported you can't change its orientation, so vertical pictures display sideways. You can use the import options to orient your photos properly.

To rotate images while importing:

1. Follow steps 1–5 of the previous task, "To import images from a digital camera."

2. The Photo Import Options dialog box appears. In the Download section, click "Some images," then click Specify.

3. The Specify Images to Import dialog box appears. Highlight any image that should be displayed vertically and rotate it left or right using the rotate arrow buttons (**Figure 12.23**). Click OK to finish.

   You can select several images at once and rotate them all at the same time in the same direction.

✔ Tip

- In OS X, iPhoto is usually set to launch automatically when you attach a digital camera. You can change this default to FileMaker. In OS 10.2, before you attach your camera, open the Image Capture application. Choose Image Capture > Preferences. When the Image Capture Preferences dialog box appears, choose Other from the Camera Preferences drop-down menu (**Figure 12.24**). Navigate to FileMaker Pro and click Open.

Figure 12.23 You can rotate the image left or right to orient it properly.

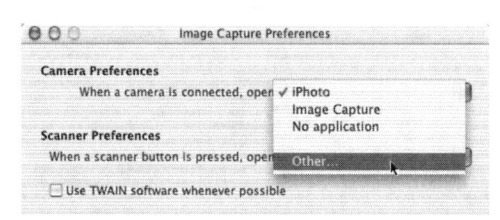

Figure 12.24 Selecting Other allows you to change the application that launches when you attach a digital camera.

Importing with Scripts

When you need to import data into a FileMaker database regularly, it makes sense to use scripts. In this example, we'll do an import and then create a script to do that same import. With this script, as long as the field names remain the same, the data will be imported into the correct fields even if the field order in the source file changes.

To import data with matching field names:

1. Open the file where you'll be importing records and choose File > Import Records > File.

2. When the Open File dialog box appears, choose the file to be imported. Click OK.

3. When the Import Field Mapping dialog box appears, choose "matching names" from the "View by" drop-down menu (**Figure 12.25**).

4. In the Map column, make sure that the fields you want to import are checked (**Figure 12.26**). Click the Import button.

5. When the Import Options dialog box appears, click the "Perform auto-enter" check box if you want the imported records to have any auto-enter or lookup fields updated (**Figure 12.27**). Click OK.

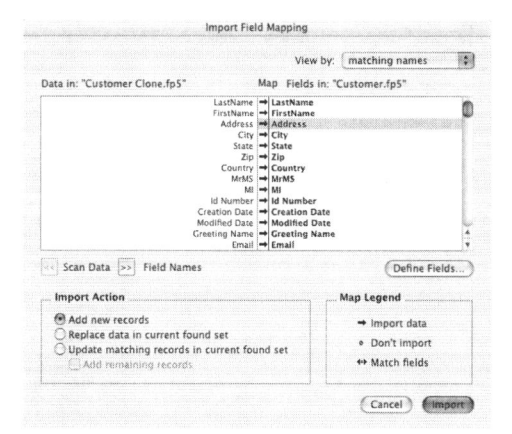

continues on next page

Figure 12.25 When the Matching Names option is chosen, the fields will automatically line up with imported fields that have the same name.

Figure 12.26 The matching fields must have an arrow in the Map column or they won't be imported.

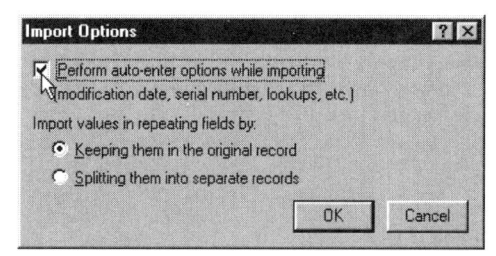

Figure 12.27 Import Options can update serial numbers and lookups if there are any in the database

Chapter 12

6. Now that the import order has been established, we'll create a script to do the same import. Choose Scripts > ScriptMaker.

7. When the Define Scripts dialog box appears, type `Import Matching` for the script name and click Create (**Figure 12.28**).

8. When the Script Definition dialog box appears, scroll down to the Records category and double-click Import Records.

9. In the Options section, leave the "Restore import order" box checked. Click "Perform without dialog," then click Specify/Specify File (**Figure 12.29**).

10. When the Open File dialog box appears, choose the file that the script will import. Click Open.

11. Click OK and then Done to finish.

Figure 12.28 Name the script Import Matching to remind you of what the script actually does.

Figure 12.29 Select "Restore import order" and "Perform without dialog" so the script will re-create the import without user input.

Setting the Next Auto-Entry Serial Number

When you import data, you can choose whether or not to update auto-enter and lookup fields. This choice is useful, but unfortunately it makes the two updates a package deal. So if you want to enter serial numbers but don't want to update the lookup fields, you'll handle the serial numbers in a separate step.

The easiest way to enter new serial numbers would be to use the Replace command. However, this simple solution could turn ugly in a multi-user environment. Imagine the mess if users were editing the new records as you tried to update their serial numbers. None of the active records would be updated.

FileMaker provides a delightful pair of script steps—GetNextSerialValue and Set Next Serial Value—to rescue us. Using these helpful friends, we can create a script that checks through the newly imported records, setting the new serial numbers and taking note if any were not updated properly because they were in use.

Because this script could itself create serious havoc if it ran on the entire database, we'll include a check to verify that there is a Find in place before it runs.

Chapter 12

This example uses Id Number as the serialized field in a database called Customer.fp5.

To specify next serial number after importing:

1. In the file where you'll be importing records, choose File > Define Fields (Control+Shift+D/Command+Shift+D).

2. In the Define Fields dialog box, type gNoSerialCount for the field name, make it a global field, and click Create.

3. When the Global Options dialog box appears, set it to Number and click OK, then click Done.

   This script will use the gNoSerialCount field to note if there are any records that are not updated.

4. Choose Scripts > ScriptMaker. When the Define Scripts dialog box appears, name the script "Serialize" and click Create.

5. The Script Definition dialog box appears, In the Control category of the step list on the left, double-click Set Error Capture and leave it set to On in the Options section (**Figure 12.30**).

6. In the step list, double-click Allow User Abort and leave it set to Off.

7. In the Fields category of the step list, double-click Set Field. In the Options section, click Specify Field.

8. When the Specify Field dialog box appears, double-click gNoSerialCount.

9. In the Options section, click Specify. When the Specify Calculation box appears, type 0. Click OK.

Figure 12.30 To trap for errors in the script and suppress the default error message, Set Error Capture must be set to On.

Importing Data

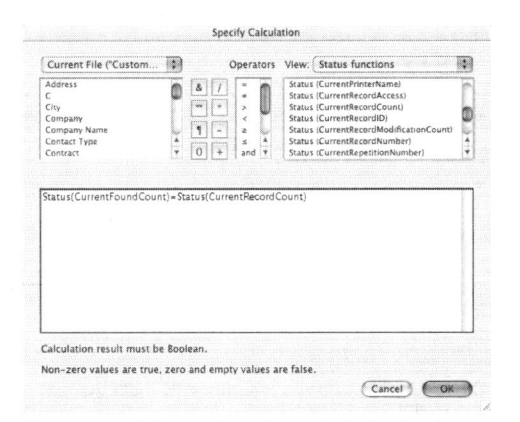

Figure 12.31 If the number of records in the database is the same as the number of records in the found set, there is no Find in use.

Figure 12.32 Since the script will end after the message is displayed, the dialog box should only offer OK as an option.

10. Now we'll check to make sure that a Find is in use. Back in the Script Definition dialog box, in the Control category of the step list, double-click If. In the Options section, click the Specify button.

11. When the Specify Calculation dialog box appears, choose "Status functions" from the View drop-down menu on the right.

12. In the function list, double-click Status (CurrentFoundCount). Click to the right of the parenthesis, then double-click the equals (=) operator.

13. In the function list on the right, double-click the Status (CurrentRecordCount) function (**Figure 12.31**). Click OK.

    This If step checks to see if the current number of found records equals the current number of records in the database. If they're the same, there is no found set.

14. Back in the Script Definition dialog box, scroll down to the Miscellaneous category of the step list. Double-click Show Message, then click Specify in the Options section.

15. In the Specify Message dialog box, type a warning message. Ours is "There is no Find in use. You don't want to run this script on the entire database."

16. In the Button Captions section, leave the First button set to OK and delete "Cancel" from the Second button box. Click OK (**Figure 12.32**).

    The Specify Message dialog box closes and the Script Definition dialog box remains.

continues on next page

SETTING THE NEXT AUTO-ENTRY SERIAL NUMBER

315

Chapter 12

17. In the Control category of the step list, double-click Exit Script.

If there is no found set, the script will exit without making any changes.

18. In the step list, double-click Set Field. Move it down below the End If step (**Figure 12.33**).

19. In the Options section, click Specify Field. In the Specify Field dialog box, double-click gNoSerialCount.

20. In the Options section of the Script Definition dialog box, click Specify. When the Specify Calculation dialog box appears, type 0 and click OK.

This Set Field step resets the gNoSerialCount field to 0.

21. In the Navigation category of the step list, double-click Go to Record/Request/Page. From the Specify drop-down menu, choose First (**Figure 12.34**).

This step sends the script to the first record in the file.

22. In the Control category of the step list, double-click Loop.

23. Scroll to the Fields category of the step list and double-click Set Field. In the Options section, click Specify Field. When the Specify Field dialog box appears, double-click Id Number (**Figure 12.35**).

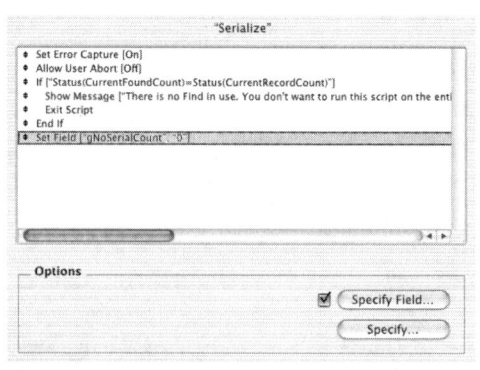

Figure 12.33 The gNoSerialCount field must be reset to 0 each time the script is run.

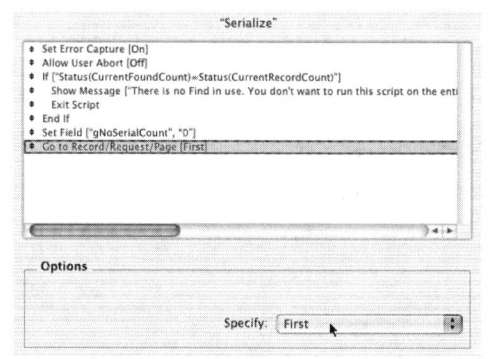

Figure 12.34 The updating must start at the first record in the found set.

Figure 12.35 Choose Id Number from the field list.

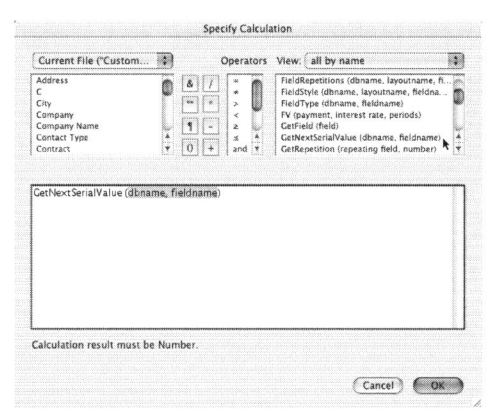

Figure 12.36 GetNextSerialValue looks at a specified database and returns the next serial number for the specified field.

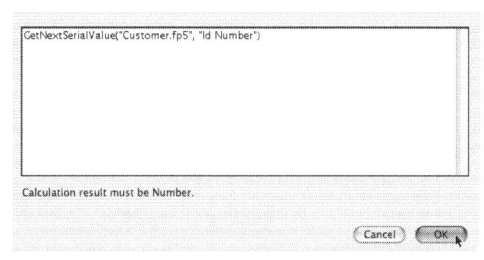

Figure 12.37 In the GetNextSerialValue function, both the database and field names must be in quotes.

Figure 12.38 If the Set Field command was successful, the current error will be 0.

24. In the Options section of the Script Definition dialog box, click Specify. When the Specify Calculation dialog box appears, double-click GetNextSerialValue in the function list (**Figure 12.36**).

25. Double-click "dbname" inside the parentheses to select it. Click the quotes button and type the name of your database inside the quotes. (We use Customer.fp5.)

26. Double-click "fieldname," click the quotes button, and select Id Number from the field list on the left. Click OK (**Figure 12.37**).

27. In the step list of the Script Definition dialog box, double-click If. In the Options section, click Specify.

28. When the Specify Calculation dialog box appears, choose "Status functions" from the View drop-down menu. Double-click Status (CurrentError).

29. Click to the right of the parenthesis and double-click the not-equal operator (≠). Type 0. Click OK (**Figure 12.38**).

If the script's attempt to set the Id Number field succeeds (the record is not in use), the Status (CurrentError) function will return 0. If it fails (the record is in use), it will move on to the next record and change nothing.

continues on next page

30. Back in the Script Definition dialog box, in the Fields category of the step list double-click Set Field. In Options, click Specify Field. In the Specify Field dialog box, choose gNoSerialCount.

31. In Options, click Specify. In the Specify Calculation dialog box, double-click gNoSerialCount in the field list. Click the plus (+) button and type 1. Click OK (**Figure 12.39**).

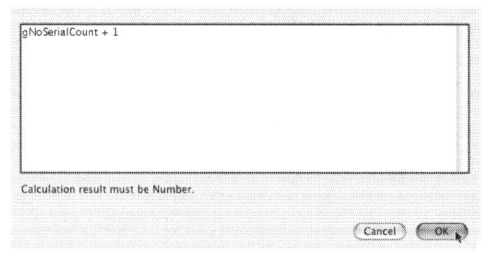

Figure 12.39 If the Set Field command was not successful, the gNoSerialCount field will be incremented by one.

32. Back in the step list of the Script Definition dialog box, scroll up to the Control category and double-click Else.

33. Scroll down to the Miscellaneous category and double-click Set Next Serial Value (**Figure 12.40**). In the Options section, click Specify Field. In the Specify Field dialog box, double-click Id Number.

34. In Options, click Specify. When the Specify Calculation dialog box appears, double-click GetNextSerialValue in the functions list.

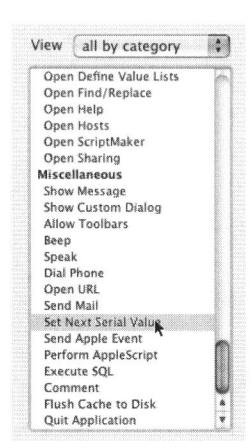

Figure 12.40 The Set Next Serial Value step allows you to update auto-enter serial numbers.

35. Double-click "dbname" inside the parentheses to select it. Click the quotes button and type the name of your database inside the quotes.

36. Double-click "fieldname," click the quotes button, and select Id Number from the field list.

37. Click to the right of the parenthesis, click the + button and type 1. Click OK (**Figure 12.41**).

This step tells the script to increment the field Id Number in our database by one.

Figure 12.41 If the Set Field command was successful, the next serial value will be incremented by one.

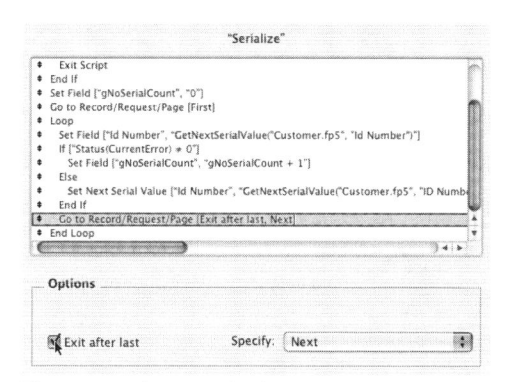

Figure 12.42 The "Exit after last" option will exit the Loop when the script reaches the last record in the found set.

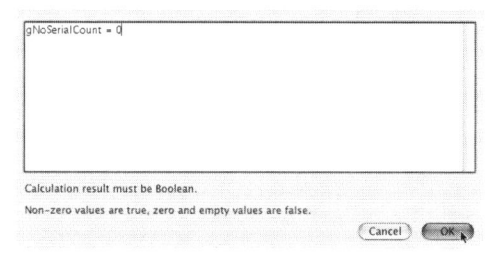

Figure 12.43 If all records were updated successfully, the gNoSerialCount field will still be 0.

38. In the Navigation category of the step list, double-click Go to Record/Request/Page. Position it between the End If and End Loop steps in the script-construction window.

39. In the Options section, choose Next from the Specify drop-down menu. Click the "Exit after last" check box (**Figure 12.42**).

    The script to this point goes to the first record and sets the Id Number field to the next serial number. If the script is successful, it increments the next serial number by one. If it is not successful, it increments the global field gNoSerialCount by one instead.

40. Now we need to test to see if there were any records that were not updated properly. Select the End Loop step in the script-construction window. In the step list, double-click If, then click Specify in the Options section.

41. When the Specify Calculation dialog box appears, double-click gNoSerialCount in the field list. Double-click the = operator and type 0. Click OK (**Figure 12.43**).

continues on next page

Chapter 12

42. In the step list, double-click Exit Script.

If there were no un-updated records, the script will end here. If not, it will continue and find the problem records.

43. In the step list, double-click Else, then scroll down to the Navigation category and double-click Enter Find Mode. Uncheck the Pause and "Restore find requests" boxes (**Figure 12.44**).

44. In the step list, double-click Set Field. In the Options section, click Specify Field.

45. When the Specify Field dialog box appears, choose Id Number. In Options, click Specify. In the Specify Calculation dialog box, click the quotes button, then double-click the = operator (**Figure 12.45**). Click OK.

46. In the Sort/Find/Print category of the step list, double-click Perform Find. Uncheck the "Restore find requests" check box (**Figure 12.46**).

The Perform Find will find all the records in which the Id Number field does not have a value.

47. In the step list, scroll down to the Miscellaneous category and double-click Show Message. In the Options section, click Specify.

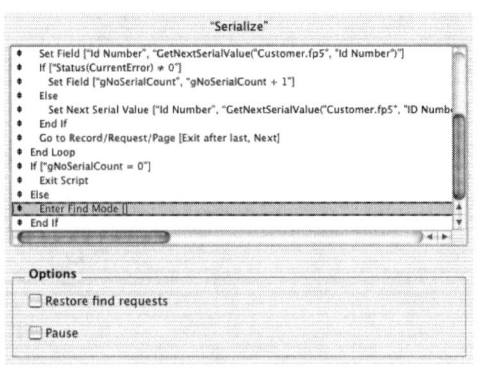

Figure 12.44 You specify Enter Find Mode to allow you to set Find criteria in the next step.

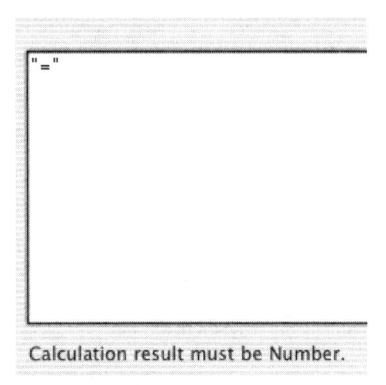

Figure 12.45 In Find Mode, setting a field to = will find any records where that field is blank.

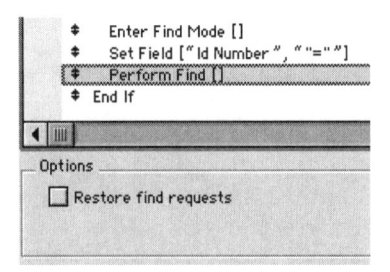

Figure 12.46 The Set field step will set the find criteria, so you don't need the Restore option.

Importing Data

Figure 12.47 This message offers no choices, so you don't need the second button.

Figure 12.48 To return to a specific layout after the script is run, use the Go to Layout step.

48. When the Specify Message dialog box appears, type:

    The current found set contains the records that were not updated properly.

49. In the Button Captions area, delete "Cancel" from the Second box (**Figure 12.47**). Click OK.

50. Back in the Script Definition dialog box, you can specify a layout to go to after the script finds unserialized records: In the Navigation category of the step list, double-click Go to Layout (**Figure 12.48**). Choose the layout from the Specify drop-down menu in Options. Click OK and then Done to finish.

321

About FileMaker Mobile

How many times have you wished you could access a FileMaker database you have on your computer while you're on the road? FileMaker Mobile lets you handle browse functions on your handheld, and keep your changes upgraded and synched with your main database. After you've set up the plug-in software to work with FileMaker Pro and installed the software on your Palm OS handheld device, you can add, delete, or modify records and easily keep both database versions up to date.

FileMaker Mobile is emphatically not a mini-version of FM Pro. Its whole purpose is to let you access your data while on the road and make updates when needed. There are limitations on the fields you can transfer to the Palm. A maximum of 50 Text, Number, Date, and Time fields can be moved, and no more than 5,000 records in all. No text field can exceed 2,000 characters, and no other type of field can exceed 255 characters. Any field that exceeds these limits will simply not be loaded. In addition, you can't define new fields, create relationships, or in any other way modify the structure of the original database from Mobile.

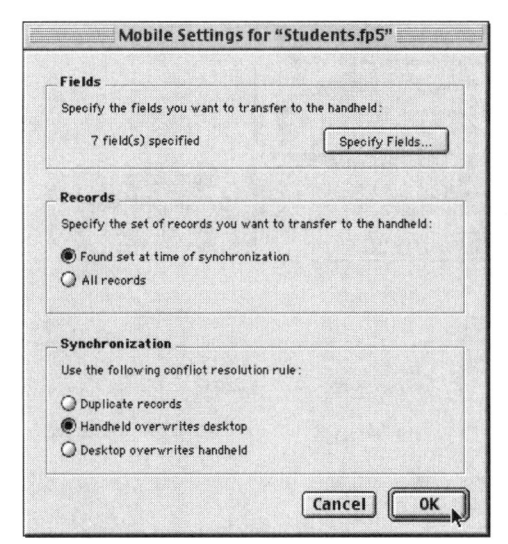

Figure 12.49 Before removing your old version of FM Mobile, update any changes you've made in the handheld data to the main database file.

Setting Up or Upgrading FileMaker Mobile

PDAs are very different from desktop computers, particularly in how you install or upgrade their software. Because they have limited memory, it isn't practical to upgrade on top of an existing version the way we've grown accustomed to on the desktop. In fact, you'll need to get rid of the first version before the bigger, better version takes its place.

First, back up your handheld database to your computer database so no recent changes will be lost. Then you must remove everything—all FileMaker Mobile handheld and application software—before you install a new version. Once that's complete, upgrading is no different from setting up from scratch.

To remove an old FM Mobile from your PDA:

1. Open the FileMaker Pro database you've been using with FM Mobile. If you've been using a found set to transfer data, re-create it.

2. Choose File (FileMaker Pro in Mac OS X) > Sharing. The File Sharing dialog box appears. In the Companion Sharing section, double-click Mobile Companion.

3. When the Mobile Settings dialog box appears, make sure the Synchronization options are set either to "Duplicate records" or "Handheld overwrites desktop." Click OK to close the dialog box (**Figure 12.49**).

4. Connect your handheld and synchronize your database, then quit the FileMaker Pro application.

continues on next page

5. Go to the handheld's Main window. In the menu bar, tap App, then tap Delete.

6. In the Delete window, find FileMaker, then tap Delete (**Figure 12.50**).

7. When the Delete Application dialog box appears, tap Yes, then tap Done to close the window.

   Once your PDA is ready, you can remove FileMaker Mobile from your computer.

8. In Windows, go to Start > Settings > Add/Remove Programs. On a Mac running a Classic OS, delete the specific file extensions (FileMaker Conduit and FileMaker Mobile.prc) from your Palm folder. From the FileMaker Extensions folder in your FileMaker Pro folder, delete the FileMaker Mobile extension. This extension is named "Mobile Companion (v2.0)" or "Mobile Companion Palm OS (v1)," depending on whether you are upgrading from version 1 or version 2.0 (**Figure 12.51**).

Figure 12.50 Deleting FileMaker Mobile deletes its databases as well.

Figure 12.51 Mac Classic users can search for these files in Sherlock and drag them to the Trash.

To set up FM Mobile with a FileMaker Pro database:

1. Make sure that you've installed the FM Mobile software and that the Mobile Companion file is in the FileMaker Extensions folder.

2. Open the database you want to transfer.

   If you want to transfer only a portion of the records, choose View > Find Mode. Enter your criteria and click Find.

3. Choose File > Sharing. When the File Sharing dialog box appears, select Single User and check Mobile Companion in the Companion Sharing area (**Figure 12.52**).

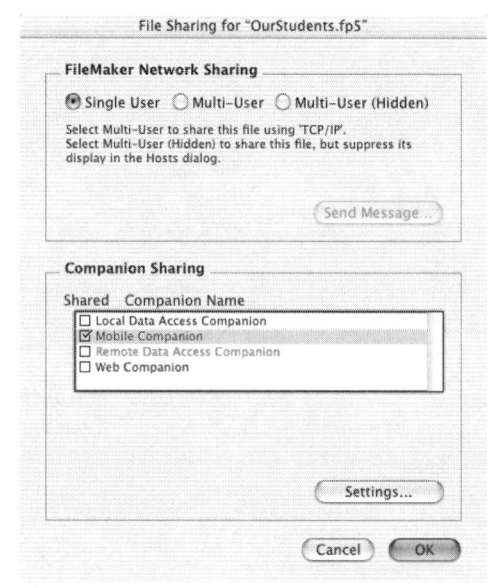

Figure 12.52 FileMaker Mobile works by sharing files between the desktop database and the handheld.

Figure 12.53 If you specify fields, you don't have to transfer an entire file to the handheld.

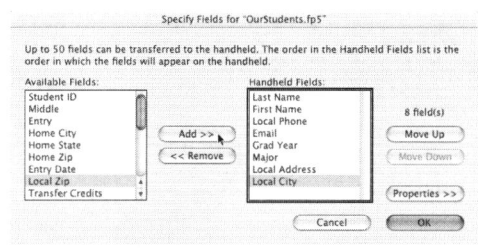

Figure 12.54 When you choose your fields, you can also set the order in which they'll appear on your handheld display.

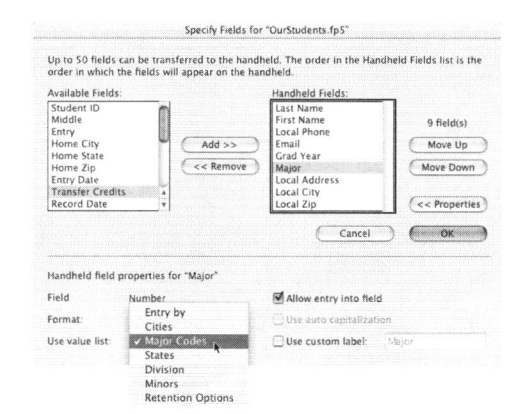

Figure 12.55 Your value list should match the value list you've been using on the original database.

4. Click the Settings button. When the Mobile Settings dialog box appears, click the Specify Fields button in the Fields portion of the dialog box (**Figure 12.53**).

5. From the list on the left of the Specify Fields dialog box, choose the fields you want to transfer to the handheld and click Add to move them (**Figure 12.54**).

   Fields can be added only one at a time, and only fields that meet Mobile's criteria are listed.

6. If a field has a value list you'd like to use, click Properties. The "Handheld field properties" section will appear at the bottom of the dialog box.

7. From the Format drop-down list, select the value list format you prefer. From the Use value list drop-down menu, select the value list associated with the field (**Figure 12.55**).

8. When you're finished, click OK to return to the Mobile Settings dialog box.

continues on next page

Chapter 12

9. If you've created a found set to transfer, click the "Found set at time of synchronization" button in the Records section (**Figure 12.56**).

10. Select a Synchronization option, then click OK, and OK again.

    The Synchronization options determine what happens when a record in FM Pro and Mobile don't match. The default is "Duplicate records." This option creates two different records so you can choose between them later.

11. HotSync your handheld (**Figure 12.57**). The files you've chosen will be transferred to it.

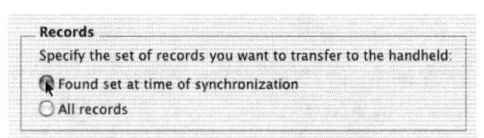

Figure 12.56 If you don't need an entire file, create a found set and choose the Found set option in the Records section.

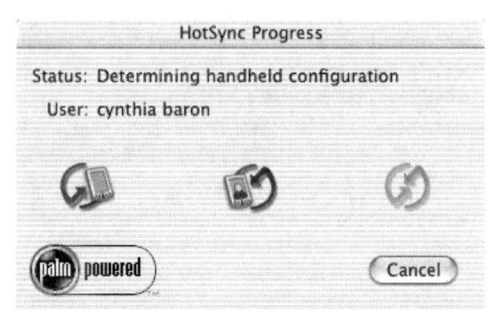

Figure 12.57 Your desktop Palm software will let you know that your files are being transferred.

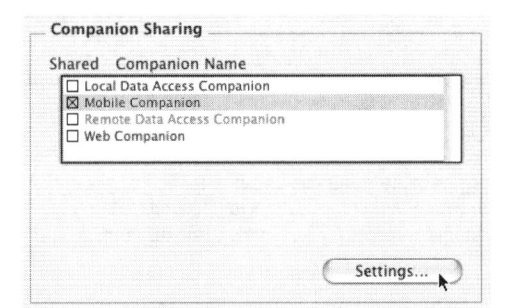

Figure 12.58 If you don't change your File Sharing options after you set up Mobile, you can go right to Settings without enabling the Companion Sharing section.

Synchronizing from Mobile to Pro

Once you've transferred a database to your handheld, you're sure to make changes and corrections as you work with it. Just as you needed to prepare the main database before you transferred it to your handheld, you'll need to prepare your Mobile database before transferring in the opposite direction.

To synchronize a FileMaker database:

1. Turn on your handheld, choose FileMaker from its main menu, and select the first database you want to synchronize.

2. On the handheld, choose Record > Show All Records.

    To make sure that all changes you've made in the handheld are transferred, your found set must be the entire database. Otherwise, only the changes in the records in the found set will be synchronized.

3. On your desktop computer, open the same FileMaker database that's open on the handheld. Check its current found set to make sure that the records you've transferred to the handheld are all included. If not, perform a find to select the right group of records or choose Record > Show All Records if both versions contain the entire database.

4. Repeat steps 2 and 3 for as many FileMaker databases as you need to synchronize.

5. On your computer, choose File > Sharing. When the File Sharing dialog box appears, check to make sure that Mobile Companion is still checked in the Companion Sharing section, then click Settings (**Figure 12.58**).

continues on next page

6. When the Mobile Settings dialog box appears, check your settings. In the Synchronization area, choose "Handheld overwrites desktop" to update the desktop database with the handheld's information. Choose "Desktop overwrites handheld" to replace the information on the handheld with the records on the computer (**Figure 12.59**).

7. HotSync your handheld.

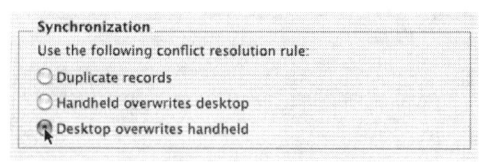

Figure 12.59 If you know you've made changes only in your handheld, you can avoid having to delete duplicate records by overwriting the desktop.

✔ **Tips**

- If you plan on using a found set to synchronize with your Palm OS handheld, create a single-step script with Perform Find (Restore) so you can easily find the set before synching. Sorting will probably take longer on the handheld, so if you'll always want your data sorted a single way, add a Sort (Restore) step as well.

- If you have multiple databases you need to transfer, be selective. Transfer only the records and fields that you're sure you'll need, and set up your most important database first. The amount of information you can carry will be limited by the amount of memory on your handheld, but even the fanciest one has only a fraction of the capacity of your computer.

- If you want to do a one-time import of an existing contact list from FileMaker Pro to your Palm's address book, you don't need FileMaker Mobile. In FileMaker, choose File > Export, navigate to your database, and select Tab-Separated Text as the file format. In your Palm Desktop software, choose File > Import and select the text file you just created. In the dialog box, choose Contacts as the type of database and match up the FileMaker field names with the Palm field names. Your database entries will be entered as Palm address book information. Sync the desktop to your handheld to transfer the information.

FileMaker Mobile, the Palm, and the Mac OS Dilemma

Many Macintosh FileMaker users are making the transition from the Mac Classic OS to OS X by putting both systems on their computer and booting into whichever one they need at the time. When moving files and information between the Classic and OS X versions of FileMaker Pro, the process is seamless. But when you use FileMaker Mobile, you add a handheld OS to the mix. Palm warns users that synchronizing data between the two Macintosh systems isn't supported, because user data is stored in different places in the two versions of the Palm desktop software.

Don't let this stop you from using FileMaker Mobile. There's a sneaky way around this problem that takes advantage of OS X's ability to understand the Classic OS. Install the Palm 4.0 software on both operating systems, accepting the installer's default folder placement. Synchronize the Palm on the Classic side. Still in Classic, go to your Documents folder and make an alias of the Palm folder. On the OS X side, navigate to the Documents folder in your home folder. You'll see a folder in Documents called Palm—drag it to the Trash. Now drop the Palm folder alias inside (**Figure 12.60**).

Now no matter which OS you use to synchronize your Palm and FileMaker Mobile data, the update will be kept in one place—the folder on the Classic side.

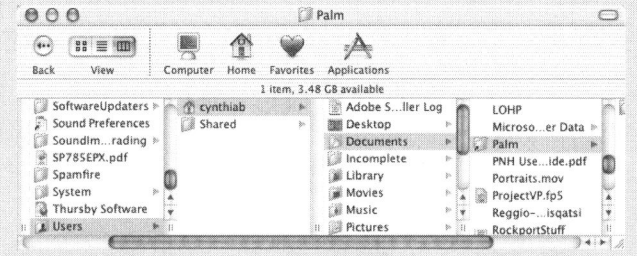

Figure 12.60 Delete the space and the word *alias* so the Palm software will always recognize the correct folder.

Once you've gotten the hang of this aliasing workaround, you'll find that you can apply it not only to the Palm desktop, but to many other software programs that share common data, like Microsoft Office and Eudora.

ODBC Import and Export

ODBC (Open Database Connectivity) is an application interface that gives all databases that support it—which is most of the databases in use today—a common "language" for record sharing. FileMaker users with access to large corporate databases like Oracle can use ODBC to access data. ODBC is also the method for importing database information from Microsoft Access files. Of course, information can go in the other direction, too. With ODBC as the translator, you can make your FileMaker databases available to corporate and Web databases as well.

That's a good thing, because setting up an ODBC database is considerably more difficult than setting up a FileMaker one, and often requires the services of a specialized programmer. It would be next to useless if it also required a programmer to mine information from the database once it's up and running. Fortunately, there's SQL (Structured Query Language)—a language designed to make that task a lot easier. FileMaker supports SQL, and helps you set up queries designed to extract very specific pieces of information from complex database files.

About FileMaker's ODBC Functions

Using SQL, FileMaker can interact with an ODBC database as both an end user and a data source. That doesn't make FileMaker itself an SQL database. FileMaker doesn't support the full range of SQL queries, and it doesn't ship with a wide variety of ODBC drivers. It supports text queries in all platforms (Windows and Mac OS X and Classic), but doesn't support Oracle 8 database drivers in Mac OS X. And it supports SQL Server 7 only in Windows.

Most important, every database you plan to pull data from or send data to has probably been constructed a little differently than you're used to in FileMaker. For example, SQL databases don't support repeating fields, and may mangle the repeated data when they receive it. Before you begin sharing information, it's a good idea to contact someone who knows about the other database's structure so you can prepare your FileMaker queries appropriately, or structure a new FileMaker database to work smoothly with the SQL database's format.

✔ Tip

- If you're using OS X and need to share ODBC data with other databases, you should definitely be using the latest OS X version and FileMaker 6.03. FileMaker's support of ODBC in OS X was very limited in version 5.5.

ODBC Import and Export

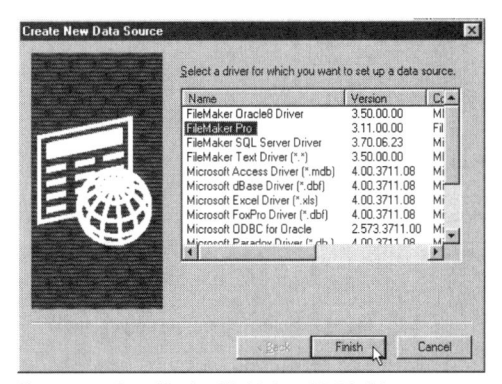

Figure 13.1 Specify the FileMaker ODBC driver to make your file available to other ODBC programs.

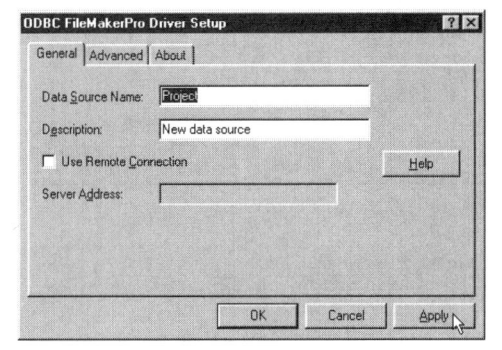

Figure 13.2 Other programs will identify your database by the name you enter.

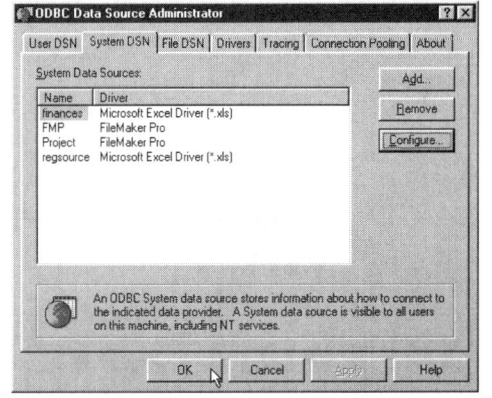

Figure 13.3 Your database will be available to other ODBC applications when it's listed as a data source.

Sharing Databases Using ODBC

You can share your FileMaker databases with ODBC client applications. To make it possible for others using ODBC to access your files, you must first register the FileMaker database on your computer as a data source, then turn on the Data Access plug-ins. The registration process is a bit different in different platforms.

To register a database in Windows:

1. Open the FileMaker database you want to register.

2. From the Windows taskbar, choose Start > Settings > Control Panel. Double-click ODBC Data Sources.

   The ODBC Data Source Administrator dialog box appears with the User DSN tab selected. You should see FileMaker listed as a user data source. If it isn't listed, click Add and follow the instructions that appear.

3. Click the System DSN tab, then click the Add button.

4. In the Create New Data Source dialog box, click the FileMaker Pro driver. Click Finish (**Figure 13.1**).

5. In the ODBC FileMaker Pro Driver Setup dialog box, type the name of your database in the Data Source Name box. You can add a description if you'd like, but it's not required (**Figure 13.2**). Click Apply and then OK.

6. Your database will now be listed in the System Data Sources window and will be available to other ODBC applications (**Figure 13.3**). Click OK to finish.

333

To register a database in the Classic Mac OS:

1. Open the FileMaker database you want to register.

2. Choose Apple Menu > Control Panels > ODBC Setup PPC.

   The ODBC Setup PPC control panel is installed with your FileMaker application.

3. The ODBC Data Source Administrator dialog box appears with the User DSN tab selected. Click Add (**Figure 13.4**).

4. In the Create New Data Source dialog box, double-click the ODBC 3.11 FileMaker Pro driver (**Figure 13.5**).

5. In the driver dialog box, type the name of your database in the Data Source Name box. You can add text in the Description box if you'd like, but it's not required (**Figure 13.6**). Click OK.

6. Your database will now be listed as a data source and will be available to other ODBC applications (**Figure 13.7**). Click OK to finish.

   The FileMaker file that you register as a data source must be open in FileMaker to be available to other programs.

Figure 13.4 This dialog box is empty if you've never used ODBC before.

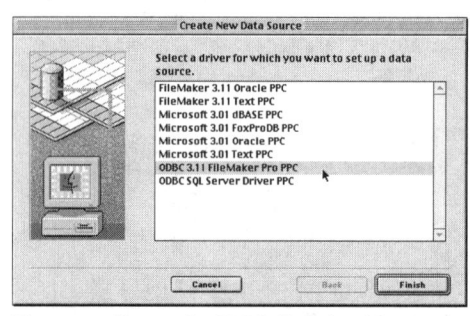

Figure 13.5 Choose the ODBC FileMaker driver.

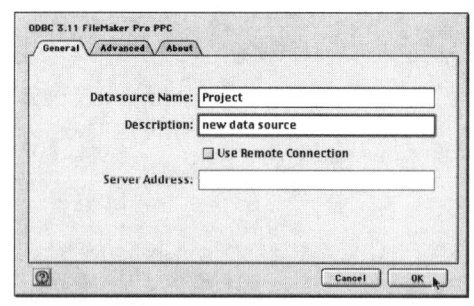

Figure 13.6 Name your database to broadcast it as an ODBC data source.

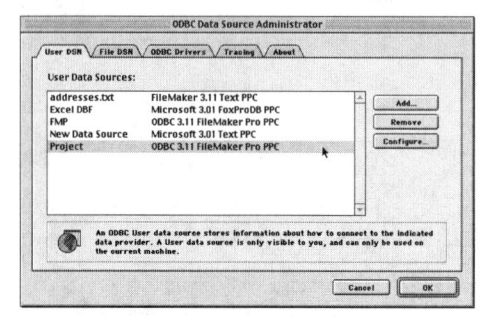

Figure 13.7 Your database is available as a data source to other applications.

ODBC Import and Export

Figure 13.8 You need to find the ODBC driver installer on your hard drive before you can use ODBC in OS X.

Figure 13.9 The ODBC driver installer creates a new folder in your Applications folder.

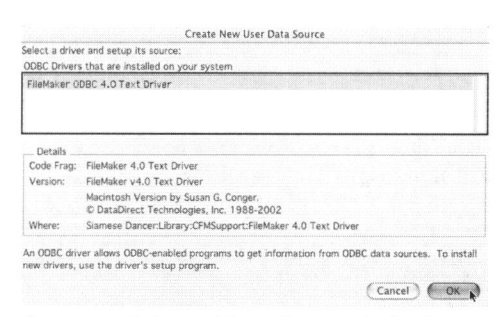

Figure 13.10 Only one driver will appear in the Create New Data Source dialog box, unless you've purchased and installed a third-party ODBC driver.

Figure 13.11 Other programs need a name by which to identify your file.

To register a database in Macintosh OS X:

1. To use ODBC in OS X, you first need to install the ODBC drivers. Go to the drive where your OS X applications reside. Navigate to Applications/FileMaker Pro 6/FileMaker ODBC drivers (**Figure 13.8**). You'll need OS X administrator access to run the installer in the folder.

2. Double-click the FileMaker Pro ODBC Drivers installer. Click Accept, then OK.

3. After the installation finishes, go to the drive where your OS X applications reside. Navigate to Applications/DataDirect ODBC folder. Double-click ODBC Configure (**Figure 13.9**).

4. The Configuration Manager dialog box appears with the User DSN tab selected. Click Add.

5. When the Create New User Data Source dialog box appears, double-click the driver (**Figure 13.10**).

   There is only one driver option in OS X.

6. When the Text Driver Configuration dialog box appears, type the name of your database in the Data Source Name box. You can add text in the Description box if you'd like, but it's not required (**Figure 13.11**).

continues on next page

335

Chapter 13

7. Click Choose Directory. When the "Choose a database folder" dialog box appears, navigate to the folder that holds the FileMaker database you want to register. Click Choose to select the database (**Figure 13.12**).

8. The path to the database will appear in the Text Driver Configuration dialog box (**Figure 13.13**). Choose a default table type, if needed, from the drop-down menu, then click OK to finish.

   The FileMaker file that you register as a data source must be open in FileMaker to be available to other programs.

To turn on Data Access plug-ins:

1. In Windows and the Classic Mac OS, choose Edit > Preferences > Application. In Mac OS X, choose FileMaker Pro 6 > Preferences > Application.

2. Click the Plug-Ins tab of the Preferences dialog box.

3. Click the check box next to Local Data Access Companion if you're going to use a program on your own computer to access FileMaker files.

4. Click the check box next to Remote Data Access Companion to allow other users on the network to access the databases (**Figure 13.14**). Click OK to save the settings.

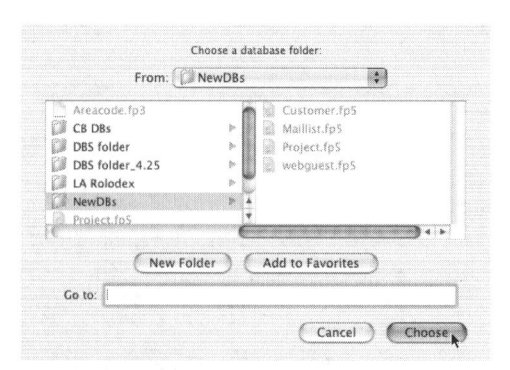

Figure 13.12 Select the database to be broadcast as an ODBC data source.

Figure 13.13 Other ODBC applications will follow this path to locate your FileMaker database.

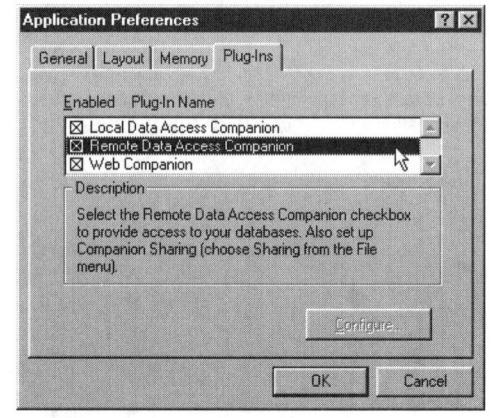

Figure 13.14 The Remote Data Access Companion plug-in creates access to your FileMaker database over a network.

About Importing ODBC Data

FileMaker allows you to use SQL commands to mine a database for very specific sets of information as well as to both import and export information between a FileMaker database and an ODBC database.

FileMaker gives you several options for incorporating ODBC data and queries into your work. You can open a database and write a query on the fly to get or give information. You can put SQL statements into text files to quickly build a query, or you can use the Execute SQL query step within a multistep script to allow users who would normally run screaming from SQL syntax to access and use ODBC data.

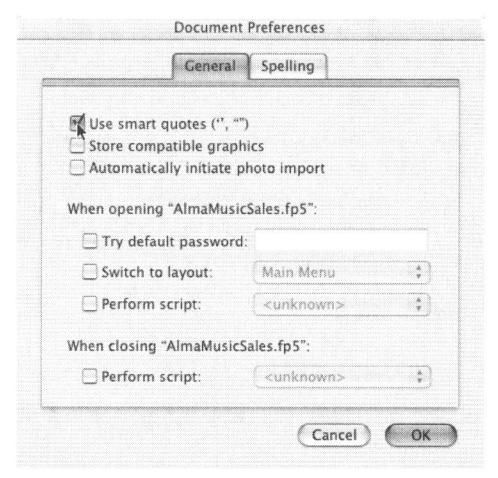

Figure 13.15 Turn off smart quotes in any file that you'll use to import or export ODBC data.

✔ Tips

- Think twice about moving to Mac OS X if you need to access an Oracle database from your Macintosh. OS X only supports the ODBC text driver. If you're working in Windows or the Classic Mac OS, FileMaker will import data from all Oracle databases through Oracle 8.

- Although smart quotes (sometimes called curly quotes) are more attractive and professional-looking in text than simple straight quotes, they can wreak havoc if they find their way into a script statement or an SQL query, because they won't be recognized properly. Go to Edit > Preferences > Document (FileMaker Pro > Preferences > Document in OS X) and uncheck "Use smart quotes" (**Figure 13.15**) before you interact with an ODBC data source.

Storing SQL Commands in Fields

SQL is not as friendly and intuitive as FileMaker—you have to become familiar with its syntax and commands to use it effectively. But it isn't particularly difficult to learn, and it's worth the effort if you need to get files from an ODBC database.

You can type an SQL query in any field, but it's not a good idea to just type the query the way you would any other piece of data. If you make even a small syntax mistake in an SQL statement, your query won't be executed. Fortunately, FileMaker has provided SQL Query Builder—a little helper tool for creating an SQL query with perfect syntax.

In this example, we'll create an SQL query to extract a subset of information from the ODBC database: the first names, last names, social security numbers, and salaries of a list of employees. Once we have the query saved, we'll create an import script to reuse this SQL query for future imports.

To store an SQL command in a field:

1. Open a database in which you want to use the ODBC data. Choose File > Define Fields (Control+Shift+D/Command+Shift+D).

2. When the Define Fields dialog box appears, type gGet Employees as the field name, make it a global field, and click Create.

3. When the Options dialog box appears, choose Text as the data type, then click OK (**Figure 13.16**). Click Done to finish.

4. Choose File > Import Records > ODBC source. When the Select ODBC Data Source dialog box appears, choose your ODBC file from the list (**Figure 13.17**).

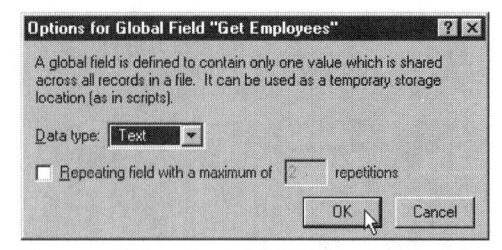

Figure 13.16 We create a global field so we can use it from any record, and make it a text field so SQL will be able to read it.

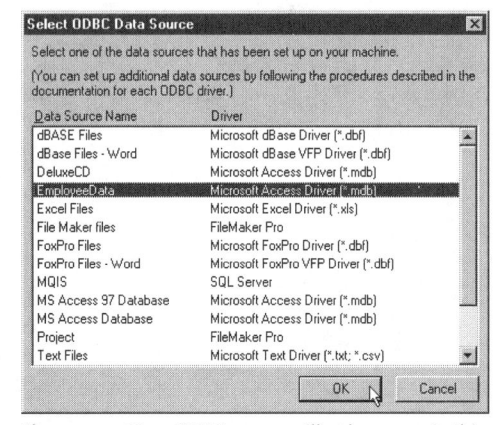

Figure 13.17 Your ODBC source will only appear in this window if you set it up first in your computer's ODBC control panel.

ODBC Import and Export

Figure 13.18 Most ODBC data sources have security settings and require a password.

5. If the data source requires a user name and password, enter them in the Enter Password dialog box. If you don't need a password, just click OK (**Figure 13.18**).

6. When the SQL Query builder appears, click to select the database table you want from the Tables listing on the left (**Figure 13.19**).

   Tables in SQL are similar to files in FileMaker. Columns are similar to FileMaker fields.

7. When the Columns list appears on the right, double-click the first field whose contents you want to import to add it to the SQL Query formula-builder section. In this example, we've chosen the SocialSecurityNumber field (**Figure 13.20**).

8. Double-click the second field whose contents you want to import (**Figure 13.21**).

   FileMaker adds the second field name to the SELECT section of the query. In our example, it's the FirstName field.

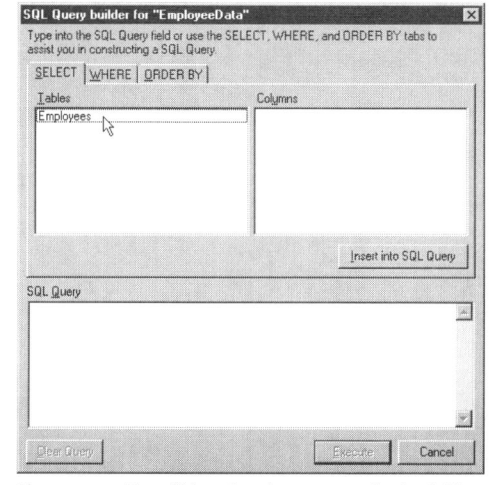

   continues on next page

Figure 13.19 Even if there's only one entry in the Tables section, you must select it to see the list of Columns.

Figure 13.20 Columns are listed alphabetically in the SQL Query builder.

Figure 13.21 As you select additional columns, they're added to the SQL query below.

STORING SQL COMMANDS IN FIELDS

339

Chapter 13

9. One at a time, select as many additional fields as you want to add to the query.

10. When you're finished adding fields to the query, click inside the SQL Query box and select the entire query. Copy the query to your clipboard, then click Execute (**Figure 13.22**).

    We continue with the Import process to set the correct field import order.

11. When the Import Field Mapping dialog box appears, match up the data from the ODBC file with the existing field names on the right (**Figure 13.23**). When you're finished, click Import.

12. Choose Records > Delete Found Records to delete the found set.

13. In Browse mode, go to a layout that holds the field you created in step 2, or enter Layout mode and add the field to a layout, then return to Browse mode.

14. Paste the SQL query you built into the gGet Employees field (**Figure 13.24**).

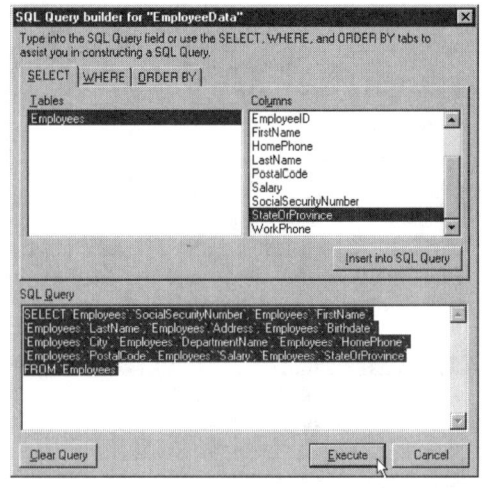

Figure 13.22 You copy the query to your clipboard so you can use it after the import. You can't step backward through the SQL Query builder to copy it later.

Figure 13.24 The SQL query is stored in a field that you can access at any time.

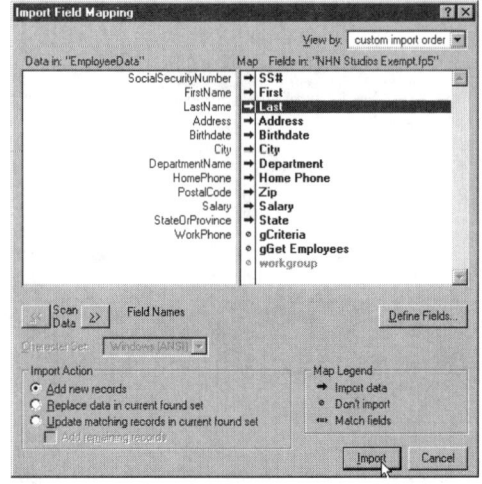

Figure 13.23 When you match up the fields, make sure that there's an arrow in the Map column for every field you want to import.

ODBC Import and Export

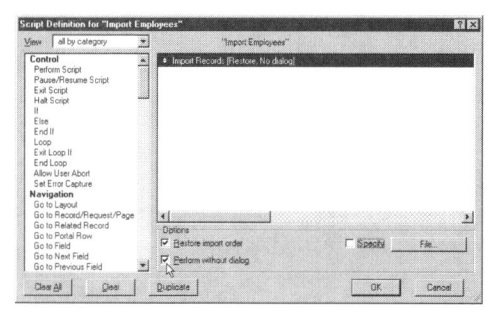

Figure 13.25 To avoid having to scroll through numerous dialog boxes every time you run the import script, choose "Perform without dialog."

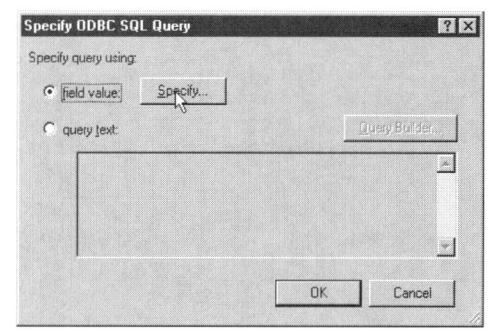

Figure 13.26 When you choose "field value," you need to specify which field contains the SQL data.

Figure 13.27 Select the global field in which you stored your SQL query.

We now have the complete, correct syntax for an SQL command with many variables, stored in a global field. You can repeat the process for any set of queries you're likely to use frequently, saving time and eliminating the possibility of syntax errors. The stored query can be rerun at any time by inserting it into an import script.

To use a stored SQL query in an import script:

1. Choose Scripts > ScriptMaker.

2. In the Define Scripts dialog box, type a name for your script and click Create.

3. The Script Definition dialog box will appear. In the step list on the left, scroll to the Records section and double-click Import Records.

4. In the Options section, check "Restore import order" and "Perform without dialog" (**Figure 13.25**).

5. Click the File button to bring up the Open File dialog box. From the "Files of type" drop-down menu, select "ODBC data sources." When the ODBC Data Source dialog box appears, select your ODBC database, then click OK.

6. When the Enter Password dialog box appears, enter your user name and password. Click the "Save user name and password" check box, then click OK.

7. When the Specify ODBC SQL Query dialog box appears, select the "field value" radio button. Click Specify (**Figure 13.26**).

8. In the Specify Field dialog box, double-click the global field in which you stored your SQL query. In our case, that's gGet Employees (**Figure 13.27**).

9. Click OK, then OK again, then Done. When you run this script, the ODBC data will automatically be found and imported into your database.

341

Chapter 13

Using Calculations to Build Complex Queries

Saving a query in a field saves lots of time and agony, especially if you aren't accustomed to using SQL regularly. If you squirrel away your most useful queries, you don't have to relearn SQL or rethink your needs every few weeks. Unfortunately, you can't run multiple SQL queries in a single script, or refine one query with additional criteria. If you want to make your SQL queries more flexible, your best tool is a calculation field. By breaking your queries into parts and recombining them with a calculation, you can quickly build more useful commands.

To create an SQL command by calculation:

1. Choose File > Define Fields (Control+Shift+D/Command+Shift+D).

2. When the Define Fields dialog box appears, type *gCriteria* as the field name, make it a global field, and click Create.

3. When the Options dialog box appears, choose Text as the data type, then click OK.

4. Repeat steps 2 and 3 for as many modular ODBC commands as you would like to store.

5. Choose File > Import Records > ODBC source.

6. When the Select ODBC Data Source dialog box appears, choose your ODBC file from the list. Enter your user name and password, or just click OK if you don't need one.

7. When the SQL Query builder appears, click to select the database table you want from the Tables list on the left, then select the ODBC data fields you want from the Columns section on the right.

ODBC Import and Export

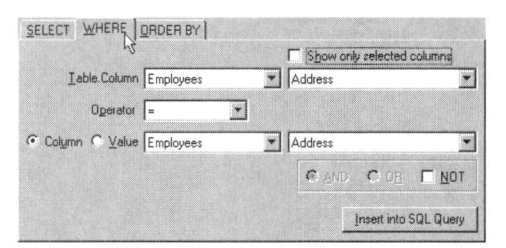

Figure 13.28 Select the Where tab to choose exactly the group of records you need.

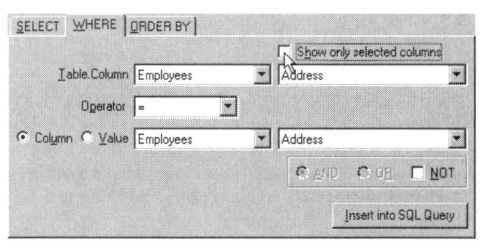

Figure 13.29 When you check "Show only selected columns," only those columns you chose to include in your query will be available in the column drop-down menu.

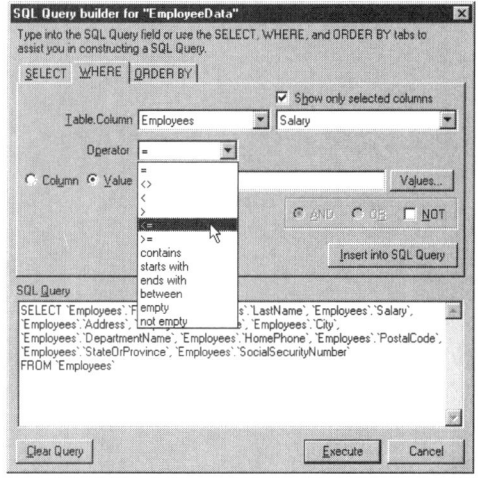

Figure 13.30 Choose an operator that matches the criterion you've selected.

8. Click to select the Where tab (**Figure 13.28**).

   In SQL you use Where to narrow the selection according to the options you choose.

9. Click the "Show only selected columns" check box to prevent choosing a criterion that isn't part of the columns you've already selected (**Figure 13.29**).

10. From the column drop-down menu on the right, select the ODBC data column you want to use to define your criterion. For this example, we choose Salary.

11. In the Operator drop-down menu, select the operator you need to define your criterion.

    In our example, we choose the less than or equal to operator (<=) because we're searching for people with salaries equal to or below a certain amount (**Figure 13.30**).

    continues on next page

USING CALCULATIONS TO BUILD COMPLEX QUERIES

343

Chapter 13

12. Choose the Column or Value radio button to finish your query. If you want to compare two different data columns, select Column. If you want to define a specific number, select Value. The dialog box will update depending on which choice you make.

    In our example, we select Value (**Figure 13.31**).

13. Type the value you want in the input box to the right of Value, or click Values to open the Column Values dialog box, where you choose a value from those in the ODBC data (**Figure 13.32**). Click OK to close the Column Values dialog box.

14. Click Insert into SQL Query to transfer your choices into the SQL Query formula box (**Figure 13.33**).

15. Select everything in the SQL Query box and copy it to the clipboard. Click Cancel to close the SQL Query builder box.

16. In your layout, select one of the global fields you created and paste the SQL query into the field.

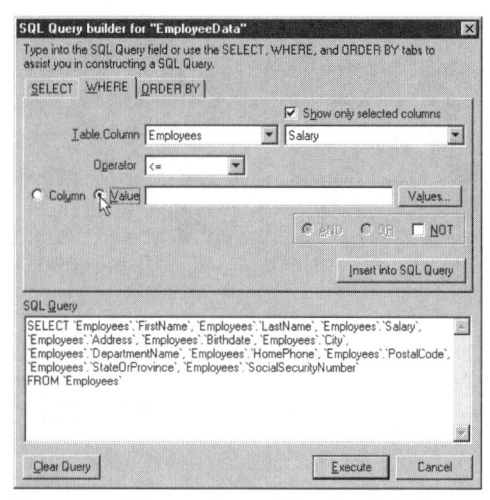

Figure 13.31 When we choose Value, the dialog box updates to show one input box instead of two drop-down menus because we won't be comparing two columns as part of our query.

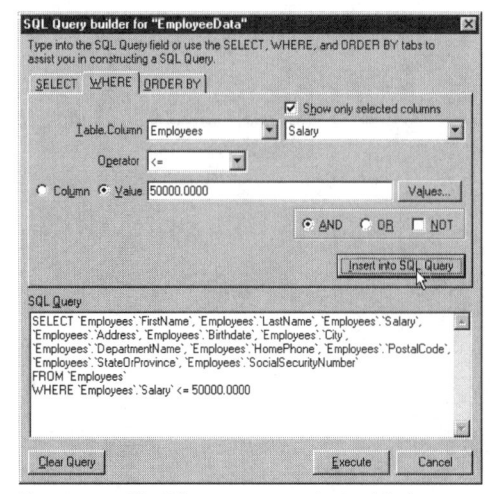

Figure 13.33 The Where statement isn't added automatically to your SQL Query—you must click the Insert button.

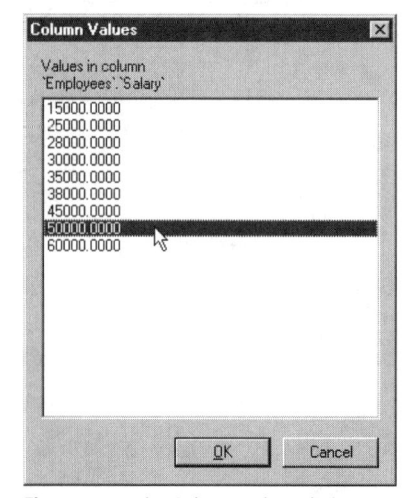

Figure 13.32 The Column Values dialog box displays only values that appear in the database.

344

ODBC Import and Export

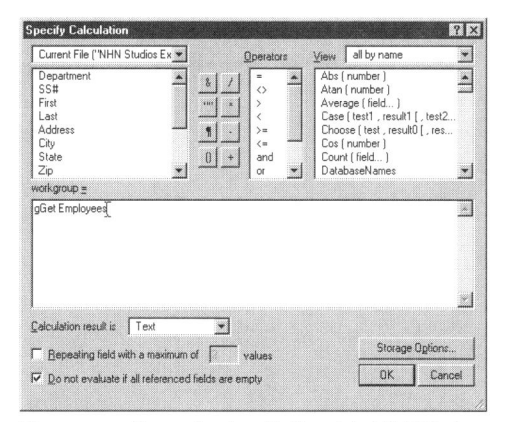

Figure 13.34 Always begin with the global field that contains the Select portion of the query.

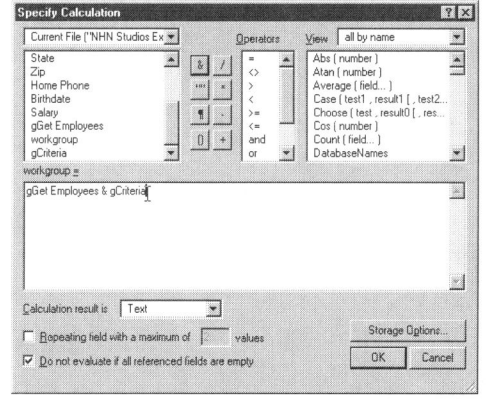

Figure 13.35 The finished calculation combines two global fields to make a complete query that selects ODBC columns based on your Where criterion and imports them into your database.

17. Copy and paste the Where section of your query into another global field.

    By dividing the query into two pieces, you make each of them modular. Without having to return to the query builder, you can vary the fields you import separately from the salary criteria you specify.

18. Choose File > Define Fields (Control+Shift+D/Command+Shift+D). When the Define Fields dialog box appears, type a new field name, make it a calculation field, and click Create.

    We call our calculation field "Workgroup." We'll use this field to combine query modules for the import script.

19. When the Specify Calculation dialog box appears, select the global field that holds the first part of the SQL query from the field list on the left (**Figure 13.34**).

    The Select portion must always come before the Where portion.

20. Click the ampersand (&) operator button, then select the global field holding the other half of the query (**Figure 13.35**).

21. Make sure that Text is selected in the "Calculation result is" menu, then click OK, then Done.

22. Delete the global fields from your layout so their text can't be changed by mistake.

    You can repeat this process to create several different combinations of selections and criteria, combining them for your most frequent SQL queries.

✔ **Tip**

- In Chapter 10, we showed you how to use the Status (CurrentError) function to determine whether something has gone wrong with a script. You can use the Status (CurrentODBCError) function in much the same way, except that it returns any ODBC errors that occur when you run a SQL query.

345

Creating Dynamic SQL Queries

Although the SQL Query builder is extremely useful for importing, it doesn't include menus for other SQL tasks. When the need arises, you'll find the Execute SQL script step invaluable. Like other script steps, you can use Execute SQL more than once in a single script, allowing you to make several changes to an ODBC database at once.

In this example, we use SQL to give raises to groups of employees in the ODBC database, then transfer the payroll records into our FileMaker database.

To run an SQL query from a script:

1. Open a file you use to work with an ODBC database. Choose Records > Sort and sort the records by the criteria you want.

2. Choose Scripts > ScriptMaker.

3. When the Define Scripts dialog box appears, name the script "Salary Increase" and click Create.

4. When the Script Definition dialog box appears, scroll down to the Miscellaneous section in the step list on the left and double-click Execute SQL. In the Options section, check "Perform without dialog," then click Specify (**Figure 13.36**).

5. When the Specify SQL dialog box appears, click Specify in the ODBC Data Source section (**Figure 13.37**).

6. When the ODBC Data Source dialog box appears, select your data source from the list and click OK.

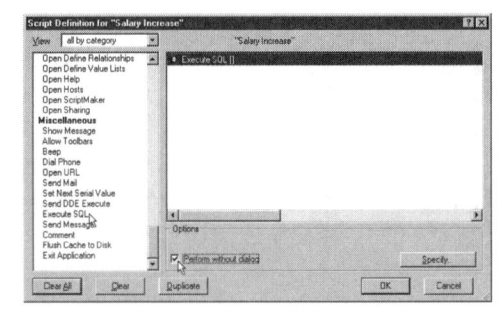

Figure 13.36 To automate your SQL query, choose "Perform without dialog."

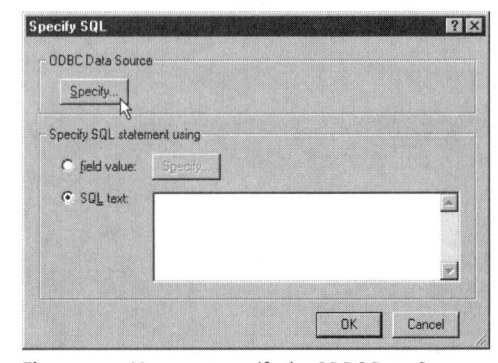

Figure 13.37 You must specify the ODBC Data Source every time you execute a different SQL script step.

ODBC Import and Export

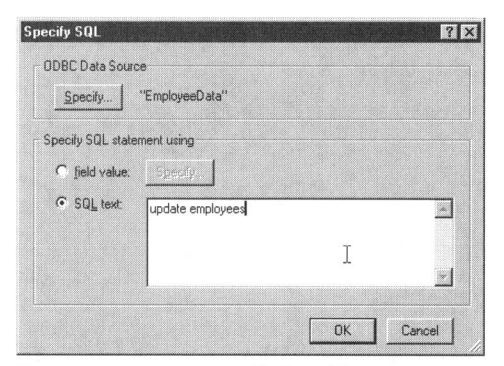

Figure 13.38 You must specify the table you want to update every time you write a different SQL query.

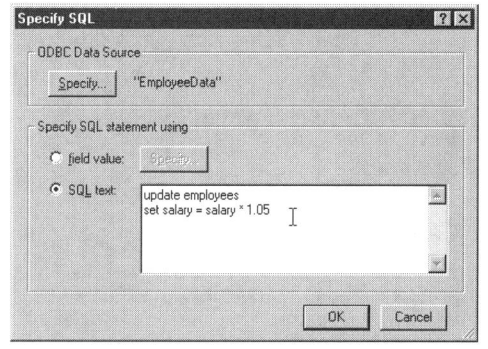

Figure 13.39 Although you don't have to type each command on a separate line, doing so makes it easier to read the query.

7. Enter your user name and password in the Enter Password dialog box, then click the "Save user name and password" check box. Click OK to return to the Specify SQL dialog box.

8. In the "Specify SQL statement using" section, select the "SQL text" radio button.

9. Enter the appropriate SQL command in the query builder box. In our example, our ODBC table is called "employees," so we type `update employees` in the query-builder box (**Figure 13.38**).

   The SQL command update changes one or more rows in the ODBC table. In this case, it will update the table called "employees" based on the criteria you specify next.

10. Enter the criteria you want to use to update the ODBC table. To change a value in a specific way, you use the SQL set command.

    We want to increase the salary for some employees by 5 percent, so we type `set salary=salary*1.05` (**Figure 13.39**). This command line says that whatever figure is currently in the salary column of the table should now be set to that figure multiplied by 105 percent.

11. If you don't want every salary to be set to the new number, you have to refine the criteria with a Where statement. Not all employees in our example will get the same increase. To specify which salaries change, we type the criterion `where salary <35000.00`.

    This portion of the SQL command modifies the Set command so that only employees whose salary is currently less than $35,000 a year will receive the 5 percent increase.

continues on next page

Chapter 13

12. Add a semicolon (;) to signify the end of the SQL query (**Figure 13.40**). Click OK to return to the Script Definition dialog box.

13. Click Duplicate to make a copy of the Execute SQL step (**Figure 13.41**), then double-click the copy to edit it.

14. When the Specify SQL dialog box appears, change the amount in the second line to 1.08.

15. Change the last line of the query to where salary >35000.00, then click OK (**Figure 13.42**).

    This statement increases by 8 percent the salary of all employees currently making more than $35,000.

16. Now we want to import the salary records into our FileMaker database. In the step list in the Script Definition dialog box, scroll to the Records section and double-click Import Records.

17. In the Options section, select "Perform without dialog" and "Restore import order" (**Figure 13.43**).

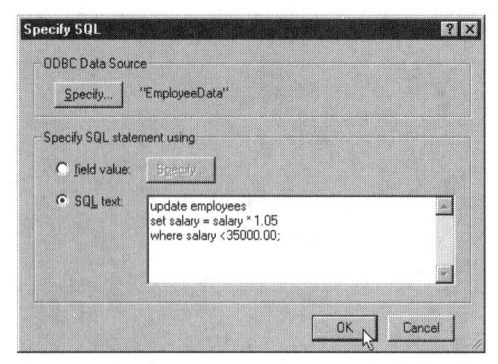

Figure 13.40 Every SQL statement you write by hand must end with a semicolon.

Figure 13.41 It's easier to avoid mistakes if you duplicate and edit an existing Execute SQL step than if you write each one from scratch.

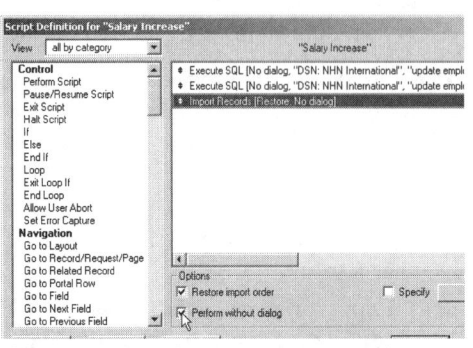

Figure 13.43 Always have a correct import order in place, and make sure to restore it in the Import Records step.

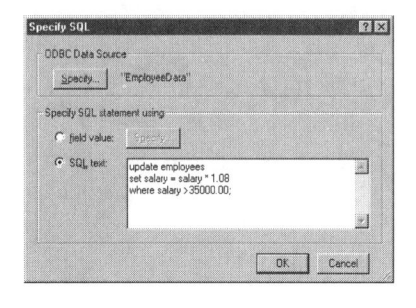

Figure 13.42 Change the last line of the original SQL text to create a slightly different statement.

ODBC Import and Export

Figure 13.44 Select either a field that holds a portion of an SQL statement or a calculation field that combines two or more pieces of statements.

Figure 13.45 Choose a layout in which to display the imported and updated records.

Figure 13.46 If you Show All Records and Sort, the new data will be displayed with the existing FileMaker records.

18. Click the File button to bring up the Open File dialog box. Select "ODBC data sources" from the "Files of type" drop-down menu. When the ODBC Data Source dialog box appears, select your ODBC database, then click OK.

19. When the Specify SQL dialog box appears, select the "field value" radio button. Click Specify.

20. In the Specify Field dialog box, double-click the calculation field you created in "To create an SQL command by calculation" earlier in this chapter (**Figure 13.44**). Click OK, then OK again.

21. If you'd like to open the data in a specific layout, back in the Script Definition dialog box, select Go to Layout in the Navigation section of the step list. Under Options, select the layout you want from the drop-down menu (**Figure 13.45**).

22. In the Sort/Find/Print section of the step list, double-click Show All Records, then double-click Sort. Make sure that "Perform without dialog" is checked in the Options section. When you're done, click OK (**Figure 13.46**), then Done.

When this script runs, it will do two separate salary increases in the ODBC database, and will then use your SQL import criteria to bring records over to FileMaker and display them with your other records.

349

Data Importing and Repairing

The world is full of information and comparatively little of it is perfect and ready to use in your database. Foreign data can be sprinkled with useless formatting and unreadable characters. Tabular text and spreadsheets may be easy to import, but often require so much editing that you're tempted to start from scratch. Perhaps you've been given the task of incorporating a file whose data overlaps with your own, but hesitate to corrupt your own files with duplications and inconsistencies. Even existing FileMaker databases can present problems. They may not have been created in a recent version, or have been so poorly designed that they need emergency care.

There are several strategies you can use to overcome these problems. Some take advantage of word processors and spreadsheets to clean up the problems before you import. Others are simple FileMaker methods that mold the new data into clean, useful records.

Cleaning Up Text Data before Importing

Sometimes the data you want to import looks promising, but the text file has a consistent quirk that is sure to cause problems. Although most people work with fairly recent versions of software, there are isolated holdouts who use programs so antiquated that their software doesn't use either of the standard delimiter characters (commas or tabs). Problems also occur with text files that contain extra return characters: The extra return produces a blank record, which can throw the database import structure off.

If you have a text file that contains extra returns or other single-character anomalies, there is a relatively painless method for removing them in Microsoft Word, before you import the file. Be sure to work on a copy of your text file, not the original, so that you can recover the original if you make a mistake. Not all of these changes are easy to undo.

Figure 14.1 To see the formatting in a text file, use Tools > Options or Preference to make the nonprinting characters visible.

Figure 14.2 These extra return characters need to be stripped out of the file before it's imported.

To delete formatting characters in Word:

1. Open the text file in Word.

2. Choose Tools > Options (Windows) or Preferences (Macintosh).

3. When the Options or Preferences dialog box appears, the View tab will be selected. Under "Nonprinting characters," click the check boxes next to "Tab characters" and "Paragraph marks" (**Figure 14.1**). (In Word 2000, the section you need in the View tab is called "Formatting marks.") Click OK.

   Tab and return characters that are usually hidden will now appear in the text file. If you see extra returns that need removing (**Figure 14.2**), choose Edit > Replace.

Data Importing and Repairing

Figure 14.3 Formatting characters are available in the Special drop-down menu.

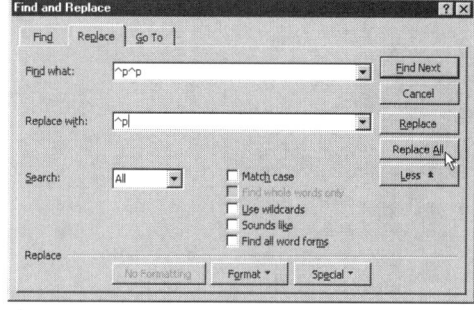

Figure 14.4 Replace All examines the entire document and replaces every double return with a single return.

4. In the Find and Replace dialog box, click the More button to display more search options.

5. Click Special and select Paragraph Mark from the drop-down menu (**Figure 14.3**). Do this a second time, so that you have two paragraph marks in the "Find what" box.

6. Tab to the "Replace with" box, click Special and select Paragraph Mark from the drop-down menu.

7. Click Replace All (**Figure 14.4**).
   Word searches for two consecutive returns and deletes one of them. Repeat the Replace All command until Word indicates that no replacements were made, then save the file.

8. You can now import the file into FileMaker without creating extra blank records.

✔ Tip

- When editing text files before importing, be very careful about deleting tabs and returns. If you accidentally remove one of these characters, you can throw off the structure of the file. If the file structure is changed, all your data from that point on could be imported into the wrong fields.

Finding and Eliminating Duplicates

Duplicate records are a constant problem in databases, particularly if you have to merge data from different sources to update or create them. Even if you're diligent in updating the unavoidable changes in contact person, address, phone, and email information, if you have duplicate records you can never be sure that you've edited the right one.

Calculated fields offer a clean and relatively simple way to find and dump the duplicates. They do, however, depend on your having a good definition of what constitutes a duplicate file. In this example, we define a duplicate by the simplest criteria: two records with the same first and last name. In a larger database, however, you'll probably want to expand that definition to include some or all of the address as well, to take into account the fact that more than one individual can have the same name.

Because setting up a calculation is time-consuming and you'll probably want to weed for duplicates periodically, we'll create a script to automate the process.

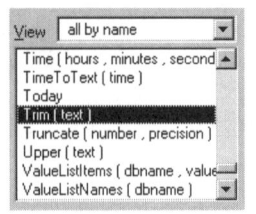

Figure 14.5 Select Trim to delete initial and trailing spaces around an entry.

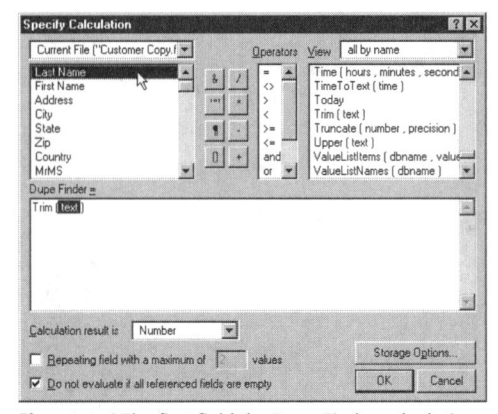

Figure 14.6 The first field the Dupe Finder calculation trims is Last Name.

To find duplicate records:

1. In the file you want to weed, choose File > Define Fields.

2. In the Define Fields dialog box, type **Dupe Finder** for the field name and click the Calculation radio button. Click Create.

3. When the Specify Calculation dialog box appears, scroll down in the function list on the right to Trim, and double-click to select it (**Figure 14.5**).

   The Trim function deletes any spaces at the beginning or end of a record.

4. In the field list on the left, double-click Last Name (**Figure 14.6**).

Data Importing and Repairing

Figure 14.7 The second half of the calculation trims the First Name field.

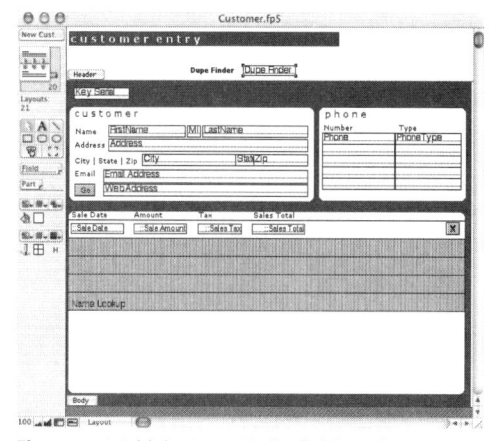

Figure 14.8 Add the Dupe Finder field to a layout.

Figure 14.9 The exclamation point is the Find symbol for duplicates.

5. Click to the right of the parentheses and click the ampersand (&) operator button.

6. Click the quotes button and type a space between the quotes.

   The space must be placed within quotes so it can be read as part of the function. Otherwise it would be ignored.

7. Click to the right of the quotes and click the ampersand operator button.

8. In the function list, double-click Trim.

9. In the field list on the left, double-click the First Name field (**Figure 14.7**).

   We chose the Last Name field before the First Name field because that's how they appear in the layout we use. You should adapt the field choices and add text characters (like commas) to fit your needs.

10. From the "Calculation result" pop-up menu, choose Text. Click OK, and then Done to finish.

11. To use this calculation, you need to put the Dupe Finder field in a layout. Go to a layout that displays the records in a form that allows you to check them. Choose View > Layout Mode (Control+L/ Command+L).

12. Drag the Field tool into the layout. When the Specify Field dialog box appears, double-click Dupe Finder. The field will be placed on your layout (**Figure 14.8**).

13. Choose View > Find Mode (Control+F/Command+F).

14. Click in the Dupe Finder field. Choose the exclamation point (duplicates) from the Symbols drop-down menu (**Figure 14.9**).

continues on next page

355

Chapter 14

15. Click the Find button.

    If there any duplicate values in the Dupe Finder field, those records will become the found set and be displayed in the layout.

16. If no records were found, make a duplicate copy of any record (Control+D/Command+D) and click Find again.

    The next step is to write a script to automate this process, and unless the search successfully locates a found set with your criteria, the script won't have any criteria to restore, and therefore won't work.

17. Choose Scripts > ScriptMaker.

18. Name the script "Dupe Finder" and click Create.

19. The Script Definition dialog box appears. In the script step list on the left, scroll down to the Sort/Find/Print section and double-click Perform Find (**Figure 14.10**). Click OK, and then Done to finish.

    You can remove the Dupe Finder from the layout because you no longer need it. If you duplicated a record to create a find criterion, delete it as well.

Figure 14.10 Use the Perform Find (Restore) step to automatically find duplicates.

✔ **Tips**

- The best way to look at the duplicate records you've found is in a column-format layout. This lets you see all the data in the same layout.

- Be careful not to choose Delete Found Records when you run the Dupe Finder. Dupe Finder will display both copies of the record so you can compare them. If you delete the found set, you delete both the duplicate and the original.

Importing Data without Duplications

Although it's good to clean up a database after you've imported records, it's even better to avoid duplication to begin with.

To compare your new data with your old data and avoid importing duplicates, you'll need to have the field and script created in "To find duplicate records" above. You'll also want to create a clone of the main file first. You can then import the data into the clone, manipulate it in perfect confidence and safety, and import the results into the main file.

To clone a database:

1. Open the main file in FileMaker.
2. Choose File > Save a Copy as.
3. In the Create Copy or "Create a copy named" dialog box, choose Clone (no records) from the "Save a" or Type drop-down menu (**Figure 14.11**). Click Save.

This clone has all the fields, scripts, and other elements from your database, but contains no records. It's a perfect place to import your new data and strip it of duplicates before adding it to the main file.

To import data without duplicates:

1. In the database clone, choose File > Define Relationships.
2. In the Define Relationships dialog box, click the New button.
3. In the Open File dialog box, navigate to your original database and double-click to open it.
4. When the Edit Relationship dialog box appears, type a name in the Relationship Name box (we use Dupes).

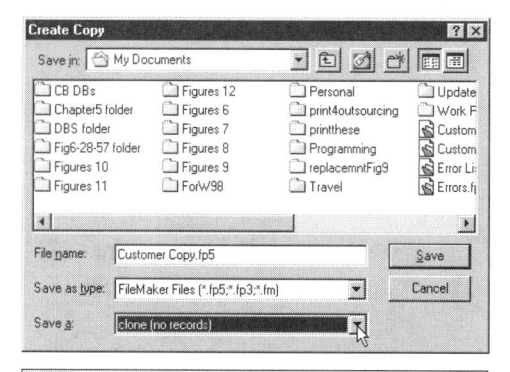

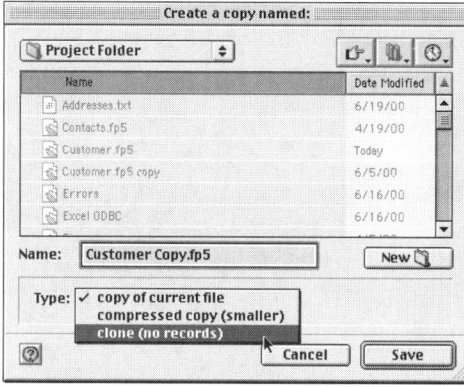

continues on next page

Figure 14.11 A saved copy (clone) will have the same structure as the original file but no records.

357

Chapter 14

5. Select the Dupe Finder field for both databases (**Figure 14.12**). Click OK and then Done to finish.

6. In the cloned file, choose File > Define Fields. In the Define Fields dialog box, name the field (ours is Dupe Lookup). Click Create.

7. In the field list, double-click Dupe Lookup to bring up the Options dialog box. In the Auto-Enter tab click the "Looked-up value" check box.

8. When the Lookup for Field dialog box appears, choose Dupes from the "Lookup a value" drop-down menu (**Figure 14.13**).

9. In the scrolling field list, click the Dupe Finder field. In the "If no exact match, then" area, verify that the "do not copy" radio button is selected (**Figure 14.14**). Click OK twice, then Done to finish.

   So far, we've created a relationship between the original and clone files that will compare the data in them based on the calculation field Dupe Finder. Only duplicate records will have a value copied to the Dupe Finder field in the clone.

10. Choose File > Import Records > File. In the Open File dialog box, navigate to the file you want to import and double-click to open it.

11. When the Field Mapping dialog box appears, follow the instructions in "To import text data files" in Chapter 12 to map the fields, then click Import.

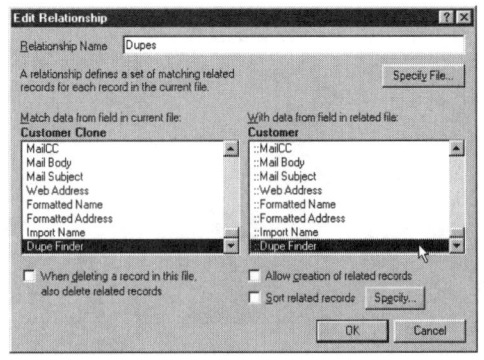

Figure 14.12 The Dupes relationship uses the Dupe Finder field in both the main and clone files.

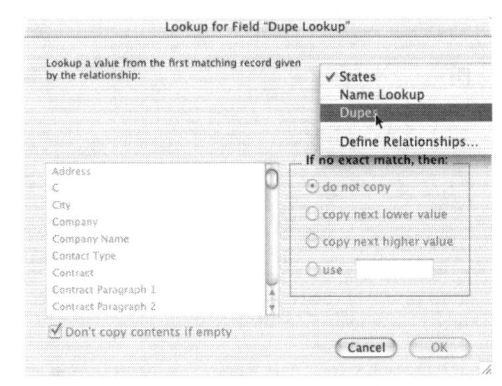

Figure 14.13 Use the Dupes relationship for the lookup in the Dupe Lookup field.

Figure 14.14 If there's no match, the "Don't copy contents if empty" option will put nothing in the Dupe Lookup field.

Data Importing and Repairing

Figure 14.15 The "Perform auto-enter" option will do the lookup when you import the data.

Figure 14.16 Before importing into the main file, find all records that don't have an entry in the Dupe Lookup field.

12. When the Import Options dialog box appears, check the "Perform auto-enter options" check box (**Figure 14.15**). Click OK.

13. Choose View > Layout Mode (Control+L/Command+L). Drag the Field tool into the layout. In the Specify Field dialog box, choose the lookup field you just created (ours is Dupe Lookup).

14. Choose File > Find Mode (Control+F/Command+F).

15. Click in the Dupe Lookup field and choose = from the Symbols drop-down menu (**Figure 14.16**). Click Find.

    The = symbol tells FileMaker to find records with no value in the Dupe Lookup field. Since the Dupe Lookup field only contains a value if it is a duplicate record, it will be blank if the imported data doesn't match any records in the main file.

16. When the find is done, none of the records in the found set are duplicates of those in the main database. Open the main database file and choose File > Import Records > File.

17. When the Open File dialog box appears, navigate to the database clone and double-click to select it as the file to import. The Import command in the main file will only import records from the clone's found set.

✔ Tip

- Although the Dupe Finder/Dupe Lookup process prevents you from importing records that duplicate your existing database, it doesn't close the door to duplicates within the data you want to import. If you suspect that the new records aren't clean, you can run the Dupe Finder script on the imported file to check it before you follow the steps to compare it to the main database.

359

Troubleshooting Problem Data

Some data problems can't be anticipated, so they find their way into your database even after you've taken basic precautions. These errors usually have to do with inconsistencies in data entry, misspellings, and missing data. FileMaker's Find/Replace command is the easiest route to fixing these imperfections when they are consistent or few in number. But with no way to access search operators or type in special characters, it's a much less useful tool than the same functions in Microsoft Word.

The Replace command is a more powerful tool that can be of immense help in correcting the problems that Find/Replace is too limited to address. The Replace command allows you to set a field in every record in the database (or in a found set) to a particular value or the result of a calculation.

To show how Replace cleans up inconsistencies, we'll use the example of inconsistent entries in a database's State field. Some records might have no state name entered, while others might have entries like "N.Y." or "n.y." when you want NY.

The Replace command cannot be undone, so before you use it, make a backup copy of your file.

To find and replace data:

1. Create a Search that finds all the versions of the state that you've observed in the records.

   You can search using Requests > Add New Request, or see Chapter 5 for ways to use search operators to fine-tune your text search. This will capture as a found set every record whose State field you want to change.

2. Enter the correct data in the field for any one of the incorrect records. In our example, we'd enter the correct state abbreviation. Leave the cursor in the field.

3. Choose Records > Replace.

4. When the Replace dialog box appears, click Replace (**Figure 14.17**). A warning box will ask if you really want to replace the records. Click OK.

5. The State field in all of the records will now contain the text you entered in step 2. You can repeat these steps for any other state, as well as any set of records with some common element, such as name or address, that you need to replace.

✔ Tip

- If you don't want to look through your data for variations on a State field, consider doing a search for a range of Zip codes instead. Since Zip codes are assigned according to state, you'll still get a found set you can work with, using the Replace command to clean up the State field.

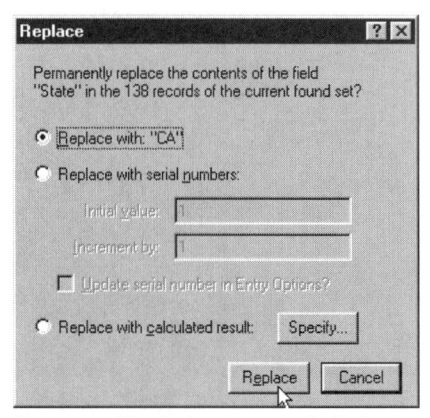

Figure 14.17 The Replace command will change all of the entries in the selected field to the data in the current record.

Replacing Inconsistent Formatting

A straight Replace puts new data where old information once was. Sometimes, however, you only want to edit a portion of a record while leaving the rest of the field contents intact. That's when you need a calculation using the Substitute function.

For example, suppose you have a State field containing a variety of formats, like NY, N.J., Ca, and R.i. Searching for each state's variations would take so long you might as well input them by hand. The Substitute function replaces a letter, word or any other piece of data with another, leaving the rest of the field intact.

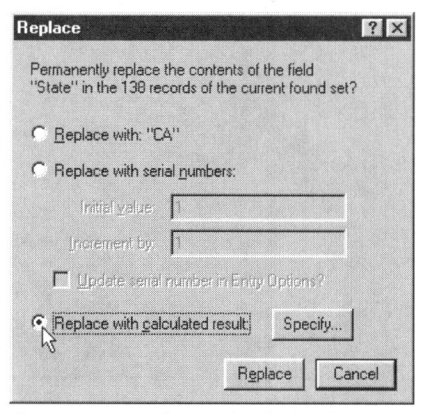

Figure 14.18 "Replace with calculated result" allows you to replace formatting, not just text.

Figure 14.19 The Upper function changes the type style to capital letters.

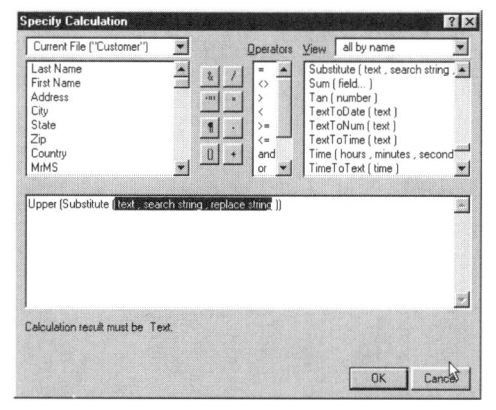

Figure 14.20 The Substitute function swaps all occurrences of one piece of information with another.

To replace inconsistent formatting:

1. Go to a layout containing the field whose data you want to improve. Click in the field. Our example uses the State field.

2. Choose Records > Replace.

3. Click the "Replace with calculated result" radio button (**Figure 14.18**).
   This option replaces the data in the field with a calculation instead of text or numbers.

4. When the Specify Calculation dialog box appears, scroll down in the function list on the right to Upper, and double-click it (**Figure 14.19**).
   The Upper function turns all text within the field you specify into uppercase characters.

5. In the function list, double-click the Substitute function (**Figure 14.20**).
   The Substitute function searches for characters in a field, then replaces them with whatever other characters you specify.

continues on next page

361

Chapter 14

6. Highlight the word "text" in the formula builder and double-click the State field in the field list (**Figure 14.21**).

   This tells the Substitute function to make its changes in the State field.

7. In the formula builder, highlight "search string" and click the quotes button. Type a period between the quotes (**Figure 14.22**).

   The Substitute function will search for periods in the State field.

8. In the formula builder, highlight "replace string" and click the quotes button. Don't type anything between the quotes (**Figure 14.23**). Click OK.

   This tells the Substitute function to delete any periods it finds in the State field.

9. In the Replace dialog box, click Replace.

   The information in the State field won't change, but it will all be in capital letters without periods.

Apply this technique to delete any characters. For instance, if you import addresses that have unwanted commas, leave out the Upper function and use a comma in the search string.

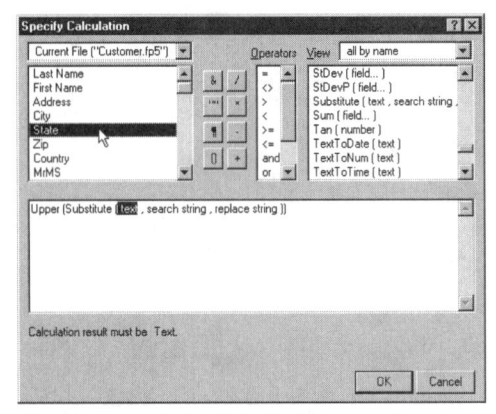

Figure 14.21 Enter the State field for the text argument.

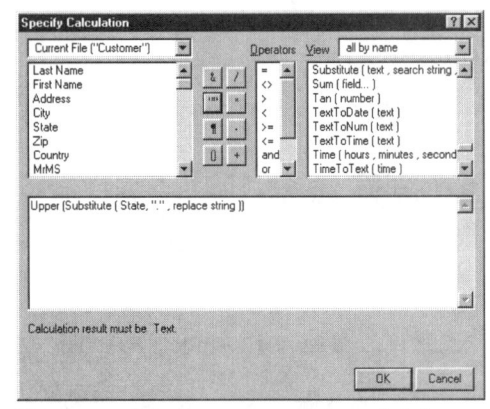

Figure 14.22 Substitute will search for periods in the field.

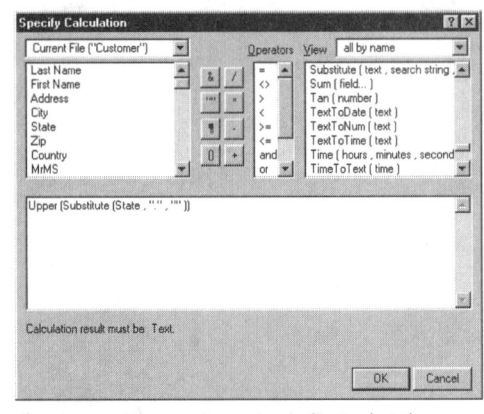

Figure 14.23 The empty quotes indicate that the periods will be deleted.

✔ Tips

- If you want to do a Find and Replace for a single record, you can do a Find to isolate that record. Then you can use a Replace with the Substitute function to search for all instances of a piece of text in a field and replace them with other text (or with nothing). This is especially handy for fields with long text blocks.

- To make Find/Replace more efficient, use it with View as List to have more records visible on-screen, and make it easier to verify that you've made all necessary changes.

- Find/Replace also works in Layout mode, so you can use it to make changes in the text in layouts.

Separating Parts of Data

If you're faced with importing a file with badly structured data, you may have to separate parts of a single field into smaller parts. For example, if your text file has a single field for first and last names or for city, state, and Zip code but your database has them as separate elements, you need to separate the data into its constituent parts. The process of doing this is called "parsing," and it can be complex because each set of text combinations can present its own problems. No one script can be used for all parsing situations, but the concept we show here is adaptable to a wide range of parsing needs. These steps show how to parse a Full Name field such as "Name = John J. Jones" into first, middle, and last names, like this: "First Name = John MI = J. Last Name = Jones."

Figure 14.24 Match the Import Name field with the full-name data.

To parse imported data:

1. Clone your main file. (See "To clone a database" earlier in this chapter.)

2. In the original database, choose File > Define Fields (Control+Shift+D/Command+Shift+D).

3. You need to create a field into which you will temporarily import the name data from the import file, so you can then parse it into separate fields. Type a name for the field (we use Import Name). Click Create and Done.

4. Open the database clone. Follow the steps in "To import text data files" in Chapter 12, matching the names (or the name field) in the import file to the Import Name field (**Figure 14.24**).

5. Choose Scripts > ScriptMaker. Type a name for the script (we use Parse Name) and click Create.

continues on next page

363

Chapter 14

6. The Script Definition dialog box appears. In the step list on the left, double-click Go to Record/Request/Page. Leave the option set to First (**Figure 14.25**).

7. In the step list on the left, double-click Loop.

8. In the step list on the left, double-click If to insert it between Loop and End Loop (**Figure 14.26**). Under Options, click Specify to bring up the Specify Calculation dialog box.

9. In the function list on the right, scroll down to WordCount and double-click it.

   The WordCount function counts the number of words in the field you choose.

10. In the field list on the left, double-click the Import Name field (**Figure 14.27**).

11. Click to the right of the parentheses and double-click the equals operator. Enter 3 (**Figure 14.28**). Click OK.

    This calculation tells the script to look at the Import Name field to see if it has three words in it.

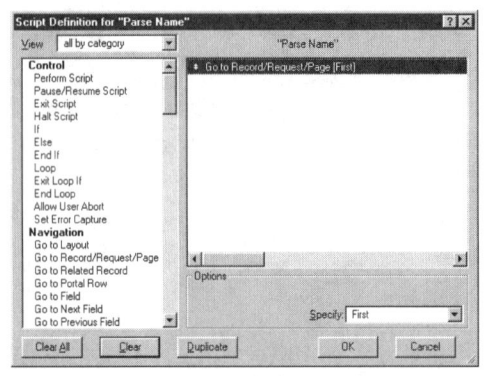

Figure 14.25 The Go to Record/Request/Page step starts the script in the first record in the database.

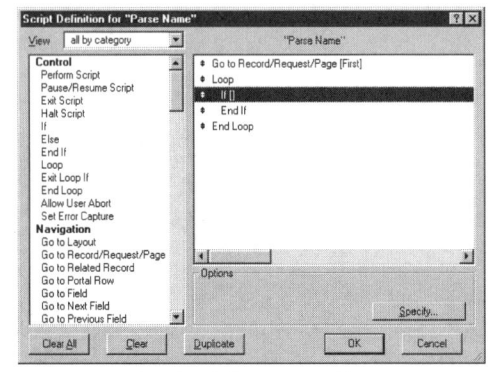

Figure 14.26 If and End If are inserted between Loop and End Loop.

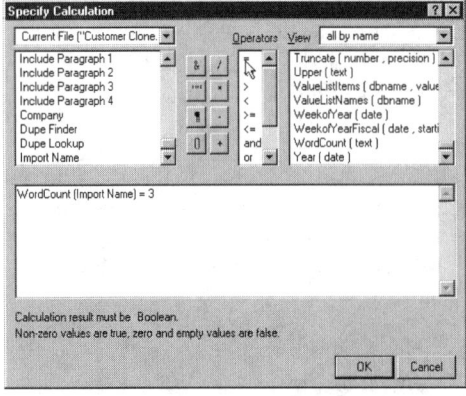

Figure 14.28 The script will act if the Import Name field has three words in it.

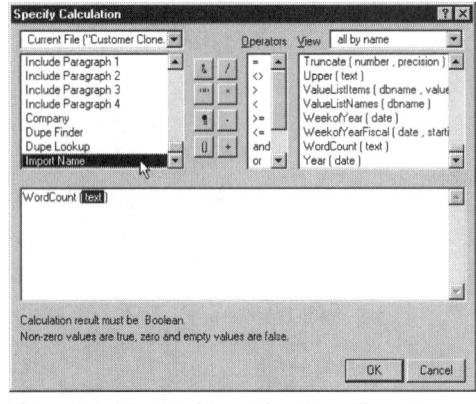

Figure 14.27 The Word Count function will count words in Import Name.

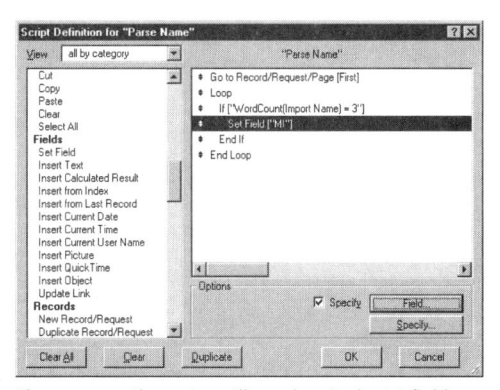

Figure 14.29 The script will put data in the MI field.

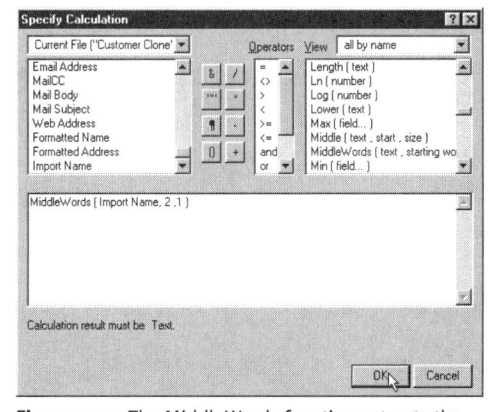

Figure 14.30 The MiddleWords function extracts the second word in the Import Name field.

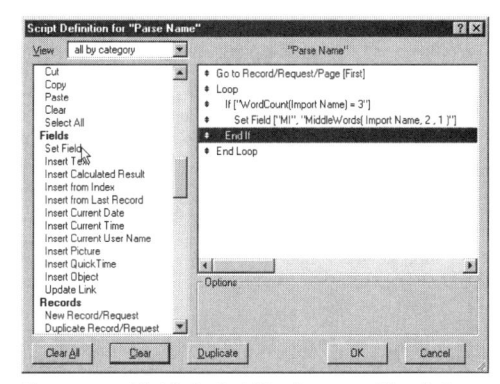

Figure 14.31 Highlight End If in the assembly window to insert the Set Field step above it.

12. In the step list, scroll down to the Fields section and double-click Set Field. Under Options, click the Field/Specify Field button (**Figure 14.29**). When the Specify Field dialog box appears, double-click MI.

13. Under Options, click the Specify button to bring up the Specify Calculation dialog box.

14. In the function list on the right, scroll down to MiddleWords and double-click.

15. In the formula box, highlight "text" inside the parentheses. In the field list, double-click Import Name.

16. In the formula box, highlight "starting word" and type 2. Highlight "number of words" and type 1 (**Figure 14.30**). Click OK.

    The script now says: If there are three words in Import Name, find word number 2 and place it into the MI field.

17. In the script assembly box, click the End If step. In the step list, double-click Set Field (**Figure 14.31**).

18. Under Options, click the Field/Specify Field button. When the Specify Field dialog box appears, double-click First Name.

19. Under Options, click the Specify button to bring up the Specify Calculation dialog box.

20. In the function list on the right, scroll down to LeftWords and double-click.

    The LeftWords function looks at the field you choose and counts from the left to find the number of words you specify.

21. In the formula box, highlight "text" inside the parentheses. In the field list, double-click Import Name.

continues on next page

Chapter 14

22. In the formula box, highlight "number of words" and type 1 (**Figure 14.32**). Click OK.

23. In the script-assembly window, click the Duplicate button to duplicate the last Set Field script step (**Figure 14.33**). Double-click the new Set Field step.

24. When the Specify Field dialog box appears, double-click Last Name.

25. Under Options, click the Specify button to bring up the Specify Calculation dialog box.

26. In the formula box, highlight "Left" in LeftWords. Type Right to change the function to RightWords (**Figure 14.34**). Click OK.

    RightWords is exactly like LeftWords, except that it counts from the right, not the left.

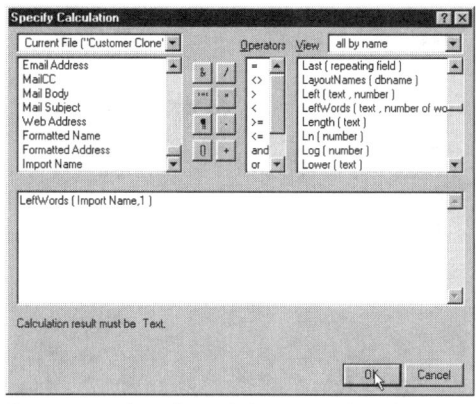

Figure 14.32 The LeftWords function will return the first word in the Import Name field.

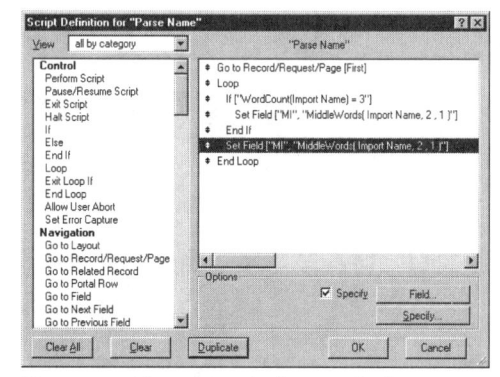

Figure 14.33 It's easier to duplicate and edit a script step with a calculation.

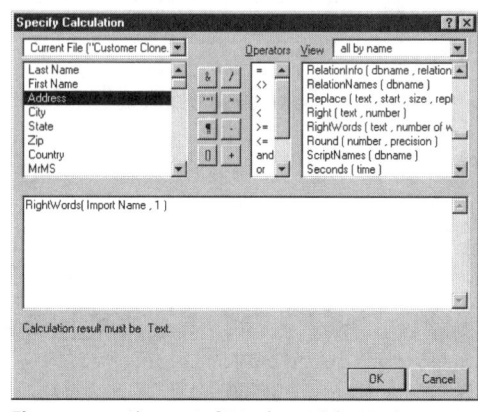

Figure 14.34 Change LeftWords to RightWords.

Data Importing and Repairing

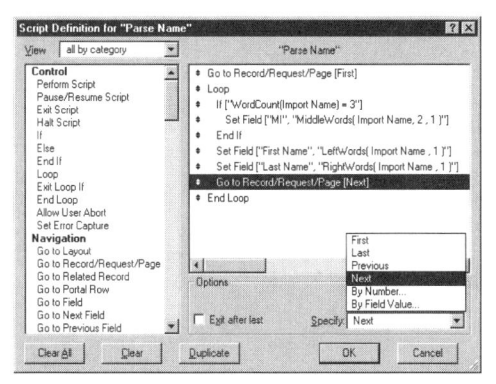

Figure 14.35 The script will go to the next record in the file until it's changed them all.

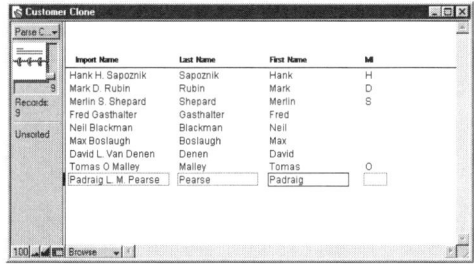

Figure 14.36 A columnar layout of the name fields makes it easy to correct any problems that the Parse Name script couldn't handle.

Figure 14.37 The number following the name of a field indicates which repetition of the field each phone number should be placed in.

27. In the step list on the left, double-click Go to Record/Request/Page. Under Options, choose Next from the Specify drop-down menu (**Figure 14.35**). Click the "Exit after last" check box.

    This step tells the script to go to the next record it finds, then stop after the last one.

28. Click OK, and then Done to finish.

When you run this script, it marches through the clone database putting the first word of Import Name into the First Name field, the last word into the Last Name Field, and, if there are three words in Import Name, the middle word into the MI field.

✔ Tips

- If any of the records have more than three words (like James J. Jones Jr.), some data won't parse correctly. To double-check your work before you import the clone data into the main database, create a column layout with the fields Import Name, First Name, MI, and Last Name. You'll quickly see which names weren't parsed correctly and can edit the records (**Figure 14.36**).

- You can adapt the script-parsing strategy for times when the data structure of the import file and main database are different. For example, many handheld devices have separate phone fields for home, work, fax, and so on, but your database may have a single phone field with several repetitions. Create several Import Phone fields (1 through however many phone repetitions you have). Keep track of which number imports into which field. Then create a script loop with a Set Field (Phone) to Import Phone 1 (the home number), Set Field (Phone/repetition 2) to Import Phone 2 (the work number), and so on (**Figure 14.37**).

SEPARATING PARTS OF DATA

367

Multi-User Files on a Network

Although many people create single-user databases for their own purposes, in general databases are maintained and used by more than one person. Frequently, that means that several users will have an urgent need to use this information at exactly the same time. If you have networked computers, no one has to wait in line. One of FileMaker Pro's strengths is its ability to allow file sharing on a network by both Windows and Macintosh users simultaneously. While one person is entering new data, another can be printing reports, as a third person is searching for particular records. This basic capability is enhanced and turbo-charged with FileMaker Server, which eliminates the major limitations placed on the standard version and supports more extensive LAN and Internet access. FileMaker Server is covered in the next chapter.

Setting Network Protocols

In order to share your database, you need to tell FileMaker what protocol your network uses. If you choose the wrong protocol you won't be able to access multi-user files or do any other network-related tasks with FileMaker. Check with your network administrator if you're not sure what protocol your network supports.

To set network protocols:

1. Choose Edit > Preferences > Application (Windows and Classic Mac OS) or FileMaker Pro > Preferences > Application (Mac OS X) to bring up the Application Preferences dialog box with the General tab displayed.

2. Click the Network Protocol drop-down menu and choose your protocol (**Figure 15.1**).

3. Click OK.

   You must quit FileMaker and start it again for the change to take effect.

✔ Tip

- Each IP (Internet Protocol) address is a unique number that identifies one computer on a TCP/IP network. If the computers on your network are already using TCP/IP, they have addresses. On the other hand, if you're setting up TCP/IP for the first time and the computers don't have an Internet connection, you can assign IP numbers to them that begin with 192.168 (following the standard IP address format, like 192.168.0.1) This series of numbers is reserved for internal computer use and isn't accessible on the Internet, but it's perfect for allowing you to test your connections before you go online, or if your FileMaker network will remain local.

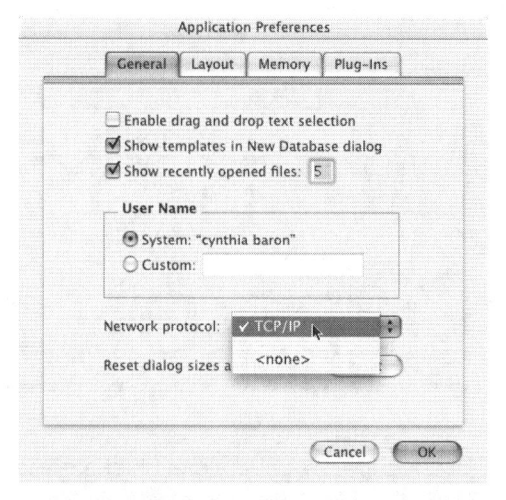

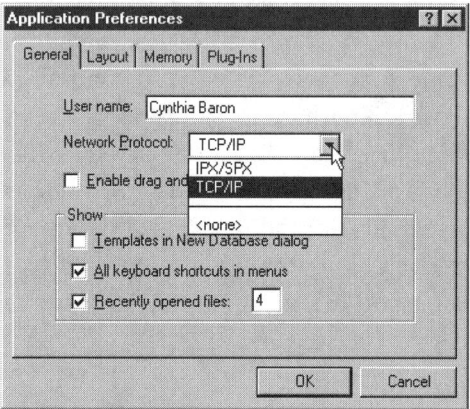

Figure 15.1 Set the network protocol by choosing it from the drop-down list.

Network Speed and Network Protocols

The more people who use your databases at the same time, the more important the network speed becomes. There are many things you can do when you configure your network to improve the way your networked FileMaker database performs.

FileMaker's minimum practical network is a 10-Base-T Ethernet architecture. If you anticipate more than 10 or 12 users, 100-Base-T is a better choice.

"Why such a high requirement?" you might ask. FileMaker is a disk-based database program. That means that data is constantly accessed from the server's disk rather than loaded into memory on each guest computer. As a result, FileMaker constantly goes back and forth between guest computer and server while a database is in use. A slow network will make people wait for their files to open, and operations like find and sort could become frustratingly slow.

Other network hardware can make a difference as well. Most small networks use a hub as their central point for sending and receiving information. If you anticipate that the number of users will grow, consider replacing the hub with a switch, which is more expensive but much faster at moving information back and forth.

Last but not least is the network protocol you choose. Protocols are like a set of language rules for computer communication. Computers that share these rules and settings are like people who share a common language—they can communicate successfully. Computers using different protocols cannot. FileMaker is capable of supporting a variety of network protocols, ranging from TCP/IP (the Internet protocol) to IPX/SPX and the Classic Mac OS's AppleTalk, but every computer that will access a FileMaker database must run the same protocol. FileMaker can use TCP/IP on any operating system. Since TCP/IP is faster on most computers than the alternatives, if you can use it as your protocol, you should. On a mixed Windows and Mac network, you won't have a choice, because it's the only protocol that both types of computers can recognize.

Chapter 15

Setting Up Multi-User Files

Once you've set your network protocols, you can either share files on your computer or access files on other computers. If your computer holds the database file, it's called the "host." If you are accessing other files, your computer is a "guest."

When you set files to be shared, FileMaker blocks both host and guest from certain actions so the integrity of the database is preserved and contradictory changes can't be made. For example, while a user of a shared database is editing a record, that record is locked. Other users can view the data but they can't edit it until the first user finishes the edit or switches to another record. Everyone can create and edit layouts and scripts, but only one user can do so at any time.

There are other actions that neither host nor guest can perform on a shared file while someone else is using it:

- Define fields
- Change the sharing status or group access privileges
- Save copies of the database

In addition, the host can't close a shared file until all other users have closed it.

To host a file:

1. Open the database that you want to share, then choose File > Sharing.

2. In the File Sharing dialog box, click the Multi-User radio button (**Figure 15.2**). Click OK.

3. Repeat steps 1 and 2 for all files that are related to the first database.

The file(s) will now be available to other users on your network.

✔ Tip

- Once a file is set to Multi-User, you may see a new dialog box (**Figure 15.3**) when you change from one view state (form, list, or table) in Browse mode to another. FileMaker is no longer automatically saving your layout changes. To return to automatic updating, you'll need to return to single-user mode.

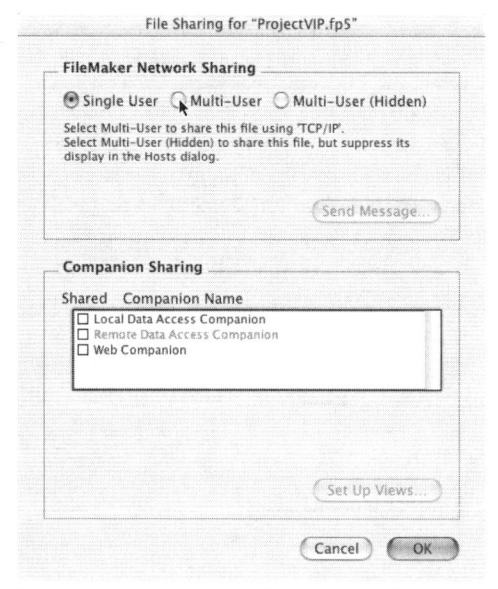

Figure 15.2 Share database files by setting them to Multi-User.

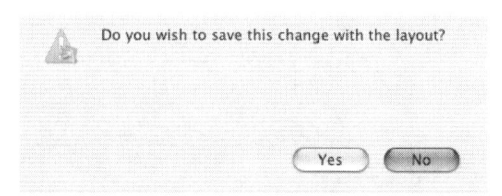

Figure 15.3 When a file is to set to Multi-User, layout changes are no longer saved automatically.

Hiding Related Files

The Hosts dialog box (refer to Figure 15.6) is fairly small, and after you've opened only a few files the window becomes full and you have to scroll to find the one you want. Rather than clutter up the Hosts dialog box with files that will be opened automatically by relationships, you can set just one file (like a Main Menu) to be visible in the Hosts dialog box and set the rest to be hidden.

To hide related files:

1. Open the related database that you want to hide, then choose File > Sharing.

2. Click the Multi-User (Hidden) radio button (**Figure 15.4**). Click OK.

3. Repeat steps 1 and 2 for all related files that you want to hide.

The related files won't appear in the Hosts file list, but they will open on guest computers along with the main file.

✔ Tip

- Make sure that you set the same passwords and access level for all related files you want to host. If you don't, the main file will open, but the related files won't be accessible. When a file is opened through a relationship, the related files accept the master file's password by default and don't require you to enter the password for each file.

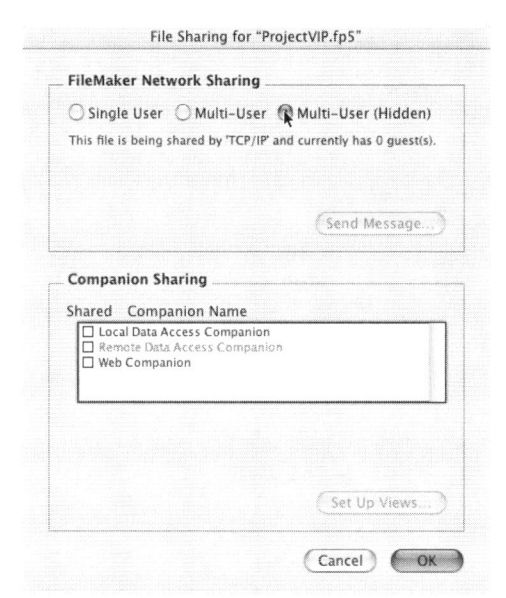

Figure 15.4 A file to set to Multi-User (Hidden) won't appear in the hosts list, but will be available if opened by a relationship or script.

Creating an Opening Script

Automating repetitive tasks is always good, particularly if they involve several steps that would keep you glued to the screen instead of doing something productive. Although you can wade through FileMaker's startup screens and dialog boxes, it's more efficient to create a single startup script to open several multi-user files automatically.

To create an opening script:

1. Start FileMaker. When the Open File dialog box appears, click Cancel. Choose File > New Database.

2. When the Create New File dialog box appears, give the new database a descriptive name like NetStart (**Figure 15.5**). Click Save.
   When the Define Fields dialog box appears, just click Done.

3. Choose File > Open Remote.

4. When the Hosts dialog box appears, make sure that all of the databases you want the script to open are available on the network (**Figure 15.6**). Open them if they're not. To close the dialog boxes, click Cancel twice.

5. Choose Scripts > ScriptMaker. In the Define Scripts dialog box, type a name for the script (ours is Opener). Click Create.

6. The Script Definition dialog box appears. In the script step list on the left, scroll down to Files and double-click Open (**Figure 15.7**). In the Options section, click the Specify or Specify File button (**Figure 15.8**).

Figure 15.5 You can create a new database that only opens files from the network.

Figure 15.6 All the files you want to open must be available before you create the script.

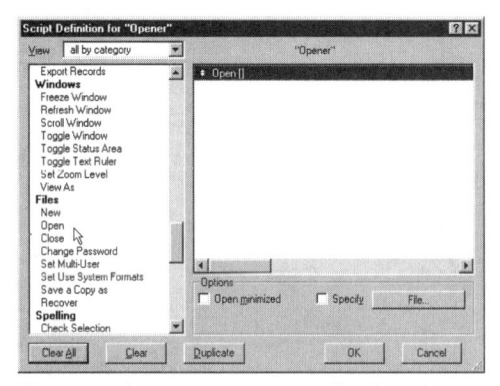

Figure 15.7 The Open step can open files from the host or server.

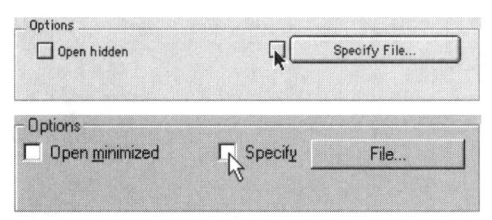

Figure 15.8 Specify the file you want to open by clicking the Specify (Windows) or Specify File (Mac) button.

Multi-User Files on a Network

Figure 15.9 In the Hosts dialog box, select files for the script to open.

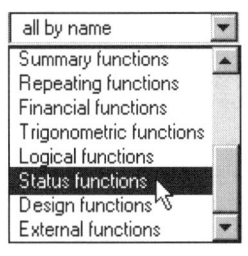

Figure 15.10 Choose Status functions from the View list to see the complete set of status functions.

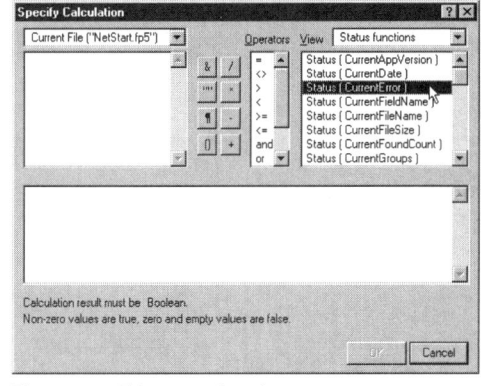

Figure 15.11 This status function captures any error FileMaker encounters while running the script.

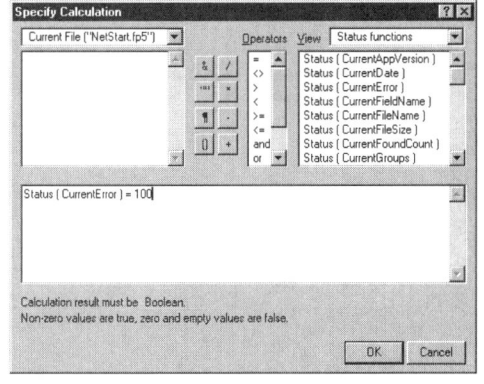

Figure 15.12 Status (CurrentError) will return error 100 if the specified file is not found on the network.

7. In the Open File dialog box, click the Hosts button. When the Hosts dialog box appears, double-click the name of the first file you want to have the script open (**Figure 15.9**).

8. In the script step list on the left, scroll up to the Control section and double-click If.

9. In the Options section, click the Specify button to bring up the Specify Calculation dialog box.

10. Click the View drop-down menu on the right and choose "Status functions" (**Figure 15.10**). In the Status functions list, double-click the Status (CurrentError) function (**Figure 15.11**).

11. Click to the right of the parentheses. In the Operators list, double-click =. Type 100 to the right of the equals sign (**Figure 15.12**). Click OK to return to the Script Definition dialog box.

    The error code 100 is the "File is missing" error.

    continues on next page

CREATING AN OPENING SCRIPT

375

Chapter 15

12. In the script step list on the left, scroll down to Files and double-click Open.

    This If statement says that if the file you want to open is missing, the Open File dialog box will appear so you can manually locate the file.

13. If there are other files you want this script to open, you can duplicate this first group of steps and edit them. Click the first step, hold the Shift key, and click the last step to select the group (**Figure 15.13**). Click the Duplicate button (**Figure 15.14**).

14. Double-click the new Open step (**Figure 15.15**). In the Open File dialog box that appears, click the Hosts button. When the Hosts dialog box appears, double-click the name of the next file you want to have the script open.

15. Repeat steps 13 and 14 for as many other files as you need to open at startup.

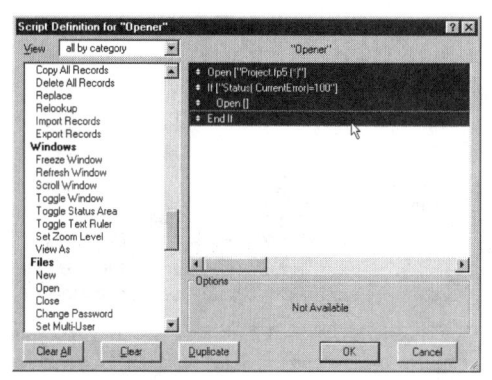

Figure 15.13 Select multiple steps by holding down the Shift key while selecting.

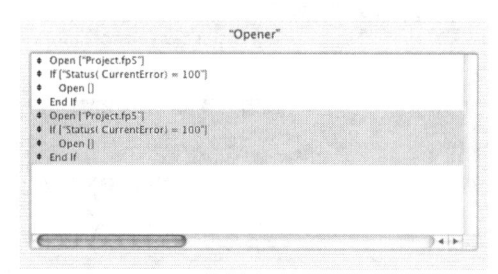

Figure 15.14 Duplicate the selected steps so you don't have to add them manually.

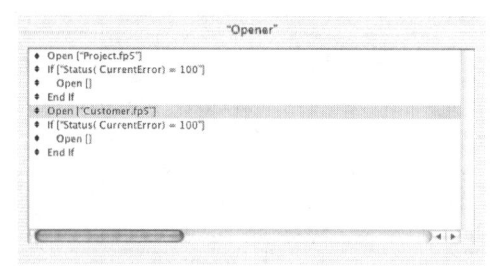

Figure 15.15 The new Open step can be edited to open another file.

Multi-User Files on a Network

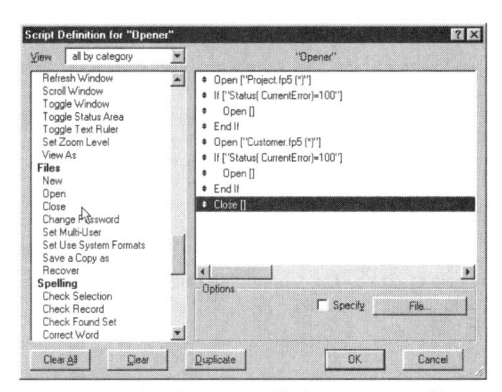

Figure 15.16 The Close step will close any open file you specify.

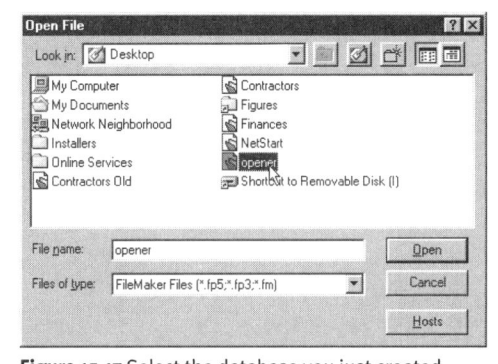

Figure 15.17 Select the database you just created.

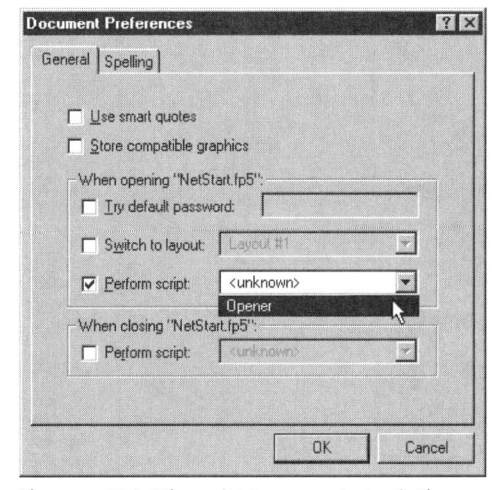

Figure 15.18 Set the script to run on startup in the Preferences > Document options.

16. In the step list on the left, scroll to the Files section and double-click Close (**Figure 15.16**).

    The Close step closes whatever file you specify. If you don't specify a file name, it closes the database of the script in which it was used.

17. In the Options section, click Specify or Specify File. When the Open Files dialog box appears, double-click the name of the new database in which you're creating the script (**Figure 15.17**).

    If you aren't sure how the script will work, you can leave out this Close script step (steps 16 and 17) so you can more easily return to the script to make changes.

18. Click OK to save the script and then Done to finish.

19. Choose Edit > Preferences > Document. The Document Preferences dialog box will appear with the General tab selected. In the "When opening" section, click "Perform script." From the script drop-down menu, choose the script you just created (**Figure 15.18**). Click OK.

When you want to open your network files, double-click to launch the database you just created. The script will run automatically, opening the specified files and then closing itself. If you open a database that has related files, the related files will open automatically, too.

377

Chapter 15

✔ Tips

- If you include the Close step but discover when the script runs that you need to change it, hit Escape (Windows) or Command+period (Macintosh) repeatedly as the database opens. This will cancel the script and leave the file open so you can access ScriptMaker. If you think this might happen frequently, you can give yourself enough time to cancel the script by inserting a short pause in the script itself.

- If you want a particular file to be the active window when all of the files are open, make it the last file to open.

- Opening a file on a host server used to be a two-step process. You had to choose File > Open (Control+O/Command+O) and then click the Hosts button in the dialog box. Now you can simply choose File > Open Remote to go directly to the Hosts dialog box. A new script step called Open Hosts offers the same convenience. When you add a server IP address to the permanent list (**Figure 15.19**), it remains there even if you no longer need it. You can edit the hosts list to remove unwanted addresses. On your computer, do a search for the file called "FileMaker Hosts." Open that file in any word processor, change the contents and replace the saved file in its original location.

Figure 15.19 You can store IP addresses for future use in the Specify Host dialog box.

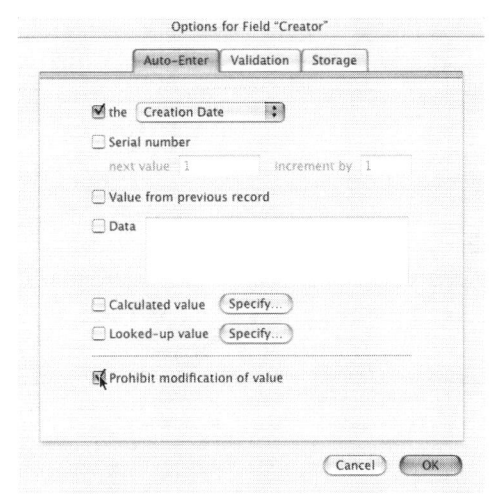

Figure 15.20 The Creator field contains the name of the user who created the record.

Figure 15.21 Select an existing password from the list on the left, or create a new one.

Restricting Access Privileges

In multi-user environments, there are many occasions when you want a user to have full control of some records but read-only or even no access to others. Using FileMaker's access privilege functions, you can exercise very specific and targeted control over each individual user's actions.

In this example, we set privileges so that users with a particular password can see any record in the database, but edit or delete only records that they created.

To set access privileges by record:

1. Choose File > Define Fields (Control+Shift+D/Command+Shift+D).

2. When the Define Fields dialog box appears, type **Creator** for the field name, choose Text as the type, and click Create.

3. Double-click the Creator field. When the Options dialog box appears, click the Auto-enter tab.

4. Click the first check box and choose Creator Name from the drop-down menu (**Figure 15.20**). Click OK and then Done. When a record is created, the name of the person who created it, based on the password used, will automatically be inserted in the Creator Name field.

5. Choose File > Access Privileges > Passwords.

6. When the Define Passwords dialog box appears (**Figure 5.21**), click the password that a user with limited access will enter (or type in a new password and click Create).

continues on next page

379

Chapter 15

7. In the Privileges section, choose Limited from the drop-down menu next to "Edit records" (**Figure 5.22**).

8. The Specify Calculation dialog box will appear. In the field list on the left, double-click the Creator field. In the Operators list, double-click the = (equals) operator.

9. From the View drop-down menu on the right, choose "Status functions" (**Figure 15.23**).

10. Double-click the Status (CurrentUserName) function (**Figure 15.24**). Click OK.

11. In the Define Passwords dialog box, choose Limited from the drop-down menu next to Delete Records, and repeat steps 8–10.

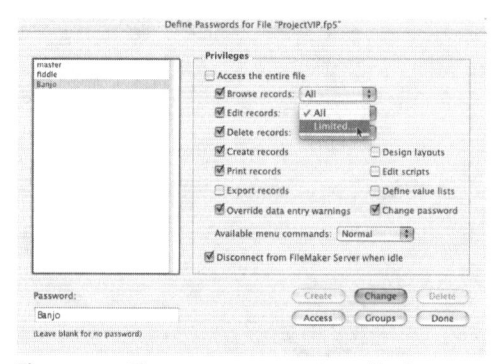

Figure 15.22 The user name auto-entered in the Creator field must match the current user name to allow them to edit a record.

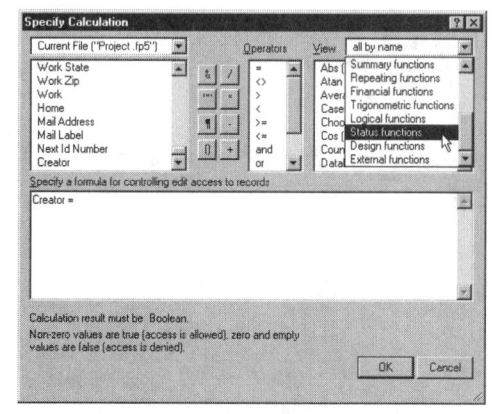

Figure 15.23 Status functions are visible in the function list only if you choose "Status functions" from the View drop-down menu.

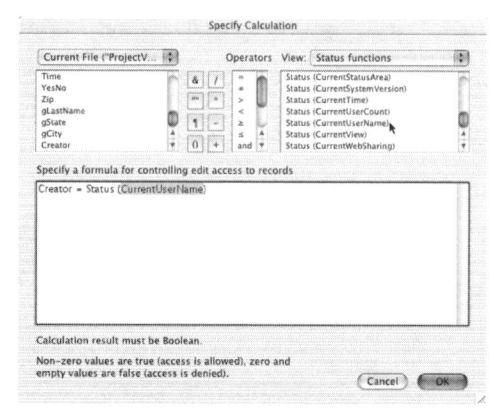

Figure 15.24 Status (CurrentUserName) returns the user name set in application preferences.

Multi-User Files on a Network

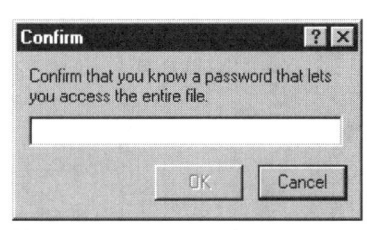

Figure 15.25 No one can change user access unless they know the file's administrator (full-access) password.

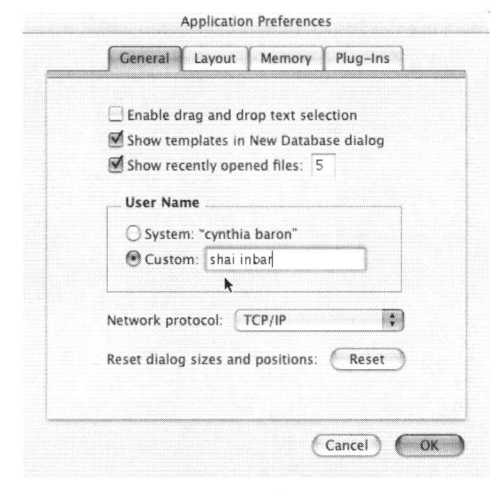

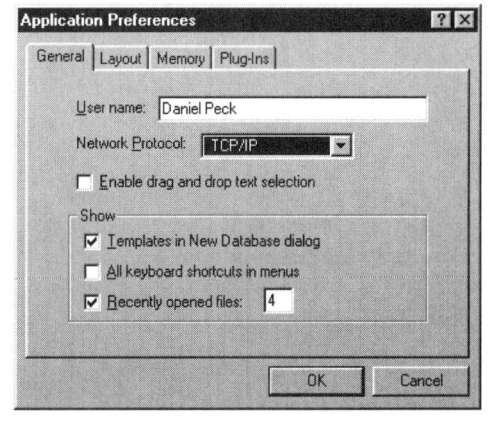

Figure 15.26 On the Macintosh, you can choose between a custom name and the system default name set in the Users system preference or the File Sharing control panel. In Windows, the User Name defaults to the name set in the Network control panel, but it can be changed.

12. Click Change and then Done to finish. You'll be prompted to enter the master (all access) password (**Figure 15.25**).

When users open the database using the password you configured, they'll be able to edit and delete only records that they created, though they can still browse records created by others. You can still access all records by opening the file with the master password.

✔ Tips

- Although we didn't do so in this example, you can follow the steps above to limit a user's ability to browse records as well.

- If you add this function to an existing database, it will work only on new records unless you go back and enter the appropriate user in each record's Creator field.

- By default, FileMaker sets the user name to the name it finds in the Network control panel (Windows), File Sharing control panel (Macintosh Classic OS), or currently logged in user (OS X). To enter a different user name, choose Edit (FileMaker Pro in OS X) > Preferences > Application. Make sure the General tab of the dialog box is showing. On the Macintosh, click the Custom button and type a new name (**Figure 15.26**). In Windows, just change the default User Name. Keep in mind that this name reflects the computer, not who is actually using the computer.

RESTRICTING ACCESS PRIVILEGES

381

Changing Password Access

If more than one user relies on a particular password, any user who changes it leaves the others up the proverbial creek. You can now limit a user's ability to change passwords.

To prevent users from changing passwords:

1. Choose File > Access Privileges > Passwords.

2. The Define Passwords dialog box appears. In the password list on the left, click the password you want to change.

3. In the Privileges section on the right, uncheck the "Change password" check box (**Figure 15.27**).

4. Click Change and then Done. Enter the master password when prompted.

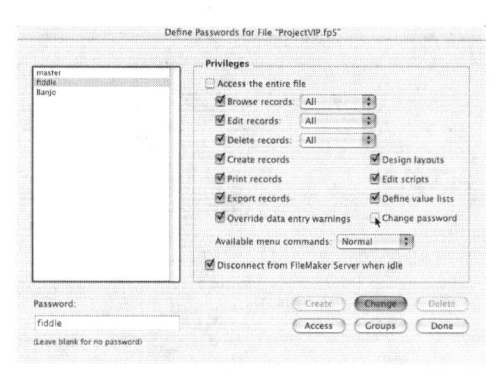

Figure 15.27 Blocking users from changing passwords can prevent access problems in a multi-user environment.

✔ Tips

- If you're installing FileMaker over a network, you probably own a volume license (a single install code that allows multiple users). If so, it's a good idea to preset options like company name, default network protocol, and install code for every installation. From the FileMaker installer CD, copy the Files Folder (Windows) or the Start Here application and the Personalization Info file (Macintosh) to a shared folder on a server. Open FileMaker Pro 6.pdf (not an Acrobat file) or Personalization Info in a text editor. Scroll to the end of the file to find instructions about setting the install options.

- Interested in preventing users from creating new databases on their local computers? One of the install options supported in FileMaker 6 allows you to do just that.

FileMaker Multi-User vs. OS File Sharing

FileMaker uses its own set of rules for sharing files. In fact, Windows or Macintosh OS File Sharing doesn't even have to be turned on for the host and guest machines to share FileMaker files.

Guests should never try to open a shared FileMaker database through their OS's File Sharing dialog boxes. They must always open files by clicking the Host button in FileMaker's Open File dialog box or by using a script that's been written to automate the process.

Figure 15.28 When you click Hosts, you look for files outside your local computer.

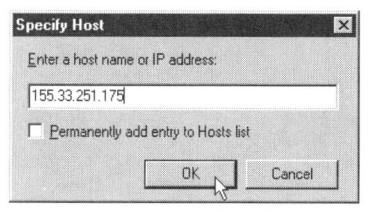

Figure 15.29 To open a FileMaker database over the Internet, enter the host computer's IP address.

Figure 15.30 When FileMaker finds the computer, it will list the host's available databases.

Accessing Databases over the Internet

You can open a FileMaker database hosted by another computer even if you aren't on the same network, as long as both the host computer and the guest are connected to the Internet and the host computer has a fixed IP address. Both host and guest machines must have FileMaker set to use TCP/IP.

To open a FileMaker database over the Internet:

1. Establish your Internet connection and start FileMaker.

2. Choose File > Open.

3. In the Open files dialog box, click Hosts.

4. In the Hosts dialog box, click Specify Host (**Figure 15.28**).

5. In the Specify Host dialog box, type the IP address of the computer hosting the database you want to open (**Figure 15.29**). Click OK.

   When you return to the Hosts dialog box, you'll see a list of all the open shared files on the host computer (**Figure 15.30**).

6. Double-click the file you want to open.

7. There will probably be a delay after you enter the IP address of the host and after you double-click the file to open (see the sidebar "Internet Speed and Internet Databases" on the following page).

continues on next page

✔ Tips

- FileMaker 6 databases can only be opened with FileMaker 5, 5.5, or 6. You have to convert databases created in earlier versions of FileMaker before they can be used in FileMaker 6. Consequently, anyone who wants to open a shared FileMaker 6 file must have one of those versions of the software installed on their computer.

- If you don't see any files listed on the host after entering an IP address, check the network settings on both computers. If the host computer's network has a firewall between the network and the Internet, you may have to have the network administrator open a port. FileMaker uses port 5003 for Internet connections.

- You've seen how easy it is to connect to a FileMaker database over the Internet. Keep in mind that anyone in the world (literally) can access your database if they know your host computer's IP address. If you host FileMaker files over an Internet connection, password protection is an absolute must.

Internet Speed and Internet Databases

There's a big difference between making a database available for searching on the Internet and having that same database be editable and shared. The first is not much different from any other Web page accessing information from an Internet server. The second is doable, but frankly less than ideal unless both host and guest computers use a high-speed connection like cable or DSL. Dial-up modems are really much too slow for satisfying communication. Opening a single file can take several minutes and large stores of patience. Finding and editing records will take noticeably longer than the same actions on a local network. Even when both computers have reasonably good bandwidth, sharing a FileMaker database over the Internet isn't zippy. For this reason, if you must share your database this way, keep your layouts as simple as possible. Don't use any unnecessary graphics or backgrounds. Avoid complex calculated fields and summary fields whenever possible.

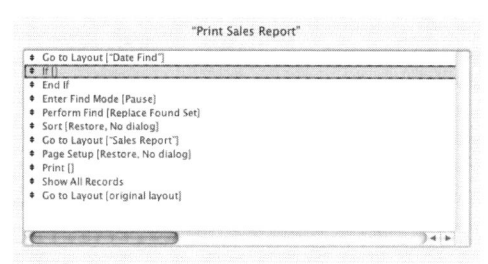

Figure 15.31 The If step allows you to test for two possible situations: the user is a group member or is not.

Figure 15.32 The If step must be placed before the rest of the script so it can test for group membership before the rest of the script runs.

Testing Scripts for Access Problems

FileMaker allows you to identify users and create groups of users to control how much access you're willing to grant to a database. However, there's a problem with this security that only arises when you use scripts. Ordinarily, if users try to go to a layout they don't have access to, they'll see an Access Denied dialog box message. Unfortunately, when this happens while running a script, FileMaker doesn't know what to do next. Sometimes the dialog box simply freezes on the screen. Other times, the script tries to continue running, fails, and then freezes. To prevent this from happening, you should include an If statement in such scripts that checks to see if the layout you've referenced is one that the individual or group running it can use.

Our example runs this test for a group, but you can substitute references to CurrentGroup with CurrentUser instead.

To test scripts for user access problems:

1. Choose Scripts > ScriptMaker. Double-click a script whose user access you want to control.

2. Click on the first line in the script-assembly box.

3. In the script step list, double-click If (**Figure 15.31**).

4. Move the If and End If steps to the top of the script assembly window so they're the first steps in the script (**Figure 15.32**). Select the If step.

continues on next page

Chapter 15

5. Under Options, click the Specify button to bring up the Specify Calculation dialog box.

6. In the function list on the right, double-click PatternCount (**Figure 15.33**).

   PatternCount searches for a string of text and tells you how many times it occurs; if it returns the number 0, the specific piece of text is not present.

7. Double-click to select "text" in the parentheses after PatternCount.

8. Click the View drop-down menu on the right and choose "Status functions." Double-click the Status (CurrentGroups) function (**Figure 15.34**).

   Status (CurrentGroups) identifies which group a user belongs to by examining the password the current user entered to log in.

9. Double-click to select "search string" in the parentheses. Click the quotes button. Type the name of the group that's allowed to access the file (**Figure 15.35**).

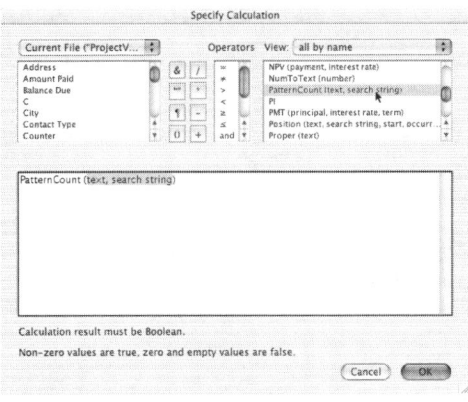

Figure 15.33 PatternCount will return the number of occurrences of a search string.

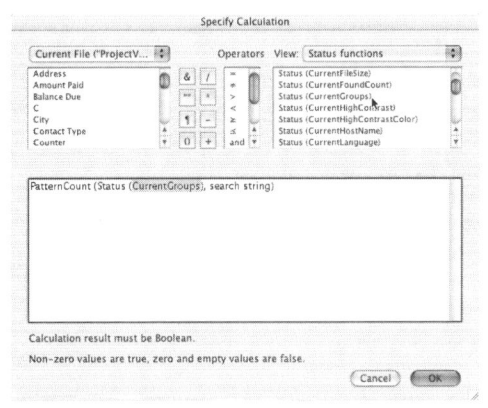

Figure 15.34 Status (CurrentGroups) returns the names of all groups associated with the current password.

Figure 15.35 For the search string, enter the name of the group that should access the script.

Multi-User Files on a Network

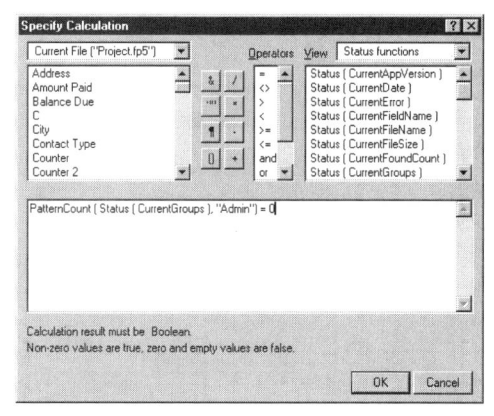

Figure 15.36 If the group name entered is not in the Status (CurrentGroups) search string, PatternCount will return 0.

Figure 15.37 Show Message will let users know why they can't get access to a script.

Figure 15.38 Specify Message lets you enter a custom message for the dialog box.

10. Click at the end of the formula. In the Operators list, select =, then type 0 (**Figure 15.36**). Click OK.

    This step looks at the password the user typed, and does whatever you specify in your next script step if the name of the group isn't the one you specified.

11. In the script step list, scroll down to the Miscellaneous section and double-click Show Message (**Figure 15.37**).

12. Under Options, click Specify. In the Specify Message dialog box, enter the message to be displayed to a user who does not have access to this script (**Figure 15.38**).

    In our example, users who aren't in the Admin group will receive this message.

    continues on next page

387

Chapter 15

13. In the Button Captions section, double-click Cancel in the Second box and press the Delete key (**Figure 15.39**). Click OK.

    We eliminate the Cancel button because the user has no alternative choices.

14. In the script step list, scroll up to the Control section and double-click Halt Script (**Figure 15.40**).

    Halt Script ends the script without running it if the user isn't a member of a group authorized to run the script.

15. Click OK and then Done to finish.

✔ Tips

- FileMaker passwords are not absolute protection for the security of a file. There are "cracker" utilities that can delve into the inner workings of a FileMaker file and reveal the password. For maximum security, proper network security procedures should be observed in addition to password-protecting the file itself.

- Group privileges take precedence over password privileges. If a user has editing privileges (set by the password), but does not have access to a field (set by the group), he or she cannot edit that field.

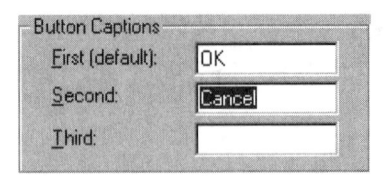

Figure 15.39 You only want to give one choice, so delete the second button text.

Figure 15.40 The Halt Script step will end the script if the user isn't a member of the right group.

USING FILEMAKER PRO SERVER

16

When there are more than five or six users accessing a shared database simultaneously, performance speed begins to degrade. Although you can partially solve this by designating one computer for file hosting, you'll find this is only a temporary solution. Instead, you should consider using FileMaker Pro Server.

FileMaker Pro Server does just one thing, but does it exceptionally well. It hosts FileMaker databases on a dedicated (single-purpose) computer and allows many users to connect to the same databases with little or no performance loss.

Although small companies or workgroups may run FileMaker Server locally, larger groups may need to integrate the application with an existing corporate network. Two important features address these needs in the Windows 2000 environment. For improved security, you can require anyone who wants to use a Server-managed FileMaker database to first log into the Windows 2000 domain. Server recognizes—and is recognized by—Windows Active Directory and other director services through LDAP (Lightweight Directory Access Protocol) support. Once registered with Active Directory, databases managed by FileMaker Server can be centrally managed through the Windows 2000 interface—a critical application requirement for corporate IS departments.

Even though FileMaker Server is called version 5.5, it will work with FileMaker Pro versions 5, 5.5, and 6. It can be installed in Windows NT and 2000 and on all Mac OS versions from 8.6 up. Server can also be installed and used under Red Hat Linux, a real boon for those who have moved to the Linux platform for their other server implementations.

Hosting Files on FileMaker Server

When hosting files, keep them in one location in the server application folder, not scattered around the disk. Centralizing files makes them easier to back up or recover, and can improve access time among files with relationships. In addition, FileMaker Pro Server will automatically open any FileMaker databases that are either in the same folder as the application or in a folder inside the Server application folder. You can also use a shortcut (Windows) or alias (Macintosh) of the databases you want to open when Server starts.

If you're running Server on any platform other than Mac Classic, you must use Remote Administration (see "Managing Server Remotely" later in this chapter) to manually open and close files, see a list of currently hosted files, and perform other administration tasks. This must be done from a computer other than the one running Server. In the Classic Mac OS, local administration is built in to the Server application.

Figure 16.1 Make a new folder for shortcuts or aliases of files you want to open automatically.

To automatically host files in FileMaker Server:

1. Open the FileMaker Pro Server application folder. Create a new folder. You can give it any name you choose (**Figure 16.1**).

2. Create shortcuts or aliases of the databases you want Server to open automatically, and move or copy them into the new folder.

3. Start FileMaker Pro Server.

continues on page 392

Getting Started with Server

Except in the Classic Mac OS, it's very important that you accept the installer's default options for Server installation. Server will not work properly if you install it in a different folder from the one the installer chooses, or if you move it to a different place on the hard drive after installation.

Although most FileMaker applications have almost identical cross-platform implementations, Server is the exception. Because the program itself had to be designed for each platform's very specific way of handling server functions, some versions of Server act like stand-alone applications, and others act as services—applications that become part of a larger server architecture.

Here's the definitive cheat sheet on how to launch the Server application:

- In the Classic Mac OS, start Server by double-clicking the Server application icon.

- In Macintosh OS X, double-click the FileMaker Server Config icon and click the Start Server button (**Figure 16.2**).

- In Windows NT, choose Start > Settings > Control Panels > Services. Choose FileMaker Server and click Start.

- In Windows 2000, choose Start > Programs > FileMaker Server Console. Click Services > Local in the Console Tree and FileMaker Server in the Details pane. Choose Action > Start.

Figure 16.2 Server is a service, not an application, and must be turned on and off from its dialog box.

Since you'll be running Server on a dedicated computer, you probably want the application to open on startup. In the Macintosh Classic OS, you can put an alias for the Server application in the Startup Items folder (in the System Folder). In Windows, you add the shortcut to the Windows > Start Menu > Programs > Startup folder. Alas, accomplishing this seemingly trivial task in Mac OS X is not so easy. As a matter of fact, it's downright burdensome. Since it involves rather extensive use of the dreaded Terminal application, it's more complicated a process than we can sensibly cover here. For complete details, refer to http://www.filemaker.com/ti/107911.html.

✔ Tips

- If you allow the computer running Server to go to sleep to save energy, the application will also shut down. To prevent this from happening, go to your computer's Control Panel or System Preferences, and set your energy-saver settings to "Never Sleep" (**Figure 16.3**).

- Avoid the temptation to toss FileMaker Pro Server on a machine that you already use for other server tasks. If your multi-user database needs are complex enough to warrant running Server, they're complex enough for havoc to arise when performance degrades and several access-intensive applications conflict.

- If you want to open several databases simultaneously, place all the files together in one folder, then select the folder in the Open Database dialog box.

- Opening a file in FileMaker Server is not the same as opening the file in FileMaker Pro. You can't use Server to access the file or make changes to it. To make changes to a FileMaker database, you must open it in FileMaker Pro.

- As long as you're the only guest in a shared file, you can make changes to the field definitions when a file is being hosted in Server. This is a wonderful improvement, since it saves you from having to go to the server computer and open the file in FileMaker Pro just to make a simple change.

Figure 16.3 Turn off the energy-saving features for the computer that's running Server, or it will quit the application every time it goes to sleep.

FileMaker Server Requirements

- FileMaker Pro Server will run on the Macintosh (Classic or X), Windows NT, and Windows 2000 operating systems. There is no version for Windows 95/98 nor, at this writing, for Windows XP.

- FileMaker Pro Server must be run on a dedicated computer. The server must not be used as a mail or Web server and should not even have file-sharing turned on.

- Ideally, the computer running FileMaker Pro Server should have the fastest hard drive (preferably SCSI) and the fastest processor you can provide. Database file serving is not a trivial task for a computer, and hardware that works beautifully for other server tasks may not be sufficient for FileMaker Server.

Figure 16.4 Adjust the number of users; add an extra three to five if you expect the number of users to grow.

Optimizing Server Settings

You can change some of the Server settings to maximize performance or make it easier for you to administer. In many cases the settings you'll need will be specific to your own database uses, hardware configuration, and number of users, so you'll probably have to experiment with some of the settings before you have everything working perfectly. Optimizing requires restarting the Server to enable your changes, so be careful to do these steps when no files are being hosted to avoid damaging database files.

The method for getting to the Server Preferences differs depending on which OS you're running.

Macintosh OS Classic: Start the FileMaker Server application. Choose Edit > Preferences.

Macintosh OS X: Start the FMServer Config application. Choose FMServer Config > Preferences.

Windows: Choose Start > Programs > FileMaker Server Console. Choose Action > Properties.

To optimize Server:

1. Open Preferences, and click the Guests tab if it isn't already active.

2. Enter the maximum number of users (or use the up or down arrows to set) that you expect to be accessing the shared databases at the same time (**Figure 16.4**). Set the number a little higher than the current number of users to allow for growth, but don't compensate too much. The more users you specify the slower your database access will be.

continues on next page

Chapter 16

3. Check the Disconnect Idle Guests check box.

   People often forget to disconnect when they leave for the day, but if they're still connected they're wasting network and server resources.

4. Enter the maximum amount of time a user connection can be idle (or use the up and down arrows to set) before the server automatically disconnects it (**Figure 16.5**).

   Don't worry that you'll accidentally cut someone off in the middle of a find. Idle time is determined by the guest's actual use of the shared file. Clicking in a field, doing a find, or switching records resets the idle time countdown to 0.

5. Click the Files tab of the Preferences dialog box.

6. Enter the maximum number of files for Server to host (**Figure 16.6**).

   The default value of 50 might be higher than you need. Lowering the value can increase performance.

7. Increase the Database Cache to 10 MB.

   The Database Cache has a default setting of 4 MB. This is the size of the memory block your operating system will dedicate to your database, but if you have sizable files that number is probably woefully small. The 10 MB we recommend is only a starting point. You'll probably have to experiment to find the right amount for your specific needs.

8. Click OK to close the Preferences dialog box when you're done.

9. Restart Server to put your changes into effect.

Figure 16.5 You can automatically disconnect users who aren't actively using the server.

Figure 16.6 Improve performance by lowering the maximum number of open files.

394

Using FileMaker Pro Server

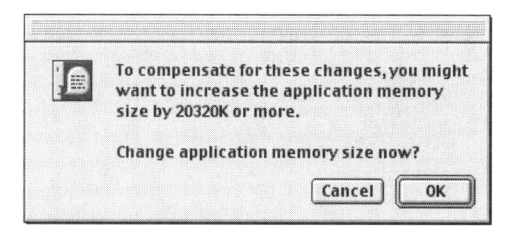

Figure 16.7 In the Classic Mac OS, you can see how much additional memory Server will need for your optimized changes.

✔ Tips

- The "Flush cache every" setting in the Files tab controls how often Server will save everything in the cache to the hard drive. A lower number (flush more often) will minimize the possibility of losing changes but can compromise performance. Practically speaking, lost changes are rare and usually limited to the most recently input record. You can usually start low and raise the Flush setting if problems arise. Like the cache setting, you can experiment to find your optimum value.

- If you check the "Allow FileMaker Server to host Single User files" check box, Server can serve files that are set to single user, so only one user at a time can use them. Hosting single-user files is useful when you want to store a file on the server, but not open it to multiple uses while it's there.

- Windows and Mac OS X handle memory assignment automatically. In earlier Macintosh OS versions, the user has the option of making changes. When you close the Preferences dialog box after optimizing FM Server, the application will tell you exactly how your changes have affected it, mention how much memory it now needs, and give you the choice of upping the memory or resetting the Server preferences (**Figure 16.7**).

- For optimal performance in the Classic Macintosh OS, don't allocate more memory to the server than it really needs. The default setting can adequately serve 25 guests and 50 files. If you think you're going beyond that or your files are few in number but very large, watch your cache hits in the Usage Statistics window (covered in the next section). Only allocate more RAM if this number drops below 90.

395

Setting Up a Usage Log

You can have Server keep track of its activity and monitor usage by enabling the Usage Log option. Usage logs note any error situations that occur and keep track of server usage. When you're trying to optimize your server, this log can be invaluable. For example, the log shows the maximum number of users who have been connected to the server at one time, as well as the average number. Since Server runs most efficiently when the number of users allowed closely matches the number of actual users the database has to support, this figure can be a great help in increasing performance. The logs are text files that can be opened in any word processor or text software.

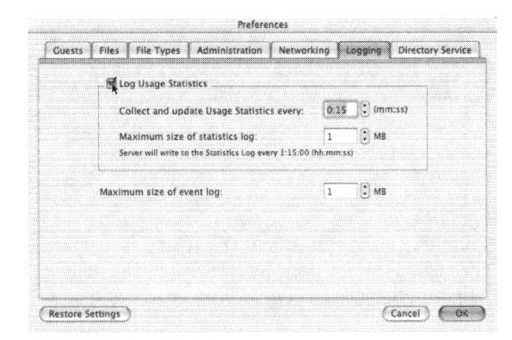

Figure 16.8 You create a log of Server activity using the Log Usage setting.

To set up a Server usage log:

1. Open Preferences, and click the Logging tab.
2. Click the Log Usage Statistics check box to create a log file (**Figure 16.8**).
   If your network has many users, you can raise the maximum size of the log from the default 1 MB.
3. When you're done, click OK.
4. Quit the Server application and restart it to enable your changes.

✔ Tip

- Make use of FileMaker's ability to convert .txt documents on the fly. Add version 6's ability to display layouts in a table, and in a snap you'll have a searchable database. Look for words like "error" or a specific file name, and you'll find analyzing the usage log much easier.

Figure 16.9 Server settings can be changed from another computer on the network if the Remote Administration setting is set on.

Managing Server Remotely

You can configure FileMaker Pro Server so that you can change its settings from another computer. There are many good reasons for not making your changes directly on the computer you're using as a server. The most important, however, is that the computer you've set up as the FileMaker Server may not be sitting right next to your desk. If you have to race around the building every time you want to tweak performance, you'll tend to let things slide instead of fixing them. Remote administration makes it much more convenient to maintain and troubleshoot networked databases.

After installing the Remote Administration plug-in (found on your Server installation CD) on any computers you want to use for Server administration, you can use FileMaker Pro to open and close files, send messages to connected users, disconnect users, and see the usage statistics. In fact, the only things you won't be able to do remotely are those functions that relate to the Server computer itself, like setting Preferences and quitting the Server application.

To set up remote administration:

1. Open Preferences, and click the Administration tab.

2. In the Remote Administration section, click the "Requires password" radio button. Enter the password you'll use to log into FM Server from another computer (**Figure 16.9**).

3. Quit the Server application and restart it to enable your changes.

4. Install the Remote Administration plug-in (on your installation CD) on any computer you'll use for remote administration.

To administer Server remotely:

1. Start FileMaker. Choose File > Open.

2. When the Open File dialog box appears, click the Hosts button.

3. In the Hosts dialog box, double-click the name of the server (**Figure 16.10**). If you've set up a password for remote administration, you'll need to type it to continue.

   FileMaker will open three databases from the Server: Server_Admin, Server_Data, and Server_Usage.

4. Choose Window > Server_Admin to open the Server_Admin window.

5. You can use the buttons in the Remote Administration window to open and close files and send messages, just as you do in the Server Admin window (**Figure 16.11**). If you click the Usage button you'll see the server's usage statistics (**Figure 16.12**).

6. When you're finished with your administration tasks, either quit FileMaker or close all three Server windows.

Figure 16.10 Choose the name of the computer you're using as your server from the Hosts dialog box.

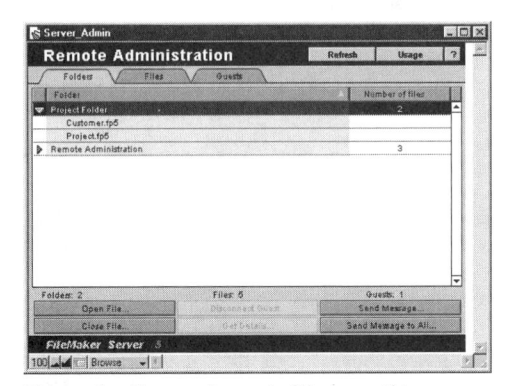

Figure 16.11 You can do most of the same things as a remote administrator that you can do right on the server.

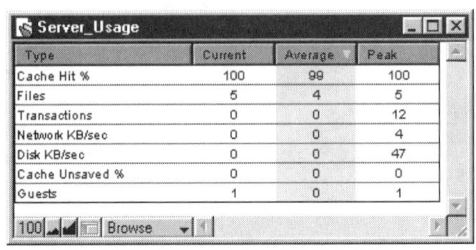

Figure 16.12 The Usage button allows you to view the usage log you created.

Using FileMaker Pro Server

✔ Tips

- Although you can't run Server on a Windows 95/98 computer, if you insert the FileMaker Pro Server installer CD in a Windows 95/98 computer, the installer will give you the option of installing the Remote Administration plug-in.

- Many FileMaker developers write database solutions that require a client machine to be running a plug-in in order to work effectively or to display material in container fields. Every time you have to download and install updates to individual plug-ins, the process becomes more irritating and time-consuming. Server will automatically download any software that individual computers need—for both Windows and Mac clients—if you simply drop it into the Server AutoUpdate folder.

Naming Your Server

Sometimes the name that's been assigned to the computer you're running FileMaker Server on isn't particularly descriptive. In large organizations, for example, computers might be called by their location number rather than by what they do. If that's the case for you, you'll want to set a different name so users can recognize the server easily.

In Preferences, in the Host Name section of the Administration tab, click the "Custom name" radio button and enter the name in the box (**Figure 16.13**). Restart the computer and the new name will broadcast as the server name.

Figure 16.13 You can set a custom name for the server on your network with the Host Name option.

MANAGING SERVER REMOTELY

399

17

WEB PUBLISHING

In Chapter 15, we used FileMaker to access FileMaker databases over the Internet. Although useful, it's actually not the best and most flexible way to combine FileMaker and the Web. FileMaker lets you use a Web browser to access your databases, which means you can make your files available to anyone even if they don't own FileMaker themselves.

If you are not a crackerjack HTML or XML programmer and your needs are simple, the best way to get your databases on the Web is by using FileMaker's Instant Web Publishing. IWP is extremely user friendly. Just by enabling one plug-in and making a few menu choices, you can put actual files on the Web with almost no prior Web experience.

When you're feeling more confident with Web publishing, you can easily suppress the IWP defaults to add your own look and feel to your Web page—or duplicate a familiar FileMaker layout—without losing the "instant" in IWP. In this chapter, we show you how to take advantage of these simple yet powerful features.

IWP is flexible and easy, but it isn't designed for incorporating FileMaker data into more complex Web pages or already-existing Web sites, or for secure data. For these things, you'll need Custom Web Publishing or XML programming instead of IWP. Both options allow you to display data, and to fully control both your FileMaker database and its visual and functional presentation. However, to use either option effectively you must already be familiar with HTML. In this chapter we cover the most important elements of using Custom Web Publishing's CDML (Claris Dynamic Markup Language).

Instant Web Publishing

Most of the same requirements we mentioned in Chapter 15 for FileMaker applications on the Internet apply for Web browsing as well. At the very least, you must have a full-time, high-speed connection to the Internet with a fixed IP address.

Consider how many users will access the database once it's published on the Web. The standard FileMaker version only allows access by 10 different computers (defined by their IP addresses) in any 12-hour period. If you limit access to just a few people, the standard version is all you need.

However, if you intend to invite the world to your database, you'll need FileMaker Pro Unlimited. This version of FileMaker is identical to the standard one, but has no upper limit on the number of people who can use it at one time.

✔ Tip

- Anyone using a dial-up connection will probably have a different IP address each time they connect. Keep this in mind if you're considering FileMaker Pro Unlimited instead of Standard, but you're not sure you absolutely need it.

Web-Savvy File Planning

If you'll be publishing a database on the Web, consider these technical requirements before you begin:

- File names should adhere to the 8.3 convention.

- File, field, and layout names should not contain spaces. Use underscores (Shift+hyphen) instead.

- Older browsers may not display pop-up lists and drop-down menus correctly, so avoid them in your layouts when possible.

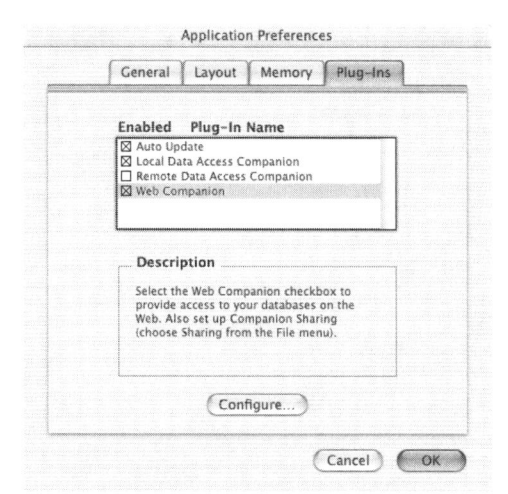

Figure 17.1 The Web Companion plug-in makes FileMaker files available over the Web.

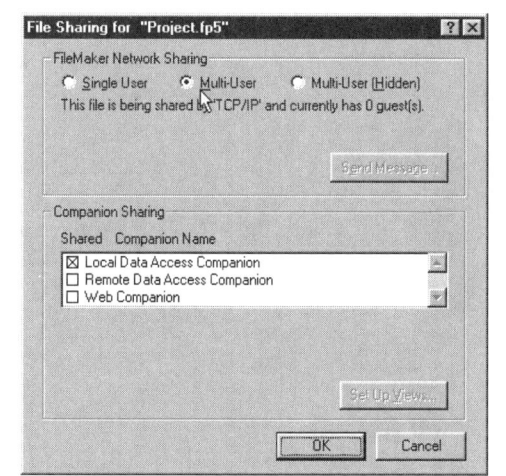

Figure 17.2 To publish a database with the Web Companion, you must specify it as Multi-User.

Configuring Databases for Web Access

The FileMaker Web Companion plug-in is your key to making databases available on the Web. This plug-in acts as a CGI, translating requests between a Web browser and FileMaker Pro into the appropriate code for each, allowing a user to interact seamlessly with your database. Once you've enabled Web Companion, you'll also need to open your files with a password that allows records to be exported.

To enable Web Companion:

1. Choose Edit (FileMaker Pro in Mac OS X) > Preferences > Application.

2. When the Application Preferences dialog box appears, click the Plug-Ins tab.

3. Click the Web Companion check box (**Figure 17.1**).

   If the Web Companion plug-in does not appear in the list, you can install it from your original FileMaker installation CD.

4. Click OK.

To configure file-sharing privileges:

1. In the database to be published on the Web, choose File > Sharing to open the File Sharing dialog box.

2. In the FileMaker Network Sharing section, click the Multi-User radio button (**Figure 17.2**).

continues on next page

403

Chapter 17

3. In the Companion Sharing area, click the Web Companion check box (**Figure 17.3**).

4. Click OK.

Repeat these steps for any other databases you want to publish and for any related databases. Your databases are now ready for Web access.

✔ Tips

- If you want to have related databases available for Web publishing but don't want them to appear as separate files, click the Multi-User (Hidden) radio button instead of Multi-User in the FileMaker Network Sharing section (**Figure 17.4**).

- Files hosted with Instant Web Publishing will obey any record-by-record access rules you have previously set up.

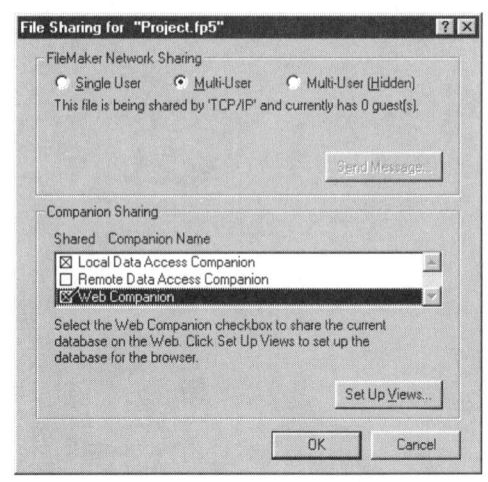

Figure 17.3 Selecting the Web Companion check box starts the Web Companion.

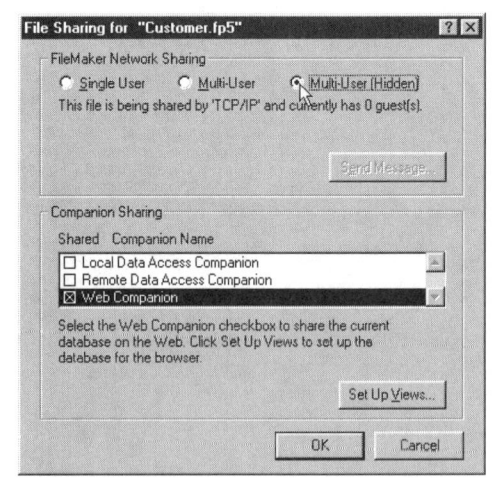

Figure 17.4 The Multi-User (Hidden) option prevents an open database from being displayed on the home page.

Web Publishing

Figure 17.5 Set Up Views lets you select Web styles for each database.

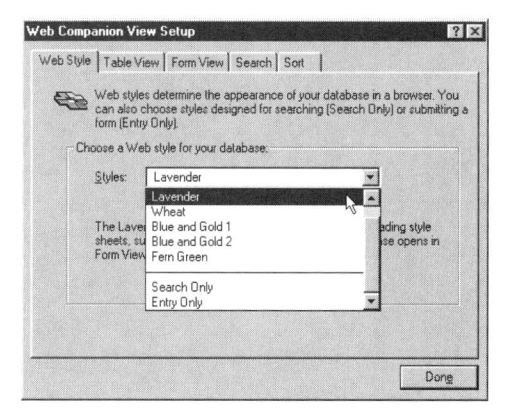

Figure 17.6 Web Style determines the colors and layout you'll see in a Web browser.

Choosing a Layout Style

Layout styles determine what your database looks like in a Web browser. Colors, text styles, and graphics are all determined by the style you select. Styles are similar in appearance to the themes that are used to create layouts in the Layout Assistant.

To choose a layout style:

1. In the database to be published, choose File > Sharing to bring up the File Sharing dialog box.
2. In the Companion Sharing area, click the Web Companion plug-in check box.
3. Click the Set Up Views button (**Figure 17.5**).
4. When the Web Companion View Setup window opens, click the Web Style tab. From the Styles drop-down menu, select the Web style you want to use for that database (**Figure 17.6**). Click Done, then OK.

continues on next page

405

✔ Tip

- While you're in Web Style, consider how you want people to use your database. You might want to choose Search Only or Entry Only. Search Only allows a user to search for and view data, but not enter new files or change old ones. Entry Only allows a user to enter a new record in the database, but not to view existing records. Entry Only comes in handy if you want visitors to add their names to a mailing list or guest book (see "Creating a Guest Book," later in this chapter). It augments FileMaker's password restriction capabilities and is an easy way to improve your Web data security.

Browser Versions and FileMaker Styles

Unfortunately, not all browsers are created equal, and some are more unequal than others. Despite their being free to download, not everyone updates Web browsers to the latest version. In fact, a surprisingly large number of people—those with older computers or slow Web access—are still using browsers that can't understand JavaScript or Cascading Style Sheets (CSS).

The range of capabilities in browsers is an important consideration when you're choosing a Web style. Styles depend on CSS to render them. If a user accesses your database with a browser that supports CSS, the layouts will appear much as they do in FileMaker itself. On the other hand, someone using an older browser will see the layouts in Fern Green. That's because all styles except Fern Green and Blue and Gold 2 depend on CSS.

If you can't be reasonably sure that the only people who will access your database are using browser versions at least as new as Internet Explorer 3 and Netscape 4, choose only one of these two "safe" styles.

Web Publishing

Figure 17.7 The IWP interface is suppressed when the Status area is set to Hide.

Suppressing Built-In Navigation in IWP

IWP exists to make creating a Web database as easy as possible. To meet this goal, FileMaker makes most of the page-creation decisions for you. If you're in a hurry or have no Web experience at all, this is a blessing. But it also allows you to leverage what you already know about FileMaker's internal interactivity and scripting to offer a Web database that looks and acts like a regular FileMaker file. To customize a Web-hosted FileMaker database, you first need to turn off the automatic IWP setup that supplies the default interactive scripts and graphic elements so you can replace them with your own. The cleanest way to accomplish this is by using a startup script that hides the Status Area.

To use a startup script:

1. In the database being hosted, choose Scripts > ScriptMaker.

2. When the Define Scripts dialog box appears, type Hide Status Area. Click Create.

3. The Script Definition dialog box appears. In the step list on the left, scroll to the Windows category and double-click Toggle Status Area.

4. In the Options section, choose Hide from the Specify drop-down menu (**Figure 17.7**).

continues on next page

407

Chapter 17

5. Click OK and then Done.

6. Choose Edit (FileMaker Pro in Mac OS X) > Preferences > Document.

7. Click the General tab. In the "When opening" section, check the "Perform script" check box.

8. Choose Hide Status Area from the "Perform script" drop-down menu (**Figure 17.8**). Click OK.

✔ **Tips**

- The Fern Green and Blue and Gold 2 Web styles do not support Cascading Style Sheets and cannot be used if you want to suppress the IWP interface.

- If you specify a startup layout in Document Preferences for a database hosted in IWP, that layout will be the first one a user sees when opening the database in a Web browser (**Figure 17.9**).

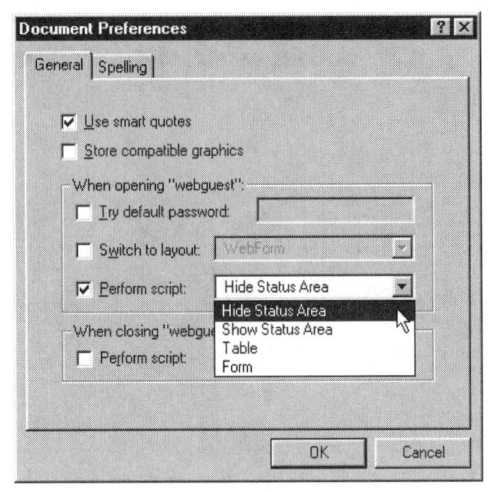

Figure 17.8 The Hide Status Area script will automatically run upon opening the database if you select it in Document Preferences.

Figure 17.9 You can set your opening Web layout at the same time that you set the opening script.

Supported Script Steps

Only a fraction of the ScriptMaker steps are supported when you use them in a Web-hosted database. Most of the supported steps cannot be combined to create more complex scripts. They are meant to be used as single-step actions that you can connect to dedicated buttons. These limitations exist because not all FileMaker functions are easily ported to the CSS and HTML protocols used on the Internet.

A few steps can be used in a single script, as long as the script doesn't contain more than three steps in all (if you duplicate a script step, it counts as a second step). Be careful not to use a step that doesn't appear in this list. If you do, your script will stop running as soon as FileMaker reaches the unsupported step. Those steps that can be combined are listed at the end of the sidebar.

Supported single script steps:

Go to Record/Request/Page [record number]
Goes to a specific record number. The number can be set with a field value or from a JavaScript prompt.

Go to Record/Request/Page [First/Last/Next/Previous]
Works the same as in FileMaker except in Table view. Go to Record in Table view will go to the first, last, next, or previous page of records. However, Go to Record by Number will work the same as in FileMaker. In Form view, Go to Record works as normal.

Go to Field [field name]
Switches view to the Edit Record layout containing the specified field. This step does not put the cursor in the specified field as it does in FileMaker.

New Record/Request []
Displays the Form View Page.

Enter Find Mode []
Displays the Search page.

Show All Records
Displays all records.

Perform Find
Submits the current request from the Find Page. Stored Find requests are not restored.

Exit Record
Submits the form.

Sort[]
Displays the Sort page.

Delete Record Request []
Deletes the current record after a confirmation.

View as [View as Table]
Displays the current page as a table.

View as [View as Form]
Displays the current page as a form.

View as [View as List]
Displays the current page as a list.

View as [Cycle]
Switches the display of the current record or page between form and table.

Enter Browse Mode[]
Displays the current page as a form. Use this to switch from Edit, Search, or New Record view to Form view without submitting the record.

continues on next page

Supported Script Steps *continued*

Open Help
Opens HTML help in a new browser window.

Open [<document name >]
Works the same as opening a hosted file from the Instant Web portal. The specified document must be open on the server.

Open URL [<URL >]
Opens the specified URL in the current browser window.

Go to Related Record [<Relationship name >]
Goes to the related record(s) from the specified relationship. The sort order is the one specified in the Web Companion View Setup dialog box for the specified database. Only records found by the relationship will be in the found set.

Supported multiple script steps:

- New Record/Request
- Go to Record/Request/Page []
- Go to Layout []
- Go to Field []
- Enter Browse Mode []
- Sort []
- Enter Find Mode []
- Show All Records
- Exit Record
- Perform Find

Creating Web Layouts

After you suppress the IWP controls for a Web-hosted database, you use FileMaker's standard tools to arrange your layout elements. Because suppressing the IWP controls means that all default interactivity is also suppressed, you must add buttons to allow users to carry out commands.

To place buttons on a Web form:

1. In the database to be hosted, go to the layout that will be used for the Form view layout. The Body section should contain the fields that the user will see.

2. If there isn't a Header part, drag the Body part down to make room. Add a header by dragging the Part tool onto the layout and choosing Header in the Part Definition dialog box (**Figure 17.10**). Click OK.

3. Drag the Header part down to make room for the buttons you'll create.

4. In the toolbar, click the Button tool. Drag the pointer in the Header to create a button.

5. When the Specify Button dialog box appears, choose the command for that button from the scrolling list (**Figure 17.11**).

    The command must be one of those listed in the Supported Script Steps sidebar. In our example, it's Go to Record/Request/Page.

6. If you want to go to a specific record or to the previous or next record in the file, specify your destination in the Options section to the right (**Figure 17.12**).

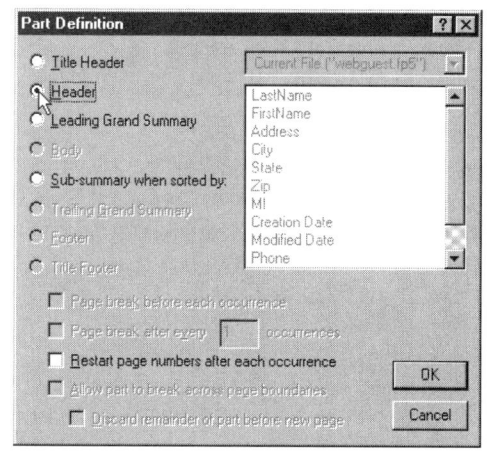

continues on next page

Figure 17.10 The Header layout part will contain the buttons for the customized interface.

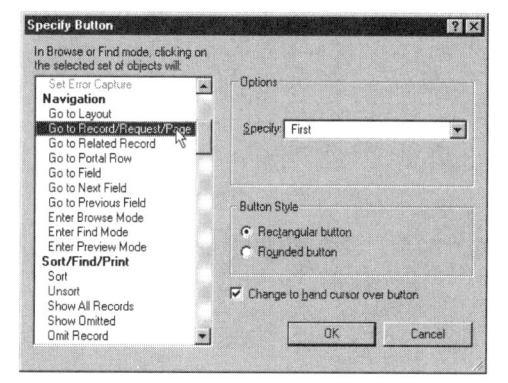

Figure 17.11 A button command must be one of the steps IWP supports.

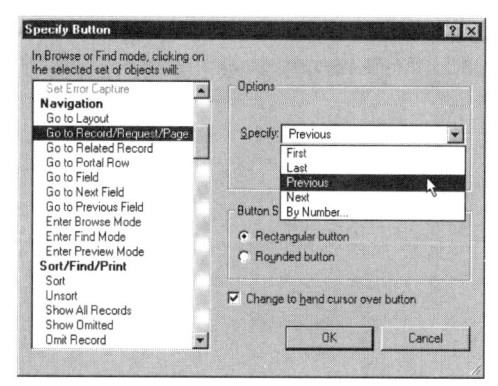

Figure 17.12 The button destination is set in the Options section.

411

Chapter 17

7. Click OK, then type a label in the button.

8. To create additional buttons, hold the Control or Option key and drag the button to duplicate it. Double-click each new button, change the command in the Specify Button dialog box, and then change the text in the layout (**Figure 17.13**).

9. Add one more button to the layout. Double-click it.

10. When the Specify Button dialog box appears, scroll down to the Records category and choose Exit Record/Request (**Figure 17.14**). Click OK.

11. In the layout, label the new button Save (**Figure 17.15**). When a user makes changes to a record, clicking this button will submit the changes and update the database (**Figure 17.16**).

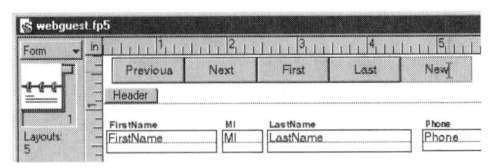

Figure 17.13 Control- or Option-dragging is a quick way to create new buttons on a layout.

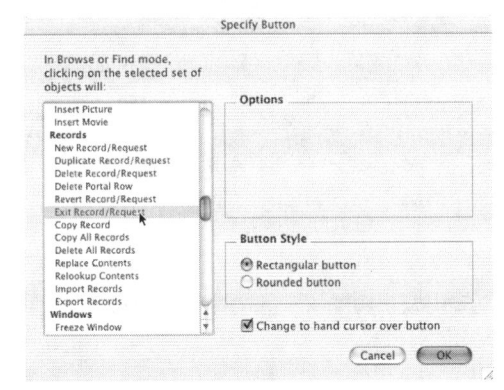

Figure 17.14 The Exit Record command submits the changes made to a record to the database.

Figure 17.15 Labeling the button that submits the record Save makes it clearer to the user what the button does.

Figure 17.16 Users must submit their changes to the database.

412

Web Publishing

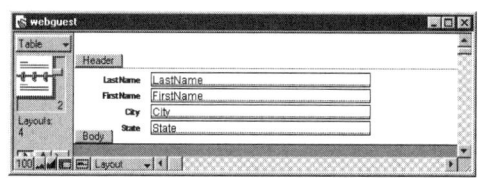

Figure 17.17 When you add fields to a layout to be displayed in Table View, they don't appear as columns in Layout mode.

Figure 17.18 Select Properties to set up your table.

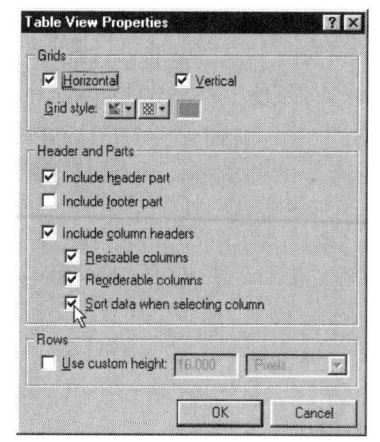

Figure 17.19 To enable users to sort the columns in Table View, select the "Sort data when selecting column" option.

To create a Table View layout:

1. In the database to be hosted, go to the layout that will be used for the Table View. Add the fields that you want to be displayed in the Table View (**Figure 17.17**).

2. Choose Layouts > Layout Setup.

3. When the Layout Setup dialog box appears, click the Views tab. Uncheck the Form View and List View boxes.

4. Click the Properties button next to Table View (**Figure 17.18**).

5. When the Table View Properties dialog box appears, make sure that, in Header and Parts, the "Include header part" and "Include column headers" boxes are checked (**Figure 17.19**).

6. Under "Include column headers," check the "Sort data when selecting column" box. This option will allow users to sort the Table View by clicking the column headers. Click OK twice to finish.

CREATING WEB LAYOUTS

413

Chapter 17

Creating a Web-Based Find Script

When you're using IWP with the defaults suppressed, running a complete Find script can look a little dicey. Users can enter the find data, but because hitting the Enter key doesn't resume the script as it does in FileMaker, they have no way to continue the script. To work around the problem, you'll need to create two scripts. The first will go the Find layout, enter Find mode, and pause to allow the user to enter the data. The second script performs the find when the user clicks the Perform Find button.

To create a Web-based Find script:

1. In the database to be hosted, go to the layout that will be used for the find.

2. Choose Scripts > ScriptMaker. In the Define Scripts dialog box, type Find Mode for the script name and click Create.

3. The Script Definition dialog box appears. In the step list on the left, double-click Go to Layout. In the Options section, select Find from the Specify drop-down menu (**Figure 17.20**).

4. In the step list on the left, scroll down to the Windows category and double-click View As.

5. In the Options section, choose View as Form from the Specify drop-down menu (**Figure 17.21**).

6. In the Navigation category of the step list on the left, double-click Enter Find Mode. Uncheck the "Restore find requests" box, but leave the Pause box checked (**Figure 17.22**). Click OK.

7. In the Define Scripts dialog box, type Perform Find for the script name and click Create.

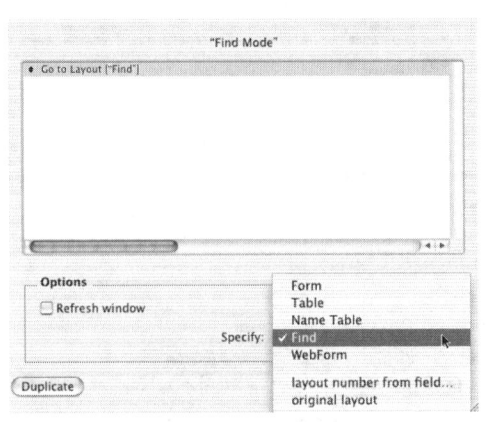

Figure 17.20 The Find layout displays the fields that will be used in the Find command.

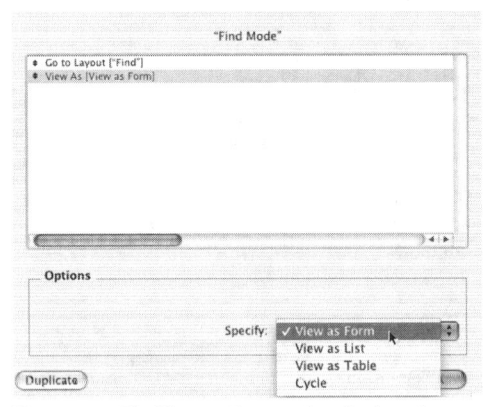

Figure 17.21 The View as Form option displays the layout as a form.

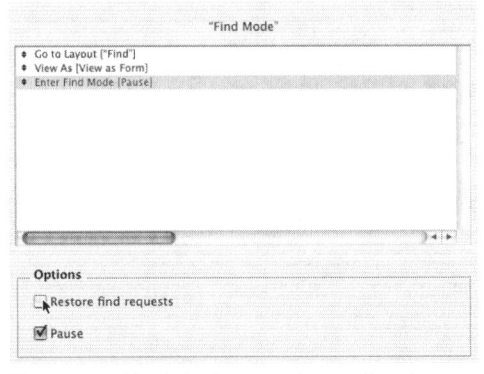

Figure 17.22 Check the Pause option to allow the user to enter data.

414

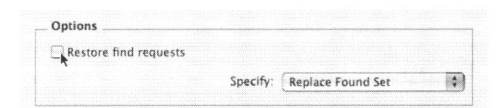

Figure 17.23 Restored finds are not supported in IWP, so this option should not be checked.

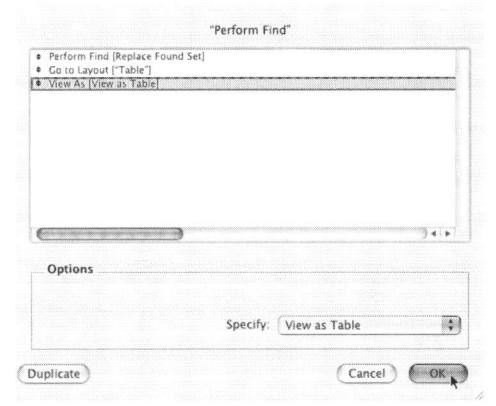

Figure 17.24 The View As option displays the layout as either a table or a form.

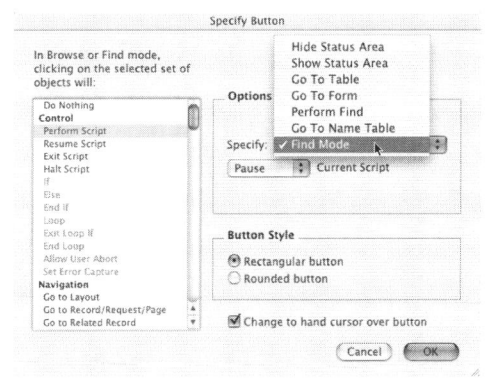

Figure 17.25 The Find Mode script switches the user to the Find layout and pauses in Find mode.

8. The Script Definition dialog box appears. In the step list on the left, scroll down to Sort/Find/Print and double-click Perform Find. Uncheck the "Restore find requests" box (**Figure 17.23**).

9. In the step list on the left, double-click Go to Layout.

10. In the Options section, choose from the Specify drop-down menu the layout that you want to appear after the find is complete.

11. In the Windows category of the step list on the left, double-click View As.

12. Choose a layout type from the Specify drop-down menu in the Options section. If the layout you chose in step 10 is a Form, choose View as Form; if it's a Table View layout, choose View as Table (**Figure 17.24**). Click OK, then Done.

13. In the Form View layout, choose View > Layout Mode.

14. Add a new button or Control- or Option-drag an existing button to duplicate it. Double-click the new button.

15. When the Specify Button dialog box appears, choose Perform Script from the list on the left. From the Specify drop-down menu, choose Find Mode (**Figure 17.25**).

continues on next page

Chapter 17

16. In the Find layout, choose View > Layout Mode. Add a button. Double-click the new button.

17. In the Specify Button dialog box, choose Perform Script. In the Options section, choose Perform Find from the Specify drop-down menu (**Figure 17.26**). Click OK.

18. Label the button Perform Find. You can add text instructions to the layout (**Figure 17.27**).

The layout will look just like a FileMaker layout, and users will have no problems creating and performing a find (**Figure 17.28**).

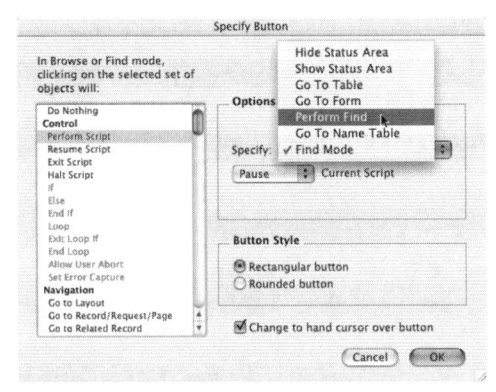

Figure 17.26 The Perform Find command carries out the find with the criteria the user enters.

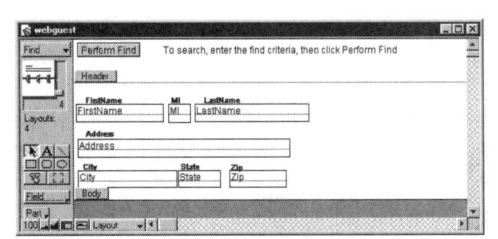

Figure 17.27 Adding text instructions helps users understand their options in a layout.

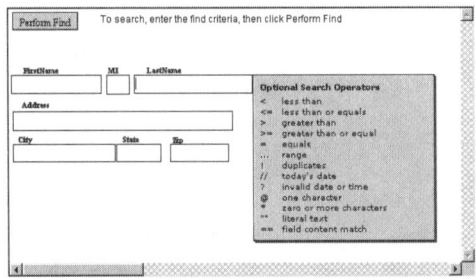

Figure 17.28 In Find mode, Web users will see an operator list when they click in a field.

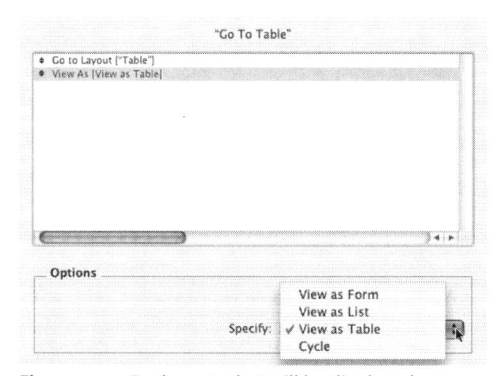

Figure 17.29 For layouts that will be displayed as tables, the View As option must be set to Table.

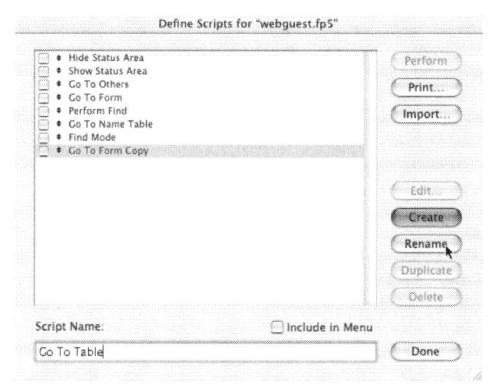

Figure 17.30 Since the step order is the same for both Go To Table and Go To Form, it's easier to duplicate and rename the first script than to create one from scratch.

Switching Layouts with a Script

IWP allows users to switch between layouts with the click of a button. The nicest part is that you need only a simple FileMaker script to provide this feature. You don't have to write a single line of HTML code.

To switch layouts with a script (without HTML):

1. In the database to be hosted, choose Scripts > ScriptMaker.

2. When the Define Scripts dialog box appears, type Go To Table for the script name and click Create.

3. The Script Definition dialog box appears. In the step list on the left, double-click Go to Layout.

4. In the Options section, choose the layout to be used for the Table View from the Specify drop-down menu.

5. In the step list on the left, scroll down to the Windows category and double-click View As.

6. In the Options section, choose View as Table from the Specify drop-down menu (**Figure 17.29**). Click OK.

7. In the Define Scripts dialog box, click to highlight the Go To Table script, and click Duplicate. Change the name to Go To Form, and click Rename (**Figure 17.30**).

8. Double-click the Go To Form script.

9. When the Script Definition dialog box appears, click the Go to Layout step in the script-assembly section on the right. In the Options section, choose Form from the Specify drop-down menu.

continues on next page

Chapter 17

10. Click the View As step in the script-assembly section. In the Options section, choose View as Form from the Specify drop-down menu (**Figure 17.31**). Click OK and then Done.

11. Go to the Form layout. Choose View > Layout Mode.

12. Create a new button. When the Specify Button dialog box appears, click Perform Script.

13. In the Options section, choose Go To Table from the Specify drop-down menu (**Figure 17.32**). Click OK. Label the button Table.

14. Go to the Table layout. Choose View > Layout Mode.

15. Create a new button. When the Specify Button dialog box appears, click Perform Script. In the Options section, choose Go To Form from the Specify drop-down menu (**Figure 17.33**). Click OK. Label the button Form.

16. Click OK and then Done.

Your layout in the Web browser will offer the Form option when viewed in Table View and the Table option when viewed in Form View. In Table view, you can click a column header to change the sort criteria, just as you would in a regular FileMaker file (**Figure 17.34**).

✔ **Tip**

■ If your hosted database has related fields, make sure that the related file has the same password and privileges as the hosted file. If a layout contains a portal, users can edit data in the portal as long as access privileges in the related database allow them to.

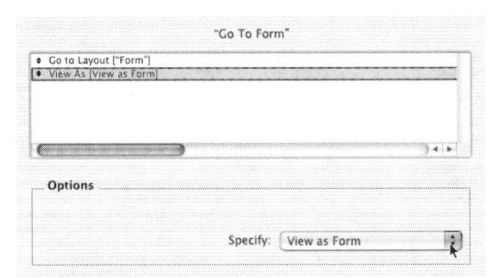

Figure 17.31 Set the View As option to match the way the layout will be displayed.

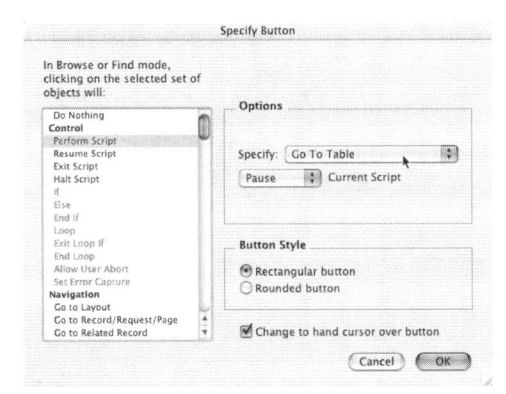

Figure 17.32 The Table button switches the user to the Table layout with a single click.

Figure 17.33 The Form button on the table layout switches the user to the Form layout.

Figure 17.34 In a Table layout, the user can click a column header to sort by that field.

418

Web Publishing

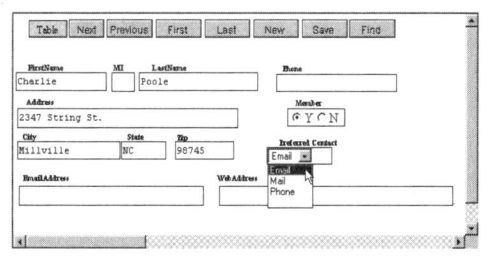

Figure 17.35 Field formats like radio buttons and drop-down lists will look the same in a Web browser as they do in FileMaker.

Web Display Considerations

Although databases on the Web may look very much the same as regular FileMaker files, their behavior and available options are slightly different:

- Value list elements like pop-up lists, check boxes, and radio buttons work perfectly on the Web, even if they're relational. They're displayed as standard HTML controls (**Figure 17.35**). However, users cannot edit value lists with the Edit option or enter new list options with the Other option.

- Repeating fields are displayed just as they are in FileMaker, but Merge fields aren't displayed at all.

- If you specify display formats for date or number fields, they'll be displayed with that format in a Web browser. If you don't specify a format, date and number fields will be displayed with the default format specified in the user's operating system.

- Container fields are displayed as a static graphic. If a container field contains a movie, the movie file must be in FileMaker's Web folder to allow users to play it in their Web browsers.

- Web browsers ignore the tab order set in FileMaker. To change the tab order, you can use the Send Backward/Bring Forward command from the Arrange menu. Web browsers will render fields in the background before fields in the foreground.

- The height of each row will be uniform even if field contents (like a graphics in container fields) are not.

419

Chapter 17

Tracking Activity and Access

You can use FileMaker's log files to keep track of who has accessed your database and when they did so. You can also track any errors that occur, which is a good way to debug a problem before too many people experience it. These three log files are in text format, which means you can easily print them out. You can also import them into FileMaker, making it possible to perform keyword searches to display errors or info on specific files. The log files are saved in the same folder as your FileMaker Pro application:

- The Access log file (access.log) records every user's IP address as well as the pages viewed (**Figure 17.36**).

- The Error log (error.log) records any errors that occur while a user is accessing the databases (**Figure 17.37**).

- The Information log (info.log) is only needed if you're using CDML replacement tags in the HTML code of a Web page. For example, the CDML tag [FMP-Log] will enter any data after the tag; [FMP-Log: Access was granted.] will enter the date and time with "Access was granted." in the info.log file.

Figure 17.36 The Access log tracks the IP address of each user who signs in to the databases.

Figure 17.37 Any errors that occur while a user is accessing your databases will be recorded in the Error log.

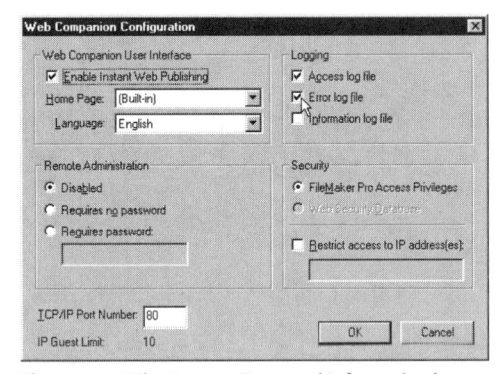

Figure 17.38 The Access, Error, and Information logs need to be enabled before they will record data.

To track activity with log files:

1. Choose Edit (FileMaker Pro in Mac OS X) > Preferences > Application.

2. In the Application Preferences dialog box, click the Plug-Ins tab.

3. In the list of Plug-Ins, click Web Companion to highlight it.

4. Click the Configure button.

5. In the Web Companion Configuration dialog box (**Figure 17.38**), click the check boxes for "Access log file," "Error log file," and/or "Information log file."

6. Click OK, then OK again to finish.

420

Web Publishing

Figure 17.39 To access published databases with a Web browser, type in the IP address of the host computer.

Figure 17.40 Unless you specify a custom home page, the built-in home page will appear when a user accesses the databases.

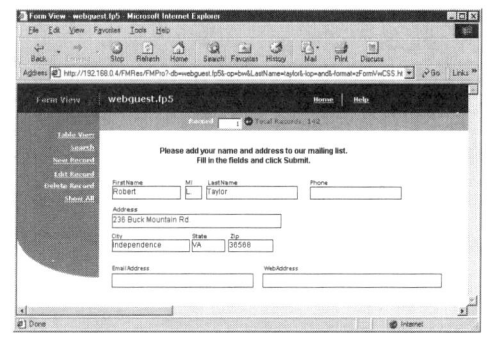

Figure 17.41 Databases are accessed by clicking the links on the home page.

Figure 17.42 If a database has a password, you'll need to enter it with your user name to gain access.

Accessing a File with a Browser

Once you've set up Instant Web Publishing, your databases are available and accessible to anyone with Internet access. All that's necessary is a basic understanding of how to use a Web browser.

To access a database with a browser:

1. In your Web browser's address box, type the IP address of the computer that's hosting the databases (**Figure 17.39**). Press Enter.

   For this example, we're using an intranet with an IP address. If your database is published using a domain name, users can enter the URL (http://domainname.com).

2. The FileMaker home page will appear (**Figure 17.40**).

3. Click any of the links displayed to access a database (**Figure 17.41**).

4. If the hosted databases are password-protected, you'll be prompted for a user name and password (**Figure 17.42**).

✔ Tip

- You can publish databases for Web access even if you open the files from FileMaker Pro Server, as long as the regular FileMaker application is running on your computer. FileMaker Pro Server alone cannot publish databases for Web access.

421

Enabling Remote Administration

You can administer your Web-published databases from computers other than the one holding your database. Remote administration allows you to open and close databases and use HTTP commands to upload and download files to your Web folder.

To enable remote administration:

1. Choose Edit (FileMaker Pro in Mac OS X) > Preferences > Application.

2. In the Application Preferences dialog box, click the Plug-Ins tab.

3. In the list of Plug-Ins, click Web Companion, then click the Configure button.

4. In the Web Companion Configuration dialog box's Remote Administration section, click the Requires Password radio button (**Figure 17.43**).

5. Type the password in the box below the radio button (**Figure 17.44**). Click OK, then OK again to finish.

✔ Tip

- Although you have the option to enable remote administration without a password, it is not a good idea. Without a password, all of your databases are open to anyone.

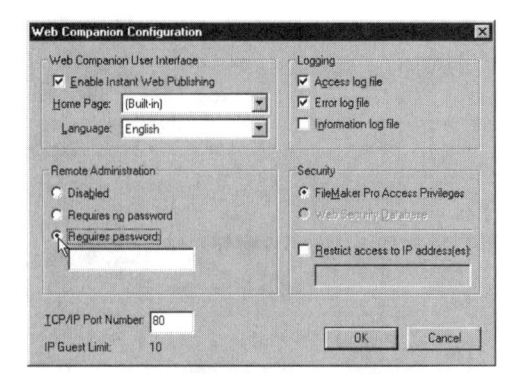

Figure 17.43 Remote administration should always be enabled with a password to protect the files.

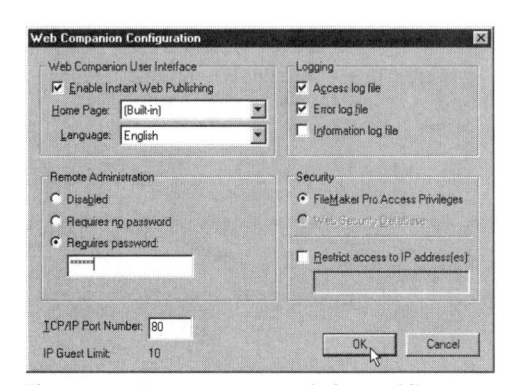

Figure 17.44 Enter your password after enabling remote administration

Web Publishing

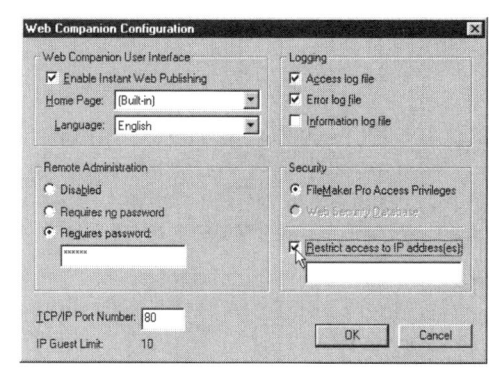

Figure 17.45 You can restrict database access to the IP addresses you enter.

Figure 17.46 By using an asterisk as a wild card, you can grant access to a range of IP addresses.

Restricting Database Access

Password protection for a FileMaker Web database is set within the application. In addition, you can limit access to your published databases to specific IP addresses. This is a handy feature if you're publishing the databases only for the use of people in your company.

To restrict access by IP address:

1. Choose Edit (FileMaker Pro in Mac OS X) > Preferences > Application.

2. In the Application Preferences dialog box, click the Plug-Ins tab.

3. In the list of Plug-Ins, click Web Companion, then click the Configure button.

4. In the Web Companion Configuration dialog box's Security section, click the "Restrict access to IP address(es)" check box (**Figure 17.45**).

5. In the box below the check box, type the IP addresses to which you want to grant access. If you want to use more than one IP address, separate the addresses with commas. If you want to allow access to a range of IP addresses, use an asterisk as a wild card (**Figure 17.46**). Click OK, then OK again to finish.

423

Creating a Custom Home Page

Unless you specify a custom home page, users accessing your database will see the default home page that FileMaker generates. Your alternative is to create a custom Web page that will serve as your gateway to the published databases.

To create a custom home page:

1. Using an HTML editing program or Web page layout program, create your custom home page.

2. To create links on the home page to the databases that you plan to publish, launch your Web browser and access the first of your published databases (refer to Figure 17.40).

3. In the browser, click the link to the first database. The URL for the database will appear in the address line. Select and copy the full address (**Figure 17.47**).

4. Paste the copied address into your HTML code as the link to that database (**Figure 17.48**).

5. Repeat steps 3 and 4 for each database that will be listed on the custom home page.

Figure 17.47 Copy the full URL from the Web browser.

Figure 17.48 For each database, paste the copied URL into your HTML code.

Web Publishing

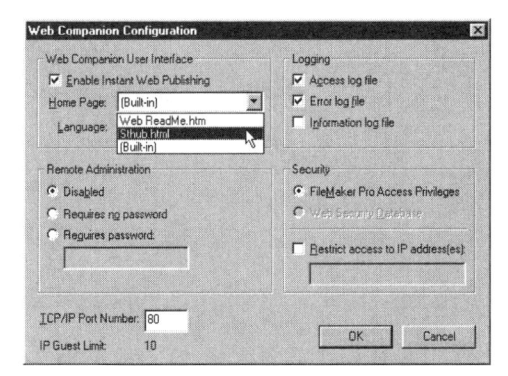

Figure 17.49 Configure FileMaker to use the custom page instead of the built-in page.

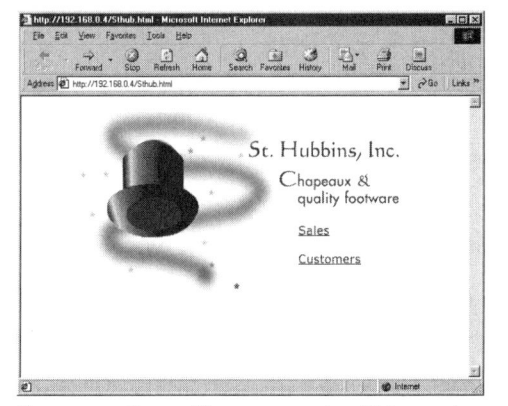

Figure 17.50 Users will see your custom Web page in their browsers.

6. After you've inserted URLs for all of your links, save the custom home page and move it to the Web folder (in the same folder as the FileMaker Pro application).

7. Choose Edit (FileMaker Pro in Mac OS X) > Preferences > Application.

8. In the Application Preferences dialog box, click the Plug-Ins tab.

9. In the Plug-In list, click Web Companion, then click the Configure button.

10. In the Web Companion Configuration dialog box's User Interface section, choose the name of your custom home page from the Home Page drop-down menu (**Figure 17.49**). Click OK, then OK again to finish.

When users accesses your databases with a browser, they'll see the custom Web page you created, rather than the default home page (**Figure 17.50**).

CREATING A CUSTOM HOME PAGE

425

Chapter 17

Creating a Guest Book

Web-published FileMaker databases are perfect for collecting names and addresses for a mailing list. In this example, visitors see a screen that allows them to enter their data, but don't see other records in the database.

When creating Web layouts for online data input, make your fields in your FileMaker layout larger than you would ordinarily. Web browsers tend to display entry fields smaller than FileMaker.

To create a guest book:

1. Create a FileMaker database with the data fields that you want visitors to fill out (**Figure 17.51**).

2. In the new database, choose View > Layout Mode.

3. Choose Layout > New Layout (Control+N/Command+N).

4. Type a name for the layout and click Blank layout (**Figure 17.52**). Click Finish.

5. Click the Header and Footer tabs and move them up until they disappear.

6. Add the fields to the Body part of the layout in the order that you want them to appear in the browser (**Figure 17.53**).

7. Choose File > Sharing to bring up the File Sharing dialog box. Make sure that the Web Companion plug-in is checked.

Figure 17.51 For best performance, add only the fields you need.

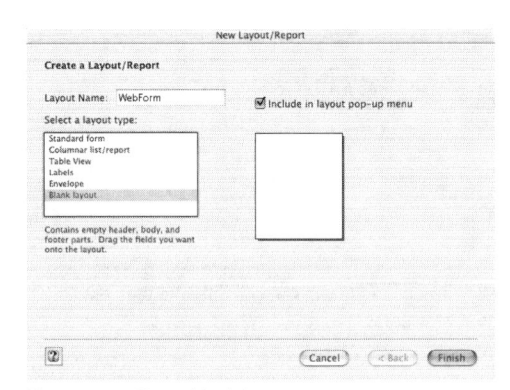

Figure 17.52 Use a blank layout to create your guest book.

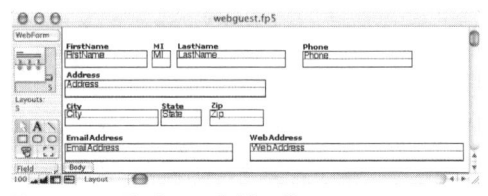

Figure 17.53 The layout fields will appear as you placed them if the browser supports CSS.

Web Publishing

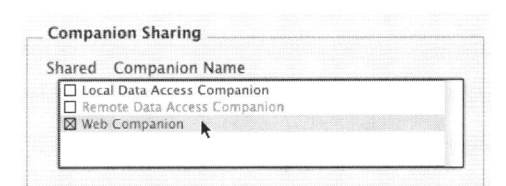

Figure 17.54 Use the Web Companion plug-in to configure the database for the Web.

Figure 17.55 The Entry Only style only lets a user enter a new record.

Figure 17.56 Form View uses the selected layout to display the layout in a browser.

Figure 17.57 When a user enters data in the fields and clicks the Submit button, a new record is created.

8. In the Companion Sharing section, double-click Web Companion (**Figure 17.54**).

9. In the Web Companion View Setup dialog box, choose Entry Only from the Styles pop-up menu (**Figure 17.55**).

10. Click the Form View tab.

11. Choose the layout you created in steps 3–6 from the Layout pop-up menu (**Figure 17.56**).

12. Click Done, then OK to finish.

To check your guest book, launch your Web browser and enter the host computer's IP address. When you click the database name in the home page, the entry form will appear. Fill in the form, click the Submit button, and the record should be added to the database (**Figure 17.57**).

✔ Tips

- If a user accesses your guest book database with an older browser that doesn't support CSS, they'll see the Fern Green style instead of the layout you created. In addition, they'll be able to see the other records entered. To deal with this weakness, import the entered records into a separate mailing list database and then delete them from the guest book. Do this frequently enough to avoid a backlog of entries.

427

Testing Your Web Database

Before you publish your databases, test them first with your own browser to make sure they work the way you expect. In fact, you should try to test them with the latest versions of both Internet Explorer and Netscape, and at least one older version. By checking with several browsers, you can make sure that no major problems will appear when a wide range of visitors access your pages.

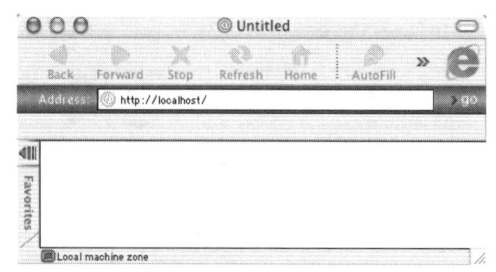

Figure 17.58 Typing Localhost instead of an IP address will access the hosted databases on the same computer you're working on.

To test published databases:

1. Open the databases configured for Web sharing in FileMaker.

2. On the same computer, start your Web browser.

3. Open a blank browser page.

4. Type http://localhost/ in the address line (**Figure 17.58**).

    The default start page (or the custom one, if designated) will appear in your browser.

5. Use your browser to view the layouts.

6. Switch back to FileMaker to make any necessary changes (like widening fields).

7. Switch back to the browser and click the Refresh or Reload button to see the changes.

About Custom Web Publishing

Instant Web Publishing is easy to set up and implement, but it can't handle sophisticated tasks. That's where Custom Web Publishing comes in. Using CDML tags, Custom Web Publishing lets you insert FileMaker data into standard Web pages. CDML tags are commands that a Web page sends to FileMaker, which interprets them through the Web Companion plug-in. Based on the requests it receives, FileMaker will either carry out a command (through CDML's action tags) or display data on the Web page (through CDML's replacement tags).

Using CDML tags, you can do much more than just display data. You can write HTML code to search, sort, and add data to a FileMaker database from a Web page.

Don't toss those IWP Styles yet, though. Although temptingly powerful, CDML is not something you can master overnight. It's somewhat similar to HTML (which should already be an old friend before you start working with CDML) but has its own, more complicated syntax. Since that syntax is worth several books on its own, this section shows you how to get your feet wet, but doesn't try to cover CDML in depth.

Setting Up Custom Web Publishing

Custom Web Publishing, like Instant Web Publishing, requires the Web Companion and a default home page. The home page can be a standard Web page, but it will require links to the format files for each action you want database users to carry out. We show you how to set up a CDML format file below.

Your home page, format files, and any other Web pages you want connected to your FileMaker database should be placed in the Web folder inside your FileMaker Pro folder.

To set up Custom Web Publishing:

1. Create your default Web page. Save or copy it to the Web folder.

2. Open the FileMaker database to be published and choose File > Sharing.

3. Make sure that the Web Companion plug-in is checked (**Figure 17.59**). Click OK.

4. Choose Edit (FileMaker Pro in Mac OS X) > Preferences > Application.

5. Click the Plug-Ins tab. Make sure the Web Companion plug-in is checked.

6. Double-click the Web Companion plug-in.

7. In the Web Companion Configuration dialog box, uncheck the Enable Instant Web Publishing check box if it is checked.

8. In the Home Page drop-down menu, choose the default home page you want to use (**Figure 17.60**). Click OK, then OK again.

Figure 17.59 The Web Companion plug-in must be enabled to use Custom Web Publishing.

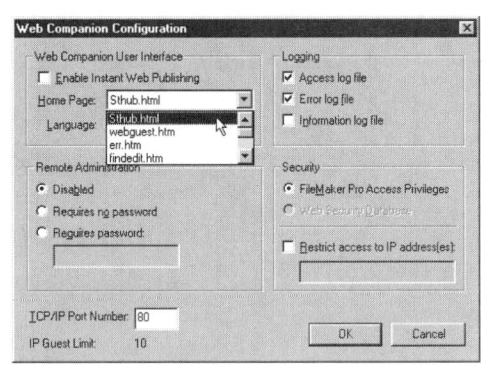

Figure 17.60 When users access your database, the default Web page will be the first thing that they see.

Web Publishing

✔ Tips

- When you publish FileMaker databases on the Web, any files placed in the Web folder can be accessed by Web users. Never put any important or sensitive files in the Web folder.

- The CDML_Format_File folder (located in the same folder as the FileMaker application) adds a new level of security to your CDML format pages. Any format pages placed in this folder will be processed by CGI requests, but can still be accessed directly by Web users. This folder only protects CDML files, not HTML or graphics files.

- If you find yourself using CDML on your Web pages, chances are pretty good that you're also working with Macromedia Dreamweaver. Dreamweaver isn't quite sure what to do with CDML code and sometimes breaks it up. When that happens, your CDML doesn't work. If you've experienced this problem, check out MacTherapy Consulting's CDML DW at www.mactherapy.co.uk/cdml. Drop the supplied tags into Dreamweaver and the incompatibilities will disappear.

CDML Tags

There are three categories of CDML tags: action tags, variable tags, and replacement tags.

- Action tags carry out commands within a database like adding, searching, and editing records.

- Variable tags are used with action tags to specify the names of database, layout, and results format files (results files are the place where the result of an action is displayed).

- Replacement tags are placeholders. They're used to display data from a FileMaker database in appropriate places on a Web page.

Action and variable tags begin with a hyphen (-):

NAME="-format"

Replacement tags are enclosed with within square brackets ([ ]):

[FMP-CurrentFormat]

Creating a Template Format File

Format files are specialized HTML pages. They determine how data from your FileMaker database appears in a Web browser. Each individual action a user needs to carry out on your database (add, edit, delete, etc.) requires an individual format file written with CDML tags.

A format file contains both CDML tags and HTML code. Most format files include two modular pieces: HTML coding for a standard Web page and HTML information that acts as a "header" to identify the FileMaker elements. Once you have these pieces, you can add custom CDML scripting to describe actions you want performed.

We'll build a complete CDML format file in two stages. First, we'll create the basic HTML for a Web page and the header information required by most of the format files we'll show you here. Second, we'll create a CDML action that prompts a user to enter information and gives feedback in response. For this example, we use the Guest Book file we created in the Instant Web Publishing example on page 426.

This is a very bare-bones, simple Web page we've created to hold our CDML heading. You can create a very complex Web page with style sheets and frames instead of this example, as long as the CDML information always appears inside the <BODY> tags.

To create a basic Web page:

1. Open a blank page in your text editor.
2. In the blank document, type the following lines, replacing "Web Page Title" with a descriptive name.

   <HTML>
   <HEAD>
   <TITLE>Web Page Title</TITLE>
   </HEAD>
   <BODY></BODY>
   </HTML>

✔ Tip

- If you use a text editor that has been designed for HTML coding (like BBEdit) it will open a new file that automatically includes all of this information. All you'll have to do is choose a title for your Web page and insert it between the <TITLE> tags (**Figure 17.61**).

Figure 17.61 BBEdit starts new Web pages with basic formatting in place.

To create a CDML form header:

1. In the HTML Web page you just created, insert your cursor between the <BODY> and </BODY> tags. Type this line of code to indicate that you'll be posting a form using FileMaker:

   `<FORM ACTION="FMPro" METHOD="POST">`

   This line must always be the first line of a Web form because it tells the browser that the next section relates to the form.

2. Although you'll add them one by one, the following four <INPUT> lines can appear in any order. The next line identifies the database you'll use:

   `<INPUT TYPE="hidden" NAME="-db" VALUE="webguest.fp5">`

3. This CDML line locates the layout in the database:

   `<INPUT TYPE="hidden" NAME="-lay" VALUE="Webform">`

4. This line tells the browser to display a standard response when the user has finished entering information. To create this response Web page, see "To create a response message format file" on page 436.

   `<INPUT TYPE="hidden" NAME="-format" VALUE="response.htm">`

5. If an error occurs while visitors are entering information, you should alert them. You'll need to create the err.htm HTML page this line requires.

   `<INPUT TYPE="hidden" NAME="-error" VALUE="err.htm">`

6. This last line is the HTML closing tag for the form (**Figure 17.62**).

   `</FORM>`

7. Save the template format file.

8. When you're ready to use this file for a project, resave the file with a descriptive name, then position your cursor just before the </FORM> tag. Additional CDML code for the form should be added just after the <INPUT TYPE> tags.

To customize this code for other projects, substitute the name of your database for "webguest.fp5" in the second line, your FileMaker layout name for "Webform" in the third line, the name of the format file you'll use to display the data for "response.htm" in the fourth line, and the name of the format file to display if an error occurs for "err.htm" in the last line of code.

✔ Tip

■ Although your HTML and CDML code will work just fine even if you run all the codes together, you'll find it a lot easier to check your code and follow what it does if you put each piece of code on its own line. HTML ignores the Return key on your keyboard, so you can organize your code without adding extra blank lines to your Web page.

```
<!DOCTYPE HTML PUBLIC "-//W3C//DTD HTML 3.2 Final//EN">
<HTML>
<HEAD>

<TITLE>Template CDML header</TITLE>

<META NAME="generator" CONTENT="BBEdit 4.5">

</HEAD>
<BODY>

<FORM ACTION="FMPRO" METHOD="POST">

<INPUT TYPE="hidden" NAME="-db" VALUE="webguest.fp5">
<INPUT TYPE="hidden" NAME="-lay" VALUE="Webform">
<INPUT TYPE="hidden" NAME="-format" VALUE="response.htm">
<INPUT TYPE="hidden" NAME="-err" VALUE="err.htm">

</FORM>

</BODY>
</HTML>
```

Figure 17.62 This Web page includes the header information needed to turn it into a CDML format file.

Prompting User Input with CDML

The database we used to set up the format file header in the previous section (webguest.fp5) contains name and address information, plus fields for email and Web addresses, in a layout named Webform. We want this format file to prompt users to fill in their contact information, so we need to input the code in the format file for this action.

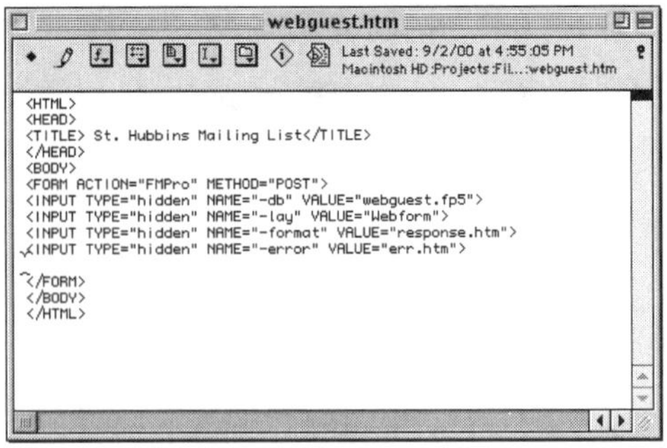

Figure 17.63 Anything that will be a part of the form must appear before the </FORM> close tag.

To prompt a user for input:

1. Open the template format file you created. Change the Web page title and save it as a new file.

2. Position your cursor just before the </FORM> tag (**Figure 17.63**) and type the HTML code for the form's instruction text:

   `<P>Please enter your information to be included in our mailing list. </P><P></P>`

3. Enter the following code to create the form's data entry fields. Since this is a Web page, all SIZE information is input in pixels. You can change these dimensions if you want.

   `<P>First Name: <INPUT TYPE="text" NAME="FirstName" SIZE=20></P>`
   `<P>MI: <INPUT TYPE="text" NAME="MI" SIZE=5></P>`
   `<P>Last Name: <INPUT TYPE="text" NAME="LastName" SIZE=20></P>`
   `<P>Address: <INPUT TYPE="text" NAME="Address" SIZE=20></P>`
   `<P>City: <INPUT TYPE="text" NAME="City" SIZE=20></P>`
   `<P>State: <INPUT TYPE="text" NAME="State" SIZE=5></P>`
   `<P>Zip: <INPUT TYPE="text" NAME="Zip" SIZE=20></P>`
   `<P>Phone: <INPUT TYPE="text" NAME="Phone" SIZE=20></P>`
   `<P>Email: <INPUT TYPE="text" NAME="EmailAddress" SIZE=20></P>`
   `<P>Web: <INPUT TYPE="text" NAME="WebAddress" SIZE=30></P>`

4. Now we'll create the CDML code to add the data entered by the user into the FileMaker database.

   `<P><INPUT TYPE="submit" NAME="-new" VALUE="submit"></P>`

   The Submit command combined with the –new tag tells FileMaker to create a new record from the information that the visitor inputs. It also adds a Submit button to the form.

5. Save this page as "webguest.htm" in your CDML_Format_File folder (**Figure 17.64**).

```
<HTML>
<HEAD>
<TITLE> St. Hubbins Mailing List</TITLE>
</HEAD>
<BODY>
<FORM ACTION="FMPro" METHOD="POST">
<INPUT TYPE="hidden" NAME="-db" VALUE="webguest.fp5">
<INPUT TYPE="hidden" NAME="-lay" VALUE="Webform">
<INPUT TYPE="hidden" NAME="-format" VALUE="response.htm">
<INPUT TYPE="hidden" NAME="-error" VALUE="err.htm">
<P>Please enter your information to be included in our mailing list.</P>
<P></P>
<P>First Name: <INPUT TYPE="text" NAME="FirstName" SIZE=20></P>
<P>MI: <INPUT TYPE="text" NAME="MI" SIZE=5></P>
<P>Last Name: <INPUT TYPE="text" NAME="LastName" SIZE=20></P>
<P>Address: <INPUT TYPE="text" NAME="Address" SIZE=20></P>
<P>City: <INPUT TYPE="text" NAME="City" SIZE=20></P>
<P>State: <INPUT TYPE="text" NAME="State" SIZE=5></P>
<P>Zip: <INPUT TYPE="text" NAME="Zip" SIZE=20></P>
<P>Phone: <INPUT TYPE="text" NAME="Phone" SIZE=20></P>
<P>Email: <INPUT TYPE="text" NAME="EmailAddress" SIZE=20></P>
<P>Web: <INPUT TYPE="text" NAME="WebAddress" SIZE=20></P>
<P><INPUT TYPE="submit" NAME="-new" VALUE="submit"></P>
<P><INPUT TYPE="reset" VALUE="Clear Form"></P>
</FORM>
</BODY>
```

Figure 17.64 After entering the code for a format file, save it in the Web folder.

Chapter 17

Providing Visitor Feedback

To provide feedback to the visitor, we need to create two more Web pages—one for display after a successful submission and another to display if an error occurs.

To create a response message format file:

1. Create a new Web page, following the steps in "To create a basic Web page" on page 432.

2. Position your cursor between the open and close <BODY> tags, and type the following HTML code (**Figure 17.65**):

   <P>Thanks. Your name has been added to our mailing list.</P>

3. You'll want to provide some way for your visitors to return to the rest of your site after they join the mailing list. We've added the following HTML code:

   <P><a href="StHub.html">Return to haberdashery</a></P>

   This line returns the visitor to our home page if they click the link.

4. Save this file as "response.htm" in the CDML_Format_File folder. It will be displayed if the record is added to the database successfully (**Figure 17.66**).

Figure 17.65 Text for the response should be inserted between the open and close <BODY> tags.

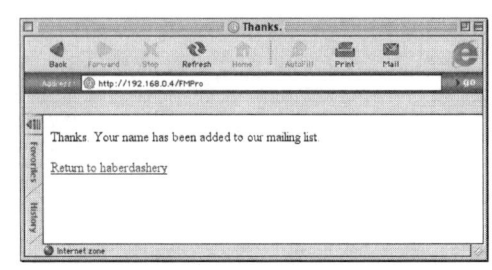

Figure 17.66 The response.htm file will be displayed after the data has been successfully entered into the database.

436

Web Publishing

Figure 17.67 If there's a problem entering the data, err.htm will be displayed.

Figure 17.68 Add a link to the default Web page to add a record with the webguest.htm format file.

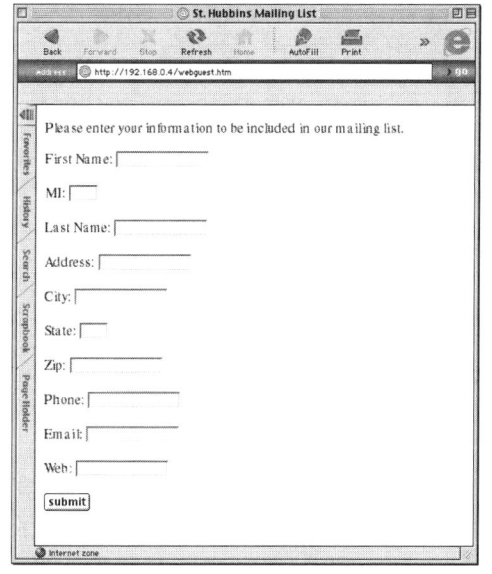

Figure 17.69 The webguest.htm file will display the fields to be added to the database.

To create an error message format file:

1. Create another Web page, following the steps in "To create a basic Web page" on page 432.

2. Position your cursor between the open and close <BODY> tags, and type the following HTML code (**Figure 17.67**):

   <P>Sorry. There seems to have been a problem. Click your Back button and try again.</P>

3. Save this file as "err.htm" in the CDML_ Format_File folder. It will be displayed if there's a problem with the submission.

You have now created the three format files needed for your visitors to enter their contact information and transfer it to the database. The last step is to create a link from your default home page to the webguest.htm format file.

To link a format file to the home page:

1. Open the default home page in your text editor.

2. Within the <BODY> tags, add a line of HTML text inviting people to join the mailing list, and providing a link to the list input page (**Figure 17.68**):

   Add your name to our exclusive <a href="webguest.htm"> Mailing List</a>

   You can, of course, customize this text with HTML coding to specify its size, position, and font.

3. Save the document.

When visitors input the URL for your home page, they'll see your default home page. When they click the link, they'll see the form your coding created (**Figure 17.69**). They can type data into the fields and click the Submit button. If all goes as planned, they see the response.htm page and the record is added to your database. If not, they see the err.htm page.

PROVIDING VISITOR FEEDBACK

437

Searching for Data with CDML

You can create a format file that searches specified fields in the published database and returns the results in another format file for editing or viewing. For this example, you'll prompt the user to search by last name or state. Users might want to do this if, for example, their contact information has changed and they need to update the information in the database.

Figure 17.70 The search format file will call the findedit.htm format file.

To create a search format file:

1. Open your text editor and follow the instructions in "To create a basic Web page" on page 432.

2. Follow the instructions in "To create a CDML form header" on page 433 to add a CDML form header. Since all of the header information is the same except for the name of the format file that will be used after the search format file, customize the information by entering a new file name in the format line (**Figure 17.70**):

   `<INPUT TYPE="hidden" NAME="-format" VALUE="findedit.htm">`

3. Position your cursor just before the </FORM> close tag and insert a line of HTML text prompting the visitor to locate his or her name in the records (**Figure 17.71**):

   `<P>Please find your name.</P>`
   `<P></P>`

4. Next we'll add the code that prompts the user for the find criteria. Right after the prompt line you just created and above the </FORM> close tag, add these lines of code (**Figure 17.72**):

   `<P><SELECT NAME="-op">`
   `<OPTION SELECTED>equals`
   `<OPTION>not equals`

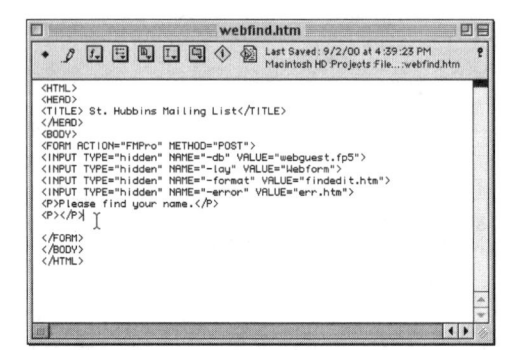

Figure 17.71 You can insert HTML text inside a </FORM> tag.

Figure 17.72 The <SELECT> HTML code creates a pop-up list of the options within it.

438

Web Publishing

Figure 17.73 Always duplicate and edit code rather than retyping it.

Figure 17.74 Once a search has finished, clearing the form allows a second search to be done.

```
<OPTION>contains
<OPTION>begins with
<OPTION>ends with
</SELECT>
Last Name: <INPUT TYPE="text"
NAME="LastName" VALUE=""
SIZE=20></P>
<P>
```

The SELECT NAME="-op" creates a pop-up list that allows the user to choose a find operator from the options that you specify with the <OPTION> tags.

5. By duplicating and editing the code, you can allow a search by State as well as by Last Name. Copy the code from step 4 and paste it in below the existing lines. Change "Last Name" to "State" and NAME="LastName" to NAME="State" (**Figure 17.73**).

6. Add this line below the second block of code:

   `<P><INPUT TYPE="submit" NAME="-find" VALUE="Find">`

   The Submit button code contains the action tag "-find", which tells FileMaker to search for the data entered in the fields and display the results in the findedit.htm file designated by the format tag in the header.

7. Add this line below the submit line (**Figure 17.74**):

   `<P><INPUT TYPE="reset" VALUE="Clear Form">`

   This input command clears the form fields of all previous data. It's the last line we add within the <FORM> tags.

8. Save the file to your CDML_Format_File folder. In this example, we've named it "webfind.htm."

You've created a format file to find a record; next you'll need one to edit the record when it's found.

439

Chapter 17

Editing Data with CDML

Once visitors have found the record that holds the desired contact information, they still need to be able to see the record itself, and then be able to edit it. For this, you need a separate format file. This format file uses replacement tags (in addition to the action and variable tags we've already seen) to display data from your database.

To create an edit format file:

1. Open your text editor and follow the instructions in "To create a basic Web page" on page 432.

2. Follow the instructions in "To create a CDML form header" on page 433.

   Since all of the header information is the same except for the name of the format file that will follow this one, customize the information by inputting a new file name in the format line (**Figure 17.75**):

   `<INPUT TYPE="hidden" NAME="-format" VALUE="editresp.htm">`

3. You need this line to tell FileMaker which record can be edited. The replacement tag [FMP-currentrecid] is a placeholder for the current record (the one in the user's found set).

   `<INPUT TYPE="hidden" NAME="-RecID" VALUE="[FMP-currentrecid]">`

4. Position your cursor just before the </FORM> close tag and insert a line of HTML text prompting visitors to edit their record (**Figure 17.76**):

   `<P>Please edit your information.</P>`
   `<P></P>`

Figure 17.75 When the current format file is completed successfully, the file named in the "-format" tag will run.

Figure 17.76 Be sure to insert your code before the </FORM> tag, or it won't appear as part of your Web page form.

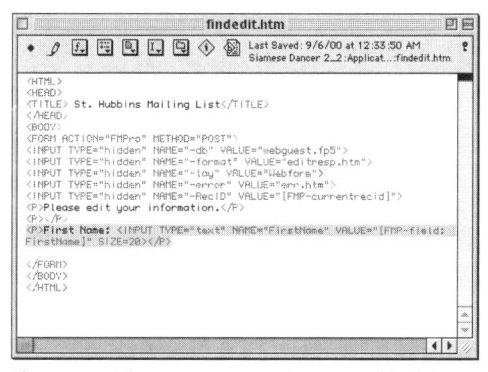

Figure 17.77 The VALUE command prompts FileMaker to display the contents of the fields from the found record in the database.

5. Next we'll add the code that displays the visitor's record in the form. Below the prompt line you just created in the previous step and above the </FORM> close tag (**Figure 17.77**), add the lines of code shown in the box below.

   These <INPUT> tag lines are basically the same as the field code for the webguest.htm format file we created in the previous section in "To create a search format file," with one exception: We add the VALUE= "[FMP-field:]" command inside the tag. To shorten the process of coding, copy the block of code in webguest.htm and paste it into this form, editing in the additional VALUE segment.

   continues on next page

```
<P>First Name: <INPUT TYPE="text" NAME="FirstName" VALUE="[FMP-Field:FirstName]"
SIZE=20></P>
<P> MI: <INPUT TYPE="text" NAME="MI" VALUE="[FMP-Field:MI]" SIZE=5></P>
<P>Last Name: <INPUT TYPE="text" NAME="LastName" VALUE="[FMP-Field:LastName]"
SIZE=20></P>
<P>Address: <INPUT TYPE="text" NAME="Address" VALUE="[FMP-Field:Address]"
SIZE=20></P>
<P> City: <INPUT TYPE="text" NAME="City" VALUE="[FMP-Field:City]" SIZE=20>
State: <INPUT TYPE="text" NAME="State" VALUE="[FMP-Field:State]" SIZE=5>
Zip: <INPUT TYPE="text" NAME="Zip" VALUE="[FMP-Field:Zip]" SIZE=20></P>
<P>Phone: <INPUT TYPE="text" NAME="Phone" VALUE="[FMP-Field:Phone]" SIZE=20></P>
<P>Email: <INPUT TYPE="text" NAME="EmailAddress" VALUE="[FMP-Field:EmailAddress]"
SIZE=20>
Web: <INPUT TYPE="text" NAME="WebAddress" VALUE="[FMP-Field:WebAddress]"
SIZE=30></P>
```

6. To create a Submit button, add this line after the <INPUT> tags:

   `<P><INPUT TYPE="submit" NAME= "-edit" VALUE="Submit"></P>`

   The -edit tag tells FileMaker to update the data in the record with the entries made in the form (**Figure 17.78**).

7. Add this line below the submit line:

   `<P><INPUT TYPE="reset" VALUE="Clear Form"></P>`

   This will clear the fields on the form, allowing the user to start over.

8. Save the file to your Web folder. We've called our example "findedit.htm."

9. You'll need a format file to tell the user that the data was updated successfully. Follow the steps in "Create a response message format file" on page 436. Replace the message text with a message that acknowledges that the changes were made successfully (**Figure 17.79**). In our example, we've inserted

   `<P>Thanks. Your changes have been added.</P>`

10. Save this file to your CDML_Format_File folder. For this example, we'll name it editresp.htm.

11. Open your default home page.

12. Add this line to create a line of text within the <BODY> tags containing a link to the find format file:

    ```
    Locate your name and
    <a href="webfind.htm"> update
    your information</a>
    ```

    Format the text line as you'd like.

Figure 17.78 The submit code automatically creates a Submit button.

Figure 17.79 The response format file is just a standard HTML page with a text message.

Web Publishing

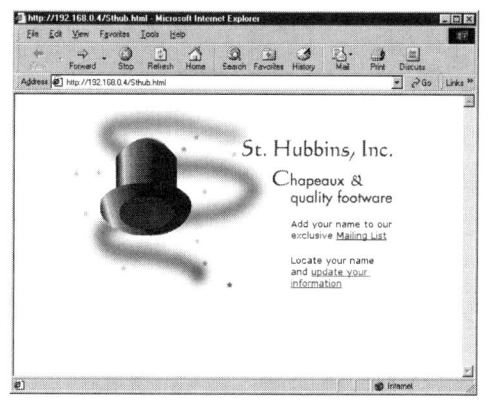

Figure 17.80 With the additional code, the default Web page displays the link to the webfind.htm format file.

Figure 17.81 The webfind.htm format file searches the database for the data a user enters.

Figure 17.82 The data in the found record is displayed in the findedit.htm format file

13. Save the default page.

    When you access the default page in your Web browser, you'll see the new choice (**Figure 17.80**).

When a visitor clicks Find, the webfind.htm format file prompts for the search criteria (**Figure 17.81**). When the visitor enters a last name and clicks the button, the findedit.htm format file displays the data from the found record (**Figure 17.82**). Visitors can make changes to the record and click Submit to update the database.

✓ Tip

- If you use a graphical Web page editor like Adobe GoLive to create Web pages, make sure that it doesn't strip out non-standard code. If it does, you can still create the basic layout of pages with the Web page editor, then use a text editor like BBEdit to add the CDML tags to the resulting code.

Browsing Records

Sometimes you don't want users to see the entire database. But what if more than one record meets the search criteria they used to find their file? To allow a user to browse your information, you need a format file that displays the database contents in a table. If you want users to be able to edit the database, you can add the code to let them choose a record from the table.

Tables themselves are regular HTML code, but by inserting CDML's replacement tags you can build a table that pulls its information from the database and displays it "on the fly."

For this example, we'll create a format file that displays 10 records at a time, with links to the next and previous pages. This file will display the Last Name, First Name, City, and State fields in a table, with a link to a separate editable format file for each record. In order to make the display neat, we'll use a table to show the data.

To create a browse format file:

1. Open your text editor and follow the instructions in "To create a basic Web page" on page 432.

    Don't enter the header data as you did in previous format files. This format file will be called from the home page with a tag.

2. To set up the format parameters of your table, add these lines right after the <BODY> tag:

    <TABLE border=1 align=center cellpadding=3>

    <P>

    <TH>Last Name</TH>

    <TH>First Name</TH>

    <TH>City</TH>

    <TH>State</TH></P>

    This code creates the headings and format for a multi-column table with a narrow border around it. The table is centered on the Web page. You can customize the look of the table in a text editor or Web page layout program (**Figure 17.83**).

3. Next, enter this line:

    [FMP-record]

    This tag tells FileMaker to repeat everything that follows it for all records until it sees a closing [/FMP-record] tag.

4. Add the following lines of HTML code and CDML replacement tags, which set up placeholders for each of the fields in the table:

    <TR>

    <TD>[FMP-FIELD:LastName]</TD>

    <TD>[FMP-FIELD:FirstName]</TD>

    <TD>[FMP-FIELD:City]</TD>

    <TD>[FMP-FIELD:State]</TD>

5. The next line of code creates a link to the database to edit a record. It tells FileMaker to display the data using the indicated layout and format file. In this example, the format file is findedit.htm and the layout is called webform.

    <TD><A HREF="[FMP-linkrecid:
    layout=webform,
    format=findedit.htm]">
    Edit</A></TD>

Figure 17.83 Basic table formatting is set in the <TABLE> HTML tag.

Figure 17.84 Page through the database in the browser by using the BACK and NEXT links.

6. Adding the following HTML and CDML tags closes all the table tags and ends the [FMP-record] repetition.

   </TR>

   [/FMP-Record]

   </table>

7. Insert these last code lines after the end of the table (**Figure 17.84**):

   <P>[FMP-linkprevious]
   BACK[/FMP-linkprevious]
   <P>[FMP-linknext]
   NEXT[/FMP-linknext]

   The [FMP-linkprevious] tags tell FileMaker to create a link to the previous page. The BACK link text won't appear on the first page. Conversely, the [FMP-linknext] tags link FileMaker to the next page. The NEXT link text doesn't appear on the last page.

8. Save the format file to your Web folder. In this example, we've called the file "browse.htm."

9. Next, we'll add a link from your home page to the browse format file. In your text editor, open your default Web page.

continues on next page

10. Add this complex code line to the link choices:

    ```
    <P><a href="FMPro?-db=Webguest.fp5&
    -Lay=webform&-Format=browse.htm&
    -Error=err.htm&-SortField=LastName&
    -SortOrder=Ascend&-Max=10&
    -FindAll">Browse</a> our records</P>
    ```

    In this example, the tag tells FileMaker to use the browse.htm format file to display all records (-FindAll) from the database Webguest.fp5, 10 at a time (-Max=10), sorted by Last Name (-SortField=LastName) in ascending order (-SortOrder=Ascend).

11. Save your default page in the CDML_Format_File folder.

If users choose the Browse option from the Web page (**Figure 17.85**), they'll see the first 10 records of the database sorted by the Last Name field. There will be links to the previous and next pages at the bottom, as well as an Edit link for each record so they can update their information (**Figure 17.86**).

✔ Tip

- You're not limited to plain-vanilla design with CDML. If you're comfortable with Web-page creation, you can replace the "BACK" and "NEXT" text links with graphic buttons or navigation bars.

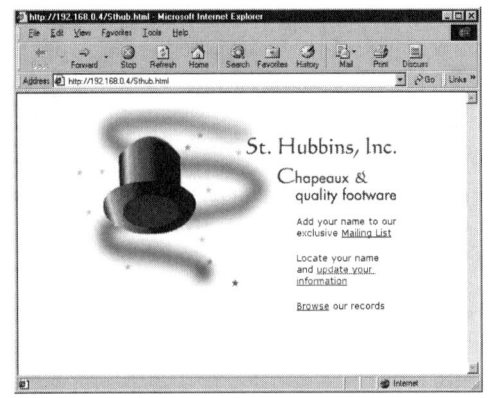

Figure 17.85 The Web page can contain links to each of your format page actions.

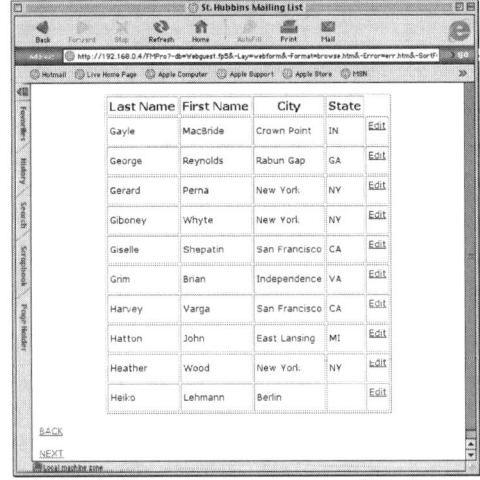

Figure 17.86 The FileMaker database looks like a regular Web table, but it pulls its information directly from the published file.

Web Publishing

Figure 17.87 Enter the name of the database (or All Databases) for which you want to set restrictions.

— Master password

Figure 17.88 The master password grants full access to the database.

— User password

Figure 17.89 Each user can have a different password and access.

Using the Web Security Database

A FileMaker database published with Custom Web Publishing can use the password settings that have already been set in the database. However, if you want more detailed control over access, you can use the Web Security database. The Web Security database doesn't work with Instant Web Publishing, only with Custom Web Publishing.

To use the Web Security database:

1. In the folder that holds your FileMaker Pro application, open the Web Security folder, then the Databases folder inside it. Double-click Web Security.fp5. Choose Records > New Record. A new blank record will appear.

2. Click the Database Name text field and type the name of your published database (**Figure 17.87**). If you want to apply the security settings to all published databases, enter All Databases.

3. Click the Database Password field. Type the master password for the published database (**Figure 17.88**).

4. If you want to set permissions and passwords for certain users, type the name under User Name and enter a password for that user in the User Password field. Click the actions you want that user to have access to (**Figure 17.89**). To apply the setting to everyone, type All Users in the User Name field.

continues on next page

447

Chapter 17

5. To restrict access to certain fields, type the name of the field you want to restrict in the Field Name field. Click the check boxes next to the field names to set the restrictions for each field (**Figure 17.90**).

6. Choose Edit (FileMaker Pro in Mac OS X) > Preferences > Application.

7. Click the Plug-Ins tab.

8. In the Plug-Ins list, double-click the Web Companion.

9. In the Web Companion Configuration dialog box's Security section, click the Web Security Database radio button (**Figure 17.91**). Click OK, then OK again.

When users access the database, the password they enter determines which actions they can perform and which fields they can access.

Figure 17.90 You can set restrictions for each field in the database.

Figure 17.91 Enable the Web Security Database to use its settings instead of the built-in password settings of the database.

✔ Tip

- The settings in the Web Security database do not override settings made in the database itself. So if an action is restricted in the passwords/groups settings, it won't be available even if you didn't restrict it in the Web Security database.

448

FM Developer's Edition

If you're doing serious Web design or advanced database programming with FileMaker, you should consider purchasing the Developer's Edition. In addition to a full copy of FileMaker 6, the Developer's Edition includes the following:

- A utility program that automates creating CDML code

- Extensive documentation for Web publishing including CDML, XML, and JDBC

- Some nifty utilities for renaming files and references

- Database Design Report, a utility that creates a FileMaker database detailing all of the major aspects of a database or group of databases, including, layouts, relationships, field definitions, and scripts

- An application that can make your FileMaker databases into stand-alone programs (so they can be run on computers that don't have FileMaker installed)

- Lots of example files demonstrating advanced programming techniques

FILEMAKER AND XML

If you've been doing any work with databases in the last few years, you have undoubtedly run across references to XML (Extensible Markup Language). It's touted by many experts as the future of database technology. But what exactly is it? This chapter will provide a brief answer to that question, but fully understanding XML and its myriad uses requires an entire book. (We recommend Elizabeth Castro's *XML: Visual QuickStart Guide* from Peachpit Press.)

XML can be used in two different ways with FileMaker. First and perhaps most useful, is FileMaker's ability to import and export data using an XML style sheet (known as an XSLT). An XSLT transforms data into a format that will work with another system. XML can also be used to deliver formatted data to Web browsers, through FileMaker's Web Companion plug-in.

About XML

You can think of XML as a Rosetta Stone for databases. It can be used to translate the data organized in one database system directly into another. Because XML is a standardized language, it can work with any combination of platforms and applications. As a result, you can not only send data between FileMaker and another program (something you can do with ODBC and an SQL query, for example), you can also maintain the original file structure.

Like FileMaker's own CDML, XML is based on SGML (Standard Generalized Markup Language, for the non-geek), the same language upon which HTML, the coding method used to create and format Web pages, is based. This common relationship means that all of these languages operate on the same basic principles and share some common formats and assumptions, which can make learning one easier if you know another. XML is potentially more powerful than CDML, because it is recognized by other applications. It allows you to work with data and the data's formatting separately, something that is not possible with HTML alone.

You can use XML to design customized markups for any data. This custom markup is referred to as a *schema* or a *grammar*. A schema is like a schematic diagram. It conveys information about the format of the data but without the data itself. A good FileMaker analogy would be if you were to make a clone of a FileMaker database. All of the records are stripped away, but the format and structure of the database remains. Here the analogy ends, because the schema can be applied to any data and recognized by any software that can read XML, making it much more useful than a FileMaker clone.

Creating a schema from scratch is a pretty daunting task, but fear not. FileMaker has not one but three schemas built into it. So you don't need a degree in advanced computing to use XML with FileMaker.

Schemas can be applied to data with the use of an XSLT (Extensible Stylesheet Language-Transformation). This is the XML equivalent of the cascading style sheets used to format font and paragraph data in HTML.

Unlike HTML, which is blessedly tolerant of minor errors, XML is a completely unforgiving language. If you make even the smallest error in syntax, your XSLT won't work. Fortunately, you shouldn't have to worry about this as long as you're creating the XML through FileMaker. It produces "well formed" XML code, so syntax should not be a problem.

Even better, you can make use of XML without ever having to learn to create schemas or XSLTs. There are many premade XSLTs available from FileMaker and other sources that will allow you to perform XML operations without getting your hands dirty creating code.

Writing Your Own XSLTs

If you're going to be using XML with FileMaker, at some point you may need an XSLT that doesn't already exist. There are a number of resources available to help you learn how to do create your own XSLT. FileMaker Developer's Edition has extensive documentation and example files. The FileMaker Web site has an entire section devoted to XML (www.filemaker.com/xml).

As with any programming language, the best way to get started learning is to look at code that others have created. You can open a style sheet in a text editor to see how it works and even adapt it for your own purposes.

Chapter 18

Exporting from FileMaker with XML

Even if you don't plan ever to create a single XSLT, XML is a valuable tool when working with FileMaker. It provides a reliable method for transferring data with a minimum of muss and fuss.

For this example, we show you how to transform contact information in FileMaker into VCF (the vCard format used by many PIMs) and transfer it to an iPod for use with the Contacts feature, which allows you to view (but not edit) name and address information. (Windows users note: iPods are now compatible with your computers as well as Macs.)

For this example, you'll need to download an XSLT called fmp_to_ipod.xsl and its accompanying documentation from www.filemaker.com/xml/xslt_library.html.

This is but one of many tasks that can be accomplished using XSLTs with your FileMaker data. Check the XML section of the FileMaker Web site for many more.

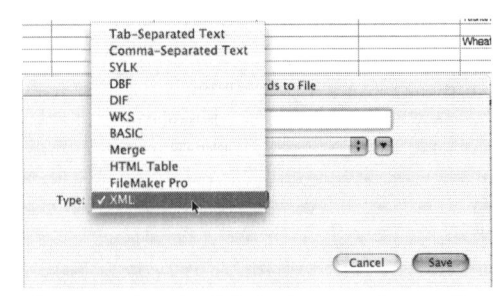

Figure 18.1 Choosing XML for the export format will create a file that can be transformed with an XSLT.

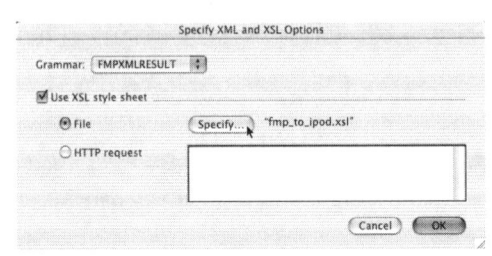

Figure 18.2 The XSLT fmp_to_ipod.xsl transforms the data from FileMaker into the .vcf format.

To export with XML:

1. Open the file containing the names and addresses you'd like to transfer to the iPod.

2. Choose File > Export Records.

3. When the Export Records to File dialog box appears, type `export.vcf` for the file name. In the Type pop-up menu, choose XML (**Figure 18.1**). Click Save.

4. When the Specify XML and XSL Options dialog box appears, click the "Use XSL style sheet" check box (**Figure 18.2**).

454

FileMaker and XML

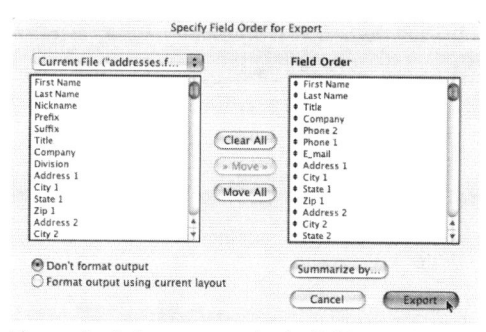

Figure 18.3 To import properly, the fields must be exported in the proper order.

Figure 18.4 Once the export.vcf file is copied to the Contacts folder its contents can be displayed in the Contacts feature of the iPod.

5. Click the Specify button. When the Open dialog box appears, navigate to the fmp_to_ipod.xsl style sheet that you downloaded. Click Open, then OK.

6. When the Specify Field Order for Export dialog box appears, double-click the fields in the left box in the following order:

   First Name
   Last Name
   Title
   Company
   Phone 2
   Phone 1
   Email
   Address 1
   City 1
   State 1
   Zip Code1
   Address 2
   City 2
   State 2
   Zip Code2
   Notes

7. Click the Export button (**Figure 18.3**).

8. Copy the export.vcf file to the Contacts folder on your iPod (**Figure 18.4**). All of that information from your FileMaker database is now available in the Contacts feature of the 'Pod.

✔ **Tip**

- The export.vcf file created above is also compatible with programs like OS X Address Book and Netscape that use the vCard format.

455

EXPORTING FROM FILEMAKER WITH XML

Importing into FileMaker with XML

Importing with XML works very much the same as exporting. You specify the file to import, choose the XSLT to do the transformation, and bring the data into the existing database. If you don't already have a database set up, an XML import into FileMaker will create one for you on the fly—reason enough to use XML as your preferred import method when possible.

For this example we'll use another XSLT available from www.filemaker.com/xml/xslt_library.html. This one, iTunes to FM (import_itunes.xslt.xsl), imports song lists that have been exported as XML from the iTunes program. Although iTunes is available only for the Macintosh, the basic steps outlined apply to any file you want to import to FileMaker with XML.

To import with XML:

1. Export a playlist or library from iTunes in XML format. Make sure that the filename ends with ".xml" (**Figure 18.5**).

2. In FileMaker, choose File > Open.

3. When the Open File dialog box appears, choose XML Source from the Show drop-down menu (**Figure 18.6**).

4. The Specify XML and XSL Options dialog box appears. In the Specify XML Data Source section, click the File radio button. Navigate to the file you exported from iTunes and double-click to select it.

5. Click the "Use XSL style sheet" check box. Click the File radio button below it.

Figure 18.5 The default file name is the playlist name plus the .XML extension.

Figure 18.6 The Open command can be used to create a new file from an XML source.

FileMaker and XML

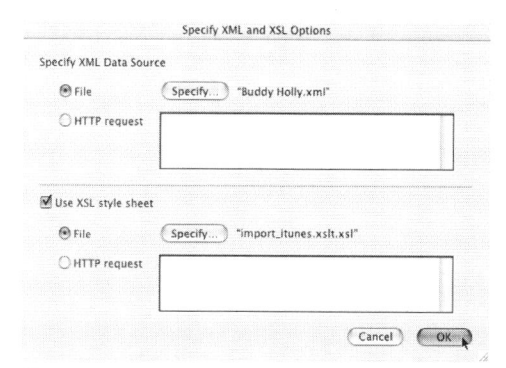

Figure 18.7 The import_itunes.xslt.xsl style sheet will transform the XML file from iTunes into a FileMaker database.

Figure 18.8 The default file name is the source file name plus "Converted.fp5."

Figure 18.9 Besides importing the data, the XML transformation creates correct field names in FileMaker.

6. When the Open dialog box appears, navigate to the import_itunes.xslt.xsl XSLT file that you downloaded from the FileMaker site. Double-click to select it and click OK (**Figure 18.7**).

7. When the "Name converted file" dialog box appears, type a name for the new database and click OK (**Figure 18.8**).

   The new database will contain all of the information that iTunes stored about each song in the exported song list (**Figure 18.9**).

✔ Tip

- The import_itunes.xslt.xsl package also includes a sample database that you can adapt to your own purposes.

457

FileMaker, XML, and the Web

Although FileMaker can serve data to Web browsers using XML, this isn't necessarily the best way to put a FileMaker database on the Web. Major problems with browser compatibility, security, and performance remain that make XML unsuitable as a conduit for multiple desktop platforms. Unless you have some very specific reason to use XML to serve FileMaker data on the Web or your implementation is for an intranet where you can control your users' desktop OS and browsers, you would be well advised to stick to Instant or Custom Web Publishing.

If you do have to employ XML for this purpose, the Developer's Edition of FileMaker has detailed documentation. Since learning XML is very tough indeed, we recommend that you only choose this route if you have prior programming or CDML experience. Another option is to choose a third-party solution that addresses some of the current implementation issues. See Appendix A for more on this option.

FileMaker and Third-Party Software

FileMaker gives you a variety of tools to construct interfaces, manipulate data, and serve databases over the Web. But, like any off-the-shelf program, there's a limit to what it can do—you don't want it to become so enormous it would overwhelm your hard drive, and so complicated that it would stop being the best choice for database users who also want to have a life. Like many savvy software developers, the folks at FileMaker have found a way to keep FileMaker easy to understand while meeting specialized user needs. They've built into the program the ability to incorporate a wide variety of plug-ins, as well as making it easy for other developers to create external programs that work seamlessly with FileMaker to make it a true database powerhouse.

Web Integration

Blue World Communications

www.blueworld.com

Lasso Professional
Macintosh OS X, Windows, Linux
List Price: $1,199

Lasso is a growing product line of tools that work smoothly with FileMaker to create database-driven Web sites that rival those based in "big iron" SQL servers. Unlike many competitors, Lasso products are completely cross-platform and work on everything from Windows 2000/XP to Mac OS X and Red Hat Linux. Lasso offers Secure Sockets Layer support, which closes some of FileMaker's security holes to provide secure Web transactions for online commerce, integration with Web servers other than FileMaker Server, and more markup tags than FileMaker's CDML.

WebFM

www.Webfm.com

WebFM
Macintosh Classic only
List Price: $395

WebFM is a FileMaker add-on designed for earlier versions of FileMaker (versions 3.0 and 4.0) that allows database access through Web servers like WebStar and Web'Ten. As with Lasso, WebFM uses custom markup tags with greater capabilities than CDML.

Beezwax Datatools

www.beezwax.net/generator.html

The XML Generator
Macintosh, Windows
List Price: starts at $99

If you need to host your FileMaker databases with XML, Beezwax offers a Web-based service that generates CGI statements from a simple set of menu choices. You can then copy the code into your existing HTML code. As a result, you enjoy the benefits of XML without having to learn much about it. The custom CGIs also add an extra layer of security to your system.

Fax and Email

Data Designs

www.datadesigns.com

FaxTool
Macintosh Classic, Windows
List Price: $199.95 Windows,
$239.95 Macintosh

FaxTool is a FileMaker add-on that employs FaxSTF (Macintosh) or WinFax Pro (Windows) to send faxes directly from a FileMaker database. It integrates smoothly with ScriptMaker, so you can automate the Fax process.

DataMail

www.datamailcorp.com

dbMailer
Windows only
List Price: $45

The dbMailer plug-in turns FileMaker Pro into a full-fledged email program. It allows you to implement email without the use of an external email application.

Plug-Ins and Utilities

New Millennium
www.newmillennium.com

DialogMagic
Macintosh, Windows
List Price: $99.95, single user; sliding-scale pricing for additional users

The DialogMagic plug-in allows you to easily script imports and exports, change all of the passwords in a series of FileMaker databases, script data entry with dialog boxes, and perform many other scripting tasks that usually require tedious step-by-step work.

ExportFM
Macintosh Classic, Windows
List Price: $99.95, single user; sliding-scale pricing for additional users

What the Batch Import function in FileMaker does for importing media, ExportFM does for exporting media. Terrific for Web-asset work, this plug-in lets you output material in container fields to fixed or relative destination folders and automatically batch-create thumbnails for Web pages.

SecureFM
Macintosh, Windows
List Price: $99 (five-user license)

Even with its recent security improvements, FileMaker doesn't offer comprehensive tools for securing database information. The Secure FM plug-in gives you precise control over the FileMaker interface itself. For example, you can determine which menus a user has access to and disable menu commands and specific dialog boxes, including Find and Replace.

Troi
www.troi.com

Troi is the best known of the companies that make FileMaker plug-ins. It offers a wide variety of add-ons that can alter and extend the FileMaker interface. Check out Troi's Web site for the full range of goodies.

File Plug-in
Macintosh, Windows
List Price: $49

File Plug-in is a file-management utility. For users of versions prior to FileMaker 6.0, it's a must-have addition for batch importing, as well as for creating and managing files. But even users of 6.0 will find it more than justifies its purchase. It can batch import from multiple folders, import parts of text files instead of the whole file, and allow users to select files and folders for import.

Coding Plug-in
Macintosh, Windows
List Price: $39

Coding Plug-in adds industrial-strength data encryption to your FileMaker files and exported and imported text. Using DES encryption technology, this plug-in provides much stronger security for your databases. If you use FileMaker to send email, it safely encrypts what you send.

Graphic Plug-in
Macintosh, Windows
List Price: $49

Graphic Plug-in gives you powerful graphic functions like thumbnail creation, screen captures, and the ability to create container fields in any RGB color.

URL Plug-in
Macintosh, Windows
List Price: $59

This handy little plug-in allows you to fill in Internet forms from within FileMaker and download the resulting data. Weather reports, listings, zip codes...the possible data you can capture is limitless.

Waves in Motion
http://wmotion.com

Analyzer
Macintosh only
List Price: $289

Analyzer is a developer's utility that creates a FileMaker database listing all of the constituent parts of an entire FileMaker solution. After running Analyzer, you have a complete database of fields, layouts, relationships, value lists, passwords, and buttons from all of the databases. Analyzer is an invaluable tool when you're trying to get a handle on large multi-file systems, and it's particularly vital when you have to take control of a complex database you didn't originally design.

eAuthorize
Macintosh, Windows
List Price: $250, single user

This add-on makes it possible to integrate credit-card authorization (through third-party systems) into a FileMaker database. It's also available as a stand-alone application.

String Functions
Macintosh, Windows
List Price: $49

String Functions provides you with new functions for controlling character strings. It can convert a text string into a desired format, extract an item from a list within a text string, distinguish between upper and lower case, and extract sub-strings without having to create complex calculations.

Interface Design

Cinco Group
www.cincogroup.com

Theme Creator
Macintosh, Windows
List Price: free for basic version; $155.55 for source code access

Theme Creator makes layout themes, automating and enhancing the formatting of FileMaker layouts. It expands upon the Layout Assistant in FileMaker Pro, enabling you to build, modify, save, and share your themes.

Krische Data Systems
www.krischesystems.com

1000 Buttons Series (vol. 1–5)
Macintosh, Windows
List Price: volumes 1 & 2, $5 each; volumes 3–5, $10 each

This collection of buttons and graphics is a great help for developers who want a professional-looking interface but don't want to take the time (or don't have the artistic flair) to design new buttons themselves.

Ascending Technologies
www.asctech.com/products.html

Calendar Monster
Macintosh
List Price: $34.95

Calendar Monster is a full-featured calendar, written entirely in FileMaker Pro (no plug-ins). It provides standard Year, Month, Week, Day, and Appointment views. It's very adaptable to existing FileMaker systems (single- or multi-user) and is licensable for distribution in custom systems.

FileMaker Resources

Books

Many fine books on FileMaker are available. Here are just a few:

Database Publishing on the Web with FileMaker Pro (Peachpit Press)
Maria Langer

FileMaker Pro and the World Wide Web (FileMaker Press)
Jesse Feiler

Although both of these books cover earlier versions of FileMaker, they're excellent resources for learning CDML and other methods of FileMaker data publishing.

Scriptology: FileMaker Pro Demystified (ISO Publishing)
Matt Petrowsky & John Mark Osborne

Scriptology is the encyclopaedia of FileMaker. It covers in detail all aspects of scripting and formula building.

For more on XML, we recommend the following:

XML for the World Wide Web: Visual QuickStart Guide (Peachpit Press)
Elizabeth Castro

Web Pages

FileMaker, Inc.
www.filemaker.com

FileMaker has always provided exemplary support for its products. Its Web pages provide access to sample files, FileMaker news, product updates, links to other Web sites, and lots more. If you're looking for FileMaker resources online, this should be your first stop.

ISO FileMaker World
www.filemakerworld.com

FileMaker World is a comprehensive Web site for FileMaker. It has links to many other FileMaker related sites, downloadable sample files, job listings, and other subjects pertaining to all aspects of FileMaker.

FMPro.org
www.fmpro.org

Like FileMaker World, FMPro offers an extensive array of links to other FileMaker sites, sample files, tips and tricks, job opportunities, information about commercial applications built with FileMaker, and many other resources.

Mailing Lists

www.blueworld.com/blueworld/lists/filemaker.html

Blue World (of Lasso fame) runs a top-notch listserv where FileMaker users and developers swap tricks and tips, post queries, and help other users solve problems. This is a fairly high-volume list (which is good), so be prepared for lots of email. A daily digest is also available.

Usenet

comp.databases.filemaker

The FileMaker newsgroup is a forum where questions, answers, and comments are posted. Although Usenet has been somewhat overshadowed by email lists, this group can be a useful resource.

Publications

FileMaker Advisor Magazine

www.advisor.com

This is the only currently available magazine that specializes in FileMaker Pro. *FileMaker Advisor* offers excellent articles on FileMaker development, a great tips column, and stories about how FileMaker is used in a variety of business applications.

ISO FileMaker Magazine

www.filemakermagazine.com

ISO FileMaker Magazine is a monthly magazine distributed as a downloadable FileMaker database. It contains useful articles, tips and tricks, and FileMaker news.

User Groups

There are many local user groups that specialize in FileMaker. User groups are a great way to meet others who are involved in FileMaker use and development.

A current list of user groups is available at *www.filemaker.com/support/usergroups.html*.

FileMaker Solutions Alliance

If you're a professional FileMaker developer, either as an independent contractor or as part of your regular job, FSA is the resource for you. FileMaker Inc. provides a private section on its Web site for FSA members offering access to news and other resources not available to the public. The annual *FileMaker Directory and Resource Guide* (included with every copy of FileMaker) lists FSA members by specialty and geographic region. FSA also runs a yearly conference for its members that presents seminars in advanced FileMaker development.

FileMaker Hosting

If you want to host your FileMaker databases online but don't have high-speed Internet access, there are companies that will host your files for you.

FMPhost.net

www.fmphost.net

World Wide Host

www.worldwidehost.com

triple8

www.triple8.net

Mad Macs

www.madmacs.net

These companies offer different hosting packages, as well as in-house FileMaker experts to help you get your databases up and running on the Internet.

INDEX

; (semicolon), 348
* (asterisk), 423
+ operator, 68
# symbol, 169

A

Access log file, 420
actions, button, 4, 27, 36
address books, 328
address labels, 69–71
administration, 397–399, 422
Adobe GoLive, 443
Allow User Abort script step, 260
And searches, 92
Apple Events, 294–295
AppleScript, 294–295
applications. *See* programs
ASCII text, 300
asterisk (*), 423
auto-entry serial numbers, 67–68, 313–321
averages, 100–101

B

batch import feature, 4, 306–310
Beep script step, 155
browse format files, 444–446
Browse mode, 59
button bars, 236–237
Button tool, 36–37, 141, 232–233
buttons
    actions, 4, 27, 36
    arranging, 238

captions, 203
custom, 36–37, 232, 248
in dialog boxes, 199–200
duplicating, 237
formatting elements as, 36–37
hiding, 236
interactive, 234
labels, 412
making fields into, 37, 140, 245
overview, 233
radio, 44
sample, 233
for scripts, 232–234, 245
using graphics as, 36–37, 232–233
on Web forms, 411–412

C

calculated match fields, 126–130
calculation fields, 61–87
    benefits of, 61–62
    combining, 74
    creating, 49
    exporting text and, 286
    labels, 49–50, 69–71
calculations, 62–66
Cascading Style Sheets (CSS), 406, 408, 426–427
CDML (Claris Dynamic Markup Language)
    browsing records, 444–446
    data searches, 438–439
    editing data with, 440–443
    prompting user input with, 434–435

Index

CDML *(continued)*
   template format files, 432–433
   vs. XML, 452
CDML form headers, 433
CDML tags, 429, 431–432
character sets, 305
characters
   deleting, 352–353, 362
   validation, 56–57
check boxes, 44, 217
Claris Dynamic Markup Language. *See* CDML
cloning databases, 39, 357
Close script step, 377–378
color
   cross-platform issues, 30
   reports, 98
   Web browsers and, 405
Color Palette, 30
columns
   described, 14
   headers, 113, 413
   layouts, 26
   SQL, 339
comments, script, 168–169
compressing files, 298
conditional script steps, 175–226
   custom dialog boxes, 198–204
   FileMaker versions and, 211–214
   If steps. *See* If steps
   Loop step, 190–194
   overview, 176
   password protection, 205–210
   status functions, 183–189
   user input and, 195–197
conditional value lists, 47–48
Constrain Found command, 90–91
contact lists, 328, 454
container fields
   creating, 38–39
   importing graphic text, 34–35
   Web display, 419
contextual menus, 2
Copy command, 58
Copy script step, 294
copying items
   buttons, 237
   databases, 39, 254, 357
   field data, 294

   formats, 31–32
   graphics into layouts, 33
   layouts, 58–59
   script steps, 165
   scripts, 151
counters, 192–194
counts
   page, 102–106
   summary layouts, 100–101
creation fields, 21
cross-platform issues, 28–32. *See also* Mac OS systems; Windows systems
   character sets, 305
   color, 30
   database transfers, 7
   dialog box text, 210
   fonts, 28–29
   Format Painter, 31–32
   status functions, 183
   window script options, 251
CSS (Cascading Style Sheets), 406, 408, 426–427
cursor, hand, 234
Custom Web Publishing, 429–431, 447–448
customization
   buttons, 36–37, 232, 248
   colors, 30
   dialog boxes, 4, 198–204, 210
   error messages, 246–249
   home pages, 424–425
   with If steps, 215–226
   letter headings, 72–76
   messages, 195–197, 248
   script messages, 195–197

D

data
   analyzing, 14–22
   breaking into smallest parts, 13
   categories, 12, 14–16
   dynamic, 10
   editing with CDML, 440–443
   entering in standard layout, 40–42
   Excel, 290–293
   exporting. *See* exporting items
   file types, 113, 300–301
   importing. *See* importing data
   inconsistent formatting, 361–362

Index

lookup. *See* lookup fields
modifying with If and Else, 181–183
organizing, 9–23
parsing, 363–367
problems with, 351
related. *See* related data
replacing, 360
replacing formatting in, 361–362
searching for. *See* searches
self-relationship, 139, 141
sort criteria, 111–112
sorting. *See* sorting items
structure, 14–17
summary. *See* summary data
troubleshooting, 360
Data Access plug-ins, 336
data reports. *See* reports
Database Design Report utility, 449
database developers, 11
databases
    accessing over Web, 383–384, 421
    cloning, 39, 357
    configuring for Web access, 403–404
    converting to FileMaker 6, 299
    copying, 39, 254, 357
    creating with Excel data, 290–291
    design guidelines, 11–12
    error trap databases, 261–269
    goal of, 11
    growth rate, 11
    layout styles, 405–406
    multi-user, 6, 369–388, 404
    names, 28
    ODBC. *See* ODBC
    opening automatically, 390
    opening simultaneously, 392
    Oracle, 337
    passwords, 421, 447–448
    publishing. *See* Web publishing
    registering in Classic Mac OS, 334–336
    registering in Mac OS X, 335–336
    registering in Windows, 333
    relational, 10, 22, 122–124
    remote administration, 422
    setting restrictions for, 423, 447–448
    shared, 324, 327, 333–336, 369–388
    sharing with ODBC, 333–336
    size of, 307
    status functions, 184
    synchronizing, 326–329
    testing, 22–23, 428
    usability considerations, 26–27
    users of, 12
    Web display considerations, 419
    Web Security, 447–448
date fields, 21
dates
    current, 189
    formatting, 419
    ranges of, 92
    status functions, 183–184
    two-digit vs. four-digit, 87
DBF format, 115, 300
debugging scripts, 270–271
Define Fields command, 118–120
Define Relationships command, 120, 128
Define Scripts dialog box, 150
deleting items
    characters, 352–353, 362
    duplicate records, 354–359
    lines, 81
    records, 235–236, 354–359
    rows, 235–236
    scripts, 151
destination files, 118–121
dialog boxes
    buttons in, 199–200
    custom, 4, 198–204, 210
    maximum text lengths in, 210
    user input in, 198–204
DIF format, 300
digital cameras, 5, 308–310
document scripts, 215–226
Dreamweaver, 431
drop-down lists, 128–130, 240–242
Duplicate Request command, 91
dynamic data, 10
dynamic SQL queries, 346–349

E

edit format files, 440–443
editing items
    with CDML, 440–443
    data, 440–443
    scripts, 152
Else script steps, 176, 180–182, 270
email, 276–282

Index

envelopes, 69–71
error codes, 263–266
Error log file, 420
error message format files, 437
error messages, 35, 246–249
error trap scripts, 261–269
errors
    description, 265–266
    displaying for files, 420
    displaying for scripts, 264–265
    file not found, 375–376
    ODBC, 345
    tracking, 420
    validation alerts, 56–57
    while running scripts, 375–376
    XML and, 453
Excel, 290–293
Execute SQL script step, 337, 346–348
EXIF data, 308–309
Exit Script step, 270–271
Export command, 286
Export Records command, 113–115, 166, 285, 289
exporting items
    data to static HTML tables, 285
    formatted fields, 289
    formatted text, 286–289
    multiple settings, 166–167
    to spreadsheets, 113–115
    sub-scripts for, 166–167
    summary data, 113–115
    with XML, 5, 454–455
Extend Found Set command, 90–91
Extensible Markup Language. *See* XML
Extensible Stylesheet Language-Transformation (XSLT), 451–457
external scripts, 170–172

F

field lists, 13
Field Order list, 113
Field tool, 79–80, 86
field types, 106
fields
    adding to layouts, 245
    calculation. *See* calculation fields
    copying contents, 294
    creation, 21, 182

date/time tracking with, 21
defining, 303
designing, 18–21
form letters, 77–81
formatted, 31–32, 128–130, 289
global, 20, 240–241
global container, 38–39
indexing, 40–41
inserting information into, 181
key, 10, 18–19, 22, 118
labels, 49–50, 54, 69–71, 133
locking, 55
lookup. *See* lookup fields
making buttons from, 37, 140, 245
mapping, 302–304, 311, 340
masks, 51–55
match. *See* match fields
merging, 62–66
modification, 21
modular, 77–81, 215–216
names, 59, 291–293, 302, 311–312, 402
in portals, 21
related, 16, 22, 122–124, 131, 418
repeating, 20, 131, 419
restricting access, 448
running scripts from, 240–245
selecting, 59, 183
sorting by, 113–115
status functions, 184
storing SQL commands in, 338–341
structure, 14–17
summary, 96–99
tab order of, 27
text, 215–216
tracking, 21
file types, 113, 300–301
FileMaker
    compatibility issues, 384
    described, 1
    determining version of, 211–214
    upgrading from pre-5.0 versions, 6
    using AppleScript with, 294–295
    versions, 2, 6, 384
FileMaker Developer's Edition, 6, 449, 453
FileMaker Mobile, 322–329
FileMaker Pro 6
    converting earlier databases to, 299
    keyboard shortcuts, 59
    migrating to, 298–300

Index

new features, 2–5
overview, 1–7
FileMaker Pro 6 Unlimited, 6, 402
FileMaker Pro Server, 389–399
   described, 369, 389
   hosting files on, 390–392
   installation of, 391
   launching, 391
   memory, 394–395
   naming, 399
   opening files in, 392
   passwords, 397–398
   performance, 389, 393–395
   remote administration, 397–399
   settings, 393–395, 397–399
   system requirements, 392
   usage log, 396
   user connections, 393–395
FileMaker Server 5.5, 6
files
   closing, 377
   compressing, 298
   destination, 118–121
   displaying errors for, 420
   format, 300, 436–446
   hiding related files, 373
   hosting, 372, 390–392, 395, 404
   importing, 4, 306–308
   key fields and, 19
   log, 420
   master, 118–121
   multi-user, 369–388
   names, 28, 402
   opening, 377–378
   opening in FileMaker Server, 392
   opening with relative paths, 173–174
   opening with scripts, 374–378
   passwords, 373, 388, 403, 422
   privileges, 403–404
   related. *See* related files
   renaming, 28
   running scripts in, 170–172
   shared, 324, 327, 372, 382, 392, 403–404
   single-user, 395
   text. *See* text data files
   unable to find, 375–376
find-and-replace functions, 3
Find layout, 228–231
Find mode, 40–41
Find/Replace command, 360, 362
Find/Replace dialog box, 3
Find scripts, 414–416
finding items. *See* searches
fonts
   cross-platform issues, 28–29
   equivalents, 29
   graphic text, 33–35
   non-standard, 33
footers, 79, 98
form letters
   formatting, 72–76
   headings, 72–76
   mailing addresses, 83–87
   modular fields in, 77–81
Format > Button command, 36
format files, 436–446
Format Painter, 3, 31–32
formatting items
   copying formats, 31–32
   dates, 419
   elements as buttons, 36–37
   envelopes, 69–71
   exporting formatted text, 286–289
   fields, 31–32, 128–130, 289
   form letters, 72–76
   global fields, 240–241
   inconsistent, 361–362
   labels, 69–71
   numbers, 51–55, 113, 419
   print formats, 257
   replacing formatting, 361–362
   text, 31–32, 286–289
   validating formats, 45–46
   value lists, 44
   Web browsers and, 406
formulas, 291
found sets, 89–91, 164–165, 326
.fp5 format, 298–299
FTP sites, 284
functions
   in calculation fields, 49–50, 52–53
   find-and-replace, 3
   ODBC, 332
   replacing with parameters, 52
   status, 183–189, 247
   summary, 136–137

Index

G

GetField function, 82–87
GetNextSerialValue function, 313, 317–318
global container fields, 38–39
global fields, 20, 240–241
Go to Related Record command, 139
GoLive, 443
grammar, 452
graphic text, 33–35
graphics. *See also* images
   reusing, 38–39
   using as buttons, 36–37, 232–233
guest books, 426–427

H

Halt Script step, 213, 267, 270–271, 388
handheld devices, 322–329, 367
hard drives
   FileMaker Server and, 392, 395
   indexing and, 40
headers
   columns, 113, 413
   form letters, 72–81
   reports, 98
   spreadsheet files, 113
home pages, 424–425, 437
host computers, 383, 398
host servers, 378, 398
hosting files, 372, 390–392, 395, 404
HTML
   data searches, 438
   tables, 285
   template format files, 432–433
   vs. XML, 452–453

I

If statements, 64, 210
If steps
   customizing with, 215–226
   Else steps and, 176, 180–182, 270
   layouts for compiled documents, 221–222
   modular text fields, 215–216
   template layouts, 217–220
   testing scripts with, 385–386
   using, 177–179
   using status functions with, 185–189

images. *See also* graphics
   digital camera, 5, 308–310
   importing, 5, 307–310
importing data, 297–329
   batch imports, 4, 306–310
   cleaning up text data, 352–353
   data with matching field names, 311–312
   Excel data, 292–293
   FileMaker Mobile, 322–329
   files, 4, 306–308
   finding/deleting duplicate records, 354–359
   graphic text, 34–35
   images, 5, 307–310
   multiple files, 4, 306–308
   ODBC data, 337–349
   parsing imported data, 363–367
   with scripts, 311–312
   setting auto-entry serial number, 313–321
   with SQL queries, 337–345
   text data files, 300–305, 307
   without duplications, 357–359
   with XML, 5, 456–457
indexing, 21, 40–42
Information log file, 420
Insert > Picture command, 35, 39
Insert From Index command, 40
Instant Web Publishing (IWP), 401–402, 407–411
interactive items
   buttons, 234
   error messages, 246–249
interface, user. *See* user interface
interface controls, 2
Internet. *See* Web
IP addresses, 370, 378–384, 402, 421, 423
iPods, 454–455
IsEmpty function, 64, 71, 75, 185
iTunes, 456–457
IWP (Instant Web Publishing), 401–402, 407–411

J

JavaScript, 406
joins, 10

Index

K
key fields, 10, 18–19, 22, 118
keyboard shortcuts, 59

L
labels
   address, 69–71
   buttons, 412
   calculation fields, 49–50, 69–71
   fields, 49–50, 54, 69–71, 133
   formatting, 69–71
Layout Assistant, 96–99
Layout mode, 59
Layout view, 3
layouts
   adding fields to, 245
   adding sub-summary parts to, 108–112
   cleaning up for printing, 42–43
   color in, 30
   columns in, 26
   for compiled documents, 221–222
   copying, 58–59
   copying graphics into, 33
   data-entry, 26
   data reports. *See* reports
   deleting extra space, 81
   described, 25
   email, 276–277
   enhancements, 25–59
   entering data in, 40–42
   Find, 228–231
   listing, 37
   Main Menu, 237–239
   to match paper sizes, 42
   names, 402
   page breaks, 81
   page size, 42–43
   planning, 26
   related fields in, 124
   reusing graphics in, 38–39
   for searching, 228–231
   standard, 40–42
   status functions, 184
   summary, 95–101
   switching with scripts, 417–418
   Table view, 413, 417–418
   templates for, 217–220
   Web, 411–413
letter ranges, 92
letters, form. *See* form letters
lines
   adding to reports, 109
   breaking, 68
   deleting, 81
   wrapping, 169
links
   to format files, 437
   to Main Menu, 239
   to URLs, 424–425
lists
   contact, 328, 454
   drop-down, 128–130, 240–242
   field, 13
   pop-up, 44
   value. *See* value lists
locking fields, 55
log files, 420
lookup fields
   creating, 122–123
   examples, 16
   problems with, 22
   self-relationships, 142–144
   uses for, 22
   vs. related data, 22, 122–124
Loop step, 190–194
looping scripts, 190–194, 259–260

M
Mac OS systems. *See also* cross-platform issues
   color and, 30
   file extensions and, 115
   file names, 28
   FileMaker 6 and, 5
   FileMaker Mobile and, 329
   FileMaker Server and, 391
   FileMaker toolbars and, 250
   fonts, 28–29
   importing images, 5, 308–310
   locking Format Painter, 32
   memory and, 5, 395
   ODBC and, 332, 337
   printing scripts, 273
   registering databases in, 334–336

471

Index

Macromedia Dreamweaver, 431
Main Menu layouts, 237–239
masks, field, 51–55
master files, 118–121
master scripts, 159–160
match fields
    calculated, 126–130
    choosing related records with, 125
    creating in master files, 120–121
    serial numbers, 118–119, 125–126
memory, 5, 394–395
menus
    contextual, 2
    Main Menu layouts, 237–239
    pop-up, 44
MER format, 115
Merge Field command, 105
merging fields, 62–66
messages
    custom, 195–197, 248
    error, 35, 246–249
    validation alerts, 56–57
Microsoft Excel, 290–293
Microsoft Word, 294–295
mobile devices, 322–329
modification fields, 21
Modify Last Find command, 90
modular document scripts, 222–226

N

navigation, 140, 407–410
Navigation step script, 258
networks
    hardware, 371
    multi-user files on, 369–388, 404
    protocols, 370–371
    sharing databases over, 369–388
    speed, 371
numbers
    format validation, 56–57
    formatting, 51–55, 113, 419
    ranges of, 92
    serial. *See* serial numbers
    Social Security, 18
    telephone, 51–57, 111

O

ODBC drivers, 333–335, 337
ODBC (Open Database Connectivity), 331–349
    errors, 345
    FileMaker ODBC functions, 332
    importing ODBC data, 337–349
    Mac OS X and, 332, 337
    sharing databases with, 333–336
one-to-many relationships, 16
Open command, 456
Open Database Connectivity. *See* ODBC
Open Hosts script step, 378
Open script step, 374–376
Open URL script step, 283
opening scripts, 374–378
operators
    frequently used, 50
    search, 92–93
    SQL queries, 343
Operators keypad, 50, 63
Or searches, 92
Oracle databases, 337
OS X. *See* Mac OS

P

page breaks, 81
page counts, 102–106
Palm devices, 322–329, 367
parameters, 52
parsing data, 363–367
Part tool, 111
passwords
    changing, 382
    databases, 421, 447–448
    FileMaker Server, 397–398
    files, 373, 388, 403, 422
    master, 447
    ODBC data, 339
    protecting scripts with, 205–210
    related files, 373, 418
    users, 379–382, 447
Paste command, 58
paths, relative, 173–174
Pause/Resume script step, 266
Pause Script step, 270–271
PDAs, 322–329, 367

Perform Script, 160–163
performance, 389, 393–395
phone numbers, 51–57, 111
photographs, digital, 308–310
Picture in Browse mode, 39
plug-ins
    Data Access, 336
    FileMaker and, 399
    Remote Administration, 397, 399
    Web Companion. *See* Web Companion plug-in
pop-up lists, 44
pop-up menus, 44
portals
    creating, 132–133
    creating related data with, 134
    described, 132
    fields in, 21
    for navigation, 140
    sorting data in, 135
pre-sets, script, 147–149, 270, 274
Print options, 149, 159–160
printing items
    cleaning up layouts for printing, 42–43
    incorrect print formats, 257
    options for, 257
    reports, 42–43, 98, 159–160, 230
    scripts, 272–273
privileges
    files, 403–404
    group, 388
    password, 388
    records, 379–381
    restricting, 379–381
problems. *See* troubleshooting
programs
    AppleScript and, 294–295
    email, 276–282
    FileMaker and, 275–295
    sending Apple Events to, 294–295
    spreadsheet, 290–295, 305
    word processors, 113, 115, 294–295
protocols, network, 370–371

Q

queries, SQL. *See* SQL queries
quotes, smart, 337
quotes operator, 63, 65, 223

R

radio buttons, 44
range operator, 92
records
    access privileges, 379–381
    browsing, 444–446
    deleting in related files, 235–236
    duplicate, 354–359
    field lists and, 13
    finding, 21, 156–157
    missing, 256
    omitting from searches, 94
    selecting, 94
    sorting, 110, 148, 157–158
    updating, 119
    wrong, 256
registering databases, 333–336
related data
    choosing with match fields, 125
    creating with portals, 134
    summarizing, 136–137
    vs. lookups, 22, 122–124
related fields, 16, 22, 122–124, 131, 418
related files
    deleting records in, 235–236
    described, 118
    hiding, 373
    passwords, 373, 418
    relating data in different files, 264–265
relational databases, 10, 22, 122–124
relationships, 117–144
    calculated match fields, 126–130
    implementing, 21–22
    lookup fields, 22, 122–124
    master files, 118–121
    match fields, 118–121
    names, 47
    one-to-many, 16
    overview, 118–119
    portals, 132–135
    related data, 22, 122–124, 136–137
    related fields, 122–125
    repeating vs. related fields, 131
    self, 138–144
    summary functions, 136–137
    using, 22
relative paths, 173–174
Relookup command, 123
Remote Administration plug-in, 397, 399

473

Index

repeating fields, 131, 419
Replace All command, 353
Replace command, 313, 360, 362
reports, 89–115
   adding lines to, 109
   averages, 100–101
   color scheme, 98
   counts, 100–101
   data searches, 92–94
   footers, 98
   found sets, 89–91, 164–165
   headers, 98
   page counts, 102–106
   printing, 42–43, 98, 159–160, 230
   running totals, 107
   scripts for, 98
   sorting records in, 97–98
   sub-summary, 108–112
   summary fields, 95–101
   summary layouts, 100–101
   summary reports, 89, 111–115
   viewing, 99
Reports field, 240–245
Restore option, 67, 147–148, 257
returns, 352–353
rows, 14, 235–236
running totals, 107

S

schemas, 452–453
Script Definition dialog box, 150
script steps. *See also* conditional script steps;
    specific script steps
   copying, 165
   order of, 270
   Web publishing, 409–410
scripting
   AppleScript and, 294–295
   described, 175
ScriptMaker, 150–152, 274
scripts
   access problems, 385–388
   adapting, 274
   buttons for, 232–234, 245
   canceling, 260
   comments, 168–169
   conditional. *See* conditional script steps
   controlling with user input, 195–197

   copying steps in, 165
   creating basic, 153–155
   creating layouts for searching, 228–231
   creating sub-scripts, 156–158
   debugging, 270–271
   deleting, 151
   duplicating, 151, 274
   editing, 152
   email, 277–282
   ending on different layouts, 258
   error trap scripts, 261–269
   errors during, 375–376
   exiting, 271
   extending interface with, 227–251
   external, 170–172
   FileMaker versions and, 211–214
   Find, 414–416
   finding/eliminating duplicates, 354–356
   found sets in, 164–165
   halting, 271
   importing with, 311–312
   looping, 190–194, 259–260
   master, 159–160
   modular document scripts, 222–226
   multiple settings in, 161–163
   names, 153, 167, 185, 274
   opening files with, 374–378
   opening URLs with, 283–284
   page counts, 102–106
   password protection for, 205–210
   pausing, 271
   planning, 146
   pre-sets, 147–149, 270, 274
   printing, 272–273
   renaming, 151–152, 274
   for reports, 98
   running from buttons, 245
   running from fields, 240–245
   running in other files, 170–172
   running other scripts with, 242–245
   running SQL queries from, 346–349
   running with Control/Command key, 152
   selecting steps in, 165
   sending email with, 276–282
   simple, 145–174
   startup, 407–408
   status functions and, 183–189
   switching layouts with, 417–418
   testing, 254–255

Index

troubleshooting. *See* troubleshooting
   using SQL queries in, 341
search format files, 438–439
searches. *See also* find-and-replace functions
   creating sub-scripts for, 156–157
   for data, 360, 438–439
   for index entries, 41
   inverted, 94
   layouts for, 228–231
   multiple finds, 161–163
   new features, 3
   omitting records from, 94
   Or searches, 92
   planning for, 21
   for records, 21, 156–157
   And searches, 92
   selecting records from, 94
   for self-relationship data, 141
   using operators in, 92–93
   Web publishing and, 406
security
   ODBC and, 339
   Web Companion, 5, 448
   Web Security database, 447–448
self-relationship data
   creating, 138
   creating lookups with, 142–144
   data display/access, 139
   searching for, 141
semicolon (;), 348
Send Mail script step, 274–279, 281–282
serial numbers
   auto-entry, 67–68, 313–321
   match fields, 118–119, 125–126
   portals, 134
   updating, 67–68
servers
   FileMaker. *See* FileMaker Pro Server
   host, 378, 398
   SQL Server, 332
Set Alignment command, 27
Set Error Capture script step, 246
Set Next Serial Value script step, 67–68, 313, 318
shared items
   databases, 324, 327, 333–336, 369–388
   FileMaker Server, 392
   files, 324, 327, 372, 382, 392, 403–404
   with ODBC, 333–336

over networks, 369–388
   Web publishing, 403–404
shortcuts, keyboard, 59
Show Custom Dialog script step, 4, 198–204
Show Message script step, 4, 195–197, 279
signatures, 81
Sliding/Printing command, 81
Social Security numbers, 18
Sort command, 67, 110, 112, 157
sort criteria, 111–112
sorting items
   default sort order, 270
   fields, 113–115
   fixing incorrect sorts, 256
   manual sorts, 270
   multiple sorts, 161–163
   planning for, 21
   in portals, 135
   records, 110, 148, 157–158
   report fields, 97–98
   sub-summary reports, 110–112
sound, 155
Specify Button dialog box, 36
Specify Calculation dialog box, 51–55, 180, 183
Specify Field dialog box, 181
spreadsheet programs, 290–295, 305
spreadsheets, 113–115, 290–293, 305
SQL commands
   creating with calculations, 342–345
   storing in fields, 338–341
   using in scripts, 341
SQL queries
   dynamic, 346–349
   FileMaker support of, 332
   importing data, 337–345
   running from scripts, 346–349
   using in scripts, 341
SQL Query builder, 339–340, 342–344
SQL Server, 332
SQL (Structured Query Language), 331
status functions, 183–189, 247
Structured Query Language. *See* SQL
style sheets, 289
sub-scripts
   combining, 159–160
   creating, 156–158
   ending scripts with, 258
   multiple export settings, 166–167

Index

sub-summary reports, 108–112
Submit button, 442
Substitute function, 361–362
summarization, 136–137
summary data, 111–115
summary fields
   averages, 100–101
   counts, 100–101
   creating, 95, 97
   creating layouts with, 96–99
   running totals, 107
summary layout parts, 95–99
summary layouts, 100–101
summary reports, 89, 111–112
synchronizing databases, 326–329
system requirements
   FileMaker Pro Server, 392
   Web publishing, 402
system settings, 184

T

tab-delimited text, 300, 305
tab order, 143–144, 419
Table View layouts, 413, 417–418
tables
   displaying data in, 444–445
   HTML, 285
   layouts displayed as, 413, 417–418
   SQL, 339
tabs, 352–353
TCP/IP, 370–371
telephone numbers, 51–57, 111
templates, layout, 217–220
testing databases, 22–23, 428
text
   ASCII, 300
   case of, 361
   exporting, 286–289
   formatted, 31–32, 286–289
   graphic, 33–35
   selecting, 59
   stringing together, 71
   tab-delimited, 300
   uneditable, 34–35
text blocks, 28
text data files
   cleaning up, 352–353
   deleting formatting characters, 352–353

   field names and, 301
   importing, 300–305, 307
text fields, 215–216
time status functions, 183–184
time fields, 21
toolbars, 250–251
Trim function, 62–63
troubleshooting, 253–274
   adapting scripts, 274
   changing scripts, 274
   common problems, 256–260
   data cleanup, 352–353
   debugging scripts, 270–271
   duplicate records, 354–356
   error trap scripts, 261–269
   incorrect print format, 257
   incorrect records, 256
   incorrect sorts, 256
   loops that won't end, 259
   missing records, 256
   printing scripts, 272–273
   problem data, 360
   script access problems, 385–388
   testing scripts and, 254–255
.txt extension, 115, 300, 396

U

upgrading FileMaker, 6
Upper function, 361–362
URLs
   links to, 424–425
   opening with scripts, 283–284, 432
user input
   controlling scripts with, 195–197
   customizing dialog boxes for, 198–204
user interface
   disabling toolbars, 250–251
   extending with scripts, 227–251
   Find layout, 228–231
   interactive buttons, 234
   interactive error messages, 246–249
   Main Menu layout, 237–239
   record deletion, 235–236
   running scripts from buttons, 232–234, 246
   running scripts from fields, 240–245
users
   access problems, 385–388
   database, 12

feedback, 436–437
FileMaker Server, 393–395
input, 434–435
passwords, 379–382, 447
tracking activity of, 420
Web access, 402

V

validation
  alerts for, 56–57
  by number of characters, 56–57
  value lists, 45–46
VALUE command, 441
value lists
  advantages, 44, 47
  altering display of, 47–48
  check boxes, 217–218
  conditional, 47–48
  creating, 44–45
  formatting, 44
  limitations, 47
  multiple, 46
  names, 47
  tips for, 46
  validating formats with, 45–46
  Web display, 419
vCard format, 454–455

W

Web browsers
  accessing databases with, 421
  display considerations, 419
  FileMaker styles and, 406
  layout styles and, 405–406, 408
  opening Web pages in, 283–284, 428, 432
  problems with, 458
  scripts for opening URLs, 283–284
  versions, 402, 406
Web Companion plug-in
  Custom Web Publishing, 430
  database access, 423
  enabling, 403
  file sharing, 403–404
  layout styles and, 405–406
  new features, 5
  remote administration, 422
  security settings, 448

Web layouts, 411–413
Web pages
  creating, 432
  for error messages, 437
  opening in browser, 283–284, 429
  opening with scripts, 283–284
  for response messages, 436
"Web palette" option, 30
Web publishing, 401–449
  CDML. See CDML
  creating Web layouts, 411–413
  Custom Web Publishing, 429–431, 447–448
  database access, 421
  display considerations, 419
  enabling Web Companion, 403
  file names and, 402
  file-sharing privileges, 403–404
  Find scripts, 414–416
  guest books, 426–427
  home pages, 424–425, 437
  IWP interface, 407–410
  layout styles, 405–406
  log files, 420
  overview, 402
  remote administration, 422
  restricting database access, 423
  script steps, 409–410
  startup scripts, 407–408
  switching layouts, 417–418
  technical requirements, 402
  template format files, 436–446
  testing databases, 428
  user access, 402
  user input, 434–435
  visitor feedback, 436–437
  XML and, 458
Web Security database, 447–448
Web sites
  home pages, 424–425, 437
  XML resources, 453
wildcard character (*), 93, 423
Windows 95/98 systems, 392, 399
Windows 2000 systems, 5, 389, 391
Windows NT systems, 391
Windows systems. See also cross-platform issues
  color and, 30
  file names, 28
  FileMaker 6 and, 5

Index

Windows systems *(continued)*
   fonts, 28–29
   memory and, 395
   printing scripts, 272
   registering databases in, 333
Windows XP systems, 5, 392
.WK1 extension, 115
WK1 file type, 113
WKS file type, 113
Word, 294–295
word processors, 113, 115, 294–295

X

XML (Extensible Markup Language)
   exporting with, 5, 454–455
   FileMaker and, 451–458
   importing with, 5, 456–457
   overview, 452–453
   vs. CDML, 452
   vs. HTML, 452–453
   Web publishing and, 458
.xml extension, 456
XSLT (Extensible Stylesheet Language-Transformation), 451–457
XTND Power Enabler, 35